Theatrical Design and Production

An Introduction to
Scene Design and Construction,
Lighting, Sound, Costume, and Makeup

FOURTH EDITION

J. Michael Gillette
University of Arizona

MAYFIELD PUBLISHING COMPANY
Mountain View, California
London • Toronto

For Joyce Ann, who will always know why

Library of Congress Cataloging-in-Publication Data

Gillette, J. Michael.
    Theatrical design and production : an introduction to scene design
  and construction, lighting, sound, costume, and makeup / J. Michael
  Gillette. — 4th ed.
      p.   cm.
    Includes bibliographical references and index.
    ISBN 0-7674-1191-9
    1. Stage management.   2. Theater—Production and direction.
  3. Theaters—Stage-setting and scenery.   I. Title.
  PN2085.G5   1999
  792'.025—dc21   99-28595
                                                         CIP

Manufactured in the United States of America
10 9 8 7 6 5 4 3 2 1

Mayfield Publishing Company
1280 Villa Street
Mountain View, CA 94041

Sponsoring editor, Janet M. Beatty; production editor, Carla White Kirschenbaum;
manuscript copyeditor, Mark Gallaher; design manager, Glenda King; art editor,
Amy Folden; text and cover design, Claire Seng-Niemoller; manufacturing manager,
Randy Hurst. The text was set in 9.5/12 Palatino by Thompson Type and printed on
45# Somerset Matte by R. R. Donnelley & Sons Company.

Cover images: makeup photo courtesy of Robert Cohen; scene by Robert Wilson
for *Four Saints in Three Acts* © Stephanie Berger; costume sketch from *The Illusion*,
Connie Strayer.

Preface

First courses in the world of theatrical design and production, like the art they introduce, come in a bewildering array of shapes, sizes, textures, and colors. Some students receive their introduction to this subject area in a general overview course that covers the design and production elements of scenery, costumes, lighting, and sound in a single semester. Other students may enjoy the luxury of an entire year in which to discuss the same material. Still others may take individual courses that specialize in the theory and craft of the separate areas that comprise the field of theatrical design and technical production. The course content is very flexible indeed.

To create a text that will serve the needs of all these courses is a distinct challenge. I've tried to rise to that challenge by organizing the material in two ways. The chapters appear in a logical sequence, but each chapter is also an island of information that can stand alone. My hope is that this organization will enable each instructor to pick and choose the type and amount of material that is appropriate for his or her particular course. This type of organization also makes the text a useful reference work for students to keep throughout their design and technical production careers.

Organization and Content

Just as a play wouldn't start without the scenery being in place, this book doesn't delve into technical procedures without first setting the stage. Chapters 1 through 4, *Production Organization and Management, The Design Process, Theatre Architecture,* and *The Stage and Its Equipment,* provide a grounding in real world issues and are appropriate for use in almost any type of technical production class.

Of special significance is Chapter 2, *The Design Process.* It contains material new to beginning technical theatre texts. It is a problem-solving and conceptual thinking model created specifically for theatrical practice. Its purpose is to increase each student's creative capacity by reducing the effects of two prime ingredients of creative dysfunction—fear and frustration. The mechanism used to effect this change is a seven-step procedure that enables students to make logical, rational, and considered decisions when making the myriad choices involved in creating a design or solving a technical challenge in any area of theatrical production.

Chapter 3, *Theatre Architecture,* provides a concise chronology, both pictorially and textually, of the history of theatre architecture. I've included this information for two reasons: the functional design of the environment in which a play is produced has always been a major factor in determining the type, style, and design of technical elements used in a production, and all too frequently student designers are not required to take courses in theatre history.

Chapter 13, *Electrical Theory and Practice,* provides a concise explanation of the nature and function of electricity and electronics and the practical use of the power formula, as well as information on wiring practices and standards.

The last three chapters in the book, *Mechanical Drafting, Perspective,* and *Drawing and Rendering,* contain specific how-to information on the drawing and rendering techniques most commonly used in theatrical production. Chapter 20, *Mechanical Drafting,* provides information about the materials and types of drafting used in the theatre and helpful hints on the process of drafting. Chapter 21, *Perspective,* offers a step-by-step procedure *with exercises* for drawing in accurate scale mechanical perspective. Chapter 22, *Drawing and Rendering,* provides an overview of the types of paints, pastels, markers, and papers commonly used in theatrical rendering as well as information on basic application techniques used with these media.

The remainder of the text provides an overview of the function and responsibilities of the scenic, lighting, costume, and sound designers. It also contains primary information about the tools and basic techniques that are used to bring each designer's concepts to the stage.

As with any art form, the basic element necessary for creating a successful design in theatre is an understanding of design principles and chosen medium. I hope that this text not only provides those basics but also offers encouragement and inspiration to create.

Features

In many ways, *Theatrical Design and Production* is a traditional introductory text for the various design and craft areas of theatrical production. A number of features, however, strive to set this text apart.

Philosophy   The underlying spirit of this text is firmly rooted in my belief that learning and creating in the various fields of theatrical design and production can be, and should be, fun. With that thought in mind, I've tried to make this text not only informative and practical but also motivating and inspirational.

Color Analysis   The sixteen-page color analysis section presents a discussion of the practical applications of color theory by analyzing the interactive effects of the color selections for the scenery, costumes, and lighting for two productions—one with a very narrow, muted palette and the other with a full-spectrum, heavily saturated color style.

Safety Tips   Safety tips are discussed throughout the text. They have been placed in special boxes adjacent to the relevant text to help readers integrate learning about a tool, material, or process with its safe use.

Running Glossary   To help students learn and remember the vocabulary of the theatre, new terms are defined in the margin on the page where they first appear.

Boxed Material   Additional material that provides further depth and practical information has been placed in boxes outside the mainstream text. This added material is included to enhance student understanding by providing insights into and solutions to real theatrical problems.

Illustration Program   An extensive photo and illustration program provides a very strong adjunct to the textual information. Photos from professional theatre productions are used to provide a model that students can strive to emulate.

New to the Fourth Edition

Once again the basic features and organizational structure of *Theatrical Design and Production* remain the same as in the previous editions. A new feature—boxed information about design inspiration—has been added to various chapters. Almost all of the chapters have been extensively revised to include new and updated information. Tools and materials that are no longer used, such as the folding rule, have been removed. Others, such as the clout nail, which is also obsolete but which holds a special place in the author's heart, have been elevated to a position of historical significance, which is duly noted. Many chapters include new photos and illustrations reflecting manufacturers' current equipment. Because the use of computers in all areas of theatrical production has become so commonplace, the material on computers has been integrated into the appropriate chapters rather than remaining in a separate chapter.

Once again, I would like to thank those students, friends, and colleagues who have offered suggestions for improving *Theatrical Design and Production*. I would particularly like to thank Jeffrey M. Gress, Denison University; Bonnie Kruger, Washington University; and Michael Rolleri, University of North Carolina, Chapel Hill for their thoughtful, close readings of the third edition. I also genuinely appreciate the comments and suggestions offered by the following reviewers of the fourth edition: Alison Ford, University of Iowa; David Martin Jacques, California State University, Long Beach; Loren Schreiber, San Diego State University; and Cheri Vasek, Central Washington University.

Brief Contents

Contents

Theatrical Design
and Production

Chapter 1
Production Organization and Management

"Great art conceals art." That statement has been attributed to Konstantin Stanislavski, founder of the Moscow Art Theatre and developer of Method acting. He was referring to the phenomenon that occurs when actors create brilliantly believable roles. Great actors don't seem to be working. They make us believe that they *are* the characters they are playing and that everything they say or do is happening spontaneously, without thought or effort. Stanislavski meant by his aphorism that a seemingly effortless job of acting is the end result of years of training, dedication, and just plain hard work.

Great art *does* conceal art, but not just the art of the actor. Imagine a male actor, wrapped in a heavy fur cape, standing in the middle of the stage and delivering a soliloquy. The stage resembles a craggy mountain peak, with an angular platform surrounded by an immense expanse of solemn purple and blue sky. The actor strides to a rocky outcropping. Under his weight the platform slowly starts to tip. The actor scrambles backward to save himself and catches the hem of his cape on another "rock." The cape comes off, and the **followspot** reveals the actor standing in his BVDs with his cape around his ankles. The spotlight operator, horrified, tries to turn off her light. But she doesn't hit the right lever and, instead of turning it off, changes its color from deep blue to brilliant white.

followspot: A lighting instrument with a high-intensity, narrow beam; mounted in a stand that allows it to tilt and swivel so the beam can "follow" an actor.

This unlikely scenario illustrates the fact that less-than-great art conceals little. It also demonstrates that Stanislavski's injunction can be just as true for the design and technical elements of the production as it is for the actors. Together, they can create the delicate illusionary reality that we call theatre. The illusion that the spectators see is just that. A great performance doesn't simply happen; it is the product of a great deal of organization, teamwork, talent, and dedication.

Theatre folk have always delighted in surrounding the process of putting on plays with an aura of mystery. This tradition stems from the probably accurate belief that a play's entertainment value increases if the audience thinks that the production just spontaneously happens. The Mickey Rooney and Judy Garland movies of the 1930s are perfect examples. Mickey, Judy, or one of their friends says, "Let's put on a show!" Someone chimes in that her uncle owns a barn. Amazingly, the barn happens to have a highly polished linoleum floor that is perfect for tap dancing, and the barn is equipped with a full orchestra, sets, lights, and spectacular costumes. The show is an astounding success.

production team: Everyone working, in any capacity, on the production of the play.

production design team: The producer, director, and scenic, costume, lighting, sound, and other designers who develop the visual and aural concept for the production.

production concept: The creative interpretation of the script, which will unify the artistic vision of producer, director, and designers.

production meeting: A conference of appropriate production personnel to share information.

supernumerary: An actor, normally not called for in the script, used in a production; an extra; a walk-on.

The real world of theatrical production isn't like that. Getting a play from the written word to the stage requires a lot of challenging work. The result of all this effort, the **production team** hopes, will be artistic and artful, but the business of making a script come alive on the stage is a process that isn't all that mysterious.

THE PRODUCTION SEQUENCE

How does a play happen? What sequence of events must occur for it to move from the pages of a script to a live performance before an audience? Every play goes through several stages of development.

Script

The overwhelming majority of theatrical productions begin with a script. This is not true, however, for every theatrical performance. The production of some plays begins with just an idea. That idea may be developed by the performing group in a variety of interesting and creative ways. Some of these concepts may evolve into written scripts, and others may remain as conceptual cores that the actors use as guides when they improvise dialogue during the actual performance.

Concept, Design, and Construction

We will assume that our hypothetical production begins with a traditional script. After the script has been selected, the producer options it, or secures the legal rights to produce it, and hires the director, designers, and actors. The members of the **production design team** read the script and then develop the **production concept,** also referred to as the "production approach."

The production concept is the central creative idea that unifies the artistic vision of the producer, director, and designers. In many ways, any production concept originates with the personal artistic "points of view" of the members of the production design team. The personality, training, and prior experiences of each team member will shape and color his or her thoughts about the play. One of the primary jobs of the director is to mold these individual artistic ideas and expressions into a unified vision—the production concept—so that, ideally, each designer's work supports the work of the other designers as well as the central artistic theme of the production. Normally, the production concept evolves during the first few **production meetings** from the combined input of the members of the production design team. The principles of the production concept are best explained by example.

Let's assume that our hypothetical production team is working on a production of Shakespeare's *The Merchant of Venice*. Most productions of this play would probably be traditional: Elizabethan costumes and a set that mimics the appearance of the Globe Theatre, the theatre most scholars think was used by Shakespeare. However, some production groups might choose, for a variety of reasons, to develop a nontraditional production concept. In a production of this play directed by Cosmo Catellano at the University of Iowa, the performance was set inside a World War II Nazi concentration camp. In this production, all of the actors in the play were portrayed as Jewish interns of the camp. **Supernumeraries,** dressed as Nazi officers and their female companions, sat in the auditorium and watched the play alongside the paying audience. Additional extras, in the uniforms of concentration-camp guards and carrying weapons, patrolled the

FIGURE 1.1
A great deal of backstage activity occurs before the production reaches the stage.

FIGURE 1.2
The director discusses a scene with
the actors.

FIGURE 1.3
Scene shifting must be carefully
organized and choreographed.

stage throughout the performance. While the script wasn't altered, the radical
production concept forced the audience to concentrate on the Jewish persecution
themes that are very much a part of the script.

After the production concept is agreed on, the sets, props, lights, costumes,
and sound are designed. Then the various diagrams, sketches, and other plans
are sent to shops for construction, fabrication, or acquisition of the production
elements (see Figure 1.1).

While the various visual elements are being built, the director and actors are
busy rehearsing (see Figure 1.2). After the rehearsal and construction period,
which usually lasts three to seven weeks, the play moves into the theatre, and
the technical and dress rehearsals begin.

Rehearsals

technical rehearsals: Run-throughs
in which the sets, lights, props, and
sound are introduced into the action
of the play.

Technical rehearsals are devoted to integrating the sets, props, lighting, and
sound with the actors into the action of the play. During this hectic period, the

FIGURE 1.4
Sound operator at work.

patterns and timing for shifting the scenery and props are established. The movements of any scenic or property elements (see Figure 1.3), regardless of whether those movements happen in front of the audience or behind a curtain, have to be choreographed or **blocked** just as are the movements of the actors. This ensures that each shift will be consistent in timing and efficiency for every performance. The shifts may be numerous or complex enough to warrant holding a separate **shift rehearsal,** in which the director, scene designer, technical director, and stage manager work with the scenery and prop crews to perfect the choreography and timing of all scenic and prop shifts.

The basic timing and intensity of the light **cues** will have been established during the **lighting rehearsal** (which precedes the first technical rehearsal). But during the tech rehearsals almost all of the light cues have to be adjusted in some way, since it is the rule rather than the exception that new lighting cues are added and old ones deleted or modified during this time. The lighting designer meets with the director and stage manager in the theatre to discuss the modifications and have a look at them. The intensity, timing, and nature of the sound cues are subjected to similar changes during the technical rehearsals (see Figure 1.4). Depending on the production schedule and the complexity of the show, there are generally one to three tech rehearsals over the course of a week or so.

The **dress rehearsals** begin toward the end of "tech week." During these rehearsals, which are a natural extension of the tech rehearsals, any adjustments to costumes and makeup are noted and corrected by the next rehearsal time (see Figure 1.5). Adjustments to the various sound, lighting, and shifting cues continue to be made during the dress rehearsals. Depending on the complexity of the production and the number of costumes and costume changes, there may be one to three dress rehearsals.

After the last dress rehearsal, there are sometimes one to ten or more preview performances (with an invited audience and/or reduced ticket prices and no critics) before the production officially opens to the public and critics.

blocking: Movement patterns, usually of actors, on the stage.

shift rehearsal: A run-through without actors to practice changing the scenery and props.

cue: A directive for action, for example, a change in the lighting.

lighting rehearsal: A run-through without the actors to look at the intensity, timing, and placement of the various lighting cues.

dress rehearsal: A run-through in which the actors wear costumes and makeup.

THEATRE ORGANIZATION

More than anything else good theatre requires good organization. Every successful production has a strong organizational structure that follows a fairly standard pattern. Figure 1.6 depicts the organization of a hypothetical, but typical, theatrical production company. Each company's structure is unique to its own needs, and it is doubtful that any two companies would be set up exactly the same.

FIGURE 1.5
Costumes must be adjusted to fit properly.

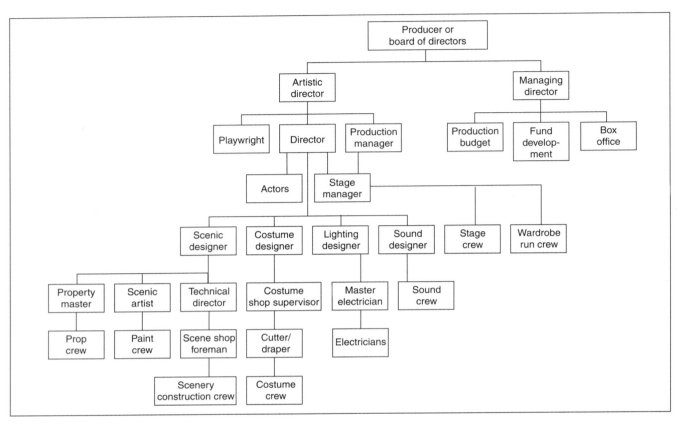

FIGURE 1.6
The organizational structure chart of a typical theatrical production company.

The functions of the various members of the company will be taken up in the next section.

The production meeting is probably the single most important device for ensuring smooth communication among the various production departments. The initial production conferences are attended by members of the production design team. Their purpose is to develop the production concept. After the designers begin to produce their drawings, sketches, and plans, the production meeting is used as a forum to keep other members of the team informed about the progress in all design areas. At this time, the stage manager normally joins in the discussions.

When the designs are approved and construction begins, the production meeting expands to include the technical director and appropriate crew heads. As construction starts, the director becomes heavily involved in rehearsals. At this time, a few adjustments are almost inevitably necessary in one or more of the design elements. These changes should be discussed and resolved at the production meeting so that all departments are aware of the progress and evolution of the production concept.

While the production concept is being developed, the production meetings are usually held as often as it is practicable and necessary—daily, or less frequently. As the meetings become less developmental and more informational, their frequency decreases to about once a week. The last meeting is usually held just before the opening of the production.

Who participates in production meetings depends, to a great extent, on the nature of the producing organization. A single-run, Broadway-type professional conference usually includes only the members of the production-design team and their assistants. A production conference at a regional professional theatre includes the production-design team and some of the other members of the permanent production staff, such as the production manager and technical director. For a professionally oriented educational theatre, the staffing of the production meeting is generally the same as for the regional professional production group and ideally will include those faculty supervisors overseeing the work of student designers, technical directors, and crew heads.

The development of advanced communication technologies and the reality that most professional designers are working on more than one project at a time often necessitate that much of the direct communication between members of the production design team take place over great geographical distances. Designs can be sent by overnight express, forwarded as e-mail attachments, or faxed. Phone or video conferences can be used in place of face-to-face meetings. While these developments speed the transfer of data and information, the isolation of the design team members from each other may break down the necessary communication flow within the group. But if everyone is aware of this potential "communication gap," it doesn't have to become a problem. More and more designers are communicating electronically, and we can expect even more "remote conferencing" in the future.

PRODUCTION JOB DESCRIPTIONS

Although the organization of any company will fit its own needs, the duties of those holding the various positions will be much the same.

Producer

The producer is the ultimate authority in the organizational structure of a theatrical production. He or she is, arguably, the most influential member of the team. The producer secures the rights to perform the play; hires the director, designers, actors, and crews; leases the theatre; and secures financial backing for the play. The specific functions of the producer can vary considerably. In the New York professional theatre, most productions are set up as individual entities. As a consequence, the producer and his or her staff are able to concentrate their efforts on each production. They will sometimes be working on the preliminary phases of a second or third production while another show is in production or in the final stages of rehearsal, but in general they concentrate on one show at a time.

Regional professional theatres such as the Guthrie Theatre in Minneapolis, the American Conservatory Theatre (ACT) in San Francisco, the Arizona Theatre Company in Tucson, the Asolo Theatre in Sarasota, Florida, and others have been set up in every section of North America over the past forty years. Generally, these theatres produce a full seven- or eight-month season of limited-run productions. Some of them have active summer programs. Because of the sweeping responsibilities imposed on the producer within these organizations, the functions of the position are generally divided between two persons, the *managing director* and the *artistic director*. The business functions of the producer—contracts, fund raising, ticket sales, box-office management—are handled by the managing director, and any artistic decisions—selection of directors, actors, and designers, for example—are made by the artistic director. The managing and artistic directors are hired by the theatre's board of directors, which is responsible for determining the long-range artistic and fiscal goals of the theatre.

In educational theatre, the department chair and administrative staff frequently function in the same capacity as the managing director. The duties of the

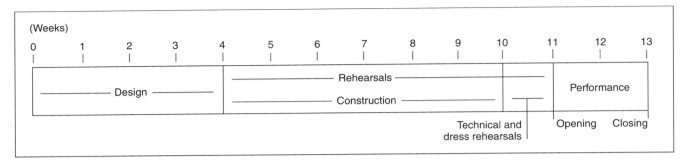

FIGURE 1.7
The production calendar shows the time line for each production from the initial production conference until the closing night.

artistic director are often assigned to a production committee, which selects the plays and is responsible for their artistic quality.

In other nonprofit theatres, such as community or church groups, the functions of the producer are usually carried out by a production committee or board of directors, which functions as previously described.

Playwright

The playwright is obviously a vital and essential link in the production chain. The playwright creates and develops the ideas that ultimately evolve into the written script. In the initial public performance of the play, he or she may be involved in the production process. The playwright frequently helps the director by explaining his or her interpretation of various plot and character developments. During this developmental process, the playwright often needs to rewrite portions of some scenes or even whole scenes or acts. If the playwright is not available for conferences or meetings, the production design team proceeds with the development and interpretation of the script on its own.

Director

The director is the artistic manager and inspirational leader of the production team. He or she coordinates the work of the actors, designers, and crews so that the production accurately expresses the production concept. Any complex activity such as the production of a play must have someone with the vision, energy, and ability to focus everyone else's efforts on the common goal. The director is this leader. He or she works closely with the other members of the production design team to develop the production concept and also works with the actors to develop their roles in a way that is consistent with the production concept. The director is ultimately responsible for the unified creative interpretation of the play as it is expressed in production.

Production Manager

The production manager must be an adept mental gymnast, because this important position has the responsibility for coordinating the complex activities associated with a multishow season. The necessity for a production manager has evolved with the development of regional professional theatres. Each production within the theatre's season requires its own logistical structure to bring it from concept to the stage. Figure 1.7 illustrates a typical period needed to develop a play from production concept to reality. Since most regional professional theatres or professionally oriented educational theatres produce eight to twelve plays a

Backstage Etiquette

Although every production company has specific rules that relate to its own production circumstances, some general rules of backstage etiquette are universal.

1. Don't talk to other crew members backstage during rehearsals or performances unless it is about the business of the production. Then talk only in a low whisper.

2. Don't talk to the actors backstage during rehearsals or performances unless it is about the business of the production. Their job—acting—takes a great deal of concentration, and they shouldn't be distracted.

3. Wear dark clothes, preferably dark blue or black, to minimize the dis-

traction to the audience if you are seen. Wear sturdy rubber-soled shoes (no tennis shoes, cowboy boots, sandals or flip-flops). Sturdy shoes will protect your feet, and the rubber soles will minimize noise.

4. Be sure to show up on time for your crew call (the time you are scheduled to arrive at the theatre ready for work). Sign the sign-in sheet, and check in with your crew head for work.

5. Don't smoke, eat, or drink backstage.

6. Do not touch props, costumes, or stage equipment that is not your responsibility.

season, frequently on several different stages, they must develop rehearsal and performance schedules for all of them simultaneously.

The production calendar shown in Figure 1.8 is used by the production manager to help keep track of the various stages of development for each play in the season. This master calendar contains all pertinent information regarding tryouts, rehearsals, design and construction deadlines, technical and dress rehearsals, and performances. From the production calendar, the production manager gleans the information necessary to coordinate the assignment of personnel and rehearsal space as well as the scheduling of the various production meetings and other necessary activities.

Stage Manager

The stage manager can be compared to a very gifted, slightly eccentric master mechanic who keeps a cantankerous, highly complex machine running at top efficiency by talking to it, soothing it, and lovingly fixing whatever is broken. The specific duties of the stage manager can be broken down into two primary categories: (1) assisting the director during rehearsals and (2) being responsible for all backstage activity after the show opens.

The stage manager is hired or assigned to the production at about the same time as the director. In the professional theatre, the stage manager must be a member of Actor's Equity, the actors' union. Sometimes the stage manager finds him- or herself in an awkward position because he or she not only assists the director but also, if elected the Equity deputy by the union actors, functions as the enforcer of the Equity rules during rehearsals and performances. Since the Equity deputy can be viewed as enforcing the union rules to save money for the producer, some stage managers decline to serve as deputy because of the potential conflict of interest. Other stage managers elect to serve as deputy since they are already in a leadership position and do not see these activities as a conflict of interest.

Production calendar Aug 20-26 | 27-2 Sept | Sept 3-9 | 10-16 | 17-23 | 24-30 | Oct 1-7 | 8-14 | 15-21 | 22-28 | 29-4 Nov | Nov 5-11 | 12-18 | 19-25 | 26-2 Dec | Dec 3-9 | 10-16 | 17-23 | 24-30 | 31-6 Jan | Jan 7-13 | 14-20 | 21-27 | 28-3 Feb

Row	Phases
School schedule	Fall semester (spanning). Markers: Labor Day, Veteran's Day, Thanksgiving, Exams, Christmas vacation
Studio I	Rehearsal & construction — Tech — Perf
Main Stage I	Rehearsal & construction — Tech — Perf
Studio II	Design — Rehearsal & construction — Tech — Perf
Main Stage II	Design — Rehearsal & construction — Tech — Perf
Studio III	Design — Rehearsal & construction — Tech — Perf
Main Stage III	Design — Rehearsal & construction
Studio IV	Design
Main Stage IV	
Summer Rep I	
Summer Rep II	
Summer Rep III	

FIGURE 1.8
A sample production calendar.

The stage manager helps the director by taking responsibility for the majority of administrative details. They include such diverse duties as making sure that the ground plan of the set is taped or chalked on the floor of the rehearsal hall, arranging for rehearsal furniture (substitute furniture for the set) as well as tables and chairs for the director and other production personnel, and writing the blocking in the stage manager's **prompt book.**

The stage manager also assists the director by keeping information flowing among the director, the designers, and the various technical shops. During the rehearsal process, the director may decide to introduce a piece of **stage business** that requires the modification of some technical element. If the director decides that an actor should bounce a ball against one of the set walls, the stage manager needs to tell the set designer that this section of the wall must be sturdy.

Until the production moves into the theatre—or until the beginning of technical rehearsals, if the play has already been rehearsing in the theatre—the stage manager usually sits beside the director to facilitate communication. When technical rehearsals begin, the stage manager moves to the location from which he or she will **call** the show. The crew members will have previously recorded what to do on their cue sheets, but they don't start the action until they receive their "go" cue from the stage manager. Stage managers have traditionally called the show from backstage, because this location kept them in close contact with the cast and crew. However, the development of new theatre conventions, environments, and equipment enables the cast to make entrances through the auditorium and allows the lighting and sound operators to be in the optimal positions for seeing and hearing the stage action. This dispersion of the actors and crew from the backstage space has freed the stage manager to call the show from whatever position provides the best overall view of the action.

When the stage manager begins to call the show, the primary focus of his or her responsibility changes from administrative support for the director to tech-

prompt book: A copy of the script with details about each actor's blocking as well as the location of all sets, props, lights, and sound cues.

stage business: A specific action, also known as a "bit," performed by an actor during the play.

call: To tell specific crew members when to perform their cues.

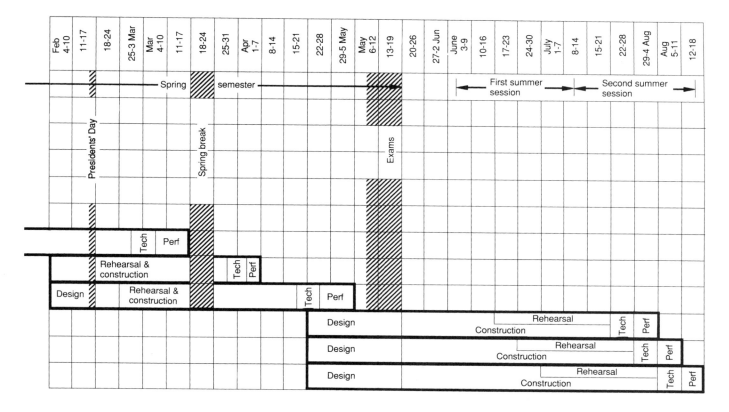

nical coordination of all production activities. The director and various designers determine the nature and timing of the cues, but it is the stage manager who is responsible for seeing that those instructions are carried out. Figure 1.9 illustrates the change in organization that takes place when the play goes into technical and dress rehearsals and performances. The designers still discuss conceptual and aesthetic issues with the director, but they usually communicate specific information related to cues that will be called by the stage manager directly to the stage manager.

The stage manager calls the show from notes written in the prompt book. Preliminary locations for many of the cues will have been noted in the book during the rehearsal period. During the tech and dress rehearsals, the location, timing, and character of these cues are adjusted. When the last dress rehearsal or preview performance is finished, the prompt book will contain a complete and accurate set of instructions for running every cue in the production.

Scenic and Property Personnel

Those who work with the scenery and props in a production are the scenic designer, the scenic artist, the paint crew, the property master and crew, the technical director, the scene-shop foreman, the construction crew, and the stage crew.

Scenic Designer The scenic designer is responsible for the visual appearance and function of the scenic and property elements used in the production. To translate the scenic design from concept to the stage, the designer produces either hand-drawn or computer-printed colored sketches or renderings of the sets and properties, scale models of the various sets, and scale mechanical drawings that

Stage Manager's Prompt Book

The stage manager's prompt book is the bible of the production. The stage manager details all pertinent information about the production in a loose-leaf notebook as shown. Each page of the prompt book contains one page of the script. The blocking is usually indicated in the wide margins of the pages with arrows showing the movement of each actor. Some stage managers prefer to place a ground plan of the set on the facing page for each page of the script. The blocking and notes are then placed on this sheet.

The nature, location, and duration of each technical cue (lights, sound, shifting) are also written in the margins. Warning cues (to prepare the appropriate personnel for any forthcoming cues) are normally placed in the prompt book about half a page before the cue location.

The prompt book also contains a ground plan of the set(s), a prop schedule detailing the placement and conditions of props ("a half-full glass of milk on the coffee table"), and a "contact sheet" listing the phone numbers and addresses of all cast members, crew members, and other production personnel.

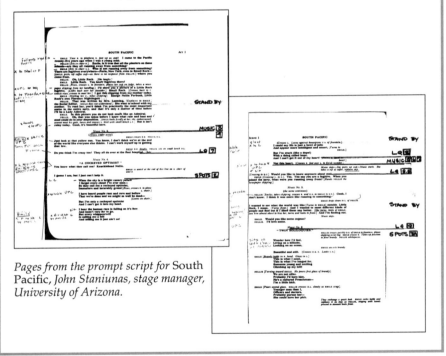

Pages from the prompt script for South Pacific, *John Staniunas, stage manager, University of Arizona.*

fully describe the settings (see Figure 1.10). When appropriate the scene designer may also produce computer animations to describe any scenic movement. The scenic designer's job will be explored in depth in Chapter 7, *Scenic Design.*

Scenic Artist   The scenic artist, under the supervision of the scenic designer, is responsible for the painting of the scenery. He or she needs to be an excellent craftsperson capable of working in a variety of media and styles. Although the scenic artist does a great deal of the actual scenic painting, he or she is also responsible for supervising the work of the paint crew.

Paint Crew   The paint crew, under the supervision of the scenic artist, paints the sets and sometimes the **properties.** This challenging job involves painting the

properties: Such elements as furniture, lamps, pictures, table linens, bric-a-brac, and window drapes that provide the finished set with visual character.

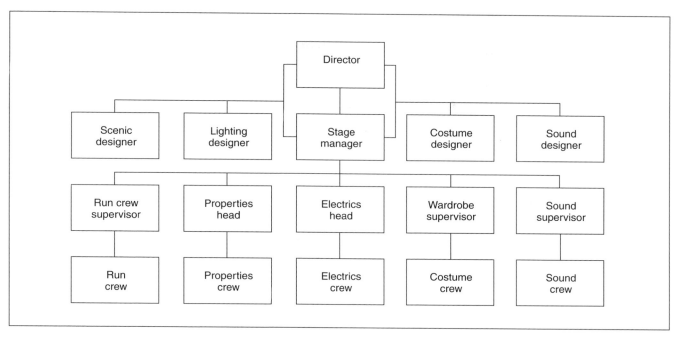

FIGURE 1.9
The organizational structure changes as a play goes from regular rehearsals into the tech/dress rehearsals and performances.

set (walls, floor, background, properties) to make it reflect the character of the design. Rarely do playwrights set their plays in freshly painted environments. More frequently than not the paint crew must make the set look old, tired, abused, and worn. Techniques for achieving these results are detailed in Chapter 10, *Scene Painting.*

Property Master   The property master is a unique artisan in the theatre. He or she must be adept at a variety of skills ranging from design to painting, sculpting, furniture construction and upholstery, welding, and electronics. The property master is responsible for the design and construction of the various decorative and functional props that are used in a production. He or she generally works under the artistic supervision of the scenic designer and works closely with the technical director and scene-shop foreman. Chapter 11, *Stage Properties,* contains information about stage-prop construction techniques.

Property Crew   The property crew, under the supervision of the property master, constructs or acquires all the props used in a production. During rehearsals and performances, the supervision of the prop crew shifts to the stage manager, who oversees its work involving the placement, shifting, and storage of the props.

Technical Director   The duties of the technical director, also known as the TD, are evolving into what currently constitutes two job descriptions with one name. In some theatres the TD basically functions as a master carpenter. In these instances, under the artistic supervision of the scenic designer, he or she is responsible for building the scenery and properties, mounting them on the stage, and overseeing the work of the scenic and property crews during rehearsals and performances. In this capacity, the primary activity of the TD is supervising the construction of all scenery and properties. To accomplish this task, the TD uses scale plans from the scenic designer. These drawings may have to be supplemented with **plates** drawn by the technical director or an assistant, showing the

plate: A sheet of mechanical drawings, drawn to scale.

FIGURE 1.10
(A) *Look Back in Anger*, scenic design by A. S. Gillette, University of Iowa. (B) *The Petrified Forest*, scenic design by Peggy Kellner, University of Arizona.

construction details and techniques that will be used to build the scenery. The TD also supervises the transporting of the scenery from the shop to the stage as well as the mounting, rigging, and maintenance of the scenery while it is in the theatre.

In theatres with heavy production programs, the TD frequently functions more as a technical administrator than a master craftsman. In these situations the TD oversees the work being done by the various crews in the wood, metal, paint, and prop shops. These busy programs frequently mount several production series simultaneously, often in multiple theatres or venues. Someone needs to facilitate communication among the production design team for each production, keep track of the construction progress on each show, oversee the budgets, and generally keep everything moving smoothly. That responsibility is frequently assigned to the technical director.

An introduction to scenic and property production (the organization, tools, and construction techniques) is contained in Chapter 8 (*Tools and Materials*) and 9 (*Scenic Production Techniques*) as well as Chapter 11 (*Stage Properties*).

Scene-Shop Foreman   The scene-shop foreman or master carpenter, under the supervision of the technical director, is responsible for the construction, mounting, and rigging of the scenery. He or she usually supervises a crew of carpenters in the actual construction. The foreman is also normally responsible for the maintenance of the scene-shop equipment and supplies.

Construction Crew   The construction crew is composed of the people who build the various pieces of scenery and properties for the production. After the set has been built and painted, they move the sets from the shop to the theatre and assemble them on the stage.

Stage Crew   The stage crew **shifts** the set during technical and dress rehearsals and during the performances. This work is accomplished under the direct supervision of the stage manager.

shift: To change the position of the scenery, props, or stage equipment.

Lighting Personnel

The lighting staff is made up of the lighting designer, the master electrician, and other electricians.

Lighting Designer   The lighting designer is responsible for the design, installation, and operation of the lighting and special electrical effects used in the production. Because light is a nontactile sculptural medium, it is all but impossible to build a model or draw a sketch of what the lighting will look like.

To present their visual ideas, lighting designers frequently draw sketches or show visual examples—paintings, photographs, and so forth—that demonstrate the type and style of lighting that they intend to create. Various computer rendering/modeling/animation programs can now be used to create virtual examples of how the lighting is going to look. With currently available programs it is possible to scan in a rendering of the set, add a character or two, then add the lighting and print the result on a color printer. As computer technology continues to improve and rendering times are reduced, digital imagery will probably become the preferred method of demonstrating the lighting designer's concepts, simply because a computer image, whether printed or seen on the monitor, provides an extremely accurate, evocative visualization of the designer's intentions— one that was unavailable prior to the development of computer imaging.

To show where the lighting equipment will be placed, the lighting designer produces a light plot, which is a scale drawing that details the placement of the lighting instruments relative to the physical structure of the theatre and the location of the set. The techniques and materials that the lighting designer uses are discussed in Chapters 12 (*Lighting Design*), 13 (*Electrical Theory and Practice*), 14 (*Lighting Production*), and 15 (*Projections*).

Assistant Lighting Designer   While the lighting designer's primary duty is to concentrate on the artistic elements of the lighting design, it is often said that a lighting design is only as good as its paperwork. Producing that paperwork is the role of the assistant lighting designer, also known as the lighting associate. This person is responsible for creating and continually updating the various types of paperwork that are an essential element of any good lighting design.

hanging: Placing lighting instruments and equipment in the designated positions on the light plot.

focusing: Directing light from the lighting instruments to a specific area.

running: Controlling or operating some aspect of production.

circuit: To connect a lighting instrument to a stage circuit.

patch: To connect a stage circuit to a dimmer circuit.

hookup sheet: A sheet containing pertinent information (hanging position, circuit, dimmer, color, lamp wattage, focusing notes) about every lighting instrument used in the production. Also known as an instrument schedule.

color media: The colored plastic, gel, or glass filters used in lighting instruments.

focus: To direct light from a lighting instrument to a specific location.

That paperwork will be explained in Chapter 12, *Lighting Design*. The assistant lighting designer may also, at the discretion of the designer, assist with focusing, organization of work, and so forth.

Master Electrician   The master electrician, under the supervision of the lighting designer, implements the lighting design. He or she is directly responsible for the acquisition, installation, and maintenance of all lighting equipment and the supervision of the crews who hang, focus, and run the lighting equipment.

Electricians   The work of the electricians can be divided into three areas: **hanging, focusing,** and **running.** The *hanging crew* places the lighting instruments and associated equipment in the positions designated by the light plot. They also **circuit** and **patch** the instruments. The circuit and dimmer for each instrument are indicated on the light plot or **hookup sheet;** or the master electrician designates the appropriate circuit and dimmer during the hanging session. The hanging crew also puts the **color media** on the lighting instruments and, under the supervision of the lighting designer, **focuses** the instruments.

The *running crew* is responsible for the operation of the lighting equipment during the rehearsals and performances. Depending on the complexity of the production, as few as one or as many as five or more electricians are needed to run the lights.

Costume Personnel

Those staff members who are responsible for the production's costumes include the costume designer, costume shop supervisor, cutter/draper, and costume construction crew.

Costume Designer   The costume designer is responsible for the visual appearance of the actors. These responsibilities will include what isn't seen as well as what is. Clothes and accessories are seen. Undergarments aren't. But undergarments can be just as important. Corsets, hoops, and boning create the distinctive silhouette and appearance that tell us much about the costumes of specific periods. Additionally, character elements such as padded stomachs, sagging bosoms, and so forth add greatly to the audience's understanding of the nature of each character. The visible costume elements include the clothes, accessories (shoes, hats, purses, canes, parasols), jewelry, wigs, and makeup worn by the actors during the performance.

Designs for theatrical costumes consist of colored sketches depicting the clothing and accessories that will be worn by the actor. In the case of complex costume designs, sketches that show more than one view may be needed. In either case, the sketches, which can be either hand- or computer-drawn and painted, normally have appropriate construction notes jotted in the margins, and small swatches of the fabrics and trims from which the costumes will be made are usually attached to the sketches. Additional information about costume and makeup design as well as costume production can be found in Chapters 16 (*Costume Design*), 17 (*Costume Construction*), and 18 (*Makeup*).

Costume Shop Supervisor   The costumer shop supervisor, also known as the costumer, is the person who, under the artistic supervision of the costume designer, builds or supervises the building of the costumes. The costumer must be able to read and translate the costume designer's sketches into working garments, be skilled in all phases of costume construction, and be able to work with the designer and actors as well as supervise the shop personnel. In many operations, the costumer is also responsible for maintaining the costume shop equipment and keeping the shop inventory of basic supplies current.

In larger costume operations, the duties of the costume shop supervisor are frequently divided into two parts—the costume shop and the craft shop. Each may have its own manager, although the craft shop sometimes is managed by an assistant to the costume shop supervisor. With this type of organization the duties are divided between the shops. The costume shop constructs the costumes—cuts, drapes, sews the fabric—while the craft shop generally creates "crafty" things—dyeing and painting fabric before it is cut and constructing shoes, accessories, millinery, jewelry, and specialty costumes such as animals, masks, and so forth.

Additional information about the work of the costumer and costume construction can be found in Chapter 17, *Costume Construction.*

Costume Crew   The costume crew can be divided into several specialty areas. Depending on the type (professional or educational) and size of the costume operation, these areas may or may not have their own heads, assistant heads, and crew members.

The *cutter/draper* is responsible for actually translating the designer's sketches into reality. He or she devises an appropriate pattern using either draping or flat-patterning methods and, generally, cuts the fabric. This is an extremely important job because not only the shape of the pattern, but how it is cut from the fabric—how the pattern is placed on the fabric in relation to the **warp and weft** or grain of the fabric—greatly affects the finished appearance of the costume. The *first hand* may also do some cutting from patterns developed by the cutter/draper, but this job is generally to supervise the construction of the costumes. Sewing of the costumes is done by *stitchers* who operate the machines and do the hand sewing that pieces the costumes together. Depending on the size of the production, there may be more than one cutter/draper on the show. If so, their responsibilities are frequently divided along gender lines, with one team (cutter/draper, first hand, stitchers) making the female costumes and another team making the male costumes.

Dyer/painters dye and paint the fabric. They select and mix the dyes to the costume designer's specifications, dye the fabric before it is cut, paint or embellish finished costumes to add dimension, and distress or age costumes to make them look old and worn.

Hats are an important accessory for many period and contemporary costumes. They are frequently made in the costume shop by the *milliner.* Wigs, like hats, are an important part of costuming. The *wigmaster* not only styles and arranges wigs but also makes them.

Although many theatres adapt modern footwear through the use of appliqúes that disguise the period of the footwear being worn, a complete costume shop frequently has the necessary equipment and expertise required to construct period footwear, or it has access to a company that produces this specialized work. The person who does this work is generally referred to as the *costume craftsperson.*

After the show moves into dress rehearsals and performances, the *wardrobe supervisor* is responsible for all costumes and accessories. Under the wardrobe supervisor's guidance, the costume crew cleans, presses, stores, and organizes the costumes, **dresses** any wigs or hairpieces to create a specific style or look, and makes any necessary costume-related repairs. The costume crew also places all costumes and accessories in their appropriate locations—actors' lockers,

warp and weft: The vertical and horizontal threads in a fabric.

dress: In this context, dress refers to the process of curling, combing, teasing, and/or brushing necessary to maintain the style of a wig or hairpiece.

quick-change dressing rooms, and so forth—before and during the dress rehearsals and performances. During dress rehearsals and performances, *dressers* may assist the actors in getting into their costumes, quick changes, and so forth.

Sound Personnel

Those who create the sound for a production include the sound designer and the sound crew.

Sound Designer   The sound designer is responsible for the design, recording, equipment setup, and playback of any sound used in the play. The sound design can vary in complexity from simple recorded music used during intermissions to meticulously designed aural special effects used to underscore the entire production. This newest design field in theatre is very challenging; it will be discussed in greater depth in Chapter 19, *Sound Design and Technology.*

sound-reinforcement system: The amplification of sound coming from the stage.

Sound Crew   Under the supervision of the sound designer, the sound crew does the actual recording, editing, and playback of sound during rehearsals and performances. The sound crew is also responsible for the running of any **sound-reinforcement systems** during the production.

Chapter 2
The Design Process

It may come as a rude shock, but design is more a process than an art. It is a series of steps through which we pursue the goal of creating what we hope will be a work of art—a scenic design, costume design, lighting design, or audio design—or the artistry of an efficiently coordinated production. The design process is a method for finding answers to questions. Although the examples and terms used in this chapter will direct your thinking toward theatrical design and production, the principles of the design process can be applied with equally productive results to acting, directing, and, for that matter, life in general. These principles and techniques can help you discover an appropriate and creative solution to virtually any design problem or challenge you may encounter. A problem-solving model for theatrical design and production consists of seven distinct phases: (1) commitment, (2) analysis, (3) research, (4) incubation, (5) selection, (6) implementation, and (7) evaluation.

Unfortunately, the design process isn't a simple, linear progression. As you move from step to step, you must check back on your previous steps to make sure that you are headed in the right direction with your proposed solution. Figure 2.1 shows the back-and-forth movement that occurs as you move through the various stages of the design process. Although Satchel Paige, the wise old pitcher, once advised, "Don't look back; something may be gaining on you," you would do well to look back during your progression through the design process, because the thing gaining on you could be a new thought, a better mousetrap.

A perceptive teacher/designer, Alison Ford, suggests that "perhaps good design is the intersection between the emotional and intellectual realms." While the process being discussed in this chapter is primarily intellectual, it is essential for you to understand that emotions are an equally important part of the design equation. Your emotional reaction to the script and the production concept will intuitively guide your design work on any project. Audience members strongly respond to the emotional content of a production—the story told by the script, the personalities of the characters and their interrelationships, as well as the scenic, costume, lighting, and sound designs. When working through any design process, you need to include your emotional reactions and personal life experiences as part of that process. This will greatly assist you in developing your own design ideas and your personal artistic point of view. Not coincidentally, your work probably will be better for it.

COMMITMENT

Commitment is probably the most important step in the whole design process. If you wholeheartedly *commit* your energies to an assignment, you are promising yourself that you will do the best work you can possibly do.

FIGURE 2.1
The design process is not simply a linear progression. As you move through the steps of the design process, you monitor your progress by continually checking back to see where you have been.

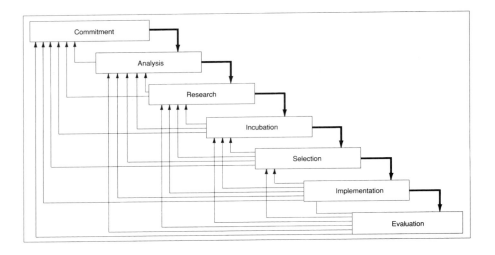

A simple semantic game may help you commit yourself to an assignment. Use the word *problem* as infrequently as possible—it has a negative connotation—and substitute the word *challenge*. Everybody likes a challenge: The word itself hints at fun, games, and competition. When your problem has been transformed into a challenge, it automatically becomes more interesting and manageable.

ANALYSIS

The analysis step in the design process has two objectives: (1) gathering information that will help clarify and refine the definition of the challenge you are facing and (2) identifying areas that will require further research. Analysis in theatrical production is primarily a search for information and an objective evaluation of the data you discover. Prime sources of this information are the script and other members of the production design team—the producer, director, and your fellow designers. In your discussions with them, you need to examine everything—production style, concepts, budgets, schedules—that is relevant to your design project. "*Who* is producing the play? *What* is the production budget? *Where* is the play being produced? *When* is the design due? *Why* are we doing this play? *How* is the scenery being moved from the shop to the theatre?" The answers to these questions will provide you with information that will further define and clarify your challenge. Each answer should also raise another question or two in your mind. Ask them. This **stream-of-consciousness questioning** can provide you with invaluable information about your challenge.

At some point in your information gathering, you will read the script. Some designers prefer to read the script before they talk to other members of the production design team; others wait until later. Either way is fine. There isn't any rule about when you should read the script. Just make sure that you discuss it and share your ideas with the other members of the production design team.

Analyzing the Script

Although it is not at all unusual for designers to read scripts many times, they usually undertake the first three readings of the script with specific objectives in mind. The arbitrarily designated "first three readings" should be considered as a somewhat allegorical reference. Information can be gathered, and emotional or evocative reactions can occur, during any reading. The important point is that

stream-of-consciousness questioning: Asking whatever relevant questions pop into your mind in the course of a discussion.

there are three related but distinct sets of information that any designer needs to glean from the script.

First Reading   The first time you sit down with the script, read it for fun. Discover the flavor of the play. Learn its general story line, the nature of its characters, their interrelationships, and your emotional response to the play. One of the first things you see when you open the script is the description of the physical environment of the play. Usually written in italics just before the opening lines, it describes the set and, occasionally, the costumes, sound, and lights. Unless you are working from an original script, these descriptions are usually taken from the stage manager's prompt book for the first major professional production of the play and explain the specific designs for that particular production. These descriptions shouldn't be thought of as the correct design solutions for the play; they are just one way that the show can be designed. Your production, along with your audience, is entitled to a fresh design treatment that will be appropriate to its personnel, time, place, and budget. To believe that you have to, or should, copy the original design is an insult to your creative ability. Use the descriptive information in the script along with the other information you gather to synthesize an original design concept.

Second Reading   During the metaphorical second reading of the script, you should be looking for specific moments and incidents within the play that stimulate your imagination and provide you with strong visual and textural images and feelings. These inspirations are random, often disconnected, thoughts, impressions, and emotions about the appearance of the various design elements. Jot them down. If they are more visual than verbal, sketch them. Carry a small notebook with you. Whenever a thought, idea, or emotion about the play pops into your mind, regardless of how inconsequential it seems, put it in your notebook. These thoughts and emotional responses can be anything relevant to the design challenge. A thought about a character's texture—"He is rough like burlap"—is an idea that should be noted. An impression that the atmosphere of the play is hot, heavy, and sticky is important. Your sense that the play is soft and curved, not sharp and hard, should also be noted.

As you continue to reread the play, you will get more ideas. Ideas will also appear when you are not reading the script. They can materialize when you are talking to the director, discussing the play with another designer, eating breakfast, or walking to class. Don't judge the ideas at this point. Gather information now, and weed later.

Third Reading   In the metaphorical third reading, you are looking for specific mechanical information rather than broadly based concepts. For example, set designers look for such things as the number of sets, whether the scene changes are going to happen in front of the audience or behind the curtain, and specific requirements such as a closet door that needs to be hinged on the upstage side. Information that affects the budgets (time and fiscal) should also be noted at this time. Such notes include any special properties, construction, costumes, or effects that will require extra time or money.

Information from the third reading is gathered not only from reading the script but also from conferences with other members of the production-design team. As with the first and second readings, all of this information needs to be put in your notebook.

The Questioning Process

Questioning is one of the keys to creativity. Your drive to create is based, to a great extent, on your perceived need for change, or your creative discontent with

Talk It Over

The most unified production concepts are developed as a result of talking. In a production of *Cabaret* at the University of Arizona, the production design team began preliminary concept discussions in early January for a production that was to open on April 25.

The director indicated at the first meeting that he wanted to stress the decadence of Berlin society. Our initial informal discussions centered on what this decadence should look like. Someone said that the cabaret should appear to be below ground level (to subliminally support the idea of descending into the hell that was about to engulf Germany). Another person mentioned that it could be useful to have four towers onstage with followspots on top, because the audience might make a connection between them and the guard towers in a concentration camp.

The director said he wanted to have the cabaret audience watching the onstage action (cabaret and noncabaret scenes) at all times. He thought that this device would add an appropriately voyeuristic quality. Ideas just seemed to pop up as we all became more excited about the project.

Within a month, we developed the production concept through our discussions at these once-a-week meetings. We all brought rough sketches, photos, and ideas to every meeting. We discussed everything—acting style, acting areas, color, visual motifs, atmosphere, history. When the deadline for final designs arrived, we all knew what everyone else was thinking and doing.

This example shows what can happen when the production design team, under the leadership and coordination of the director, works together to evolve the production concept. For a variety of reasons, however, it frequently isn't possible for the director and designers to sit around a table and work together to develop the production concept. When this happens, a good director usually adopts a more authoritarian posture in the development of the production concept. He or she develops a primary production concept and discusses it in individual meetings with the designers. The designers then work toward this concept.

The two methods work equally well. Quality productions can be achieved with either method. The common denominator is communication. A good production concept can evolve only if the director and designers talk to one another and share their ideas, thoughts, and imagination.

the status quo. If you are satisfied with everything in your world, you will see no need to change, modify, or create anything.

To analyze effectively, it is necessary to shed fear—fear of criticism, fear of making mistakes, fear of seeming less than brilliant, fear of being thought a fool or somehow different. Fear inhibits thinking and makes us afraid to ask questions. All too frequently I hear students in my classes say, "I don't want to ask a dumb question, but . . ." As far as I am concerned, the only dumb question is one that isn't asked.

Analyze the script, question the director, question the other members of the production design team, and question the producer. Learn what they are thinking, feeling, and planning for the production. Analyze what they say. See how it fits in with your reactions and plans. The more information you receive, the more source material you will have to draw on when you finally begin to design.

RESEARCH

As you gather information, you will discover small pockets of knowledge in which your personal experience and background are weak. List them in your notebook as the areas in which research is necessary. You will be doing both background research and conceptual research.

Background Research

Designers have to study the historical background of each production they design. This type of research involves searching the library for books, catalogs, paintings, periodicals, and other sources of information about the era.

How Did It Look?

A number of references are helpful in any search for visual information. Photo magazines such as *Life* and *National Geographic* contain excellent pictures of costumes, furniture, props, and decoration for plays set in the twentieth century. Department-store catalogs can provide additional visual information for the turn of the century and earlier. Visual information about earlier eras must usually be gleaned from paintings, sculpture, and engravings. Art history books have photographs of these items.

The ultimate use of these visual references is up to the individual designer. Some designers faithfully reproduce a costume or piece of furniture so that they can be sure the "look" they have achieved is authentic for the desired period. Other designers study a variety of sources and then design something new that reflects the general style of the period.

Your historical research should include reading about previous productions of the play and *may* include looking at photos, sketches, and models of those prior productions. But don't think that you *must* look at any visual references of prior productions. If you choose to look at them, simply use them as references for one way that the play was once produced. Don't fall prey to the temptation to copy someone else's work. That stifles your own creativity and, more pragmatically, is illegal in most states. While you shouldn't copy someone else's work, you should also be sure that you don't try to create something so original that it blinds you to the playwright's intention. Remember, the root of any viable design is based in the script.

Additional background research in the field of color will also be necessary for all designers. A thorough understanding of this extremely important area will enable the designer to match and blend colors in pigment and light. Addi-

Historical Relevance for Design

Although each designer must look at visual material relevant to his or her design area, all designers should also study the history of the period. As an example, the costume designer needs to know the history and style of dress of the era of the play. This study could begin with a look at a text on costume history to get a general understanding of the style of the time. More detailed study will also be necessary. You can look at paintings, photos, museum displays, catalogs, and any other sources that illustrate the fashion of dress for the period.

An understanding of the socioeconomic background of the play's environment is also useful, because clothing styles are usually a reflection of the morals and economics of the time. Throughout the major periods of fashion, there have been subtle, and sometimes not so subtle, shifts of style based on the socioeconomic status of the individual. Servants have rarely dressed like their employers, and it has usually been fairly easy to differentiate between classes based on the cut and quality of their clothes.

Additional research into the arts (painting, sculpture, literature, music) and history of the playwright's era can provide information on the world that shaped the author's thinking. Essays and critical reviews of the playwright's work are another good source of background information.

Unblocking Your Thinking

How can we get rid of our perceptual blocks? By eliminating the cause, we can usually eliminate the block. Proper identification of the real challenge is extremely important. Many times challenges are not what they first seem to be. If a play requires three sets, one of the design challenges would be to devise ways to shift among them. To most of us that would mean finding ways to move the sets. We see sets shifted in this way all the time—it's normal. But couldn't the challenge be solved just as well by putting all three locales on a unit set and shifting the audience's attention by lighting only the part of the set that we want it to see? or by using three separate theatres, each with its own set, and having the audience move? or by having two of the sets hidden behind the upstage wall of the third set and moving sections of the wall to reveal the appropriate set? These additional solutions to the challenge are the result of nothing more than a careful examination of the specific question being posed in the challenge.

Define Your Challenge More Broadly

If you thought about the traditional ways of shifting between sets in the previous problem, you were defining the challenge too closely. By unconsciously limiting your quest for possible solutions to the traditionally accepted methods, you were shutting off a whole realm of new, potentially effective solutions to the challenge. Think creatively about the elements of the challenge, and don't accept only the commonplace answers to the questions posed in the challenge.

Overcome Tunnel Vision

When working on a design it is very easy, and egocentrically convenient, to fall into the trap of not seeing your assignment from the viewpoint of others involved in the challenge. When designing scenery, it is very easy to put a ceiling on the set without worrying about how this is going to affect the lighting design. Similarly, when determining the width of doors to be used on your set, it is easy to forget that the costume designer is planning to use hoop skirts that measure four feet in diameter at the hem.

Tunnel vision can be avoided if members of the production design team discuss their ideas in production meetings. By conferring on a regular basis, the director and designers can remain aware of everyone else's work as it progresses from conception to completion.

Avoid Visual Stereotyping

Visual stereotyping refers to seeing what you expect to see rather than what is actually in front of you. It limits your ability to conceive of existing elements in new combinations. If you expect to see casters attached to the bottom of a stage wagon, it may be difficult for you to envision turning the casters upside down and attaching them to the stage floor. But that "inverted" thinking may provide an effective solution to the problem of shifting scenery for a complex show when you don't have enough casters to accomplish the task in the more conventional manner.

Remember Details Selectively

People remember things selectively. If we decide that something doesn't have great personal significance, we tend to forget it. To demonstrate this principle try to draw, from memory, a detailed sketch of the front door of your house, apartment, or dorm room. Most people can't do it. We see and use the door several times every day, but most of us never look at it very closely.

All of us remember details that we have determined will be important for us to recall. Albert Einstein was reputed not to have known his own telephone number. When asked why, he reportedly said that he didn't want to clutter up his mind with information he could look up.

Although it is very important for a designer or technician to have a thorough knowledge of the various subjects that make up his or her field of expertise, it is equally important to follow Einstein's dictum and not clutter up your mind with details that can be found fairly easily in a reference work.

tionally, by studying the psychology of color, you will be able to design color keys that help the audience understand the primary character motivations and relationships in the play. Color is discussed in Chapter 6.

Conceptual Research

Conceptual research involves devising multiple solutions to specific design challenges. In reading a script, for example, you may discover that the heroine leaves the stage at the end of Act I in a beautiful gown and reappears at the start of Act II with the same dress in tatters. Your conceptual research would be to figure out as many ways as possible to solve this challenge.

A snag frequently encountered during conceptual research is our apparently natural inability to conceive of any more than two or three possible solutions to any given challenge. Too often our brains go numb and refuse to dream up new ideas. In psychology this type of nonthinking state is referred to as a perceptual block. If the perceptual block can be eliminated, our ability to devise, or create, additional solutions to any given problem is greatly improved. In other words, the removal of perceptual blocks increases our personal creative ability.

INCUBATION

How many times, having left the room after finishing an exam, have you suddenly remembered the answer to a question that eluded you while you were writing the test? How many times have you come up with the solution to a problem after having "slept on it"? In both of these cases, the information necessary to answer the questions was locked in your subconscious and only needed time and stress reduction to allow the answer to float into your consciousness.

Incubation provides you with time to let ideas hatch. During this time, you should basically forget about the project. Your subconscious mind will use the time to sort through the information you've gathered in the previous steps and may construct a solution to the challenge or point you in a valid direction.

Give yourself enough time to let your subconscious mind mull over the data that you have absorbed. How much time is enough? That depends on the scope or size of the project and, realistically, the amount of time remaining until the project is due. "Enough time" can be anywhere from a few hours to several days. It simply isn't possible to do your best work if you wait for the deadline and then rush through the assignment. You are more likely to produce quality work if you allow time for incubation.

SELECTION

Selection is the step in the design process in which you sift through all of the data you've accumulated and decide on your specific design concept. Because the choices of each designer affect the work of all members of the production design team, everyone's designs need to be discussed in another production meeting.

The scenic designer draws as many **thumbnail sketches** as necessary to explain the scenic concepts for the production (see Figure 2.2). If the sets for the play are complex or the sketches do not fully explain the concepts, then a **functional model** of each set idea may be constructed. Alternatively, a computer model of the set can be constructed. These virtual models can be viewed from a variety of angles and help to fully communicate the scenic designer's intentions. If there is a lot of scenic movement—wagons sliding on and off stage, set elements rotating, drops flying in or out, and so forth—an animated computer presentation can be used to clearly show their timing and scope.

The scenic designer also provides an indication of the intended color scheme with the thumbnail sketches. This can be done by coloring on them or by accompanying them with color sample cards (paint chips).

The costume designer provides hand- or computer-drawn sketches or pictures of the intended costumes. Although the costume designer attaches fabric swatches to the final costume renderings, these preliminary sketches require only an indication of the color and type of fabric that will be used (see Figure 2.3).

The lighting designer submits sketches or computer presentations showing the general characteristics of the concept for the lighting design, if such sketches are appropriate. At the least, he or she presents the intended palette and a verbal description of the atmospheric effect of the lighting during the production

thumbnail sketch: A small, quick, rough drawing, usually done in pencil, that shows the major outline, character, and feeling of the object but does not have much detail.

functional model: A three-dimensional thumbnail sketch of the scenic design; normally built on a scale of one-half or one-quarter inch to one foot; usually made from illustration board, Bristol board, file folders or similar cardboard; also known as a white model.

FIGURE 2.2
Thumbnail sketches for the University of Arizona Department of Drama's production of *Nicholas Nickleby,* scenic design by Tom Benson, directed by Harold Dixon and Dianne Winslow. The first sketch (A) shows a basically symmetrical platform arrangement flowing from the upstage center high point down toward the edges of the proscenium. The set has an elaborate gridwork behind the platforms and a planked wooden floor. (B) The directors and designer made notes and sketches on a copy of the design as they discussed modifications to the set. (C) The stage right platforms were then opened to make the space underneath more usable, and the downstage left staircase was curled further onto the stage, making the set asymmetrical and more dynamic. The background gridwork was also abstracted, and the planked floor was eliminated to make the central floor more visually useful. In the final sketch (D), some of the background gridwork was angled to create a more dynamic line, and the lighting instruments were included as a scenic element.

FIGURE 2.3
The costume designer uses preliminary pencil sketches as a visual notebook to record ideas that may ultimately find their way into a finished costume design. Preliminary costume designs by Peggy Kellner for *MacBeth*, produced at the Old Globe Theatre, San Diego, California.

meeting. The sound designer discusses the sound scoring—the types of background and specific sound and musical effects—as well as the location and function of the various speakers' setups.

The selection phase of the design process is finished when the director feels satisfied that all design areas support the production design concept.

IMPLEMENTATION

The implementation phase begins when you stop planning and start doing. At this time the designers produce all drawings, models, plans, and instructions necessary to construct the scenic, lighting, costume, and sound designs.

The scenic designer makes the final color renderings for each set of the production and, if necessary, constructs **production models** of the sets. He or she also drafts the plans that describe, to scale, all the details of how the set should look (see Figure 2.4). After completing the paperwork for the design, the scenic designer monitors the progress of the construction of the set(s) and properties to make sure that they are completed according to plan, on time, and within budget.

The lighting designer draws the light plot as well as the other paperwork associated with the lighting design (see Figure 2.5). He or she then supervises the hanging and focusing of the lights and determines the intensity levels and timing for all lighting cues.

The costume designer produces colored renderings for each costume, complete with notes and sketches that fully describe the accessories as well as the

production model: A scale model, similar to the functional model but fully painted and complete with all furniture and decorative props.

FIGURE 2.4
Finished scenic design for *Nicholas Nickleby.* (A) The production model, (B) the ground plan, (C) (on page 32) some construction drawings.

(A)

(B)

(continued)

FIGURE 2.4
(continued)

(C)

general style, period, and feeling of the costume (see Figure 2.6). Fabric samples and trims are attached to each sketch to indicate the various materials to be used. These designs are turned over to the costume shop. The costume designer maintains close contact with the shop to determine that the costumes are being built as planned and will be completed on time and within budget.

The sound designer completes the **sound plot** and begins gathering and recording the various musical and effects cues, as well as assembling the necessary playback equipment and speaker systems. During the technical and dress

sound plot: A list describing each sound cue in the production.

FIGURE 2.5
The light plot for *Nicholas Nickleby.*
The lighting designer uses the light
plot to codify his or her design.

The Gobo Trick

A lot of art is the result of happy accident. While sitting in the auditorium during technical rehearsals for some forgotten production, I noticed that one area of the stage floor seemed to have a rough texture. I went up on stage and looked more closely. The floor didn't have any texture; it was painted a smooth, flat color. Then I looked up at the lights. One of the instruments had a gobo (a thin metal template that creates a shadow pattern) left in it from a previous production. That instrument was creating the texture. Although I took the gobo out of the instrument, I remembered the effect. Now whenever I want to create a textured atmosphere I put gobos in the instruments.

The moral? Always evaluate what you've done, even if you think it's a "mistake." Just because something isn't right for one situation doesn't mean it won't be right for another.

rehearsals, the sound designer determines the appropriate loudness levels for each sound cue and does any necessary rerecording or reediting.

At this time, the technical director completes the production calendar, makes any necessary construction drawings, orders the materials for construction of all sets and props, organizes the crews, and begins construction. During rehearsals the director's view of the production concept will probably change or evolve as the actors become involved. Minor changes should be expected as part of the process of putting a production together. Production meetings during the implementation phase help to ensure that the information keeps flowing.

FIGURE 2.6
The costume designer provides annotated colored sketches of the costumes, complete with samples of the fabrics to be used, to the costume shop for construction of the costumes. Costume design for *Two Gentlemen of Verona* by Peggy Kellner, Old Globe Theatre, San Diego, California.

EVALUATION

Evaluation takes place within each step of the design process, and it also occurs when the project is completed. This final evaluation, or review, is not so much a back-patting session as an examination of the methods and materials used in the final design goal. All designers evaluate their selections to see if they were appropriate and to determine if they could be used in the future in another context.

All members of the production design team look objectively at the interchanges and communication process that took place inside and outside the various production conferences to see if they can improve the communication the next time around. The designers also evaluate the judgments they made to see if anything that might have helped was left out, ignored, or rejected.

As you become more familiar with the design process, you will discover that your own work is more creative and that you can produce it faster and more easily. The design process described here is a valuable, efficient, time-saving, and frustration-reducing tool. Use it and enjoy.

Chapter 3
Theatre Architecture

"Last night the curtain rose at the . . ." could have begun almost any theatrical critic's review during the 1940s or 1950s. Interestingly, the curtain rises on few productions these days, not for a lack of productions but because two of the three current styles of stage configuration don't use a front curtain. Of the three types of theatrical space used in the modern theatre—**proscenium, thrust,** and **arena** (see Figure 3.1)—only one, the proscenium, has a front curtain. Each of these spaces has its own set of design and staging requirements, but they have all evolved from the same common heritage: the theatres of ancient Greece.

GREEK THEATRE

Our knowledge of Greek or Roman theatres is based almost exclusively on archaeological studies and educated guessing. No one can say with authority that "this is the way it was." My summary offers the same disclaimers.

In practical reality, there was no single style or type of Greek theatre. A number of elements, however, seem to have been common to almost all the ones we know. The typical Greek amphitheatre illustrated in Figure 3.2 is a composite reconstruction based on a number of theatres dating from the fifth century B.C.

The steeply raked seating area for the audience, called the auditorium, or *theatron,* surrounded on three sides the circular playing area, known as the *orchestra.* Immediately in back of the orchestra was the *skene* (skee'-nee), or stage house. The front wall of the skene probably had several doors or arches through which actors made their entrances. The exact purpose of the skene isn't known, but since it hid the actors from the audience's view and contained a number of rooms, it is assumed that it served various functions such as housing for stage machinery, storage for props, and possibly space for dressing rooms. The *paraskenia* were long, high walls that extended on either side of and parallel with the skene. It is believed that a low platform, about a foot high, extended across the front of the *paraskenia.* On later Greek theatres, they did not extend directly from the skene but were placed closer to the audience. A natural byproduct of this relocation was to extend the low platform across the front of the skene to create a platformed stage. A columned arch, the *proskenium,* was located at the rear of this stage and just in front of the skene. It served to support a porchlike projection from the second story of the skene.

proscenium: A stage configuration in which the spectators watch the action through a rectangular opening (the proscenium arch) that resembles a picture frame.

thrust stage: A stage projecting into, and surrounded on three sides by, the audience.

arena stage: A stage completely surrounded by the audience.

FIGURE 3.1
Examples of (A) proscenium,
(B) thrust, and (C) arena theatres.

(A)

(B)

(C)

FIGURE 3.2
A typical Greek theatre.

ROMAN THEATRE

Roman architects tinkered with Greek designs, but most of their theatres were simply modifications of the basic Greek form. The most conspicuous Roman development was the compression of the three separate parts of the traditional Greek theatre (orchestra, auditorium, and skene) into one structure. The integration of these elements caused some interesting developments in the structure of the Roman theatre, as shown in Figure 3.3. The auditorium (called a *cavea*) was limited to a semicircular configuration. In many of the theatres, the *cavea* was separated from the orchestra by a short wall. The orchestra became a semicircle extending outward from the stage area, which was framed by the proscenium. The *skene* was transformed into an elaborately decorated single facade called the *scaenae frons.* Its height generally matched the height of the *cavea.*

A number of subtle changes were also brought about by the development of the consolidated Roman theatre structure. The theatres were usually built on level ground instead of the hillside sites favored by the Greeks. In addition, a roofing system was developed for a number of the theatres. The roof extended from the *scaenae frons* to the edge of the proscenium. Some of the theatres even had an awning, known as a *velum,* covering the entire seating area.

With the fall of the Roman Empire in A.D. 364, these grand theatres, which were also the sites of circuses, gladiatorial fights, and lion feedings (Christians and slaves being the primary food), were essentially abandoned, silent relics of a lost era. For approximately five hundred years after the empire fell, the formal theatre was virtually dead. Yet the theatrical tradition was kept alive by bands of traveling entertainers, primarily actors and jugglers. These vagabonds surreptitiously performed wherever they could find an audience—in courtyards, village squares, and other temporary stage locations.

MEDIEVAL THEATRE

During the Middle Ages, the suppression of theatrical activities was a direct result of the church's opposition to secular drama. Yet the same church that denied the sacraments to actors was also responsible for the revival of the theatre. Sometime during the tenth century, clerics began to use dramatized scenes to help convey their lessons and church doctrine to congregations. During the

FIGURE 3.3
A typical Roman theatre.

thirteenth century, many of these interludes became too complex to be staged inside the churches, so they were moved outdoors. Staging techniques naturally varied from church to church and location to location. Platform stages were generally constructed adjacent to the church, and the audience stood in the town square (see Figure 3.4). In some cases, the platforms were mounted on wagons, appropriately called *pageant wagons* (Figure 3.5), which were pulled from town to town to perform the plays.

All of these productions shared some common characteristics. The sets were identical, in concept if not detail, and followed the conventions that had been developed by the clergy for the church productions. The sets were composed of small buildings called *mansions,* or stations, that depicted locations appropriate to the biblical stories dramatized in the productions (see Figure 3.6).

The mansions for heaven and hell were on opposite ends of the stage, with the other mansions sandwiched between them. There was a common playing area, called a *platea,* located in front of the mansions, where most of the play's action took place.

One interesting byproduct of the medieval theatre was the development of a large number of relatively realistic special effects. Stage machinery, fittingly called *secrets,* included trap doors and a wide variety of rigging that was used to move people and objects about the stages. In one account of "a play staged at Mons [a city in southwestern Belgium] in 1501, technicians were hired to

FIGURE 3.4
A platform stage.

FIGURE 3.5
A pageant wagon.

FIGURE 3.6
A typical medieval mansion stage.

construct the secrets, and seventeen people were needed to operate the hell machinery alone; five men were paid to paint the scenery, and four actor-prompters were employed both to act and to help with the staging."[1]

RENAISSANCE THEATRE

With the Renaissance, the theatre became a central part of the cultural reawakening that quickly spread throughout Europe. Although church-sanctioned pageants continued, secular drama reemerged and became the dominant theatrical form. Theatres, which hadn't been permitted or constructed for over a thousand years, sprang up all over Europe. Because of the strong interest in classical forms

Stage Machinery

Although most of the scenes in Greek plays were set outdoors, the Greeks used several devices to move or change scenery. The *eccyclema*, a wheeled platform, was apparently used in a variety of ways. If a scene called for a throne, the central doors in the *skene* were opened and the *eccyclema*, with a throne on top, was rolled forward. One of the Greeks' theatrical conventions dictated that violent deaths take place offstage, but the bodies were later revealed onstage. The *eccyclema*, this time piled with corpses, was again rolled onto the stage.

Periaktoi, which probably date from the fourth century B.C., were tall, three-sided forms that rotated on a central pivot. Each side was painted with a different scene. Although their exact use isn't known, they were probably placed in the background, and when a change of scene was desired, the *periaktoi* were rotated to reveal another face.

Possibly the most interesting machine was the *machina* (ma-kee'-na). This was a basket or platform that was lowered to the orchestra level from the second story of the *skene*. Many plays called for intervention by the gods, and the *machina* was used to help the gods descend to, or rise from, the earth.

1. Oscar G. Brockett, *The Theatre: An Introduction,* 4th ed. (New York: Holt, Rinehart and Winston, 1979), p. 106.

FIGURE 3.7
The Teatro Olympico.

and structures, the basic shape of almost all these theatres corresponded with the description of Greek and Roman theatres contained in the architectural writings of Vitruvius. Although the theatres were patterned after the classical forms, their designers made many interesting, and clever, adaptations.

The Teatro Olympico in Vicenza, Italy, was one of these theatres (see Figure 3.7). Built between 1580 and 1585, it was designed in the style of the ancient Roman theatres. Probably the most significant change was that the theatre finally moved indoors, with the entire structure enclosed in a building. The *cavea*, or auditorium, was designed not as an exact semicircle but as an ellipse, and this minor change dramatically improved the sight lines in the theatre. The *scaenae frons* was no longer a single decorated wall but was broken by several arches; elaborate permanent sets of street scenes were built, in **forced perspective,** on a **raked stage** floor in back of the arches. In many Renaissance theatres, the stage floors were raked to improve the visual effects of the scenery. The actors normally performed on a flat playing space in front of the raked stage.

A second minor Renaissance innovation in southern Europe was the introduction of elaborately painted scenery. The use of **stock sets**—usually painted **drops** of the "comic scene," the "tragic scene," the "satyric scene," and so on— necessitated the evolution of the proscenium, or picture frame, stage. Drops were usually hung at the upstage edge of the stage.

forced perspective: A visual-distortion technique that increases the apparent depth of an object.

raked stage: A stage floor that is higher at the back than the front.

stock set: Scenery designed to visually support a generalized location (garden, city street, palace, interior) rather than a specific one; commonly used from the Renaissance through the early twentieth century and still in use today in some theatres.

drop: A large expanse of cloth, usually muslin or canvas, on which something (a landscape, sky, street, room) is painted.

ELIZABETHAN THEATRE

At approximately the same time, drama in England was being produced in a different type of structure. A number of theatres had been constructed just outside London by 1600. Probably the most famous was the Globe (1599–1632), the home theatre of William Shakespeare (see Figure 3.8). Although these theatres differed in detail, their basic shape was similar.

The stage of a typical Elizabethan theatre was a large, open-air platform generally raised from four to six feet off the ground (see Figure 3.9). The platform was surrounded by a yard, or *pit*, which served as the space for the lower-class audience—the groundlings—to stand. At the upstage end of the stage platform was the area that formed the *inner below*. There is some dispute about the shape of this structure. One theory maintains that it was a curtained alcove recessed into the upstage wall. Another hypothesis holds that it was a roofed structure, curtained on three sides, that projected a little way onto the stage platform. A final theory contends that there was no inner below at all. Depending on the

Inner below

Inner above

Pit

Stage

FIGURE 3.9
The stage of the Globe Theatre.

theory to which you subscribe, the *inner above* was an area above the inner below on the back wall, or the acting area provided by the roof of the structure that projected onto the stage, or an area that didn't exist as a playing space. In any case, separate entrances apparently flanked either side of the inner below to provide access to the stage.

The stage, the pit, and the wall behind the stage were surrounded by the outside of the building, a three-story structure that housed the galleries and private boxes for the wealthier patrons and nobles.

Little scenery seems to have been associated with Elizabethan productions, although contemporary records do indicate that a number of props—rocks, trees, and the like—were associated with the theatres.

RESTORATION THEATRE

The interest in spectacle and visual effects that began in Italy in the mid-1500s moved rapidly northward across Europe during the next 100 years. By about

Function Follows Form

The structure and equipment of theatres has affected theatrical conventions through history. The funeral marches so prominent in Shakespearean tragedies were simply expedient methods to clear bodies from the stage. The Elizabethan theatres didn't have a curtain to hide the stage, and the plays were held in the daytime, so the stage was always lit. This precluded any artful, or semibelievable, method for getting rid of the bodies. Hence the funeral marches.

In the Restoration and eighteenth-century theatres, entrances were made from doors on either side of the apron, because the raked stage was cluttered with scenery and the actors' intrusion there would have distorted the illusion of depth carefully designed into the forced-perspective scenery.

apron: The flat extension of the stage floor that projects from the proscenium arch toward the audience.

wings: In scenic terms, either tall, cloth-covered frames or narrow, unframed drops placed on either side of the stage, parallel with the proscenium arch, to prevent the audience from seeing backstage; were usually painted to match the scene on the upstage drop.

borders: Wide, short, framed or unframed cloth drops suspended to prevent the audience from seeing above the stage; normally match the decorative treatment of the wings and drops in wing and drop sets.

1660, the architectural style of theatre buildings and the types of scenery used in them were fairly standardized throughout England and the rest of Europe.

The theatres were primarily rectangular, with the stage set at one end of the building, as shown in Figure 3.10. The raked stage was framed by the proscenium arch, and the **apron** thrust toward the auditorium. Like its historical antecedents, the forestage of the Elizabethan stage and the *platea* of the medieval theatre, the apron was the site of the majority of the action of the play.

Although the scenery had become more elaborate by this time, with more locations depicted, it still followed the tradition of providing a visual background for the play rather than an environment in which the action of the play could happen. It was painted in perspective on movable drops, **wings,** and **borders** and was placed on the raked stage, where the inclined floor greatly added to the sense of depth created by the perspective painting of the scenery. Most of the plays took place in a generalized location (drawing room, courtyard, palace, garden, and so on), so each theatre owned stock sets that depicted these various scenes. When the action of the play took place in a library, the library set was used. If the theatre didn't happen to have a library set, another stock interior set, such as the drawing room, was substituted.

The auditoriums of these theatres also followed a traditional arrangement (see Figure 3.11): multitiered boxes (for dignitaries and other notables), galleries

FIGURE 3.10
A typical Restoration theatre.

FIGURE 3.11
The auditorium structure of a typical late seventeenth through late nineteenth century theatre.

(for those who could afford the extra charge), and the pit (for those who wanted to see the play but couldn't afford, or weren't permitted, a better seat). This style of proscenium theatre was essentially modern. Some theatres continued to install raked stages, but more and more new structures were built with flat stages. Theatres were constructed in this style until the late nineteenth century.

MODERN THEATRE STRUCTURES

A revolution in the style of theatre began in the late 1800s and continued into the early twentieth century. The work of a number of theatre artists was taking a decidedly different turn from the declamatory style of earlier theatre. The new theatre was devoted to a more realistic and naturalistic type of drama and stressed the previously unheard-of concepts of unity of style for all elements of the production. The Théâtre Libre, founded by André Antoine in Paris, and the Moscow Art Theatre, founded by Konstantin Stanislavski and Vladimir Nemerovich-Danchenko, were but two of the leading groups in this movement toward a more naturalistic and unified style.

As the productions became more realistic, it was natural for the shape of the theatres to change to support this new form. The new plays required that the settings become environments for the action of the drama rather than backgrounds. Consequently, as the action of the play moved onto the stage from the apron, the depth of the apron shrank. When this happened, it became difficult to see all of the action from the boxes and gallery seats adjacent to the proscenium, so the shape of the auditorium began to evolve. The side seats were eliminated, and the remaining seats faced the stage.

Everything speeded up in the twentieth century. Almost as quickly as the realistic movement became the dominant mode of theatre, splinter groups broke off from it to create a number of antirealistic movements. These movements rose, fell, and evolved so rapidly that most of them didn't have a chance to develop distinctive types of theatre structures. Actually, most of these movements didn't need to change the basic shape of the proscenium theatre or its machinery, because the existing theatres provided a workable environment for their divergent styles.

From the Boxes to the Pits

Throughout history the various shapes of theatre have been determined, to a large extent, by the mores of the sponsoring society. In ancient Greece, everyone (except the slaves) was considered of equal rank, so the seating was similarly democratic and unsegregated. In the southern Renaissance and in Europe for the ensuing 200 years, the majority of theatres were built by the aristocracy for their own amusement. The visual illusions of forced-perspective scenery were best seen from a single point in the center of the auditorium. This ideal location, subsequently known as "the Duke's seat," was usually found in the second-level box at the back of the auditorium.

The theatres of Elizabethan England, such as the Globe, also had elevated boxes surrounding the stage. The aristocracy, and those others who could afford the higher ticket prices, sat in the boxes. The common people stood in the pit. About the time of the French Revolution, seats began to appear in the pit throughout European theatres as the various societies became more democratic.

In the United States, the Little Theatre movement of the 1920s and 1930s was an effort to establish quality productions outside of New York City. It also gave new playwrights a chance to improve their craft and have their works produced in an environment that was less critical than the supercharged atmosphere of Broadway. This movement continued and expanded throughout the country. Its crowning glory has been the establishment of a number of excellent contemporary regional professional theatre companies in such cities as San Francisco, Dallas, Denver, Hartford, Washington, San Diego, Minneapolis, Tucson, and Sarasota.

A ripple effect of the Little Theatre movement was that fledgling companies, funded more by inspiration and lofty intentions than money, began to produce theatre in "found" spaces. Existing barns, churches, feed stores, grocery stores, libraries, old movie houses, and other large, relatively open buildings were all candidates for takeover. Many of these groups relished the enforced intimacy between the actors and audience that shoehorning theatres into these cramped spaces provided. Whether by accident or design, many of these converted theatre spaces didn't have the room to erect a proscenium stage and auditorium. For whatever reasons, thrust and arena stages sprang up all over the country.

The form and structure of the physical theatre have gone through a great many developments. Any number of people have attempted to "improve" the spatial relationship between the stage and auditorium. It is doubtful, however, that anyone will ever devise any genuinely new developments in this relationship, simply because the theatrical experience is based on the premise that the actors need a space in which to perform and the audience must be in a position to see and hear them. When the form of the physical theatre is thought of in this context, it becomes apparent that there are no different types of theatre, only variations on a basic theme.

Chapter 4
The Stage and Its Equipment

Theatrical performing spaces have undergone an interesting evolution since about 1960. Influenced by a number of experimental theatre movements as well as economic pressure to make theatres usable for dance groups, symphony concerts, and esoterica such as car, home, and boat shows, companies are changing the shapes of theatres and playing spaces.

Probably the most dominant trend in this evolution is the reduction of the physical and psychological barriers that separate the audience from the production. The New York production of *Cats* was indicative of this change. The set, a stylized representation of an incredibly cluttered junkyard, did not just sedately sit behind the proscenium arch. It negated the concept of the **picture frame stage** by placing elements of the set not only on the stage and apron but also in and on the **orchestra pit,** up the walls of the auditorium, around the balcony rail, and up into the ceiling of the auditorium (see Figure 4.1). The actors made entrances through the house, touched members of the audience, and talked directly to them. This exciting style of theatre doesn't let the audience simply sit and observe but directly involves them in the production.

Innovative productions like *Cats* have been happening with increasing regularity throughout the country, and the theatre spaces being designed today are reflecting these production trends. Although an ingenious production concept and large budget can radically alter the appearance of almost any stage-auditorium relationship, it is still true that there are three primary stage configurations—*proscenium, thrust,* and *arena*—that dominate the world of theatre.

picture frame stage: A configuration in which the spectators watch the action of the play through a rectangular opening; synonym for proscenium-arch stage.

orchestra pit: The space between the stage and the auditorium, usually below stage level, that holds the orchestra.

PROSCENIUM STAGE

As we have seen, the proscenium stage is also known as the picture-frame stage, because the spectators observe the action of the play through the frame of the proscenium arch (Figure 4.2). Although there is debate among theatre artists regarding the appropriateness of using what some describe as an aloof stage that forcefully separates the audience from the action, the fact remains that the proscenium stage and its machinery have, for 300 years, been the dominant mode of presentation. The reason is simple: Designs that work needn't be tinkered with.

Proscenium Arch

The proscenium arch, which gives this type of stage its name, is a direct descendant of the *proskenium* and *skene* of the Greek theatres (see Figure 4.3). This

FIGURE 4.1
Cats, New York production, produced by Cameron Mackintosh, The Really Useful Company Limited, David Geffen, and the Shubert Organization. Photo by Martha Swope.

FIGURE 4.2
Proscenium stage, Gammage Auditorium, Arizona State University, Tempe.

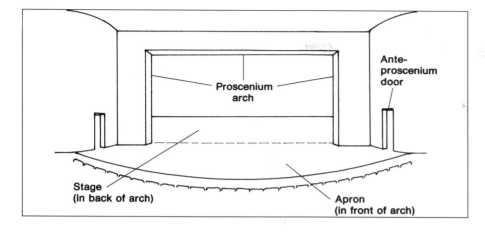

FIGURE 4.3
The parts of a proscenium stage.

arch, which separates the stage from the auditorium, can vary in both height and width. The average theatre (with 300 to 500 seats) has a proscenium arch that is eighteen to twenty-two feet high and thirty-six to forty feet wide.

Stage

The playing area behind, or upstage, of the proscenium arch is referred to as the stage (see Figure 4.4). A stage floor is a working surface that serves a number of diverse functions. For the actors, it must provide a firm, resilient, nonskid (but not too sticky) surface that facilitates movement. For scenic purposes, a stage floor needs to be paintable. It should also be reasonably resistant to splintering and gouging caused by heavy stage wagons and other scenic pieces, and it should slightly muffle the sound of footfalls and shifting scenery.

Although some directors choose to move the action of their productions forward onto the apron to bring the play closer to the audience, the primary playing area for many proscenium productions is behind the proscenium arch.

Wings

The spaces on either side of the stage are called the wings. Wings are primarily used for storage. During a multiscene production, all sorts of scenic elements, props, and other equipment are stored in the wings until needed on stage.

FIGURE 4.4
The proscenium stage and wings.

Stage Directions

It can be frustrating trying to tell an actor what direction to move or telling a technician that "I want the sofa a little further to the left." "My left?" he asks. "No, that way. Over there." Through the years, a system of stage directions has evolved to help clear up these problems.

On the American proscenium and thrust stages, stage directions are understood to mean that you are standing on the stage and looking into the auditorium. Stage left is to your left and stage right is to your right. Upstage is behind you, and downstage is in front of you. The terms *upstage* and *downstage* probably evolved in the sixteenth or seventeenth century during the era of raked stages, when you literally moved up the slope of the stage when moving upstage.

Stage directions in Europe are noted in a slightly different manner. Upstage and downstage are the same, but right and left are reversed from the American system, being given in reference to the auditorium rather than the stage.

Stage directions for arena stages cannot use this system, since the audience surrounds the stage. When this happens, it is much easier to describe the stage directions by referring to one direction as north, and then remaining directions are understood to be south, east, and west.

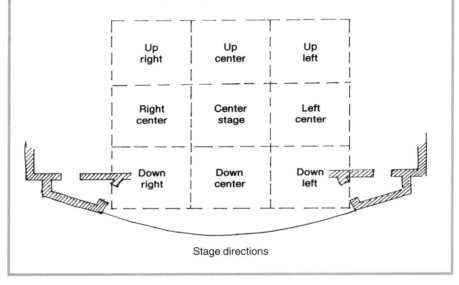

Stage directions

Apron

The apron, or forestage, is an extension of the stage from the proscenium arch toward the audience. It stretches across the proscenium arch to the walls of the auditorium and can vary in depth from a narrow sliver only three or four feet deep to as much as ten or fifteen feet. It generally extends for five to fifteen feet beyond either end of the proscenium arch.

Orchestra Pit

Many proscenium theatres have an orchestra pit, which is almost always placed between the apron and the audience. It is used to hold the pit band, or orchestra, during performances that need live music. To hold an orchestra, the pit obviously needs to be fairly large. Most pits extend the full width of the proscenium and their upstage-to-downstage dimensions are roughly eight to twelve feet. The

FIGURE 4.5
The orchestra pit usually occupies part of the apron.

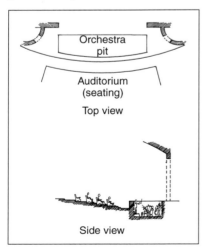

Stage Floors

A good stage floor is actually composed of several layers. The subfloor should be made of soft wood such as pine or plywood. These materials are resilient and tough and will hold nails and other fasteners. Traditionally, a heavy, canvas groundcloth covered the subfloor. But a groundcloth can wrinkle or tear when heavy scenery is moved over it, can be painted only a few times before it starts to deteriorate, and is lousy for tap dancing. Quarter-inch tempered Masonite has all of the qualities needed for a good stage floor surface. It has the added advantage of being fairly inexpensive, and individual sections of the floor can be replaced as needed. The one drawback to this fiberboard floor is that it has a tendency to warp when first painted. This problem can be significantly reduced if the sheets are painted *on both sides* before being nailed to the subfloor. (Stand the fiberboard on edge, and paint both sides simultaneously.)

Detail of a typical stage floor. 2 × 3 sleepers are on 16" centers. Sleepers and sleeper pads are not attached to concrete slab. Floor detail courtesy of Landry & Bogen, Theatre Consultants.

depth of the pit varies, but a good pit is deep enough so that the orchestra won't interfere with the spectators' view of the stage.

Obviously, the size of the orchestra pit imposes a formidable gulf between the audience and stage when it is not in use. Various solutions have been adopted to remedy this situation (see Figure 4.5). In some theatres, the orchestra pit is hidden beneath removable floor panels under the apron; when the pit is needed for a production, the floor panels are removed. In other theatres, the pit is placed beneath the auditorium floor. When not in use it is covered with removable panels, and auditorium seats are placed on top. This method has the obvious advantage that additional tickets can be sold when the pit isn't being used.

In some theatres, the entire forestage area (apron, orchestra pit, front of the auditorium) is composed of one or more hydraulic lifts. With their great lifting power, it is possible to raise or lower whole sections of the stage. When more than one lift is used, they are able to shape the forestage into a variety of configurations, as shown in Figure 4.6.

Bally's Hotel in Las Vegas has created what may be the ultimate answer to the orchestra pit: There isn't any. In the Jubilee Room (a 2500-seat theatre), the orchestra plays in a room in the basement of the theatre complex while watching the production on closed-circuit television. Each section of the orchestra is **miked,** and the sound is **mixed** and **balanced** with that of the singers before it is amplified and sent into the auditorium. Although this solution works well in the high-tech atmosphere of Las Vegas, it is doubtful that every musical director would feel comfortable working in this remote and disconnected manner.

mike: To place one or more microphones in proximity to a sound source (instrument, voice).

mix: To blend the electronic signals created by several sound sources.

balance: To adjust the loudness levels of individual signals while mixing, to achieve an appropriate blend.

FIGURE 4.6
Hydraulic lifts can provide a variety of interesting auditorium/stage arrangements.

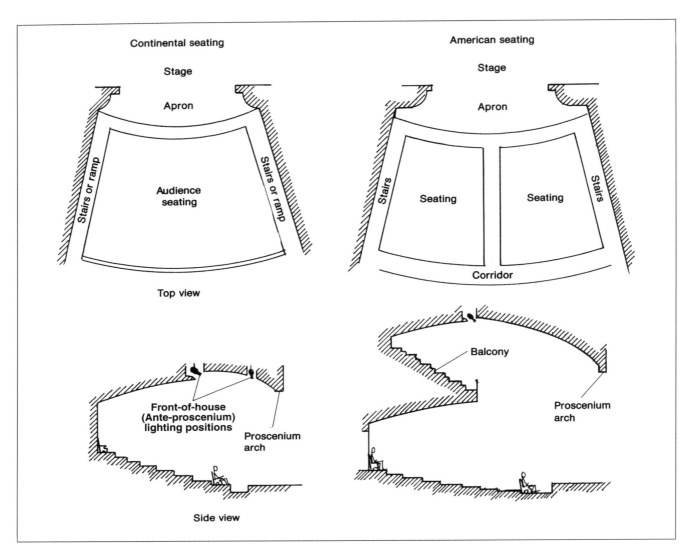

FIGURE 4.7
Types of seating configurations.

Auditorium

The shape of the typical proscenium theatre auditorium, or house, is roughly rectangular, with the proscenium arch located on one of the narrow ends of the rectangle (see Figure 4.7). Normally, each seat is approximately perpendicular to the proscenium arch. To reduce the reflection of sound waves in an auditorium, none of its finished surfaces (walls, ceiling, floor) should be parallel with any others. Thus, the side walls of most auditoriums angle out from the proscenium arch in the shape of a slightly opened fan. The rear wall of the auditorium is usually curved, and the ceiling generally slopes toward the rear of the house.

The floor of the auditorium is raked, or inclined, from the stage to the rear of the house. Angling of the house floor improves not only the acoustics of the theatre but also the view of the stage, by elevating each successive row.

The lighting control booth is generally located at the back of the auditorium. It normally has one or more large windows to provide the light-board operator(s) with an unobstructed view of the stage. Although a sound booth with a large window (which can be opened) is usually located in a similar back-of-house location, the sound operator frequently runs the **sound mixer** from a position in

sound mixer: An electronic device used to adjust the loudness and tone levels of several sources, such as microphones and tape decks.

FIGURE 4.8
Stage traps provide access to the area beneath the stage.

the auditorium so that he or she can hear what the audience is hearing and balance all the sound sources accordingly. The resulting sound "picture" has a focal point, usually the voice of the actor or singer.

Proscenium Stage Equipment

Several interesting pieces of permanent stage equipment are frequently associated with proscenium theatres.

Traps   Many theatres have traps cut into the stage floor. These removable sections provide access to the space beneath the stage (see Figure 4.8). These holes can be filled with stairs, an elevator, or a slide, or can be left open, depending on the desired visual and physical effect. Ideally, the majority of a stage floor is trapped. If only a few traps have been installed, Murphy's Law indicates that they will almost always be in the wrong places. Although traps are more frequently found in proscenium theatres, there is nothing to prevent this useful piece of equipment from being installed on either thrust or arena stages.

Revolve   The revolve, also called a turntable or revolving stage, provides a visually interesting and efficient manner of shifting scenery (see Figure 4.9). Some theatres have revolves built into the stage floor. Depending on the size of the revolve, part or all of a multiset design can be fit onto it and rotated to bring other scenic elements into view.

Slipstage   The slipstage is a huge stage wagon large enough to cover the full width of the proscenium arch (see Figure 4.10). When not in use, the slipstage is stored in one of the wings. Entire sets can be mounted on the slipstage. When needed, it is simply rolled into place on stage.

Revolves and slipstages are permanent features of a theatre's stage. Smaller, temporary versions can be constructed to meet the needs of individual productions. Construction techniques for making these smaller versions are discussed in Chapter 9, *Scenic Production Techniques.*

Fly Loft

The area directly over the stage is called the fly loft (see Figure 4.11). The fly loft, also referred to as "the flies," is usually quite tall, minimally two and a half times the height of the proscenium arch, to allow the scenery to be raised out of sight

FIGURE 4.9
A revolving stage is sometimes built into the stage floor.

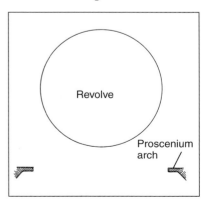

FIGURE 4.10
A slipstage is
designed to hold
an entire set.

grid: A network of steel I beams supporting elements of the system used to
raise and lower scenery.

fly: To raise an object or person above
the stage floor with ropes or cables.

batten: A thick wooden dowel or metal
pipe (generally 1¼ to 1½ inches in diameter) from which are suspended
scenery and lighting instruments.

loft blocks: A grooved pulley, mounted
on top of the grid, used to change the
direction in which a rope or cable
travels.

stage house: The physical structure
enclosing the area above the stage and
wings.

head block: A multisheave block with
two or more pulley wheels, used to
change the direction of all the ropes or
cables that support the batten.

of the audience. The **grid,** or gridiron, is located just below the roof of the fly loft.
It serves as a platform to hold some of the equipment used to **fly** scenery, as well
as providing the primary support for the weight of the scenery and curtains
being flown.

Fly Systems

Several systems are used to fly scenery. The two primary methods, rope set and
counterweight, work on the same operating principle: counterbalancing.

   The oldest method of flying is with rope and pulley. The pulley is attached
to the grid, and the rope is fed through it and tied to the scenery. A stagehand
pulls on the free end of the rope and raises the scenery. If the load is too heavy, a
sandbag is tied to the free end of the rope as a counterbalance.

Rope Set   The rope-set system operates exactly like a rope and pulley, except it
has three or more lines instead of one (see Figure 4.12). The ropes, usually three-
quarter-inch manila, support a **batten.** From the batten they run to the grid,
where they pass over **loft blocks,** which direct them toward the side of the **stage
house.** At the edge of the grid, the lines pass over the **head block** and then down

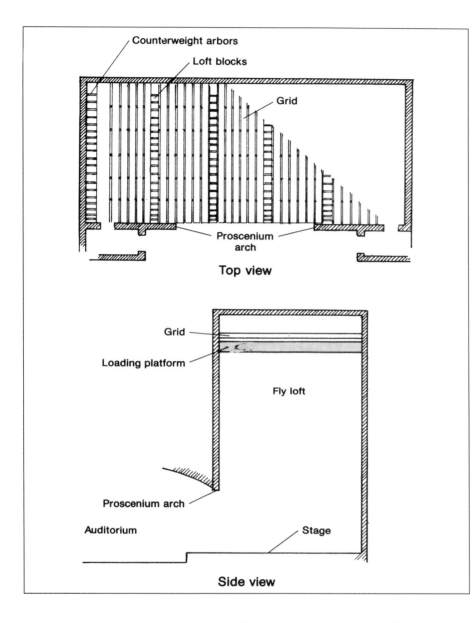

Counterweight arbors

Loft blocks

Grid

Proscenium arch

Top view

Grid

Loading platform

Fly loft

Proscenium arch

Auditorium

Stage

Side view

FIGURE 4.11
The fly loft and grid are integral parts of any flying system. Scenery and equipment can be flown for storage in the fly loft, while the grid supports the loft blocks.

to the **fly gallery,** where they are tied off on the **pin rail.** The fly gallery is generally located fifteen to twenty feet above the stage floor to give the flypersons, or operators of the flying system, a clear view of the stage.

The rope set is archaic and dangerous if not properly maintained and operated. For this reason it is rarely used today. Although seldom used, it is included here to show the evolution of flying techniques.

Counterweight System The counterweight system works on the same principle as the rope-set system and is much safer. As shown in Figure 4.13, the support ropes for the battens have been replaced with steel cables. The cables are attached to the batten, and they run up to the loft blocks and over to the head block. But instead of being tied off at the pin rail, they are secured to the top of a **counterweight arbor,** or carriage. The counterweights in the arbor balance the weight of the scenery that is attached to the batten. When the batten is lowered to the stage level, the arbor raises to the level of the **loading platform** just below

fly gallery: The elevated walkway where the pin rail is located.

pin rail: A horizontal pipe or rail studded with belaying pins; the ropes of the rope-set system are wrapped around the belaying pins to hold the batten at a specific height.

counterweight arbor: A metal cradle that holds the counterbalancing weights used in a counterweight flying system.

loading platform: A walkway, suspended just below the grid, where counterweights are loaded onto the arbor.

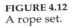

FIGURE 4.12
A rope set.

Safety Tip

Rope-Set Systems

Although the rope-set system is fairly simple, it is not particularly safe. The ropes, which are made from manila fiber, and sandbags, which are made of heavyweight canvas, are subject to constant—and all but impossible to detect—stress and deterioration. They must be continually inspected for cuts, nicks, and other indications of wear. The ropes should be replaced as soon as any abrasions or cuts are noticed. Even if no deterioration is noted, they should be replaced at least once a year if the system is used with any frequency and more frequently if it is used heavily. The sandbags should also be replaced at least once every five years or immediately if any damage is noticed.

The scenery must be raised to its high trim mark (the height at which it will be stored) before the counterweight sandbag can be attached to the free end of the rope. Finally, the system must always be batten heavy (the scenery must always be heavier than the counterweight) so that the scenery can be lowered without having to attach special ropes to pull it down.

Head block

¼" Steel cable

Loft block

Grid

Trim chain

Pipe batten

Loading
platform

Turnbuckle

¾" Manila operating line

Counterweight arbor

T-bar track

Rope lock

Locking rail

Tension pulley

Cable
clamps
Trim
chain

FIGURE 4.13
A counterweight system.

the grid. This allows the counterweights to be loaded onto the arbor while the scenery is still resting safely on the stage.

The system is controlled by an operating line of three-quarter-inch manila rope. (Parallel-core polyester rope can be used as a substitute for the manila operating line.) The operating line is attached to the top of the arbor, runs over a head block, down through a rope lock to a tension pulley, and then back to the bottom of the counterweight arbor. To lower the batten, you pull down on the part of the line that is closest to you. To raise the batten, you pull down on the offstage part of the line. The **locking rail** is located on the stage floor against the stage-house wall. Although this arrangement is convenient, it does take up floor space that could be used for other purposes.

In theatres with limited offstage space, the use of a multiple-speed counterweight system solves the problem by raising the locking rail off the stage floor.

locking rail: A rail that holds the rope locks for each counterweight set.

Safety Tip ⚠

Counterweight Systems

It isn't difficult to make a counterweight system safe to operate. A few basic rules need to be observed.

1. Make sure that everybody clears the stage area under the loading platform when counterweights are being loaded onto, or unloaded from, the arbor.

2. Don't stack counterweights above the lip of the loading platform or anywhere where they might be knocked off of the platform.

3. When working on the grid, loading platform, or pin rail, don't carry anything in your pockets other than the tools you are going to use. Extra tools, pencils, or keys might fall on someone, causing serious injury.

4. Inspect all flying hardware, and repair or replace *any* defective equipment.

5. Bolt in place the hardware supporting all flown units. Nails or screws can pull out of the wood.

6. Always attach the scenery to the batten first, then load the counterweights.

7. When removing (striking) flown scenery, always unload the counterweights first, then remove the scenery from the batten.

8. Any unit other than a very light flat should be flown under compression. This means that the lines supporting the piece are attached to the bottom of the unit rather than the top.

The three-quarter-inch manila operating line should be inspected for abuse or unusual wear at least once a year. If any nicks or abrasions are noticed, replace the rope at once. Routinely replace the rope every five years. The cable clamps securing the cable to the batten and arbor should be inspected and tightened at least every six months. Any bent or otherwise broken or abused batten pipes should be replaced immediately. The entire rigging system should be inspected by a reputable professional rigger at least once every five years.

This type of system, shown in Figure 4.14, creates a mechanical advantage (2 to 1) that allows the batten to move twice as far as the counterweight arbor. The drawback to this system is that twice as much weight must be loaded onto the arbor to balance the weight of the scenery.

Motorized systems increasingly are being used for flying. These vary from simple systems that drive the operating line of a regular counterweight set to complex designs of great electronic sophistication, as shown in Figure 4.15.

Stage Drapes

The proscenium stage uses more types of stage drapery than does either the thrust or arena stage. Although they have specific functions, all stage drapes are designed to **mask** backstage areas from the spectators. Stage drapes are usually made of black, light-absorbing material such as heavyweight velour or similar material (commando cloth, duvetyn, rep). Typical hanging positions for the various types of stage drape are shown in Figure 4.16.

Grand Drape   The purpose of the grand drape (also known as the main curtain, main drape, or grand rag) is to cover the proscenium opening. In theatres that have a fly loft, the grand drape, which is usually made from heavy-weight velour, can normally be flown or **traveled.**

mask: To block the audience's view—generally, of backstage equipment and space.

travel: To move horizontally relative to the stage floor, as with a drape that opens in the middle and is pulled to the sides.

FIGURE 4.14
A multispeed counterweight system.

Grand Valance   The grand valance normally is located just downstage of the grand drape. It is made of the same material as the grand drape but is much shorter, usually only eight to twelve feet high. It is used to mask the equipment and scenery that are flown immediately upstage of the proscenium.

False Proscenium   The false proscenium (Figure 4.17) is located immediately upstage of the grand drape and grand valance. It is normally mounted on a rigid framework. The **flat** structures of both the **hard teaser** and **tormentors** are usually covered with thin (one-eighth-inch to three-sixteenths-inch plywood), which is then covered with black velour or some similar type of black, light-absorbing material. The primary purpose of the false "pro" is to provide masking. The tormentors mask the sides of the stage, and the hard teaser provides primary

flat: A framework, normally made of wood or metal; frequently covered with thin plywood or fabric, although a variety of other covering materials may be used.

hard teaser: The horizontal element of the false proscenium; usually hung from a counterweighted batten so that its height can easily be adjusted.

tormentor: The vertical flats that form the side elements of the false proscenium.

Mechanical Advantage

Certain mechanical systems can provide a power-multiplying effect known as mechanical advantage. A 2:1 mechanical advantage means that you can move twice the weight, with the same amount of force, that you can with a system providing no mechanical advantage.

The single whip illustrated in the first figure doesn't create any mechanical advantage, because it is just changing the direction of pull on the operating line. If, however, we attached one end of the rope to a strong beam in the ceiling, as shown in the second figure, attached the pulley to the weight we were trying to raise, and then pulled *up* on the rope, we would create a 2:1 mechanical advantage. This system is called a running block.

It is fairly easy to determine the mechanical advantage of any tackle-rigging configuration. Simply count the number of lines that pass through the block. Don't count the operating line if it is hanging down from the last pass through the block (the housing for the pulley wheels). The total number of lines will be equal to the mechanical advantage for that particular block-and-tackle system. Friction reduces the actual efficiency of any block-and-tackle arrangement by 10 percent for each pulley sheave in the system.

With block and tackle you create increased lifting power, but you do so by losing speed. For example, with a double whip (2:1 mechanical advantage) the load moves half the distance that the operating line travels, whereas the watch tackle (3:1 mechanical advantage) moves the load one-third the distance that the operating line travels.

Single whip
(no mechanical advantage)

Running block
(2 to 1 mechanical advantage)

Double whip
(2 to 1 mechanical advantage)

Watch tackle
(3 to 1 mechanical advantage)

Four common tackle rigs.

FIGURE 4.15
A motorized winch system. The
winch drives cables over standard
loft blocks positioned on the grid.
Illustration courtesy of the Peter
Albrecht Corporation.

masking for the flies. Since both the tormentors and hard teaser are movable, they can also be used to shrink the apparent size of the proscenium opening.

A **show portal** (Figure 4.18) is a false proscenium designed for a specific production. It masks the stage and provides a picture frame for the set.

Legs and Borders Legs are narrow, vertical stage drapes that are used to mask the sides of the stage upstage of the proscenium arch. They are generally made of the same light-absorbing material as other stage drapes. Borders, also called

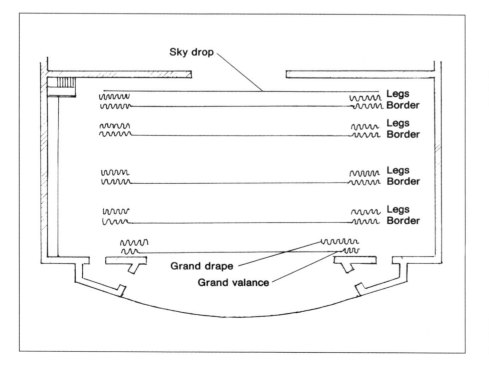

show portal: A false proscenium that visually supports the style and color palette of a particular production.

FIGURE 4.16
Standard hanging positions for stage draperies.

FIGURE 4.17
A false proscenium.

False proscenium

Proscenium arch
Front view

Pipe batten

Snatch lines

Hanger irons

Rear view

FIGURE 4.18
A show portal.

Show portal

Proscenium
arch

grommet: A circular metal eyelet used
to reinforce holes in fabric.

teasers, are short, wide, horizontal draperies, normally four to ten feet tall, used to mask the flies. Legs and borders usually have long strings, called ties, either sewn to the jute tape at the top of the drape or slipped through brass **grommets,** which are fixed to the jute tape so that they can be tied to a supporting batten. Ties are usually made from thirty-six-inch pieces of half-inch-wide cotton tape, although thirty-six-inch shoestrings work very well.

Borders are normally used in conjunction with a set of legs (two legs) to provide a complete framework of masking for the stage, as shown in Figure 4.19. If the theatre is equipped with a counterweight system, borders and legs are rarely hung on the same batten, because the trim height of the borders needs to be variable, whereas the legs should be trimmed so that the lower hem barely

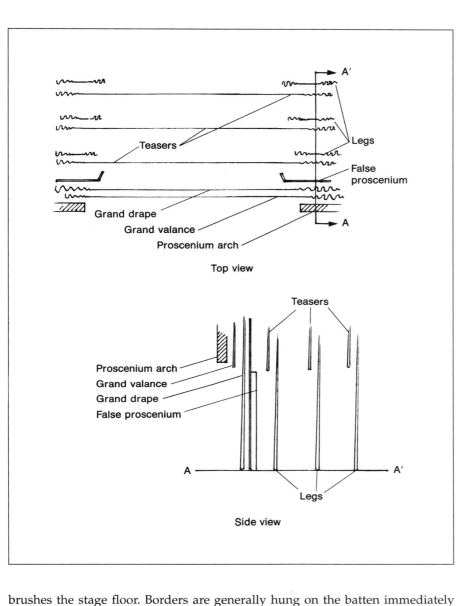

FIGURE 4.19
Hanging positions for legs and teasers.

brushes the stage floor. Borders are generally hung on the batten immediately downstage of the one holding the legs. If the theatre doesn't have a counterweight or adjustable height rigging system, the legs and borders are frequently hung on the same batten.

Sky Drop   The sky drop (Figure 4.20), also known as a sky tab, is, as its name implies, used to simulate the sky. It is a large, flat curtain, without fullness, normally made of muslin or scenic canvas. It is usually hung on a batten as far upstage as possible.

Prior to the early 1960s, the sky drop was traditionally dyed a uniform blue to help simulate the color of the sky. Current practice suggests that the sky drop should be made of unbleached fabric, which is off-white. This neutral color allows the lighting designer to create a sky color that is appropriate to the mood and concept of the production.

Cyclorama   The cyclorama, or "cyc" (Figure 4.21), is an expansion on the concept of the sky drop. Although the sky drop works very well for productions that require only a small patch of sky, it doesn't surround the set with the illusion of

FIGURE 4.20
A sky drop.

vast expanses of open sky. Historically, when plays began making this type of scenic demand, technicians responded by hanging two more sky drops at almost right angles to the original curtain to provide a wraparound expanse of sky, as shown in Figure 4.21B. Where the drops met, they were overlapped to prevent gaps in the smooth expanse of simulated sky.

The **fly cyc** (Figure 4.21C) is made from one unbroken expanse of cloth. It is hung on a counterweighted pipe located outside the other counterweighted battens to reduce any possible interference between the two systems.

fly cyc: A single drop, hung on a U-shaped pipe, that surrounds the stage on three sides.

Safety Tip

Fire Protection

Over the years, fire has destroyed more theatres than any other cause. The traditional mainstay of fire safety for the proscenium stage has been the asbestos curtain. This fireproof curtain is located immediately upstage of the proscenium arch. Its purpose is not to put out the fire but to contain it. When a fire starts, the asbestos curtain is lowered, effectively isolating the auditorium from the stage. Although recent research has shown that inhalation of asbestos fibers is hazardous, almost all proscenium theatres built before 1965 frequently still have an asbestos curtain as their primary line of fire safety. Some theatre owners have replaced their asbestos curtains with either sprinkler systems or curtains made of fire-retardant synthetic materials.

Nonproscenium-stage theatres, and newer proscenium theatres, are now also being protected by sprinkler systems. These systems flood the stage, wings, and auditorium with a heavy mist of water in the event of a fire. They are much more effective than the asbestos curtain.

Regardless of the primary method of fire protection, portable fire extinguishers should be located in easily accessible and clearly identified locations in all shops, on the stage, and in the control booths.

A final suggestion: Always check your local fire codes. Become familiar with them. Know them. Follow them.

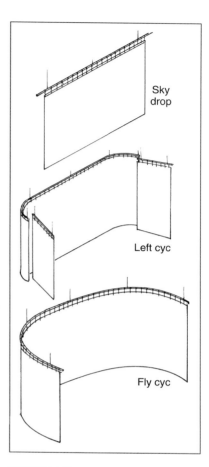

FIGURE 4.21
A sky drop and two types of cycloramas.

Sometimes sharkstooth **scrims** are used in conjunction with both sky drops and cycloramas. Sharkstooth scrim is a knit fabric that is actually composed of more open spaces than thread. Because of this structure, the fabric possesses some very interesting properties. When light is projected onto the front of sharkstooth scrim, it is reflected back toward the viewer, and the fabric appears to be opaque. When the front light is turned off and any objects behind the scrim are lit, the sharkstooth scrim becomes transparent, and the objects in back of it are clearly visible. When those same objects are lit, and light also strikes the scrim, it becomes translucent, and the objects, while still visible, are hazy and less distinct.

A white scrim hung in front of the cyc helps smooth out any wrinkles, dirty spots, and imperfections on the cyc. If the scrim is hung on a batten a foot or two downstage of the cyc, additional lights can be focused onto the scrim to provide very interesting, and sometimes spectacular, multilayer cyclorama lighting.

A black sharkstooth scrim can also be used to enhance the sky drop or cyc lighting. Used in the same manner as the white scrim, it improves aerial perspective by reducing the intensity and saturation of objects that are lit behind it.

A great deal of stage-lighting equipment could be considered a part of the permanent stage equipment. It will be discussed in Chapter 14, *Lighting Production*.

THRUST STAGE

As we saw in the last chapter, the thrust stage (see Figure 4.22) isn't a new development. Medieval audiences gathered on three sides of the pageant wagons and platform stages to watch passion plays, and research indicates that the Globe Theatre also had a thrust stage. The thrust stage was rediscovered by directors who wanted to move the action of the play out of what they felt were the artificial

scrim: A drop made from translucent or transparent material.

FIGURE 4.22
A typical thrust-stage arrangement.

lighting grid: A network of pipes from which lighting instruments are hung.

hanging position: A location where lighting instruments are placed.

dead hang: To suspend without means of raising or lowering.

ratchet winch: A device, used for hoisting, with a crank attached to a drum; one end of a rope or cable is attached to the drum, the other end to the load; turning the crank moves the load; a ratchet gear prevents the drum from spinning backward.

and limiting confines of the proscenium stage. Thus, the mid-twentieth century saw the birth of a large number of thrust stage theatres in the United States.

The stage of the thrust theatre projects into, and is surrounded on three sides by, the audience, so tall flats, drops, and vertical masking cannot be used where they would interfere with the spectators' view of the stage (see Figure 4.23). But on the fourth, or upstage, side of the stage, drops and flats can be placed to help describe the play's location. Entrances are frequently made through openings in the upstage wall, but the house is also used for this purpose.

The **lighting grid** in a thrust theatre is usually suspended over the entire stage and auditorium space, so instruments can be hung wherever necessary to effectively light the playing area. Lighting grids vary in complexity from designs that hide the lighting instruments from the spectators' view to simple pipe grids from which the lights are hung in full view, as shown in Figure 4.24.

Access to the simpler pipe grids is usually from a rolling ladder placed on the stage. The more complex grids frequently have walkways above the pipes to allow electricians to adjust the lighting instruments from above. In addition to the grid, there are usually some additional **hanging positions** above the house, either open pipes or some type of semiconcealed location.

Some thrust theatres retain a vestigial proscenium arch on the upstage wall as well as a small backstage area. Although battens are frequently **dead hung** above this backstage space, some theatres have installed **ratchet winches,** rope sets, or counterweight sets so the battens can be raised and lowered.

The lighting and sound booths are generally located at the back of the house directly facing the stage, although nothing stronger than tradition prevents them from being placed at any location in the auditorium that provides an unobstructed view of the stage. Again, as in the proscenium theatre, and for the same reasons, the sound operator frequently chooses to run the mixing board from a position in the house rather than from the sound booth.

FIGURE 4.23
Thrust theatre. Tyrone Guthrie Theater, Minneapolis, Minnesota. Seating an audience of 1,441, no seat is farther than 52 feet from the stage. Photo by Robert Ashley Wilson.

FIGURE 4.24
Lighting grids for thrust theatres are frequently exposed pipe grids. The Contemporary Theatre, Seattle, Washington. Photo by Chris Bennion.

ARENA STAGE

The arena stage (Figure 4.25) is another step in the development of an intimate actor-audience theatre. The audience surrounds the stage and is much closer to the action of the play than in either the proscenium or thrust theatres (see Figure 4.26).

The scenery used on an arena stage is extremely minimal. Because the audience surrounds the stage, designing for the arena theatre provides a challenge to all the designers. Anything used on an arena stage—sets, costumes, makeup, props—must be carefully selected to clearly specify the period, mood, and feeling of the play. Additionally, everything must be well constructed, because the audience sits almost on top of the stage and can see every construction detail.

As in the thrust stage theatre, the space above the arena stage has a lighting grid rather than a fly loft. The lighting grid frequently covers not only the stage but the auditorium as well.

The stage manager and the lighting and sound operators need to have a clear view of the stage. Many arena theatres have an elevated deck running around the perimeter of the auditorium to provide these people with a variety of

FIGURE 4.25
A typical arena theatre configuration.

FIGURE 4.26
Arena theatre. The interior of the 827-seat Arena Stage in Washington, D.C.

potential work locations. Some arena theatres have a traditional lighting booth and sound-control booth rather than flexible work stations.

BLACK BOX THEATRES

The flexible staging of black box theatres—so named because they are usually painted black and have a simple rectangular shape—encourages, and demands, ingenuity from the production design team. These design-it-yourself performance spaces are a direct result of a number of experimental theatre movements that sought to break down the visual and psychological barriers created by the proscenium stage.

In black box theatres the seating is generally located on movable bleacherlike modules that can be arranged in any number of ways around the playing space. Although the space can be set up in traditional proscenium, thrust, or arena configurations, it can also be aligned into excitingly different staging arrangements that support the production concept for particular productions. This type of theatre is fun to work in, and every production creates a challenge to the ingenuity of the production design team.

The black box theatre was developed partially as a reaction against the artistic confines of more formal types of stage space. Consequently, there isn't a great deal of specific stage equipment associated with it. However, there is a lighting grid, similar to that of the arena theatre, located above the stage and auditorium space, and there is usually a variety of additional hanging locations.

"FOUND" THEATRE SPACES

Found theatre spaces lend a great deal of credence to the statement that all theatre needs is "two boards and a passion." These theatres are housed in structures that were originally designed for some other purpose. Almost every conceivable type of space has been, or could be, converted for use as a theatre. In Tucson, Arizona between 1970 and 1985 a supermarket, movie house, lumberyard, feed store, office building, and restaurant were converted into theatres. The found theatre space conversions experienced in Tucson were not unique. The Lafayette Square Theatre in New York City houses five theatres in what used to be a library. The only criteria for conversion seem to be sufficient square footage to house a stage and its audience and nearby parking or public transportation.

Found theatre spaces are frequently converted into black box theatres, but a number of converting companies have opted for the more traditional arena or thrust stage configurations (see Figure 4.27). For some producing groups, the appeal of the converted space lies in the intimacy of the audience-actor relationship that is inherent in these generally small theatres. For others, the lower production costs of the smaller, more intimate theatre forms are an asset. For all of them, the fact that these spaces were considerably less expensive than building a new structure was a boon.

FIGURE 4.27
Converted theatre space. The stage/auditorium of the Yale Repertory Theatre, housed in a former church.

Chapter 5
Style, Composition, and Design

A designer needs to communicate, to share his or her information and ideas both verbally and visually. In Chapter 2, you were introduced to the verbal language of the designer—that is, the questioning process and the dynamics of group discussion, which are vital to the interaction among members of the production design team. In this chapter, you are introduced to the other, equally important language of the designer—the visual language.

STYLE AND STYLIZATION IN THEATRICAL DESIGN

What is style? In conversation we might refer to a particular "style" of clothing such as blue jeans or evening wear. When we refer to a "style" of car, we often use the word to differentiate between models that have significantly different appearances, such as sports cars and sedans. Narrowly defined, style refers to the compositional characteristics that distinguish the appearance of one type of thing from another. Style can be more generally defined as a "reflection of the social and political history of the times, . . . that . . . are eventually reflected in the patterns and shifting artistic trends of the period."[1] Combining both definitions provides a definition of style useful in theatrical design: a recognizable pattern of compositional elements that provides a distinctive reflection of the social and political history of the time. This definition can be used to identify particular compositional features that are reflective of a moment in history, such as the long, sweeping lines generally characteristic of women's clothing in the Late Gothic period (Figure 5.1) or the mechanistically based repetitive patterns of German expressionism.

PRODUCTION STYLE

production style: A manner of producing a play in which all production elements (costumes, scenery, lights, acting) adhere to a common set of artistic/philosophical characteristics (e.g., expressionism).

A definition of **production style,** while including the previously discussed definition of design style, must include acting and directing as well. Thus, production style can be viewed as the central stylistic theme on which the world of the production is based. It is a recognizable pattern of visual and intellectual elements, based on social and political history, used to create the production environment for a particular play.

1. Douglas A. Russell, *Stage Costume Design*, 2nd ed. (Prentice-Hall, 1985), p. 170.

The identification of a particular production style, which derives in part from a careful and creative interpretation of the script, is the single most important step in the development of a play's production concept.

DESIGN STYLES AND DESIGN PERIODS

It is convenient to refer to specific design styles, such as romanticism or naturalism, and design periods, such as Elizabethan or Late Nineteenth Century. However, neither styles nor periods exist within narrowly prescribed time frames. They are merely indicative of major stylistic elements that are common during a particular period of time. Romanticism did not stop on one day and naturalism begin the next. Nor did the style of Elizabethan clothing abruptly begin with the coronation of Elizabeth I and end with her death. Both styles evolved from those that preceded them and into those that followed. Naturalism began as a reaction against what its practitioners viewed as the stylistic excesses of romanticism. As more artists followed the stylistic leaders of the naturalistic movement, naturalism became the dominant artistic style. Realism began as a reaction against what a few artists viewed as the rigid dictates of the naturalistic style. Again, a new style emerged and became dominant as another declined.

FIGURE 5.1
Long sweeping lines are a characteristic style of Late Gothic gowns.

Stylization

It is difficult, if not impossible, and of no theatrical value, to create an absolutely accurate historical period or style on stage. The reasons are twofold: (1) the impact that contemporary stylistic and practical influences have on the designers and (2) the expectations of the audience. To illustrate the point, let's assume that we're producing a hypothetical play set in 1820 England. If contemporary fashion, which to a great extent determines audience reaction, dictates that the hair styles of 1820 England were ugly, silly, or funny looking, any costume designer would be ill-advised to insist on absolute historical accuracy of the hair design for the young female romantic lead in the play. Why? Simply because the audience is supposed to like her. If her hair style seems ugly or silly, it will be difficult for the audience to empathize with her character. Under these circumstances, a modification of the design, based on the historical research, would be more appropriate. It is frequently impossible to find historically accurate fabrics from which to make costumes. It is also a bit bizarre to think that the walls of the set for the library scene in our play would have to be made with historically accurate bricks, mortar, lath, and plaster; that the library shelves would have to be made from oak that has been painted with historically correct stains and varnishes; and that the books on those shelves would have to all have been published prior to 1820!

Instead of slavishly copying historical designs, designers stylize. Stylization refers to the use of specific compositional elements characteristic of a particular style or period to create the essence of that style or period. Designers use the degree of stylization of the scenic, costume, and lighting designs to communicate the level of reality of the production to the audience. Costumes, set, and furniture designs that are minimally stylized—that closely duplicate the line, mass, texture, and color of a particular style or period—normally will be interpreted by most audiences as being historically accurate and realistic. As designs depart further from visual reality—exaggerate or simplify line, shape, mass, texture, and/or color—audience interpretation becomes harder to project. A wide variety of demographic information, such as cultural background and values, as well as the audience's level of theatrical experience, come into play. A theatrically

value: Relative lightness or darkness.

sophisticated audience may think that heavily stylized scenic and costume designs reinforce the psychological reality of a play, while the same production may seem totally bizarre to others.

Literary Style and Theatrical Design

Another type of style that influences theatrical design is literary style. The style in which a script is written provides major clues for the designer. Verse drama has a majesty and sweep that cannot be duplicated in prose. The world of the verse play frequently seems more noble, simply because the story is written in verse. The scenic, costume, and lighting designs should mirror this noble quality. To reinforce this feeling, costume designers might choose to work in "noble" fabrics: rich velvets, brocades, and similar aristocratic materials and colors. Scenic designers would probably choose to work in a particular style that projects aristocratic, rather than middle-class, tastes.

The same criterion that visual style should respond to literary style can be applied to plays in which the dialogue is written in short, choppy prose. To reflect the rough flavor of this literary style, the scenic and costume designers might choose to work with short, choppy lines and harsh angles to create realistic forms.

ELEMENTS OF DESIGN

Design can be described as the process of conceiving and executing a plan. In the theatre, design involves creating a stylistic plan for the production concept and developing the necessary sketches, patterns, and other visualizations of the design concept(s), as well as overseeing the production of the sets, costumes, lights, and sound.

The drawings produced by every designer (scenic, costume, lighting, and to a certain extent, sound) need to be guided by the elements of design: line, shape, mass, measure, position, color, and texture. An understanding of the definition, characteristics, and function of each element, and how they work in combination, can lead to the creation of compositions that imply specific meanings, which is the ultimate purpose of all theatrical design.

Line

Line can be defined as a mark that connects two points. The properties that define the characteristics of that "connecting mark" are dimension, quality, and character.

Dimension   Dimension refers to the length and width of a line.

Quality   The quality of a line refers to several intrinsic characteristics: its shape, its **value,** and its contrast with surrounding objects. Lines can be straight, curvilinear, angled, jagged, serpentine, or any combination of these characteristics.

Character   The character of a line refers to its emotionally evocative characteristics.

We notice lines because of their dimension and quality. We attach meaning to their character. Lines attract attention as their complexity increases, as shown in Figure 5.2. Long straight lines are more noticeable than short straight ones (Figure 5.2A). Lines that contrast strongly with their surroundings or backgrounds draw more attention than those that don't (Figure 5.2B). Curved lines

(A)

(B)

(C)

FIGURE 5.2
(A) Long lines are more noticeable than short ones. (B) Lines that contrast with their surroundings are more noticeable than those that don't. (C) Curved lines are more distinctive than straight lines of the same length.

are more distinctive than straight lines of the same length (Figure 5.2C). Scenic and costume designers understand and utilize these principles. Notice that the boldest lines in the costume design in Figure 5.3 are those that outline the silhouette of the gown. The lines revealing trim details are of lower value and contrast.

Shape

Any line that encloses a space creates a shape. The quality of the line creating the shape strongly influences the connotative meaning of that shape (Figure 5.4). In scenic design, shape defines the form of large elements such as walls, platforms, and so forth, as well as defining the outline of such details as windows, doors, and furniture (Figure 5.5A). Similarly, in costume design shape refers to the outline of the garment, whether it is the silhouette of the whole garment or the form of some trim element (Figure 5.5B).

Mass

Mass is the three-dimensional manifestation of shape. It creates an awareness of depth and spatial arrangements. Mass creates a feeling of depth in sketches of scenic elements such as platforms, walls, and furniture. Individual costume sketches depict the mass of each garment. While costume designers don't produce sketches depicting costumes in relation to the whole stage picture, they need to be aware of how their designs will function within the spatial arrangement of the stage.

Measure

Largely an intuitive skill, and closely related to proportion (discussed later in this chapter), measure refers to the ability to judge the size of objects and the relative distance between them without the aid of measuring devices.

Position

Position refers to the relative location of adjacent shapes or masses. This definition encompasses both the distance between objects and their placement relative to forms around them.

Color

Color is one of the most important and complex of the design elements. It generates complex responses in the viewer based on psychological and cultural reactions. Because of its complexity, color will be discussed separately in Chapter 6.

Texture

Texture refers to the visual or tactile surface characteristics or appearance of an object. In costume, where the primary visual element is fabric, the texture of a fabric's surface plays a vital role in creating the audience's response to, and understanding of, the nature and personality of the character wearing the costume. Hard-surfaced fabrics, such as satins, taffeta, and metallics, reflect light. Soft, fuzzy-surfaced materials, such as wool, flannel, and velour, absorb light. Audience responses to specific fabric surfaces vary depending on the personalities of the individual audience members and the mix of textures in the design, so it is

FIGURE 5.3
Costume design for Myra by Kathi Perkowski Mills, in the American Southwest Theatre Company production of *Hayfever*.

FIGURE 5.4
The quality of the line creating the shape determines the quality of the shape.

THE WINSLOW BOY   —A Gillette

(A)

FIGURE 5.5
Any line that encloses a space creates a shape such as a window, door, or wall. (A) *The Winslow Boy,* scenic design by A. S. Gillette. (B) Costume design for Irina by Kathi Perkowski Mills, in the American Southwest Theatre Company production of *Three Sisters.*

Irina
IV.

(B)

gobo: A thin metal template inserted into an ellipsoidal reflector spotlight to project a shadow pattern of light.

difficult to draw any generalizations about "meanings" for specific fabric surface textures. However, expensive cloth has always been the province of those who could afford it, such as the nobility and the upper class. Therefore, the surface textures, and light reflective qualities, of expensive fabrics, such as satins and brocades, can be loosely associated with the wealthy and upper class. Similar comparisons can be drawn with those fabrics worn by the middle and lower classes.

In a similar manner, scenic designers have traditionally used texture to provide visual reference to the play's psychological environment. Although it is difficult to describe texture without reference to other design elements such as line, shape, and mass, certain associative reactions to texture are reasonably uniform. Generally speaking, smooth surfaces reflect a finished, orderly type of environment when compared with the harsher, less polished atmosphere created by rough textures.

In lighting design, **gobos** are used to create texture by breaking up the otherwise smooth output of the lighting instrument into shadow patterns. (See Chapter 14, *Lighting Production,* for more information on gobos.) These patterns provide an effective tool to increase the dramatic tension in the lighting by providing the only effective means of creating texture in lighting.

PRINCIPLES OF COMPOSITION

To be an effective designer you must understand the basic principles of composition. They can guide you to an understanding of how the elements of design are coordinated. Good composition usually results when the elements of design are arranged in a cohesive and unified manner according to the following guidelines.

Unity

Unity in design can be described as the creation of a stylistic plan to which all parts of the design subscribe. The production concept is that plan. It is the conceptual core of the production. In practice, unity in design means that each part of a design should have some type of logical connection with the production concept. In scenic design, unity is achieved when the arrangement of flowers on a table, the design of a door, or the library and living room sets for Act I and Act II of a hypothetical play, all subscribe to the guiding principles of the production concept. Unity in costume design is achieved when the elements used in the design of individual costumes, as well as those groups of costumes that are on stage at the same time, have some type of logical connection to the production concept. Similarly, there must be a conceptual thread that ties together the various elements of the lighting and sound designs. That conceptual thread is the production concept.

Harmony

Harmony is the sense of blending and unity that is obtained when all elements of a design fit together to create an orderly, congruous whole. Harmony is achieved when a combination of design elements seem to naturally blend or flow together, avoiding discordant or incompatible contrasts.

Although harmony is primarily concerned with congruity, it doesn't require that all lines, forms, masses, values, and colors within a design be of one particular style, shape, or character. What it does mean is that those elements should be chosen to complement one another. For example, the **profile,** or **silhouette,** for the walls of the set of *The Member of the Wedding* (Figure 5.6) is actually composed of two basic lines. The more apparent is the slightly jagged silhouette of the short, vertical cuts. The second is the long, gentle sweep of the silhouette itself. The jagged line was chosen for two reasons, one aesthetic, the other logical. The jagged line is evocative of the emotional stress that is felt by Frankie, the play's main character. The more mundane reason for selecting this line is that the short, vertical breaks can be thought of as the ends of the clapboards that cover the outside of the house. The long, sweeping line was chosen to reinforce the romantic, nostalgic nature of the play.

Lest you think that harmony is a goal always to be sought, you need to realize that too much harmony can be monotonous, as when a motif, such as the harmony of angle and measure shown in Figure 5.7, is repeated too often.

profile (silhouette): The outline of a form, which determines the form's quality and character.

FIGURE 5.6
The profile, or cutout line, affects visual meaning. *The Member of the Wedding,* scenic design by J. Michael Gillette.

FIGURE 5.7
Too much harmony can be
monotonous.

FIGURE 5.8
The use of an interesting silhouette
can increase visual interest and connotative meaning in a scenic design.

Monotonous harmony can also be achieved when too many closely related colors
are used in the same design.

All designs don't necessarily have to be harmonious. Some designs might
provide an accurate reflection of the mood and spirit of play by being deliber-
ately unharmonious. The degree of harmony to be pursued in the design depends on the designer's interpretation of the production concept.

Contrast

Contrast in composition can be defined as the juxtaposition of dissimilar design
elements. To be effective, contrast must work in opposition to the major, or dominant, visual theme in a composition. But too much contrast can destroy that
visual theme, and too little (too much harmony) will be monotonous. The obvious design ideal is to create compositions that provide a proper balance of harmony and contrast reflective of the production style. In scenic design, visual
contrast frequently mirrors the psychological stress levels of the play—tragedies
and plays with serious themes frequently have greater visual contrast than comedies do. In costume design, the personality of the character wearing the costume
is a prime determinant of the amount of contrast used in the design of an individual costume. As a general guideline, the costumes of flamboyant characters employ greater contrast than do those of their more retiring compatriots.

Manipulation of contrast affects meaning. Note the change in "personality"
between the two versions of the scenic design shown in Figure 5.8. The curved
cutout lines used in Figure 5.8A create a new visual personality for the design by
contrasting with the dominant vertical and horizontal lines of the "noncutout"
design pictured in Figure 5.8B. The sensuous line makes the entire design seem
more relaxed, less formal and austere.

Variation

When too much harmony in a design produces monotony, variation of the monotonous elements can introduce visual interest. A simple pattern repeated many
times (Figure 5.9A) can be monotonous, but by varying the shape of every second
or third object in the design (Figure 5.9B) visual interest in the whole design is
heightened. Similar effects are achieved by varying any of the design elements
(line, shape, texture, and so forth) in a repetitive pattern, as shown in Figure 5.9C
and D.

FIGURE 5.9
Variation creates visual interest.
(A) Repetition of a simple pattern
can be monotonous. (B) Varying the
width of every second shape in the
pattern creates visual interest.
(C and D) Alternating patterns
heighten visual interest.

Terminal Accents

(A)

(B)

Carefully selected terminal accents—the lines that define the profile, or silhouette, of a form or mass—can be used to help portray emotional quality. In some productions, the upper parts of the set walls are cut off (Figure A). The quality and character of the line chosen to form this terminal accent on the upper edge of the wall (form) can help shape the audience's understanding of the emotional atmosphere of the play. If the play is a light comedy, a "fun" sort of curlicue line will reinforce the happy nature of the play. If the production is more romantic, a gentle, sensuous line may be more appropriate. If the play is serious and heavy, straight lines with sharp, angular corners are probably more appropriate.

The same effect can be achieved in costume design, where the character of the line chosen to create the silhouette of a costume helps shape the emotional quality of the gown (Figure B).

The emotional quality of the terminal accent can also be used to good advantage in costume design. The hems of the sleeves and skirts of witches' costumes are frequently designed with sharp points (dags) to visually support the menacing nature of the characters wearing those costumes. The unadorned neckline of a collarless smock provides a visual clue to the stiff, unyielding nature of its wearer. But add a soft, frilly, lace collar to that same dress, and our perception of its wearer will similarly be softened.

(A) Scenic design for The Birthday Party *by J. Michael Gillette. (B) Costume designs for Elise Darling in* Very Good Eddie *(left) and Queen Elinor in Shakespeare's* King John *(right) by Paul D. Reinhardt.*

FIGURE 5.10
Symmetrical balance results when the left side of a design is a mirror image of the right side, as in this scene design for *Lady Precious Stream* by A. S. Gillette.

symmetrical balance: Correspondence in size, form, and relative position of parts on either side of a center dividing line; mirror-image balance.

asymmetrical balance: A sense of equipoise achieved through dynamic tension created by the juxtaposition of dissimilar design elements (line, form, mass, value, color).

FIGURE 5.11
Asymmetrical balance occurs when dissimilar forms appear to be balanced within the framework of the composition.

Balance

Balance can be achieved by arranging the design elements to give a sense of restfulness, stability, or equilibrium to the design. There are two types of balance: symmetrical and asymmetrical. In **symmetrical balance,** if you were to draw a line down the center of a design, the objects on the left side of a design would be the mirror image of the objects on the right, as shown in Figure 5.10. In **asymmetrical balance,** the left side of the design does not mirror the right. Balance is achieved by creating a pattern in which the juxtaposition of the various design elements creates a sense of restfulness, stability, or equilibrium, as shown in Figure 5.11. In this illustration, the white circle on the left of the design is dynamically balanced by the larger expanse of dark space to its right. This type of "nonmirror" balance presents many more ways for the designer to create dynamic balance through the manipulation of the elements of design.

The design of individual costumes is much more likely to involve the use of symmetrical balance (Figure 5.12A), in which the left side of the costume mirrors the right. However, a dynamic visual statement can be made about a character through the use of asymmetrical elements such as diagonal sashes, asymmetrical modular blocks of color, or asymmetrical draping (Figure 5.12B). Additionally, the overall balance of the costume design for the entire production is normally asymmetrical because the ebb and flow of the stage picture will rarely, if ever, contain any moments in which the left side of the stage picture will be a mirror image of the right. The majority of scenic designs employ asymmetrical balance because its dynamic nature presents more opportunities for the personality of the play to be visually described in the scenery, as shown in Figure 5.13.

Proportion

Proportion involves the harmonious relationship of the parts of an object to each other or to the whole. A significant portion of our understanding of beauty is based on proportion. Facial beauty, for example, is predominantly based on proportion. We normally think of a face as beautiful if all of its parts seem to "match" or "fit together." But if the nose or ears seem too big or too small, or if the spacing of the eyes is too wide or too narrow, what we are really discussing is proportion. The criteria that determine what is too big or too small are intuitive, culturally based, and vary considerably from person to person. This situation makes it all but impossible to create a definition of "proper proportion." But if some part of a scenic, costume, or lighting design appeals to our sense of beauty, a significant portion of that beauty derives from our personal definition of "proper proportion."

Emphasis

Emphasis in theatrical design involves directing the audience's attention to a specific place. In scenic and lighting design, those focal points are normally in the **acting areas.** The actor's face and upper torso should be the focal point in costume design. In a quality costume design, the entire ensemble—clothing, hair, hat, shoes, accessories—will create an appropriate initial impact, but then the eye should be drawn to the upper torso and face. Why draw the audience's attention to the actor's face? Because of an old, and true, theatre adage: If you can't see 'em, you can't hear 'em. If audience members cannot see the actor's face, or if their attention is drawn to some area of visual emphasis other than the actor's face, they will have trouble understanding what the actor is saying.

Emphasis is achieved in a variety of ways. A color accent—a throw pillow on a sofa, a flower in the hair, a shaft of light—draws the audience's attention to the accent area. Similarly, converging lines or a change of texture can direct the audience's attention to a specific location, whether on an individual costume or on the set.

DESIGN ANALYSIS OF *THE KITCHEN*

A working knowledge of the elements of composition and the techniques used to create interesting and meaningful designs is essential for all theatrical designers. An analysis of the author's scenic design for Arnold Wesker's *The Kitchen* (Figure 5.14) should help explain one way that all of these elements can be combined to create a design. In this analysis, a discussion of the individual elements of design—line, shape, mass, measure, position, color, and texture—would not be of particular value, since their visual meaning is contingent on their relationships with one another in the design. Of more importance is a discussion of how the principles of composition are applied in the design.

Because all of the principles of composition are intertwined, you'll notice that it is difficult to focus on a single principle of composition without discussing one or more additional principles. The contrast of a composition can't be discussed without discussing its harmony, variation, and so forth. With this understanding that the areas of discussion will overlap, let's begin the analysis.

Unity

Unity in design is achieved when all elements of the design subscribe to a plan—the production concept. The production concept for this production of *The Kitchen* centered on three concerns: the idea that everything in the work area of the kitchen had to be, or appear to be, real; the view that what happens in a restaurant kitchen is a microcosmic view of the real world; a sense of the transitory nature of human relationships.

(A)

(B)

FIGURE 5.12
(A) Balance in costume design: symmetrical balance. (B) Balance in costume design: asymmetrical balance. Costume designs by Peggy Kellner.

acting area: *Those areas of the stage on which specific scenes, or parts of scenes, are played.*

FIGURE 5.13
Asymmetrical balance helps create visual character. Scenic design by James Billings for the American Southwest Theatre Company production of *True West*.

Harmony

Harmony is achieved when all elements of the design fit together in an orderly, congruous whole. The exact nature of the harmony is shaped by the production concept. The dominant lines in this design are the straight horizontals and verticals used to form the outline of the set and to define its interior space and furnishings. The sharp angularity of these lines is occasionally softened by sweeping curves. The character of the sharply etched horizontal and vertical lines supports the harsh view of life that is implicit in the script. The broad curves defining the cutout line of the walls and the central archway soften some of this starkness and suggest that there may be some gentleness in the play. The sweeping curves of the cutout lines are echoed in the curved lines that define the warming shelf-support brackets on the stoves and the well covers on the steam tables.

Contrast

Contrast implies that one or more design elements are working in opposition to the dominant visual theme in the design. As previously discussed, the dominant visual theme of this design is long vertical and horizontal lines. The dominant visual motif—the upstage wall—is composed of long vertical and horizontal lines that define the shape of the wall, as well as the door and window openings. The curved lines that define the central archway and the side walls work in contrast with the dominant horizontal/vertical theme. The downstage elements of the design—the stoves and worktables—provide additional visual contrast in two ways: (1) Their mass is composed almost exclusively of short, right-angled, intersecting lines, and (2) the long axis of each unit—stoves and worktables—fan out from the upstage wall at nonperpendicular angles.

This design also makes use of color contrast. The lower portion of the walls was finished with off-white ceramic tile wainscoting. Above the dirty-looking

FIGURE 5.14
The Kitchen, produced at the University of Arizona, directed by Robert C. Burroughs, scenic and lighting design by J. Michael Gillette.

wainscoting the kitchen walls were finished to look as though they had started out white years ago but had accumulated successive layers of smoke and grease. The walls of the short central hallway were painted medium green to help make that area recede in visual importance. The floor was finished with dull red to resemble the floor tiles frequently found in older commercial kitchens. The stoves along the outside walls were finished with a low-sheen black, and the worktables were brushed stainless steel. This color scheme resulted in visual emphasis being placed in the downstage areas, which is where the majority of the play's action took place.

Contrasting surface textures—slick ceramic tiles, dull-black cast-iron stoves, brushed stainless steel, flat off-white and green walls, dull-red floor tiles—add to the visual interest of the design.

Variation

Repetition of a regular pattern produces monotony. Variation of that pattern introduces visual interest. This design exhibits several repetitive patterns: the door-and-window-trim motif, the height of the ceramic wainscoting, the shapes of the stoves. Variation is introduced in the door and window trim by varying the height and width of the openings. The horizontal line created by the top of the ceramic wainscoting would be visually boring if it were not interrupted by the door and window openings. While the design of the stoves remains the same on both sides of the stage, the pattern is varied by having three stoves on stage left and four on stage right. This variation is further enhanced by adding a double oven to the upstage end of the stoves on stage right.

Balance

Balance refers to the arrangement of design elements to provide a sense of restfulness, stability, or equilibrium. This design appears to be symmetrically balanced, but closer scrutiny reveals that it doesn't possess the requisite mirror-image balance. There are three stoves and a little work sink on the stage-left wall, while there are four stoves plus a double oven on the right. There are three work stations on stage left and only two on stage right. The center archway is slightly stage left of the center line of the set. While the set isn't symmetrical, the placement of the various elements creates a sense of dynamic equilibrium. The "slightly asymmetrical" design was created to support the idea that everything in the world of *The Kitchen* is a little bit "off"—is not quite what it seems.

Proportion

Closely related to balance, proportion refers to the harmonious relationship of the parts of an object to each other or to the whole. There is a harmonious balance of mass and color in this design. The up-center wall creates a solid backdrop, and the walls, appliances, and work stations cascade out, down, and around to encircle the primary playing area. The layout of the major color blocks—the dirty off-white up-center wall, green and mahogany up-center hallway, black stoves, and silver work stations—is essentially symmetrical and provides a nice sense of balance and harmony to the design.

Emphasis

Emphasis refers to creating areas of visual interest that the audience will look at before they look at anything else. In scenic design, emphasis is normally placed on the acting area(s). In this design, emphasis was directed toward the primary down-center acting area in several ways. The black void surrounding the set doesn't give the audience anything to look at, effectively forcing them to direct their attention toward the set. The cutaway walls further reduce nonessential visual elements, requiring the audience to look at what remains. The essentially symmetrical design of the set dictates that a sense of equilibrium or balance is achieved only when you are looking at the approximate center of the set. The color design further focuses the audience's attention on the down-center area of the set. The dirty-white up-center wall provides an effective primary point of focus, but it was several shades darker than the white costumes of the cooks, so the wall didn't steal focus from the actors. The chrome and brushed stainless steel of the work stations provided two points of emphasis that effectively framed either side of the primary playing area. The stoves, placed further from the primary playing area, were finished in burnished metallic black to effectively recede into the black void surrounding the set. The medium green walls and dark mahogany doors of the up-center hallway diminished the visual importance of that prominent position, again focusing attention further downstage.

The foregoing example employed scenic design to explain the uses of the various principles of composition. An understanding of these tools of the designer will provide you with the basic artistic resources to be able to create effective designs in not only scenic design but costumes, lighting, and sound as well.

Chapter 6
Color

Color is easily the most noticeable of the design elements and is arguably the most dominant. It is also the least understood. We grow up with color all around us, and we see and use it every day. It is probably because of our constant contact with color that we accept it without really thinking about it. This chapter attempts to help you understand the complex subject of color.

DEFINING COLOR

Color has a variety of definitions. It can be defined as a perception created in the brain as a result of stimulation of the retina by light waves of a certain length. It can also be thought of as the intrinsic physical properties of specific objects that allow those objects to reflect and absorb light waves of a certain length. The common denominator for any definition of color is light, because the visual perception of all color is derived from light. The phenomenon that we call light is actually the very narrow portion of the spectrum of electromagnetic radiation that is visible to the human eye. Figure 6.1 shows the position of visible light on this spectrum, as well as that of some of the other types of radiation. The visible spectrum stretches in frequency from approximately 750 nanometers to 400. (A nanometer is one billionth of a meter.) Figure 6.2 shows the approximate wavelengths for the various colors of the visible spectrum.

Color Terminology

Without a specific set of terms to describe the various properties of color, almost any discussion of it would quickly degenerate into rather meaningless comparisons. An example will help explain this phenomenon. If you provided each member of a group of twenty people with one hundred **paint chips,** all yellow, but each slightly different, and asked them to identify canary yellow, they would probably select twenty different chips. This is because the connection between the description of any specific color, such as canary yellow, and the brain's understanding of the physical appearance of that color differs, sometimes significantly, from person to person.

The terms that we will be using in our discussion of color are as follows:

Hue   Hue is the quality that differentiates one color from another, such as blue from green or red from yellow.

Saturation   Saturation, also known as chroma, refers to the amount, or percentage, of a particular hue in a color mixture. Fire-engine red has a high, or strong, saturation, because there is a lot of fully saturated color in the mixture.

paint chip: A small rectangle of paper or thin cardboard painted in a specific hue.

FIGURE 6.1
The frequency range of selected energy forms contained in the electromagnetic radiation spectrum.

10^{22}Hz	Cosmic rays
10^{21}Hz	Gamma rays
10^{20}Hz	
10^{19}Hz	
10^{18}Hz	X-rays
10^{17}Hz	
10^{16}Hz	Ultraviolet
10^{15}Hz	
10^{14}Hz	Visible light
10^{13}Hz	Infrared
10^{12}Hz	
10^{11}Hz	
10^{10}Hz	
10^{9}Hz	Radar
10^{8}Hz	Television
10^{7}Hz	
10^{6}Hz	Commercial radio
10^{5}Hz	

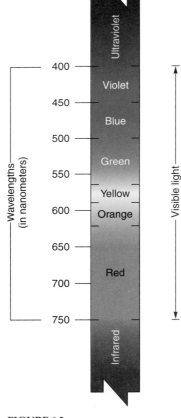

FIGURE 6.2
The frequency range of visible light.

Dusty rose, in contrast, has a low, or weak, saturation, because there isn't a lot of fully saturated color in the mixture; instead, the majority is white or gray.

Value   The relative lightness or darkness of a color is referred to as value. Pale blue has a high value, and dark brown has a low value.

Tint   A color with a high value is referred to as a tint. It is usually achieved by mixing a hue with either white pigment or white light.

Shade   A color with a low value is known as a shade. It is usually created by a mixture of one or more hues and black.

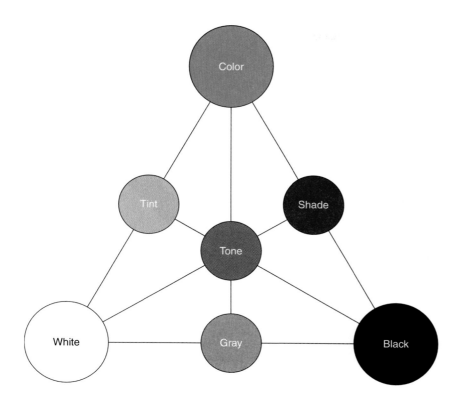

FIGURE 6.3
The color triangle is a visual representation of the relationships that exist between color, shade, tint, and tone.

Tone   A color of middle value is frequently referred to as a tone. It is a mixture of a hue with black *and* white. The addition of a **complementary** hue tones a color.

The color triangle in Figure 6.3 shows the relationships among hue, white, black, gray (the product of mixing black and white), tint, shade, and tone.

SEEING COLOR

Before we learn how color works, we should understand how we see color. Human sight comprises a complex series of events. When you look at an object, elements within your eye are stimulated by the light being emitted by, or reflected from, the viewed object. An electrochemical reaction occurs in specialized nerve cells in the retina. Two distinct types of light-receptor nerves, **rods** and **cones,** emit minute charges of electricity that are relayed to your brain, where the received data are interpreted as a "picture" that you have seen. The cones are divided into three primary groups: those that respond to the wavelengths of light that correspond to red, blue, and green, respectively.

If a red light enters the eye, the red-responsive cones are stimulated but the others are not. If a light that contains both red and blue wavelengths enters the eye, both the red- and blue-responsive cones are stimulated. In this case, the message that is sent to the brain corresponds to the ratio of red and blue light contained in the light mixture that the eye receives. If the light contains more red than blue light, that information is transmitted.

Notice that the eye can only send information to the brain corresponding to the input it has received. The brain is the organ that does the interpretative mixing of the colors. In the example of the red and blue light, the amount of red and blue in the mixture will be interpreted by the brain to be a particular color such as violet, magenta, or purple.

complementary: Two hues that, when combined, yield white in light or black in pigment; colors that are opposite each other on the color wheel.

rods: Nerve cells in the retina that are sensitive to faint light.

cones: Nerve cells in the retina that are sensitive to bright light; they respond to red, or to blue, or to green light.

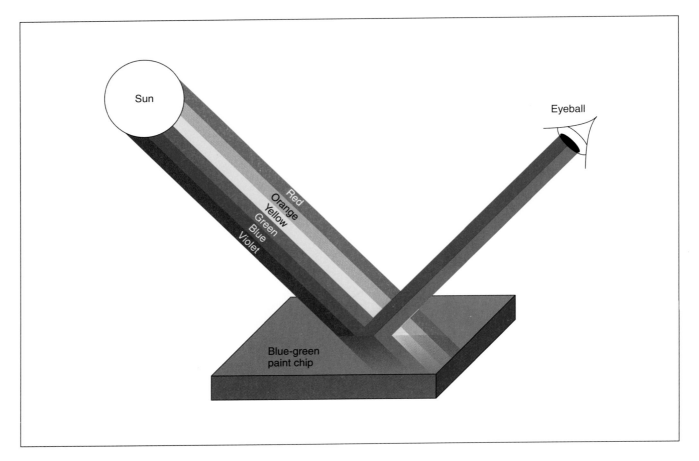

Sun

Eyeball

Red
Orange
Yellow
Green
Blue
Violet

Blue-green
paint chip

FIGURE 6.4
The brain interprets the neurological information it receives from the eye to be a specific hue.

All perceived color is transmitted to the eye by light. If the light is dim, the cones (color sensors) do not function. The best way to demonstrate this effect is by standing outside on a moonlit night and looking at your surroundings. Everything you see will be a monochromatic gray, with perhaps a slight tint of blue or green if the moonlight is sufficiently bright. You will see no vibrant reds, blues, or greens, because the cones require more light than is being transmitted to your eye. If you look at the same scene during the daytime, the bright sunlight will activate the cones in your eye. Unless your eye has some physical dysfunction or the color-interpretative segment of your brain is impaired, you will see colors.

To further illustrate how the eye sees and the brain interprets color, let's assume that you are standing outside in the sunlight looking at a turquoise (blue-green) color chip, as shown in Figure 6.4. The sunlight, which contains all of the electromagnetic wavelengths of the visible spectrum, strikes the blue-green surface of the color chip. Some of that light is reflected, and some of it is absorbed by the pigment on the paint chip. The majority of those wavelengths of light that correspond to the color of the chip (blue and green) are reflected. The majority of all other wavelengths of light are absorbed by the paint chip. The reflected blue and green light is received by the eye. The blue and green cones are stimulated by the light, causing them to send electrical impulses to the brain. The relative strength of these signals from the blue and green cones is proportionate to the specific amount of blue and green in the color mix. When the color-sensitive area of the brain is stimulated by these impulses, it interprets that information as a specific color known to that particular brain as turquoise.

COLOR MIXING

Before examining color mixing, we must understand some additional terms.

Primary Colors

Primary colors are those hues that cannot be derived or blended from any other hues. In light, the primary colors are closely related to the color sensitivity of the red, blue, and green cones in the eye.

Secondary Colors

Secondary hues are the result of mixing two primary colors. In the color wheel for light (Figure 6.5A), the mixing of adjacent primaries creates the secondary hues yellow, magenta, and cyan (blue-green). The primary colors in **pigment** (Figure 6.5B) are red, blue, and yellow. The secondary colors in pigment are purple, green, and orange.

pigment: A material that imparts color to a paint or dye.

Complementary Colors

Complementary colors can be described as any two hues that, when combined, yield white in light or black in pigment. They can also be described as colors opposite each other on a color wheel. The color wheel for light (Figure 6.5A) shows that the complementary hue for red is cyan. When the two are combined, they form white light. In the color wheel for pigment (Figure 6.5B), the complementary of red is green. When the two are mixed, they form black.

Filtered Light

When white light passes through any type of filtering material, such as glass, plastic, or air, a certain portion of the spectrum is absorbed. To fully understand

FIGURE 6.5
Color wheels for (A) light and (B) pigment.

(A)

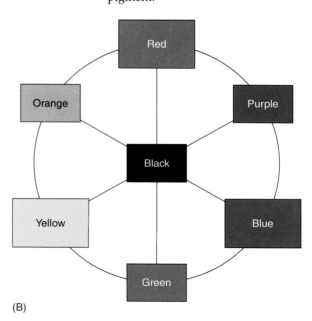

(B)

Theoretical Versus Practical Color Mixing

According to color theory, the combination of complementary pigments yields black. The reason is straightforward. Each pigment reflects the wavelengths of light that correspond to its own hue and absorbs all others, as shown in Figure 6.6. Complementary hues are composed of one primary color and a secondary color. The secondary color is created from a mixture of the other two primary hues. The resultant blend of all three primaries should, theoretically, absorb all light that strikes it. This absence of reflected color means no light, which is the same as blackness.

In the practical mixing of pigments, you will be dealing with paints that are not pure colors. There are fillers, extenders, and impure colors in every commercially prepared paint. These impurities and surface diffusion—the scattering of light caused by the texture of the reflecting surface—will result in a deep gray instead of the theoretically correct black when mixing complementary hues.

this type of absorption, you need a little background about the nature of light and energy.

Light, as we have seen, is a form of radiant energy (part of the electromagnetic spectrum). According to the laws of physics, energy can be neither created nor destroyed, but its form can be changed or converted. This principle can be

FIGURE 6.6
Color reflection and absorption are determined by the hue of the pigment. Each hue will reflect its own color and absorb all others.

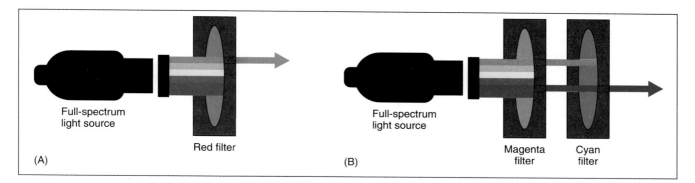

(A)

Full-spectrum
light source

Red filter

(B)

Full-spectrum
light source

Magenta
filter

Cyan
filter

FIGURE 6.7
Subtractive color mixing in light.
A colored filter will allow its own
color to pass but will absorb all
others.

demonstrated by touching a window through which the sun is shining. The glass
will be warmer than a similar window that isn't in the direct sunlight. This is
because the energy being absorbed by the glass is being converted from light into
heat.

Subtractive Color Mixing in Light If the glass in the window mentioned
earlier is colored, another type of filtering takes place. Colored filters allow only
their own hue to pass through the filtering medium; they absorb all other wavelengths of light.

Figure 6.7A shows a red filter placed in front of a full-spectrum light source.
The white light emitted by the lamp is composed of wavelengths from all portions of the visible spectrum. The red filter allows only the wavelengths of light
that correspond to its own color to pass. All other light is stopped by the filter
and converted into heat.

When two or more filters, such as the secondary hues magenta and cyan, are
placed in front of a single source (Figure 6.7B), each filter removes all but its own
segment of the spectrum. The resulting blue light is caused by successive filtration. The magenta filter allows only red and blue light to pass through it. The
cyan filter absorbs the red portion of the magenta light but allows the blue portion to pass. In practical application, it is usually preferable to use a single filter,
rather than multiple filters. By selectively removing portions of the visible spectrum, subtractive color mixing actually reduces the intensity of the output of the
source. A yellow or amber color medium of minimal saturation may reduce
intensity by about 5 percent, for example, and a heavily saturated dark blue may
reduce it by as much as 95 percent. If more than one filter is used, the output of
the source can be significantly reduced.

Additive Color Mixing in Light When several individual hues are transmitted
to the eye, added together, and interpreted by the brain, the process is called
additive color mixing. Figure 6.8 illustrates color mixing in light. The beams of
the three lights are being projected onto a neutral or white surface. When a
primary hue, such as red, is mixed with an adjacent primary, such as green, a
secondary hue, yellow, is created. (It is interesting to realize that this hue is *not*
created on the projection surface but is the result of the red and green cones in
our eye being stimulated by the red and green light and our brain interpreting
this neurological information as the hue yellow.) This same phenomenon occurs
when any two or more hues are additively mixed.

All color is perceived in the same way. The subtle tones, tints, and shades of
the various hues that you see are all determined by the level of stimulation that
the red, blue, and green cones receive from the light reflected to your eye and by
your brain's interpretation of that information.

FIGURE 6.8
Additive color mixing in light. The eye sees each separate color; the brain interprets the ratio of the color mix to be a specific hue.

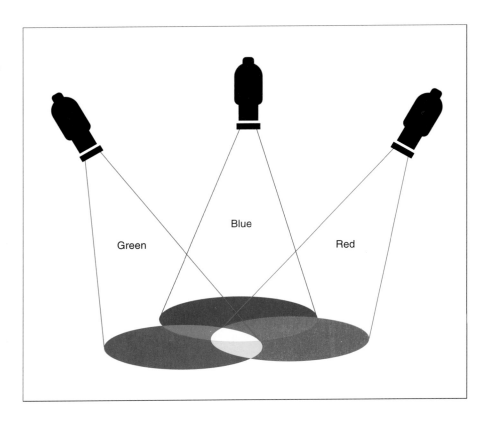

Color Mixing in Paint

Color mixing in light and paint rely on the same principles of color reflection and absorption. Color mixing in paint is primarily a subtractive process, because pigments and dyes of specific hues reflect the wavelengths of light that correspond to their own hue and absorb all others. The primary hue blue provides a good example of how this subtractive process of color absorption works. When the white light strikes the blue surface illustrated in Figure 6.9, the various wavelengths of light are either reflected or absorbed depending on the particular hue of blue paint. Since the dominant color of the surface is blue, the blue light is reflected to your eye, and the other wavelengths of light are either reflected or absorbed according to their proportions in the blue paint.

The selective absorption characteristics of the individual hues in a paint mix cause a reduction in the saturation, or chroma, of the resultant hue. If yellow and red paint are mixed, for example, the result is an orange. But since the yellow pigment absorbs some of the red light and the red pigment absorbs some of the yellow light, the resultant orange paint is not so fully saturated as either original color.

Integrated Color Wheel

Sir Isaac Newton demonstrated that six principal hues (violet, blue, green, yellow, orange, and red) can be generated when sunlight is passed through a prism. These hues can be placed on a color wheel, as shown in Figure 6.10. Additional hues, which are full chroma equivalents to a mixture of adjacent original hues, can be created and placed between the six principal colors to create a color wheel with twelve specific, fully saturated, hues.

This integrated color wheel can help clarify the interrelationships between pigment and light. For years a semantic problem has hindered easy understand-

FIGURE 6.9
Selective reflection and absorption.
A pigment will reflect its own color
and absorb all others.

ing of these relationships. The use of the same words to describe some of the primary and secondary hues for pigment and light has tended to create some confusion. Although the words red, blue, green, and yellow are used to describe colors in both pigment and light, the specific hues are not identical. The integrated color wheel resolves this problem by renaming the primary colors in light to more accurately reflect the true color relationship that exists between the various hues in pigment and light.

Fully saturated colors don't all have the same value. The twelve principal hues of the integrated color wheel have been arranged in Figure 6.11 in their appropriate relationships to a value scale.

A wide variety of interesting and useful tones can be created by mixing complementary pigments with black and white. Figure 6.12 demonstrates this effect with the complementary hues red and green. The value and saturation (chroma) of the resultant hues change as they are mixed with either black or white. **Neutralization** occurs in mixing complementary hues of the same value.

A Practical Postscript to Color Theory

Any discussion of color theory necessarily revolves around hues of 100 percent purity and saturation. Colors of this strength and value are not used in theatrical work, for two primary reasons: They would be incredibly expensive, and the use of fully saturated colors isn't particularly appropriate in the theatre, simply because the colors would visually dominate anything else on the stage.

neutralization: Subtractive color mixing; the selective absorption of light as the result of mixing complementary pigment hues; the creation of gray.

APPLICATION OF COLOR IN THE THEATRE

In any discussion of color, there is bound to be a disparity between theoretical principles and practical results. Although the principles of color theory are certainly applicable in the practical use of color, the end results of mixing paints,

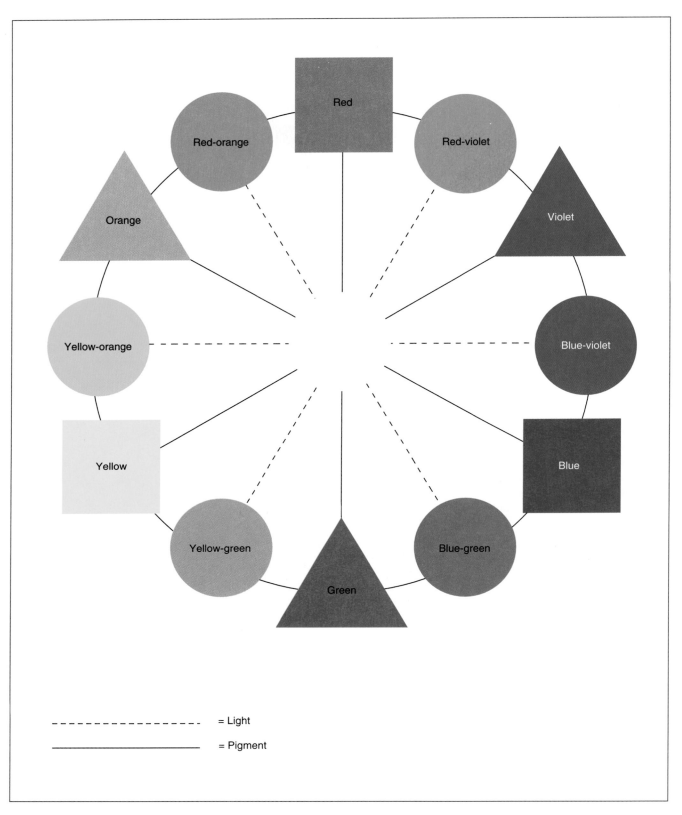

FIGURE 6.10
Integrated color wheel. This device is used to help clarify the relationships that exist between the primary and secondary hues in both pigment and light.

FIGURE 6.11
A hue-value relationship chart (left). Since fully saturated colors do not all have the same value, this chart helps explain the relative values of the indicated colors. The values of the colors on the outside columns correspond with the values of the adjacent gray blocks on the center gray-scale column.

FIGURE 6.12
Complementary hue-tone relationships (right). The value of a specific hue changes as white or black is added to it. The values of the resultant tints and shades on the outside columns correspond with the values of the adjacent gray blocks of the central gray scale.

dyes, or lights will be somewhat different from the results projected by the theory. This is because of the impurities and contaminants found in all stage paints, dyes, lamps, and color media.

Meaning of Color

People react to color. Sometimes that response is subtle and subconscious, and at other times it is overtly physical. Doctors and drug-rehabilitation counselors have discovered that an extremely violent patient will often become calm and manageable in about fifteen or twenty minutes if placed in an all-pink environment. Many hospitals now have "pink rooms" in which everything—the floor, ceiling, walls, doors—is painted the same hue of pink.

The meanings of color are constantly changing. Color meanings are influenced by many factors: cultural background, age, personality, adjoining colors, and individual mood. The variability of these factors is the primary reason that the following list of affective meanings is necessarily ambiguous. Moreover, these definitions are simply common interpretations of the meaning of specific colors and should not be thought of as being the "correct" ones.

yellow: stimulating, cheerful, exciting, joyful, serene, unpleasant, aggressive, hostile

orange: warm, happy, merry, exciting, stimulating, hot, disturbed, distressed, unpleasant red: happy, affectionate, loving, exciting, striking, active, intense, defiant, powerful, masterful, strong, aggressive, hostile

green: youthful, fresh, leisurely, secure, calm, peaceful, emotionally controlled, ill

blue: pleasant, cool, secure, comfortable, tender, soothing, social, dignified, sad, strong, full, great

violet: dignified, stately, vigorous, disagreeable, sad, despondent, melancholy, unhappy, depressing

black: sad, melancholy, vague, unhappy, dignified, stately, strong, powerful, hostile, distressed, fearful, old

white: pure, tender, soothing, solemn, empty

brown: secure, comfortable, full, sad, disagreeable

Practical Color Use

Designers in the theatre normally follow some general color guidelines. The following discussion provides a survey of examples and general practices. Any competent designer will advise you that there are many occasions when it is appropriate, logical, and right to ignore the normal and the conventional if doing so will support the visualization of the production concept.

Pigment   Scenic designers generally use hues of medium saturation and value, because most sets serve as a background environment for the action of the play, and the set needs to recede from the audience's consciousness after it has made its original visual statement. For the same reason, costume designers generally work in a less constricted palette. Colors of full saturation and brilliance will direct the audience's attention to the actors. Generally, the only proviso for their use is that the hue and value be an appropriate reflection of the actor's character.

Color proximity—the placement and relationship of specific hues—has a great impact on the spectators' perception of a scene. Strongly contrasting colors create a greater dynamic tension than do less conflicting hues. A set that had a highly saturated yellow sofa placed in front of a brilliant blue wall would be visually shocking. The startling color contrast would indicate that the owner of that particular apartment was dynamic, eccentric, possibly volatile, and probably wacko. Similarly, a man dressed in an electric blue suit with a brilliant yellow vest would also be thought of in the same basically antisocial way. But if the saturation of those contrasting colors was reduced and modified—a soft-yellow, floral-print sofa against a dusty powder-blue wall of the same or similar value— our perception of the owner of that apartment would be similarly softened.

Accent colors, which are basically small touches of contrasting colors, are continually used by both scenic and costume designers. The color dynamics of an otherwise lifeless set can be enhanced by setting a vase of colorful flowers on a table, hanging a painting on the wall, or accenting a table through the use of a white or color-coordinated tablecloth. Costumers frequently provide accent colors in their designs with accessories such as jewelry, scarves, purses, and shoes. Accent colors generally are interpreted in the same way as other contrasting colors: Greater contrast creates increased dynamic tension.

Light   There are some very pragmatic reasons for using colored light onstage. The light from theatre spotlights is rather bright and harsh. In its uncolored state, and at close to full intensity, it will tend to bleach any color out of the scenery, costumes, and makeup. If colors that are compatible with the scenery and cos-

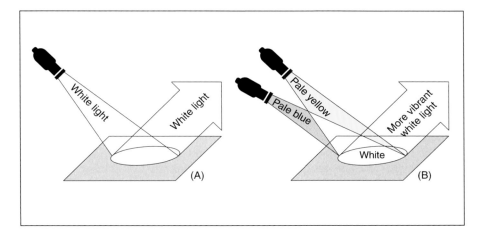

FIGURE 6.13
The use of an additive mix of complementary tints results in a more lively, vibrant light.

tumes are used to filter the stage lights, however, the scenic designer's and costume designer's color palettes and values will be maintained.

As we have seen, the mixing of complementary hues creates white light. In the discussion on color theory, this principle was demonstrated with fully saturated hues. In practical application, fully saturated hues are rarely used because of their adverse effect on the other designers' palettes and on actors' skin tones. Complementary hues of low chroma are frequently used, however, because pigments lit with additively mixed white light are enhanced rather than bleached. This color enhancement is caused by the brain's interpretation of retinal stimulation, as demonstrated in Figure 6.13. Figure 6.13A shows white light striking a white surface. Since the white light is composed of all wavelengths of light, the white surface simply reflects all the light rather than absorbing or filtering out any specific portion of the spectrum. Figure 6.13B shows two complementary hues of low saturation (light blue and light yellow) striking the same white surface. These low-saturation hues emphasize a relatively narrow portion of the spectrum (blue and yellow), although there is still a large proportion of the full spectrum (white light) in the mix. The white surface reflects the pale blue and pale yellow, as well as the white light, to your eye. Because blue and yellow are complementary, your brain interprets the mixture of those two lights as white. However, the cones are more strongly stimulated by the blue and yellow light than they would be with plain white light. Interestingly, the brain interprets this stronger color stimulation as a richer, more vibrant color. This phenomenon works for all complementary color mixes. Although the specific color reflectivity and absorption of any colored light from any particular costume or set color will depend on the characteristics of that particular hue, the principles of color vibrancy remain constant.

The palettes used by the scenic and costume designers generally dictate the specific complementary hues that are chosen by a lighting designer. The lighting designer usually selects specific hues that will enhance the primary palettes of the other designers, using the guideline that every hue heightens its own color and suppresses its complementary. If the scenic or costume designer is using a full-spectrum palette, the lighting designer may combine three or more colors to create white light. When more specific hues are used to create the white light mix, the range of hues affected by the color-enrichment characteristics of a complementary mix are similarly broadened.

The lighting designer can also produce a white light mix that is not exactly complementary—either slightly warm or cool—to create a corresponding warming or cooling of the stage environment. This type of not-quite-complementary color mixing is very helpful in establishing an atmospheric feeling of heat or cold on the stage.

An audience can only see objects as a result of those objects reflecting or emitting light. Since the overwhelming majority of objects in a play (actors, costumes, sets, props) reflect rather than emit light, an analysis of the use of color in a design concept would logically stem from an analysis of the effects of the hues used in the lighting design on the various other elements of the total design for the production.

The two sections that follow will analyze the use of color in two distinctly different types of color designs: a muted, predominantly low-saturation, closely coordinated palette in the University of Arizona production of Ted Tally's *Terra Nova*; and a vibrant, highly saturated, full-range color design for the University of Arizona production of the Masteroff/Kander/Ebb musical *Cabaret*.

COLOR ANALYSIS OF *TERRA NOVA* AND *CABARET*

*Terra Nova**

The Environment of the Play   The primary location is the vast frozen whiteness of Antarctica, but numerous vignettes take place in a variety of other locations: an English country garden in spring, a banquet hall, and several nonspecific memory locations. It is essential for the continuity of the play that scenes flow smoothly from location to location without a break in the action.

The Scenic Design   The color design helped to create the cinematic flow required for the production. To bring to life the vast coldness of Antarctica, the set, which was a jumble of platforms arranged to create an abstraction of the ruptured surface of an ice floe, was painted an off-white (Figure 6.14). On the upstage side of the platforms a large expanse of unpainted, unbleached muslin was suspended from an abstracted ship's spar (Figure 6.15). This sail was used as a projection surface for color washes, visual effects, and photographic images of Scott's ill-fated expedition to the South Pole. The entire set was surrounded by a black cyclorama to help focus the audience's attention on the set and actors.

The Costume Design   The costumes and properties were ultrarealistic. The natural earth tones (primarily shades of browns and grays) of the properties and the men's costumes stood out in strong contrast against the whiteness of the set. Scott's wife, the only woman in the play, was seen only in Scott's memory scenes of home. She was dressed in a warmly colored floral print (Figure 6.16) to present a stark contrast with the muted patterns and solids that were worn by the men.

Lighting Design   The lighting used color as a primary device to create psychological keys in support of the emotional content of the various scenes. Figure 6.17 provides a color key of the lighting used in this production indicating the direction and color of the various light sources. (Note that the numbers indicate Roscolux color numbers.) Figures 6.18–6.21 show how the various design elements (scenic, costume, properties, lighting) blended to create the color impact of the production design.

*Director: Harold Dixon; scenic and lighting design: J. Michael Gillette; costume design: Jerry D. Allen; property design: Peter Wexler—the properties were designed and constructed for the original production of *Terra Nova* at the Mark Taper Forum in Los Angeles, produced by the Center Theatre Group.

FIGURE 6.14
The color of the set and sail (white) was selected for two reasons: (1) antarctica is overwhelmingly white; (2) the highly reflective neutral color makes an excellent projection surface for the various colors and images that make up a large segment of the design concept.

The scenes in Antarctica were lit with almost painfully brilliant white light (Figure 6.18), which resulted in the colors of the costumes and properties being portrayed very closely to their true hues.

The memory scenes were lit with textured top lights and color washes selected for their psychological impact: deep blue for Scott's heavier memories (Figure 6.19); soft pastels for the romantic memories of his wife (Figure 6.20); amber candlelight for the banquet scene (Figure 6.21).

The use of low-saturation complementary colors to light the acting areas from the front and sides significantly reduced the color-shifting effects of the stage lights on costumes and skin tones. The clear, textured top lights, when used in conjunction with the heavily saturated top washes, created significant changes in the visual appearance of the set. These elements, working together, created a subtly effective color design that worked for the support of the production.

FIGURE 6.15
The sail was backlit with color washes (left) to provide primary atmospheric and psychological keys about the nature of the individual scenes. It was also used as a projection surface for black-and-white slides of Scott's actual expedition (right).

FIGURE 6.16
The warmly colored, floral-print summer dress worn by Scott's wife provided a strong color contrast with the predominantly muted patterns of gray and brown worn by the men.

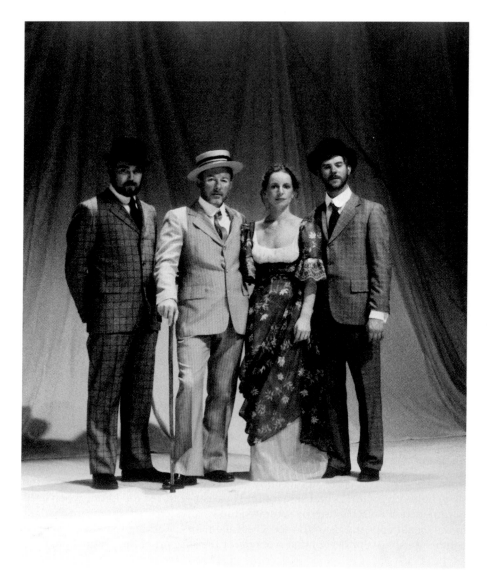

Explanations of how the color palettes of the various design elements (scenic, costume, property, and lighting) interacted are contained in the captions for each illustration.

Cabaret*

The Environment of the Play   The primary location of this musical is a seedy, second-rate night club, the Kit Kat Klub, in Berlin, Germany, in the years 1929–30. Additional scenes take place in several other locations: a railroad car, various rooms in a rooming house, and a fruit shop.

The Scenic Design   The scenic design for *Cabaret* created a startling contrast through the juxtaposition of line, color, and finish (Figure 6.22). The strong contrast was appropriate because it helped to heighten the dramatic tension inherent

*Director and choreographer: Richard Hanson; scenic design: Tom Benson; costume design: Peggy Kellner; lighting design: J. Michael Gillette.

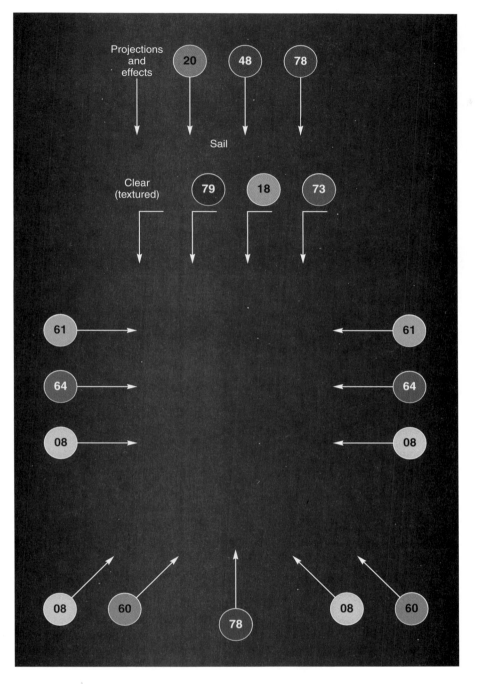

FIGURE 6.17
Color key for the *Terra Nova* lighting
design. The arrows indicate the direction from which the light is
traveling toward the stage. The horizontal flags on the arrows at the
upper part of the illustration indicate that those lights are coming
from above, rather than behind, the
actors.

in the script and the production concept. The dominant element of the design
was the Kit Kat Klub, which was painted in medium-saturation earth tones.
However, the color was applied in an erratically angular pattern on the vertical
face of the runway as well as on the floor of the audience portion of the nightclub.
The zigzag motif was continued with the busy herringbone pattern on the floor
of the runway and the rest of the stage.

The floor and four upstage columns were finished with a high-gloss glaze to
heighten the contrast between those elements and the remainder of the set, which
was painted with a traditional matte finish. The shimmering aluminized Mylar

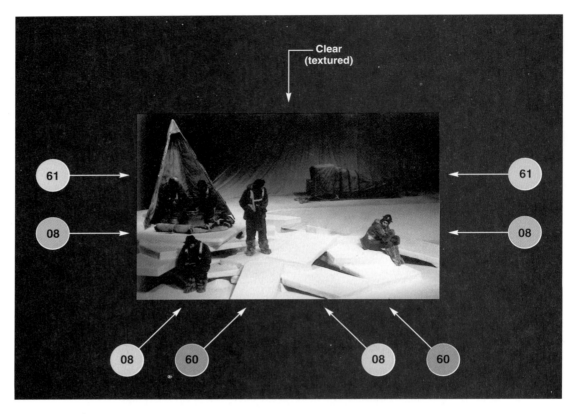

Clear
(textured)

61

08

61

08

08   60

08   60

FIGURE 6.18 ▲
Complementary colors (Roscolux 08
and 60 from the front and 08 and 61
from the sides) were used at high (but
equal) intensity to provide a white,
very bright, slightly cool color mix.
The clear (white) top light helped to
edge the actors' heads and shoulders
with white as well as wash out any
color shadows created by the individual hues in the front and side lights.
The rendering of the skin tones as well
as costumes and property colors was
slightly cooler than if white light (as
opposed to the complementary mix)
had been used. The "cooler" look was
a desired effect.

FIGURE 6.19 ▶
The textured light was created by
bathing the stage with saturated blue
(78 and 79) from the front and top.
The texture was created by introduc-
ing the clear, textured top light at
relatively low intensity. Scott's face
was framed with a low-intensity followspot whose beam diameter was
only shoulder wide. Skin tones and
upper-torso costume colors were
rendered naturally by the warm followspot (at low intensity the light
from the uncolored beam is naturally
warm) combining with, and overrid-
ing the effects of, the deep blue.

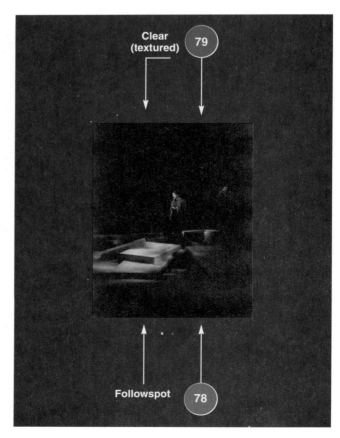

Clear
(textured)   79

Followspot   78

FIGURE 6.20
The atmosphere of England was created by using textured top lights colored in warm, soft hues (18 and 73) and the back lights on the sail (20 and 48) to provide a striking contrast with the blue-white coldness of the lights for Antarctica. Scott and his wife (down stage) were lit with warm-white combinations of 08 and 60 from the front and 08 and 61 from the sides. The figure in the background was side lit with a warm, dim, front/side light. The warm-white light on Scott and his wife provided accurate color rendering of their costumes. The warm light striking the background figure created a fairly accurate color rendering of his tuxedo.

FIGURE 6.21
Primary color for this scene was provided by the warm amber (20) on the sail in the background. The banquet table was lit with a warm-white blend of 08 and 61 from the sides and 08 from the front and uncolored, textured top light. A little blue top light (79) was used to enhance the edging effect of the top light on the black tuxedos. This created a candle-lit feeling with warm skin tones, tablecloth and floor, and black tuxedos.

curtain (Figure 6.23) provided another dazzling type of contrast during one of the production numbers.

Small white light bulbs were used to spell CABARET and outline the arches. These little pinpoints of light played against the black void created by the surrounding black cyclorama to create another type of emphatic contrast.

The fully saturated secondary colors (amber, cyan, and magenta) used in the double rows of vertical striplights on either side of the stage, and the six-inch Fresnel spotlights hung from the upper-level railings of the set, created another jarring note of color contrast.

The color and contrast treatment of the other locations, which slid in on a shuttle stage just upstage of the nightclub runway, were more muted than those of the Kit Kat Klub because, in general, scenes that took place in the other locations were emotionally "softer" and more intimate.

The Costume Design   Contrast was also readily evident in the costume design. The designs for the Kit Kat Girls were based on vibrant, fully saturated colors (Figure 6.24) and high-sheen fabrics. A powerful statement was made by the contrast between the actresses' pale skin and the skimpy, heavily saturated, highly reflective surfaces of the costumes.

FIGURE 6.22
Scenic design for *Cabaret*, by Tom
Benson. A number of hues were
used on this production, but they
were all in a fairly close tonal range.
Contrast was achieved primarily by
pattern variation and gloss finish
coats applied to selected elements
of the set.

The costumes for Sally (the two on the left and the two on the right in Figure
6.25) used a change in saturation and hue as a device to mirror her emotional
progression through the play. In the beginning, she was dressed in the vibrant,
shocking colors and styles of the Kit Kat Girls. As she fell in love with Cliff, she
dressed in softer, more muted tones. When Sally chose to stay in Germany as
Cliff left, her reimmersion in the world of the cabaret was mirrored in the high
contrast of a floor-length black sequin evening dress that she wore in the final
scene.

The men's costumes, while being faithful to the period, also mimicked the
emotionally based use of high contrast employed for the women's costumes. The
Master of Ceremonies and the cabaret ensemble men were costumed in black-
and-white evening wear, while Cliff and Herr Schultz were dressed in suits of
muted hues selected to mirror their emotional warmth.

Lighting Design   The colors selected for the lighting design were dictated by
three primary considerations: (1) the full-spectrum colors of the costumes and
set; (2) the heavy, smoke-filled, sensuous atmosphere needed for the cabaret; and
(3) the need for a lighter, more realistic atmosphere for those scenes outside the
cabaret (Figure 6.26).

FIGURE 6.23
The aluminized Mylar curtain provided a startling contrast with the black background immediately upstage of the curtain and created a spectacular reflective surface for the fully saturated hues in the vertical striplights on either side of the stage.

Complementary colors of light-to-moderate saturation (Roscolux 62 and 02) were selected for the front lights for the acting areas because they would be appropriately neutral for both the cabaret scenes and those more intimate scenes outside the cabaret. However, those colors had enough saturation to enhance the costume and set colors in both locations. By balancing the color mix between the 02 and 62, the stage could be made neutral, cool, or warm as appropriate. The full saturation necessary for the scenes inside the cabaret was supplied by the Roscolux 20, 57, and 93 used on the vertical striplights and Fresnels on either side of the stage. These saturated color washes, used in conjunction with the acting-area lights, enhanced the full-spectrum, strongly colored palettes of the costumes and scenery used in the cabaret scenes, as well as creating the heavy atmosphere necessary within the cabaret. (Specific hues of strongly saturated light create an impression of more vibrant color than do similar hues of less saturation. If two or more of these relatively saturated hues are additively mixed to create a white light, the resultant white light will create a similar vibrant color reaction from the full color spectrum.)

During production numbers, the set was generally lit with psychologically appropriate color washes, and the six followspots, using white or lightly tinted light, were used to highlight the various leads.

The downstage area of the cabaret audience was lit with a top wash of textured white light to support the concept that the area was lit by the individual table lamps. During the out-of-the-cabaret scenes, the textured top wash was combined with a deep blue wash to reduce the area's apparent visibility. (The deep blue looks like a shadow color but allows the "real" audience to see the shadow detail.)

FIGURE 6.24
Costume designs by Peggy Kellner. The full-saturation, high-contrast "glitzy" materials of the Kit Kat Girls' costumes were enhanced by the strongly saturated hues used to light the cabaret scenes.

FIGURE 6.25
Costume designs by Peggy Kellner. The color progression of Sally's costumes mirrored her emotional progression through the production. See text for details.

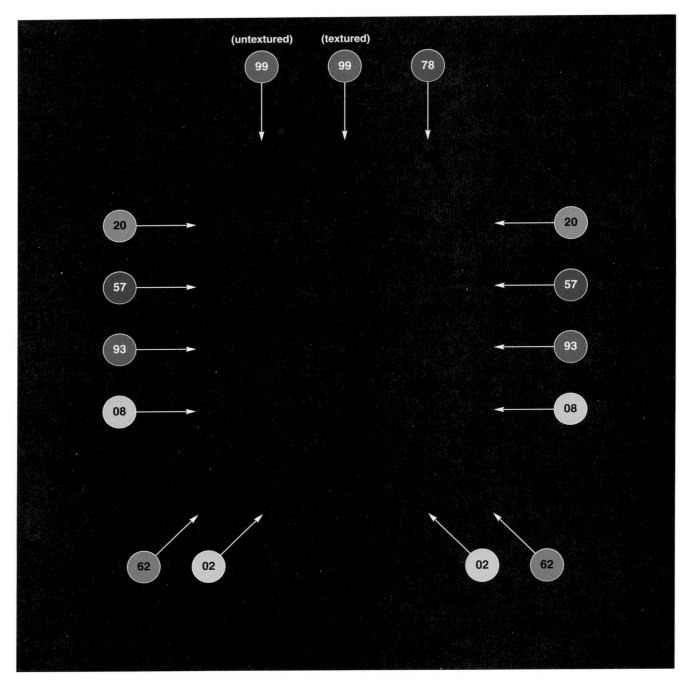

FIGURE 6.26
Color key for the lighting design. Low-saturation colors (02, 62, 08, 99) were used for general acting-area lights, while strong-saturation color washes (20, 57, 93, 78) were added for psychological emphasis. See text for details.

The difference between the theory and practice of color mixing is only a matter of degree, not principle. Although an understanding of the laws of physics that govern the mixing of color is very helpful in using color in the theatre, the only way that a designer can develop any real understanding of, and facility in, the use of color is through experimentation and experience. Additional information on the practical application of color can be found in Chapters 10 (*Scene Painting*), 12 (*Lighting Design*), and 22 (*Drawing and Rendering*).

Chapter 7
Scenic Design

Scenery helps the audience understand and enjoy a play by providing a visual reinforcement of the production concept. However, the scenery hasn't always been designed with a production concept in mind.

Before about 1875, no one paid any great attention to specifying the elements (period, country, locale, socioeconomic status, and mood) that most contemporary designers believe make up a well-conceived stage setting. Greek and Roman productions were performed out of doors with little or no scenery. Medieval drama used standardized scenic elements (heaven, hell, the courtyard, and so on) that represented the various locations needed for almost all productions. The Renaissance was a period of evolutionary development in scenery. Some theatres had permanent sets built as part of the theatre architecture (Teatro Olympico). Other theatres (the Globe) had bare, open stages with no scenic elements. From the Restoration (1660) until the mid-nineteenth century, plays were performed in front of stock sets. Only in the past 100 years has scenery evolved into its present form.

CONSIDERATIONS FOR THE SCENIC DESIGNER

Before we look at the various elements that must be considered to create a quality scenic design, a cautionary digression seems appropriate. Beware of any so-called rules of design. There aren't any. What works in one design situation may not work in another. If every design choice we make is a rational, considered decision, there is no need for rules such as "Never paint a set white," "Don't use green light," "Never wear taffeta on stage," and so forth. In terms of creativity, these rules are debilitating, because they arbitrarily limit our ability to select from the full breadth of our knowledge and experience. Having said that, I'm now going to contradict myself. There is one guideline that *does* apply to all scenic designs: The design should create an environment for the play that is supportive of the production concept.

Although we should be wary of arbitrary rules, most good scenic designs do comply with a majority of the principles discussed in this section.

In addition to the scenery, the scenic designer is frequently responsible for designing the stage properties. Props are an important element of the stage picture, and they subscribe to all of the qualities discussed in this section. In black-box and arena theatres, furniture props take on added significance as the primary visual elements of the scenic design, since flats, drops, and other vertical elements of scenery generally aren't used. Additional information on stage properties appears in Chapter 11, *Stage Properties*.

FIGURE 7.1
Scenic designs can provide reinforcement of the mood and spirit of the play. (A) *Flea in Her Ear,* Florida State University; scene design by Park Warne, costume design by Abby Lillethun, lighting design by Michael Murphy; photo by Robert M. O'Lary. (B) John Bottom and Ben Halley, Jr., in *Endgame,* produced by the American Repertory Theatre (Cambridge, Massachusetts); scene design by Douglas Stein, costume design by Kurt Wilhelm, lighting by Jennifer Tipton; photo by Richard Feldman.

(A)

(B)

Mood and Spirit of the Play

One guideline works for all plays: the design should be expressive of the **mood** and **spirit** of the play. Within this context, mood usually refers to the dominant emotional quality of the production. Spirit is generally interpreted to refer to the production concept—the way in which the production design team (producer, director, and scenic, costume, lighting, and sound designers) decide that the play is going to be presented.

For the design to effectively express mood and spirit, the designer needs to incorporate some elements that suggest the emotional characteristics of the play, as shown in Figure 7.1. If the play is a gentle romance, it might be appropriate to use soft curves to define the outline of the set, and the scenery could be painted with delicate pastel to reinforce the romantic qualities of the play. If the play is

mood: The feeling of a play—comic, tragic, happy, and so forth.

spirit: The manner and style in which a play is presented to the audience.

an intense tragedy, hard lines, sharp angles, and a palette of dark colors would express the heavy mood that the production concept seeks to project.

Assume that an old melodrama is being considered for production. The play has many situations that are essentially serious (the heroine, her widowed mother, and her seriously ill little brother are being thrown out of their house for nonpayment of rent), and most of the characters are likable people who just happen to be down on their luck. Unhappiness, sadness, and despair seem to be the general emotional qualities of the play. Instead of emphasizing these depressing qualities, however, the director decides to change the emotional tone of the play. He or she chooses to concentrate on the comic aspects. The serious and dramatic situations are exaggerated to the point that they no longer seem believable, and the whole spirit of the production changes.

The design work should mirror this change in the mood and spirit of the production. For the original mood, the settings could appropriately have been realistic and depressing, and the color palette would logically have been muted and somber. For the reinterpretation, the settings can be simplified and exaggerated in a cartoon style that supports the same spirit of overemphasis and artificiality that is evident in the acting and business of the play.

Historical Period of the Play

A caveat: The following discussions of period, locale, socioeconomic status, and season all assume that the design style chosen by the production team is based in realism. If your production concept is nonrealistic, then the primary visual clues probably will be much more sharply guided by the evocative/emotional content of the script and production concept.

If the design style for the production is going to be based in realism, the scenic designer will probably want to provide historically accurate visual clues that will help the audience identify the period of the play. To provide these clues, the designer needs to do historical research.

Historical research may mean that the set designer looks at furniture, rooms, knickknacks, and buildings from the period of the play. Or the designer may search the library for pictures of furniture, room design and decoration, architecture, landscape photos, paintings, and so forth, in books and periodicals. Such background research is extremely important, because the style of the trim, furniture, and furnishings, as well as their arrangement within the room or building, varies tremendously from generation to generation and from one geographic area to another. It is this change of appearance that helps the audience identify the period, country, and locale of the play, as shown in Figure 7.2.

Although it is vital that you do historical research, don't assume that your design must adhere to every stylistic quirk of the period in which you are working. It isn't necessary to make exact copies of furniture pieces and trim styles. You will need to understand the general motifs and idiosyncrasies of the period and use them in a way that creates a faithful visual representation. But you don't have to duplicate every variation and nuance. A scenic design is not a reproduction; it should be a creation that mirrors the essence of a period to provide a physical environment that will enhance the mood and spirit of the play.

Locale of the Play

Geography has a significant impact on the design of buildings and their furnishings. In the days before air conditioning and central heat, climate shaped the buildings. For example, steeply pitched gables helped the snow slide off the roofs of houses built in the North. Homes in the warmer climates had lower-pitched

FIGURE 7.2
Historical detail helps provide visual keys to the period of the play. (A) John A. McQuiggan's production of *The Foreigner* at the Astor Place Theatre (New York); scenic design by Karen Schulz, costume design by Rita Ryack, lighting by Paul Gallo; photo by Van Williams. (B) Asolo Theatre (Sarasota, Florida) production of *Misalliance;* scenic design by Jack Doepp; photo by Gary W. Sweetman Photography.

(A)

(B)

roofs and large overhanging eaves to keep the summer sun off the walls and out of the windows. By using these and similar visual keys, the scenic designer can help the audience identify the play's location.

Styles in the design of houses and business structures change rapidly. These changes stem more often from socioeconomic circumstances than from architects' aesthetic yearnings. Thus, the oil crisis of the 1970s strongly influenced American architecture. As the cost of heating oil, natural gas, and electricity rose, the size of the average residential dwelling decreased accordingly. The all-glass designs for commercial buildings of the 1960s and early 1970s were replaced by structures that could be heated and cooled more economically.

Even more noticeable than the differences in the exterior design of houses and buildings are the differences in interiors. Depending on the historical period and the socioeconomic status of the occupants, ceilings may be high or low. Walls may be plain, painted, or covered with wallpaper. They may contain window arrangements, recessed bookcases, or ornamental niches. The only guideline for their inclusion in the design is that they be appropriate for the period of the play and the social status of the characters.

The walls of the room in which the action of the play takes place may be made from rough logs, finished boards, or lath and plaster. They may also have a variety of decorative trim, for example, baseboards, wainscoting, chair rails, plate rails, picture rails, or cornices (see Figure 7.3). Depending on the type of room and the period of the play, there may be a fireplace. The fireplace may be built into the wall, or it may project into the room and be surrounded by a plain or decorative hearth.

In addition to the shape, arrangement, and details of the walls, the furnishings also provide the scenic designer with an excellent opportunity to help create an appropriate environment for the play. In selecting furniture, the designer should study the types of arrangement appropriate for the period and adapt them to the **blocking** needs of the play. In selecting the appropriate number of chairs, sofas, or other seats to be used on a set, for example, a good rule of thumb is to have enough places for everyone to sit if all the principal actors are on stage at the same time.

blocking: The actors' movements on the stage.

Decorative properties can also aid in creating a believable environment. Decorative props, also called stage dressing, are generally considered to be those furnishings that aren't used by the actors and serve no specific purpose in the business of the play but that help project atmosphere and feeling. Small pieces of furniture and stage dressing, such as occasional chairs and end tables, pictures, wall hangings, rugs, knickknacks, lamps, lighting fixtures, and similar decorative articles, all fall into the category of decorative properties.

The floor needs to be considered when doing historical research. It provides a unifying visual element that ties the whole set together and can provide the foundation for the color scheme for the entire design. In many arena and thrust stages, the audience is seated above the stage floor. In these theatres the floor treatment becomes even more important because of the visual dominance that it has over other elements of the design. The stage floor can be covered with one-quarter-inch Masonite fairly inexpensively, and it can be painted in whatever treatment (boards, earth, stone) is appropriate for the design. Rugs or some similarly individualized, movable treatment can be used for the individual scenes of a multiset production.

FIGURE 7.3
Various types of wall trim.

Socioeconomic Level and Personality of the Characters

Most realistic sets give some indication of what sort of characters will inhabit the environment of the play. The designer normally uses set and decorative props as tools to achieve this effect. A living room that is decorated with inexpensive but reasonably tasteful furnishings suggests one type of occupant, and the same room furnished with expensive but incredibly gaudy things indicates that a completely different sort of person lives in the room. If either of the preceding rooms were littered with a month's accumulation of dirty dishes, clothes, and other junk, it would seem likely that a completely different type of character was living there.

Selecting furniture can be a bit complex, simply because so many factors can influence what furniture should be used. The status of the "owners" of the furniture greatly affects not only the style but also the amount of furniture. If the principal character is a "pack rat" type, it is usually appropriate to have more furniture on the set than if the lead is a more fastidious type.

There are, of course, many production situations that prevent a scenic designer from giving any indication of the socioeconomic level or personalities of the characters. Examples of this type of situation would include "studio productions," in which a series of neutrally painted blocks are used for the furniture, as well as those low-budget productions that depend on borrowed furniture and props. But when the circumstances permit, furniture selection is another means by which the designer can enhance the audience's understanding and enjoyment of the play.

Season of the Year

Normally, it is difficult for the scenic designer to provide anything other than a cursory indication of the season in which the play is happening. If the play takes place in summer, the designer can suggest heat by having the doors and windows open and using screen doors and windows. The selection of light colors and fabrics for any upholstery and curtains can help create a feeling of summer, but by and large the projection of seasonal atmosphere is usually left to the lighting and costume designers.

Elements of Composition

Full discussions of composition and color were presented in Chapters 5 and 6. However, this is an appropriate time to remind you that scenic, property, and costume designers must be able to draw freely and easily. This is a skill that can be learned, and instructions for basic perspective drawing and sketching are included in Chapter 21, *Perspective,* and Chapter 22, *Drawing and Rendering.* Although these instructions will provide you with a beginning point, the best way to become adept at drawing and painting is to take art classes.

Manipulation of the compositional elements (line, form, mass, value, and color), as we have seen in Chapter 5, is the root of any design. We will now explore the applicability of this principle to scenic design.

Line   Line defines form. The characteristics of any line are defined by its physical properties (dimension, quality, and character). These properties, especially character, give any particular line its emotional content.

Cartooning is almost always based on the principle of line simplification. Walt Disney's cartoon characters Mickey Mouse and Donald Duck are simplified outlines of a mouse and a duck. There is no mistaking the objects for anything else, yet their simplicity gives them distinctive personalities that are uniquely their own.

Simplifying or altering the line of a natural form within a scenic design creates the same type of unique character definition as does line simplification in cartooning. The personality of the object created by this process is directly related to the emotional quality of the line style chosen by the designer. Generally, an object drawn with strong (heavy, sharply angular, bold) lines creates an emotional response that the object is more powerful, dominant, and purposeful than if it were drawn with weak (soft, curvilinear, lightweight) lines.

Form   In compositional terms, form refers to a space enclosed by a line. The evocative characteristics of the line defining any form will dictate the emotional qualities of that form. The character of the chosen line (heavy, light, straight, squiggly, softly curving, sharply angled) will create a perceptual key that helps explain the psychological nature of the object being depicted (Figure 7.4).

FIGURE 7.4
Peter Pan, produced at Florida State University; scenic design by Robert Barnes, costume design by Erin Wertenberger of Costume Crafters, Inc., lighting design by Lauren Schoemaker.

Mass   Within the context of composition, mass is defined as the three-dimensional manifestation of an enclosed form, and the perceived meanings of mass are closely related to those of form. The exaggeration of either form or mass can be used to stylize a design. By exaggerating the height, width, or depth of the natural dimensions of an object, we can change the character of that object. The illustrations from almost any book or cartoon version of *Alice's Adventures in Wonderland* serve to illustrate this point. Once Alice encounters the March Hare and enters the strange land ruled by the Queen of Hearts, hardly anything is seen in its normal size or shape.

Value   Value refers to the relative lightness or darkness of a line, form, or mass. The emotional reaction to the value or reflectance of an object has become ingrained in the core of Western thought, although no one is sure why white has come to symbolize purity, truth, and honor. Its opposite in terms of reflectance or brilliance, black, has similarly come to symbolize evil, dishonesty, and dishonor. These evocative differences can be used by the scenic designer when selecting the color palette for use in a production. Although the values of white, gray, and black are obvious, the value differences within specific hues—pink, medium red, and deep red, for example—are more subtle but have the same emotional effect on the audience. The color pink generally evokes a response that is allied to the emotional response to white—purity, truth, honor. Its counterpart—dark red—evokes an emotional reaction that is more closely related to black—evil, dishonesty, dishonor.

Color   Although scenic objects are normally painted to appear as they are in life, interesting results can be achieved by substituting an unexpected hue for the natural color. Any production of the musical *Brigadoon,* which centers on time travel of the hero to the mythical pseudo-Scottish country of Brigadoon, needs a set to show the countryside of Brigadoon for several of the scenes. The drop for this scene usually shows a typical Scottish glen complete with hills, heather, and

---

Good Design: A Checklist

Here is a concise list of those qualities that can be found in a good design. It is equally applicable to scenic, property, costume, and lighting design.

Does the design support the work of the other designers? Does the design express

- the mood and spirit of the play?
- the historical period of the play?
- the locale of the play?
- the socioeconomic status and personality of the characters?

- the season of the year?

Is the design based on the elements of good composition? Practically, does the design meet

- the needs of the director?
- the needs of the actors?
- the technical demands of the production?
- the fiscal and time budgets?

---

sylvan glade. The audience will be alerted that all is not quite normal in Brigadoon if, rather than natural colors, the hillside is painted in a gaily colored plaid.

Practicality of the Setting

A sketch for a scenic design can be both absolutely beautiful and totally worthless, because a design doesn't exist just on paper. It must also be practical. Any scenic design must fulfill utilitarian functions before it can be considered anything more than a pretty picture. The designer must take into consideration the needs of the director and actors, the demands of construction, and budgets of money and time.

Needs of the Director   The set design must meet the needs of the director. The form of the setting(s) must be designed to accommodate the blocking and other stage business that the director has in mind. If the director wants the heroine to make a grand entrance down a flight of stairs, it is the responsibility of the scenic designer to place the stairs in a prominent position. The director and scenic designer discuss these directorial needs during the early production conferences so that they can help to shape the set in the scenic designer's mind.

Needs of the Actors   To fulfill the actors' needs, the set must function properly, efficiently, and as planned. It must also provide a safe environment. Actors have to be able to concentrate in order to perform their roles properly. The last thing that they need is anything that would break that concentration, such as slippery floors, doors that won't open or stay closed, windows that jam shut, and supposedly solid floors that wiggle.

Construction Demands of the Design   Every scenic design presents certain technical demands when it is constructed. Their complexity is directly related to the intricacy of the design. Elements within the design, such as a spinning staircase or a cantilevered platform, may create construction challenges that cannot be solved by ordinary scenic-construction techniques. The designer must be aware of these and must determine how these pieces can be constructed and rigged. It can be disastrous for a production if the designer and director plan on a specific piece of equipment, such as an elevator or a large wagon or a revolve,

Designing for Stock Scenery and Found Objects

Many theatres maintain an inventory of standard-sized flats and platforms. This inventory is referred to as stock scenery. Found objects are simply that: objects retrieved from a salvage yard, a garbage can, or a dark corner of the prop room.

Designing for stock scenery or found objects can be cost-efficient and sometimes even inspirational. If your budget is small, using stock flats for the walls of the set will allow you to save money. If the flats aren't the right height, small flats called headers can be attached to the top of the stock flats to increase their height. Jogs, which are narrow flats less than a foot wide, can be made to modify the width of the flats. Stock platforms, which are normally four feet wide by eight feet long, are another cost-efficient scenic element. Although the shape of a raised stage area may be irregular, the majority of the elevated platform can be constructed using the four-foot-by-eight-foot platform modules. The remaining spaces can be filled in with irregular platforms specifically constructed for the production.

Designing for found objects requires that you look at utilitarian objects in a slightly different way. Jim Gray sculpts dinosaurs of amazing anatomical accuracy from old auto parts. He looks at a junkyard and doesn't see piles of broken cars but rather the bones of long-vanished animals waiting to be resurrected.

Using this same kind of different vision, Peter Wexler created a backdrop for the Theatre Center Group's production of *Godspell* from old doors, pipe, and chain-link fencing. Designing for found objects can be fun, effective, and cost-efficient.

Other people's junk can be turned into art. Twentieth Century Dinosaurs sculpted by Jim Gray. Photo by Tova Navarra courtesy of the San Francisco Chronicle.

Scenic design for Godspell, *produced by the Center Theatre Group at the Mark Taper Forum, Los Angeles. Scenery designed by Peter Wexler.*

and then discover during the technical or dress rehearsals that the unit won't function as planned.

Additional technical demands are imposed because scenery must be portable, and the scenic designer needs to specify how the sets should be broken down into manageable units. Even the scenery for plays that require a single set must be portable, since the scenery is usually built in one place and transported to the stage for setup. The unit breakdown of the scenery for a multiscene production must be carefully planned to ensure that there will be room to store everything in the wings and flies.

Before construction starts, the scenic designer reviews the plans with the lighting designer to be sure that the set can be lit as effectively as possible. Sometimes, portions of the scene design are slightly rearranged or modified to give the lighting designer room to hang and focus the lighting instruments. Sets with full ceilings normally preclude the use of top and side light, but if the scenic designer can include a beam or similar architectural feature in the ceiling, an opening can be cut on the upstage side of the beam and the instruments focused through the slot.

Time and Fiscal Budgets   The administration of the actual construction schedules and fiscal budgets varies from organization to organization, but the scenic designer is ultimately responsible for the timely construction of the scenery and properties. It is the designer's responsibility to produce the best possible design that the budgets will allow.

In the commercial theatre, the scenic costs and construction schedules are determined in a fairly straightforward manner. The scenic designer submits the plans to the producer, who approves the plans and then solicits bids for the construction and painting of the scenery and properties from a number of independent scenic studios. The contract is generally awarded to the lowest bidder. If the actual costs of the scenery are above the estimated budget for scenic construction, the producer and scenic designer discuss cost-cutting procedures. These generally involve eliminating some part of the design or redesigning various elements to reduce their construction costs.

In regional professional companies that construct their own scenery, and in educational and community theatres, the responsibility for formulating cost and time estimates varies. Generally, the producer, managing director, or production manager determines the estimated budget, and the scenic designer and technical director work within those estimates to determine the actual time and fiscal budgets for the construction, finishing, and mounting of the scenic and property elements. To accomplish this relatively complex task, the scenic designer is in almost constant communication with the technical director during the design phase. The whole process of budgeting is immeasurably improved if the scenic designer can produce fairly accurate estimates of costs and construction time.

VISUAL PRESENTATION OF SCENIC DESIGNS

To communicate effectively, the scenic designer must be able to present his or her visual concepts to the other members of the production design team in some clearly understandable manner. Two methods are used to fulfill this vital function: sketches and models.

Sketches

Thumbnail sketches and renderings are the two basic types of sketch that the scenic designer produces.

Thumbnail Sketches   Thumbnail sketches (Figure 7.5) are rough drawings, usually made in pencil, that show the general composition of the set but very little detail. They are generally made while the designer is developing various concepts for the set while doing conceptual research.

FIGURE 7.5
Thumbnail sketches.

The Design Process in Scenic Design

Commitment

As in any other design field, you have to make a commitment to yourself to do your best possible work on the assignment.

Analysis

To help clarify the challenge of scenic design, you need to read the script, talk to other members of the production design team, and ask questions. Find out everything you can about the play (see the material on script analysis in Chapter 2), the director's production concept, and the production circumstances (type of stage, budget, and so forth).

A ground plan and center-line sectional of the theatre in which the play will be produced provide information regarding the stage configuration, sight lines, general stage equipment, and other aspects of the physical structure of the theatre. Many times these drawings are accompanied by a specification sheet that provides other pertinent data regarding the auditorium, stage equipment, and policies. The producer or theatre manager should be able to supply you with these drawings and specification sheets.

While you are running around asking questions, you will identify areas that require additional research. For example, if you are designing *Terra Nova*, which is set in Antarctica, you will have to know what that frozen continent looks like. Because the chances are pretty good that you've never been there, you will have to study the geography, climate, and appearance of that continent. This kind of information is usually available in books and periodicals at the library.

Research

Background research in scenic design involves several things. If the production concept requires a realistic setting, the scenic designer must delve into the architectural, sociological, and cultural background of the environment of the play. If the setting is to be nonrealistic, it may not be necessary to probe as deeply into these details. You may need to examine the psychological roots of the play more closely, however, because a nonrepresentational setting ideally should be a physical extension of the psychological environment of the play.

This research will necessitate several trips to the library or museum(s) to look at books, periodicals, paintings, and other sources that provide visual information about homes, buildings, furniture, and other details of the period of the play.

Up to this point in the design process, your primary function has been the stockpiling of information, which has helped clarify the challenge and pointed out areas requiring further research. In the next phase of the design process—conceptual research—you start to synthesize and utilize the information you have been gathering.

The object of conceptual research is to create as many potential solutions to the design challenge as possible. Now is the time to start producing thumbnail sketches or functional models based on a synthesis of your information. It is also appropriate, and almost inevitable, that you experiment with differing combinations of elements from the various design concepts you have evolved. This sort of experimentation is the key to a creatively vital design, because creativity in theatrical design is basically the combination of existing forms and elements into new arrangements or orders.

Incubation

After you have conjured up as many solutions to the design challenge as possible, you need to set the whole project aside for a while and go do something else.

Selection

The next phase of the design process involves selecting the one solution that seems to best fit the parameters of the design challenge. In actual practice, the solution that you finally settle on will undoubtedly be a combination of bits and pieces from several of the design concepts that you evolved during the conceptual research phase.

Implementation

During the implementation phase, you produce the plans, drawings, and models that will allow the design idea you have selected to be constructed. At this time, you produce the rendering of the set(s), build the presentation model(s), and prepare the ground plan, front elevations, detail drawings, painter's elevations, prop dressing lists, prop sketches, and any other drawings or notes that will help the shop to build the set and properties as they were conceived.

Evaluation

In the evaluation phase of the design process, you take an objective look at how the scenic design worked in relation to the production concept and objectively review the communication that took place between yourself and the other members of the production design team. You need to examine the methods that you used, as well as the materials that you selected to reach the goal of your scenic design. You also need to evaluate your communication with the other members of the production design team. Did you do everything you could have to foster good communication? Did you consult with the other designers when you made adjustments to your design after construction had begun?

Thumbnail sketches are almost always unfinished drawings. Their purpose is to provide a rough visualization of the various scenic concepts on which the designer is working. They are drawn rapidly for two primary reasons. The quick sketching seems to lessen the inhibitions that other members of the production design team feel when suggesting changes in the various elements of the design; and the lack of time spent on the drawing also seems to keep the designer from getting locked into one particular design concept too soon.

Storyboards provide another use for thumbnail sketches. In motion picture production, storyboards are used to provide a clear visualization of the action before the film is shot. Their use in the theatre is much the same. A series of thumbnail sketches can be drawn of any moment in the play in which complex scenic action occurs in order to provide a clear picture of "what is happening" within that particular scene.

Renderings   Renderings are finished color sketches of the set. They are normally drawn to scale in **mechanical perspective** so that they are an accurate representation of the actual size, shape, and color of the setting. The renderings are also complete in terms of the type, style, and location of any furniture, as well as all trim and decorative touches that will be used on the setting. Quality renderings also show the scenic designer's thoughts regarding the lighting for the set. These sketches generally include a figure or figures to help the viewer determine the scale of the design.

Renderings can be produced using any media, but watercolor and acrylic paints, pastels, colored pencils, and markers are used most frequently. Specific "how-to" information on scale drawing, perspective drawing, and rendering techniques is contained in Chapters 20 (*Mechanical Drafting*), 21 (*Perspective*), and 22 (*Drawing and Rendering*).

Models

Two specific types of scenic models are used to present the visual ideas of the scenic designer: functional models and production models. Scenic models are attractive, interesting, and fun to look at, but they are most useful when they are placed within an accurate scale model of the stage space (proscenium, thrust, or arena) for which they are designed. The scale model of the theatre needs to be used because it is difficult to understand the relationship between the set, stage, and audience unless those spaces are clearly defined.

Functional Models   The functional model is the three-dimensional equivalent of a thumbnail sketch. Its purpose is to help the scenic designer and other members of the production design team visualize the basic composition of the scenic design. It is usually quickly constructed from Bristol board, white card stock, or stiff paper and held together with tape or glue. It is made to scale (usually one-quarter or one-half inch to one foot) so that it will be an accurate representation of the finished set.

Because the purpose of the functional model (Figure 7.6) is to show the general shape and form of the set and not the detail, any indication of trim and decoration is usually limited to pencil sketches indicating the location and general style of the major architectural trim elements. The functional model is rarely painted.

The functional model is an excellent aid to the scenic designer. Most designers begin the execution step of the design process with a series of thumbnail sketches. Then they frequently construct functional models of these sketches as a means of verifying and solidifying their design concepts. It is important to

mechanical perspective: A drafting technique that provides an illusion of depth.

FIGURE 7.6
The functional model is usually constructed from thin cardboard, and any detail is drawn with pencil or pen and ink. *As You Like It: The Forest,* produced at the MacLeod Theatre, Southern Illinois University; designed by Darwin Reid Payne. This illustration and Figure 7.7A are from *Theory and Craft of the Scenographic Model* by Darwin Reid Payne, copyright 1985 by the Board of Trustees, Southern Illinois University, Carbondale. Reprinted by permission of the publisher.

remember that functional models are the three-dimensional equivalent of thumbnail sketches. As the scenic design is being developed, a series of these models may need to be constructed to provide a clear visualization of the evolving design concept.

The use of a functional model is particularly important when working on a design that is difficult to represent with a sketch, such as a setting that is more sculptural than decorative. The functional model is also a great aid when dealing with any set that makes use of forced perspective, because it is much easier to see the effect of the visual distortion on the model than it is in a drawing. Additionally, it is very easy to create the exact angle of desired distortion by cutting down, or adding to, the height and angle of the thin cardboard walls of the model.

The functional model also provides an excellent method of presenting visual concepts to other members of the production design team. It is usually much easier for everyone to understand the scenic designer's concept and intentions when a model is used to supplement the scenic sketches.

The director can use the functional model as a visual aid while explaining the set concept to the actors. Furthermore, he or she can use it when planning the blocking for the production.

The scenic designer and technical director use the functional model to help plan complicated scene shifts. Problems of limited storage space or complex movements of the various scenic units can be solved with its aid.

To check on the accuracy of plans after they have been drawn, simply glue the plans onto thin cardboard, and make a functional model from the plans. If no errors have been made in drawing the plans, the model should fit together perfectly.

Production Models   The production model (Figure 7.7) provides a complete visualization of the scenic designer's concept. The production model is also built to scale (usually one-quarter or one-half inch to one foot), is fully painted, and completely decorated with all of the furniture, props, and set dressing that will be used during the production.

Because it is complete in every detail, the production model provides an excellent method of explaining the full scenic concept to the other members of the production design team. For the same reason, it is also used by the property master to help guide the design and selection of props and set dressing for the production.

The production model also provides a good means of keeping a record of the scenic design for the production. When security permits, it can also be used during the production as a decorative display in the lobby of the theatre.

Computer Presentations

While watercolor renderings and models are the traditional methods of depicting the scenic designer's concepts, they are not the only ones used. Computer drafting, rendering, and animation software packages have opened a whole new world of visual-presentation techniques. More and more frequently, scenic designers are using computer-based demonstrations to aid in presenting their ideas to other members of the production design team. Perspective **wireframe** models of the set can be rotated to show what the set will look like from any position in the house. The **sight lines** can be checked to determine that the whole set is visible for all seats in the auditorium and that the masking prevents the audience from seeing backstage. With current technology it is both fast and easy to produce color renderings of three-dimensional computer models of sets. The color

wireframe: Lines used to define the shape of an object.

sight line: A sighting extending from any seat in the house to any position on stage; used to determine how much of the stage and backstage area will be visible from that auditorium seat.

FIGURE 7.7
The production model is painted and furnished to provide an accurate miniature version of the finished set. (A) *Suddenly Last Summer,* scenic design by Darwin Reid Payne. (B) *The Member of the Wedding,* scenic design by J. Michael Gillette.

(A)

(B)

and texture of these sets can be modified to show what other color combinations might look like. It isn't necessary or essential that you render the set on the computer. The wireframe model of the design can be printed and rendered with pencils, pastels, and/or markers to create a treatment not available in the software program. Animation software can be used to show the choreography of shift changes.

A frequent by-product of these computer presentations is the number of "what if" conversations that they spawn among the production team—"What if the stage left wall was a little darker?" "What if it was a little taller?" "What if, during that second scene shift, that small wagon moved left instead of right?" A few mouse clicks and the team can see the answers to their "what if" questions. The exciting possibilities that computer imaging now offer the designer are just beginning to be explored.

Other Presentation Techniques

More traditional artistic techniques such as **collage** and **photomontage** can be used with either sketches/renderings or models. Copy machines produce excellent black-line reproductions of sketches on either white or colored stock. They can be colored with pencils or colored markers. If the copies are made on rag paper, water-based media can be used to color them. If these reproductions are printed in multiple copies, all appropriate personnel can be given a copy. Color copiers can also be used, although the color reproduction may not be totally accurate. If a sketch is made on **tracing paper,** blueline copies can be made using a blueprint machine. Some blueprint machines can print on **card stock,** which is available in a variety of colors. Like copy-machine prints, blueline copies can also be rendered with color using colored pencils, pastels, or markers.

These sketches and models are tools, not end products. The thumbnail sketches, renderings, and models that are made by the scenic designer help him or her discover workable solutions to specific design challenges. They are also the primary tools used to communicate those solutions to other interested members of the production team. They are, to a very real degree, working drawings.

Designer's Plans

The colored sketch or production model for a scenic design may be a thing of beauty, and it may give a clear picture of the designer's intentions, but it does not give the technical director or carpenters all of the information they need to build the set. This information is contained in a series of mechanical drawings, called designer's plans, that depict every detail of the set as well as providing exact measurements of its components. These plans are prepared by the set designer and consist of a ground plan, front elevations, detail drawings, full-scale drawings, sight-line drawings, and painter's elevations.

Ground Plan   The ground plan (Figure 7.8) is the key drawing on which the remainder of the designer's plans are based. It is a scale mechanical drawing showing the top view of a setting in its proper position on the stage. It clearly shows the form of the set and its relationship to the physical structure of the theatre. The location and measurements are given for all architectural features of the set, onstage and off, such as doors, windows, fireplaces, columns, stairs, and ramps. Additionally, the position and measurements for all **backing, ground rows,** wings, borders, and cycloramas are indicated.

A majority of the work done in planning a production depends on the information provided by the ground plan. During the rehearsal period, the director has the stage manager, using the ground plan as a guide, tape or chalk the outline of the design onto the rehearsal room floor. Then the actors can rehearse and perfect their blocking in a space that corresponds to the actual set.

The lighting designer, when drawing the light plot, uses the ground plan to provide information about the shape and placement of the set within the theatre. This type of information is needed when making decisions about the **hanging positions** for the various instruments that will light the production.

The technical director uses the ground plan for a wide variety of functions. Together with the **center-line section,** it tells the TD where the set will sit on the stage and where to place the masking. It also indicates a great deal of information about the amount of materials that will be needed to construct the set(s).

Information on how to draw a ground plan, as well as the other drawings that make up the designer's plans, is contained in Chapter 20, *Mechanical Drafting.*

collage: A picture made of various materials (e.g., paper, cloth) glued on a surface; can include drawn or photographic images as well.

photomontage: A composite picture made by combining several separate pictures; can include nonphotographic images as well.

tracing paper: Translucent paper used for drafting.

card stock: A thin cardboard, similar in thickness to 3 × 5 notecards and/or file folders.

backing: Flats, drops, or draperies on the offstage side of doors and similar openings to prevent the audience from seeing backstage.

ground row: Low, horizontal flats used to mask the base of cycs or drops; frequently painted to resemble rows of buildings, hedges, or similar visual elements.

hanging positions: The various locations around the stage and auditorium where lighting instruments will be placed.

sectional: A drawing, usually in scale, of an object that shows what it would look like if cut straight through at a given plane.

center-line section: A sectional drawing whose cutting plane is the center line of the stage and auditorium, showing the height of the various elements of the theatre; usually drawn in the same scale as the ground plan.

FIGURE 7.8
Ground plan for *Blithe Spirit*, produced at the University of Arizona, scenic design by K. Pistor.

Front Elevations   Front elevations (Figure 7.9) show a front view of the set as if it were flattened into a single plane. The main purpose of these scale drawings (normally one-half inch to one foot) is to indicate all of the vertical measurements that cannot be shown on the ground plan. These dimensions include the height of walls, doors, and windows as well as the location of any features on the walls such as baseboards, wainscoting, chair rails, cornices, paintings, or other decorative features.

Even if the scenic designer has constructed a functional model of the set, he or she will actually be designing as much when drafting the elevations as when producing the thumbnail sketches, renderings, or models, because what appears on the elevations is actually a proportional reduction of the appearance of the finished set. If the designer wants to change or adjust any element, it is fairly easy to erase and redraw the elevations. A corresponding change needs to be made on the ground plan whenever the changes made on the elevations, such as widening or moving a flat, affect its accuracy.

The primary purpose of the front elevations is to describe the appearance of the set; they don't tell how to build it. For this reason, no attempt is made to indicate the width of the individual flats that will be used to construct the various

FIGURE 7.9
Front elevations for *Blithe Spirit,*
produced at the University of Arizona; scenic design by K. Pistor.

wall units. This breakdown of the wall segments into manageable units is the
responsibility of the technical director or, in the professional theatre, the scene
shop foreman. The construction of the flats is made from rear elevations, which
are drawings that show the reverse side of the flats depicted in the front elevations. These scale drawings show the framework of the flat, including the placement and dimensions of all its various parts. The structure and nomenclature of
flats will be discussed in Chapter 9, *Scenic Production Techniques,* and the drawing
of rear elevations is taken up in Chapter 20, *Mechanical Drafting.*

Detail Drawings   The scale of one-half inch to one foot normally used in drawing the front elevations reduces the size of some of the smaller features to the
point that it is difficult, if not impossible, to draw all of their details. Detailed
pieces, such as an elaborate fireplace or an intricately designed stained-glass
panel, need to be drawn in a larger scale (Figure 7.10).

Many features of a setting cannot be fully described by drawing them in top
and front (or rear) views only. Three-dimensional objects often require a third
view to supplement the other two. There are several methods of drafting (orthographic projection, isometric drawing, oblique drawing, and cabinet drawing)
that show more than two sides of an object. The techniques of these methods of
drafting are discussed in Chapter 20, *Mechanical Drafting.*

Full-Scale Drawings   A few of the smallest features of a set should be drawn
in full scale, or actual size. If the design is unusually intricate or the object rather
small, such as the pattern for a turned bannister or a wallpaper pattern, it is
usually both easier and faster to draw it in full scale. It is also easier to construct
something from a full-scale drawing than one that has been proportionally
reduced.

FIGURE 7.10
Portions of a detail drawing for Metropolitan Opera Association production of *Les Troyens,* produced at the Metropolitan Opera House, Lincoln Center, New York; scenic, costume, and visual effects (film) designed by Peter Wexler.

FIGURE 7.11
Plan view and vertical section of the Jule Styne and Joe Kipness production of *Jockeys*, produced at the Promenade Theatre, New York City; scenery, lighting, and costumes designed by Peter Wexler.

Design Inspiration: Scenic Design

The following discussion is based on and quotes extensively from "Onstage Magic With Water," by Mel Gussow (New York Times, July 28, 1998, pp. E1, E3).

The setting for Twelfth Night is an Oriental fantasy of the mind. As far as the eye can see, there is a road winding through water. At the front of the Vivian Beaumont stage, actors are lolling on the stage, surrounded by burning candles and incense. Nearby is a pool for swimming and dunking. Later in the play there will be a rainstorm. In Bob Crowley's scenic design for Nicholas Hytner's production, water is the central motif—more than 10,000 gallons is used at every performance.

"This is literally and metaphorically a waterlogged play," Mr. Crowley said. "It begins with a shipwreck, and the water imagery is in virtually every other scene. There is also the narcissism of the characters, constantly looking at their own reflections. The idea of water being the first mirror, the twinning of things—all that has resonance."

"And," he said, "there is a liquidity about the theatrical floor plan." The set is "all curved."

This is an unusual design for *Twelfth Night,* which is generally presented as alternating between the Duke's palace and Olivia's home, with Viola disguised as the Duke's male messenger plying a path between the two. Seldom is the play presented completely alfresco as in this Lincoln Center Theatre production.

Mr. Crowley, who was born in Ireland, studied painting and sculpture before going to drama school and deciding to be a scenic designer.

Mr. Hytner, who has frequently worked with Mr. Crowley in theatre and opera over the last ten years, said about his collaborator: "He always responds poetically to a play. His sets are often painterly. My taste, which is influenced by Bob, is not toward

sight-line drawings: A scale drawing (plan and section views) of sightings that extend from the extreme seats (usually the outside seats on the front and last rows of the auditorium) to any position on the stage; used to determine how much of the stage and backstage will be visible from specific auditorium seats.

Sight-Line Drawings An improperly or inadequately masked set is a sign of a second-rate production. Most people come to the theatre to be entertained, to escape into the world of the play. When they can see backstage and watch actors waiting for their cues, stagehands lounging around, or any of the backstage paraphernalia, their concentration on the substance of the play is broken. All of these unnecessary distractions can be avoided if the scenic designer takes the time to draft some **sight-line drawings.**

The sight lines of any set can be checked through the use of two drawings, a ground plan and a vertical section of the stage and auditorium, with the set in its proper position on the stage (Figure 7.11). The horizontal section, or plan view, shows the view of the stage, or sight line, of the people sitting in the extreme side seats of the first and last rows of the auditorium. The vertical section shows a side view of the sight line for the same seats.

architectural literalism or social realism. The kind of worlds we like to create are worlds of the imagination."

Mr. Crowley specializes in creating magical environments. To the director as to the designer, Shakespeare's Illyria in "Twelfth Night" meant, in Mr. Hytner's words, "not here, not now, somewhere different, a world where romantic impossibilities are made possible—a midsummer madness that can be resolved through the power of the stage."

As usual, Mr. Crowley began his research in a museum. In creating the New England background for *Carousel,* he was inspired by the paintings of Andrew Wyeth and Winslow Homer. With *Twelfth Night,* he drew upon two exhibitions at the Metropolitan Museum of Art: one of Oriental carpets, the other of illustrated pages from an Indian manuscript. Mr. Crowley made clear that he had not tried to reproduce anything in the exhibitions for *Twelfth Night,* but approached them for their atmospheric emanations.

The environment is generically Eastern, stressing the play's fabulistic side. "We talked about the hallucinogenic nature of the piece and the obsessive nature of the people who occupy the place," Mr. Crowley said. The aim was to give "people's desire and dreams—and the language—room to breathe." The approach, as with all his Shakespeare designs, is to keep it "fairly free and abstract" and not to "straitjacket it into a certain time, place, or period."

Another of Mr. Crowley's design inspirations were pictures of the Alhambra gardens in Granada, Spain. He was struck by the way that light filtered through the space so that things were only half visible. Avoiding solid scenery, he wanted the setting to have a translucent quality, so that people could be glimpsed on the wing. Intentionally, the feeling is cinematic, with crosscuts between scenes. As one scene finishes downstage, another begins upstage. "If the characters met," he said, "they would recognize each other and the play would finish. Instead, they take the opposite road like we all do in life, and life goes on."

Mr. Crowley's concept of design may seem somewhat heretical: He does not like scenery. At least not an abundance of it. Whenever possible he chooses the simplest setting. In this production, there are a bench and at one point a wall, both of which pop out of the floor. "I hate moving furniture onstage," he said, "and it is even harder to move it offstage." Only cushions are carried on and off.

"I would rather look at a beautifully lit backstage with a great actor in the middle of it than a great production with fifty-five tons of naturalistic living rooms flying in and out," Mr. Crowley said. In his eyes, an empty stage can be a design choice, and it can be exquisite, if properly lighted. "I'm putting myself out of work, aren't I?" he said with a laugh.

Pointing to Peter Brook's production of *The Cherry Orchard,* in which there were carpets and an absolute minimum of furniture, he said there was no such thing as something not being designed: "As Brook says in *The Empty Space,* the minute an actor walks across the stage and somebody looks at him, that is the beginning of a piece of theatre."

But where does the designer come in? Mr. Crowley responded with questions: "Is the floor wooden or is it a piece of canvas? Is it covered in dirt? Does it need sweeping? What's illuminating the actor? Those are all design decisions."

The little time required to draft sight-line drawings is time well spent. Too often the scenery is built, painted, and assembled on stage before the sight lines are checked. The sight lines may be perfectly satisfactory, but occasionally some area of the set is out of sight of the audience, the backing flats are too small, or the masking drapes have been hung in the wrong position. Sight-line drawings can reveal any potential problems with masking in sufficient time to correct them.

Painter's Elevations   Painter's elevations are front elevations of the set, but they are drawn on watercolor board and painted to show not only the colors but also the painting techniques that will be used in finishing the set. The painter's elevations (Figure 7.12) are the renderings that the scenic artist and paint crew use when painting the set. The scenic artist mixes the colors to match the palette

FIGURE 7.12
Painter's elevations for *Blithe Spirit*, produced at the University of Arizona; scenic design by K. Pistor.

used on the painter's elevations, and the crew applies the paint using techniques that will duplicate the style illustrated in the painter's elevations. Information on the materials and techniques of scene painting is contained in Chapter 10, *Scene Painting*.

Scenic design is both a demanding and a rewarding practical craft. In order to create a quality scenic design you have to use your imagination, sketch, paint, construct scale models, and produce accurate mechanical drawings. Although this process may seem to be an almost overwhelming task, seeing your design standing on the stage as tangible proof of a viable production concept is an extremely rewarding experience.

Chapter 8
Tools and Materials

Almost any material can be used to make scenery. Wood, fabric, metal, and plastics are commonly used, but almost anything else can be, or has been, used in scenic construction. The majority of these nontraditional construction materials are generally applied to a basic scenic form as decoration. Most basic scenery is made by constructing a supporting form from wood or metal and covering that structure with wood, fabric, or both. These structures will be covered in Chapter 9, *Scenic Production Techniques.* This chapter introduces the tools and materials used in scenic and property construction. The following list isn't intended to be exhaustive. Rather, it is intended to be representative of the types of tools and materials that can be found in a typical scene shop.

HAND TOOLS

Almost any type of scenery can be built with just a few hand tools; after all, people were building scenery long before the discovery of electricity and the development of power tools. The only advantages that power tools provide are speed and reduced effort.

Measuring Tools

Measuring tools are used to measure dimensions and angles.

Tape Measure   Metal tape measures (Figure 8.1A) are housed in either a plastic or a metal case. Most have a self-return spring to retract the tape into the case. They should have a lock to hold the extended tape in position. Available in a variety of tape lengths from six feet to twenty-five feet, they are appropriate for general scenic measuring. The steel tape (Figure 8.1B), which comes in lengths between fifty feet and two hundred feet, is manually retracted into the case with a built-in crank. It is used for measuring long distances, as when laying out the dimensions of the set on the stage floor.

Tri Square   A tri square is a small, rigid, hand square with a steel blade and a steel, composition, or wooden handle, as shown in Figure 8.1C. It is used as a guide for marking ninety-degree angles across narrow (under six inches wide) materials.

Combination Square   The larger combination square is a twelve-inch steel rule with a movable handle angled at forty-five and ninety degrees, as shown in Figure 8.1D. It is used for marking those two angles, and the steel rule can also be used for measuring.

FIGURE 8.1
Measuring tools.
(A) Tape measure
(B) 50′ Steel tape
(C) Tri square
(D) Combination square
(E) Bevel protractor
(F) Framing square
(G) Bevel set
(H) Carpenter's level

End view

Bevel Protractor The bevel protractor is similar to a combination square, except the angle is adjustable, allowing it to be set anywhere between zero and ninety degrees (Figure 8.1E).

Framing Square The framing square is a large steel L (Figure 8.1F), typically sixteen inches long on the bottom leg and twenty-four inches on the vertical leg. It is normally used for checking the accuracy of ninety-degree corner joints in flat construction.

Bevel Set The bevel set (Figure 8.1G) has a combination wood and metal case housing a movable metal blade that can be locked in position at any angle. It is also called a bevel gauge. The set is used for transferring angles from one piece of work to another.

Carpenter's Level The carpenter's level is used to determine true horizontal and vertical angles. A two- to four-foot-long carpenter's level, as shown in Figure 8.1H, is appropriate for stage use.

Marking Tools

Marking tools are used in conjunction with measuring tools to mark dimensions and angles.

Pencils Pencils—either carpenter's pencils or number two yellow pencils—are the preferred marking medium. Pens shouldn't be used because the ink can bleed or discolor subsequent paint jobs. Wax pencils, also called china markers, and soapstone are used to mark metal while wax pencils are used on lighting color media.

Scribe Also called a scratch awl, the scribe (Figure 8.2A) has a sharp metal point and is used for marking on wood, metal, and plastic. It can also be used for enlarging smaller holes or making **starter holes** for wood screws.

Chalk Line A tool used to mark straight lines is the chalk line (Figure 8.2B). A metal or plastic housing holds a length of cotton twine on a reel. The housing is filled with dry scenic pigment, which coats the twine. The twine is stretched between two points and lightly snapped to leave the straight line.

Hammers

Hammers are used for nailing and starting screws, as well as shaping and forming metal.

Scribe

(A)

Chalk line

(B)

FIGURE 8.2
Marking tools.

starter hole: A small hole bored into a piece of wood to hold the tip of a screw or drill bit; also called a pilot hole.

Safety Tip !

Using Hammers

Claw hammers and rip hammers should be used only for nailing, because their face may chip if they are used for pounding metals that are harder than nails. These chips can cut your hands or cause serious eye damage. The ball peen hammer has a hardened face that won't chip when used for beating metal.

FIGURE 8.3
Hammers.
(A) Claw hammer
(B) Rip hammer
(C) Ball peen hammer
(D) Mechanic's hammer
(E) Tack hammer
(F) Mallet

Claw Hammer Designed for inserting and removing nails, the claw hammer has two sharply curved claws projecting from the back of its head, as shown in Figure 8.3A. The curved claws facilitate nail removal. Claw hammers are available with a variety of head weights and shaft and grip compositions.

Rip Hammer Sometimes referred to as a straight claw hammer, the rip hammer (Figure 8.3B) has straighter claws than the claw hammer. They can be used for prying or ripping apart previously nailed wood. This hammer is also available in a number of head weights and shaft and grip compositions.

Ball Peen Hammer Primarily used for bending and shaping metal and seating rivets, instead of pounding nails, the ball peen hammer (Figure 8.3C) is made of harder steel than the claw or rip hammer and has a rounded striking face instead of claws on the back of the head.

Mechanic's Hammer Also known as a blacksmith's or heavy-duty hammer, the mechanic's hammer (Figure 8.3D) has a heavy head (one to three pounds). It is used for shaping metal.

Tack Hammer Used for inserting tacks, the lightweight tack hammer (Figure 8.3E) has two faces. The smaller face is magnetized to hold the tacks for insertion, and the larger face is used to seat the tacks.

Mallet A mallet (Figure 8.3F) can have a wooden, plastic, or hard rubber head. The wooden and hard plastic mallets are generally used for driving chisels. All

FIGURE 8.4
Saws.
(A) Crosscut saw
(B) Rip saw
(C) Backsaw and miter box
(D) Keyhole saw
(E) Coping saw
(F) Hacksaw

three can be used for shaping thin sheet metal when you don't want to leave hammer marks on the work.

Cutting Tools

Saws   Saws are used to cut such materials as wood, metal, and plastic. The material that a saw is supposed to cut generally depends on the number of teeth per inch in the blade, with wood-cutting blades having the fewest teeth.

Crosscut Saw   The crosscut saw (Figure 8.4A) is used to cut across the grain of wood. Alternate teeth on the blade are bent outward so that the **kerf** is wider than the width of the blade. This is done to prevent the blade from binding. A

kerf: The width of the cut made by a saw blade.

miter: An angle that is cut in a piece of work, usually in pairs to form a corner.

½"   ¾"   1"

FIGURE 8.5
Miscellaneous cutting tools.
(A) Utility knife
(B) Scissors
(C) Tin snips
(D) Wood chisels
(E) Cold chisels

saw with a twenty-six-inch blade and ten to twelve teeth per inch is suitable for most scenic purposes. (A blade with a higher number of teeth per inch will give a smoother cut.)

Rip Saw   Similar in appearance to the crosscut saw, the rip saw (Figure 8.4B) is designed to cut parallel with the grain of the wood. It has fewer teeth per inch—usually around six—and the teeth are filed straight across the blade to give a chisel-like cut.

Backsaw and Miter Box   The backsaw (Figure 8.4C) is a fine-toothed (twelve to fourteen teeth per inch) crosscut saw with a strong spine on its back. The spine stiffens the blade for more accurate cuts and also fits into a guide on the **miter** box. The miter box is a guide for making accurate cuts at forty-five- and ninety-degree angles. Some miter boxes have adjustable guides to permit cutting other angles.

Keyhole Saw   With its narrow, tapering blade of ten to twelve teeth per inch, the keyhole saw (Figure 8.4D) is used for making curvilinear cuts in stock lumber or plywood.

Coping Saw   The lightweight coping saw (Figure 8.4E) is used for making fine, curvilinear cuts in thin plywood. The replaceable blades have sixteen to eighteen teeth per inch and are easily broken. For making interior cuts, the blade can be snapped out of the frame, inserted through a hole in the work, and reinserted in the frame.

Hacksaw   The hacksaw is an adjustable frame saw for cutting metal (Figure 8.4F). The extremely fine-toothed (20–25 per inch), replaceable blades are available in a number of configurations for cutting mild steel and nonferrous metals such as copper and aluminum.

Utility Knife   Also called a matte knife, the utility knife (Figure 8.5A) has a replaceable blade. It is generally used to trim excess muslin from the edges of flats but can also be used for cutting out stencils and for other light-duty cutting or carving projects.

Scissors   Heavy-duty scissors (Figure 8.5B) are used for cutting a wide variety of papers and fabrics that are commonly used in scenic construction.

Tin Snips   There is a variety of tin snips, some that cut on a straight line (Figure 8.5C) and others that cut either left- or right-hand curves. Compound-leverage snips multiply the force that is applied to them with your hand. All snips are designed for the same purpose: to cut thin (generally under eighteen-gauge) ferrous and nonferrous strap and sheet metals. Snips should not be used to cut nails, wire, or similar small objects, because the small surface area of the object may pit or nick the cutting edge of the blades.

Wood Chisel   The wood chisel's steel blade, sharpened at a thirty-degree angle, is used for gouging, paring, or smoothing wood (Figure 8.5D). It has either a wooden or plastic handle. The chisel is struck lightly with a mallet or the heel of the hand. It is available in a variety of blade widths, with the one-half, three-quarter, and one-inch widths the most useful in scenic-construction work.

Cold Chisel   The cold chisel, made of very hard steel, is used for cutting through, or shearing, mild steel and nonferrous metals (Figure 8.5E). It is struck with a ball peen or mechanic's hammer.

Planes   Planes are knife-bladed tools used to smooth or round the edges or corners of wood. The lumber being planed must be firmly anchored in a vise or clamped to a solid surface like a workbench.

Block Plane   The small block plane (Figure 8.6A) is used to smooth the ends (across the grain) of boards. The blade is set at an angle of approximately fifteen degrees to the plane's **sole** (this angle varies with the manufacturer). The depth of the cut can be adjusted by raising or lowering the blade.

Smoothing Plane   Larger and heavier than the block plane, the smoothing plane (Figure 8.6B) is applied parallel to the grain of the wood. The blade is set at a steeper angle (approximately 25 to 30 degrees), and the depth of cut can be adjusted.

Spoke Shave   Whereas the block and smoothing planes are pushed across the wood to make their cuts, the spoke shave (Figure 8.6C) is pulled across the surface of the work. It has an adjustable blade to regulate the depth of cut, and the blade angle is approximately twenty to twenty-five degrees. The sole is slightly rounded rather than flat, since the spoke shave is used to soften or round sharp edges rather than to smooth flat surfaces.

Surform Tools   The trademarked Surform tools (Figure 8.6D) fall between the cracks of traditional definitions: They aren't really planes, and they aren't really files. They are based on the Surform blade, a thin, disposable strip of spring steel honeycombed with sharpened protrusions projecting from the surface. The Surform tool is pushed across the work, cross-grain or parallel with the grain. The serrated blade face doesn't leave a smooth finish, so the work generally has to be smoothed after the tool has been used.

Files   Files are used to rasp or grind wood, metal, plastic, and other materials. The teeth of a file are formed in diagonal ridges or rows across its face, with the more coarsely grained files having distinctly individual teeth. The spacing and height of the teeth determine the type of material for which the file is designed. Coarse teeth are used with wood, medium teeth with wood and plastic, and fine teeth with metal and some plastics.

Wood Rasp   An extremely coarse-toothed file, with individually discernible teeth, the wood rasp (Figure 8.7A) is usually flat on one face and curved on the other. It is used for rough shaping of wood.

Wood File   The wood file (Figure 8.7B) has smaller teeth than the wood rasp. It is available in three cross-sectional configurations: flat on both faces, flat on one surface and curved on the other, and round. It is used for smoothing wooden and plastic surfaces.

Rat-Tail File   The rat-tail file (Figure 8.7C) is also known as a round file. It is available in a variety of surface finishes and diameters appropriate for use with wood, plastic, and metal.

Metal File   Metal files have very fine teeth for use on metal. As shown in Figure 8.7D, they are available in a variety of configurations.

Drilling Tools

Several tools provide the motive force to spin the bits for drilling holes in wood, plastic, and metal. When drilling you usually need to make a starter hole, so the hole will be drilled exactly where you want it. When working in wood, you can make the starter or pilot hole with a nail and hammer or a push drill (described

sole: The bottom plate of a plane, with a slot through which the tip of the blade projects.

(A)

(B)

Front
(C)

Bottom

(D)

FIGURE 8.6
Planes.
(A) Block plane
(B) Smoothing plane
(C) Spoke shave
(D) Surform tools

FIGURE 8.7
Files.
(A) Wood rasp
(B) Wood file
(C) Rat-tail file
(D) Metal files

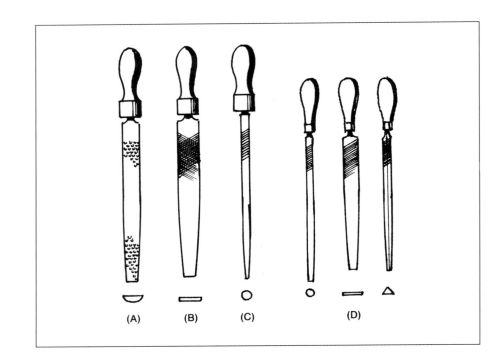

(A)   (B)   (C)   (D)

center punch: A pointed tool made from a similar type of hard steel as the cold chisel and used for indenting shallow holes in wood and metal.

chuck: The adjustable jawed clamp at the end of a drill that holds the drill bits.

later in this section). With steel the starter hole is usually made with a **center punch.**

Hand Drill   The hand drill is a cranked device (Figure 8.8A) for making small-diameter holes in wood. The bit is inserted into the **chuck,** which is driven by a small geared crank. The chuck will accept only bits that have a shaft diameter of one-quarter inch or smaller.

Brace   The brace, another hand-cranked drill for wood (Figure 8.8B), is used for holes larger than one-quarter inch in diameter. The wood bits are held by the chuck, which is driven by an offset handle. The handle works as a lever to increase the twisting power applied to the bit.

Push Drill   The push drill (Figure 8.8C) has a spring-loaded shaft that spins the chuck as you push downward on the drill handle. Designed for light usage, it can accept bits from $\frac{1}{64}$ to $\frac{3}{16}$ inch in diameter. The push drill is very useful for making starter holes.

Bits

Twist-Drill Bits   Twist-drill bits (Figure 8.9A) are designed for use with either wood or metal and are available in a variety of sizes from $\frac{1}{64}$ to approximately $\frac{3}{8}$ inch in diameter. When these bits are used in metal (mild to medium steel and common nonferrous metals), the work should be lubricated with cutting oil. The cutting oil not only lubricates the bit and the work but also helps to dissipate friction-generated heat, which would otherwise quickly dull the bits.

Wood Bits   Paddle-shaped wood bits, sometimes called spade bits (Figure 8.9B), are designed for use in wood, although they can be used in some soft plastics. They must be used with power hand drills or drill presses, because they require high-speed rotation to do their work. They are generally available in diameters from $\frac{1}{4}$ to $1\frac{1}{4}$ inches.

Chuck

(A)

(B)

Chuck

(C)

FIGURE 8.8
Types of hand drills.
(A) Hand drill
(B) Brace
(C) Push drill

(A)

(B)

1¼"   ½"   ¼"

Expansion bit

(C)

(D)

(E)

FIGURE 8.9
Drill bits.
(A) Twist-drill bit
(B) Wood bits for power drill
(C) Auger bits
(D) Push-drill bit
(E) Hole saw

Auger Bits Designed to be used with the brace for cutting holes in wood, auger bits (Figure 8.9C) are available in diameters from ¼ to 1 inch. A modification of the auger bit, the expansion bit, has an adjustable cutting head that can be set to drill holes with 1- to 2½-inch diameters.

Push-Drill Bits Push-drill bits (Figure 8.9D) have very sharp points and straight, fluted indentions running up the side of the bit shaft to carry away the wood chips loosened during drilling. Because of the very narrow bit diameter (1/64 to 1/8 inch) and the strong downward pressure on the drill itself, push-drill bits seem to punch rather than drill holes in the wood.

Hole Saws Although not really bits, hole saws (Figure 8.9E) are saw-toothed cylinders of hardened steel with a drill bit in the center that is used to center the hole saw in the work. Generally available in sets of six to eight diameters, hole saws are used to cut holes up to 2 inches in diameter in wood that is 1½ inches thick or less and in thin, mild steel.

Clamping Tools

Clamping tools cover a wide variety of devices, ranging all the way from vises to pliers to C clamps. Regardless of the type of clamp, they are designed to firmly hold wood, metal, or plastic.

Carpenter's Vise The carpenter's vise (Figure 8.10A) is attached to the edge of a workbench and is designed for holding wood. One or both faces are covered with hardwood to prevent the vise from scratching, denting, or marring the surface of the work.

Machinist's Vise Used to clamp and hold metal, the machinist's vise (Figure 8.10B) has toothed steel faces to help grip the work. The machinist's vise can be

FIGURE 8.10
Clamping tools.
(A) Carpenter's vise
(B) Machinist's vise
(C) Adjustable wood clamp
(D) Belt clamp
(E) Pipe clamp
(F) Bar clamp
(G) C clamp

(A)

(B)

(C)

15' Reserve of
1" wide nylon belt

Belt lock

Style
12

Turn to
tighten loop

Front view

Working loop

Release to loosen
working loop

Rear view

(D)

(E)

(F)

(G)

used for clamping and holding wood, but it will score or mar the surface of the work unless protective blocks of wood are used to sandwich the object.

Adjustable Wood Clamp   The adjustable wood clamp (Figure 8.10C) is a versatile tool used primarily in furniture construction. The two jaws can be adjusted to a variety of angles that are useful in holding various parts of furniture frames together while the glued joints are drying.

Belt Clamp   A belt clamp (Figure 8.10D) is a woven nylon belt that can be used to clamp irregularly shaped pieces together. It uses a ratchet device to tighten the belt after it has been placed around the object. It is very helpful in furniture construction. Some belt clamps substitute a nylon rope for the web belt.

Pipe Clamp   Pipe clamps (Figure 8.10E) are composed of a threaded pipe, a movable end plate, and an adjustable head plate. The bar clamp (Figure 8.10F) is the same as the pipe clamp except that a notched bar is substituted for the pipe. Both pipe and bar clamps are used to clamp furniture frames, table tops, and similar wide objects together while their glue joints dry.

C Clamp   C clamps are available in an almost bewildering array of configurations (Figure 8.10G). The most useful sizes for scenic and property construction have an opening from 4 to 8 inches and a minimum throat depth of 2½ inches. They are used for a wide variety of jobs, such as holding work together while the parts are being assembled or while glue joints are drying.

Pliers   Pliers are used for a variety of gripping, clamping, bending, and cutting jobs in scenic and property construction. There are almost as many styles and types of pliers as there are potential uses.

Slip-Joint Pliers   Slip-joint pliers (Figure 8.11A) are very common. They have an adjustable pivot point that provides two ranges of jaw openings. They can be used for clamping, gripping, bending, and cutting light wire.

Long-Nose Pliers   Extremely useful for holding small objects in hard-to-reach locations, long-nose, or needle-nose, pliers (Figure 8.11B) should not be used for bending anything other than the lightest wire, because the jaws can be forced out of alignment very easily.

Adjustable Arc-Joint Pliers   Known by a variety of other names, such as slip-joint pliers and alligator pliers, arc-joint pliers are truly versatile (Figure 8.11C). They have a series of jaw ranges that allows them to be used for a wide variety of purposes. The jaw design and long handles enable the worker to grip both square and round objects with a great deal of leverage. These pliers are used for holding metal pipe and tubing and for similar gripping jobs.

Locking Pliers   Generally known by its trade name of Vise Grip, locking pliers (Figure 8.11D) are available in a number of configurations to fit a variety of shapes. Their primary function is to grasp, lock, and hold almost any object. The size of the jaw opening and the amount of pressure applied by the jaws are adjustable by the screw at the base of the handle.
   The welding clamp (Figure 8.11E) is a variation of the locking plier that can be used to clamp almost any combination of metal shapes together.

Diagonal Cutters   Available in a variety of sizes, diagonal cutters (Figure 8.11F) are primarily used by electricians for cutting soft wire.

FIGURE 8.11
Types of pliers.
(A) Slip-joint pliers
(B) Long-nose pliers
(C) Adjustable arc-joint
    pliers
(D) Locking pliers
(E) Welding clamp
(F) Diagonal cutters
(G) Wire strippers
(H) Wire crimper

FIGURE 8.12
Types of wrenches.
(A) Open-end wrench
(B) Box-end wrench
(C) Adjustable-end wrench
(D) Monkey wrench
(E) Pipe wrench
(F) Ratchet and socket

Wire Strippers   Wire strippers (Figure 8.11G) are used for stripping insulation from electrical wires without cutting the wire.

Wire-Crimping Tool   The wire crimper (Figure 8.11H) is used to pressure-clamp solderless connectors to electrical wire.

Wrenches   Many wrenches are useful in the scene shop. They are used to tighten nuts and bolts.

Open-End Wrench   Nonadjustable open-end wrenches have smooth jaws (Figure 8.12A). These wrenches are designed to fit nuts of a specific standard or metric diameter.

Box-End Wrench   Also made in standard and metric sizes, box-end wrenches have a closed, toothed head that must be fit over the nut. The head of the box-end wrench is frequently offset, as shown in Figure 8.12B.

Adjustable-End Wrench   Also known by the trade name Crescent Wrench, the adjustable-end wrench (Figure 8.12C) has smooth jaws that adapt to fit almost any small- to medium-sized nut. The six-, eight-, and ten-inch sizes are the most suitable for stage work.

Monkey Wrench   The monkey wrench is a heavyweight, smooth-jawed, adjustable wrench (Figure 8.12D) for use on large nuts and work that is too large for adjustable-end wrenches.

Pipe Wrench   Similar in shape to the monkey wrench, the pipe wrench (Figure 8.12E) has jaws that are serrated to bite into the soft metal of pipes. It is used to hold or twist pipes and their associated couplings.

FIGURE 8.13
Types of screwdrivers.
(A) Slotted screwdrivers
(B) Phillips screwdriver
(C) Nut driver

Socket Set and Ratchet Handle   Sockets are cylindrical wrenches used with a ratchet handle (Figure 8.12F). The design of the reversible ratchet handle allows you to tighten or loosen nuts without removing the socket from the nut. The tool is useful for working in confined spaces.

A deep-throated nine-sixteenth-inch socket is useful in attaching or removing platform legs that have been bolted with three-eighth-inch carriage bolts.

Screwdrivers

Screwdrivers are used for inserting and removing screws. They are available in a variety of configurations and sizes.

Standard Screwdriver   The standard, or slotted, screwdriver (Figure 8.13A) is available in sizes from approximately three inches long with a blade width of one-eighth inch to large screwdrivers sixteen inches long with a blade width of one-half inch or larger. The handle is usually made of wood or plastic and sometimes has a thin jacket of rubber to provide electrical insulation. The smaller screwdrivers are useful for working on electronic devices and for similar lightweight applications. The largest screwdrivers are primarily for uses other than scenic construction. Screwdrivers six and eight inches long with one-quarter-inch tips are the most useful for scenic construction.

Phillips Screwdriver   The Phillips-head screwdriver (Figure 8.13B) has a four-flanged tip that matches the crossed slots on Phillips-head screws. The design of the Phillips screw allows more rotational force to be exerted on it when seating it in wood or metal. The six- and eight-inch sizes are most useful in the scene shop.

Nut Driver   Similar in appearance to a screwdriver, with a cylindrical socket instead of a slot or Phillips head, the nut driver (Figure 8.13C) is used for tightening small hex nuts (six-sided nuts) on bolts. It is available in a variety of socket sizes from approximately one-eighth to three-eighths inch in diameter.

Miscellaneous Hand Tools

There are several useful hand tools that don't fit conveniently into any particular category.

Sandpaper   Various weights of sandpaper are useful for smoothing wood, metal, and plastic before painting or varnishing. Garnet- or silicon-grit sandpapers with fine (220), medium (120), and coarse (80) ratings are the ones most often used in the scene shop. Garnet- and silicon-grit papers work equally well, but garnet-grit paper lasts a little longer because its pores better resist clogging with wood dust.

Wrecking Bars   Various tools are used to pry wood apart and remove nails (Figure 8.14A). The crowbar and pinch bar have flattened metal claws that can be used to pry wood apart. The claws have V's cut in them so that they can be used as nail pullers. The rip bar has slightly rounded tips that provide a little more leverage when it is inserted between pieces of nailed wood. All three wrecking bars are extremely useful for prying nailed boards apart and dismantling platforms.

Nail Puller   The nail puller (Figure 8.14B) is a tool for extracting nails that have been driven flush with the surface of the wood. The sliding handle is used as a

FIGURE 8.14
Miscellaneous hand tools.
(A) Wrecking bars
(B) Nail pullers
(C) Grommet set
(D) Oil stone
(E) Staple gun

hammer to drive the jaws into the wood to grasp the nail. The handle is then used as a lever to pull the nail out.

Grommet Set The grommet set (Figure 8.14C) consists of a hole punch, a small anvil, and a crimping tool. The set is used to seat grommets, which are brass reinforcing rings, on drops, stage draperies, and the like.

Oil Stone The oil stone (Figure 8.14D) is an indispensable part of a shop inventory. It is used to sharpen knives, chisels, and other cutting tools. It is usually made of silicon carbide, has coarse and fine faces, and should be lubricated with oil when it is being used.

Staple Gun The staple gun (Figure 8.14E), also known as a hand stapler, uses a spring-driven piston to drive staples. The staple legs vary in length from three-sixteenths to five-eighths of an inch. The stapler is used for attaching muslin to flat frames and fabric to furniture, and for similar jobs.

Metalworking Hand Tools

Although many of the basic woodworking tools are equally useful when working with metal, there are a few additional tools designed specifically for metalwork.

Anvil A heavyweight anvil (Figure 8.15A) is an essential tool for bending metal. It is a solid metal device with varying shaped faces. Strap metal and rod can be

FIGURE 8.15
Metalworking hand tools.
(A) Anvil
(B) Conduit bender
(C) Center punch
(D) Bolt cutter
(E) Pipe cutter
(F) Tubing cutter
(G) Tap and die set

shaped by bending it around these faces. Sheet metal, rod, and strap can also be formed by holding the material against the anvil and pounding it with a blacksmith's or mechanic's hammer. The metal will take on the shape of the particular facet on which it is being worked.

Conduit Bender   Thin-wall conduit (used in nonscenic construction as a housing for electrical wires) can be bent into curves with a conduit bender (Figure 8.15B). The notch at the end of the curved face of the conduit bender holds the conduit, and the bend is made by pulling on the pipe handle of the conduit bender.

Center Punch   Made of hardened steel, the center punch (Figure 8.15C) is used to make small indentations in metal that can be used as hole starters for drill bits in both metal and wood.

Bolt Cutter   Bolt cutters (Figure 8.15D) are heavy-duty shears that use a great deal of leverage to cut through mild-steel bolts and round stock up to one-half inch in diameter.

Pipe Cutter   A pipe cutter (Figure 8.15E) is used to make clean, right-angle cuts through steel pipe of half-inch and larger diameters. A smaller version, called a tubing cutter (Figure 8.15F), is designed for cutting half-inch and smaller tubing.

Tap and Dies   Tap and dies (Figure 8.15G) are used to cut threads on pipe and rod stock. The tap is used to cut threads on the inside of pipes (internal threads), and the die is used to cut threads on the outside of pipe and rod stock (external threads). Dies used to cut threads on pipes three-quarters of an inch in diameter and larger are also called pipe threaders.

POWER TOOLS

Power tools by and large perform the same function as hand tools. But they usually do it quicker and with less effort. However, the use of power tools does increase the safety hazards that are present in the shop. Before you work with any power tool, you must be certain that you have received thorough instructions in its safe operation. As a general safety rule, you should remember that any power tool, if improperly used, has the potential to cause severe injury.

Although almost all power hand tools are commonly available with 120-volt electric motors, many are also made with pneumatic drives (pneumatic tools are discussed later in this chapter), and due to advances in battery technology, most of these power hand tools are now run very efficiently and effectively on rechargeable batteries.

Stationary Power Saws

Stationary power saws are mounted on a stand and are normally located in a fixed position in the shop.

Table Saw   The circular blade of the table saw (Figure 8.16A) projects through a slot in the table of the saw. The height and angle of the saw blade can be adjusted. Primarily used for ripping lumber, the table saw also can be equipped with a **dado head** to cut wide slots (technically, a dado cut runs across the grain of the wood, whereas a groove runs parallel with the grain) or a **molding cutter head**

dado head: A saw accessory consisting of a set of toothed blades that sandwich a chisel-like chipper; the blades smooth-cut the outside edges of the kerf while the chipper gouges out the wood between the blades; the distance between the blades is variable.

molding cutter head: A heavy cylindrical arbor in which a variety of matched cutter blades or knives can be fit.

for making a variety of decorative moldings. Blade diameters vary between seven and twelve inches. Commercial-quality table saws with ten- or twelve-inch blades are appropriate for almost all scenic work.

Safety Tip !

Wood Dust, Wood Dust, and More Wood Dust

Power woodworking tools create copious amounts of sawdust and wood chips. Safe woodworking practice requires keeping as much of this wood dust out of the air as possible. Clean air in the shop environment is also required by Occupational Safety and Health Administration (OSHA) regulation. Every power saw should be fitted with some type of dust-collecting system. Most power woodworking tools manufactured since 1990 have some type of integral dust/chip chute that is connected to either a dust bag or power vacuum. Handheld power tools, like belt sanders, typically use a bag collector. Larger tools, like table saws, are typically connected to a power vacuum via a flexible hose.

Professional scenic woodworking shops typically have a centralized vacuum system connected to all stationary power tools via ductwork and flexible hoses. Sometimes stationary power tools are mounted on castered benches or platforms so they can be moved around the shop. In these installations, portable shop vacuums—shop vacs—are typically attached to the platforms and connected via flexible hose to the dust chute of the power tool.

Because of the static electricity generated within these shop vacuum systems, and the potential explosiveness of airborne wood dust, great care must be taken to properly install and ground all shop vacuum systems. Be sure to check with appropriate authorities to determine that the system is properly installed and grounded before operating it.

FIGURE 8.16
Stationary power tools.
(A) Table saw
(B) Radial-arm saw
(C) Bandsaw

(A)   (B)   (C)

Radial-Arm Saw   The radial-arm, or pullover, saw (Figure 8.16B) is probably the most versatile power tool in the scene shop. The housing containing the circular blade and motor is suspended from an arm above the surface of the work table. The height of the blade is adjusted by raising or lowering this supporting arm. The angle of the cut can be adjusted by swinging the arm or rotating the angle of the housing. Although primarily used for cross cutting and angle

Safety Tip ⚠

Stationary Power Tools

Table and radial-arm saws should be equipped with protective blade guards. Before operating these saws, be sure that the blade guards are in place, are in good operating condition, and do not bind on either the blade or the wood that you are cutting.

Before using any power saw, be sure that the blade is sharp. A dull blade can bind and kick the wood back toward the operator. To avoid kickback when using a table saw, be sure that you feed the wood into the blade without twisting or forcing.

Keep your hands well away from the operating blades. Use a push stick when feeding small pieces into a table saw.

Keep your eyes, and your attention, on the saw and the work. Don't talk to anyone when operating a power tool.

Always maintain your balance when working with a saw. Don't lean toward the saw.

Be sure to wear goggles or a face mask when you are working with any power tool to protect your eyes from flying chips.

When working with any power tool be sure to tie back, pin up, or secure long hair under a cap. Don't wear loose clothing such as baggy shirts or neckties.

Be sure to unplug any power tool before changing the blade or bit.

Use a push stick to keep hands away from the blade of a table saw.

⚠ Safety Tip

Power Hand Tools

There are several commonsense safety tips for working with any hand-held power tools:

1. Watch what you are doing.
2. Don't talk to anyone or allow yourself to become distracted when operating the tool.
3. Keep long hair tied up or pulled back so that it doesn't get tangled in the tool.
4. Don't operate the tool when you or the electrical cord is in contact with water or something that is very damp.
5. Wear some type of eye protection.
6. Be sure work is properly supported so that the blade or bit won't bind (become stuck).
7. Before cutting be sure the path of the intended cut is clear so that the blade or bit won't cut sawhorses, extension cords, nails, and the like.

FIGURE 8.17
Power handsaws.
(A) Circular handsaw
(B) Saber saw
(C) Cut Awl

cutting, the radial-arm saw can also be used for ripping. Commercial-quality saws with blade diameters of ten or twelve inches are appropriate for theatrical work. Accessories are available for converting this saw for use as a router, planer, or grinder.

Bandsaw   Whereas the table saw and radial-arm saw are used to make straight cuts in lumber, the bandsaw (Figure 8.16C) is used to make curvilinear cuts. The narrow, continuous loop (or band) blade passes through a table that supports the work to be cut. If the bandsaw has either mechanical or electronic speed-reduction capability, an appropriate blade can be substituted for the wood-cutting blade, and the bandsaw can be used to cut mild steel, nonferrous metals, and plastic.

Power Handsaws

Some power saws are hand held rather than being mounted on a bench or stand.

Circular Saw   The portable circular saw (Figure 8.17A) normally has a blade diameter between seven and eight inches. The angle and depth of cut can be adjusted, and the saw has a guard that completely covers the blade when it is removed from the work. The portable circular saw is used for straight-line cross cutting and angle cutting as well as ripping of stock lumber, plywood, and composition board.

Saber Saw   The saber saw (Figure 8.17B) uses a reciprocating action with stiff, narrow blades to make curvilinear cuts. With a speed control and appropriate blades, the saber saw can cut metal and plastic as well as wood. It is excellent for cutting curved lines in plywood, composition board, and stock.

Cut Awl   Also used for making curvilinear cuts, the Cut Awl (a registered trade name) combines reciprocating cutting action with a swiveling blade mount (Figure 8.17C). Available with both toothed and knife-edged blades, the Cut Awl can

FIGURE 8.18
Power drilling tools.
(A) Drill press
(B) Electric hand drill
(C) Heavy-duty electric drill

be used to make very intricate, smooth-edged cuts in wood, plywood, and composition board as well as plastic, paper, and cloth.

Power Drilling Tools

Power drills speed the process of drilling holes.

Drill Press Mounted on a stand or bench, the drill press (Figure 8.18A) has variable speeds and is very accurate. The chuck usually accepts bit shanks up to one-half inch in diameter as well as a variety of accessories that enable the operator to polish and sand as well as cut mortise and tenon joints for furniture construction.

Electric Hand Drill The electric hand drill (Figure 8.18B) is a lightweight, hand-held drill that accepts bits up to one-quarter or three-eighths of an inch in diameter. Many electric hand drills have variable speed and reverse controls. The electric drill is generally used for light-duty drilling on lumber 1½ inches thick or less and on light metals.

Heavy-Duty Hand Drill Heavy-duty hand-held drills (Figure 8.18C) generally have more powerful motors and a lower gear ratio (which turns the chuck more slowly). They can accept drill-bit shanks up to one-half inch in diameter. They are used for heavier work such as drilling through multiple layers of wood, three-sixteenth-inch and thicker mild steel, and concrete.

Battery-Powered Tools

The advancement of rechargeable battery technology has made life easier for the shop technician. Almost gone are the days when you had to drag a power cord behind you when using a powered hand tool. Almost all powered hand tools—drills, screwdrivers, circular saws, sanders, and so forth—are now available with rechargeable batteries. The higher voltages of today's rechargeable batteries—typically 12 to 18 volts—are much more powerful, and hold their charges much longer, than their predecessors. While power and life-between-charges issues dictate that most sanders and circular saws are still powered with 120-volt motors, most scene shops now utilize battery-powered screwdrivers and drills almost exclusively.

Pneumatic Tools

Pneumatic tools perform the same functions as electrically powered tools, but they are driven by air pressure. To effectively use pneumatic tools, a shop needs to have a large-capacity compressor and air tank as well as an efficiently designed system for distributing the compressed air to convenient locations around the shop and stage.

Pneumatic Stapler   The pneumatic stapler (Figure 8.19A) uses air pressure to drive the staples. The length of the staple legs that can be used with pneumatic staplers varies from about ¼ to 2 inches depending on the manufacturer. Staples are available in a variety of styles: Straight-leg staples go straight into the work; coated-leg staples have a heat-activated adhesive; and the legs of divergent-leg staples spread in opposite directions when they enter the wood. The pneumatic stapler is used for the same types of jobs as a hammer and nails. It can be used for assembling flat framing, putting tops on platforms, and performing similar functions.

FIGURE 8.19
Pneumatic tools.
(A) Pneumatic stapler
(B) Pneumatic nailer
(C) Pneumatic impact wrench

Pneumatic Nailer   The pneumatic nailer (Figure 8.19B) uses clips of coated nails in much the same manner that the pneumatic stapler uses staples. It can be used for rapid assembly of platforms and similar structures.

Impact Wrench   The pneumatic impact wrench (Figure 8.19C) uses air pressure to tighten or loosen nuts. If you have ever watched someone change a tire in a service station, you have probably seen a pneumatic impact wrench in action. In the scene shop, this device is useful when you are "legging" (bolting legs onto) platforms. The impact wrench is also available in an electrically powered version.

Other pneumatically driven tools, such as sanders, grinders, and drills, work exactly as their electrically powered counterparts do.

Metalworking Power Tools

Welders   Several types of welders are used for fusing metal in the scene shop.

Oxyacetylene Welder   The oxyacetylene welder (Figure 8.20A) combines oxygen and acetylene to produce a very hot flame (approximately 6000°F) capable of melting most metals. The oxygen and acetylene are stored under pressure in steel tanks. The amount of each gas in the mixture is controlled by pressure regulators attached to the top of each tank. The gas is fed to the torch, where the mixture is again adjusted with the small valves at the end of the torch.

A cutting torch (Figure 8.20B) has an extra lever that introduces more oxygen into the mix, enabling the flame to burn through the metal. (See Chapter 9, *Scenic Production Techniques*, for a discussion of using welding equipment.)

Arc Welder   The arc welder (Figure 8.20C) consists of a power housing unit, cables, and a welding handle. It works by creating an electrical arc that melts the metals being welded. There are several power settings, which can be adjusted for the heat range that is appropriate to the composition and thickness of the metal being welded.

Mig Welder   The MIG (metal insert gas) welder (Figure 8.20D) is an arc welder that focuses a flow of inert gas (usually carbon dioxide or argon) on the welding zone as the weld is being made. The electrode of the MIG welder is a thin piece of wire that is automatically fed through the welding handle from a spool stored in the housing of the power unit.

Soldering Equipment   Soldering provides a low-strength bond between most common metals such as steel, copper, and brass. It is frequently used to bond wires together in an electrical circuit. Aluminum can be soldered, but it requires high heat and a special **flux.**

Various soldering pencils, guns, and irons are used to heat solder to its melting point. Soldering pencils (25 to 40 watts) are used for lightweight projects such as working on the circuitry of electronic equipment (Figure 8.21A). Soldering guns (50 to 200 watts) are trigger-operated, rapid-heating, medium- to heavy-usage devices (Figure 8.21B). Soldering irons (Figure 8.21C) are larger versions of soldering pencils with proportionally higher wattages (80 to 500). They are used for heavy-duty soldering projects in which the iron is required to heat a relatively large mass of metal.

flux: A chemical that reduces surface oxidation, which would prevent the solder or filler rod (welding) and the metal being soldered or welded from flowing together.

Propane Torch   The propane torch (Figure 8.21D) consists of a small bottle of propane gas and a nozzle with a number of fittings designed to produce different flame shapes. The heat produced by the torch is sufficient for soldering most heavy-duty scenic jobs. It is also useful for heating thin-gauge steel for bending or shaping.

Power Hacksaw   A motorized gear assembly provides the forward and backward movement necessary for the blade of the motorized hacksaw (Figure 8.22A) to cut through various types of metal stock.

FIGURE 8.20
Welding equipment.
(A) Oxyacetylene welder
(B) Cutting torch
(C) Arc welder
(D) MIG welder

FIGURE 8.21
Soldering equipment.
(A) Soldering pencil
(B) Soldering gun
(C) Soldering iron
(D) Propane torch

Cutoff Saw   Also called a motorized miter box, the cutoff saw (Figure 8.22B), equipped with a wood-cutting blade, can also be equipped with a metal-cutting blade to make either straight or angle cuts through various types of metal stock.

Power Pipe Cutter   The power pipe cutter (Figure 8.22C) performs the same functions as the manual pipe cutting tools: cutting and threading metal pipes with diameters from approximately one-half to two inches.

Miscellaneous Power Tools

Some additional power tools cannot be neatly placed into any particular category.

Router   A router (Figure 8.23A) is a hand-held, motor-driven tool used for shaping wood. The chisel-like rotating bit is driven at extremely high speed (generally 25,000 revolutions per minute) to shape or carve designs from the surface or edge of the piece of wood. It is primarily used for shaping decorative moldings and trim pieces.

FIGURE 8.22
Metal-cutting power tools.
(A) Power hacksaw
(B) Cutoff saw
(C) Power pipe cutter

FIGURE 8.23
Miscellaneous power tools.
(A) Router
(B) Wood lathe
(C) Bench sander
(D) Electric screwdriver
(E) Bench grinder
(F) Hand power grinder
(G) Hand power sander
(H) Belt sander
(I) Hot-melt glue gun

Wood Lathe   The wood lathe (Figure 8.23B) is a bench-mounted tool that holds and spins wood rapidly so that it can be shaped by carving. Special wood-turning chisels are used to carve the wood. The speed is variable and is controlled by either mechanical or electronic means. In the scene shop, the lathe is used for turning bannisters, table legs, and the like. The wood lathe can also be modified for use in turning Styrofoam.

Bench Sander   A variety of sanders is available, but the bench sander (Figure 8.23C) is normally mounted and is usually a combination of belt sander and disk sander. It is used to bevel or smooth the surface or edges of wood and some plastics.

Electric Screwdriver   One very handy tool bears a strong visual resemblance to an electric hand drill, but instead of holding drill bits its special chuck holds the magnetized tip of a Phillips screwdriver. Electric screwdrivers (Figure 8.23D) have variable-speed motors, so the screws can be started slowly, and a clutch that stops the chuck from turning when the screw is fully seated. It is designed for use with case-hardened Phillips screws that work equally well in wood and metal with no starter hole. The electric screwdriver is used for assembling flats and platforms and in similar situations where assembly and the strength of a screw fastener are needed.

Bench Grinder   The bench grinder (Figure 8.23E) is used for grinding and sharpening metal. It is normally equipped with a grinding wheel and a wire brush (for polishing), although a cloth buffing wheel can be used for polishing metal to a high luster.

Hand Power Grinder   A portable version of the bench grinder is the hand power grinder (Figure 8.23F). It is particularly useful for pieces that are too heavy or awkward to be worked on the bench grinder.

Hand Power Sander   Basically a slightly less powerful version of the hand power grinder, the hand power sander (Figure 8.23G) uses a rotating disk of sandpaper to sand wood, metal, and plastic.

Belt Sander   The powerful belt sander (Figure 8.23H) uses belts of sandpaper for rapid sanding of (primarily) wood.

Hot-Melt Glue Gun   One of the most versatile tools in the shop, the hot-melt glue gun (Figure 8.23I) uses sticks of heat-activated adhesive for making rapid-hold glue bonds on and between just about every type of material—wood, plastic, paper, cloth, metal, dirt, sand, and so on.

WOOD

Three categories of wood are used in scenic construction: stock lumber, moldings, and sheet goods.

Stock Lumber

To be appropriate for use in scenic construction, stock lumber must possess the following characteristics. It should be strong, lightweight, free of knots, splinter resistant, easily worked, and fairly inexpensive. White pine, a generic name applicable to a number of separate species of pine grown in the western United States, generally satisfies these requirements. White pine is normally used to build the frames of flats and in similar lightweight construction projects.

Unfortunately for the theatrical technician, white pine isn't always called white pine. The name varies considerably depending on the locale. Because of these regional name variations, it isn't possible to simply call up your friendly lumber store and order "white pine." First, visit the lumberyard and look for the wood that has the required characteristics. Then, find out what it's called.

Another commonly used wood in scenic construction is Douglas fir. This wood is heavier than white pine, is stronger, and generally sells for one-half to one-third the cost of white pine. It is normally used for heavier construction projects such as weight-bearing structures and platform legs.

All stock lumber is graded. There are two primary grades of wood, *select* and *common*. Each of these categories is further subdivided.

A Select   "A select" wood is free of all knots, blemishes, erratic graining, and warps.

B Select   Also known as "B or Better," "B select" wood is primarily the same as A select except that the grain can be less uniform and the wood can contain more pitch, which increases its weight.

C Select   "C select" wood can have a few tight knots (that will not fall out) of less than one-half inch in diameter, slightly less uniform graining, and still more pitch.

D Select   "D select" wood can have more tight knots (still only one-half inch in diameter), an occasional pitch pocket, and some warping.

No. 1 Common   No. 1 common lumber can have knots up to 1½ inches in diameter. The knots do not have to be tight; in other words, they may fall out, leaving a knothole in the plank. Warping and twisting are more prevalent in this grade of lumber.

No. 2 Common   The knots in No. 2 common lumber can be greater than 1½ inches in diameter, and the edges can show an occasional strip of bark. The wood will probably be warped and twisted.

The cost of lumber goes down as you move down the scale from A select to No. 2 common. It is difficult to find A select in most lumberyards. When it is available, it is almost always very expensive. Most stage construction can be accomplished by using C select or D select. The occasional knot, split end, or slight warp that will be found in these grades can usually be trimmed to prevent it from interfering with the construction project. The common grades of lumber are not particularly suitable for stage purposes, although they can be used for applications where their appearance and structural weakness would not adversely affect the appearance or safety of the set.

Dimensions of Stock Lumber   The Department of Agriculture determines the standards for the thickness, width, and length of all stock lumber sold in the United States. Since the sizing of lumber is done before the boards are milled to a smooth surface, the actual dimensions of the lumber that we buy are smaller than the indicated size, as shown in Figure 8.24. Slight variations in the actual dimensions of the lumber can be measured on almost any piece of stock because

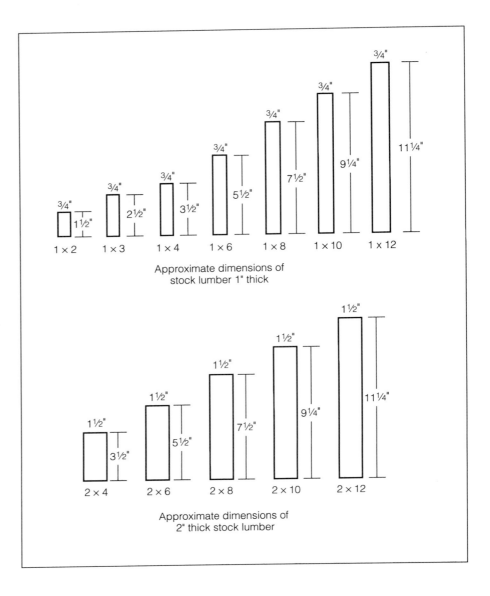

FIGURE 8.24
Standard lumber dimensions.

of milling variations and shrinkage. Because of these discrepancies, it is a good practice to measure the width of every piece of lumber before you use it. The typical scenic uses of the various sizes of lumber are described in Table 8.1.

Molding and Trim

In addition to stock lumber, there are a number of standard trims and moldings (Figure 8.25) that can be used in theatrical production. Decorative moldings are normally manufactured from white pine and are used extensively for architectural trim on and around door and window casings as well as to provide visual interest on baseboards, chair rails, cornices, wall panels, and similar locations.

Sheet Stock

Various materials fall into the general classification of sheet stock, or lumber products that are manufactured in sheet form.

TABLE 8.1
Standard Uses of Lumber in Scenic Construction

Indicated Size (cross section)	Actual Size	Typical Stage Uses
1 × 2	¾ inch × 1½ inches	small flats; lightweight corner bracing of flats
1 × 3	¾ inch × 2½ inches	standard flat framing (6–14 feet); diagonal bracing of platform legs
1 × 4	¾ inch × 3½ inches	large flat framing (over 14 feet)
1 × 6	¾ inch × 5½ inches	door and window frames and similar architectural trim work; narrow sweeps
1 × 8	¾ inch × 7½ inches	
1 × 10	¾ inch × 9¼ inches	stair treads, sweeps, profile cutouts, furniture
1 × 12	¾ inch × 11¼ inches	
2 × 4	1½ inches × 3½ inches	platform framing, platform legs, and similar weight-bearing structures
2 × 6	1½ inches × 5½ inches	
2 × 8	1½ inches × 7½ inches	
2 × 10	1½ inches × 9¼ inches	temporary scaffolding; some stair carriages
2 × 12	1½ inches × 11¼ inches	not normally used for stage scenery

Plywood Plywood is made by laminating several layers of wood. Most plywood used in the theatre is composed of either three or five layers of wood. The direction of the grain of each successive layer lies at a ninety-degree angle to the layers immediately above and below it, as shown in Figure 8.26. Because the strength of wood lies across its grain, plywood is much stronger than solid wood of a similar thickness.

Plywood is manufactured in interior and exterior grades. The only difference between them is that the exterior grade is laminated with a waterproof glue, whereas the interior grade uses a glue that is water-soluble.

Plywood is available in most lumberyards in thicknesses of ⅛, ³⁄₁₆, ¼, ⅜, ½, ⅝, and ¾ inch. Almost all plywood, unless precut by the lumberyard, is sold in 4-by-8-foot sheets. Generally, the only exception to this 4-by-8-foot rule involves ⅛-inch **luan,** or Philippine mahogany, plywood. While luan plywood is available in 4-by-8-foot and 4-by-10-foot **paper clad** sheets, in both ⅛-inch and ¼-inch thicknesses, it is also sold as "door skin" in which the ⅛-inch-thick sheets are 3-foot-by-6-foot-9-inch or 7-foot.

Plywood is graded according to its surface finish, as shown in Table 8.2. Although there are other grades of plywood, those listed in the table are the most common and are readily available.

AD plywood, despite the fact that it has **plugs,** small knotholes, and grain irregularities on one face, is the standard grade for almost all theatrical construction purposes. The AA grade is rarely used because of its high cost. **Keystones** and **cornerblocks** are made from one-quarter-inch AD plywood. Sweeps, profile pieces, and other curvilinear forms can be cut from any appropriate thickness of AD plywood. Three-quarter-inch AD plywood (A side up) is often used to make platform tops. CD plywood costs less than AD, and its inherent strength is not reduced by its surface imperfections. As the price of AD plywood has risen, more and more technicians are opting to use ACX as their plywood of choice. ACX

luan: Also known as Philippine mahogany. This one-eighth-inch luan plywood is strong and quite flexible. Commonly used as a flat-covering material and for covering curved-surface forms.

paper clad: Both sides covered with paper.

plug: A wooden insert used to replace a knothole or other imperfection in the surface layer of a sheet of plywood.

keystones and cornerblocks: Pieces of one-quarter-inch AD plywood used to reinforce joints in the construction of stage flats.

FIGURE 8.25
Specialty-cut lumber and moldings.

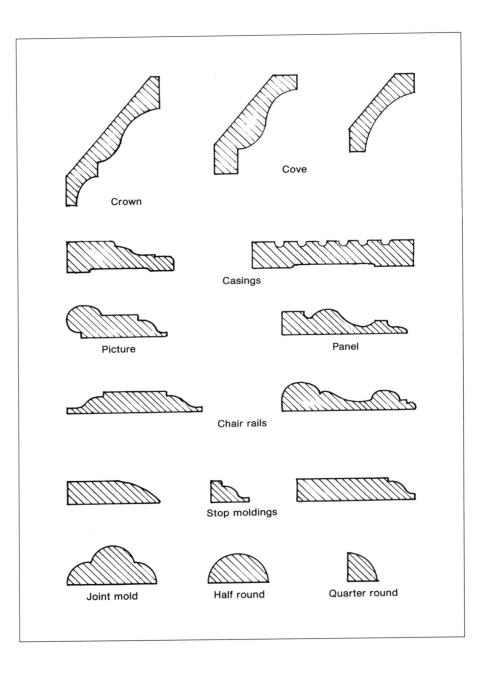

plywood has almost the same characteristics as AD. The D face is upgraded to C, it is made with exterior glue, and it is frequently easier to find than AD. CD or CDX plywood can be used instead of AD or ADX for platform tops if the rough surface is going to be covered with some other material or if it is not going to be seen by the audience.

Furniture-grade plywood is manufactured with higher-quality filler layers. The outer surfaces are usually AA or AD and are made from hardwoods such as mahogany, birch, oak, or walnut. There is also a wide variety of plywoods, usually three-sixteenth- or one-quarter-inch thickness, that have prefinished, painted, or hardwood veneer surfaces. These prefinished panels can be used to cover flats as well as in other applications.

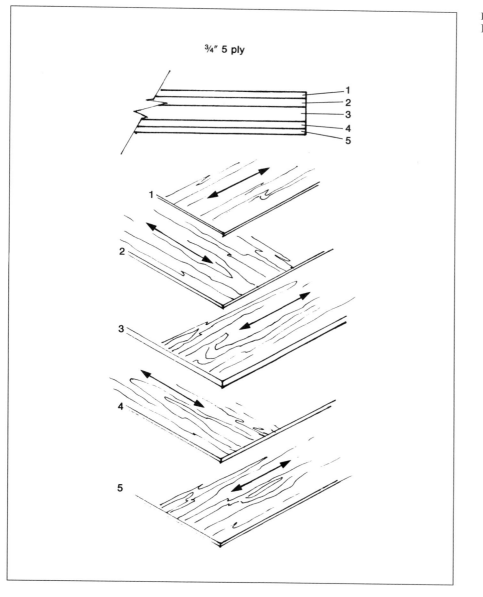

FIGURE 8.26
Plywood laminations.

TABLE 8.2

Plywood Grading System

Grade	Surface Appearance
AA	smooth sanded on both sides; both faces free from knots, plugs, or grain irregularities
AD	smooth sanded on both sides; one face (A) is free from imperfections, and the other (D) is not
CD	rough sanded on both sides; each face may have many surface imperfections, some open knotholes, and grain irregularities; whole sheet may be slightly warped

FIGURE 8.27
Closeup views of (A) particle board
and (B) wafer board.

(A)   (B)

Particle Board   Particle board (Figure 8.27A) is composed of wood chips and
sawdust mixed with a glue binder and compressed into four-by-eight-foot sheets.
Particle board is usually available in three-eighth-, one-half-, five-eighth-, and
three-quarter-inch thicknesses. It is much heavier than plywood of similar thickness and isn't nearly so strong, but it can be used for subflooring, cabinet shelves,
and similar structures.

Wafer Board   Similar to particle board but composed of much larger chips,
wafer board (Figure 8.27B) is actually as strong as plywood and is lighter and
cheaper. It is finished with one smooth face and one that has a slight texture.
Because it is more "springy" than plywood of similar thickness, wafer board (also
called strand board) generally isn't used as platform-topping material. Other
construction uses, such as the web material for the wooden I beams used as joists
and rafters, are continually being discovered.

Hardboard   Hardboard, frequently called Masonite, a registered trade name, is
manufactured from wood pulp that is compressed into four-by-eight sheets of
one-eighth-, one-quarter-, and three-eighth-inch thickness. It is available in two
degrees of hardness, untempered and tempered. Untempered hardboard, which
is light brown, has a soft, easily gouged surface. Tempered Masonite is dark
brown and has an extremely hard surface.
    Although hardboard is brittle and can be broken easily with a sharp blow,
the one-eighth-inch board can be used as a facing surface for counters, stair risers,
and other vertical surfaces that may receive moderate physical abuse during the
production. It is flexible enough to be bent around slightly curved forms. Either
one-quarter- or three-eighth-inch tempered Masonite can be used to cover the
permanent wooden stage floor, because the hard surface resists the abuse caused
by heavy stage equipment and can easily be painted with casein, latex, or acrylic
paint.

Upson Board   Upson board is basically paper pulp and binder that have been
mixed and compressed into four-by-eight sheets. It is available in thicknesses of
one-eighth, three-sixteenths, and one-quarter inch. The material is fairly flexible

and has little inherent strength. Unless the edge of a piece of Upson board is supported by a wooden framework, it can be easily bent, broken, or frayed.

Upson board one-eighth-inch thick, also known by the trade name of Easy Curve, is used to cover fairly sharply curved surfaces such as columns or curved walls. The three-sixteenth- and one-quarter-inch Upson board can be used as a hard cover for flats or profile cutouts if they won't be subject to too much physical abuse.

Fabrics that are normally used for covering scenery are discussed in Chapter 9, *Scenic Production Techniques,* and typical drapery and upholstery materials are dealt with in Chapter 11, *Stage Properties.*

Manufactured Wood

An ever-increasing number of wood-like construction materials made from wood byproducts (chips, strands, sawdust, and so forth) are finding their way into scenic construction. One significant advantage to these products is their dimensional stability. They are milled to much closer tolerances than stock lumber and generally don't swell or shrink as much as stock lumber. In larger sizes they are also cheaper than stock lumber. Lumberlam (a trade name) is a laminated, engineered material used as a replacement/substitute for stock lumber. Glue-lam beams are laminated beams made from relatively short pieces of stock lumber. They can be used to span openings of up to 18 to 20 feet and still have sufficient load capacity to support platforming on top. Other stock lumber substitutes are molded by subjecting a slurry of sawdust and high-tech adhesives to heat and high pressure.

Theatrical uses for these products will undoubtedly expand as more types and variations are introduced and more technicians try them.

METAL

Metal is being used with increasing frequency in scenic construction. This popularity can be attributed to three specific factors: (1) The increasing cost of wood has eliminated what was once a significant cost difference between wood and steel; (2) metal is inherently stronger than wood; and (3) with proper tools, metal can be worked as easily as wood.

The greater strength of metal allows the construction of frameworks for platforms and large flats that are as strong as or stronger than, but weigh less than, similarly sized wooden units. Additionally, metal's strength encourages its use in the fabrication of delicate or irregular shapes that would be impossible to duplicate in wood.

Safety Tip

Heating Galvanized Coatings

Galvanized finishes—the mottled, silvery finish frequently found on steel water pipes, rigid and thin wall conduit, water/paint buckets, and thin steel sheet colloquially known as "galvanized tin"—emit noxious fumes when the galvanized finish is drilled, welded, or flame-cut. Be sure to work with these materials in well-ventilated areas or outdoors and to wear a proper respirator.

Although there are literally hundreds of metals and alloys, only two types—mild steel and aluminum—are used extensively in scenic construction. Other metals, most notably bronze, brass, and copper, are occasionally used in prop construction, but their relatively high cost and working characteristics argue against their being used for other than decorative purposes.

Mild Steel

Mild steel, officially known as AISI (American Iron and Steel Institute) C-1020, is the most commonly used type of steel in theatrical construction. It is malleable and is fairly easy to cut, bend, drill, and weld, and its strength is sufficient for most general scenic uses such as flat and platform frameworks.

AISI C-1020 is manufactured in two primary forms: *structural* and *merchant bar*. Structural steel has a uniform chemical composition throughout, complete internal soundness (no air pockets, cracks, nonuniform crystallization formations, or other weaknesses that would affect its strength), and no significant surface flaws. Merchant bar may have internal defects that would affect the material's strength and more apparent surface flaws. Because of its questionable strength, merchant bar shouldn't be used for critical weight-bearing structures.

Mild steel is finished at the mill with several different surfaces. The two most common finishes are *plain oxide* and a treatment called *oiled and pickled*. Plain oxide is the most common and least expensive finish. The steel is covered with a gray oxide that naturally forms as the steel cools and has some **scale** and a light coating of rust. For welding, brazing, or painting, the contaminants (oxide, scale, and rust) must be removed, usually by wire-brushing or grinding. An oiled and pickled finish provides a clean surface to the steel. At the mill, the steel receives an acid bath and a neutralizing rinse while it is still hot. It is then coated with oil to prevent the natural formation of oxide as it cools. The oil coat also prevents the formation of rust. Steel that has been *plated* or *painted* is also available from the factory. Generally, it isn't used in scenic construction because of its higher cost. But a galvanized finish has a bright silvery finish that is difficult to duplicate with paint and may be appropriate for some applications.

Mild steel is readily available from steel suppliers in the shapes illustrated in Figure 8.28 as well as in sheets of varying sizes and thicknesses.

Typical scenic-construction uses of the various shapes of steel are listed below.

Square and rectangular tubing   Square and rectangular tubing are arguably the most used and useful shapes of steel for theatrical construction. Rectangular tubing is frequently used for platform framing and similar weight-bearing structures, whereas square tubing is more typically used for flat framing and other lightweight forms that will be covered with cloth or thin hard coverings (plywood, Upson board, Masonite, etc.).

Rectangular tubing is available in sizes ranging from slightly under 1" × 2" up to 6" × 12" with a variety of wall thicknesses ranging from about .035" up to ½". Square-tubing sizes range in ⅛" increments from ⅜" to 1¼" with wall thicknesses ranging between .035" and .065". For small- to medium-sized platforms and flats, 1" × 2" rectangular and 1" square tubing with wall thicknesses of .035" to .065" are typical.

Tubing or pipe   One of the most common uses of pipe is for electrical conduit. There are two types of conduit, rigid and EMT (electrical metallic tubing). Rigid conduit is sold with internal diameters ranging from ½ inch to 6 inches. EMT, commonly known as thin-wall conduit, is available in sizes ranging from ⅜ inch

scale: A black scaly coat that forms on iron when it is heated for processing.

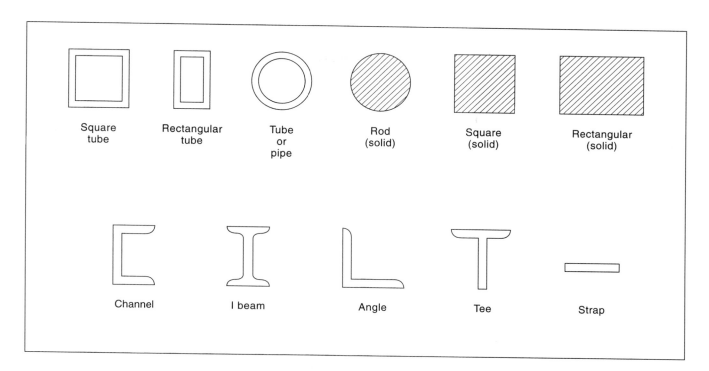

FIGURE 8.28
Basic forms of metal.

to 2 inches. Thin-wall conduit can be bent in fairly intricate shapes with a pipe or conduit bender and is primarily used for decorative elements. Before bending thin-wall conduit, be sure to fill the pipe with sand to prevent the walls of the pipe from collapsing. Neither type of conduit is strong enough to be used for weight-bearing structures.

Thicker-walled pipe, such as the "black pipe" used for gas lines, is more typically used for structural purposes such as platform legs and battens.

Channel   Channel is most typically used in structures requiring significant strength, such as the framework for large platforms or wagons.

Angle   Angle, or angle iron, is frequently used in those situations requiring less strength than rectangular or square tubing provides—lightweight frames, braces, and stiffeners.

Strap   Strap is used to strengthen or brace existing wooden structures. Its most apparent use is as the sill iron that spans the bottom of door openings in wooden framed flats.

Proprietary Structural Systems

Several companies manufacture steel structural systems that can be used like giant Erector sets to construct a wide variety of structural and scenic items ranging from lighting grids to stairways, platforms, scaffolds, flat frames, and open frameworks. The advantage of these systems is the speed with which structures can be assembled and the reusability of the materials. The disadvantage lies primarily in the increased cost of the materials and specialized fastening hardware.

FIGURE 8.29
(A) Unistrut metal framing. (B) Joining requires special hardware. (Courtesy of Unistrut Corporation.)

(A)

(B)

Unistrut This system consists of U-shaped channels of differing sizes, as shown in Figure 8.29A. The Unistrut system requires only that the channels be cut to length and bolted together with the specialized hardware (Figure 8.29B).

Telespar Also manufactured by the Unistrut Company, Telespar (Figure 8.30) is a system of telescoping square steel tubing. Tubing with ⅜-inch holes on **1-inch centers** punched into all four faces of each section of tubing is available in sizes ranging between 1½ and 2½ inches. Telescoping plain-tube sizes range between

1-inch centers: The centers of adjacent elements, such as holes, are spaced 1 inch apart.

1 inch and 2½ inches. The telescoping feature allows the length to be adjusted without cutting.

Slotted Angle   Slotted angle (Figure 8.31) is manufactured with a variety of holes and slots punched into both faces of the stock. These holes permit the slotted angle stock to be bolted together without additional drilling. The slotted angle is cut to length and fastened together using standard bolts, washers, and nuts.

This listing of shapes and uses of steel materials is far from exhaustive, but it does provide an introduction to the use of mild steel in theatrical construction. A trip to your local steel distributor can show you the materials available in your area. A trip to your metal scrap junkyard can be equally illuminating.

Aluminum

Aluminum is manufactured in the same shapes as mild steel. Additionally, decorative panels made of aluminum can be purchased in many hardware or lumber stores.

Aluminum is not used as extensively as mild steel, primarily because it is more expensive and is more difficult to weld than steel. It is used mainly for decorative purposes in scenic construction.

PLASTICS

Various plastics are useful in technical production, but more substantial safety hazards are involved in forming and processing plastics than in dealing with any other common construction material.

Friction between a saw or knife blade and plastic creates heat. This heat liberates gases from the plastic. Some of these fumes simply smell bad; some are noxious, or unhealthy; others are toxic, or poisonous; and still others can be lethal.

Because it is frequently difficult to determine the level of toxicity of these various fumes, it is vital that you work with plastics only in a well-ventilated area. If your workshop isn't equipped with a good fresh-air circulation system, create your own. Set up a cross-ventilation pattern, illustrated in Figure 8.32, between outside windows and doors. Use box fans or similar large-bladed fans set on high speed to move a large volume of air. When you first open the windows or doors, check the natural direction of the air flow and reinforce it with your fans. However, be sure that you ventilate the fumes to the outdoors rather than simply blowing them into another part of the building. If your shop doesn't have direct access to outside fresh air, don't work on plastics in the shop. Work on them outdoors, or if that isn't possible, appropriate a room that can be

FIGURE 8.30
Telespar is square telescoping tubing. (Courtesy of Unistrut Corporation.)

FIGURE 8.31
Slotted angle.

Safety Tip ⚠

Urethane Plastics

If at all possible, completely avoid using urethane foams. When the formed foam is heated, either with a saw blade or an open flame, it emits a toxic gas. The same gas is emitted as the pour-in-place foams set up and cure. If you must use this material, be absolutely sure to wear a respirator and have a high volume of fresh-air ventilation in the workplace.

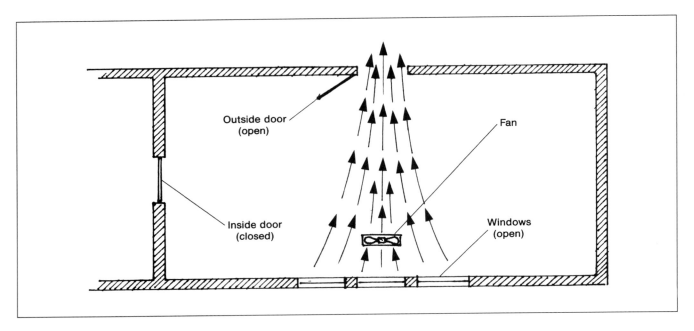

FIGURE 8.32
Cross-ventilation air-flow pattern
for a shop.

properly ventilated. The necessity for a high volume of air movement cannot be stressed too much. Your physical health, and the health of everyone else in the shop, depends on it.

When working with plastics, be sure to wear a respirator specifically designed for use with the plastic with which you are working. This mask filters the air through appropriate materials that remove the harmful elements from the air. The use of a respirator and an effective fresh-air ventilation system, when combined with the commonsense rules of shop safety, can make working with plastics safe.

Acrylic

Frequently identified by one of its trade names, Plexiglas, acrylic is available in rigid sheets of varying sizes and thicknesses in clear, translucent, textured, and

---

Safety Tip   ⚠

OSHA requires manufacturers to provide a Material Safety Data Sheet (MSDS) for each of their products. MSDS's are available by calling the manufacturer or by accessing the manufacturer's home page on the Internet.

The MSDS provides all pertinent safety information about the product: hazardous materials the product contains; known health hazards associated with the product; required protective equipment (gloves, type of respirator, and so forth) for working with the product; first-aid procedures to be used when product overexposure occurs; emergency contact phone numbers for information about the product.[1]

Everyone working in any shop should be familiar with the safe handling of any materials to which they will be exposed. The MSDS for each product provides you with that information.

[1]Chris Minik, "Hazardous Chemicals in the Workshop," *Fine Woodworking*, June 1999, pp. 117–118.

colored finishes. It is also available in rods, tubes, and bars and in a liquid form for use as a **casting resin.** It is commonly used as a glass substitute, and the casting resin can be used to make decorative baubles for costumes, props, and stained glass. The sheets, rods, and tubes can be formed by heating and bending the material to the desired shape.

Epoxy

Epoxies are available in a variety of formulations to suit a number of purposes, but in theatrical construction the most commonly used types are those for adhesives and casting resins. All epoxies are extremely durable and moisture resistant. Depending on the particular formulation, epoxies can be worked with either wood- or metal-cutting tools.

Epoxy adhesive is useful for scenic and property construction projects that require strength or water resistance. Epoxy auto-body putty is useful for molding and sculpting decorative detail on sets and props. The casting resin can be used to make objects that are much stronger than those cast with either acrylic or polyester casting resins.

Fluorocarbons

Teflon is probably the best-known trade name in this family of tough, durable, low-friction, nonstick plastics. Although it is commercially available in a variety of forms, the most useful for theatrical purposes are the sheets and tapes.

Teflon makes an excellent bearing surface because of its extremely slippery qualities. It can be used for turntables or for covering the tracks and runners of **skids.**

Polyesters

There are two types of polyester, saturated and unsaturated. All polyesters have a characteristically smooth surface and great tensile strength.

Saturated Polyesters   Saturated polyesters are used to form the fiber from which polyester fabrics such as Dacron are made. Saturated polyesters are also used to manufacture films such as Mylar.

Polyester fabrics have a variety of uses in both scenic and costume construction, and they can be worked with normal fabric-cutting tools. The film, which is available in a variety of textures, treatments, and colors, has many uses in the scene shop. Aluminized Mylar film is frequently used as a lightweight, unbreakable stage mirror, and Mylar film is used as the base material for several lines of lighting-instrument color media as well as audio and video recording tape.

Unsaturated Polyesters   Unsaturated polyesters can be used in casting or to create the multipurpose material known as fiberglass.

The unsaturated polyester casting resin can be used for the same purposes as the acrylic and epoxy casting resins. Fiberglass, also called glass-fiber plastic, is used in situations where its great strength and flexibility of form are an advantage.

Unsaturated polyesters can be worked with both woodworking and metalworking tools. A basic introduction to working with glass-fiber plastics can be found in Chapter 11, *Stage Properties.*

casting resin: Any of a number of liquid plastics used for casting forms in molds.

skid: A low-profile substitute for a wagon; usually a piece of three-quarter-inch plywood on which some small scenic element is placed.

Polyethylene

Polyethylene plastics are available in a variety of formulations, but the forms most commonly used in the theatre are film and foam. All polyethylenes have a characteristically slick, waxy surface.

Polyethylene film, generally available in black, white, and clear, can be used for such things as drop cloths and projection screens. Polyethylene foam, generally known by the trade name Ethafoam, is very flexible and is generally available in sheets and rods. It is frequently used for architectural trim and similar nonstructural functions. It rejects every type of paint except acrylic, and even acrylic will chip off if the surface of the foam is flexed. Ethafoam can be painted if, after it is applied to the scenery, it is coated with Sculptural Arts Coatings' Sculpt or Coat or Rosco's Flexcoat or it is covered with several layers of cheesecloth that have been coated with white glue. Sheets of polyethylene foam, sold under the trade name of Bubble Board, make excellent rear-screen projection surfaces.

Polystyrene

As with other plastics, the strength of polystyrene is directly dependent on the density of its molecular structure. High-impact polystyrene has a fairly dense molecular structure and a hard surface and is moderately flexible, fairly strong, and somewhat brittle. It becomes very limp when heated, and it is the primary plastic used in vacuum forming (to be discussed in Chapter 11).

Polystyrene foam, commonly known by the trade name Styrofoam, does not have a dense molecular structure, yet it retains the basic characteristics of all polystyrenes—a hard surface, moderate flexibility, strength, and brittleness. It is frequently used for making decorative trim such as cornices and statuary. Techniques for carving Styrofoam will be discussed in Chapter 11.

Polyvinyl Chloride

Although there are probably more formulations of vinyls than any other family of plastics, arguably the most useful formulations for stage purposes are those members of the polyvinyl chloride group. Characteristically, polyvinyl chlorides (PVCs) are strong, lightweight, and rigid.

PVC pipe has those characteristics. Normally used in lawn sprinkler systems, it can also be used for a variety of decorative scenic purposes. PVC is available in a variety of other forms (sheet, rod, and so forth) that are useful for the theatre artisan.

PVC pipe, and its other forms, can be formed using heat. Heat forming will be discussed in Chapter 11.

Pyroxylin

Felt treated with pyroxylin is sold under the trade name Celastic. The material becomes extremely limp and flexible when dipped in acetone and can be formed into a wide variety of shapes. When the acetone evaporates, the Celastic becomes rigid again.

Urethanes

Urethane plastics have a number of uses in technical production. Flexible urethane foam is commonly used for cushions and padding in furniture. The rigid foam, which has a tighter cell structure than polystyrene foam, is used as the modeling block in floral displays and has also been used as an insulation material in building construction. Urethane is also available as a casting resin.

Kits for hand-mixing rigid or flexible foams can be purchased from building-insulation companies and scenic or plastics supply houses. Two types of kits are generally available. The hand-mix, or pour-in-place forms are two-part compounds that are mixed together and poured into molds. Spray-pack foams, such as the Insta-Foam Froth Pak, are also two-part formulations, but they are automatically mixed as they are sprayed. Both molds and casting techniques are discussed in Chapter 11.

FASTENERS

Fasteners in a variety of forms are used in scenic and property construction.

FIGURE 8.33
Standard nails.

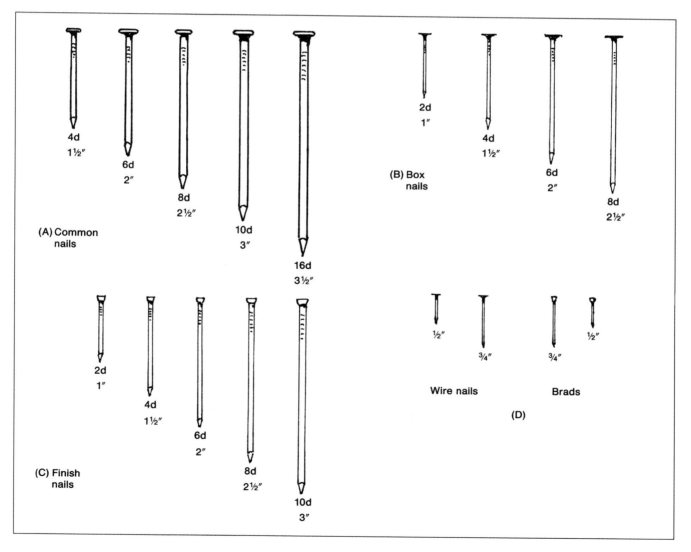

Nails

Nails are the most commonly used mechanical fasteners. They are driven into two or more pieces of wood with a hammer to hold them together. The strength of the fastening depends on the gripping pressure that the wood exerts on the shaft of the nail.

The size of nails is designated by the term *penny,* which is symbolized by the letter *d.* There is a rough equivalency between the length of the shaft, or shank, of a nail and the penny designation: the higher the number, the longer the shaft.

All of the nails, screws, and bolts listed in this section are commonly used in nontheatrical construction and are readily available at lumberyards.

Common Nail   The common nail (Figure 8.33A) has a large head and thick shank. It is used for heavier general construction—platforms, bracing, and the like.

Box Nail   Similar in shape to the common nail, the box nail (Figure 8.33B) has a narrower shaft that reduces the chance of splitting the lumber.

Coated Box Nail   Similar to the box nail but with a slightly narrower shaft, the coated box nail has an adhesive applied to the shaft. The friction generated when the nail is driven activates the adhesive to tightly bond the nail to the wood.

Finish Nail   The finish nail (Figure 8.33C) has a slender shaft and a very narrow, almost nonexistent head. It is designed so that the head can be driven below the surface of the wood and the resultant hole filled with putty or filler. The finish nail is not normally used in general scenic construction but is employed in the building of props or furniture and at any time that it is desirable to hide the nail head.

Wire Nail and Brad   Wire nails and brads (Figure 8.33D) are small (under one inch long) finish or box nails with very slender shafts. They are used in property construction or for attaching delicate decorative moldings or panels to larger scenic elements.

Double-Headed Nail   Double-headed nails (Figure 8.34A) are also known as scaffolding nails. They are driven into the wood until the lower head is flush with the surface, leaving the upper head exposed so that it can be pulled out easily. As the secondary name implies, these nails are used for scaffolding or any temporary structure that you may want to dismantle quickly.

Screw Nail   The screw nail (Figure 8.34B) has a threaded shank that rotates as it is driven into the wood. It has more holding power than a common nail and is used for attaching platform tops and for similar jobs where the greater holding power would be useful.

Clout Nail   The specialty nail known as the clout nail (Figure 8.34C), once used in flat construction, is included here primarily as a historical reference as power-driven screws and pneumatic staplers and nailers, which provide equal or greater gripping power with a lot less fuss, muss, and bother, have relegated the clout nail to hardware heaven. Made from soft iron, the wedge-shaped clout nail was about 1¼ inches long and was used to attach cornerblocks and keystones to the framing of a flat. It was driven through the wood onto a steel backing plate,

(A)   (B)

Front   Side

Flat side of clout nail
at right angle to wood grain
to prevent splitting

(C)

FIGURE 8.34
Specialty nails.
(A) Double-headed nail
(B) Screw nail
(C) Clout nail

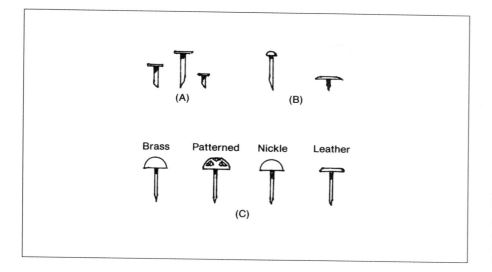

FIGURE 8.35
Tacks.
(A) Carpet tacks
(B) Gimp tack (left) and thumbtack
(right)
(C) Upholstery tacks

which curled the end of the nail back into the lumber. This process, called clinching, is what gave the nail its strong grip.

Tack   Various tacks are used in scenic construction. Carpet tacks (Figure 8.35A) have very wide heads and tapered shafts varying from approximately three-eighths to three-quarters of an inch in length. Carpet, gimp, and thumb tacks (Figure 8.35B) are generally used for attaching fabric to some type of wooden backing, for example, tacking carpeting to the floor, upholstery fabric to furniture frames, and so forth. Decorative tacks have rounded heads and straight shanks, as shown in Figure 8.35C. Although they do hold upholstery fabric to its wooden frame, their primary purpose is simply decoration. They are also very useful to the property master in the decoration, or "glitzing," of various stage props.

Corrugated Fastener   Corrugated strips of metal about ⅝ inch tall and 1⅛ inches wide, shown in Figure 8.36, are primarily used to hold lightweight frames together.

Staple   Staples are U-shaped fasteners sharpened at both ends. Fence, screen, and poultry staples (Figure 8.37) are driven with a hammer and can be used to attach wire, rope, cording, chicken wire, screening, and similar materials to supporting wooden frameworks.

Spring-powered and electrically powered staple guns use short-legged staples (¼ to ½ inch) to attach fabric to wooden frames. Relatively long-legged

FIGURE 8.36
Corrugated fastener.

FIGURE 8.37
Staples.

Screen
staple

Cable
staple

Fence
staple

Automatic
stop

Cable
staple

Poultry
staple

FIGURE 8.38
Types of screw heads.
(A) Standard or slotted
(B) Phillips
(C) Allen
(D) Slotted flex
(E) Square

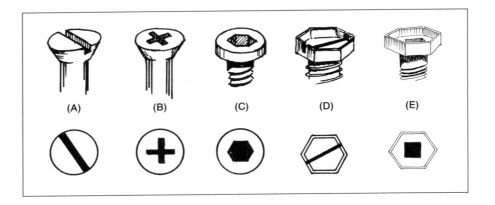

staples (¾ to ½ inch), when driven by a pneumatic stapler, are used to fasten various types of wooden structures together.

Screws

Screws provide a stronger method of joining than nails, because their augerlike thread digs into the material on the sides of the screw hole to mechanically bind them to the material. Various screws are used in scenic construction. The type of screw appropriate for an individual job depends on the type and thickness of the material being worked and the strength needed in the particular joint. Most screws are designed with either a standard or slotted or a Phillips head (Figure 8.38A and B), although some are manufactured for use with an **Allen wrench** (Figure 8.38C) or have a combination slotted hex head or square head (Figure 8.38D and E).

Allen wrench: An L-shaped piece of steel rod with a hexagonal cross-sectional shape; used for working with Allen-head screws and bolts.

Flat-Head Wood Screw   The flat-head wood screw (FHWS), with the possible exception of the drywall screw, is probably the most common type of screw used in the scene shop (Figure 8.39A). It has a flat head that is beveled on the under-side to easily dig into the wood. This countersinking action allows the upper face of the head to be flush with the surface of the work. Common uses for the FHWS

FIGURE 8.39
Screws.
(A) Flat-head wood screw
(B) Round-head wood screw
(C) Drywall screw
(D) Pan-head sheet-metal screw
(E) Hex-head sheet-metal screw
(F) Lag screws

Starter, or Pilot, Holes

Unless you are using a power screwdriver, a screw is much easier to use if you drill a starter, or pilot, hole. Ideally this hole should be the same diameter as the solid shaft of the threaded portion of the screw (not counting the flange of the screw thread).

Specialty drill bits called screw starters, designed for use with electric drills, can drill starter and countersink holes in the same action. They are available for most common sizes of screws.

The starter hole for a bolt should be the same diameter as the full diameter of the bolt (including the screw flange).

are attaching hardware (hinges, doorknobs) and joining various wooden elements together. FHWS's range in length from about ½ inch to 3 inches, although the most common sizes used in the shop vary from ¾ to about 1¼ or 1½ inches, with a screw shank diameter of No. 8 or No. 9. (The numerical rating of screw shank sizes is roughly dependent on their diameter: the higher the number, the larger the diameter.)

Round-Head Wood Screw   Identical in most respects with the FHWS, the round-head wood screw (RHWS) has a head with a flat underside and a rounded upper surface (Figure 8.39B). The RHWS is used in those situations in which you do not want to have the top of the screw flush with the surface of the work, such as when you are attaching thin metal or fabric to a wooden frame.

Drywall Screws   Drywall screws are used in construction to attach gypsum board or drywall to wooden wall and ceiling studs (Figure 8.39C).

The screws are coarse-threaded, Phillips-head, self-starting (which means they don't require a pilot hole) and are designed to be driven with a power screwdriver. Drywall screws have excellent gripping power and can be quickly attached and easily removed. They do, however, have a disconcerting habit of shearing or breaking when being driven into thick or particularly dense wood. The yellow zinc screw has the same shape and characteristics as the dark grey drywall screw, but the brass-colored metal is much stronger than the regular drywall screw.

When paired with the latest generation of power screwdrivers that utilize replaceable/rechargeable battery technology, drywall screws are the fastener of choice for many types of wooden scenic construction. One note of caution: The points of drywall screws are extremely sharp. Use caution when picking them up.

Sheet-Metal Screw   As the name implies, sheet-metal screws are used for joining sheets of metal. They are commonly available with either a pan head (Figure 8.39D) or a hex head (Figure 8.39E). Most jobs using sheet-metal screws in the scenic or property shop require shank lengths between one-quarter and three-quarters of an inch.

When pieces are to be joined with the use of a hand-driven screw, the metal must be predrilled with a hole slightly narrower than the width of the screw shank. If a power screwdriver is used, it is not necessary to predrill the work.

Lag Screw   Lag screws are very large wood screws with hexagonal or square heads (Figure 8.39F). They are used where the lack of access to both sides of the

FIGURE 8.40
Bolts are the strongest form of
mechanical fastener.

work prevents the use of bolts, such as when attaching something to a wall or the floor. Shaft diameters range from one-quarter to one-half inch with shaft lengths varying from one to six inches. A washer should be used under the head of the lag screw to increase the bearing area and prevent the head from biting into the surface of the work.

Bolts

Bolts are used when you want the strongest type of mechanical fastening. In using a bolt, a hole is drilled in both members of the work, the appropriate type and size of bolt is inserted into the hole, a washer is slipped onto the bolt shaft, and a nut is threaded onto the bolt shaft and tightened (Figure 8.40).

Carriage Bolt The upper face of a carriage-bolt head has a rounded surface, and the underside has a slightly tapered square collar a little wider than the diameter of the bolt shaft, as shown in Figure 8.41A. The carriage bolt is used to join either wood to wood or wood to metal. After the bolt has been inserted into the hole, the head is struck with a hammer to make the square collar seat, or bite into, the surface of the wood to prevent it from turning. This type of bolt is commonly used to fasten legs to platform frames and in similar types of work. Carriage bolts range in diameter from one-quarter to three-quarters of an inch and in length from one to twenty-four inches.

Machine Bolt Machine bolts are designed to join metal to metal, although they can be used to join wood to wood if a washer is used under the head of the bolt as well as under the nut. Machine bolts are manufactured with both square and hexagonal heads (Figure 8.41B). The bolt shaft diameters range from one-quarter to one inch and the lengths from one to six inches.

Stove Bolt Stove bolts (Figure 8.41C) are smaller than carriage or machine bolts and have threads on the entire length of the shaft. They have head shapes identical to flat- and round-head wood screws to serve similar purposes. Sizes appropriate for general scenic purposes range from diameters of one-eighth to five-sixteenths of an inch, with shaft lengths ranging between one and six inches. Much smaller stove bolts (shaft diameters less than one-eighth of an inch and lengths under one inch) are available from hobby or electronic stores.

Stove bolts are generally used for attaching stage hardware, hinges, and similar items in situations that might require the extra fastening strength available with the use of bolts instead of screws.

FIGURE 8.41
Bolts.
(A) Carriage bolt
(B) Machine bolts
(C) Stove bolts

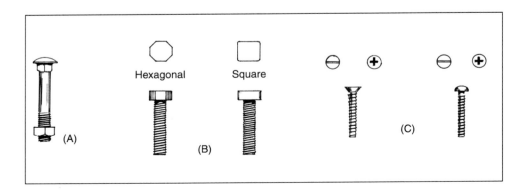

Washers

Washers are flat steel disks with a center hole cut for the bolt shaft. When placed between either the nut or the head of the bolt and the material being joined, a washer (Figure 8.42A) increases the bearing surface of the nut or bolt head and prevents the head from cutting into the surface of the work. Lock washers (Figure 8.42B) are made from spring steel and are cut and slightly spread apart to form a compression tension when the nut is tightened. The purpose of the lock washer is to hold the nut in place after it has been tightened.

Torque washers (Figure 8.42C) are designed to prevent carriage bolts from twisting once they have been seated. The torque washer is slipped onto the shaft of the carriage bolt before it is inserted into the predrilled bolt hole. The square collar on the underside of the bolt head fits into the square hole on the face of the torque washer. When the bolt is seated, the four prongs bite into the surface of the wood. By firmly seating the head of the carriage bolt in the wood, the torque washer allows more torque, or pressure, to be applied when tightening the nut.

Nuts

Nuts are applied to the threaded ends of bolts to close and tighten this type of fastener. Nuts designed to be tightened with wrenches are generally either square (Figure 8.43A) or hexagonally shaped (Figure 8.43B). The wing nut (Figure 8.43C) is designed to be tightened with your fingers. Nuts are available in sizes and metallic compositions identical to the shaft diameters and composition or coating of their corresponding bolts.

GLUES AND ADHESIVES

Myriad glues and adhesives are manufactured today, and many of them have applications in theatrical work, particularly in the area of property construction. Although the following list is certainly far from exhaustive, it does introduce you to the glues and adhesives commonly used in scenic and property construction.

There are general guidelines for using all glues and adhesives. Be sure that the faces being glued are clean, dry, and free from oil and dust. Most glues, except contact cement, require some type of clamping. The amount of pressure and the time that it must be maintained depend on heat and humidity as well as the type of glue being used. The working characteristics of each glue and adhesive are discussed in the following sections.

Glues

Glue is made of, or primarily derived from, natural substances.

Animal Glue   Animal glue is just what the name implies. A byproduct of the meat-packing industry, it is purchased in a dry form (granular or flaked) and must be prepared in the theatre shop before it can be used. The dry glue is poured into an electric glue pot or double boiler, covered with water, and soaked (no heat added) until it becomes a gelatinous mass (about six to ten hours). It is then heated until it reaches the consistency of syrup, at which time it is ready for use. It is one of the prime ingredients of scenic glue, which is one of the formulas used to glue muslin or canvas to flats and other scenic elements. It is also used as a binder in the mixing of scene paint. These formulas are discussed in the section of Chapter 9, *Scenic Production Techniques,* on covering flats.

FIGURE 8.42
Washers.
(A) Washer
(B) Lock washer
(C) Torque washer

FIGURE 8.43
Nuts.
(A) Square nut
(B) Hex nut
(C) Wing nut

Animal glue can be used to join most natural substances—wood, paper, cloth. When dry it has a glossy, smooth surface that is stiff and brittle. It is not effective for any project that requires a flexible joint. It can be purchased from scenic paint and supply houses as well as some paint and hardware stores. Animal glue sets when it cools. If it is diluted with water, the drying time varies between one and four hours depending on the heat and humidity.

Flexible Glue   Flexible glue is animal glue with glycerine added. It must be prepared in the same manner as animal glue and can be used for projects requiring flexibility. It is available from scenic supply and paint houses. The drying characteristics of flexible glue are the same as those of animal glue.

Wheat Paste   Wheat paste is made from a mixture of unrefined wheat flour and water. Although it looks like flour, wheat paste shouldn't be used for cooking, because it is usually laced with rat poison to prevent it from being eaten when it is in storage. It is used for hanging wallpaper, as the glue in papier-mâché, and as one of the ingredients in the glue used for attaching **dutchmen** to wall units. After wheat paste has dried, it is reasonably flexible and has a dull, or matte, surface finish. It can be purchased at paint and wallpaper stores, hardware stores, and lumberyards.

Adhesives

Adhesives perform the same functions as glues but are primarily composed of synthetic materials. They have a distinct advantage over natural glues in that they will not spoil, rot, or turn sour, and they generally come in ready-to-use formulations.

Drying and curing times for adhesives vary considerably depending on type and manufacturer. Read the label of the specific product to determine its particular characteristics.

White Glue   White glue (widely known by the trade name of Elmer's Glue-All) is a synthetic glue that is used extensively in scenic construction. It is reasonably fast drying, is slightly flexible, and adheres to wood, paper, cloth, Styrofoam, and some other plastics as well. When dry, it leaves a slightly glossy surface. It can be purchased from almost any lumber, paint, or hardware store. White glue dries in about one or two hours depending on heat, humidity, and air circulation around the glue joint, but for the joint to develop strength, the glue must be allowed to cure for about twenty-four hours.

Carpenter's Glue   Carpenter's glue is another readily available synthetic glue extensively used in woodworking. Similar in many respects to white glue, carpenter's glue is yellow when liquid but dries almost clear. It is stronger and generally dries more quickly than white glue.

Latex Cement   A milky-white, flexible cement commercially used in laying carpet, latex cement can be used whenever a very flexible glue joint is required. It adheres to cloth, paper, wood, and many other materials and can be purchased from many carpet shops, some furniture stores, and scenic supply houses.

Contact Cement   Contact cement is an adhesive for bonding nonporous surfaces together. As the name implies, the surfaces being joined are bonded as soon as they come in contact with each other. Each surface to be joined is spread with a light coating of the contact cement and allowed to dry for a few minutes; then

dutchman: A five- to six-inch-wide strip of cloth of the same material as the flat covering; applied over joints between flats to give the appearance of a smooth, unbroken wall unit.

the pieces are brought together and are immediately bonded. There are two basic types of contact cement: One has a highly volatile, extremely flammable base, and the other has a water-soluble latex base. The volatile-base contact cement dissolves most foamed products, such as Styrofoam. Additionally, while the adhesion of the volatile-base cement appears to be slightly better, in the interest of safety it is recommended that the latex-base contact cement be used whenever possible.

Polyvinyl Glue   A white liquid adhesive that resembles white glue in appearance, polyvinyl glue is a synthetic with excellent adhesion to porous surfaces and good flexibility. It can be used for a number of jobs, ranging from furniture repair and construction to use as the binder for scene paint.

Cyanoacrylate Cement   Cyanoacrylate cements are a relatively new family of very powerful adhesives that will bond almost any porous or nonporous surface to almost anything else. Therein lie their strengths and dangers. Sold under trade names such as Super Glue, Krazy Glue, and so on, these powerful adhesives are too expensive for use in general scenic construction but are excellent for use in property construction. Like contact cement, cyanoacrylate cements bond very rapidly. However, they also bond skin to skin or skin to anything else just as rapidly. When using cyanoacrylate cements, be sure to follow the instructions very carefully.

Epoxy Resin Adhesive   Two-part epoxy resin adhesive is available in a number of formulations that enable the user to do gluing, filling, and painting. The bond created by an epoxy adhesive is extremely strong and waterproof. It is used in the shop in situations where its strength can be an advantage, such as furniture construction and property work.

Almost all of the adhesives discussed in this section can be purchased at any well-stocked hardware store. If you are involved in scenic construction, particularly property construction, it would be to your advantage to spend some time wandering around a hardware store familiarizing yourself with the vast range of adhesives.

HARDWARE

A great deal of hardware is used in the construction of stage scenery. Most of this hardware is also used in building construction and can be purchased at a lumberyard or hardware store. The specialized hardware designed for specific stage applications is usually not available locally and must be purchased from a scenic supply house.

Construction Hardware

Eye Bolt   Eye bolts (Figure 8.44A) can be used for almost any situation that requires attaching lines or ropes to an object, such as the pull rope for a stage wagon or a guide for the piano wire or cable on a piece of flying scenery. The diameter of the steel rod used to manufacture the eye bolt varies from approximately one-eighth to three-eighths of an inch. The shaft length varies from about one to six inches.

Screw Eye   Screw eyes (Figure 8.44B) are similar to eye bolts but are used when the additional strength of the bolt fastener isn't necessary or when the back of

FIGURE 8.44
Common construction hardware.
(A) Eye bolt
(B) Screw eye
(C) Screw hook
(D) U bolt
(E) Cable clamp
(F) Nicopress and sleeve
(G) Cable thimble
(H) Turnbuckle
(I) Swivel snap
(J) Spring snap

the surface to which the screw eye is being attached cannot be reached. Screw eyes are available in a wide range of sizes: Shaft diameters vary from about one-sixteenth to three-eighths of an inch and lengths from one-half inch to four inches.

Screw Hook Screw hooks (Figure 8.44C) are similar to screw eyes but have a hook instead of an eye so that items hung from the hook can be removed quickly. Size variations are similar to those of screw eyes.

U Bolt U bolts (Figure 8.44D) are made from metal rod that has been bent in a U shape and threaded on both ends. They are typically used to secure or fasten pipe, tube, or rod to a flat surface.

Cable Clamp Another type of U bolt, the cable clamp (Figure 8.44E), also known as a cable clip, has a grooved metal clamp that fits over the bolt shafts. The size of the grooves corresponds to the diameter of the wire rope or cable that

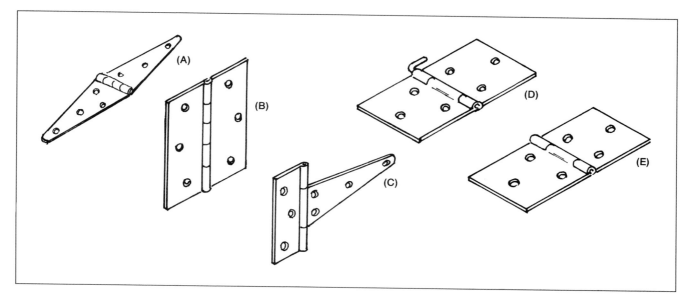

FIGURE 8.45
Hinges.
(A) Strap hinge
(B) Butt hinge
(C) T-strap hinge
(D) Loose-pin back-flap hinge
(E) Tight-pin back-flap hinge

is used to hang scenery and battens. For safety reasons, cable clamps should always be used in pairs.

Nicopress Tool   Another cable fastener, the Nicopress tool (Figure 8.44F), provides a permanent, nonremovable friction clamp for wire rope or cable. Nicopress sleeves, which are thin, soft metal tubes approximately one-half to three-quarters of an inch long, are designed for specific diameters of cable and must be crimped or tightened with a Nicopress tool. Like the sleeves, the Nicopress tools are designed to work with only one diameter of cable.

Thimble   The thimble (Figure 8.44G) is a narrow, grooved, teardrop-shaped piece of sheet metal used to protect wire rope or cable from sharp bends or kinks when the cable is attached to a ring or similar device.

Turnbuckle   A turnbuckle (Figure 8.44H) has a long, oval body with a threaded eye bolt protruding from either end. When attached as a link in a cable, it can be used to lengthen or shorten that line system. This property makes it an excellent device to place between a flying line and a flown piece of scenery to adjust the trim of the flown unit. When using these in a flying system, be sure to securely twist 12-gauge wire around the threaded ends of both eye bolts so they cannot become uncoupled from the turnbuckle body.

Snaps   There are various types of snaps—some with swivel bases (Figure 8.44I), some designed for use with rope, and others intended for use with cable, chain, and curtains (Figure 8.44J). But they all have the same purpose—they provide a quick means of attaching a line to its associated load.

Hinges   A hinge is composed of two joined metal plates that swing around a pivot point. A number of types of hinges have applications in scenic construction.

Strap Hinge   Strap hinges (Figure 8.45A) are composed of two tapering leaves that are joined by either a loose or a fixed pin. Strap hinge **leaves** vary in length from 2½ to 8 inches. Each leaf is drilled and countersunk to accept flat-head wood screws or stove bolts. They are commonly used to hinge stage doors by bending

leaf: The movable flap of a hinge.

one leaf, attaching it to the depth piece of the casing, and attaching the straight leaf to the back of the door.

Butt Hinge   Butt hinges (Figure 8.45B) are available in a wide variety of sizes and finishes, but they are all used for the same general purpose—hanging doors. They are composed of rectangular leaves joined by either a fixed or a loose pin. The holes are countersunk to accept flat-head wood screws or stove bolts.

T-Strap Hinge   A combination of one leaf from a strap hinge and an elongated leaf from a butt hinge, the T-strap hinge (Figure 8.45C) is used for hanging doors, gates, and box lids.

Loose-Pin Back-Flap Hinge   Loose-pin back-flap hinges (Figure 8.45D) have square leaves in sizes ranging from approximately 1¼ to 2½ inches in width. The 1½- and 2-inch sizes are the most commonly used in scenic construction. These hinges can be used as "regular" hinges, but in scenic construction they are primarily used for joining scenery. The individual hinge leaves are attached to the separate pieces of scenery, and the pin is inserted to hold the unit together. The pin can be removed whenever it is necessary to break the unit into its component elements for shifting or storage.

Tight-Pin Back-Flap Hinge   The tight-pin back-flap hinge (Figure 8.45E) is primarily used for the same purposes as its loose-pin companion whenever a permanent joining is desired. It is frequently used when two or more flats are joined to form an unbroken expanse of wall. Details of this type of wall construction are covered in Chapter 9, *Scenic Production Techniques.*

Stage Hardware

Lashing Hardware   Lashing, the technique of joining flats together by a process that is closely akin to lacing your shoes, requires some very specific stage hardware. Lashing is done with a lash line, which is a piece of one-quarter-inch cotton clothesline approximately eighteen inches longer than the height of the flats being lashed together. The location of lashing hardware is illustrated in Figure 8.46. For safety purposes, all lashing hardware should be attached to the flats with one-inch (No. 8 or 9) flat-head wood screws or stove bolts.

Lash-Line Eye   The lash-line eye (Figure 8.47A) is used to attach the lash line to the flat. It is placed on the inside edge of the **stile** just beneath the cornerblock.

Lash-Line Cleat   The lash-line cleat (Figure 8.47B) is attached to the flat so that its pointed end projects over the inside edge of the stile. The lash-line cleat is used to hold the rope in place so that the flats can be lashed together.

Lash-Line Hook   The lash-line hook (Figure 8.47C) serves the same purpose as the cleat. However, it is used when the construction of the flat prevents the use of a cleat, as when the stile is extra wide or is next to an opening in the flat (window, doorway) or some type of projection. It can also be used in place of a tie-off cleat.

Tie-Off Cleat   Tie-off cleats (Figure 8.47D) are used in pairs approximately thirty inches above the stage level to tie off the line after the flats have been lashed together. Regular cleats or hooks can also be used for this purpose.

Stop Cleat   Stop cleats (Figure 8.47E) are attached to the back of the flats with their ends projecting three-quarters of an inch past the outside edge of the stiles to prevent the flats from slipping past each other when they are being lashed together in an outside corner configuration.

stile: A vertical side member of a flat.

FIGURE 8.46
Locations for lashing hardware.

Lash-line
eye

Stop block

Lash-line attached
to corner block

Lash-line cleat

Brace cleat

Stage brace

Stop cleat

Tie-off cleat

Foot iron

Placement for lashing and
bracing hardware

Stop Block   Although it is not an actual piece of lashing hardware, a stop block (Figure 8.47F) is a small piece of scrap wood that is attached to the stile of a flat to prevent flats from slipping past each other when they are being lashed together in an inside corner configuration.

Flying Hardware   Several pieces of stage hardware aid in flying scenery and stabilizing flown scenery. For reasons of safety, all flying hardware should be attached with bolts (or screws if the scenery is reasonably light).

Hanger Iron   The hanger iron (Figure 8.48A) is a metal strap with a D ring at the top. It is attached to the stile at the top of the flat in a position that keeps the D ring hidden behind the top of the flat. The hanger iron, also called a top hanger iron, is used in conjunction with a bottom hanger iron for flying heavy scenery, but it can be used by itself for flying lightweight pieces.

Bottom Hanger Iron   The bottom hanger iron (Figure 8.48B) is a metal strap with a hooked foot at the bottom and a D ring at the top. The bottom hanger iron,

FIGURE 8.47 ▲
Lashing hardware.
(A) Lash-line eye
(B) Lash-line cleat
(C) Lash-line hook
(D) Tie-off cleat
(E) Stop cleat
(F) Stop block

FIGURE 8.48
Flying hardware.
(A) Hanger iron
(B) Bottom hanger iron
(C) Ceiling plate

also called the hook hanger iron, is attached so the bottom of the flat rests on the hooked foot. The flying line is attached to the D ring so that the flat will, in effect, be picked up from the bottom or lifted under compression.

When rigging a heavy or tall flat for flying, use the bottom hanger iron in conjunction with a hanger iron. The hanger iron is attached to the top of the flat in a line directly above the bottom hanger iron. The flying line is fed through the D ring of the hanger iron and attached to the D ring of the bottom hanger iron. If the flat is very small, a screw eye can be substituted for the top hanger iron.

Ceiling Plate   The ceiling plate (Figure 8.48C) is bolted to primary structural members of the ceiling to provide a means of attaching the flying lines to the ceiling.

Bracing Hardware   Most flats need some type of external support to be able to stand up. If the flats don't need support to stand, they will probably need some type of bracing to prevent them from wiggling. The normal positions for placing these pieces of hardware are shown in Figure 8.46.

Stage Brace   The stage brace is the mainstay of scenic bracing. It is an adjustable wooden (Figure 8.49A) or aluminum (Figure 8.49B) pole that can be quickly attached to a brace cleat on the back of a flat. The other end of the stage brace is secured to the stage floor by one of the several methods to be described.

Brace Cleat   Attached to the stile of a flat with the end projecting past the inside edge of the stile, a brace cleat (Figure 8.49C) provides a point of attachment between the scenery and the stage brace.

Rigid Foot Iron   The rigid foot iron (Figure 8.49D) is an L-shaped piece of metal. The long leg is attached to the bottom of the scenery with screws or bolts. The horizontal foot sticks out and is secured to the stage floor with a stage screw inserted through the ring at the end of the foot.

Hinged Foot Iron   The hinged foot iron is similar to the rigid foot iron. Its horizontal foot (Figure 8.49E) is hinged to fold out of the way when the scenic unit is being shifted or flown.

Stage Screw   The stage screw is a large, coarse-threaded, hand-driven screw used to anchor a foot iron or the foot of a stage brace to the wooden stage floor. Although stage screws (Figure 8.49F) provide an effective means of anchoring stage braces, they leave ragged holes and splinters wherever they are used.

Improved Stage Screw   The improved stage screw (Figure 8.49G) doesn't tear up the stage floor nearly so much as its unrefined cousin does. A steel plug, threaded on the outside and inside, is inserted into an appropriately sized hole that has been drilled into the stage floor. The improved stage screw screws into the plug. When the production is over, the plug can be removed from the floor, and the hole patched by gluing a small piece of hardwood **dowel** into the hole.

Floor Plate   It is rather difficult to use either a stage screw or an improved stage screw if your stage floor is concrete or if the building owner or administrator has said, "Thou shalt not put any holes in the stage floor." Fortunately, all is not lost, because a floor plate (Figure 8.49H) can come to the rescue.

The lower end of the stage brace is secured to the floor plate, which is a block of wood with a nonskid material (foam, rubber) attached to the bottom. Sandbags or counterweights are piled on the plate to anchor it to the floor.

FIGURE 8.49
Bracing hardware.
(A) Extension stage brace
(B) Lightweight stage brace
(C) Brace cleat
(D) Rigid foot iron
(E) Hinged foot iron
(F) Stage screw
(G) Improved stage screw
(H) Floor plate
(I) S hook

dowel: A short cylinder of hardwood (usually birch).

FIGURE 8.50
Miscellaneous stage hardware.
(A) Corner plate
(B) Tee plate
(C) Picture hook and eye
(D) Casket lock

S Hook   Also known as a latch keeper, the S hook (Figure 8.49I) is used to hold stiffening battens on the back of wall units that are made up of two or more flats. Normally used on flats that must have the stiffening battens removed for shifting, S hooks can be purchased or made in the shop from ⅛- or ³⁄₃₂-by-1-inch mild-steel strap.

Miscellaneous Hardware   There are several additional pieces of stage hardware that cannot be neatly categorized because their use is not necessarily limited to a single purpose.

Corner Plate   The corner plate (Figure 8.50A) is an L-shaped piece of one-sixteenth-inch galvanized steel, available in a variety of sizes. Each leg is pre-drilled, or tapped, for use with No. 8 or No. 9 flat-heat wood screws. Corner plates are used to reinforce the corners of doors, windows, door or window casings, and picture frames and in similar applications.

Tee Plate   Made of the same galvanized steel as the corner plate, the tee plate (Figure 8.50B) can be used as a substitute for keystones or in similar applications.

Picture Hook and Eye   Picture hooks and eyes (Figure 8.50C) are shop-made pieces (³⁄₃₂-by-¾-inch or 1-inch mild-steel strap) that facilitate the rapid hanging and removal of decorative draperies on a set. They are used in sets of two or more. The sockets are attached to the face of the flat with screws or bolts, and the hooks are similarly attached to the drapery rod.

Casket Lock   The casket lock (Figure 8.50D) is a heavy-duty hidden lock that is used to hold platforms together or in similar applications. Its use as a platform lock is detailed in Chapter 9, *Scenic Production Techniques.*

Casters   Casters come in a bewildering array of sizes, styles, and load ratings. To be useful for stage purposes, casters should meet a few specific requirements. They should have hard rubber tires, should have a load rating of at least 300 pounds, and should be sturdily constructed. Although stage casters can be pur-

Air seal

Load

Air flow

Route of air through bearing

Circular air bearing
locked to platform

Shape of larger
air bearings

Inflated
Section A–A'

Deflated
Section A–A'

Attachment clip for
locking bearing
in place

(A)

(B)

(C)

FIGURE 8.51
Types of casters.
(A) Swivel caster
(B) Rigid caster
(C) Air caster

chased from theatrical-equipment supply houses, it is sometimes advantageous to buy your casters at a local building-equipment supply firm.

Swivel casters (Figure 8.51A) are mounted on a bearing plate that allows the wheel to pivot around a vertical axis. To turn easily under a load, the pivot should be supported by ball bearings. For use with stage wagons, the overall height of the caster should be four to five inches. The tires on a swivel caster should be made of rubber to reduce the rumble that inevitably accompanies the movement of a stage platform. The wheel of the caster should be metal, and it should have some type of bearing (ball, tube) to decrease the friction between the axle and the wheel. The axle should be removable so that a metal strap can be attached to the axle and the platform to lock the swivel caster in a stationary position. Some swivel casters are equipped with built-in pins that can be used to hold the caster stationary.

Rigid casters (Figure 8.51B) are permanently locked in position so that they cannot pivot. The specifications for the swivel caster regarding the structure of the tire, wheel, axle, height, and load rating are applicable to the stationary caster.

Furniture casters do not have the same rigorous specifications as stage casters. They should be sturdily constructed, but because they are often seen by the audience, they need to look as if they belong to the period being depicted in the production. Furniture casters can be purchased at furniture and hardware stores.

A revolutionary type of compressed-air lifter literally floats heavy objects on a thin cushion of air. The *air caster* or *air bearing* (Figure 8.51C) is an inflatable saucer-shaped disk of rubberized fabric. The air caster works as follows: Compressed air inflates the doughnut-shaped bearing to raise the load; the compressed air continues to flow, creating an air cushion under the bearing. Three or four air casters are needed to raise an object. Although they are available in a variety of diameters ranging from one to four feet, the one-foot size, which is load rated at approximately 2,000 pounds, is adequate for almost any theatrical use. Air casters don't work well if the stage floor isn't perfectly smooth. Another drawback to the air caster is the noise of the compressor needed to supply the low-compression, high-volume air. The noise problem can be solved, however, if the compressor (a shop vacuum cleaner works well) is located in an adjacent space (not on stage) and air hoses are run to the casters.

ROPE, CABLE, AND WIRE

Several types of ropes are used for a variety of purposes in the theatre.

Manila Rope

Manila is the primary type of rope used for raising and suspending loads (scenery, equipment) in the theatre. It is used as the operating line for counterweight systems and for rope-set (sandbag counterweight) systems. Manila rope is strong and flexible, but it is affected by humidity, which causes it to stretch when the weather is damp and shrink when it becomes drier. Table 8.3 provides some information about the relative strengths of differing diameters of manila.

You will probably notice that there is a discrepancy between the information in this table and the general guideline of using the ten-to-one safety margin recommended in the accompanying box. The information in this table is calculated for unused manila rope, whereas the safety factor is a "guesstimate" that takes into account the wide range of rope types, uses, and conditions.

Sisal Rope

Sisal looks like manila, but the fibers are much stiffer, and the rope deteriorates rapidly when subjected to the sharp-angle bending caused by running it over pulleys and tying it in knots. For these reasons, it should not be used as a substitute for manila.

Clothesline

Clothesline is a braided cotton rope that should never be used to raise a load over the stage. It simply isn't strong enough for that type of use. It can and

TABLE 8.3
Manila Rope Data

Diameter	Feet per Pound	New Rope Breaking Point (pounds)	Working Load (pounds)
¼ inch	50.0	540	54
⅜ inch	24.0	1,215	122
½ inch	13.0	2,385	264
⅝ inch	7.5	3,960	496
¾ inch	6.0	4,860	695

Safety Tip

Rope

Regardless of the type of rope being used, there are several general safety rules. Any rope that is suspending a load over the stage should have a breaking strength at least ten times the weight of the load that it is required to bear. Any rope should be carefully inspected before use—at least annually and more frequently if the rope is part of a permanent system (counterweight, rope set and the like) or is in constant use—for signs of abrasion, cuts, gouges, seriously worn or broken fibers, discoloration, kinks, or twists. If any of these conditions is evident, the rope should be replaced. Any rope used as the operating line for a counterweight system should be replaced at least every three years, even if it appears to be in good condition. The strain that has been placed on the rope during those years will have broken down the fibers enough to significantly decrease its effective working strength.

should, however, be used as the operating line on **travelers** and as the line for lashing flats together.

traveler: Any drapery that moves horizontally; generally, travelers are composed of two sections of stage drapes that split in the middle, with each section retracting in an opposite offstage direction.

Nylon Rope

While very strong, nylon and other synthetic ropes generally stretch too much or are too expensive to be used for most applications in the theatre.

Monofilament Line

Commonly sold in sporting goods stores as fishing line, monofilament line is basically a single-strand plastic string. It is transparent, comes in a variety of breaking strengths ranging from two to over one hundred pounds, and is used whenever an "invisible" or "trick" line is needed.

Aircraft Cable

Aircraft cable is frequently used in the theatre, because it is very flexible and very strong. One-eighth-inch aircraft cable is often used for flying heavy stage scenery because its breaking strength is approximately one ton.

Wire

Wire is used for a variety of purposes in both scenic and property construction.

Stovepipe Wire   Soft-iron stovepipe wire is approximately one-sixteenth of an inch in diameter and is generally colored black. It is quite flexible but has very little tensile strength. It is normally used for tying or wiring things together. It shouldn't be used for flying scenery, because it isn't strong enough to support a load. Stovepipe wire of slightly greater diameter is known as baling wire. Soft-iron, or stovepipe, wire is also manufactured with a galvanized finish to prevent rust.

Piano Wire   Piano wire is made from spring steel and is frequently used to fly scenery because of its remarkable tensile strength in comparison with its diameter. Care should be taken to avoid making sharp bends in piano wire, because kinking greatly reduces its strength.

BLOCK AND TACKLE

The term *block and tackle* refers generically to arrangements of pulleys and ropes that provide a mechanical advantage. A pulley has one specific job: It changes the direction of travel of the rope passing through it. An ideal pulley accomplishes this task with no friction and little noise. Unfortunately, this ideal pulley doesn't exist. All pulleys create friction and make noise. But, as in all things, some pulleys are better than others. The small galvanized pulleys found in a hardware store can be used for lightweight applications such as the curtain pull for some decorative set drapes, but they are rather noisy. A better solution can be found in the marine-hardware section of a boat supply shop. These stores usually stock high-quality pulleys that are very quiet and have relatively little friction loss.

For heavy-duty use, the best pulleys are available from scenic supply houses or, sometimes, from well-stocked hardware stores. These pulleys have wooden bodies, have well-matched sheaves (wheels) and axles, and are fairly quiet in operation. Three common tackle rigs are illustrated and explained in Chapter 4.

SAFETY EQUIPMENT

There is a variety of protective equipment for working in the shop. The specific device depends on the materials with which you are working.

Clear-lensed goggles, safety glasses, and face shields will protect your eyes from flying wood and metal chips as well as from chemical splashes. Specially tinted eye shields such as welding goggles or (preferably) welding masks need to be worn when welding.

A **dust mask** should be worn when working with any material that produces dust. A **respirator,** equipped with an appropriate type of filter, should be worn any time that you are working with materials which produce fumes or vapors.

Proper hand protection is necessary to prevent possible injury: chemically resistant rubberized gloves for working with chemicals; heavy leather gloves for welding; heat-resistant gloves (not asbestos) for handling heated objects; and regular light leather or cotton work gloves for handling manila rope such as that found on the operating lines of the counterweight system.

When working with noise-producing objects, wear hearing protectors such as noise-abatement earmuffs or earplugs. When working with heavy objects such as metal pipe, tubing, or sheet or when moving or building large stage platforms, you should wear steel-toed shoes or steel shoe caps. When there is any danger of something being dropped from above the stage floor, all personnel should wear protective headgear, such as a plastic helmet that meets or exceeds the minimum federal standards.

There are a variety of other safety-related issues that need to be addressed in the shop. Most of the following have specific OSHA guidelines that dictate minimum levels of acceptability. Check with appropriate school or city/county authorities to determine if your shop is in compliance. The air in the shop should be run through some type of recirculating filtering system to meet OSHA guidelines for clean air. As mentioned earlier, every power tool that generates wood dust or chips should have some type of collection system, either a vacuum draw or collector bag. There should be an OSHA-approved eye wash station in the

dust mask: A device covering the nose and mouth that filters particulate matter from the air.

respirator: A mask covering the nose and mouth that filters out gases as well as particulate matter.

shop area. Fire extinguishers should be placed in strategic locations around both the shop and stage. Make sure that they are *always* accessible and fully charged. First-aid kits should be clearly visible in the shop and stage areas. Their contents should be kept up-to-date and fully stocked. Do not place or lean anything in front of, or on, either fire extinguishers or first-aid kits.

Use common sense in the shop. It is filled with equipment and materials that can injure or kill. But if you are careful and abide by common-sense safety practices and OSHA-prescribed safety regulations, it can be a safe and enjoyable work environment.

This chapter has outlined the tools and materials used in the construction of scenery and properties. Chapter 9, *Scenic Production Techniques,* will discuss basic techniques of scenic construction, and Chapter 11, *Stage Properties,* will take up some of the more specialized techniques and materials used to make stage properties.

Chapter 9
Scenic Production Techniques

Playwrights have set their plays in almost every imaginable environment. Thousands of plays have been set in ordinary rooms in homes or buildings, and thousands more have been set in representational settings like caves, mountaintops, river beds, lakesides, wheat fields, war zones, and even the gondolas of hot air balloons. Nonrepresentational scenery can be, and frequently is, beautifully imaginative, evocative, and representative of the emotional content of the play. Whether wheat field or moonscape, representational or nonrepresentational, the setting must work as conceived by the scenic designer and director—and it's the technical director's job to see that it does.

Technical production refers to the broad field concerned with the processes and techniques used in taking the design from conception to reality. Specifically, the field encompasses the construction and painting of the scenery and properties, the assembly of the set(s) onstage, the shifting of those sets and props during the production, and the tools that are used to accomplish those tasks. The specific organization and assigned responsibilities vary considerably depending on the type of producing unit.

In the commercial theatre, the personnel are hired for a single production. After the producer has approved the construction bids, the designs are constructed and finished by independent professional scenic and property studios. During construction and painting, the scenic designer is in frequent contact with the scene-shop foreman to answer artistic and practical questions about the scenery. When the scenery is completed, it is moved from the studio to the theatre and set up on the stage. This **load-in** is carried out by union stagehands under the supervision of the production's stage manager. The scenic designer and the

technical production: All organizational and procedural aspects of the construction, painting, and operation of scenery and properties.

load-in: The moving of scenery and associated equipment into the theatre and the positioning of them on the stage.

The Production Calendar

The production calendar (see Figure 1.8) helps the technical director keep track of progress on the various productions. It specifies pertinent information (tryouts, design due dates, construction and painting schedules, rehearsals, and performances) for every play being produced by the theatre during the season. It also provides a visual reference that shows at a glance the status of each production. The production calendar is usually developed by the technical director in conjunction with the producer or managing and artistic directors with input from the resident directors and designers.

stage manager work together to choreograph any scene shifts, and the stage manager is responsible for supervising the work of the union crews that will be shifting the scenery.

The Broadway theatre's single-production concept is the exception rather than the rule in the American theatre. Most theatre in the United States is produced on a limited-run, multiple-production basis by colleges, universities, community theatres, and regional professional theatre groups. Almost all of these theatres produce three or more productions a year. They are almost always working on more than one production at any given time. This situation creates a definite need for some very specific organization to keep all of the production activity flowing smoothly. The primary organizer of the technical aspects of production is the technical director. Probably the most important skills that the TD must possess are the ability to effectively organize time and resources and the ability to manage people. The technical director is an expediter. He or she needs to know the current status of the work being produced by every member of the production team. This task is compounded because most technical directors are keeping track of two, three, or more productions simultaneously.

The technical director's work on scenic and property construction cannot begin until the designer provides plans (ground plan, front elevations, detail sheets, functional models, painter's elevations) for the production. After studying the plans, the technical director or an assistant draws any necessary rear elevations or construction drawings that will facilitate the building of the scenery and props, then orders the construction materials. At this same time, he or she also creates a construction calendar. This calendar specifies the amount of time scheduled for the construction, painting, and assembling of the individual elements of the sets.

SCENIC CONSTRUCTION TECHNIQUES

Although the overall construction plan, as well as the specific methods used to build each piece of scenery, should be guided by the basic tenets of the design process (see Chapter 2), some fairly standardized construction techniques are used to fabricate stage scenery.

Scenic Construction Priorities

It takes a tremendous number of hours to construct the scenery for even a simple production. The following list provides a construction sequence that makes very efficient use of available construction time.

1. Build practical elements of the set that will be needed by the actors in the early rehearsals.

2. Build and hang flying units, including any masking, that either will be flown over the set or will use counterweighted battens hanging above the set.

3. Build anything that will have a complicated or time-consuming paint job.

4. Base the construction schedule for any remaining scenic elements on the complexity of the item. The least complex scenic elements, such as flats, should be built last.

5. Allow some time at the end of the construction sequence for adjustments, repairs, and the inevitable changes that will be made in the set.

Construction Drawings

Construction drawings or rear elevations are scale mechanical drawings that show the back of the flats depicted on the front elevations. These drawings:

1. show the construction details of the framework of the flats.

2. indicate which flats are to be joined to form wall units.

3. show the unusual construction challenges.

In professional scene shops, the foreman is responsible for drawing any rear elevations. In practice very few are drawn, because the carpenters working in these scenic studios are very knowledgeable about construction methods and techniques.

In educational theatres, however, the construction crews are usually students who are just learning how to build scenery. Rear elevations should be drawn to provide the student carpenters with all of the information needed to build the scenery.

Front elevation   Rear elevation

Rear elevations show the framework of a flat.

Woodworking

Wood is used extensively for building two- and three-dimensional scenery. It is relatively inexpensive and can be worked easily with a variety of tools, which were described in Chapter 8.

Various wood joints are used. The following are most common in scenic and property construction.

Butt Joint   The butt joint is made when two pieces of wood are cut square at the end and fitted together, as shown in Figure 9.1A–D. Because the area of contact between the two pieces of wood is relatively small, a butt joint isn't very strong unless some type of reinforcement is applied.

FIGURE 9.1
Standard wood joints.
(A) Butt joint
(B) Butt joint
(C) Butt joint
(D) Butt joint
(E) Lap joint
(F) Battened butt joint
(G) Butt joint reinforced with a cornerblock
(H) Butt joint reinforced with a keystone
(I) Miter joint

Construction Calendar

The complexity of the construction calendar depends on the complexity of the play. A single-set production will not be so difficult or time consuming as a multiset musical. The following construction calendar shows a reasonable work schedule for a production of a single-set show.

February	27	Receive designer's plans. Begin analysis of the plans. Order any special building materials. (This calendar assumes that the theatre shop maintains an inventory of standard building materials in the scene shop at all times. If all building materials are ordered on a per-show basis, additional time will be needed at the beginning of the calendar to allow for their delivery.)
	28	Begin drafting working drawings.
	29	Finish drafting working drawings.
March	1	Begin construction: platforms, properties.
	2	Construction: platforms, stairs, properties.
	3–4	Weekend (no work)
	5	Construction: platforms, stairs, properties. Hang flying units and masking above area occupied by the set.
	6	Construction: same as preceding day. Hang and circuit lights above set.
	7	Construction: same as preceding day.
	8	Construction: same as preceding day. Erect platforms; begin platform facings.
	9	Construction: platforms, stairs complete. Build facings, railings.
	10–11	Weekend
	12	Construction: same as preceding day. Begin painting offstage. Hang lights.
	13	Construction: same as preceding day.
	14	Construction: same as preceding day.
	15	Construction: major construction complete. Paint floor. Build and paint props.
	16	Construction: same as preceding day.
	17–18	Weekend
	19	Construction: all scenic construction complete. Focus lights. Paint props.
	20	Construction: same as preceding day.
	21	Construction: all set and prop construction and painting complete. Lighting rehearsal.
	22	Touch-up and detail work. Decorate set. Adjust lights. Load in sound.
	23	Detail work. Final property adjustments.
	24	Technical rehearsal: make necessary adjustments.
	25	Sunday (no work)
	26	Dress rehearsal: make necessary adjustments.
	27	Dress rehearsal: make necessary adjustments.
	28	Dress rehearsal: make necessary adjustments.
	29	Opening of play.

Lap Joint   A lap joint (Figure 9.1E) is probably the simplest of all joints. Two pieces of lumber are joined face to face and fastened together. This type of self-reinforcing joint is used when attaching legs to platforms.

Battened Butt Joint   A battened butt joint (Figure 9.1F) is created when two pieces of stock lumber are butted end to end, and an eighteen- to twenty-four-inch piece of lumber of similar width is attached directly over the joint with glue and screws. Specialized battened butt joints (Figure 9.1G and H) are used in flat construction. Cornerblocks of one-quarter-inch plywood are used to reinforce the butt joints at the corners of the flats. Keystones, also made from one-quarter-inch plywood, are used to reinforce the butt joints made for any internal bracing on the flats.

Miter Joint   A miter joint (Figure 9.1I) is a type of butt joint. The only difference is that the wood being joined is cut on an angle instead of square. A miter joint is used when making **irregular flats** and picture frames.

Dado Joint   A dado joint (Figure 9.2A) is made by cutting a slot across the face of one piece of lumber to receive the edge of another. The slot is cut only halfway

irregular flat: A flat having non-square corners.

FIGURE 9.2
Specialty wood joints.
(A) Dado joint
(B) Halved joint
(C) Halved joint
(D) Notched joint
(E) Scarf joint

through the depth ofthe lumber. Fastened with glue and nails, the dado joint is frequently used for shelving and similar applications.

The dado slot can be cut with several passes of a regular blade in a radial-arm saw or with a dado blade. The width of the kerf on the dado blade can be adjusted so that the dado slot can be made in a single pass.

Halved Joint A halved joint (Figure 9.2B and C), also called a halved lap joint, is made by removing half of the thickness of each piece of lumber from the area to be joined so that the thickness of the finished joint will be no greater than the stock from which it is made. This is a very strong joint when secured with glue and nails, screws, or staples, and it can be cut fairly easily with a dado blade. It is used in making the **muntins** and **mullions** of windows and in similar applications.

Notched Joint A notched joint (Figure 9.2D) is created when the edge or face of one board is inserted into a notch cut in another. The size of the notch is determined by the width and thickness of the piece that the notch will receive. The notched joint is used for shelving and similar applications.

muntin: A horizontal crossbar in a window.

mullion: A vertical crossbar in a window.

Safety Tip ⚠

The Scene Shop

Any workplace that uses electricity, flammable and toxic materials, and tools capable of cutting, gouging, and sawing is an inherently dangerous environment. With a healthy dose of common sense and a few safety rules, however, working in the scene shop can be safe, efficient, and enjoyable.

1. Wear clothing suited to the work: long pants, short- or long-sleeve shirt, and hard-toe, hard-sole shoes (not sandals or sneakers). Clothing should be reasonably close fitting. Don't wear flowing robes—they might get caught in power equipment.

2. Tie back, put under a cap, or otherwise contain long hair so that it won't get caught in a power tool. For the same reasons, don't wear jewelry.

3. Always get instructions before operating any power or hand tool. Be sure you know what you're doing before you do it.

4. Pay attention to what you are doing. Don't operate any tool unless you are giving it your undivided attention. Watch your work area for potential hazards such as wood with protruding nails and potential fire or electrical hazards. Either correct the hazard (if you know how) or report it to your supervisor.

5. Keep your work space clean. If the shop is kept neat, clean, and organized, accidents are reduced and you can find the tools and supplies you need.

6. Know where the first-aid materials are kept. Disinfect all cuts and splinters, and bandage even minor cuts. Report all accidents to your supervisor.

7. When working with materials that emit dust or fumes, make sure that the work area is well ventilated and that you wear an appropriate mask.

Scarf Joint   The scarf joint (Figure 9.2E) is used to make one long board from two short ones with no increase in the thickness of the lumber. The angled surface of the joint should be at least eighteen inches long. It can be cut using a band saw (with a wide, newly sharpened blade to rough-cut the diagonal cut). A plane or power sander should be used to smooth the surface of the cut so that the faces of the joint will be **flush** when joined. Each face is coated with glue, and the unit is clamped together and fastened with screws or bolts and allowed to dry.

Mortise and Tenon Joint   A square hole, the mortise, can be chiseled into one of the pieces to be joined. This is much easier than it sounds if a **mortise drill bit,** which drills square holes, is used. The other piece of wood has the edges cut back to create the tenon. The tenon must snuggly fit into the mortise. The mortise and tenon joint (Figure 9.3A and B) is normally secured only with glue.

An open mortise and tenon joint has the tenon exposed; a closed mortise and tenon joint looks from the outside just like a butt joint. Because of their strength, both the opened and closed mortise and tenon joints are used extensively in furniture construction.

Doweled Joint   A doweled joint is a butt joint that is reinforced with small pieces of hardwood dowel. An open doweled joint (Figure 9.3C) has the end of the dowel exposed; a closed doweled joint (Figure 9.3D) shows no outside evidence of its existence.

flush: Smooth, level, even.

mortise drill bit: A drill bit housed inside of a square hollow chisel; used with a drill press to make square holes; available in a variety of diameters.

Welding

Welding is the process of fusing metal by heating the pieces being joined to their melting temperature and inducing the metal to flow together before it cools. During this high-temperature process, a certain amount of the metal is vaporized or otherwise lost. The **filler rod** is used to replace the lost metal.

Surface Preparation   Before welding, the surface of the metal must be cleaned of all oil, grease, paint, rust, and any other contaminants. This can be done by polishing the welding zone with a wire brush, by sanding, by grinding, or by cleaning with commercial chemical removers.

Welding Techniques   Several welding techniques have been developed to use with the various types of welders (see Chapter 8 for a description of welding equipment).

FIGURE 9.3
Internally supported wood joints.
(A) Closed mortise and tenon joint
(B) Open mortise and tenon joint
(C) Open doweled joint
(D) Closed doweled joint

filler rod: Metal piece, of the same composition as material being welded, used to replace the metal lost during the welding process or to fill a hole or groove in the work.

> ## Safety Tip ⚠
>
> ### Guidelines for Welding
>
> According to OSHA guidelines, welders shall be required to wear (1) nonflammable gloves with gauntlets, (2) shoes, boots, or leggings, (3) leather aprons, (4) shirts with sleeves and collars, (5) face shields or helmets suitable for head protection, (6) suitable eye protection, and (7) respiratory protection.
>
> The necessity to protect your body from being burned from the sparks of molten metal generated at the welding zone is obvious. What isn't so obvious is the necessity to protect your eyes and respiratory system.
>
> Gas and arc welding generate differing levels of visible and ultraviolet light. Ultraviolet (UV) light can cause temporary and/or permanent diminution or loss of sight. Be sure to wear the type of protective lens appropriate to the type of welding in which you're engaged. If you aren't sure whether your eye protection is correct for the type of welding you're doing, don't weld.
>
> Various metal compositions and/or finishes, such as the silvery coating used to galvanize steel, emit noxious or toxic gases when heated or burned. High volume ventilation and the use of an appropriate respirator will eliminate this health risk. OSHA regulations state that there must be a 100-CFM (cubic feet per minute) airflow in a welder's breathing zone or that an appropriate respirator must be worn. Whenever you weld, be sure you have adequate ventilation.

two-handed welding: A technique in which the torch or welding handle is held in one hand and the filler rod in the other.

arc: An electric current that leaps the gap between two closely placed electrodes.

welding rod: A rod, usually covered with flux, that serves as the positive electrode in arc welding.

single-hand welding: A technique in which one hand holds the welding handle and the other hand is not used.

Oxyacetylene Welding   Oxyacetylene welding uses the **two-handed welding** technique. With this method, the welder holds the torch or welding handle in one hand and the copper-clad filler rod in the other. As the flame melts the pieces being joined, the operator feeds the filler rod into the welding zone. The rod melts, flows into the joint, and replaces the lost metal.

In oxyacetylene welding (Figure 9.4), the strength of the weld depends on a chemically neutral flame. This neutral flame is achieved through a proper mix of the oxygen and acetylene gas. After the torch flame has been lit (using acetylene gas only), oxygen is introduced to the mix. When the oxygen is first introduced, a small white cone appears at the base of, and inside, the flame. At first this cone is rather long. Sometimes it is a double cone. As more oxygen is added, the cone gets smaller. A neutral flame is produced when this white cone is short and slightly rounded. An oxidizing flame, which will burn the molten metal, is produced when more oxygen is added to a neutral flame.

A cutting torch (see Chapter 8) is equipped with a lever-actuated valve that introduces additional oxygen to the flame, creating an oxidizing flame. This flame burns the metal, resulting in a cut.

Arc Welding   The arc welder utilizes electricity to generate an **arc** that has a temperature of approximately 13,000°F. This extremely high heat almost instantaneously melts most common types of metal.

To use an arc welder, you attach the ground cable from the welding machine to the work, effectively turning the work into an electrode. When a flux-coated **welding rod,** which is connected to the power side of the welding machine, comes into close proximity with the work, an arc is formed across the gap. The resultant heat melts the metal, and the weld is made. The electrode, which also acts as a filler rod, is consumed in the welding process. Since the welding handle is held with only one hand, the process is called **single-hand welding.**

The MIG (metal inert gas) welder (discussed in Chapter 8) is another single-hand arc welder. It differs from the arc welder in that the welding handle focuses

FIGURE 9.4
Oxyacetylene welding technique. For portability the oxygen (tall) and acetylene tanks are normally secured to a rolling cart (A). To light the welding torch, close the valves on the handle of the torch, then turn on the oxygen (B) to approximately 30–35 pounds and the acetylene (C) to 5–7 pounds. (The pressure settings will vary with the composition and thickness of metals.) Open the acetylene valve on the torch handle and light the torch (D). Adjust the acetylene flame until the base of the flame just touches the tip of the torch (E), then slowly open the oxygen valve on the torch and adjust the flame until the small inner cone at the base of the flame is approximately ¼″ long (F). Be sure to wear protective clothing and use welding goggles or a welding mask (G) when you weld.

(A)

(B)

(C)

(D)

(E)

(F)

(G)

FIGURE 9.5
MIG (metal inert gas) welding technique. (A) Adjust the power setting of the welder to suit the composition and thickness of the metal being welded (consult the welding machine's instruction book). (B) Attach the ground cable to the welding table or the work. (C) Turn on the gas (carbon dioxide or argon) to 5–9 pounds (consult the welder's instruction book for appropriate setting for your specific equipment). (D) Bring the welding wire close to the welding zone, press the trigger, and weld. Be sure to wear appropriate protective clothing.

(A)   (B)

(C)   (D)

oxidation: A chemical reaction between the metal and air that forms a very thin, discolored "skin" over the metal; this skin effectively prevents heat transfer and reduces the strength and conductivity of the joint.

a flow of inert gas on the welding zone (as shown in Figure 9.5) as the weld is being made, and it has a wire electrode. The inert gas reduces **oxidation,** which can substantially weaken the weld. The thin wire electrode of the MIG welder is automatically fed to the handle from a spool in the housing of the power unit. A flux coating for the wire electrode isn't used because of the oxidation-reducing properties of the shielding gas.

When equipped with a steel wire electrode and carbon dioxide or argon gas, the MIG welder does an excellent job of welding steel. It can be used for welding aluminum if aluminum wire and argon gas are used.

Although the single-hand welding technique used with the arc and MIG welder is the same, the MIG welder is easier to use. It is probably the easiest welder on which to learn how to weld, because the electrode is automatically fed to the welding zone, and the shielding gas yields a substantially better weld than does either an arc or an oxyacetylene welder.

The TIG (tungsten inert gas) welder uses a nonconsumable tungsten rod as the electrode and requires a two-handed welding technique. A filler rod of the same composition as the materials being welded is held in the other hand and fed into the welding zone as the weld is being made.

Types of Welds   Common welding joints are described below and illustrated in Figure 9.6.

Butt Weld   The butt weld is probably the most common, and strongest, type. The edges of the materials to be joined are clamped edge to edge with a narrow

FIGURE 9.6
Types of welded joints.
(A) Butt weld
(B) Flange weld
(C) Lap weld
(D) Fillet weld

Before welding

After welding

(A)

(B)

(C)

(D)

space (one-sixteenth to one-eighth inch) between them. If the material is between three-sixteenths and one-half inch thick, the edges should be ground to form a V, as shown in Figure 9.6A. If the metal is less than three-sixteenths of an inch thick, the V will not be needed.

Flange Weld   A flange weld is similar to a butt weld, except the edges of the material being joined are bent up, as shown in Figure 9.6B, before the sheets are clamped in place. The weld is made by melting the upturned flanges. Although it is necessary to apply flux to the welding zone, the flange weld can frequently be made without the use of a filler rod.

Lap Weld   A lap weld is made when two pieces are overlapped, as shown in Figure 9.6C. Both overlapped edges must be welded.

Fillet Weld   A fillet weld (Figure 9.6D) is made when the edge of one piece is joined to the face of another. Both sides of the angled piece should be welded to create the strongest possible weld.

Soldering

solder: A metal alloy of lead and tin.

Soldering is the process of heating metal (usually lightweight steel, copper, or brass) until it is hot enough to melt **solder.** The solder flows over the surface of the metal and bonds the pieces together. For an effective soldering bond to be made, there must be a good mechanical connection between the parts being soldered. The parts must be clean and free of grease, oxidation, and other contaminants.

Soldering flux is applied to further clean the metal and prevent oxidation when the joint is heated. Flux is manufactured in solid, powder, paste, and liquid forms. The type of flux used depends on the project. Rosin flux is noncorrosive and should be used on all electrical work. Soldering wire with a rosin-flux core can be purchased at almost any hardware store. Acid fluxes are very effective, but the acid is corrosive, so the work must be washed with warm water to prevent corrosion. Be sure to wait for the solder joint to cool before you wash it.

If you aren't using a soldering wire with a flux core, it will be necessary to apply flux to the joint before it is heated. After the joint has been fluxed, heat is applied to the work. The solder should be melted by touching it to the work, not the iron. The melted solder should freely flow over and through the joint where the hot solder bonds with the surface of the metal and fuses the joint together.

Making a Good Solder Joint

A good solder joint can be made only if you heat the work to the melting point of the solder. If the work is not heated sufficiently and the solder is melted by touching it to the soldering iron, the solder will just sit on top of the work rather than bonding with its surface. This produces what is known as a "cold" solder joint. A cold solder joint isn't very strong, and it doesn't conduct electricity very well. A cold solder joint can be identified by its appearance. The solder looks dull, whereas a good solder joint will appear bright and shiny. A cold solder joint can generally be fixed by adding a little flux to the joint and reheating the work until it is sufficiently hot to make the solder flow freely.

TWO-DIMENSIONAL SCENERY

Two-dimensional scenery can be divided into two basic subgroups: hard scenery and soft scenery. Hard scenery generally refers to flats, and soft scenery to unframed units such as drops and draperies.

Flats

Flats are lightweight frames made of wood or steel tubing. They are normally covered with muslin or, when the circumstances require, with plywood, Upson board, paper, Masonite, velour, or other fabrics and materials.

The various pieces that make up the framework of a flat have specific names, as shown in Figure 9.7. The top and bottom horizontal members are called **rails,** the outside vertical elements are called **stiles,** and the interior horizontal members are referred to as **toggle bars. Corner braces** are located in the upper and lower corners of the same side of flats over three feet wide.

There are three general styles or types of flats: soft flats, studio flats, metal-framed flats.

rail: A top or bottom framing member of a flat.

stile: A vertical side member of a flat.

toggle bar: An interior horizontal framing member of a flat.

corner brace: A diagonal internal framing member that helps keep a flat square.

Rail

Diagonal brace

Keystone

Toggle bar

Stile

Cornerblock

FIGURE 9.7
The parts of a flat.

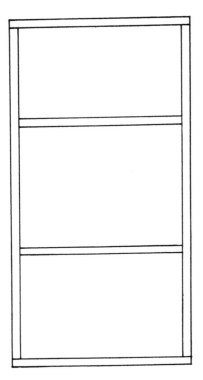

FIGURE 9.8
Positioning of butt joints on a flat.

stock: Regular-sized lumber that can be purchased from a lumberyard.

jog: A flat less than two feet wide.

FIGURE 9.9
The placement of cornerblocks on a flat.

Soft Flats   Soft flats generally refer to wooden-framed flats covered with some type of fabric. Soft flats can be designed to be almost any size and shape, but the vast majority resemble tall rectangles from one to six feet wide and eight to sixteen feet high. The wooden framework for a flat up to fourteen feet tall is usually made of 1 × 3 white pine ("B or better" or "C select"). This wood needs to be light in weight, straight grained, fairly free of knots, and most importantly, straight.

Flats over 14 feet tall will probably need the additional strength offered by ⁵⁄₄ × 4 **stock.** ("Five-quarter" stock is lumber that is 1¼ inches thick; thus, ⁵⁄₄ × 4 stock actually measures 1¼ inches thick by 3½ inches wide.) Because five-quarter stock is comparatively expensive, outsized flats are frequently built from 18-gauge, one-inch-square steel tubing. The face of the steel frame is covered with ¼- or ⅛-inch plywood that is attached with power-driven, self-tapping screws, and the hard surface is covered with appropriate cloth material.

Toggle bars are used to keep the stiles parallel. If toggle bars were not used, fabric shrinkage (caused when the flat is painted) would cause the stiles to twist and bow in toward each other. Toggles should be spaced approximately four to five feet from the nearest toggle bar or rail.

Any flat wider than six feet is awkward to handle and takes up a lot of storage space. Flats less than two feet wide are generally referred to as **jogs,** and jogs less than one foot wide are normally made from solid stock rather than fabric covered framework. The solid jog is covered with the same fabric as other flats so that it will look the same when painted.

Building Flats   To build a standard wooden flat fourteen feet tall and four feet wide, you can follow a standard procedure outlined in fifteen steps:

1. Select good, straight white pine 1 × 3 ("B or better" or "C select") for the rails, stiles, and toggle bars.
2. Trim and square the end of one of the boards, and cut two pieces four feet long for the rails. (Note that the rails are cut the full width of the flat.)
3. Trim and square the boards, and cut the two stiles fourteen feet (the height of the flat) minus the combined width of the two rails.
4. Square the boards, and cut two toggle bars four feet (the width of the flat) minus the combined width of the two stiles.

Keystones and Cornerblocks

Keystones and cornerblocks are used as reinforcement for the butt joints commonly used in flat construction.

The *cornerblock* is a triangle of one-quarter-inch AD plywood with eight- to ten-inch legs. To provide effective reinforcement, position the cornerblock so that its grain runs perpendicular to the joint between the rail and the stile.

Also made of one-quarter-inch AD plywood, the *keystone* is six inches long and shaped like a keystone of an arch. The small end is slightly narrower (one-half inch) than the width of the toggle bar that it is covering; the wide end is approximately one-half inch wider than the toggle bar.

Some technicians prefer rectangular strips of plywood, called straps, to keystones. These straps should be cut approximately one-half inch narrower than the width of the toggle bar. Both keystones and rectangular straps provide about the same amount of bracing for the joint, but many technicians think that keystones are prettier, so they continue to use them in preference to the plywood straps.

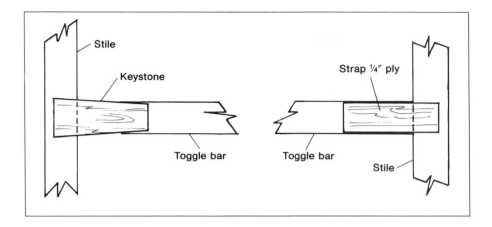

FIGURE 9.10
The placement of keystones on
a flat.

5. Before you begin to assemble the flat, cut the keystones and cornerblocks.

6. Although a flat can be assembled using mortise and tenon or halved joints
    for extra strength, most shops use butt joints when putting flats together.
    Butt the stiles against the edge of the top and bottom rails, as shown in
    Figure 9.8. Assembling the flat in this manner means that the rail will be the
    only framing element making contact with the floor when the finished flat
    is set upright. If the flat were assembled with the end of the stile touching
    the floor, it would be splintered and broken whenever the flat was moved
    or skidded along the floor.

7. Use a framing square to make sure that the corner joint between the rail and
    stile is square. Lay a cornerblock on top of the joint with its grain running
    perpendicular to the line of the joint (parallel to the grain of the stile), and
    inset three-quarters of an inch from the outside edge of both the rail and
    stile, as shown in Figure 9.9. Secure the cornerblocks (as well as the key-
    stones or straps) with clout nails and a clinch plate, coated staples, or
    screws. This routine is repeated for each corner of the flat.

8. Center the toggle bars at four feet eight inches and nine feet four inches so
    that they will be equidistant from the top and bottom of the flat and from
    each other, as shown in Figure 9.8. Use the framing square to make sure that
    the toggle bars are square to the stile, and secure them with keystones that
    are also inset three-quarters of an inch from the edges of the stiles, as shown
    in Figure 9.10.

9. When the flat is wider than three feet, diagonal corner braces made of 1 × 2
    are placed in the upper and lower corners of the same side of the flat. Se-
    cure these corner braces with plywood straps ripped in half and angle cut
    so that they can be inset three-quarters of an inch from the outside edge of
    the flat, as illustrated in Figure 9.11.

10. To cover the flat, you will need to turn it over so that it is lying on the
    cornerblocks and keystones (Figure 9.12A). Stretch a piece of heavyweight
    muslin (128- or 140-thread count) over the frame (see the box on page 204).
    The muslin should be slightly larger than the height and width of the flat,
    as shown in Figure 9.12B. Using a hand stapler, attach the muslin along the
    inside edge of the face of one of the stiles. Place the staples about one foot
    apart.

11. Move to the center of the other stile, and pull the muslin until it barely sags
    across the face of the flat. Staple it on the inside edge of the face of that
    stile. Be sure that you don't stretch the muslin until it is tight; you need to

FIGURE 9.11
The placement of reinforcement for
diagonal braces on a flat. Be sure
that all cornerblocks, keystones, and
straps are placed with their outside
edges ¾" from the outside edge of
the flat.

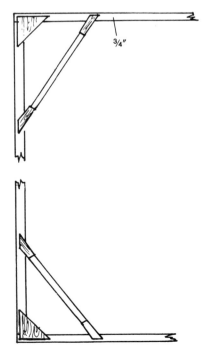

FIGURE 9.12
Flat-covering technique. (A) The smooth front side of a flat frame. (B) Lay fabric slightly wider and taller than the flat frame over the frame. (C) Staple the fabric to the inside edge of the face of the flat. (D) Glue the fabric to the frame, and smooth the fabric onto the frame with your hands (E) or a small block of wood. Trim the excess fabric with a matte knife (F) after the glue has dried. (G) The finished flat.

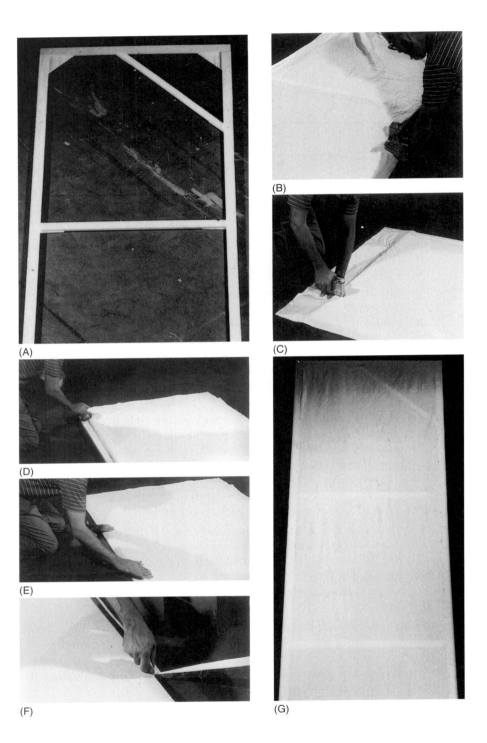

allow room for fabric shrinkage when you paint the muslin. (On a four-by-fourteen-foot flat, the completely tacked muslin should just brush the work surface underneath it.) Work your way toward the end of the flat, alternately pulling and stapling the material. Do this in both directions from the staple that you placed in the center of the stile.

12. In a similar fashion, pull and staple the fabric to the inside edge of the face of both rails, as shown in Figure 9.12C. If there are any wrinkles or puckers

in the fabric, the staples should be pulled and the fabric restretched until the wrinkles are removed.

13. To finish covering the flat, you need to glue the muslin to the frame. Regardless of the shape of the flat, you should glue the covering only to the face of the rails and stiles. If the covering fabric is not glued to any internal pieces (toggle bars, corner braces), it will be able to shrink evenly when the flat is painted. This uniform shrinkage will result in fewer wrinkles on the face of the finished flat.

14. To glue the cloth to the flat, turn back the flap of muslin around the edge of the flat and apply a light coating of glue to the face of the stiles and rails, as shown in Figure 9.12D. Be sure that you use a thorough but *light* coating, because if it soaks through the muslin, it may discolor or darken the ensuing paint job. Fold the muslin back onto the wood, and carefully smooth out any wrinkles with your hand (Figure 9.12E) or a small block of wood.

15. After the glue has dried, you will need to trim the excess fabric from the flat. The easiest way to do this is to pull the fabric tight and run a matte knife down the edge of the flat, as shown in Figure 9.12F.

Studio Flats   Studio flats, also called Hollywood-style flats, are framed flats that are covered with a hard material such as plywood. They are constructed using the same general framing layout as a soft flat with one major exception: The framing wood is placed on edge rather than flat. The wood is placed on edge for a simple reason: strength. To illustrate: If you pick up the end of a ten or twelve foot 1 × 4, you'll notice that the board flexes and bounces up and down quite freely. This is because the movement is being countered only by the force generated by the ¾-inch thickness of the plank. But if you turn the board on edge it barely flexes up and down. This is because the wood countering the up-and-down movement is now 3½ inches rather than ¾ inch thick.

In a soft flat the frame is designed so the 3½-inch width of the lumber counters the force created by the shrinkage of the covering fabric. Plywood, the covering material for studio flats, flexes in only one direction—perpendicular to its thickness. Therefore, in a studio flat the framing lumber is placed on edge so the 3½-inch width of the lumber counters any flexing of the covering plywood.

When several studio flats are used to create a wall unit, bolts and nuts are most frequently used to join the flats together. Holes are drilled approximately one-quarter of the distance down from the top and up from the bottom of the stiles of adjacent flats, then bolts are inserted and snugged down with nuts.

Metal-Framed Flats   The process of constructing a flat from square metal tubing instead of 1 × 3 lumber is almost identical. Eighteen-gauge, 1 inch × 1 inch square tubing is used instead of lumber. The stiles are still placed inside the rails, and the toggle bars are spaced using the same formula. All joints between the rails, stiles, and toggle bars are welded, preferably with a MIG welder. Because of the strength of the welded joints, keystones and cornerblocks are not needed. The surface of the flat is generally covered with some type of sheet stock such as ⅛-, ³⁄₁₆-, or ¼-inch plywood. The plywood is attached to the frame using self-tapping screws and a power screwdriver. The screws should be spaced between twelve and eighteen inches apart. The plywood is then covered with an appropriate type of fabric or covering.

Door and Window Flats   All wooden and metal-framed flats can be constructed and covered using the general principles previously listed. The stiles of all flats (regular, irregular, door, window) are always placed inside their

FIGURE 9.13
Standard door flats.

FIGURE 9.14
Standard window flats.

sill iron: A strap of mild steel attached to the bottom of a door flat to brace it where the rail has been cut out.

Flat-Covering Fabrics

A variety of fabrics can be used to cover flats.

Unbleached Muslin

Heavyweight unbleached muslin is an excellent, low-cost flat-covering material. It is available in a variety of widths—72, 81, 90, and 108 inches and 33 feet. The narrower widths are used for flat covering, and the 33-foot material is usually used for making seamless drops and cycloramas.

This type of muslin, which is available from scenic supply houses, has a high-thread count—128 or 140 threads to the inch—which gives sufficient strength for flat covering and most other scenic uses. Muslin accepts all scenic paints well and has a uniform shrinkage rate.

Although bleached muslin is available in fabric stores, it isn't particularly useful for scenic purposes, because the bleaching process weakens its fibers, it normally isn't available in sizes wider than forty-eight inches, and it is more expensive.

Linen Canvas

Linen canvas is an excellent flat-covering material, because it is extremely durable and has a coarse weave similar to artist's canvas. The fabric is sixty-nine to seventy-two inches wide and weighs twelve to sixteen ounces per square yard. It accepts paint well and doesn't shrink much. Unfortunately, it is also the most expensive of the flat-covering materials, is not always available, and can be purchased only from scenic or fabric supply houses.

Cotton Canvas

Cotton canvas is an excellent substitute for linen canvas, because it has many of the same properties, is approximately the same weight (nine to sixteen ounces), is readily available, and is much less expensive. It is the preferred type of canvas for making platform covers and ground cloths.

Cotton canvas is available in widths up to seventy-two inches, is sometimes available from tent and awning suppliers, and can also be purchased from scenic or fabric supply houses.

Cotton Duck

Cotton duck is a lighter weight—five- to eight-ounce—cotton canvas. It has the same properties as cotton canvas and is generally available locally, although it may be difficult to find in sizes wide enough for stage purposes (generally sixty-nine inches or wider). It is available from local fabric stores, tent and awning suppliers, and scenic-fabric supply houses.

respective rails to prevent splintering of the stiles (if wood is used). The sizes of any interior openings in the flats (doors, windows, and so forth) are determined by the position of the toggle bars and door or window stiles, as shown in Figures 9.13 and 9.14.

Door flats have one construction variation. The bottom rail across the door opening of a wooden framed flat is removed and replaced with a **sill iron,** which is a mild-steel strap three-sixteenths or one-quarter of an inch thick and three-quarters of an inch wide, as shown in Figure 9.15. The sill iron should extend at least one foot beyond either side of the doorway. For maximum strength, the sill iron should run to the outer edges of the door flat, bend at right angles, and run up the outside edge of the stiles a minimum of six to eight inches. With either method, a thin strip of wood the thickness of the sill iron needs to be removed from the bottom of the rail and/or the outside edge of the stile to maintain the overall height and width of the flat. The sill iron is attached with 1- or 1¼-inch No. 8 or 9 flat-head screws or yellow zinc drywall screws. On metal-framed door flats, unless the door opening is quite wide, the sill iron isn't needed.

Arches and irregular openings in flats are made by insetting **sweeps** in regular door and window openings, as shown in Figure 9.16. Sweeps can be made from three-quarter-inch stock or plywood. Stock is preferable, because it will

sweep: A wooden curvilinear form, generally used to outline an arch or irregular form in door- and window-flat openings.

Scenic Canvas and Muslin Glue Formulas

There are several effective methods of gluing covering fabric to flats.

Paint

Probably the easiest method of gluing muslin to a flat frame is with casein, acrylic, or latex paint. When using paint, either select white paint (which is close to the color of muslin) or mix a color that closely approximates the prime coat that you will be using to paint the set. Simply paint the stiles and rails with the paint, apply a very light coat of paint to the underside of the fabric flap, flop the fabric back onto the wood, and smooth it out. The binders in the paint will glue the fabric to the wood. This method works well if the flat is going to be used for a single production, as the binders in the paint are not strong enough to permanently bond the fabric to the flat. If the flat is going to be reused, one of the following glues would be more appropriate.

Animal Glue and Whiting

Animal glue is combined with whiting (a thickening agent made of low-grade chalk) in the ratio of one part prepared animal glue (see Chapter 8 for instructions) to one part whiting paste. To make whiting paste, put the dry whiting in a container and stir in enough water to make a paste the consistency of sour cream. Add the glue to the whiting paste, and use while it is hot. The mixture dries when it cools, but it can be reheated in a double boiler or glue pot to make it workable again.

White Glue and Water

A mixture of two parts of white glue thinned with one part of water makes a good muslin glue. Take care to use a light coat of glue, because if the white glue bleeds through to the surface of the fabric, it can leave a glaze coat that may discolor any subsequent coats of paint.

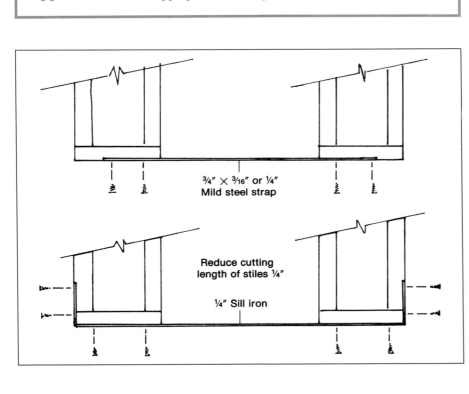

¾" × ³⁄₁₆" or ¼"
Mild steel strap

Reduce cutting length of stiles ¼"

¼" Sill iron

FIGURE 9.15
A sill iron is used to replace the bottom rail that is cut out when constructing a door flat.

FIGURE 9.16
Sweeps are used to create irregularly shaped openings in door and window flats.

FIGURE 9.17
Depth pieces, or reveals, help create the illusion of wall thickness.

FIGURE 9.18
Dependent doors and windows.

Standard Door Dimensions

Although the appearance of any door is the province of the scenic designer, certain dimensions and characteristics of doors are fairly standard.

1. Doors that people will pass through need to be at least two feet six inches wide. Set doors normally vary in width from two and a half to three and a half feet, depending on the height and style of the door. Closet doors are often narrower. Double doors are usually five to seven feet wide.

2. Door heights vary between six feet nine inches and seven feet six inches.

3. Doorknobs are generally placed about three feet above the floor, although certain European styles place the doorknob closer to four feet.

4. Doors normally swing offstage. They are usually hinged on the upstage side of the doorway unless other needs (stage business, architectural faithfulness) dictate that the door be hung in some other manner.

better hold the nails driven into its edge to support the depth pieces, also known as reveals. Sweeps that are used to create arches in either doors or windows should be notched into the door or window stiles approximately one-half to three-quarters of an inch. If they aren't, the end of the sweep will have to be cut to a feather edge, and the chances of breaking that slivered end will be very good.

Trim enhances the realistic appearance of a door or window flat. Depth pieces create the illusion that the flat has actual thickness. Straight-line depth pieces can be made from 1 × 6 stock, one-quarter-inch Masonite, or similarly rigid material, as shown in Figure 9.17; curved depth pieces can be made from one-eighth-inch Easy Curve, three-sixteenth-inch Upson board, or one-eighth-inch Masonite. The actual depth of the door or window depends entirely on the style and architectural period chosen by the scenic designer. The appearance of the window or door is similarly dependent on its architectural model.

There are two types of stage windows and doors: dependent and independent. The basic difference between the two is that the dependent unit is fixed to the flat, whereas the independent unit is largely self-contained and can easily be attached to or removed from the flat. Figure 9.18 shows exploded views of dependent doors and windows, and Figure 9.19 shows similar illustrations of independent doors and windows.

There isn't really a single, "correct" way to build either stage doors or windows. The appearance and function of doors and windows are determined by the scenic designer, and their appearance largely determines how they need to be built.

It is fairly standard practice to design doors to pivot on their upstage side and swing offstage (Figure 9.20), because, with this arrangement, they are self-masking. Self-masking doors block the spectators' view of the backstage area, they don't mask the actors' entrances, and they don't cut off the spectators' view of any part of the set. Because doors usually swing offstage, the spectators normally see only one side of them. For this reason, it is fairly common to build them on a base piece of one-quarter-inch plywood. Decorative trim can be applied to the face of the plywood (Figure 9.21). If both sides of the door are going to be seen, the same type of trim is applied to the back.

FIGURE 9.19
Independent doors and windows.

FIGURE 9.20
Stage doors are usually hinged to swing offstage.

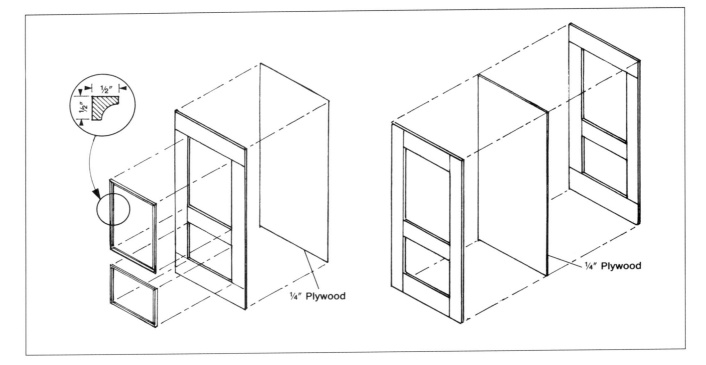

FIGURE 9.21
Trim is attached to a plywood door to provide appropriate decoration.

FIGURE 9.22
Flats can be joined together to create a wall unit.

Joining Flats Up to this point, the discussion has been confined to constructing individual flats no more than six feet wide. But most designs call for walls that are considerably wider. To construct such a larger wall, you join individual flats. As shown in Figure 9.22, varying styles of door, window, and plain flats can be joined to form a wall unit.

FIGURE 9.23
Rigid flat-joining techniques.

prime coat: The first coat of paint applied to the flats, to develop a relatively uniform color and surface to the wall units.

stiffening batten: A length of 1 × 3 attached to a multiflat wall unit to keep it from wiggling.

book: To fold hinged flats together (so that they resemble a book).

tumbler: A ¾-inch-thick-by-1-inch-wide (or 1 × 3) piece of stock used as a spacer when three or more flats are going to be booked.

header: A small flat that can be placed between two standard-sized flats to create a doorway or window.

book ceiling: Two large flats about the same width as the proscenium arch, stored in a booked position in the flies; when needed to create a ceiling, they are opened and lowered onto the walls of the set.

FIGURE 9.24
An effective stiffening batten can be made from two 1 × 3s.

FIGURE 9.25
S hooks can be used to hold removable stiffening battens.

There are two primary methods of joining flats to form wall units: rigid and flexible. The rigid joining method is used when the wall unit doesn't have to be folded for shifting or storage. The flexible method is used when it is necessary to fold the wall.

Rigid Joining   If the multiflat wall does not need to fold, the flats can be joined to form a rigid unit (Figure 9.23) in the following manner:

1. Lay the flats face up in their proper order. Where adjacent flats butt together, attach tight-pin hinges to the stiles, as shown in Figure 9.23.

2. Cover the joint and hinges with a dutchman. Fray one-quarter inch of the edges of a five- to six-inch-wide strip of cloth (the same material as the flat covering), and attach it to the flat by coating one side of it and the stiles with latex, acrylic, or vinyl paint the same color as the **prime coat.** Apply the dutchman to the joint, smooth out any wrinkles, and allow to dry. (You don't have to put the dutchman on at this time. You can wait until you are doing the other painting.)

3. Turn the hinged wall unit onto its back, and attach **stiffening battens.** Stiffening battens are 1 × 3s, on edge, that are attached to the back of a multiflat wall as stabilizers. The stiffening battens are held in place with tight-pin hinges. One flap of the hinge is attached to the batten and the other to a stile or toggle bar of the flat. To keep the stiffening batten in the proper position, the hinges are attached alternately to opposite sides of the batten.

Some technicians prefer to lay the stiffening battens on their sides and attach them to the flats with screws. Although this method holds the flats together, it does not provide nearly the stiffening effect that is supplied by the 1 × 3 standing on edge. However, if another 1 × 3 is screwed to the edge of the stiffening batten, as shown in Figure 9.24, the stiffening effect will be regained.

Flexible Joining   Flexible joining uses the same principles as rigid joining, with the exception that the stiffening batten is removable. The flats are joined with tight-pin hinges on the faces of the flats, and the joint is covered with a dutchman. To make the stiffening batten removable, attach it with loose-pin hinges. To remove the batten, take the pins out of the hinges. S hooks provide another method of attaching a removable batten, as shown in Figure 9.25.

If more than two flats are going to be **booked,** you will have to use a **tumbler.** A tumbler is basically a miniflat. It is a piece of three-quarter-inch stock the full height of the flats but only one inch wide. A tumbler can also be made from a 1 × 3. It acts as a spacer between two flats and allows the flats to be fully closed, as shown in Figure 9.26. It is attached to the other flats with tight-pin hinges and covered with a dutchman.

When joining flats, you can use **headers** to create doors or archways simply by placing them between two regular-sized flats, as shown in Figure 9.27.

Ceilings   Ceilings for sets are primarily used on proscenium stages. They are really large, horizontal flats, but they do provide some special challenges simply because of their size. The **book ceiling** (Figure 9.28) is a permanent piece of stage equipment in many proscenium theatres. It is composed of two large flats approximately the same width as the proscenium arch. The depth of the opened book ceiling is normally about sixteen to twenty feet. It can be stored on a single counterweight line.

Irregular ceiling pieces (Figure 9.29) that do not completely cover the set can be built just as any other flat is. They are normally built of 1 × 4 stock for additional strength. Spot lines of piano wire can be dropped from the grid or a batten to support the downstage edge of the ceiling.

Soft Scenery

Soft scenery refers to unframed fabric units such as drops and draperies, which are usually suspended from the grid, a batten, or some type of structure capable of supporting their weight.

Drops   Drops are large, flat curtains that have no fullness. There are two primary methods of attaching drops to their respective supporting battens: ties and batten clamps.

Tie-Supported Drops   Probably the easiest way of hanging a drop is to tie it to the batten. Ties (which can be made from strips of scrap muslin, one-half-inch heavy cotton tape, thirty-six-inch shoelaces, or similar materials) are attached to the top of the drop and then tied to the batten. Cotton-tape ties can be sewn to the four-inch jute backing tape at the top hem of the drop, as shown in

FIGURE 9.26
A tumbler permits the flats being booked to fold completely.

FIGURE 9.27
A header can be used to create a doorway.

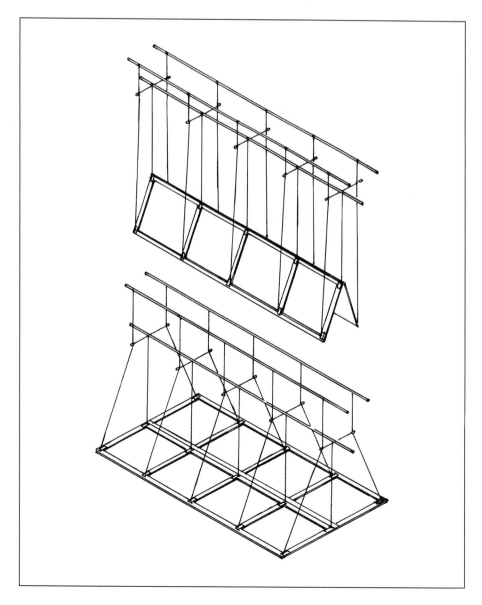

FIGURE 9.28
A book ceiling.

FIGURE 9.29
An irregular ceiling.

FIGURE 9.30
Methods of attaching drops to battens.

Figure 9.30. The other kinds of ties are used in conjunction with grommets in the jute-tape backing of the drop. The grommet-reinforced holes are usually spaced on one-foot centers across the width of the drop. The ties (ideally thirty-six to forty inches long) are looped through the grommet holes and tied to the batten.

Batten-Clamp Drops   Drops are sometimes attached to a counterweight batten with batten clamps. The batten clamp facilitates rapid hanging or removal of a drop from the batten. The top of the drop is sandwiched between two 1 × 3s, as shown in Figure 9.31. The batten clamp is designed to hold the wooden batten "sandwich" without touching the drop.

A variety of effects can be achieved with drops. Drops are generally hung on an upstage batten and provide a background such as a forest, street scene, or the upstage wall of a ballroom. To an extent, the effects the drops create are dependent on the type of material from which the drop is made and the manner in which it is painted and lit.

Opaque Drops   Commonly made of heavyweight muslin, opaque drops are painted with opaque paints (scene paint, casein, latex, acrylic, and so on) and are lit from the front. The audience cannot see through them.

Translucent Drops   Made of heavyweight muslin, translucent drops are painted with dyes or a combination of dye and opaque paint and are lit from both front and back. This makes the areas that have been dyed translucent, increasing the apparent depth of the scene. Since any seams would show when such drops were back-lit, they are frequently made from seamless muslin thirty-three feet wide. If the translucent area is fairly small, the drop can sometimes be made so that any seams fall in the opaque painted areas.

Scrim Drops   Made from sharkstooth scrim or theatrical gauze, scrim drops have the unique ability to become transparent when the scene behind the drop is

Scenic Specialty Fabrics

A variety of fabrics can be used for special scenic-construction purposes. These fabrics are not normally available in local fabric stores and must be purchased from scenic supply houses.

Sharkstooth Scrim

The thirty-foot-wide, seamless cotton material called sharkstooth scrim has a unique property. When lit from the front, the material is opaque. When light is taken off the fabric and objects behind it are lit, the scrim becomes transparent because the material has a very open weave that creates rectangles of open space about 3/16 inch wide by 3/16 inch high.

A close-up view of sharkstooth scrim.

It is available from scenic-fabric supply houses in natural (a creamy white), white, and black. It can be painted with dye or paint, although if paint is used, care must be taken to avoid filling the open spaces.

Sharkstooth scrim is used for transparent drops, in illusion effects, and in similar applications. It can also be used as a diffusion drop (a drop that softens light) for cyc lighting. If sharkstooth scrim is hung in front of a muslin cyc, it diffuses and softens the effects of the cyc lighting and creates a greater illusion of depth.

Bobbinet

Another thirty-foot-wide, open-weave cotton material is bobbinet. It is lighter in weight than sharkstooth scrim, is more transparent, and has a hexagonal weave. It is also available from scenic supply houses in natural, white, or black. It can be used as a substitute for glass in windows, as a diffusion drop for cyc lighting, as net backing for cut-out drops, and in similar applications.

A close-up view of bobbinet.

Theatrical Gauze

Theatrical gauze is a cotton fabric with a fine-mesh weave similar to cheese-cloth, but its threads are thicker and the weave is slightly tighter. It is seventy-two inches wide and can be purchased from scenic-fabric supply houses in natural, black, and a limited range of colors. Its applications are similar to those of sharkstooth scrim with the exception of those situations where the seams every six feet would prove objectionable.

A close-up view of theatrical gauze.

Safety Tip

Strength of Welds

The strength of any weight-bearing welded structure depends on the strength of its welds. Before attempting to construct any metal platforming or other structures on which actors are going to stand, be sure to practice enough so that you are sure you are producing high-quality welds. Have your work checked by an instructor so that you know your welds will be strong.

FIGURE 9.31
A drop that has to be quickly
removed from the batten can be
supported with batten clamps.

lit. The material can be painted with dyes or thinned paint. Be sure that the paint
does not fill the large holes in the fabric.

Cutout Drops   Cutout drops have sections or pieces of the drop actually cut out
of the material. The sense of depth in a design can be greatly enhanced by the
use of a series of cutout drops placed in back of one another. The drops are
painted before they are cut to keep the cut edges from curling. Bobbinet or similar
loose-weave netting can be glued to the back of the drop to support the cut-out
areas if necessary.

Draperies   The two types of draperies used in the theatre are discussed elsewhere in this book. Stage draperies are covered in Chapter 4, and the drapes and
curtains used to decorate sets will be discussed in Chapter 11, *Stage Properties.*

THREE-DIMENSIONAL SCENERY

Although flats and architectural trim actually have three dimensions, the term
three-dimensional scenery generally refers to the construction of platforms, stairs,
and similar objects.

Stage Platforming

Directors love multilevel stage floors, because they make it easy to create interesting blocking pictures. Platforms are used to create these levels. There are several types of platforms and a number of techniques for joining them.

Rigid Wooden Platform   Probably the easiest stage platform to build, the rigid
wooden platform, is also the least expensive. An added bonus is that the legs are
detachable, so its height can be varied easily.

FIGURE 9.32
A rigid wooden platform consists of
a top and a ladderlike supporting
structure.

Labels on figure:
¾" plywood top (attach to frame with power-driven screws)

Predrilled caster plates (to match hole pattern on caster flange)

1" × 2" 16-gauge tubing

8'-0"

4'-0"

Leg plate (matches pattern on caster plate)

Leg

FIGURE 9.33
Steel tube platforms are similar in appearance to rigid wooden platforms.

The framing for a rigid platform is generally made of 2 × 4 although 1 × 6 or 2 × 6 can also be used. The frame is a ladderlike construction with the rungs, or **joists,** spaced no more than two feet apart, as shown in Figure 9.32. Rigid platforms can be easily constructed in almost any irregular shape, but standard rigid platforms that are kept in a theatre's inventory of stock scenery are normally four feet wide by eight feet long.

Rigid Steel-Tubing Platform   Steel tubing can also be used to fabricate rigid platforms, as shown in Figure 9.33.[1] The framework is made from sixteen-gauge 1 × 2 steel tubing, and the top from three-quarter-inch plywood. **Gussets** inset into each corner of the frame, or steel plates one-quarter inch thick designed to accept casters or legs, are welded to the frame. These are predrilled in a pattern that matches the hole pattern on a caster flange or shop-built leg base. Casket locks are attached to the underside of the platform in a uniform pattern so that the platform can be locked to an adjacent unit.

Rigid Platform Legs   Legs for rigid platforms can be fabricated from a variety of materials, as shown in Figure 9.34. All platform legs over eighteen inches tall should be braced, regardless of whether they are wooden or metal, because the sideways forces exerted on the platform by the movement of the actors can easily break either the joint between the leg and the platform or, possibly, the leg itself.

Braces should be placed so that they form a triangle between the leg and the rail to take advantage of the structural strength of the triangular form, as shown in Figure 9.35A. Braces will be effective if placed at any angle between thirty and sixty degrees, as shown in Figure 9.35B, although forty-five degrees provides the maximum strength. There should be no more than four feet between bracing support points, as shown in Figure 9.35C.

The strength of the rigid wooden platform is primarily based on the depth of the wood used to construct the frame. There are pragmatic limits to the size of a rigid wooden platform that are loosely based on the weight of the assembled

joists: Parallel beams that support flooring.

gusset: A triangular piece of material used to reinforce a corner joint.

1. This design is based on Stancil Campbell, "Steel Framed Stock Platforming," *Theatre Design and Technology* (Summer 1984): 16–20.

FIGURE 9.34
Types of platform legs and methods of attachment.

platform and the platform storage space available in the theatre. Rigid platforms are generally made no larger than four by eight feet.

Stressed-Skin Platform Stressed-skin construction involves securely gluing and screwing plywood **skins** to an internal framework that is nailed and glued, as shown in Figure 9.36. In this type of construction, in which the frame and covering are interlocked, the load is distributed over the entire unit instead of just on the joists. Since the skins can be **laminated** from two sheets of easily warped one-quarter-inch plywood, stressed-skin construction can be used for making curved-surface platforms. With this technique, platforms longer than eight feet can be made that require support only at the platform ends.

skin: A plywood covering. In this case, the top or bottom plywood covering for a platform.

laminate: To build up an object from several layers.

1'-6" or taller (A)

30°
45°
60°
(B)

8'-0"
4'-0"

Anchor legs to stage floor
(C)

FIGURE 9.35
Platform-leg bracing techniques.

½" plywood
(glue and screw to frame)

2" × 2" frame
(all joints glued)

½" plywood
(glue and screw to frame)

FIGURE 9.36
Stressed-skin construction
techniques.

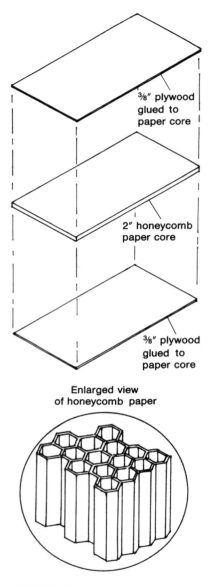

FIGURE 9.37
Honeycomb-laminate platform construction techniques.

honeycomb paper: A manufactured paper product with a hexagonal structure similar to a honeycomb.

cure: To harden and reach full strength (in reference to glue).

hardboard: Generic term for composition sheet goods such as Masonite and particle board.

butcher paper: A medium-weight brown paper, available in thirty-six-inch-wide rolls; also known by its trade name, Kraft paper.

The strength of stressed-skin construction depends on the secure interlocking of all the components, so it is essential that all the edges of the plywood skins be supported by the internal framework.

Honeycomb-Paper Lamination   Another lamination method is based on the principles used to fabricate the extremely strong, lightweight wings of supersonic aircraft. The strength of the platform depends on a continuous glue bond between the **honeycomb paper** and its covering skins.

These platforms are made by sandwiching honeycomb paper between two sheets of plywood, as shown in Figure 9.37. A liberal coat of a strong adhesive such as polyvinyl glue, foaming polyurethane glue, or white glue must be applied to the inside faces of both the top and bottom skins as the platform is being assembled.

To further ensure uniform bonding, pressure has to be maintained on the platform until the adhesive dries. Large pieces of one-quarter-inch steel plate that completely cover the platform's surface can be placed on top of it. Counterweights can be used if the steel plate isn't available. Vacuum pressure can be used instead of weights. To vacuum clamp, the assembled platform is covered with heavyweight plastic sheeting, the plastic is taped to the shop floor with gaffer's (duct) tape, and a vacuum pump is used to remove the air under the cover.

Clamping pressure, whether from weights or vacuum, must be maintained on the platform for at least two hours or until the glue has set. The glue has usually **cured** enough after twenty-four hours, so the units can be moved, but no weight or stress should be placed on the platforms for at least thirty-six to forty-eight hours. The curing time depends on a number of variables, such as the type of glue, relative humidity, and the shop temperature.

After the glue has cured at least overnight, a facing of stock lumber, plywood, or **hardboard** should be attached to the edge of the platform to protect the paper core from possible damage. If the core is damaged—ripped/punctured/bent—the strength of the platform may be compromised.

To make platforms larger than four by eight feet, the top and bottom skins can be laminated from two thicknesses of plywood. When making these laminated skins, be sure that the butt joints between sheets in adjacent layers are separated by at least eighteen inches, as shown in Figure 9.38.

The flexibility of the honeycomb paper encourages its use for the development of free-form, curvilinear platforms.[2] Basic forms can be developed by laminating several layers of **butcher paper** and gluing the honeycomb paper to it. This form can be draped, honeycomb paper up, over forms until the desired shape is achieved. Additional layers of butcher paper are laminated to the top of the honeycomb paper to make a rigid structure. If necessary, after the unit has dried, it can be covered with fiberglass (see Chapter 11, *Stage Properties*, for a discussion of application techniques) to make it strong enough to walk on.

Honeycomb-laminate platforms present an additional advantage: They are quiet. The vibrations of footsteps and caster rumbling are absorbed by the honeycomb paper, which significantly reduces the "drumming" phenomenon associated with other types of platforming.

Parallels   Another type of platforming, the parallel, comes in two varieties: standard and continental. In both the top is removable, the framework (made of 1 × 3) folds for compact storage, and the height of the framework is not variable.

2. Tom Corbett, "Laminating Stage Platforms Using Honeycomb Paper," *Theatre Design and Technology* (Winter 1980): 24–25; 57–58.

Design Inspiration: Scenic Production

The following discussion is based on and quotes from "Hooping It Up," by Si Morse (Stage Directions, *March 1999, pp. 9–11*).

Design inspiration—the inspiration for any good design solution—is just as important for a technician as it is for a designer.

In the Seattle Children's Theatre production of *The Former One-on-One Basketball Champion* by Israel Horovitz, technical director Si Morse devised an inspired solution to a very real problem. The play tells the story of a junior-high basketball hotshot who encounters a depressed former basketball star at a city playground. The kid challenges the star, and they exchange views on life while playing one-on-one. The action of the play requires the two actors to play basketball—dribbling, jumping, and actually making shots.

The design challenge for the technical director came from the "booming" sound that the platformed court made as the actors dribbled, jumped, and cut.

Morse's first thoughts were to cover the platform with carpet. "But the carpet absorbed not only sound energy," Morse said, "it also absorbed some of the ball's rebound energy. Similarly, any kind of plastic foam (with a layer of plywood on top) absorbed rebound as well as sound energy." Morse

thought of using multiple layers of particle board. Experimentation showed that five or six layers of particle board deadened the sound, but the cost exceeded the available budget.

An inspired potential solution presented itself at a building supply store. "I noticed bags of 'cold-patch,' granular asphalt for tamping into pot holes in a driveway," Morse said. He built a two-foot by four-foot wooden box and tamped the cold patch into a two-inch layer on top. "Even with the box propped across 2 × 4s, the ball rebounded normally, and while it 'thwacked' on the asphalt, that was a much shorter and quieter sound—there was no 'boom.'"

Morse "cut a deal" with a neighborhood paving company. The platform-cum-basketball court was paved with 1½ inches of asphalt and hand-rolled in about an hour.

"By the next day, all the fans in the building had removed the odor, and the asphalt had cooled so the designer could paint stripes and 'dirt' on it."

Striking the court wasn't a problem. The asphalt was easily pried up with large steel bars, and the same company that "paved the stage" hauled the material away.

The lesson to be learned from this example is *Don't overlook the obvious.* Many of us become focused on "building it theatrically." Sometimes the real thing works even better.

The folding patterns of the two types are different, and the center support of the continental parallel is removable. Although parallels can be built in almost any size, they are normally four feet by eight feet.

Standard Parallel   The standard parallel is hinged to fold like a giant parallelogram (see Figure 9.39). This is done by placing the hinges in the specific pattern shown in Figure 9.40. The framework for the standard parallel is locked open with the 1 × 3 **cleats** on the underside of the top. These cleats fit snugly into the corners of the framework and prevent it from moving. The standard parallel can be set up or moved fairly quickly, because after the top is removed, the framework collapses into a single unit.

Continental Parallel   The continental parallel is hinged differently than the standard parallel, as shown in Figure 9.41. Although it folds into a more compact unit than does the standard parallel, its center support frames must be removed

cleat: A piece of wood used to brace, block, or reinforce.

FIGURE 9.38
Skins for large honeycomb-laminate platforms are made by laminating two thicknesses of plywood.

Separate joints by 1'-6" or more

¼" Plywood

FIGURE 9.39
The standard-parallel hinging pattern.

Partly folded

Second central support prevents parallel from folding flat

2

1

FIGURE 9.40
A standard parallel.

Construct with mortise and tenon joints or butt joints reinforced with cornerblocks or keystones

FIGURE 9.41
A continental parallel.

Folding pattern (note position of hinges)

before it can be collapsed. The framework is locked open in the same manner (with cleats on the underside of the top preventing the hinges from moving).

Platform and Parallel Tops   Platform and parallel tops are usually made from three-quarter-inch AD plywood or five-eighth-inch waferboard. The top can also be made of 1 × 6 white pine tongue and groove, but most TDs prefer to use plywood or waferboard, because these sheet stocks are stronger, are less likely to squeak, and take less time to construct.

To help muffle noise, it may be appropriate to cover the platform top with some type of padded surface. Old rugging (either jute- or foam-backed) or jute rug padding (not foam) can be tacked or stapled to the upper face of the top, as shown in Figure 9.42. The rugging is covered with scenic canvas. Muslin—even heavy-weight muslin—should not be used, because it will not stand up to the physical abuse the platform tops are likely to receive. When you are covering the platform top, the scenic canvas should be stretched over the outside edge of the top, pulled around to the underside, and tacked with heavy carpet tacks.

Care should be taken that all platform tops are covered with rugging or padding that is the same thickness, to avoid the possibility of creating an uneven floor when several platforms are joined together to be used as a unit. If a hard, shiny surface is needed, the platform tops can be covered with Masonite, as discussed in Chapter 4.

Another effective sound muffling technique is to sandwich a layer of ½-inch Celotex, a loosely bonded composition board, between the plywood platform top and a covering of tempered hardboard. The Celotex absorbs most sounds generated by traffic—actors, wagons, and so forth—on the platform.

Connecting Platforms   When more than one platform is used to create a new floor level, the platforms must be connected to improve the lateral stability of the unit. Fastening them together can be accomplished in a number of ways.

Bolting   Wooden platforms or parallels can be bolted together by drilling through the framing members of adjacent units and using three-eighth-by-four-inch bolts, as shown in Figure 9.43. Two or three bolts per long side and one at each end are usually sufficient.

Clamping   If the platforms or parallels need to be shifted during the production, C clamps can be substituted for the bolts described in the process above, as illustrated in Figure 9.44.

Casket Locks   Casket locks can be inset into the framing members of rigid wooden platforms or parallels, as shown in Figure 9.45, to tie the platforms together. Casket locks can also be welded to the bottom of the frame on steel-framed platforms.

If casket locks are attached to every stock platform in a standard pattern (Figure 9.46), it will be easy and quick to lock any platform to an adjacent unit of the same height. Because platforms equipped with casket locks can be locked or unlocked quickly, they can be used for either permanent or temporary staging.

Stairs

Two basic types of stairs are used in scenic construction: dependent and independent. The dependent units require support from some other element, usually a platform, for support; the independent units are self-supporting, as shown in Figure 9.47. Although the primary difference between independent and

FIGURE 9.42
A platform-top padding technique.

FIGURE 9.43
Platform modules can be bolted together to create a larger platform.

FIGURE 9.44
Platforms can be temporarily joined together with C clamps.

Size of Joists

A rule of thumb for estimating wooden joist spans such as the longitudinal, or lengthwise, joists of a rigid platform is

$$\text{span} = 24 \times \text{joist depth}$$

For example, if you build a rigid platform frame from 2 × 4, the practical limit for the length of the platform would be eight feet:

$$24 \times 4 = 96 \text{ inches, or 8 feet}$$

Other factors—such as the spacing between joists, the number of support points (legs), and the load and type of activity that will be imposed on the platform—must be factored in to help determine the design of the platform. But the preceding formula provides a rough guide for determining the size of wood that should be used for the construction of a rigid platform.

FIGURE 9.45
Casket locks can be used for permanent or temporary platform locking.

carriage: The part of a stair unit that supports the tread and risers.

tread: The horizontal surface of a stair.

riser: The vertical face of a stair unit.

score: To cut partially through.

dependent staircases is in their method of support, the actual units are built in much the same manner.

The **carriage** can be built in a variety of ways, as shown in Figure 9.48. Carriages can be cut from 1 × 12 for stair runs of less than six feet. For runs over six feet or in those instances where the stairs must support an unusual amount of weight, 2 × 12 should be used.

The **treads** can be made from three-quarter-inch stock or plywood. They should be cut with the grain running parallel with the long side of the tread (Figure 9.49A) to take advantage of the strength of the wood. For safety reasons, the unsupported span of a tread should never exceed two feet six inches. **Risers** are usually made from one-quarter-inch tempered Masonite or plywood. If the riser has to curve, one-eighth-inch Masonite or plywood can be used, and the back of the quarter-inch sheet stock can be **scored** so that the wood can be bent more easily. Scoring can be done by adjusting the blade height of the radial-arm

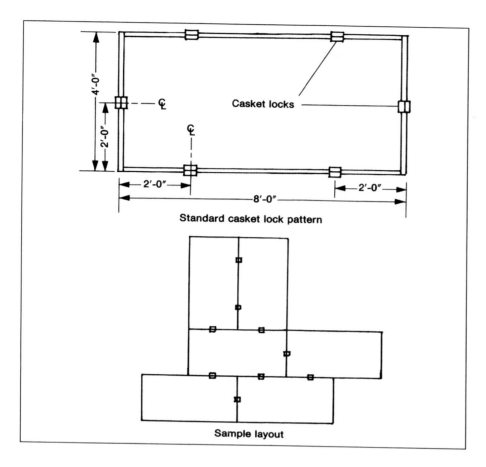

FIGURE 9.46
A standard casket lock pattern.

saw so that it cuts about halfway through the wood. Depending on the arc of the anticipated bend, cuts are spaced between three-eighths and one inch apart.

Although the size of treads and risers varies considerably, ten to twelve inches could be considered a fairly normal tread depth, and a riser of six to seven inches would be typical and appropriate.

FIGURE 9.47
Dependent and independent stair units.

FIGURE 9.49
Tread construction.

FIGURE 9.50
Methods of attaching banisters to
stair units.

FIGURE 9.48
Carriages can be built in a variety of ways.

Another way of thinking about riser height and tread width is known as "the rule of 18." The design of a staircase is considered comfortable and easy to use for most people if the total of the riser height plus the tread width equals eighteen inches. For example, a 12-inch tread with a 6-inch riser subscribes to "the rule of 18," as would a 10-inch tread with an 8-inch riser. While useful, it is important to remember that "the rule of 18" is a guideline and not an absolute. Ultimately, the scenic designer determines the riser height and tread width for any design. The important point is that the stairs work within the context of the scenic design and that the actors need to be comfortable and secure when moving on the stairs. Figure 9.49B shows the usual construction method of butting the treads into the bottom of the risers.

Staircase Railings

Although the design of any staircase railing is the province of the scenic designer, some seemingly universal challenges are encountered in the construction of these units. Unless **handrails, banister,** and **newel posts** are firmly anchored to the stair unit, they will wiggle and detract from the action of the play. For this reason, it is generally preferable to securely attach at least every other banister post to the stair riser with screws or bolts, as shown in Figure 9.50A. If the design indicates that the banisters and lower newel post cannot be butted against the risers, the base of the banister posts should be extended through the tread and screwed or bolted to the carriage, as shown in Figure 9.50B.

The lower newel post should be firmly anchored to the bottom tread, and the top newel post and handrail should be solidly attached to the flat at the top of the stairs, as shown in Figure 9.51.

Wagons

Wagons are usually rigid platforms (although parallels can be used) that rest on casters instead of legs (Figure 9.52). They can vary in size from very small (one foot square or less) to very large. (The slipstage is a huge wagon slightly larger than the normal playing area of the stage. It can hold an entire set.)

Casters, either rigid or swivel, are usually bolted onto caster plates attached to the underside of the platform (Figure 9.53). The caster plates should be sufficiently tall to create ½ to ¾ of an inch of clearance between the bottom edge of the platform and the stage floor. Unless the platform framing is very stiff (2 × 6 or 2 × 4 reinforced with 1½- to 2-inch by $\frac{3}{16}$ inch or ¼ inch mild-steel strap—see

handrail: The part of the stair railing that is grabbed with the hand; supported by the banister and newel post.

banister: The vertical member that supports the handrail of a staircase railing.

newel post: The post at the bottom or top of a flight of stairs that terminates the handrail.

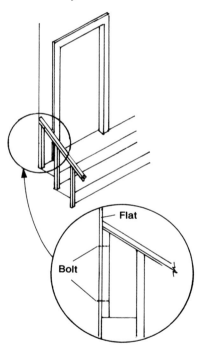

FIGURE 9.51
The top newel post and handrail must be firmly anchored.

FIGURE 9.52
Wagons.

FIGURE 9.53 ▶
Caster mounting techniques for
rigid platforms.

FIGURE 9.54
Reinforcing a 2 × 4 frame with
strap steel decreases the springiness
of a wagon.

FIGURE 9.55
Caster mounting techniques for
stressed-skin and honeycomb-
laminate platforms.

FIGURE 9.56
Principles of truss bracing and
types of trusses.

Figure 9.54), the casters should be spaced no more than 48 inches apart to prevent the platform from bouncing when it is walked on.

Wagons can also be made from stressed-skin and honeycomb-laminate platforms. With both types of platforms, the mounting bolts for the casters will have to penetrate both skins to ensure a strong attachment, as shown in Figure 9.55A. Figure 9.55B shows a caster-mounting jig and bearing plate that can be used to increase the strength of the caster mount.

Trusses

Many times it is necessary to bridge a large span between supporting points. A wooden or welded-steel truss (Figure 9.56A) offers another solution to this challenge.

The truss derives its strength from a redistribution of forces, as shown in Figure 9.56B. The downward force on the truss is channeled and redirected into a horizontal force by the legs of the triangle. Since the truss is composed of a

FIGURE 9.57
Revolve construction principles.

FIGURE 9.58
Revolve edge-finishing techniques.

series of interlocking triangles, a downward force anywhere on its top will be distributed over its full width.

Trusses, as noted, can be made from either wood or metal. Wooden trusses can be made by sandwiching the vertical and diagonal support pieces between the two longitudinal joists, as shown in Figure 9.56C. A more easily constructed, but heavier and more expensive, wooden truss can be made by substituting three-eighth-inch plywood for the diagonal bracing. Be sure that the grain of the plywood runs vertically, as shown in Figure 9.56D. The top and bottom rails of the truss can also be made by sandwiching 2 × 4 rails with the diagonal and vertical elements, as shown in Figure 9.56E. All joints in any type of wooden truss should be fastened with a high-quality synthetic adhesive (polyvinyl or epoxy glue) and nails, screws, bolts, or staples.

Metal trusses can be made by using bar stock for the diagonal supports and angle stock for longitudinal rails, as shown in Figure 9.56F. Again, to keep the truss from twisting, the rails should sandwich the diagonal bar stock. Metal trusses can also be made from square tubing, as illustrated in Figure 9.56G. In the interests of making strong and safe welds, use an arc welder (preferably MIG), rather than oxyacetylene for this type of weight-bearing, welded structure.

Trusses should be spaced no farther than two feet apart if the **decking** attached to the top of the truss is three-quarter-inch plywood. If the truss is to be decked with rigid, stressed-skin, or honeycomb-laminate platforms, the spacing

decking: The covering surface of a structure on which people will walk.

shim: Scrap wood or metal used to raise adjacent parts so that they are level or fit together as designed. (See Figure 9.60.)

between the trusses can be varied accordingly. The design of any weight-bearing truss should be checked with a structural engineer to ensure that it will be safe to use and will perform as intended.

Revolves

Revolves, also called turntables, are large, circular platforms that pivot on their central axis. The primary challenges in constructing a smooth-turning revolve are (1) attaching the casters so that the wheels are absolutely perpendicular to the radii of the turntable and (2) placing the pivot in the exact center of the revolve.

Revolves can be built using any of the standard platform-construction techniques, although the rigid platform method, shown in Figure 9.57, seems to work best, particularly if the scenery that will be placed on the revolve requires that you cut through its surface for support points.

If the revolve is going to be rotated with a winch drive (discussed later in the chapter), the outer edge of the revolve will have to be smoothly finished to provide a uniform bearing surface for the cable. Figure 9.58 shows a method that can be used to finish the edge of the revolve. The curved 2 × 8 sweeps create a smooth bearing surface for the drive cable, and the curved one-quarter-inch-plywood sweeps that form the three-quarter- to one-inch lip around the lower edge of the revolve prevent the drive cable from falling off.

Skids

Skids are low-profile, casterless substitutes for wagons. They are generally pieces of one-half- or three-quarter-inch plywood that are "skidded" across the stage. Although skids (Figure 9.59) can be pushed across the stage with a pole or pulled with a monofilament fishing line, they are frequently propelled by a winch and cable system. Skids are normally used to shift lightweight scenic pieces such as chairs and tables or small set elements.

Winch-Drive Systems

Figure 9.60 shows designs for hand-cranked or motorized winches that can be used in scene shifting. Figure 9.60A is a hand-cranked version, and Figure 9.60B illustrates a version that uses a variable-speed motor. The drum can also be mounted horizontally.

When working with a cable-drive system, it is important to provide some means of adjusting the tension on the cable, because a loose cable might tangle, wrap around a pulley, or otherwise foul up the works. Figure 9.60C shows a technique that makes adjusting the cable fairly easy.

To turn a small revolve, a plastic-covered steel cable is served around the circumference of the revolve and attached to the winch drum, as illustrated in Figure 9.61. The plastic covering on the steel cable increases the friction on the finished edge of the revolve, reducing slippage. By constructing a false floor with stock platforms, as shown in Figure 9.62, you can feed cable through the slot and attach it to steel tongues extending from the underside of the wagon or skid.

Platform-Anchoring Techniques

Large, three-dimensional scenic elements are frequently mounted on wagons to facilitate shifting. Once the wagon is in place, however, the casters will still wiggle or roll unless the wagon is anchored. Figure 9.63 illustrates a number of methods that can be used to anchor platforms.

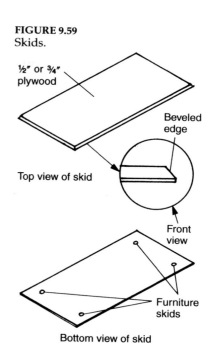

FIGURE 9.59
Skids.

½" or ¾" plywood

Beveled edge

Top view of skid

Front view

Furniture skids

Bottom view of skid

FIGURE 9.60 ▲
Hand-cranked and motorized winches.

FIGURE 9.61 ▼
Cable drive for a small revolve.

FIGURE 9.62 ▼
Winch-driven wagons and skids.

234

FIGURE 9.63
Wedges and blocks.

FIGURE 9.64
Lift jacks.

Lift Jack   The lift jack (Figure 9.64) is another platform-anchoring technique. The casters are placed in contact with the stage floor when the platform needs to be moved, but the platform rests directly on the stage floor when it is stationary. Lift jacks are normally equipped with swivel casters.

Tip Jack   The tip jack (Figure 9.65) can be used when a large wall unit cannot be conveniently shifted in another manner. The tip jack is simply two large interconnected jacks that are fitted with swivel casters. When the flat is tied into the rest of the set, the casters don't touch the stage floor. But when the lashing is released, the wall unit leans back, and the weight of the flat rests on the casters for easy shifting.

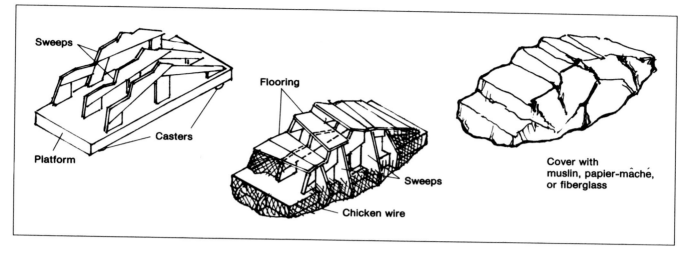

Rocks, Irregular Platforms, and 3-D Trees

Rocks, irregular platforms, and three-dimensional trees are all built in approximately the same manner. The basic principles of platform construction (three-quarter-inch plywood top, 1 × 4 or 2 × 4 framing, 2 × 4 legs) are followed when building stage rocks and other irregular platforms, as shown in Figure 9.66. Although the actual shape of these units will be determined by the scenic designer, the only significant construction difference is that surfaces of the rocks and irregular platforms are not straight, square, and level. The irregular quality is achieved by tilting the platform tops and covering the vertical faces of the units

FIGURE 9.66
Rigid platforms can be modified to look like rocks.

FIGURE 9.67
A three-dimensional tree.

with chicken wire and papier-mâché or some more-substantial covering material such as Celastic or fiberglass. The chicken wire is supported by a basic armature of plywood or stock sweeps. Techniques for working with papier-mâché, Celastic, and fiberglass are discussed in Chapter 11, *Stage Properties.*

Three-dimensional trees are built on a basic framework that utilizes the principles of flat construction. Plywood or stock sweeps are attached to the framework (Figure 9.67), which is subsequently covered with chicken wire, papier-mâché, and burlap or some similar rough-weave fabric to give the appearance of bark. The character of the bark can be created by forming the burlap into ridges that resemble the type of bark that you are simulating.

The frame can also be covered with heavy paper and chicken wire then sprayed with foam. It is probably best in terms of safety and cost effectiveness to job the foam-spraying out to a roofing contractor who does this type of work. After the foam has cured, it can be carved into the desired "bark-like" appearance and either painted directly with acrylic paint or coated with Sculptural Arts Coatings' Sculpt or Coat, Rosco's Foam Coat, or Rose Brand's Aqua-Resin to create a smoother surface and then painted.

Chapter 10
Scene Painting

Scene painting is the crowning touch on the realization of any scenic design. Through the techniques and materials described in this chapter, the scenic artist can make the various elements of the set—walls, floors, furniture, beaches, rocks, trees—look as if they belong to the play. Scene painting is the primary method used to create character in the set. Like any other craft field, scene painting can be divided into two primary areas: materials and techniques.

MATERIALS

The basic materials that are used in scene painting can, in turn, be divided into two main areas: paints and applicators.

Scenic Paints

Experience has proven certain types of paint to be more effective for theatre work than others are. All paints are composed of four elements: **pigment, filler, vehicle,** and **binder.** The pigment is that portion of the mixture that provides the paint with color. The type and amount of filler and, to a certain extent, the hue of the pigment determine the opacity of the paint. The vehicle is the liquid in which the pigment, filler, and binder are suspended. The binder is the adhesive that bonds the pigment and filler to the painted surface.

When the paint is mixed, the pigment, filler, and binder are suspended in the vehicle. When you paint something, the vehicle evaporates, and the binder bonds the pigment and filler to the painted surface.

Almost all paints used for general scenic purposes are water-vehicle (water-base) paints, because they are generally nonflammable, less expensive, easier to mix, quicker to dry, lighter in weight, and easier to clean up than their oil-base counterparts. However, some oil- and lacquer-base paints are used in scene painting for specific applications, such as creating metallic trim and highlights.

Dry Pigment and Binder   A safety caveat is required before beginning this discussion of dry pigment and binder. While the chemicals in some dry pigments are relatively inert, others are highly toxic. Because of the very light, dust-like texture of dry pigments, it is easy to inhale them. *Always* wear an appropriate respirator when mixing or handling any dry pigments. Consult the Manufacturer's Safety Data Sheet (MSDS) for the appropriate respirator to be worn with the pigments you're using.

Dry pigment and binder, otherwise known as scene paint, is probably the oldest type of scene paint. The pigment and filler are premixed at the factory. To create scene paint, you mix this powder with **size water** in the shop. With some

pigment: A material that imparts color to a paint or dye.

filler: A material that creates opacity (covering power) in paint.

vehicle: The liquid medium—water, oil, lacquer, and the like—in which pigments, fillers, and binders are suspended to create a paint mixture; after the paint is applied, the vehicle evaporates.

binder: An adhesive in paint that "glues" the pigment and fillers to the painted material after the vehicle has evaporated.

size water: A mixture of one cup of hot animal glue and one tablespoon of Lysol per gallon of warm water; white glue can be substituted for the animal glue in approximately equal measure.

pigments—generally the fully saturated mineral colors—a little more glue will have to be added to the mix. The exact water–glue ratio varies from pigment to pigment, because the amount of binder needed in the mix is related to the weight of the pigment and the amount of pigment used in the paint mix. The best way of determining the correct amount of glue in the paint is with the "finger test." After the paint has been mixed, dip your finger and thumb in the mix and then touch them together. If they feel slightly tacky or sticky, you have enough binder; if they don't, add some more.

Dry pigments are available in a wide range of hues, as shown in Table 10.1. They are inexpensive in comparison with the other types of scenic paint and will store indefinitely. These scene paints have moderate covering properties and a matte finish. More glue added to the size water will make the finish become slightly glossy.

A major drawback to using scene paint is the relatively rapid spoilage of the size water binder. Size water will spoil within one to several days depending on the heat and humidity of the environment in which it is stored. When dry pigment and binder paint spoils, it smells positively awful. The following caveat cannot be emphasized too much: *Do not use spoiled paint. Throw it away.* If you paint with spoiled dry pigment and binder, the repulsive smell will remain even when the paint is dry!

Dry pigment and binder, although still quite serviceable for many applications, is becoming somewhat obsolete. This is primarily because other types of paint are easier and less messy to mix and apply, cover better, and do not spoil as quickly.

Casein Paint Casein is a water-base paint with a soy protein- or milk-base binder. Anyone who has tried to clean dried milk out of the bottom of a glass has had firsthand contact with the bonding properties of casein. It is generally available in one- and two-gallon cans of concentrate that is diluted approximately two to one with water.

Casein is easily mixed, has excellent covering properties, and yields a matte finish. When fully dry it is water repellent, so it can be used on outdoor scenery. A primary drawback to casein is that the concentrate can spoil relatively quickly after the can has been opened. Paint made with the diluted concentrate also spoils relatively quickly. As with dry pigment and binder, if you paint with spoiled casein, the really revolting odor—like super-sour milk—will remain after the paint has dried.

Latex Paint Although water-base, latex-binder paint is not often thought of as a scenic paint, it serves that purpose very well. Latex is a synthetic liquid plastic with the flexible qualities of natural latex, or rubber. It not only bonds well but is reasonably flexible too. White latex paint is available at a reasonably low cost in five-gallon buckets and provides a very workable base for mixing tints with the more saturated paints. Dry pigment, **aniline dyes,** casein, and highly saturated

aniline dye: A transparent pigment made from aniline, a poisonous derivative of benzene; characterized by brilliant hues and full saturation.

Safety Tip ⚠

Mixing Dry Pigment

When mixing dry pigment and, especially, aniline dye, be sure to wear a dust mask or respirator that will filter out any airborne particles. The colors are made or respirator from a variety of chemicals that can be injurious if inhaled.

TABLE 10.1

A Representative Listing of Scene Paints

	Dry Pigments		Protein Paints		Latex, Acrylic, and Vinyl Paints		
	Gothic Scenic Colors*	Iddings Deep Colors	Gothic Casein Fresco Paints	Flo-Paint Scenic-Decorator Colors (vinyl)	Cal-Western Show & Display Colors (acrylic)	Rosco Paint Super Saturated (vinyl acrylic)
Whites	Permanent white 171 Danish whiting	Priming white 5550 White 5551	White	White gloss 5055 White flat 5033	White 520 Blockout white 565 Texture white 568 Hi gloss white 5119	White base 6002
Black	Ivory black 169 Hercules black 170	Black 5552	Black	Black gloss 5079 Black flat 5034	Black 519 Hi gloss black 5120	Velour black 6003
Yellows	Lt. chrome yellow 103 Med. chrome yellow 104	Lemon yellow 5566 Golden yellow 5567	Lemon yellow Golden yellow	Lemon yellow flat 5050 Lt. yellow gloss 5075 Golden yellow flat 5051 Med. yellow gloss 5069	Acacia 506	Chrome yellow 5981
Oranges	French orange mineral 110	Orange 5563	Orange	Orange flat 5052 Orange gloss 5068	Orange 507	Moly orange 5984
Reds	Turkey red lake 121 American vermilion red 113 Solferino red 126 Lt. maroon 127 Dk. maroon 124	Bright red 5562 Red 5560 Dark red 5561 Magenta 5569	Bright red Red Dark red Magenta	Bright red Flat 5044 Gloss 5076 Deep red Flat 5054 Gloss 5077 Magenta Flat 5048 Gloss 5065	Phthalo red 533 Fire red 503 Magenta 502	Red 5965 Spectrum red 5977 Magenta 5975
Violets	Purple lake 130 Royal purple 132	Purple 5568	Purple		Violet 505	

(continued)

TABLE 10.1
(continued)

	Dry Pigments	Protein Paints		Latex, Acrylic, and Vinyl Paints		
	Gothic Scenic Colors*	Iddings Deep Colors	Gothic Casein Fresco Paints	Flo-Paint Scenic-Decorator Colors (vinyl)	Cal-Western Show & Display Colors (acrylic)	Rosco Paint Super Saturated (vinyl acrylic)
Blues	American ultramarine blue 141 French cobalt blue 142 Italian blue 143 Prussian blue 144 Celestial blue 146	Turquoise blue 5570 Cerulean blue 5572 Ultramarine blue 5559 Navy blue 5573	Turquoise blue Cerulean blue Ultramarine blue Navy blue	Cerulean blue flat 5049 Medium blue gloss 5067 Ultramarine blue flat 5045 Navy blue flat 5047 Dark blue gloss 5066	Ultramarine blue 538 Phthalo blue 508	Green shade blue 5968 Ultramarine blue 5969
Greens	Lt. chrome green 150 Med. chrome green 152 Dk. chrome green 153 Emerald green 151 Hanover green 154	Emerald green 5564 Chrome oxide green 5565 Dark green 5571	Emerald green Chrome oxide green Dark green	Emerald green flat 5088 Light green gloss 5060 Chrome oxide green flat 5037 Medium green gloss 5061 Dark green flat 5039 Deep green gloss 5063	Phthalo green 504 Green oxide 501	Chrome green 5971 Phthalo green 5973
Earth colors	French yellow ochre 160 Golden ochre 161 Italian raw sienna 165 Italian burnt sienna 164 Raw turkey umber 163 Burnt turkey umber 162 Van Dyke brown 166 Eng. venetian red 123	Yellow ochre 5553 Raw sienna 5555 Burst sienna 5556 Raw umber 5557 Burnt umber 5554 Van Dyke brown 5558	Yellow ochre Raw sienna Burnt sienna Raw umber Burnt umber	Raw sienna Flat 5040 Gloss 5056 Burnt sienna Flat 5041 Gloss 5057 Raw umber Flat 5042 Gloss 5058 Burnt umber Flat 5043 Gloss 5059	Raw sienna 517 Burnt sienna 516 Raw umber 514 Burnt umber 515 Venetian red 513	Yellow ochre 5982 Burnt sienna 5987 Raw umber 5986 Burnt umber 5985 Iron red 5980

TABLE 10.1
(continued)

| | Dry Pigments | Protein Paints | | Latex, Acrylic, and Vinyl Paints | | |
	Gothic Scenic Colors*	Iddings Deep Colors	Gothic Casein Fresco Paints	Flo-Paint Scenic-Decorator Colors (vinyl)	Cal-Western Show & Display Colors (acrylic)	Rosco Paint Super Saturated (vinyl acrylic)
Other		Acrylic/latex gloss 5580 Acrylic/latex flat 5581		Clear gloss 5080 Clear flat 5053 Krom-o-key blue 5046 Peel paste 5083 Strip coat 5084 Heat resistant blue-white 5027 Battleship gray Flat 5035 Gloss 5064	Clear acrylic glaze 574 Acrylic artist paste 588 Acrylic gel (hi gloss) 539 Five fluorescent colors Four metallic finishes	Gloss medium

*This is an incomplete listing of Gothic Dry Pigments but indicates the range of colors available.
Source: Richard L. Arnold, *Scene Technology,* © 1985, pp. 150–151. Reprinted by permission of Allyn & Bacon.

vinyl acrylic concentrates can be used to tint latex paint. The dry pigment or dye is mixed into a little water and a couple tablespoons of wood alcohol to form a paste about the consistency of sour cream. The paste is stirred into the latex paint. The acrylic concentrates can be stirred directly into the paint. Fully saturated colors and custom-mixed hues are available from most paint stores. Latex paint formulated for use as an interior wall paint adheres to wood and fabric very well and has a matte finish when dry.

Vinyl Acrylic Paint   This is another water-base paint that has a vinyl acrylic binder. It has excellent adhesion, is extremely flexible, and is suitable for painting wood, fabric, and most metals and plastics. After the paint has dried for approximately twenty-four hours, it becomes quite water-resistant.

The paint is mixed by combining the concentrated, fully saturated pigments with either a clear or white base. If a fully saturated hue is desired, the pigment is mixed with the clear base; if a tint is needed, the white base is used. Two parts of concentrated pigment are normally mixed with one part of water before being mixed with the base. To create a transparent wash, or **glaze,** you can dilute the mixed paint (pigment and base) with eight to ten parts of water. The clear base can be used to provide a matte-finish glaze coat over painted scenery.

Aniline Dye

Another safety caveat is essential before beginning this discussion of aniline dyes. Many aniline dyes are carcinogenic. All are toxic. Appropriate safety equipment—respirator, gloves, eyewear—must be worn when handling or mixing any aniline dye. Consult the MSDS for the aniline dyes with which you are working for appropriate safety equipment.

vinyl acrylic concentrate: A highly saturated pigment with a vinyl acrylic binder; mixed with an opaque base (for tints) or a transparent base (for fully saturated hues) to create a working paint.

glaze: A transparent, usually lightly tinted, slightly glossy coating.

Aniline powders form transparent, brilliant, saturated dyes when mixed with water. A very strong dye solution can be made by mixing approximately one teaspoon of dye with a quart of boiling water. This concentrated dye solution is reduced with additional water to make less saturated colors.

Aniline dyes can be used by themselves to paint scrims and muslin drops or cycs. They can also be used to tint water-base scene paints. To keep the dye from **bleeding,** or **spreading,** by capillary action, add a binder such as starch, white flex glue, animal glue size, or clear vinyl acrylic base to the dye solution.

bleeding (spreading): Capillary action causes the dye solution to spread past the edge of the painted brush line.

Varnish   Varnish is a transparent coating made of synthetic or natural resinous materials suspended in an oil (oil varnish), alcohol (spirit varnish), or synthetic (polyurethane, vinyl acrylic) vehicle. It is used to provide a sealing coat over other types of finish. In the world outside the theatre, varnish is frequently used as a finish coat on stained wooden furniture and other woodwork. In the theatre, it is used in this way and also as a satin- or gloss-finish glaze coat over matte-finish scene paint.

Varnish is formulated in matte, satin, and glossy finishes. The amount of gloss on the finished surface can be controlled in two ways: by mixing portions of the various finish types together or by increasing the amount of thinner in the mix (more thinner lessens the gloss).

Varnish is thinned with—and the equipment used to apply it must be cleaned with—an appropriate type of solvent: mineral spirits or paint thinner for oil- or polyurethane-base, alcohol for alcohol-base, and water for vinyl acrylic. The polymer-base varnishes, such as polyurethane varnish, are generally better for stage use because they are easier to apply and dry faster than their oil-base counterparts.

Shellac   Shellac is a transparent finish coating made of resinous material (lac—the secretions of certain scale insects) suspended in alcohol. Similar in appearance to high-gloss varnish, shellac must be thinned with wood alcohol, usually about two parts to one. Because of the extreme volatility of wood alcohol, great care must be exercised when working with the shellac.

Shellac can be used as a high-gloss finish for painted floors and furniture. It is also used as a sealing coat to prevent previous coatings of aniline dyes, and certain pigments that have dyes in their chemical structure (such as cerulean blue), from bleeding through successive coats of scene paint, varnish, or enamel. Knots in pine boards can also be sealed with shellac to prevent the resin in the knots from bleeding through the finish coat. Shellac can also be used as the vehicle and binder for the application of bronzing powders (metallic powders—aluminum, bronze, gold, and the like) to impart a metallic appearance to smooth-finish surfaces.

Lacquer   Lacquer is a form of shellac or varnish (depending on the type of resinous material used as the binder and filler) that has been diluted with alcohol or other quick-drying solvents. It is used for the same purposes as shellac.

Polyester Resin   Although not an actual paint, polyester resin is the plastic coating that is used with glass-fiber reinforcement to form those materials generically known as fiberglass. When cured, the resin has a very smooth, high-gloss, metallic finish. Dry pigment, bronzing powders, and commercial colorants can be added to the resin to give it color. Almost any natural material (dirt, sand, sawdust) can be added to impart texture. Polyester resin is probably the quickest finishing method available that will cover the grain of wood to give it a realistic metallic appearance.

Safety Tip ⚠

Flammable-Base Paints

Any of the oil-, alcohol-, and lacquer-base paints and some synthetic-base paints are flammable. Polyester resin and its catalysts are also flammable. The volatile liquids used for thinning and cleaning these materials—turpentine, mineral spirits, alcohol, acetone—are extremely flammable. Fire codes require that any flammable liquids (including aerosol spray paints) be stored in a special fire-resistant metal cabinet.

Be sure to work carefully with these materials. Never use them in the vicinity of an open flame. Absolutely never smoke while working with them; make sure the area in which you are working is well ventilated, and if at all possible, work with them outdoors. Also be sure to read the MSDS's for appropriate safety equipment to be used when working with these paints.

Polyester resin must be mixed with the catalyst-hardener methylethylketone (MEK) to harden. Since the amount of MEK added to the polyester resin determines the time it takes the resin to "set," or harden, pay particularly close attention to the instructions on the resin container. Always mix the resin and hardener in wax-coated paper or metal containers. Don't use Styrofoam, because the resin will melt it. Be sure to use disposable containers, because the resin is all but impossible to remove after it has begun to cure.

Enamel Enamel is an opaque paint with an oil, lacquer, or synthetic base. It has a hard surface and excellent covering power. Enamel is usually formulated so that it dries with a smooth satin or gloss finish. It is used to paint any surface on which this type of hard finish is needed or desired (furniture, door and window casings, and so on).

Any object that is to be enameled should first be painted with enamel undercoat so the surface will be properly sealed. If the surface isn't sealed, the finish of the enamel will not have the desired smooth, softly glowing appearance.

Applicators

A number of different types of applicators are used in scene painting.

Brush Good-quality scene-painting brushes are expensive. But it is also axiomatic that good scene painting demands good brushes.

Brushes that are to be used with the various types of water-base scene paint should have 100 percent natural bristles of the highest available quality. These bristles are fairly long and have good springiness when wet. Scene-painting brushes generally have to be ordered from scenic supply houses.

There are three general types of scene-painting brushes: priming, lay-in, and detail, as shown in Figure 10.1. The priming brush is used for applying the prime coat, or first covering coat, of paint. It is quite large (six to seven inches wide), so it can carry a great deal of paint. The lay-in brush is used to apply the base coat, which follows the prime coat. This brush is smaller (four to five inches wide), because the application techniques frequently used with base coats require quick manipulation of the brush, and it is much easier to change the position of a smaller and lighter brush. The detail brushes (one-quarter to two inches wide) are used for fine work such as painting lines and leaves.

FIGURE 10.1
Paint applicators.

A push broom can be effectively used for painting floors. Paint is simply poured directly onto the floor and pushed around and smoothed out with the broom.

Several specialty brushes are extremely useful to the scenic artist. The wood-graining brush is actually several small brushes in one. Each of the approximately six China-bristle artist's brushes are flexibly mounted in a four-inch-wide ferrule (the metal cap that binds the bristles to the handle). As the brush is used, the individual tips move independently of one another to give a random wood-grain appearance. The badger brush is made with the very limber bristles of the badger. Rather than being used to apply paint, it is used to feather and blend paint applied with other techniques. Lettering brushes, which can be purchased at most art stores, are very useful for lettering and similar sign-work applications.

Sponges   Both natural and synthetic sponges have many uses in scene painting. Natural sponges, which hold a great deal of paint, can be gently pressed against the scenery to create an irregularly textured pattern. Synthetic sponges are also used for texturing, and they can be cut into a pattern (using a bandsaw, scissors, or knife), mounted on a backing board such as a small piece of plywood with latex contact cement, and used as a stencil to form a repetitive pattern. A sponge mop—the type used to wash kitchen floors—works extremely well for applying streaky undercoats to floors and other large, smooth, hard surfaces as part of a woodgraining paint job.

Brushes: Dos and Don'ts

You'll need to follow several suggestions to help your brushes last a long time and provide you with the best possible results.

Dos

1. Always thoroughly clean the brush in the appropriate type of solvent. Water-base paints are cleaned with warm water and liquid dish soap. The appropriate solvent for non–water-base paints will be printed on the container label. To remove the paint from the ferrule, load the brush with solvent and repeatedly press the bristles sideways in alternate directions.

2. After cleaning, hang your brushes to dry in a clean, well-ventilated place (preferably a brush cabinet) with the bristles pointing down. Lay-in and priming brushes usually have a hole in the handle for this purpose. Detail brushes don't. Either drill a hole in the end of the brush or hang it vertically with a spring-loaded clip.

3. Use the right kind of bristle for the job. Natural bristles (white China bristles) are best for detail work (lining, foliage) with water-base paints. High-quality polyester bristles are good for lay-in and priming brushes (four to seven inches wide). General-purpose brushes (one to three inches wide) can have either natural or polyester bristles.

4. Use natural-bristle brushes only when working with polyester resin. The resin will melt most synthetic bristles into a useless blob.

Don'ts

1. Don't use a natural-bristle watercolor brush (liner, foliage brush) in anything but water-base paints. The solvents in oil- or lacquer-base paints will deteriorate the bristle spine and make the brush floppy and basically useless.

2. Don't use synthetic-bristle brushes in polyester resin.

3. After cleaning your brushes, don't put them anywhere where the bristles will be bent.

Rollers Paint rollers, with extending handles, can be helpful for a variety of scene-painting jobs, ranging from floor painting to detail work on drops. Generally, the wider rollers are used for applications on large areas, such as floors and similar hard surfaces, and the narrower rollers are used for detail work. Regardless of the application technique, the rollers should be covered with quality material designed for use with water-base paints.

Aerosol Spray Can Spray cans of paint are amazingly useful items for the scenic artist. Available in a wide range of metallic and nonmetallic colors, these paints are useful for painting props, plastics, and metals, and they can be used to apply highlights and shadows to decorative elements on the sets. Aerosol fabric sprays are frequently used in the costume shop to **distress,** or age, costumes and costume accessories. When working with aerosol sprays, be sure to consult the MSDS's for essential safety equipment, ventilation, and other safety considerations.

distress: To create a worn or aged appearance, as with fabric, wood, or metal.

Spray Gun Compressed-air spray guns can be used in a variety of ways for scene painting. They are used for painting furniture and applying a dusting of shadow or highlight color to both drops and scenery. When working with compressed air sprayers, be sure to consult the MSDS's for the spraying equipment

spattering: A technique of applying a relatively smooth covering of evenly spaced small droplets of paint to a surface.

as well as the materials being sprayed for appropriate safety equipment and handling techniques.

Garden sprayers can also be used for applying glaze coats, fire-retardant solutions, and **spattering**. You will need to use a high-quality sprayer for spattering, simply because these more expensive models produce a fairly smooth pattern from one edge of the spray cone to the other.

Auxiliary Scene-Painting Tools

A number of other tools are also part of the craft of scene painting.

Charcoal and Chalk   Although hardly unique to scene painting, charcoal and white or lightly colored chalk are invaluable tools for drawing parts of the design on the scenery during various phases of the painting process. The choice between charcoal and chalk is usually dictated by whether the background color on the item to be painted is light or dark.

Handle Extender   Handle extenders can be made for almost every scene-painting brush to allow you to paint scenery that is lying on the stage floor while you are standing up. The extenders, generally three feet long, are frequently made from bamboo. The end of the bamboo is split so that it will slide over the end of the handle. The extender is then secured to the brush handle with either heavyweight rubber bands or tape. If bamboo isn't locally available, broom handles or similar three-quarter- to one-inch-diameter dowels taped to the handle of the brush make acceptable extenders. Broom handles with threaded tips can be used as extenders for roller handles, or you can purchase extendable handles in paint stores.

Bucket   Small, lightweight, one-gallon plastic buckets are useful for carrying small amounts of scene paint. (Number 10 tin cans are good, usually free, substitutes for these buckets.)

Larger buckets (over one gallon) should be made from either heavyweight plastic with a wire-reinforced lip or galvanized metal, simply because the weight of the paint will break a lightweight plastic bucket. Casein, latex, and vinyl acrylic paint are often sold in heavyweight one- or two-gallon plastic pails that make ideal paint buckets. The sturdy five-gallon metal or plastic buckets in which interior latex wall paint is sold are perfect for mixing large batches of paint.

Straightedge   A straightedge is used as a guide while painting straight lines. Although it can be made in any length, it is normally 3 to 6 feet long and about 2½ inches wide. A handle is attached to the center of the straightedge (Figure 10.2) so that you can balance it while working. The underside of the straightedge should be beveled to prevent the paint from creeping under it. A long handle can be attached to the straightedge to facilitate painting on the floor or deck.

Chalk Line   The chalk line, also called a snap line, is a tool borrowed from the carpenters (see Chapter 8 for details). When used in scenic painting, the chalk line should be loaded with charcoal or dry pigment rather than carpenter's chalk. The bow snap line, which looks like an archery bow, is a shorter version of the chalk line that can be used easily by one person. Dry pigment is rubbed on the snap line, the bow is held in place with one hand, and the line is snapped with the other hand.

FIGURE 10.2
Painting accessories.

Paint Cart   When painting detail work, it is usually necessary to mix a little bit of a number of different color paints to achieve the right hue. The paint cart (Figure 10.2) provides a convenient method of carrying those different colors, as well as the other paraphernalia used by the scene painter.

Electric Glue Pot   The electric glue pot (Figure 10.2) is an indispensable tool for melting animal glue, which is an essential ingredient in the previously mentioned formula for size water. A good-quality glue pot is thermostatically controlled to heat the glue to its melting point without burning or scorching. Although animal glue can be melted in a double boiler or by placing the container of glue in a water-filled pan on top of a hot plate, the electric glue pot all but eliminates the potential fire and horrendous odor hazards associated with these improvised solutions.

Immersion Heater   An electric immersion heater is a handy device for heating water for any of the paint-mixing chores that require hot water (starch mixtures, aniline dye, flameproofing, and so on). It is simply inserted into the bucketful of water and turned on. It can heat the water to boiling fairly quickly.

When using an immersion heater, you must take care that it is always in excellent working condition—that the electrical cord, plug, and watertight seal between the unit and the cord are not damaged in any way. After using be sure that the heater is placed on a heat-resistant surface in a location where no one will accidentally touch it.

Stirrers   A variety of stirring sticks are used when mixing paints. Wooden stirring sticks can be obtained from paint shops or made in the shop. Large whisks, the same as used in cooking, can be obtained from restaurant supply stores and kitchen specialty shops. Large batches of paint—3 to 5 gallons—can most easily be stirred using one of the many stirring attachments available for power drills. These can be purchased in most paint stores and home supply centers.

box: To pour paint back and forth between buckets to ensure a complete
and uniform mix.

When the amount of paint you're mixing requires that you use two or more
buckets, be sure to **box** the paint to obtain a uniform color in every bucket. To
box the paint, pour the paint into several buckets. Don't fill any bucket more than
halfway. Pouring from one of the buckets, fill another bucket to a few inches
below the top. Then pour from that bucket into a third bucket. Repeat the process
until the paint is thoroughly mixed among all of the buckets.

PREPARING SCENERY FOR PAINTING

A certain amount of preparation needs to be done before scenery can be painted.

Repairing Holes

Any holes in the fabric covering of the flats should be repaired. First, fray the
fabric for about one-quarter of an inch back from the edge of the hole. Then cut
out a piece of the same type of material (muslin, scenic canvas) approximately
twice as large as the hole. Cover the patch with animal glue, casein, or vinyl
acrylic paint, and place it over the hole *on the back* of the flat. On the face of the
flat, smooth the frayed edges of the hole, and blend them into the surface of the
patch.

Applying Dutchmen

As we have seen, dutchmen are four- to six-inch-wide strips of muslin used to
cover the joints between flats in a single wall section. Fray about one-quarter of
an inch along the edges of the dutchman. Paint the joint (the full width of the
dutchman) with a compound made of three parts water and one part hot glue.
(This compound won't bleed through the dutchman to stain the finished paint
job.) Quickly apply the dutchman over the joint, and smooth the frayed edges to
blend into the surface of the flats. Be sure to select dutchman material that is of
the same composition and condition as the flats that it is covering.

Flameproofing

All scenery needs to be flameproofed. Although more and more items that are
used for building scenery and props are being flameproofed at the factory, it is a
good precaution to apply a flame-retardant solution to all scenery constructed in
the shop. There are a variety of commercially manufactured flameproofing solutions, but a formula that has been used for years, and is generally effective, is as
follows: one pound of borax, one pound of sal ammoniac, one-half pint of
vinegar, and one gallon of hot water. This solution is liberally sprayed, brushed,
or rolled onto both the fabric and wood of the scenery before any coats of paint
are applied. The materials for this flameproofing solution are generally available
locally. When this shop-built flameproofing solution is used, its effectiveness
should be tested and the results verified by the local fire inspector. Washing or
dry cleaning removes the salts that give any flameproofing solution its effectiveness, so scenery that is cleaned will have to be treated again.

Horizontal and Vertical Painting

Traditionally, two-dimensional scenery has been painted while lying flat. There
are several advantages to this method of painting: A number of painters can
work simultaneously; all portions of the set are accessible; some texturing tech-

FIGURE 10.3
Vertical scene-painting tools.

niques are more suited to this horizontal application; washes, glazes, and water-color-like techniques are more easily produced with horizontal painting; and a wooden floor provides excellent uniform support for drops and other unframed scenery. But horizontal painting has some disadvantages: It requires a lot of floor space; you have to walk on the fabric to get to the center of a large piece; the toggle bars in flats may leave horizontal drying lines if the paint is applied heavily; if the humidity is high, drying time for a drop is lengthened (although warm air forced under the drop will solve this challenge); and unless the shop is equipped with a loft or some elevated vantage point, it is difficult to move away from the paint job to see what it looks like.

Vertical painting is usually done on a paint frame (Figure 10.3A). The frame is either permanently fixed to one wall or counterweighted and lowered into a paint well. In either case, the framed or unframed scenery is nailed to the paint frame. If the frame is permanently mounted, painting above floor level is done from ladders or a multilevel rolling platform called a boomerang (Figure 10.3B). The counterweighted paint frame is lowered into the paint well to bring the upper parts of the scenery to the painter's eye level. Almost all painting techniques can be used when the scenery is in a vertical position; it just takes a little more care and skill to avoid drips and runs.

PRELIMINARY COATING

Two basic coatings are normally applied to scenery before the application of the specialized texture and detail coats of scene paint. Preparing fabric for painting with an aniline dye is discussed a little later.

Size Coat

If the muslin or other fabric covering has never been painted, you will need to size it before proceeding with the rest of the paint job. Sizing does two things: (1) It shrinks the fabric, which tightens it on the flat frame, and (2) it fills the surface of the cloth, which prepares the fabric for the ensuing coats of paint. The sizing can be brushed or sprayed onto the fabric.

Sizing can be made from water and hot glue (sixteen to one), with whiting and a little pigment added to let you see where you've painted. It can also be made by thinning inexpensive latex interior paint with water (approximately two to one).

If you want to create a translucent effect when painting with dye, size the fabric with cornstarch (about one pound of starch in one gallon of hot water). A semitranslucent effect can be created with dyes if you do not size the fabric before painting. However, you will need to brush the material with water first to tighten it on the flat.

Prime Coat

The prime coat, also called the ground coat, is the first layer of paint that is applied to all of the scenery to provide a uniform base for the rest of the paint job. If the scenery is going to be painted with casein or vinyl acrylic paints, the prime coat can be eliminated as long as the colors on the previously painted parts of the set are not too wildly divergent in hue or brilliance.

The prime coat provides a golden opportunity to use any **garbage paint** that may be in the shop. Garbage paint is composed of those remnants of paint that are inevitably left after a paint job has been completed. As long as the paint hasn't

garbage paint: Any paint left over from previous paint jobs; the various hues are mixed to create a (usually) rather ugly light-brown color.

Preventing Bleedthrough

If you are painting over scenery that has been previously painted with dry pigment and binder, you can prevent bleedthrough (caused when the moisture from the new paint loosens the binder in the old paint, allowing the two coats to blend) by mixing about one-quarter cup of alum per gallon of paint. A mixture of approximately fifteen parts water to one part white glue can also help prevent bleeding.

If small areas of the undercoat continue to bleed through, or if a persistent stain won't stay covered with the alum or white glue coat, you can brush the offending area with white shellac. White shellac will also stop the staining caused by pine knots. Zerolac, a commercially available product, also does an excellent job of sealing.

spoiled and the various hues are not too saturated, these remnants can be mixed together, neutralized to a medium gray or brown by adding a complementary pigment, and used as the prime coat.

PAINT-MIXING TECHNIQUES

Several techniques are used in mixing the various types of paint.

Dry Pigment and Binder

The only real way of determining the amount of pigment needed per gallon of paint is based on the particular situation (new versus old material, type of previously applied paint, and so on). Generally speaking, however, the paint is "right" when it is the consistency of coffee cream.

Some general guidelines may help you mix this type of paint. Mix a little alcohol and water with the pigment to form a paste the consistency of sour cream. (The alcohol helps the pigments go into solution.) Add enough size water to the paste to get it to painting consistency.

Casein

Although the exact ratio varies with hue, manufacturer, and specific application, one part of paste is generally mixed with two to four parts of water.

Latex

Most frequently used in its undiluted state, latex paint can be extended with up to approximately one pint of water to one gallon of paint before its covering power is adversely affected.

Vinyl Acrylic

The many techniques for mixing vinyl acrylic paint were covered under the discussion of this extremely versatile paint earlier in this chapter.

No paints look the same wet as they do dry. Dry pigment and binder looks much lighter when it's dry than when wet. For this reason, mix the pigments to match the painter's elevations before you add the size water. The variations between the wet and dry appearance of the other paints aren't quite so dramatic, but it is still necessary to make dry test samples (chips) and check them against the painter's elevations whenever you are mixing colors. (A hand-held hair dryer speeds the drying process immeasurably.)

SCENE PAINTER'S PALETTE

The scene painter's color palette (Figure 10.4) provides a practical guide to the use of readily available scenic paints. (A full-color version of the same palette can be found in Chapter 6.) As we have seen, complementary colors produce the greatest contrast in a comparison between any two hues on a color wheel. Additionally, if complementary colors are mixed in equal proportion, the resultant hue will be a neutral gray. (Theoretically, the mix should produce black, but impurities in the paints prevent a theoretically perfect mix.) Many scene painters prefer to mix gray this way, because a gray mixed with complementary hues has

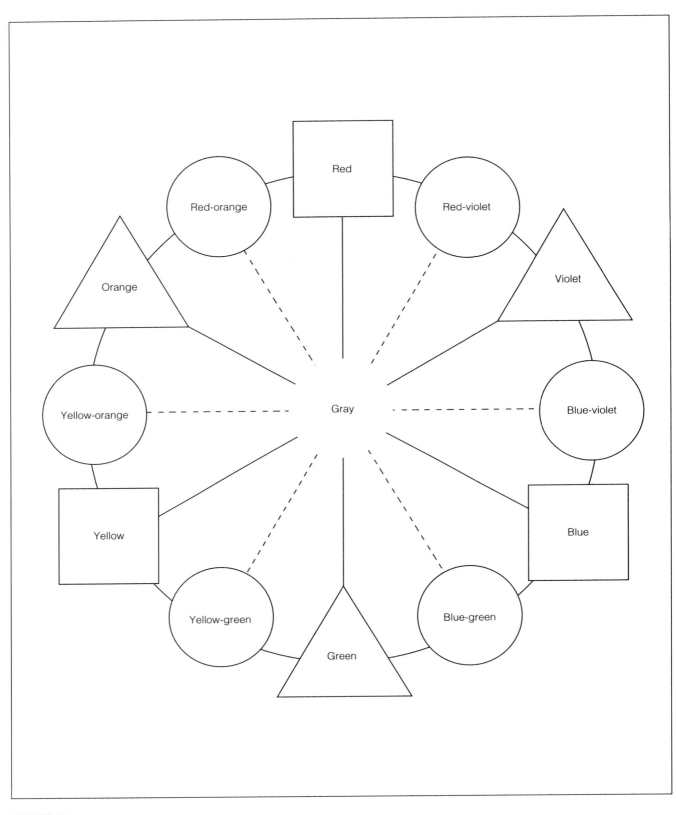

FIGURE 10.4
Scene painter's color palette. (See the full-color version on page 90.)

more visual vibrancy and life than does a gray produced from a black and white mix. When **analogous** (or **related**) **colors** are mixed, they produce a hue that is an approximate average of the two original hues. However, this resultant hue has a lower value than either of the original colors. Mixtures of hues other than complementary or related will create colors that fall somewhere between these two extremes.

The mixing of colors to match the various hues on the painter's elevation is a very specialized craft that has to be practiced to be learned. The principles of color theory discussed in Chapter 6 provide the base from which all practical pigment mixing stems. However, there are a few practical hints that may help as you try to translate theory into practice.

1. Be sure that all individual component paints are thoroughly stirred and all lumps of color completely dissolved before you start mixing the final paint.

2. To reduce the value or saturation of any hue, add a complementary hue, add a less saturated pigment of the same color, or, as a last resort, add black. The addition of black should be done very carefully, and only to hues of relatively low value (shades: dark blue, dark green, purple, and the like), because the black has a tendency to kill the vibrancy and life in any color. It will turn tints (light yellow, pink, and the like) into ugly mud colors.

3. To increase the value of a color, add a pigment of the same hue but higher value, or add white. The addition of white should also be done judiciously. If added to hues of relatively low value, it will tend to bleach out the color and make them look chalky. When it is added to tints, the "bleaching" effects are less dramatic, but still prevalent. To counteract the reduction in saturation caused by the addition of white, add a small amount of a more fully saturated version of the original color to restore the level of saturation.

4. If the hue that you are mixing is of high value, start mixing with the lightest pigment and slowly add the other components.

5. When mixing dark colors, start with the darkest hue and slowly add the lighter colors.

6. If mixing a batch of paint that fills more than one bucket, be sure to box the paint.

7. Almost all paints appear lighter when they are dry than when they are wet. Make test patches of the various hues on the same type of material that is to be painted. Use a hair dryer or a heat gun to speed up the drying process.

Regardless of how many helpful hints you can get from a textbook, the only way that you will learn the craft of color mixing is to go into the paint shop and actually mix paint. A little practice and experimentation will show you that it probably isn't so difficult as you originally thought.

analogous (related) colors: *Colors that are adjacent to each other on the color wheel.*

PAINTING TECHNIQUES

A variety of painting techniques are traditionally used in scene painting. Almost all of them are fairly simple, but as with most seemingly easy craft skills they generally take a good deal of practice to master.

Base Coats

The base coat is the foundation for the remainder of the paint job, so it is imperative that it match, as closely as possible, the hue and value of the desired

FIGURE 10.5
Applying a smooth base coat is normally done with a cross-hatch technique.

finished color of the set. The specific hue of the base coat, and any other color used in the scenic design, should be mixed using the scenic designer's painter's elevations as the color guide. The method used to apply a base coat can be varied to create different visual effects.

Smooth Base Coat   A smooth base coat results from a uniform coat of paint of a specific hue and value being applied to the scenery, as shown in Figure 10.5. There are several guidelines that should help you to apply a smooth base coat.

1. It is generally more efficient to begin painting vertical scenery such as flats at the top. This way, you pick up any drips and splashes as you work your way down the scenery. Begin painting horizontal scenery (platform tops, floors) at a narrow edge or corner, and work your way across the surface.

2. Keep the brush fully loaded with paint. Don't dip more than three-quarters of the length of the bristles into the paint, and lightly press the brush against the inside wall of the bucket to remove any excess paint. Think of the paint as flowing from the tips of the bristles onto the surface that you're painting. When the bristles begin to drag across the surface, reload your brush.

3. Keep a wet edge. If the edge of the paint is allowed to dry, it will generally show up as a line or a slight darkening in the finished color. If it becomes necessary to stop painting in the middle of a surface, feather the edge, as shown in Figure 10.5. When you start again, begin painting in an unpainted area of the surface, and feather back into the previously painted surface.

4. Don't scrub the surface with your brush. Scrubbing can loosen old paint and cause a variation on the finished surface of the base coat.

(A)   (B)   (C)

FIGURE 10.6
A graded base coat. The pigments to be blended are painted in proximity to each other (A). Using a separate brush for each pigment and working quickly so that the paint will stay moist, the painter brings the edges of the dark and light pigments together and merges them (B), to yield a smoothly blended coat of paint (C).

5. When using dry pigment and binder, apply the paint in a cross-hatch pattern, as shown in Figure 10.5, to significantly reduce the chances of having any brush marks appear on the finished surface of the base coat. Cross-hatching isn't quite so important when using casein, latex, or vinyl acrylic paints, simply because they are generally more opaque than dry pigment and binder paints and don't show brush marks so easily.

Graded Base Coat   A graded base coat is one that gradually changes hue or value over the height or width of the painted surface, as shown in Figure 10.6. Graded base coats are frequently used to help make a set look used and worn with age.

The secret to a good graded base coat is speed. The blending must be done while the paint is still wet. Use a separate brush for each color, work rapidly, blend a small area at a time, and progressively work your way around the set.

Scumbling   Scumbling is similar to a graded base coat in that it involves the blending of several hues. Scumbling provides the illusion of texture by creating an irregular, multihued (or multivalued) base. Instead of creating a smooth blending from one area to the next, scumbling yields a roughly blended base coat of fairly indistinct pattern, as shown in the examples illustrated in Figure 10.7. The type of pattern created is primarily dependent on the style and number of brush strokes used when scumbling. Any type or combination of large or small, circular, swirling, cross-hatch, straight, or curved strokes can be used. Actually, any manipulation of the brushes that slightly blends the varying hues or values of paint is a valid scumbling technique. For scumbling to be effective, you will need to follow these two general guidelines:

1. Use a separate brush for each color, in order to maintain the integrity of the individual hues.
2. Work rapidly, because the paints must be wet for the blending to take place.

Depending on the hue and value of paints and the type of brush strokes used when blending them, scumbling can be used to create the appearance of rough plaster, wood, stone, dirt, and a myriad of other surfaces.

(A)

(B)

(C)   (D)

FIGURE 10.7
Scumbling techniques. (A) A
sharply textured, high-contrast curvilinear scumble created by using
separate brushes for each pigment
and not blending the pigments. (B)
A softly textured, low-contrast curvilinear scumble created by using
separate brushes for each pigment
and overbrushing the surface to
blend and merge the separate pigments. (C) A high-contrast linear
scumble created by applying separate pigments with a linear brush
stroke. (D) A low-contrast linear
scumble created by overbrushing
the separate pigments.

Painting Techniques with Aniline Dye

Aniline dyes differ from the other types of paints in that they provide very
intense, transparent colors. They are frequently used to paint transparent and
translucent drops made of sharkstooth scrim or muslin. They can also be used to
paint "regular" two- and three-dimensional scenery when their characteristically
clear colors will be of benefit. The water-soluble aniline colors can also be used
to tint all water-base paints, while the oil-soluble hues can be used to tint oil-base
finishes such as varnish.

Mixing aniline dyes is a little different from mixing paint. Traditionally, a
strong dye solution is made by mixing one teaspoon of aniline dye in a quart of
boiling water. If boiling water is unavailable, add a little vinegar or alcohol to the
aniline crystals or powder to make a paste, then add hot water to make the dye
solution. Custom colors are created by mixing these concentrated dye solutions,
not by mixing dry aniline powders or crystals.

Aniline is a dye, not a paint. It penetrates, rather than coats, the surface to
which it is applied. This characteristic can lead to bleeding or spreading. To
prevent bleeding, you need to prevent the dye from easily penetrating the surface
of the painted object. To do this, add a little liquid binder (starch, glue size, white
flex glue, or clear vinyl [flat or gloss]) to the dye solution. An alternative "fix" is
to size the fabric with a starch or clear vinyl size prior to painting it with the dye.
The size should be mixed ten parts water to one part liquid binder. If dry starch
is used, mix it with enough water to make a paste prior to mixing with the ten
parts of water.

When using aniline dyes to paint surfaces where the dye can't easily penetrate the material—primed or starched fabrics, primed or raw wood—dilute the
concentrated dye using a solution of eight parts water mixed with one part clear
vinyl. This size will help the dye adhere to the surface of the material. To paint

---

Safety Tip   ⚠

Dry Aniline Powders

Wear a respirator when working with dry aniline powders or crystals. Inhalation of
even small amounts of these powders can be injurious to your health.

nonporous surfaces such as sheet acrylic (Plexiglas) or glass, use a diluting mixture of three parts water to one part clear vinyl to cut the concentrated dye solution.

Spraying Techniques

Spraying is the fastest method of applying paint. It is ideal for applying a base coat to ornate forms such as wicker chairs, picket fences, and wrought-iron forms. It can also be very effectively used to apply a graded base coat.

The texture of the **spray cone** of most **spray guns** can be adjusted from a fine mist to light droplets. The width of the cone pattern can also be adjusted from narrow to wide.

A spraying system is composed of three separate parts: the spray gun, the paint container, and the compressor. The regular spray gun has a one-quart paint reservoir and is designed for continuous-duty applications—painting flats, floors, houses, and so forth. Touch-up guns have much smaller containers (two to six ounces) and are designed for light-duty jobs such as painting chairs and picture frames and for situations in which the color will have to be changed frequently. Air brushes are equipped with small paint containers (one-half to two ounces) and are used for fine detail and lining work. Most air brushes can be varied to spray a hard- or soft-edged line as well as a typical misty cone.

Compressors provide the motive power for most spray guns. The smallest serviceable compressor for general theatrical spraying would have an electric motor of approximately one horsepower and a ten-gallon air tank. The larger, permanent compressor systems found in many shops provide an excellent air source for spray painting. Much smaller one-eighth- or one-sixteenth-horsepower compressors, as well as disposable compressed-air cans, are frequently used to power air brushes. Small electrically powered airless spray guns such as the

spray cone: *The pattern of paint emitted from the nozzle of a spray gun.*

spray gun: *A pistol-like device that shoots out a cone of paint.*

compressor: *A pump, typically electric- or gasoline-powered, that drives air into a tank; output pressure from the tank is controlled by a valve called a regulator.*

Spray-Painting Tips

If these general guidelines are followed, you should find that your spray-painting experiences will be productive and relatively trouble free.

1. Always rinse the spray gun before using it to make sure that there is no dust or grit which could clog the nozzle in the gun or paint container.

2. Be sure to strain the paint with a commercial strainer or small-mesh nylon, such as the material in stockings or pantyhose. Straining the paint will remove any little globs of paint that might clog the nozzle.

3. Run a momentary blast of compressed air through the hoses before attaching them to the gun to remove any dust or grit from the hoses.

4. Don't "fan" the gun at the work; keep the gun a uniform distance from the work, and move it parallel with the surface to deposit a uniform coat of paint.

5. Be sure to wear an appropriate respirator to filter out the atomized paint from the air you breathe; wear goggles to keep the airborne paint out of your eyes. Consult the MSDS's for the materials with which you are working for specific information about required safety equipment and other safety considerations.

6. Be sure to keep the compressor pressure within the recommended levels for the gun and type of paint you're using.

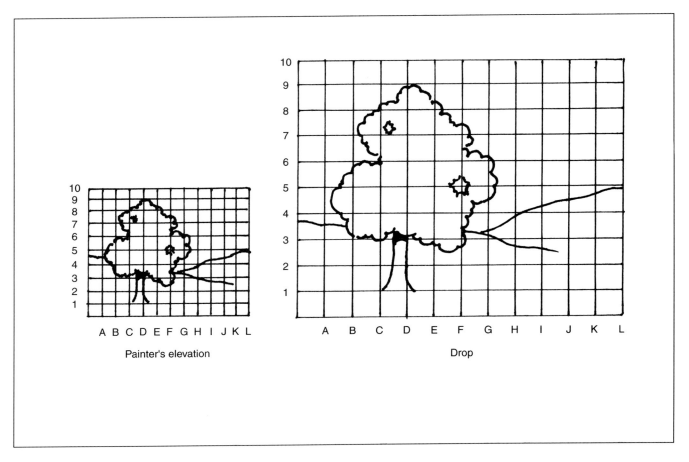

FIGURE 10.8
Grid-transfer technique.

Wagner Power Painter can be used in most theatrical applications as an effective substitute for the more expensive compressed-air systems.

Cartooning

Some scenic designs have a great deal of detail that must be transferred to the scenery after the prime and base coats have been applied. Cartooning refers to the process of making these transfers. Large, simple designs can usually be applied simply by taking scale measurements of the object on the painter's elevation and transferring them to the scenery. Any further details can usually be duplicated by freehand sketching with frequent references back to the painter's elevation. If the object is quite detailed, one of the following methods can be used to duplicate it accurately on the scenery.

Grid Transfer   In the appropriate scale, draw a one-foot-square grid on the painter's elevation. (To preserve the elevation, cover it with a sheet of acetate, and use a fine-point acetate marker or well-sharpened grease pencil to draw the grid.) Also draw a full-scale one-foot-square grid on the scenery, as shown in Figure 10.8. If the scenery is small, this grid can be drawn using a straightedge and charcoal or chalk. If the scenery is large, the grid can be created by tacking four-penny box nails, one foot apart, around the edge of the scenery. String is laced back and forth between the nails to create the grid. Be sure to use the same beginning point for both grids, such as the lower left corner or some other readily identifiable point, on both the painter's elevation and the scenery.

If the horizontal grid lines on both the painter's elevation and the drop grid are designated with letters and the vertical lines with numbers, as shown in Figure 10.8, it becomes a fairly rapid process to accurately transfer the points of intersection between the drawing on the elevation and the elevation's grid to the full-scale grid on the scenery. When those points have been located, connect the dots using a piece of charcoal or chalk to complete the transfer of the design to the scenery.

Projection Transfer   An opaque projector can also be used to project the painter's elevation onto the scenery. The projector is placed far enough from the scenery to project a full-scale image of the object onto the scenery, and the design is traced in charcoal or chalk.

There are two drawbacks to this method: The shop needs to be dark while the projection transfer is being made; and unless the projector is placed perpendicular to the center point of the drop or flat, **keystoning** will occur. (A full discussion of keystoning and how to avoid it is contained in Chapter 15, *Projections*.) If you can avoid these two pitfalls, projection cartooning is generally much faster and more accurate than a grid transfer.

The computer has opened up worlds of new transfer methods based on video projection of computer files. Images can be scanned in or created in the computer, manipulated as desired, then projected onto the scenery for copying by the scenic artist or paint crew. While exciting, there is the very real issue of bringing this high-tech, high-priced equipment into the rather dirty environment of the shop. It would be a rather expensive "oops" if a bucket of paint were inadvertently dumped on either a video projector or computer. However, instead of direct video projection of the files, the files can be printed on either paper or acetate, and these prints can be projected with either an opaque or overhead projector.

The computer can also be used to create full-scale layout patterns such as wallpaper patterns or drop details. Generally, these pieces need to be printed on a plotter as they are normally too large to be printed on the paper used in an ordinary desktop printer. For a really large piece, or if a plotter isn't available, the original drawing can be broken into segments, the segments can be printed, then the various pieces taped together to create the full pattern. These patterns can then be transferred to the scenery.

Standard Texture Coats

The following techniques are normally applied on top of the base coat to provide visual interest, variety, depth, and patina to the scenery.

Spattering   As mentioned earlier spattering is the process of applying small drops of paint to a surface. Spattering is done over the base coat to help age the paint job, slightly alter the hue, or smooth out any apparent irregularities in an unevenly applied base coat. Spattering can be done either by hand or with a garden sprayer (the Hudson brand is preferred by many professionals) and with the scenery in either a vertical or a horizontal position. It is a very effective painting technique that can be mastered with a little practice.

Hand spattering is done by slapping a lightly loaded paintbrush against the heel of your hand. Dip only the tips of the brush in the paint, and scrape most of the paint off on the lip of the bucket. Stand three to five feet from the surface, and slap the **ferrule** of the brush against the heel of your hand. As the bristles snap forward, they throw tiny paint droplets at the scenery. The amount of paint in the brush and the distance that you stand from the object being spattered will

keystoning: The distortion that occurs in a projected image when the projector is placed at some angle other than perpendicular to the center of the projection surface.

ferrule: The metal part of a brush that binds the bristles to the handle.

FIGURE 10.9
Spattering is created when drops of
paint are applied to a surface. This
is an example of a two-tone spatter.

FIGURE 10.10
Stippling with a brush (A), with
a sponge (B), and with a feather
duster (C). Stippling is frequently
used to create the appearance of
surface texture.

(A)   (B)   (C)

determine the size and density of the individual droplets. By constantly changing
the relative position of the brush, you will make a cross-hatch design that creates
an appropriately neutral spatter pattern, as shown in Figure 10.9.

A garden sprayer can also be used to spatter. The nozzle of the sprayer can
be adjusted to spray a pattern that varies in density from a fine mist to medium-
sized droplets. The sprayer handle should be moved in a circular pattern as you
spatter to avoid any tendency to create a linear pattern. To avoid clogging the
nozzle, strain the paint through cheesecloth, window screening, or commercially
available paint strainers before putting it into the sprayer. Be sure to thoroughly
clean the sprayer after each use.

Stippling   Although similar to spattering, stippling applies a heavier texture to
the scenery. As shown in Figure 10.10, stippling can be done with the tip of a

brush, a sponge, or a feather duster. It can also be done with the frayed end of a rope or the edge of a piece of burlap.

Stippling is accomplished by loading one of these applicators with paint and touching it to the scenery. To avoid making an obvious pattern, you need to constantly change the position of the applicator and the pressure with which you apply it to the scenery.

Dry Brushing   Dry brushing is painting with a brush that holds very little paint. Just the tip of the brush is dipped in the paint. Any paint that has been picked up by the bristles is scraped off on the lip of the bucket. The brush is then lightly drawn across the surface to deposit a linear, irregular pattern of paint (see Figure 10.11).

Dry brushing is very effective in creating the appearance of wood. If the dry-brushing paint(s) is fairly close in hue and value to the color of the base coat, the result will look like smooth wood. If the contrast between the hue and value of the base and dry-brush paints is greater, the result will look more rough hewn.

Lining   Lining involves painting narrow, straight lines of varying width. The lines are painted with lining brushes, which were illustrated in Figure 10.1, with larger brushes creating wider lines. A straightedge is used in conjunction with the lining brush, as shown in Figure 10.12A.

Lining can be used to create the appearance of depth, as shown in Figure 10.12B and C. The illusion is primarily achieved through the use of highlight and shadow lines. The effect of the **source light** on an object will determine where the highlight and shadow lines need to be painted. On the bricks, notice the highlight at the top edge and the shadows below. On the paneling, see how the placement of the highlight and shadow lines creates the illusion of depth. Both of these examples are effective because the highlight and shadows look as if they were created by some specific source light. The location of the source light should appear to be some specific source within the design—either a practical onstage lamp or a specific position and angle (agreed on by the scenic and lighting designers) for an offstage, unseen source such as the sun.

Applications of Painting Techniques

Figure 10.13 shows a potpourri of fairly standard applications of the various painting techniques that have been discussed in this section. Careful study of the

FIGURE 10.11
Dry brushing is often used to create the appearance of wood grain. The tip of the brush is dipped in paint, scraped across the lip of the bucket (to remove excess paint), and lightly dragged across the surface of the work.

source light: The apparent source of light that is illuminating a scene or an object.

(A)

(B)

(C)

FIGURE 10.12
Lining is accomplished with a straightedge and a lining brush (A). It is frequently used to create the illusion of highlight and shadow, as shown in B and C.

FIGURE 10.13
Scene-painting techniques can be combined to create a variety of realistic forms. Wood grain (A) is primarily accomplished with successive layers of dry brushing in (generally) two or three tones of paint and an overcoat of glaze(s) in one or more tints. Stone (B) is usually created by scumbling two or three tones of a similar hue with a light, uneven overlay of stippled or spattered highlight and shadow to provide a slightly rougher texture. Marble (C) is created by wet-blending (scumbling with a lot of paint) several tones or related hues in a loose, vaguely linear pattern and overspattering with large drops of the same paint. Foliage (D) uses a combination of all techniques; the tree trunk and branches are created by scumbling and dry-brushing, the foliage and grass with scumbling, stippling, and spattering, and the distant bushes with stippling and a light spatter.

(A)

(B)

(C)

(D)

whiting: A white powder extender, basically low-grade chalk, used to increase the covering power of dry pigment and binder paint.

individual pictures can be helpful in understanding how the images were created.

Specialized Finishing Techniques

The following techniques are not used so frequently as the previously discussed methods of painting, but when the design opportunity presents itself, they can provide dazzling and effective results.

Texturing   Texturing refers to the use of additives in paint to give depth and texture to the surface being painted. Anything can be used for texturing, but organic materials such as sawdust, shreaded newspaper or tissue paper, wood shavings, **whiting,** and sand are commonly used. An alternative form of texturing is to build up a surface using papier-mâché (see Chapter 11, *Stage Properties,* for how-to information on papier-mâché) or some other method and then paint that surface with textured or untextured paint.

A variety of surface textures and forms (bricks, stone, stucco, adobe, tree bark) can be created using the texturing techniques described above. The secret to creating a realistic texture is to carefully study an example of the real thing and then duplicate its general shape, surface quality, and color.

Stenciling   Stencils are large cut patterns that facilitate the creation of repetitive, intricate designs such as wallpaper patterns. The stencil can be cut from

stencil paper, a commercial product made of heavy, stiff paper impregnated or coated with oils that make the paper water-resistant. Stencil paper can be made in the shop by painting thin illustration board with a water-resisting coating such as shellac, lacquer, or spray varnish. Be sure to coat the paper *after* you have cut the design. The high-impact polystyrene plastic used for **vacuforming** is completely waterproof and is excellent for use as stencil material.

After the stencil is cut, it is normally framed with 1 × 2 stock to hold it flat and make it easier to handle. The paint can be applied with a brush, **stencil brush,** roller, paint sprayer, or sponge, as shown in Figure 10.14. Generally, spraying works best, simply because it is gentler on the stencil. Regardless of the application tool used, the stencil will have to be cleaned frequently to remove any excess paint that could be accidentally transferred to the scenery.

Front-Back Painting   An incredible depth can be created when you paint, and light, both the front and back of muslin-covered scenery. Although this technique, also called translucent painting, is normally used with drops, equally effective results can be achieved on flats and other framed scenery.

Imagine you are painting a landscape on a small drop that will be hung upstage of a window of an interior set. The normal tendency is to paint the entire scene with paint and light in from the front. However, if you paint the solid objects (ground and trees) with paint and the translucent or transparent items (sky and clouds) with dye, you can light the drop from both the front and the back. The apparent depth that is created with this technique is really amazing.

The technique is particularly effective if the scene involves a sunset effect. If the front lights are dimmed and the back lights are up, the painted areas will appear in silhouette. The hue of the backlights, and projections, can be used to create spectacular sunset or night-sky effects.

Translucent painting can also be used to create stained-glass windows and similar effects. Be sure to work with the paint before the dye, because the paint will act as a "dam" to prevent the dye from creeping into other areas of the fabric.

Glazing   Glazing is simply applying a clear top coat to an existing finish. The finish of the glaze coat is usually satin or gloss, but it can also be matte. Stain and gloss glazes are generally used on furniture and natural woods, and matte glazes are frequently used to protect painted designs. However, there aren't any laws that dictate the particular uses of glaze coats. Use the type of finish that is appropriate to the specific design need.

Glazing can be done with a variety of materials. Extra-strength size water (one part animal glue to eight parts water), thinned white glue, clear vinyl acrylic, lacquer, shellac, and polyurethane varnish are all frequently used for glazing. The choice of which material to use is predicated on the use that the particular piece will receive. Finishes that are more water- and scratch-resistant (shellac, clear vinyl acrylic, polyurethane varnish) should be used for those objects that may be subjected to water or abrasive physical treatment.

Glaze coats can also be tinted with pigment or dye to tone down the brilliance or slightly change the hue of the undercoat over which they are being applied. They are frequently used to add shadow details to the set.

Metallic Finishes   The types of material that can be used to create metallic finishes have been discussed in various other sections of this chapter. Briefly, bronzing powders, which are powdered metal (available from scenic supply houses or well-stocked art stores), are mixed with a vehicle and applied to the work. High-gloss materials such as shellac, clear vinyl acrylic, varnish, and polyester resin all work very well as vehicles for the bronzing powders. Bronzing

stencil paper: Stiff, water-resistant paper used for making stencils.

vacuforming: The process of shaping heated plastic, usually high-impact polystyrene, around a mold through the use of vacuum pressure.

stencil brush: A short, squat brush with a circular pattern of short, stiff bristles; the bristles are pressed onto, rather than stroked across, the work, to prevent the paint from bleeding under the edges of the stencil.

FIGURE 10.14
Stencils are often used to apply repetitive patterns, such as for wallpaper.

powders are highly toxic. The standard safety caveat applies: Read, and follow, the information contained in the MSDS's for the products with which you are working.

The secret to a good metallic finish is the undercoat. The wood, plastic, or fabric to which you are applying your alchemy must be filled until there is absolutely no evidence of any wood grain or other texture. The best undercoat is polyester resin. Generally, one coat of resin will fill any but the roughest surface.

After the undercoat has dried or cured, the bronzing powders or colorants are mixed with vehicle and applied to the work. For small areas, metallic spray paints create a nice metallic appearance if they are used on top of a smooth undercoat.

Wallpapering

As an alternative to painting, particularly in theatres where the audience is sitting very close to the stage, real wallpaper can be used. Although wallpaper can be applied to muslin-covered flats, the finished job will look much better if the flat is covered with a hard covering such as Upson board, Masonite, or plywood. The wallpaper is applied with vinyl acrylic wallpaper paste or wheat paste.

FIGURE 10.15
Temporary drop stretcher.

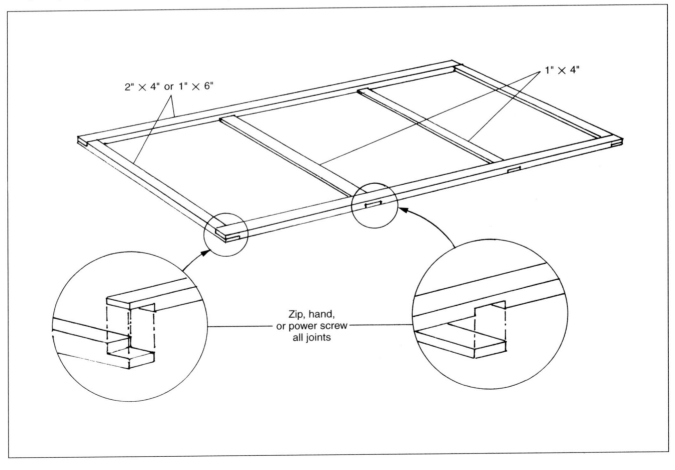

Drop Painting Techniques

Drops need to be stretched and framed in some manner before they can be painted. The stretching not only produces a smooth surface on which to paint but also minimizes shrinkage. The drop can be stretched on a vertical paint frame by

1. nailing a framework of boards the same width and height as the drop to the paint frame.

2. attaching the drop to the framework. Staples with one-half-inch legs, spaced three to four inches apart, normally secure any muslin drop to the framework. If the drop is going to be saturated with dyes or paint (which causes it to shrink a great deal), it will be better to secure it with staples spaced one to two inches apart.

Some painting techniques are more easily executed with the drop in a horizontal position. In these cases, the drop will need to be stretched and secured on a wooden floor with staples spaced on three- to four-inch centers. (Partially seating the staples will make them easier to remove.) Again, if the drop is going to be heavily saturated, space the staples one to two inches apart to prevent scalloped edges on the drop. Be sure to put a layer of **bogus paper** under the drop to absorb the dye or paint. Place a layer of Kraft or butcher paper underneath the bogus paper. (If the bogus/butcher paper backing isn't used, the paints or dyes may stain the floor or the drop may pick up some staining from old paint or dye already on the floor.)

If you do not have a wooden floor large enough to accommodate the size of the drop, you will need to build a temporary frame large enough to stretch the drop. The frame can be made of notched 2 × 4 or 1 × 6 so that it will hold its shape against the strong force created when the fabric shrinks. As shown in Figure 10.15, the toggle bars of this oversized frame are made of 1 × 4s. Be certain that the drop frame is square. After painting, the drop will shrink to the shape of the frame. If the frame is out of square, the drop will also be out of square and may be impossible to hang or trim properly. Finally, before you stretch the drop and staple it to the framework, don't forget to cover the area under the drop with the aforementioned layers of bogus and butcher paper.

In the final analysis, the quality of any scenic paint job depends on the talent and ingenuity of the scenic artist. The materials and techniques suggested in this chapter provide only a beginning point for the scene-painting artist. Although each of the materials has specific properties, there aren't any artistic "rules" to which the painter must adhere. Experimentation, trial and error, and learning from your happy accidents are the only guidelines that need to be followed as you work to develop your skill in the challenging field of scene painting.

bogus paper: A heavy, soft, absorbent paper. Similar to blotter paper.

Chapter 11
Stage Properties

In the proscenium theatre, the stage properties are the icing on the scenic designer's cake. Although the set usually creates the dominant visual motif, the properties are coequal design elements. They are generally the primary design tool used to provide clues about the personality and socioeconomic status of the inhabitants of the set. Figure 11.1 demonstrates these principles. Figure 11.1 is a rather nondescript living room that is furnished in three different ways. In Figure 11.1A, it is furnished with utilitarian props that don't provide many indications of the nature and character of the inhabitants or to the period of the play. Figure 11.1B illustrates how changing the style of the properties to late Victorian changes our perception of the social class and characteristics of the room's inhabitants. Additionally, it suggests a fairly clear idea of the period of the play. These visual clues are again demonstrated in Figure 11.1C, where the absence of any furnishings other than the stacked boxes, broom, and a crumpled newspaper suggests that the room's inhabitants are either moving in or moving out.

The visual importance of stage properties increases significantly when the play is produced in either a thrust or arena theatre or any of the other configurations that preclude or restrict the use of vertical scenic elements such as flats and drops. In these intimate theatre spaces where the audience is usually sitting close to the stage, the furniture and decorative props are frequently the major visual elements of the scenic design.

Although the duties and responsibilities of the members of the prop department were covered in Chapter 1, it bears repeating that the property master needs to have a detailed working knowledge of every craft area in theatre; woodworking, metalworking, electrical wiring and electronics, mold making, ceramics, sewing, upholstery, furniture construction, and scene painting are but a few of the craft areas in which a true property master will be competent.

When you understand the impact of properties on the appearance of a design and the scope of knowledge that a prop master must possess, it becomes obvious that a full discussion of how to construct stage properties cannot be contained in this chapter. Probably more than in any other single craft area in theatre production, someone who is interested in property design and construction needs to know it all—the history of fashion, architecture, furniture, and decoration; design theory and practice; and craft construction techniques.

WHAT IS A PROP?

Stage properties have traditionally been divided into three categories: (1) set props, (2) hand props, and (3) decorative props.

Set Props

Set props are generally defined as larger movable items, not built into the set, that are used in some way by the actors. This group would include such things as furniture, floor lamps, rugs, stoves, tree stumps, swings, and so forth.

Hand Props

Hand props refer to small items that are handled or carried by the actors. This group includes plates, cups, letters, books, fans, lanterns, and similar items.

Decorative Props

Into the category of decorative props fall all the things that are used to enhance the setting visually but are not specifically touched by the actors. Such items as window curtains, pictures, doilies, table lamps, bric-a-brac, and the books in a bookcase are typical of decorative, or dress, props.

PROPERTY DESIGN

In the commercial and educational theatre, properties are normally designed by the scenic designer (Figure 11.2). In the commercial theatre, properties are either purchased from stores or constructed by studios that specialize in property construction. In educational theatres, props are also bought, but they are frequently borrowed or rented, and if they are built, they are usually constructed in the organization's own shops. The scenic designer does background research by studying books, paintings, and other sources that contain pictures of the objects needed for the production. If there is a museum in the area that has examples of the actual objects from the period, the scenic designer may investigate that source as well. After researching the appearance of the objects, the scenic designer provides the prop master with all necessary sketches and mechanical drawings, as well as furniture and dressing lists. The prop master then builds, buys, rents, or borrows the props for the production.

Real or Fake?

If an actor is going to touch or pick up a prop, it should feel real. For example, assuming that you are trying to project a realistic or naturalistic appearance, a book should look and feel like a real book and, if it is going to be opened, it should have pages. The scenic designer and the property master may want to alter the appearance of the book by painting or staining the cover, covering it with cloth or leather, or hot-gluing jewels or appliqués to it.

Props can be faked if they aren't going to be used by the actors. If the prop book just discussed isn't going to be touched by an actor, it may simply be a cigar box or piece of wood that is painted and decorated to look like a book. Frequently, the books in a bookshelf are the spines of books that have been attached to a frame. Other types of props can be treated in the same way.

Property Acquisition

To create an aura of authenticity, property masters frequently try to find actual objects appropriate to the period of the play to use as props. For a contemporary production, props can usually be purchased or borrowed from local stores. For a play set twenty or thirty years ago, it is fairly easy to find most props in junk shops or used-furniture stores. However, when producing a period play such as *Amadeus*, which moves in time between 1780 and 1820 and is set in Vienna, it is very difficult to find actual furniture or decorative props of that period. Even if you could find them, you wouldn't want to put them on the stage for fear that they might be damaged. In these situations, the property master frequently builds the props or acquires reproductions.

Borrowing or Renting Props   Some special challenges need to be considered when borrowing props. Any type of prop used in the theatre is subject to unusual stresses and wear. Furniture, which is designed to sit in one location in a room in someone's house and occasionally be moved for cleaning, will be moved around the stage as the scenery is shifted. Even if it isn't moved, the director may block someone to stand on it, flop on it, run across it, or spill a drink on it. It should be obvious that if any of these things are going to take place, the furniture involved shouldn't be borrowed or rented.

If you are borrowing furniture, you should be able to assure the lending party that it will be returned intact. Lenders are frequently more at ease if a lending agreement (Figure 11.3) is executed. This agreement stipulates the use of the item, that the object will be returned in good condition, and that the borrower will be responsible for any necessary repairs resulting from accidental damage. If the borrowed prop is expensive or rare, the borrowing organization should investigate the cost of insurance to cover any possible repairs or replacement. Finally, if the producing organization cannot afford to replace the prop, it should not be borrowed in the first place.

Building Props   Some props, such as antiques, are best not used on stage. It is usually more appropriate either to use a reproduction or to build the piece in the shop. Other props such as fantasy pieces and antiques, for which there are no reproductions, will have to be built.

ORGANIZING PROPS FOR A PRODUCTION

If properties are going to be an effective addition to a production, they must be consistently placed in their proper locations on or around the set. If a floor lamp that is supposed to be placed next to a specific chair is misplaced, the concentration of the actor who is supposed to turn it on at a crucial moment in the play will undoubtedly be broken. Similarly, if an actor is supposed to pick up a book from a stack of books on an end table, the specific book must always be placed in the same position and location in or on the stack so that the actor can pick it up without having to look for it. A little thought, preparation, and organization will smoothly integrate the use of properties into the flow of the production.

Depending on the personnel structure of the producing organization, the technical director, property master, or property crew head will carefully organize and orchestrate the storage, placement, and use of all properties.

Hand props and small set props, such as lamps, pictures, radios, and so forth, should be locked in storage cabinets adjacent to the stage area between rehearsals and performances. Many theatres have lockable storage bins in the wings for this purpose. Other organizations use small lockable storage rooms. Valuable and borrowed props should always be stored in a secure area. Ideally, all props will be stored under lock and key. However, some pieces may be too large and/or cumbersome to move into the locked storage area. These items should be moved off the set, if possible, and covered with muslin dust covers and marked with a sign stating: "Theatrical Property. Do Not Use or Remove."

A written list, including a map or location indicator, detailing the onstage placement of all set props *must* be created by the appropriate person in charge of the properties. This list should also indicate where each item is stored between rehearsals and performances. The exact placement of the set props will be determined by the scenic designer, and any electrical connections will be coordinated with the master electrician. During rehearsals and performances the property crew, under the guidance of the property crew head, will place the set props in their appropriate locations. Depending on the union rules, if any, affecting the producing organization, any electrical connections will be made by either electricians or members of the prop crew.

The organization of hand props must be equally exact. The prop crew head creates a precise, written master list of what props are handled by the actors during each scene. This list includes the secure location where these items will

FIGURE 11.2
Property designs for the Metropolitan Opera Association's production of *Les Troyens*, produced at the Metropolitan Opera House, Lincoln Center, New York. Scenery, costumes, and visual effects (film) designed by Peter Wexler.

GOLD

GOLD

RED MARIBU

RED COCK
FEATHERS AND
ROPE

RED ROPE MACRAME

RED FEATHER

10'0"

GOLD

SOLDIER'S
MAX. REQ'D 38
- DISCUSS -

OFFICER'S
MAX. REQ'D 12
- DISCUSS -

TROJAN SPEARS

GOLD CHAIN TO GO
OVER BODY & ACROSS
SHOULDER

GOLD

GOLD

CASE MATCH
COSTUME
FABRIC

FRONT   SIDE
SHEATH

STEEL

DAGGER

TRUNCATED CONE
BELOW

3 PRONGED
SPEAR POINT

120°

PLAN OF TWO SPEARS
TO LEFT
(CAN REDUCE TO 1 PLATE)

FIGURE 11.3
A lending agreement form.

LENDING AGREEMENT FORM

1. Old Time Productions agrees to return the below listed borrowed items in the same condition in which they were borrowed.

2. If any item is damaged while in the possession of the theatre, Old Time Productions will be responsible for its repair.

3. The items will be borrowed on _____ and returned no later than _____ .

4. The prop will be used in the following manner: _____
_____ .

ITEMS

_____

For Old Time Productions: _____   Date: _____

Lender: _____   Date: _____

be stored between rehearsals and performances. If the show is complex or multi-scene, a separate list should be compiled for each scene in the play.

A hand-prop list normally includes the identity of all handled props; the location of each prop at the beginning of the scene, and if that location is different from the preceding scene (thus necessitating re-placement by the prop crew); the condition of the prop if it is functional (wine glasses full or empty, book opened or closed, and so forth); where the prop is to be left by the actor (on- or offstage location); and any other pertinent information.

A **prop table,** on which all hand props are placed, is normally set up in the wings adjacent to the stage. To aid in organizing the props, this large table is frequently covered with brown butcher paper and "mapped" with names of specific props, such as "Act I, Scene 2, tray/4 glasses" for the silver tray and four stemmed glasses that the butler carries onto the set during Act I, Scene 2. The tray and glasses are placed just above or below the caption. If there are a lot of props, or if the actors make entrances and exits from a variety of directions, it may be helpful to have more than one prop table.

Because it is so easy to misplace small hand props such as eyeglasses, snuff boxes, and the like, it is essential that the location of all props be carefully tracked and that prop crew members be responsible for placing all props in their appropriate locations and for retrieving them from the actors when they leave the stage, if the actor does not have time to return the item to the prop table.

Sometimes, as during productions that do not use an act curtain, the prop crew will move the props as the audience watches. At other times, the crew may be required to shift the props during a **blackout.** Frequently, the prop crew accomplishes its work with the act curtain down and the stage worklights on.

prop table: A table, normally located in the wings, on which hand props are stored when not in use onstage.

blackout: When the stage is completely dark. The stage lights are out and no other lights are on.

Regardless of the circumstances under which the crew works, it is essential that the prop crew head hold specific rehearsals to train the prop crew in the coordinated, speedy, and accurate placement of all props (both set and hand) in their appropriate locations about the stage.

CRAFT TECHNIQUES

Many props can be built using the construction methods that were explained in Chapter 9. A number of additional construction techniques primarily used in building stage properties are discussed in the rest of this chapter.

Furniture

Furniture construction, alteration, and upholstery aren't as difficult as they seem. Carpenter-style furniture (Figure 11.4) can be built using ordinary woodworking tools and techniques. The illustrated table will be very strong if it is assembled with open doweled joints. Because of its strength and ease of fabrication, the open doweled joint can be used for reinforcing almost any joint in furniture construction.

FIGURE 11.4
Exploded view of a carpenter-style table and the finished product.

FIGURE 11.5
Changing the upholstery can change the apparent period of a furniture piece.

Upholstery

Many times the apparent age or period of a fabric-covered piece can be altered simply by changing the upholstery fabric. For example, the relatively square silhouette of the tuxedo-style sofa (Figure 11.5) has been in continuous fashion since the 1920s. Although the dust ruffle has been in and out of vogue and floral prints have come and gone, the basic style and shape of the sofa have remained basically unchanged. The fabric covering for **stock furniture** is normally altered in two ways: by slipcovers or reupholstery.

Slipcovers   A slipcover is upholstery fabric that is tailored to fit a particular piece or type of furniture and is applied over existing upholstery. Slipcovers are normally used on fully upholstered furniture rather than on pieces that have exposed wood. They should be used only if the underlying fabric, padding, and frame are in good condition. Slipcovers can be used on borrowed furniture, since the existing upholstery material is left in place.

Reupholstery   Reupholstery involves removing the existing fabric covering and replacing it with new fabric. The existing fabric should be carefully removed, as shown in Figure 11.6, so that it can be used as a pattern to cut the new material. Once the old fabric is removed, the padding, springs, and webbing should be examined and repaired as necessary. Depending on the age of the piece, the padding may be urethane foam, cotton batting, or horsehair. Any damaged or compressed padding should be replaced with the same type of material if possible.

Before applying the new upholstery fabric, you should cover the padding with muslin. The muslin holds the padding in place, allows the upholstery fabric to move freely without snagging the padding, and serves as a base for any future reupholstery jobs.

Decorative Curtains and Draperies

Decorative curtains are used by the scenic designer to help **dress** the set. The type and style of drapery or curtain selected should be dictated by the period that is being represented in the design. Background research is done by looking at paintings, drawings, or photographs that show drapery styles of the period being represented. Figure 11.7 illustrates several typical styles of curtains.

A variety of materials are used in making draperies. The specific type of material is dictated by where it is used in the drape. The **valance, drapes** (also

stock furniture: Items owned by the producing organization and held in storage until they are needed for a production.

dress: To place decorative props such as curtains, doilies, knickknacks, or magazines on the set to help make the environment look lived-in and provide clues to the personality of the set's inhabitants.

valance: A horizontal element at the top of a drapery arrangement that covers the curtain rod.

drape: A vertical element of heavy fabric that frames the sides of a window or archway; can usually be pulled across the opening.

(A) (B) (C)

(D)

(E) (F) (G)

FIGURE 11.6
Basic reupholstery technique. (A) A chair in need of reupholstery. (B) Carefully remove and save the old fabric and torn elements of padding. (C) Apply new padding. (D) Use the old fabric as a pattern. (E) Cover the padding with muslin to hold the padding in place and to provide a smooth surface over which the covering fabric can slip. (F) Attach the new fabric with staples or decorative tacks. (G) The finished chair.

called overdrapes), and **sheers** are the primary elements of any window-curtain arrangement. The valance is generally made from heavy drapery material, although it can be made of wood painted or covered with fabric. A wooden valance is called a valance box. Heavy, soft drapery materials like those used for stage drapes (velour, velveteen, corduroy, commando) are generally used for the drapes, and lightweight, translucent materials such as chiffon and netting (see Chapter 16, *Costume Design*) are used for making sheers.

sheer: A thin gauze curtain that hangs across the opening of a window to soften the "sunlight" and obscure the view into a room.

Papier-Mâché

Papier-mâché is one of the oldest craft techniques used in the theatre. It is also one of the cheapest. It is used to make, or cover, a wide variety of shapes and objects that range from logs to statues, clubs, and various types of fake food.

Papier-mâché is made by building up a form with successive layers of paper that are bound together with a wheat-paste binder. The normal method of working with it is to tear newspaper into strips about one inch wide, dip them in the wheat-paste mixture, and form them over the mold. Between three and six layers of paper are usually applied to the form. After the object has dried (usually twenty-four to forty-eight hours), it can be painted with any of the paints used in the shop.

Craft stores frequently sell a prepared mixture of very finely shredded paper and wheat paste. You only need to add water to this papier-mâché mix to create

Open Doweled Joints

The extremely strong doweled joint, which was introduced in Chapter 9, is used extensively in the furniture industry. The closed, rather than open, doweled joint is preferred for assembling fine furniture, because the dowel is hidden inside the wood. The open doweled joint is just as strong and is very easily made, as shown in the accompanying illustrations.

The open doweled technique can be used for making any joint in furniture construction. Even if the joint is on exposed wood, the dowels will rarely be noticed, even in arena productions, because the spectators won't be close enough to see the exposed dowel, particularly if the joint has been sanded, filled with wood putty, stained, grained, and varnished.

Open doweled joint   Closed doweled joint

(A)

(B)

(C)

(D)

Open doweled construction technique. Clamp together the parts to be joined (A), and drill a hole through the top piece and approximately 1 to 1½ inches into the second piece (B). Squirt glue into the hole and insert a dowel the same diameter as the hole (C). The finished open dowel joint (D) creates a very strong joint.

FIGURE 11.7
Several styles of curtains.

a pastelike substance that can be used for sculpture or as a smooth finish coat over rough objects. It can also be formed in molds.

Vacuum Forming

Vacuum forming, or vacuforming, is the process of shaping plastics through the application of heat and vacuum pressure. Shapes can be formed with a vacuforming table of the type shown in Figure 11.8.

The vacuum-forming machine consists of a heating oven, a forming table, and a pump to evacuate air from a tank to create a vacuum reservoir. A sheet of plastic is heated by the oven until it becomes limber. While it is still hot, it is placed over a mold on the forming table, and the valve to the vacuum reservoir is released. The pressure of the outside air trying to reach the vacuum reservoir forms the plastic around the mold. When the thermoplastic cools (in a few seconds), it retains the shape of the mold.

This very flexible system can be used to form a variety of shapes such as banisters, decorative cornices, wall panels, and masks, as shown in Figure 11.9.

High-impact polystyrene .020 inch thick is the most commonly used material in vacuum forming, because it is thick enough to be reasonably strong after it has been stretched over the mold during forming. The material can be painted with acrylic vinyl, casein, and most oil- or lacquer-base paints. Other types of plastic that can be vacuum formed include thin sheets (.010 to .025 inch thick) of acrylic, vinyl, and cellulose acetate butyrate (CAB). (See Chapter 8 for a discussion of the various types of plastics.) Nicholas Bryson's book *Thermoplastic Scenery for Theatre*

Drapery and Upholstery Materials

All materials used for stage draperies have roughly the same characteristics. They generally have a soft, nonreflective surface and are available in a variety of colors. Upholstery and decorative drapery materials are not nearly so limited. They are available in a variety of finishes and a panoply of colors.

Factory flame-retardant treatment for the stage drapery materials is essential; it is also desirable for any other materials that are used on the stage. If the materials aren't flameproofed when you buy them, they will have to be treated by hand, and most flameproofing solutions, if applied by hand, will darken the fabric in an uneven pattern.

Velour

Velour is a cotton-backed material with a deep surface pile generally made from cotton, rayon, or nylon. It is available in a variety of weights ranging from twelve to twenty-five ounces per square yard and widths from forty-five to fifty-four inches. The material is available in a wide variety of colors, has a rich, lustrous appearance, and absorbs light well. It is generally the preferred material for stage drapes as well as rich, heavy decorative curtains and some upholstery applications. Crushed velour, in which the nap is compressed to create an irregular textural pattern, is a common upholstery material.

Velveteen

Velveteen possesses the same general characteristics as velour does, but it is much lighter—six to eight ounces. It has a lustrous pile finish and is generally available in forty-five- to forty-eight-inch widths from local fabric stores. It is normally used for decorative curtains and upholstery. The material, which wrinkles easily, is not durable enough to be used for stage drapes.

Plush

The pile of plush is softer and longer than that of velveteen but has the same characteristically silklike sheen. Available in a variety of colors and widths from forty-five to fifty-four inches, plush can be purchased from local fabric and upholstery shops. It is used as an upholstery or drapery material.

Commando

Commando cloth, also known as duvetyn, is a lightweight cotton fabric with a very short, feltlike, almost matted pile. It is available in two widths and weights: thirty-six-inch (lightweight) and forty-eight-inch (heavyweight). The heavy-weight material is good for stage drapes but is a little stiff to be used for decorative drapes. The lightweight is suitable for decorative drapes but is a little too delicate for the rugged treatment that most stage drapes receive. Neither type is particularly appropriate for upholstery applications. Commando cloth is available in a variety of colors and can be purchased from scenic-fabric supply houses.

Cotton Rep

Cotton rep is a tough cotton fabric with a ribbed finish that is similar to a very-narrow-wale corduroy. It reflects light more than other drapery materials do. Rep is available in a wide range of colors from scenic-fabric supply houses. It can be used for stage or decorative drapes.

Damask

Damask achieves its rich appearance from the raised patterns of high-luster yarn that are normally woven into the matte finish of the background cloth. The heavy material is available from local fabric houses in a wide range of colors and in widths ranging between forty-five and fifty-four inches. It is primarily used for decorative drapes and upholstery.

Brocade

Brocade is similar to damask but lighter in weight. The pattern, which can be either raised or flat, is generally created through the use of high-luster yarn that contrasts with the matte finish of the background. Forty-five to fifty-four inches wide, brocade is available in a wide range of colors and patterns in fabric and drapery shops. It is primarily used for decorative drapes and upholstery.

Satin

Satin is a heavy, stiff fabric with a smooth, shiny finish on the front and a dull finish on the back. If it is patterned, the design is generally printed on, rather than woven into, the fabric. Available in a wide range of colors and pattern designs, it is normally between forty-five and fifty-four inches wide and can be purchased at local fabric and drapery shops. It is used for decorative drapes and upholstery.

Corduroy

Corduroy is a cotton material whose pile ridges, called wales, alternate with a low-luster backing. The width of the wale varies from only one-thirty-second to approximately three-sixteenths of an inch. The weight of the material also varies considerably, with the lighter-weight versions suitable for costumes and the heavier weights more appropriate for upholstery. Corduroy is available in a wide selection of colors and in fabric widths from forty-five to fifty-four inches. It can be purchased from local fabric and upholstery shops. Waleless corduroy (similar to a very-short-nap velour) or very-narrow-wale corduroy can be used as a substitute for velvet in draperies, costumes, and upholstery; the wide-wale fabrics are primarily used for upholstery purposes.

FIGURE 11.8
A vacuforming table.

FIGURE 11.9
A variety of forms can be created by vacuforming. Photo by Nick Bryson, Gerriets International.

FIGURE 11.10
Rigid (top) and flexible (bottom) molds.

provides a wealth of information about the various thermoplastic materials, as well as detailed plans for the construction of a vacuum-forming machine.

Molds

In scenic and property construction, molds are generally used to create multiple copies of a wide variety of items such as fake loaves of bread, decorative panels for cornice molding, and costume jewels.

Molds can be divided into two categories—open and closed. The only significant difference between the two is that the open mold has an open top or port, whereas the closed mold is enclosed on all sides and has one or more ports into which the casting material is poured.

Molds can further be subdivided into rigid and flexible. Rigid molds (Figure 11.10 top) are generally made from such materials as wood, plaster of paris, fiberglass, or rigid urethane foam. Flexible molds (Figure 11.10 bottom) can be made from a variety of synthetic materials such as room-temperature-vulcanizing (RTV) silicone rubber. RTV silicone rubber and other mold-making materials can usually be found at local craft or art supply shops. Instructions for their use are found on the material containers.

In order to remove the cast object from the mold, the inside of the mold must have been treated with a release agent before being filled with the casting material. The release agent needs to be compatible with the type of material being cast. A silicone release agent, commercially available in spray cans, will work well for polyester, acrylic, and epoxy resins, but the heat generated by the urethane casting resins requires that a urethane mold release be used with both pour-in-place and spray foams. Both types of release agent are generally available at craft or hobby shops.

Making a Mold   Rigid molds of objects that don't have a great deal of detail can be made fairly quickly by coating the **model** with a urethane release agent and then covering it with either pour-in-place or spray urethane foam (rigid formulation), as shown in Figure 11.11. This type of mold works well for objects that

model: An object that is being used as the subject of a mold casting.

(A)

(B)

(C)

(D)

are free from **undercuts,** such as bricks and planks. Rigid molds can also be made in the same manner from plaster of paris or fiberglass.

If there are undercuts on the object being cast, a flexible mold is needed. This type of mold can be made with RTV silicone rubber, as shown in Figure 11.12.

A flexible mold that reveals a great deal of detail of the object being cast can be made by coating the model with silicone release, followed by several layers of liquid latex. Three to five coats are generally required. After the latex has dried, the inside of the box is coated with urethane release agent or lined with polyethylene film (urethane won't adhere to polyethylene), and flexible urethane foam is poured into the mold box. The flexible urethane foam will bond with, and provide a strong backing for, the latex mold.

Casting Molded Objects   It is fairly easy to cast objects from molds. The inside of the mold is coated with an appropriate release agent, and the molding material is poured into the mold and allowed to dry or set. After the material has cured (the time required varies depending on the material, heat, and humidity), the cast object is taken out of the mold. Depending on the complexity of the mold and the material being cast, some finishing details such as sanding or trimming may be required.

In order to paint the cast object, you will generally need to remove all traces of the release agent. Read the label on the release agent's container to determine the type of cleaner that will be needed.

Foam Carving

Expanded polystyrene foam, generally referred to by its trade name, Styrofoam, is frequently used in the fabrication of statues, columns, cornices, and other types of appliqués. Styrofoam is available from almost any lumber or insulation dealer

FIGURE 11.11
Rigid mold-making technique.
(A) The object being cast: a brick.
(B) Attach a collar to create a box for the mold, and coat the brick and box with a silicone release agent. (C) Coat the brick and box with spray urethane foam (rigid formula). (D) The finished mold.

undercut: An indentation in a form that leaves an overhang or concave profile—for example, the nostrils in a mask of a face.

(A)

(B)

(C)

(D)

FIGURE 11.12 ▲
Flexible mold-making technique.
(A) The object being cast: a brooch.
(B) Place the brooch in a cardboard
box, and spray both with a silicone
release agent. (C) Pour RTV rubber
into the box until it covers the top
of the brooch to a depth of about
⅛ inch. (D) The finished mold and
the brooch.

Nichrome wire or thin
spring steel strap

Heavy-duty variable transformer
such as an arc welder

FIGURE 11.13
Hot-wire cutters.

"tubed" building adhesive: An adhesive product, such as Liquid Nails,
packaged in a caulking tube and designed to be dispensed with a caulking
gun.

in thicknesses ranging from one-half to two inches. The light-blue Styrofoam is
fire-resistant, but the white variety is not. Thicker blocks can be made by laminating sheets with polyvinyl glue, latex contact cement, or several different types
of **"tubed" building adhesive.**

Styrofoam is easily cut with any power saw. Knives with serrated edges seem
to work better than those with smooth cutting edges. Soaping the blades will

Safety Tip

Foam Carving

Several notes of caution must be considered when carving foam:

1. Do not use a hot-wire cutter to work urethane foam. The heat from the cutter liberates toxic gases from the foam.

2. If possible, avoid using power tools to work either flexible or rigid urethane foam. The heat generated by the friction may produce the same toxic gases. If it becomes absolutely necessary to use power saws to cut urethane foam, soap the blade to reduce friction and push the work through the saw very slowly.

3. Always wear a respirator when carving any type of foam to prevent inhalation of fumes and small pieces of foam.

4. Wear goggles to prevent foam chips from getting in your eyes.

5. Carve foam only in a well-ventilated area. If at all possible, work outdoors.

help to reduce friction and possible scorching or melting of the foam. The foam can also be shaped with **hot-wire cutters** of the types shown in Figure 11.13. Keep in mind that heating any plastic such as Styrofoam—whether through friction, hot wire, or flame—liberates gasses (off-gassing) from the plastic. These gasses are frequently toxic. Be sure to consult the MSDS's for the materials with which you are working and follow their recommendations regarding safety equipment, shop ventilation, and safe handling.

The molding jig can be used to cut cornices or other architectural trim by shaping the cutter into the appropriate cross-sectional outline of the desired finished form. The block of foam is then slowly pushed through the jig, and the foam is cut into the finished shape.

Foam can also be cut into irregular forms by the direct application of heat with a propane torch or hot-air gun; by a soldering iron; or by a solvent such as mineral spirits, acetone, or lacquer thinner.

When the Styrofoam has been carved to the desired shape, it can be finished in a variety of ways. The soft surface will normally need to be protected in some manner. A coating of white glue will slightly toughen it, and cheesecloth glued to it will make it quite durable. To create a smooth, reasonably durable surface, you can coat the foam with two or three coats of acrylic **gesso** or plaster of paris. If the foam-carved object is going to be subject to a good deal of physical abuse, it should be covered with auto-body putty. Styrofoam and all of the above-mentioned finishing materials can be painted with latex or vinyl acrylic water-base paints and most oil- or lacquer-base paints.

hot-wire cutter: A tool for cutting foam that consists of a wire heated to incandescence.

gesso: Plaster of paris in a semiliquid state approximately the consistency of sour cream; dries to a hard plaster finish.

Heat Forming

Heat forming generally refers to warming plastic until it becomes flexible enough to bend. Sheet and rod acrylic or PVC can be heated and formed without any preparatory work. Tubes should be filled with sand before they are heated, to prevent them from crimping or collapsing as they are being bent.

If the pieces of acrylic or PVC are small enough, it will be possible to heat the plastic in the oven of a kitchen stove. Remove any paper or protective covering from the plastic, and put the plastic on a cookie sheet. Preheat the oven to 300 degrees, and heat the plastic for a couple of minutes, or until it is limber enough to bend. The plastic can be formed over a mold or clamped in position until it has cooled. Be sure to wear heavy gloves when heat-forming plastics.

(A)   (B)   (C)   (D)

FIGURE 11.14
Fiberglass construction techniques. (A) "Flesh out" a wooden skeleton with newspaper to create the basic form. (B) Cover the armature with aluminum foil, and (C) drape fiberglass cloth over it to create the line of the sculpture, and coat it with catalyzed resin. (D) The finished form. It can be reinforced with additional coats of glass cloth or mat as necessary and painted or finished as desired.

armature: A basic skeletal form that holds the covering materials in the desired shape or alignment.

Fiberglass

Fiberglass is formed by coating glass-fiber reinforcement with polyester or epoxy resin, as illustrated in Figure 11.14. Polyester resin is normally used, because it is less expensive. The most common types of glass reinforcement are (1) a woven glass-fiber cloth in either sheet or tape form and (2) a glass mat that closely resembles felt cloth. The great strength of fiberglass results from the tensile strength of the glass reinforcement being locked into place by the resin.

For most applications in property construction, the cloth or mat is draped over an **armature** and held in place with clothespins, wire, or tape. It is also possible to form the fiberglass by using molds.

When the glass-fiber cloth is formed, it is saturated with a coating of catalyzed resin. A second layer of cloth or mat can be added for additional strength after the resin has cured for twelve to twenty-four hours. Be sure to lightly sand the surface between coats. Generally, two to three coats will be strong enough for most scenic or property applications.

Most water-base paints won't adhere directly to cured fiberglass. If you first paint it with an automotive-type primer, however, you will be able to finish it with any scene paint except dry pigment and binder.

Catalyzed Polyester Resin

Polyester resin does not dry the way paint or varnish does. It will remain in its liquid state until a catalyzing agent, methylethylketone (MEK), is added and thoroughly stirred into the resin. The catalyst initiates a change in the molecular structure of the resin from liquid to solid. MEK is highly toxic. Be sure to read, and follow, the MSDS regarding appropriate safety equipment, working procedures, and shop ventilation when working with this chemical.

When the resin "kicks off" (begins to change its physical state), heat is released. If you carefully follow the suggested recipe that is printed on the resin container, you should have between ten and twenty minutes to work with the catalyzed resin. When the resin kicks off, it turns to a jellylike consistency very quickly. From this point, it will take twelve to twenty-four hours for it to fully cure.

Disposable paper cups make excellent mixing containers for resin, since you can throw them away after the resin has kicked off. Apply the resin with natural-bristle brushes, because it will dissolve synthetic bristles. Thoroughly clean any application equipment with acetone before the catalyzed resin gels; you won't be able to clean it after the resin has begun to cure.

Safety Tip

The Wood Lathe

A wood lathe is inherently dangerous. However, the following precautions should make working with a lathe safe.

1. Never wear loose clothing. It might get caught in the spinning wood.
2. Wear goggles or a face shield.
3. Be sure the wood doesn't have any defects (knots, weak spots) that might cause it to break while spinning.
4. Be sure that all glue joints on stock that is going to be turned are very carefully and thoroughly made and that the glue is completely dry before turning.
5. Center the work, and be sure that it is securely mounted between the spindles.
6. Keep the tool rest as close to the stock as possible. Before starting the motor, revolve the stock by hand to make sure it doesn't hit the tool rest. Adjust the position of the tool rest to keep it close to the stock as the turning progresses.
7. Turn stock over six inches in diameter at a slow speed, that from three to six inches at medium speed, and that under three inches a little faster.
8. Don't make any adjustments to the tool rest or other mechanical elements of the lathe while the motor is running.
9. Run all stock at the slowest possible speed until it is rounded.
10. Hold tools firmly with both hands.
11. Remove the tool rest before sanding or polishing the work. If you don't, your fingers may become caught between the stock and the tool rest.

Wood Turning

Wood turning is done on a lathe. Various prop and scenic items such as banisters, newels, and chair and sofa legs are frequently turned on a lathe.

Because hardwoods such as walnut, oak, mahogany, and cherry have a fairly dense structure, they are usually considered the best candidates for turning, although carefully selected, knot-free, tight-grained pine or fir can be used. To turn wood securely, mount it in the lathe, and as the lathe spins the stock, carve it using special chisels called turning tools.

Foam can be turned on a wood lathe by using a slow speed and using sandpaper rather than cutting tools. It can also be shaped with a hot-wire cutter. Urethane foam shouldn't be turned because of the toxic gas it emits when heated. Styrofoam sheets will probably have to be laminated to provide stock of sufficient thickness. Since Styrofoam is not very dense, pieces of one-quarter-inch plywood of the same size as the ends of the work will need to be securely glued to the ends so that the lathe's **spindle chucks** will have something to bite into to hold the work in the lathe. If the foam turnings are to be very narrow, a wooden armature (a ⅜-inch or ½-inch dowel or ¾-by-¾-inch white-pine stock) may need to be sandwiched into the foam laminate to provide sufficient strength for the unit to be turned. Be sure that the wooden armature is absolutely straight.

The design and construction of stage properties is a genuinely fascinating field. If your interest in this field has been piqued, you should undertake further study of the almost innumerable design and craft areas such as painting, furniture construction, upholstery, electricity, metalworking, ceramics, and sewing that are part of this theatrical specialty.

spindle chuck: A device used to hold wood in a lathe.

Chapter 12
Lighting Design

Any dramatic production, unless it is performed outdoors in the daytime, needs some kind of artificial light. On the other hand, if illumination were the only function of stage lighting, you could hang a bank of fluorescent lights over the stage and forget about all the dimmers, control boards, cables, instruments, and other complicated paraphernalia of stage lighting.

Obviously, there is something more to stage lighting than simply bathing the stage with light. Effective stage lighting not only lets the spectators see the action of the play but also ties together all the visual elements of the production and helps create an appropriate mood and atmosphere that heighten the audience's understanding and enjoyment of the play.

CONTROLLABLE QUALITIES OF LIGHT

Tharon Musser, a prominent professional lighting designer, has said, "If you ask most people who walk in and tell you they want to be lighting designers, what kind of weather we are having—what's it like outside?—half of them won't know how to describe it, if they remember it at all. They simply don't know how to see."[1] Learning how to see—to understand how light shapes and modifies people and objects—is absolutely essential in learning to understand lighting design.

A lighting designer can "see" how the lighting should look for a production only if he or she has an understanding of the controllable qualities of the medium. The qualities of light that the lighting designer can control are divided into four categories: distribution, intensity, movement, and color.

Distribution

Distribution is a catchall term that refers to several elements: (1) the direction from which the light approaches an area, actor, or object; (2) the shape and size of the area that the light is covering; and (3) the quality of the light—its diffusion or clarity.

Intensity

Intensity is the actual amount, or level of brightness, of light that strikes the stage or actor. Intensity can range from total darkness to painfully brilliant white light.

1. "Tharon Musser," *Lighting Dimensions* 1(1977):16.

Movement

Movement can be divided into three general categories: (1) the timed duration of the light cues; (2) the movement of onstage lights, such as a lantern or candle that an actress carries across the stage; and (3) the movement of an offstage light source, such as a **followspot** or kinetic/moving lights.

Color

Color, which was discussed at length in Chapter 6, is an extremely powerful tool of the designer. The judicious use of appropriately tinted light can greatly assist the audience's understanding of, and reaction to, the play.

followspot: A lighting instrument with a high-intensity, narrow beam; mounted in a stand that allows it to tilt and swivel so that the beam can "follow" an actor.

FUNCTIONS OF STAGE LIGHT

To increase the audience's understanding and appreciation of a play, stage lighting needs to perform several basic functions.

Visibility

A reasonably accurate adage in the theatre holds that "if you can't see 'em, you can't hear 'em." Stage lighting needs to make everything on stage—the actors, costumes, and setting—clearly visible to the spectators. At the same time, however, the concept of "designed," or controlled, visibility dictates that those actors and objects be seen only in the manner that the designer and director intend. One of the real challenges of lighting design is to create a selective visibility that subtly directs the spectators' attention. The number of lighting instruments and other sources used to light a scene, the color of those lights, and their direction and intensity all affect visibility.

Selective Focus

Selective focus means directing the spectators' attention to a specific place. The lighting designer can selectively focus attention in a number of ways, but the primary method is by manipulating our instinctive response to light. Everybody has a strong instinct to look at an area of brightness or movement in an otherwise neutral scene. By simply making one part of the stage brighter than the rest of the set, the lighting designer forces the spectators to look there (Figure 12.1). This technique of emphatic focus is amply demonstrated, for example, whenever a followspot is used in a musical number.

Modeling

Modeling is the revealing of the form of an object through the pattern of highlight and shadow that is reflected from that object to the eye. The distribution and intensity of the light will, to a great extent, determine our visual understanding of that object. Anyone who has ever yelped, "But that doesn't look like me!" when confronted by a flash snapshot of himself has just had a demonstration of this effect. The light from a camera-mounted flashbulb or strobe approaches us from a very unnatural angle—straight from the front and parallel with the floor. Light coming from this direction fills in the areas where we normally expect to see shadows—under the eyebrows, cheekbones, nose, and jaw line. It also puts highlights in rather unexpected places. Because of this redirection of the expected

FIGURE 12.1
Selective focus with light. Notice how your attention moves from person to person in the photo on the left, whereas your attention is directed to the highlighted actress in the photo on the right.

pattern of highlight and shadow, the picture doesn't look like the face that we remember.

Direction is the primary element used in modeling, although intensity, movement, and color all affect modeling to a lesser degree. A change in any or all of these variables will inevitably result in an apparent change of form and feeling of the object being lit.

Mood

Creating a mood with light is one of the easiest and, at the same time, most difficult aspects of stage lighting. It is relatively easy to create a spectacular sunset effect or a sinister feeling of lurking terror; the difficulty comes in integrating these impressive effects with the other elements of the production. Effective stage lighting is subtle and rarely noticed. Although it is fun to create a sunset or similar breathtaking visual display, the opportunity to do so legitimately does not present itself in many plays. Within the parameters of the production concept, stage lighting is usually designed to enhance the mood of the play as unobtrusively as possible.

DESIGNING WITH LIGHT

Before you can create with light, you have to *see* the light. Let's explore (with visual aids) the effects that can be achieved by manipulating the first two controllable qualities of light—distribution and intensity—to affect the four functions of light: visibility, selective focus, modeling, and mood.

The series of photographs in Figure 12.2 illustrates how varying the direction of light affects the face of an actress. Each photograph is accompanied by a drawing that shows the relative **plan angle** of the light. The **sectional angle** of the light is forty-five degrees and shows the angle of the light relative to the actor's face.

Surrounding an actor with a number of light sources provides the potential for modeling with light. In Figure 12.3 the direction of the light varies, but the intensity remains the same. A front light (Figure 12.3A) by itself is unflattering; it tends to flatten and compress facial and bodily features. Both side lights (Figure 12.3B) and top lights (Figure 12.3C) create highlights along the edges of the head and body but cause deep shadows across the face and front of the body. A

plan angle: The ground-plan view of an object.

sectional angle: The angle of intersection between the axis of the cone of light emitted by an instrument and the working height—usually the height of an average actor's face (about five feet six inches)—of the lighting area.

FIGURE 12.2
Effects of varying the direction of light.

combination of side and top lights (Figure 12.3D), together with a front light that fills in the shadows created by the side and top lights, reveals the form of the model by surrounding her with light.

When lit from the side-front at about forty-five degrees in both plan and section (Figure 12.3E), the model is smoothly illuminated, but her facial and bodily features are slightly compressed. If a top light or back light is added to the side-front light (Figure 12.3F), the resultant rim or edge light creates a highlight that adds depth to the face and body. As you can see, the greatest potential for modeling is achieved when the model is surrounded with light.

FIGURE 12.3
Surrounding an actor with light creates the most potential for modeling.

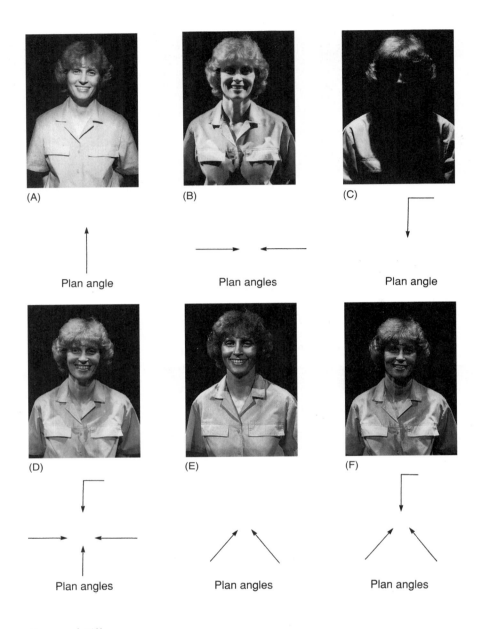

Key and Fill

The terms *key light* and *fill light* (borrowed from film and television) are frequently used to describe the relationship between the direction and relative intensity of light striking an object. The key light is the brightest light on the scene, and the fill light is used to fill the shadows created by the key light.

Psychological Effects of Light

In lighting design, just as in literature, the concepts of good and evil are often associated with light and darkness. When a scene is lit with dark and murky shadows, most people instinctively react with a sense of foreboding. The suspicion that something could be lurking unseen in the shadows is almost universal. When a scene is brightly lit, we instinctively relax, because we realize that nothing can sneak up on us unseen.

Design Inspiration: Lighting Design

The following discussion is based on and quotes extensively from "Thomas Lynch: Far East Marks This Designer's Latest Scenic Transformation," by Arnold Wengrow (Entertainment Design, March 1999, pp. 38–41). Photo by Thomas Lynch.

*Thomas Lynch, scenic designer of the 1998 revival of Ah, Wilderness! pro-*duced by Lincoln Center Theatre at the Mitzi Newhouse Theatre in New York City, says, "I'm interested in storytelling, and I'm interested in kinetic scenery, moving the scenery through an evening in a way that helps tell the story, which is different from just putting a drawing room onstage."

For *Ah, Wilderness!*, Lynch and director Daniel Sullivan stripped the gingerbread—and the walls—from the play's turn-of-the-century rooms. Lynch let his interiors breathe against horizontal swathes suggesting forest, ocean, and sky. The setting's visual purity was like sherbet against the sweetness of Eugene O'Neill's sentimental comedy.

Even pared to basics, the rooms exposed on the Newhouse's open stage had to change without impeding the dramatic flow. Lynch also believed that the play's progression demanded specificity. "You have to go to all those places, you can't just skip them. The porch is not the beach. Really you're on the porch. Really you're in the bar. Then, really, you're inside. And then, really, you're at the beach. It's hard to imagine the play, given the language, being simplified all the way down to a unit set. On the other hand, it seems to me that the play is often overburdened with scenic description. You just want to take a machete to it all."

"The transformation into the beach," Lynch said, "was kind of cool. The black band across the bottom at the back was made out of slanted veins covered in Merlin cloth that is 10 times as black as black velour. So actors could come in and out of a seemingly complete blackness. The platform, with its furniture from the porch, could track and swivel, the boat flipped out of the deck downstage right. As that occurred, there was a trade of drops. The green drop rose out of the way, and the ocean drop with the moon was there."

To divert the audience's attention, Lynch and Sullivan sent the story's young protagonist riding on a bicycle in the front of the black strip, as if going to the beach. Lighting completed the illusion. "At the moment of getting to the beach, a feeling of sand was created on the carpeted floor with some blacklight highlights, and the boat was picked up very subtly with blacklight. And then we were just there. It was in seconds, in this big space, so you felt you were looking at everything, but you didn't know how it was being done."

The design included a large, deceptively simple green drop that was actually quite complex. "The big green drop looks like a simple thing. It was not," Lynch said. "It was a very, very complicated thing. It could be front-lit, it could be backlit, and it had opaque painting on the back. Peter Kaczarowski [lighting designer for the production] could do many things on that drop and on this whole set that could give a lusciousness that isn't totally apparent in the bare bones of the scenery pieces. Boy, was I counting on Peter."

The direction from which light strikes an object has a direct effect on our perception of that object. Light striking a face from a low angle (Figure 12.4A) effectively creates a "monster" light, because such light does not occur in nature. Any light that places the face in heavy shadow, such as the back light shown in Figure 12.4B, will create an uneasy reaction in viewers, because they cannot see the facial expression of the person in the shadows and so cannot read his or her intentions.

Those who are interested in learning more about lighting design should become more fully aware of these instinctive, and learned, responses. More information on the psychology of color can be found in Chapter 6, *Color.*

THE LIGHT PLOT AND RELATED PAPERWORK

Because the product of lighting design—light—is probably the most intangible and abstract of all the theatrical design elements, some specialized paperwork is needed to help in carrying out the design.

To get the painterly density that he wanted on the drop, Lynch specified filled scrim for its lush, velvety weave. But it did not take backlighting well. Kaczarowski suggested backing the drop with rear-projection material. "We needed an RP material which would allow a good deal of transmission and color acceptance," Kaczarowski said. "We were using a lot of patterns—trees and leaves and quite a lot of fireworks effects—and all of that had to go onto a material that would maintain the integrity of the image, rather than diffusing it into one blobby, blurry thing. It had to have clarity and yet prevent us from seeing the lights that did it." After experimenting at Lincoln Center with various materials, they decided on Review, manufactured by Gerriets. In addition to the scrim, the floor and costumes became a canvas for Kaczarowski's light. Colors and patterns were layered onto the neutral floor around the set's central platform.

"There were shadows that had colors in them," said Kaczarowski, "and there was a great variance of color within the shadows. We did a daytime into sunset where the folds in the costumes and the shadows on the floor filled in starting with medium reds and yellows and oranges, going into deeper versions. Then it segued into cool colors for the evening. There was this always-changing, layered picture.

"Tom [Lynch] is interested in oddities," Kaczarowski said, "things that have an effect that you don't generally see on the stage, even if it's only momentary, like the blacklight in *Ah, Wilderness!*. It wasn't something that could stay onstage for very long, but it was a brief moment of great beauty. It was surprising."

Director Dan Sullivan recalls another moment of Lynchian surprise in *Ah, Wilderness!*: "When we got into tech and went to the beach scene, the dark space which had always been there below, butted against the black silhouette of the land above. That negative space itself turned into water, which was fascinating. Looking at the model, I hadn't known that was going to happen." Did the designer know it was going to happen? Sullivan laughs. "I asked Tom if he did, and he said of course he did."

The Light Plot

The light plot is a scale mechanical drawing—a "road map"—that indicates where the lighting instruments should be placed (Figure 12.5, pp. 296–297). More specifically, it is a "horizontal offset section in which the cutting plane intersects the theatre at whatever level gives the most descriptive view of the instrumentation in the stage configuration,"[2] according to the 1991 United States Institute for Theatre Technology's (USITT) graphic standards for stage lighting.

Although there is no universally accepted style of drafting light plots, some general information must always be included. Depicting the location of all lighting instruments being used in the production is the primary purpose of the light plot. The lighting designer specifies, to scale (usually one-half or one-quarter inch to one foot), where the instruments should be placed. The master electrician uses this scale drawing as a guide in **hanging** and circuiting the plot.

hanging: The process of placing lighting instruments in their specified locations.

2. Gill, Patrick, et al., "Revised Standard Graphic Language for Lighting Design," *Theatrical Design and Technology,* Fall 1991, p. 61.

The Legend

A legend, or instrument key (Figure 12.6), provides complete identification information about each instrument used on the plot. In addition to identifying the particular type or style of instrument that is denoted by each symbol, the legend should also contain an explanation of the peripheral information (Figure 12.7) that is associated with each instrument symbol. The USITT-recommended standards for this type of instrument notation are shown in the box "Lighting Symbols" on page 299. The types of peripheral information that can be used with each lighting instrument symbol are explained below.

Instrument Number   Each instrument needs to be assigned an identification number so that it can be cross-referenced with the **instrument schedule,** or hookup sheet. Figure 12.8 shows how lighting instruments are numbered on the light plot. The specific number recorded for each lighting instrument on the instrument schedule is determined by two factors: (1) its hanging location and (2) its position relative to the other instruments on that **pipe.** The first segment of the number is an abbreviation of its hanging location. The number "1E," illustrated in Figure 12.9, indicates that the instrument is hanging on the **first electric.** The second part of the number indicates the instrument's sequential position on the pipe. In a proscenium theatre, the numbering of any **electric** starts at the left end of the pipe when viewed as if you were standing with your back against the upstage wall of the stage house. The box "Drafting for Lighting Design" on page 314 explains the USITT-recommended method for numbering instruments for all of the hanging locations in the theatre.

Focus Area   The focus area for each instrument is identified by a letter placed in front of the lens housing of the symbol for that instrument. This letter corresponds to the same letter that identifies a specific lighting area on the light plot.

Circuit Number   The circuit number identifies the stage circuit into which the lighting instrument should be plugged. Although the lighting designer may assign the circuit number for each instrument, this particular decision is usually left up to the master electrician.

Dimmer Number   The **dimmer** number identifies the specific dimmer that will control the instrument. The assignment of the dimmer is frequently determined by the lighting designer, although this decision may also be left to the discretion of the master electrician.

Channel Number   The channel number identifies the control channel to which the dimmer will be assigned on a computer board. The assignment of the control channel is normally left up to the electrician, although it may be specified by the designer.

Instrument Color   The instrument color number refers to the specific color media that will be used with that particular instrument.

The Vertical Lighting Section

The vertical lighting section is a scale drawing, usually drawn in the same scale as the light plot, that isn't really a sectional drawing at all. It is actually a

instrument schedule: A form used to record all of the technical data about each instrument used in the production; also known as a hookup sheet.

pipe: A counterweighted batten or fixed metal pipe that holds lighting instruments.

first electric: The onstage pipe for lighting instruments that is closest to the proscenium arch.

electric: Any pipe that is used to hold lighting instruments.

dimmer: An electrical device that controls the intensity of a light source connected to it.

(A)

(B)

FIGURE 12.4
Psychological effects of varying the angle of light.

FIGURE 12.5
The light plot from *Jockeys* for the Jule Styne and Joe Kipness production at the Promenade Theatre, New York. Designed by Peter Wexler.

FIGURE 12.6
A sample legend.

FIGURE 12.7 ▼
Peripheral information notation standard.

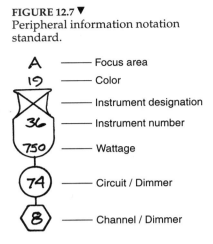

A ———— Focus area

19 ———— Color

———— Instrument designation

———— Instrument number

36

750 ———— Wattage

74 ———— Circuit / Dimmer

8 ———— Channel / Dimmer

FIGURE 12.8
Instruments are numbered according to two factors: the pipe on which they are hanging and their position relative to other instruments on the pipe.

composite side view of the set, masking, and lighting instruments (Figure 12.10). It is used for several purposes: (1) to check sight lines of the lighting instruments, (2) to assist in determining the appropriate trim height for the horizontal masking, and (3) to ensure that the lighting instruments will not interfere with any scenic elements and vice versa. (See Appendix B: "A Revised Standard Graphic Language for Lighting Design" for complete information on drafting style and symbology.)

The Instrument Schedule

The instrument schedule, also known as the hookup sheet, is a specification sheet that contains everything you might want or need to know about every instrument that is used on the production (Figure 12.11). It identifies each instrument by its instrument number and specifies its type, hanging location, focus area, circuit, dimmer, lamp wattage, and color. A section for special remarks is used to note anything else that might be appropriate, such as focusing notes, auxiliary equipment that needs to be attached to the instrument, and so forth.

All of the paperwork required in connection with a lighting design can be generated with various computer programs. Numerous drafting programs can be used to draw the light plot and vertical lighting sectional. Database programs can be used to create the instrument schedule or hookup sheet. If a software program has been specifically developed for lighting design, it may link these two elements. With a linked program, if you change anything—instrument location, color, channel, circuit number, and so forth—on either the plot or hookup sheet, the program will automatically change the same data on the other. The data contained on the instrument schedule can also be used to generate a wealth of other information such as **cut lists, hanging cards,** and so forth.

cut list: A
used in the
frame size,
Roscolux O

hanging c
plot, by po
Used by el
plot.

THE IMAGE OF LIGHT

The image of light is a picture or concept of what the light should look like for a production. The following discussion makes reference to the image of light as a pictorial vision. For the majority of lighting designers these images are pictorial, but they can also be auditory or emotional. It is essential that you develop some

FIGURE 12.9
Details of instrument-notation technique.

1E1		
1E12	8"	
1E13	6×12	
1E14	6×9	
1E15	6" F	
1E16	6×12	

FIGURE 12.10
The lighting section for *Jockeys;*
designed by Peter Wexler.

type of core image. The mental manifestation of that concept isn't nearly so important.

The analysis of the image of light for its distribution and intensity is probably the prime creative factor in determining the hanging positions for the lighting instruments. To analyze the image of light for its distribution and intensity, you have to see the image of light and then analyze its appearance to determine the angles and relative intensities of the various sources that are illuminating that image. However, all is not lost if you cannot actually see some type of image in your mind's eye. You can create a nonvisual image (a phrase, a melody, some set of stimuli) that provides you with a central thought or concept that can then be analyzed for its quality (mood, texture, color, intensity) of light.

Lighting Symbols

Because so much data must be included on a light plot or vertical lighting section, the United States Institute for Theatre Technology has developed a system of symbols for use on these drawings. The following information on lighting symbols is based on those recommendations.

Instrument Notation

The normal procedure in drawing a light plot is to use symbols to represent the various types of lighting instrument being used. The USITT-recommended symbols are illustrated in the following figure. A great deal of information is usually associated with each lighting symbol.

Lighting Templates

Lighting templates are used to help in drawing the various symbols for the stage lighting instruments and practical lamps used in most productions. The accompanying photo shows examples of both plan and sectional lighting templates.

Templates are readily available in scales of one-quarter inch to one foot and one-half inch to one foot (which are the most commonly used scales for drafting light plots).

Lettering

The lettering used on the drawings associated with lighting design needs to follow the same criteria of clarity and uniformity outlined in Chapter 20, *Mechanical Drafting*.

Lighting templates.

Show: THE TUNNEL		INSTRUMENT SCHEDULE					Page 4 of 4	
Inst #	Type	Location	Area	Circuit	Dimmer	Color	Lamp	Remarks
1 E13	30°	1ST ELEC	L	64	12	61	500w	
1 E14	30°	"	M	67	64	21	500w	SHUTTER ON ARCH EDGES
1 E15	6×16	"	SIGN SPEC	68	65	02	750w	SHUTTER ON SIGN
1 E16	8"F	"	C	69	27	79	1000w	BARNDOOR
2 E1	30°	2ND ELEC	R	128	21	61	500w	
2 E2	30°	"	R	129	22	18	500w	
2 E3	8"F	"	I	130	28	79	1000w	BARNDOOR
2 E4	30°	"	S	131	23	61	500w	
2 E5	30°	"	S	132	24	18	500w	
Boom 1R1	6×9	DR Boom	A-C	165				
1R2	6×9	"	A-C	166				
1R3	6×9	"	A-C	167				
Boom 2R1	6×9	RC Boom	F-H	185	44	18	500w	OVERLAP THROUGHOUT F-H
2R2	6×9	"	F-H	186	45	51	500w	
2R3	6×9	"	F-H	187	46	62	500w	

FIGURE 12.11
The instrument schedule contains all the technical data about each instrument used in the production.

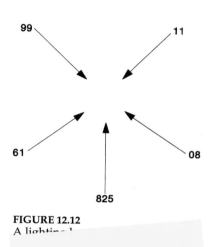

99   11

61   08

825

FIGURE 12.12
A lighting l

RESEARCH

Fl
A

(A) Acting area

Analysis of the image of light for its component colors is easier than the analysis for distribution, if for no other reason than that people usually have an emotional reaction to a play that can be translated into specific colors.

With the notable exception of productions that use intelligent or kinetic light fixtures, movement is probably the most easily adjusted of the qualities of light. The timing of the cues is customarily conceptualized during the design period, implemented during the lighting rehearsal, and adjusted during the technical and dress rehearsals. It normally isn't of primary concern to the designer during the selection phase of the design process.

The Lighting Key

The analysis of the image of light to determine its controllable qualities is not just an idle intellectual exercise. The lighting designer codifies that information to create a very pragmatic tool called the lighting key. The lighting key (Figure 12.12) is a drawing that indicates the plan angle and color of the various sources that illuminate the image of light. The lighting key is used by the designer as the primary guide for locating the hanging positions of the lighting instruments.

Acting and Lighting Areas   To fully understand the purpose and function of a lighting key, it will be necessary to digress momentarily and discuss acting areas and lighting areas. Acting areas are those spaces on the stage where specific scenes, or parts of scenes, are played. The shape and size of an acting area (Figure 12.13A), although roughly determined by the shape of the setting, are specifically determined by the blocking patterns used by the actors. A lighting area (Figure 12.13B) is a cylindrical space approximately eight to twelve feet in diameter and seven feet tall.

7'-0"

8'-0" to 12' 0"

(B) Lighting area

FIGURE 12.14
Lighting areas are overlapped in an acting area to facilitate the creation of a smooth wash of light.

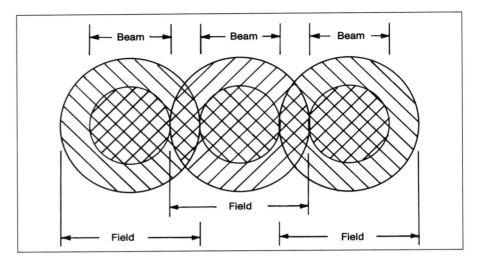

beam angle: That point in the cone of light emitted by an instrument where the light is diminished by 50 percent when compared with the output of the center of the beam.

field angle: That point in the cone of light where the output diminishes to 10 percent of the output of the center of the beam.

To achieve a smooth wash of light throughout an acting area, it is necessary to overlap individual lighting areas by approximately one-third, as shown in Figure 12.14. This overlapping of adjacent areas takes advantage of the optical properties of the **beam angle** and **field angle** of the stage lighting instruments to create a smooth wash of light throughout the acting area.

Creating the Lighting Key   The process of converting the image of light into a lighting key is best explained through example. To illustrate this process, we will create a lighting key for *The Playboy of the Western World* by John Millington Synge.

Let's assume that the image of light for this production could be stated as "a bright, twinkling Irish morning." Our analysis of this statement leads us to the conclusion that to achieve the concept of a bright, twinkling Irish morning on the stage it will be necessary to create the following: (1) a light and cheery atmosphere, (2) no shadows, and (3) thin tints of springlike colors.

If an actor in our play were surrounded with light, as shown in Figure 12.15, we would have achieved one of our stated objectives—no shadows. If we adjusted the dimmers that control those lights to a fairly bright setting, we would achieve another of our objectives—a bright atmosphere. By selecting happy, springtime, pastel colors, we would also meet the third objective—a cheery springlike atmosphere.

With this brief analysis of the image of light, we have already determined a great deal of the information that is needed for completing the basic lighting key for our production. Specifically, we have determined the distribution for the basic lighting of each lighting area (four diagonal cross lights) and the basic range of the color palette (pastel tints). Let me hasten to add that this particular solution is not the "correct" analysis of the image of light. There are myriad other possibilities, all of them equally "correct." You could have light from more or fewer directions (Figure 12.16A and B). You could also interpret the concept of "springtime pastel colors" to mean thin tints of cool colors as opposed to warm—it just depends on your personal understanding of the idea of a springtime atmosphere.

FIGURE 12.15
Four-source lighting key for *The Playboy of the Western World.*

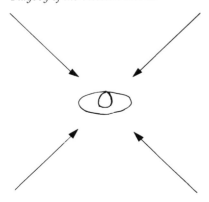

With the foregoing proviso firmly in mind, we make the conscious decision that our lighting key is going to be based on a five-sided distribution pattern (Figure 12.17). We made this decision because this pattern will provide a smooth, shadowless light that will support our interpretation of the image of light. Additionally, the top or back light (the arrow at the top of the pentagon) will provide a nice rim or halo light around the head and shoulders of the actors to prevent them from blending into the set.

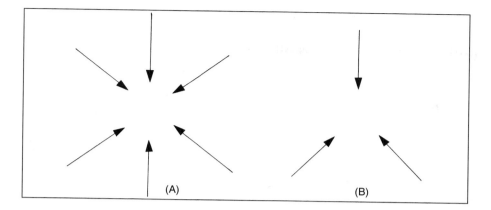

(A)   (B)

FIGURE 12.16
Six- and three-source lighting keys
for *The Playboy of the Western World.*

Before selecting specific colors for the lighting instruments, you must study the color palettes of the scenic and costume designers. This "color study" normally occurs during the various production conferences as each designer (scenic, costume, lighting) presents his or her design and color concepts. The reason that the lighting designer must know what colors the other designers are using is fairly simple. Colored light can drastically alter the apparent color of the sets and costumes, and it isn't in the interests of a unified production concept (or the lighting designer's physical well-being) to change the other designers' work without their knowledge and consent.

During the initial conferences of our hypothetical *Playboy* production, the design team decided that the play would be produced in a realistic style. Based on this concept, the lighting designer will want the set to appear as though it were being lit by the source lights that are located on the set. To determine the nature of these sources, and their locations, it will be necessary to look at a scenic rendering or model of the set. The scenic sketch (Figure 12.18) shows that there are oil lamps on the counter and each table, there is a peat fire glowing in the fireplace, and the window and door are open. Each of these sources would provide light of differing hues. The sunlight, according to our analysis of the image of light, is cool-white, bright, and cheerful. The fireplace is warmer and redder than the sunlight, and the oil lamps give off a soft, amber glow.

Using this analysis and information as a guide, Roscolux 61, Mist Blue, is selected to represent the bright, clean sunlight. Roscolux 02, Bastard Amber, is chosen for the firelight, and Roscolux 09, Pale Amber Gold, is selected to represent the color emitted by the oil lamps. (Roscolux colors, a common brand of theatrical lighting-instrument media, are being used to identify the specific hues

FIGURE 12.17
Five-source lighting key for *The Playboy of the Western World.*

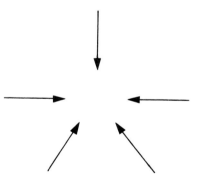

Beam and Field Angles

The field angle for an ellipsoidal reflector spotlight (the most commonly used stage lighting instrument) is approximately twice the beam angle for any given design or make of instrument. In practical terms, this relationship between the beam and field angles means that when the lighting areas are overlapped by one-third, the beam angle of each instrument lights the central, or "un-overlapped," portion of each lighting area, and the field angles of adjacent lighting areas overlap. The result is an additive effect that brings up the intensity level of the overlapped areas to approximately that of the area covered by the beam angle.

FIGURE 12.18
The set design for *The Playboy of the Western World.*

FIGURE 12.19
Five-source lighting key, with color, for *The Playboy of the Western World.*

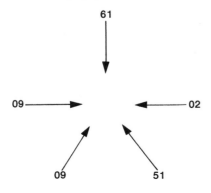

selected for this exercise. These colors are identified by the manufacturer with a name and number.)

Now that the colors have been selected to represent the various sources, they need to be applied to the lighting key. The application of color to the basic distribution pattern of the lighting key should support the thesis that the source lights are providing the light for the environment of the play. To achieve this goal, the lighting designer should color the light from stage left to represent the fireplace color, Bastard Amber, because the fireplace is on the stage-left side of the set. The oil-lamp color (Pale Amber Gold) is used from a direction (stage right) that supports the visual impression that the oil lamps are primarily on the downstage-right part of the set. The light approaching the stage from an upstage direction should represent the sunlight (Mist Blue), because the window and doorway are on the upstage wall of the set.

Figure 12.19 shows the colors assigned to the specific distribution pattern that we had previously determined from our analysis of the image of light. The stage-left side light is assigned Bastard Amber, to support the concept that the fireplace is lighting the room from this direction. The top-back light is colored with Roscolux 61, Mist Blue, because this supports the idea that any light approaching the stage from this direction would be sunlight coming through the window or door. The stage-right side light and the stage-right front light are colored with Pale Amber Gold, to support the notion that the primary source light for this side of the stage comes from the oil lamps.

This leaves the stage-left front light as the only uncolored instrument. Since there is no specific source light coming from this direction, it will be necessary to refer back to the image of light to determine the appropriate color for this instrument. The image of light specifies that the atmosphere should resemble a "twinkling spring morning." Roscolux 51, Surprise Pink, is selected for use from this direction, because this bright, cheerful color will blend with the Pale Amber Gold (used in the other front light) to produce a warm white light that supports the concept of a cheery morning that is dictated by the image of light.

Using the Lighting Key to Draw the Light Plot

The lighting key is the primary tool in drawing the light plot. The shape of the acting areas determines the number and arrangement of the lighting areas. In our hypothetical production of *The Playboy of the Western World*, the whole set is a single acting area. In order to draw the light plot, it will be necessary to subdivide that acting area into lighting areas, as shown in Figure 12.20.

(A)

(B)

FIGURE 12.20
Acting (top) and lighting areas for
The Playboy of the Western World.

To create a smooth wash of light over the entire acting area, the lighting designer needs to replicate the lighting key in each of the lighting areas. This process of duplication is demonstrated for a single lighting area in Figure 12.21.

Unfortunately, it isn't always possible to achieve an exact duplication of the lighting key in every lighting area, because the walls of the set prevent the use of side light in the lighting areas that are adjacent to the walls, and the ceiling interferes with a great deal of the top and back light. More challenges are imposed by the physical limitations of the auditorium, which generally inhibit some of the front-of-house hanging positions.

When a situation occurs that makes it difficult to place an instrument exactly where it is needed, the lighting designer must make a design decision. If the light can't be placed in a position where it will replicate the angle specified in the lighting key, the compromise solution should be guided by the principles outlined in the lighting key and the designer's interpretation of the image of light. For example, it isn't possible to use direct stage-left side light for Area J (see Figure 12.22), because the wall gets in the way. Two possible compromise solutions to this challenge might be: (1) Put an instrument on the stage-left end of the first electric, as shown in Figure 12.22. (2) Eliminate the instrument. The choice of which solution to use should be guided by your interpretation of the image of light and the lighting key.

To complete the basic, or first, layer of the lighting design, it will be necessary to duplicate, as closely as possible, the lighting key in every lighting area. This process of replication results in a basic light plot that creates the atmosphere and look dictated by the image of light.

Layering

A lighting design exists in time as well as space. It ebbs and flows as the mood of the play changes. Creating a temporal development in the lighting design re-

FIGURE 12.21
Replication of the lighting key in a lighting area for *The Playboy of the Western World.*

FIGURE 12.22
Replication of the lighting key for
The Playboy of the Western World in a
lighting area that is difficult to light.

quires that some method of creating that time-based element be designed into the light plot.

Layering is primarily an organizational tool of the lighting designer. It refers specifically to the process of designing layers of light.

The first layer of light for our hypothetical production of *Playboy* was created when we implemented our interpretation of the image of light—"a bright, twinkling Irish morning." This image works well for Acts II and III, which take place in the morning and afternoon, respectively. However, Act I takes place in the early evening. The "twinkling morning" look simply doesn't translate as night. To create an appropriate look of early evening for Act I, it will be necessary to do one of two things: (1) Create a completely separate lighting key and design for Act I, or (2) create some supplemental "early evening" lighting that can be used in conjunction with the basic "twinkling Irish morning" lights.

From an aesthetic standpoint, a completely separate plot for Act I would be the preferred solution, but a separate design would necessitate a very large instrument inventory.

The supplemental lighting solution would achieve relatively similar results with a considerably smaller number of instruments. The instruments used to create this second layer of light need to be positioned and colored to create the look of "indoor evening" in the pub, where the principal sources of light are oil lamps and the peat fire. Any light coming in the window and door should have the appearance of "night light" rather than daylight.

Since this second layer of light needs to be integrated with the "twinkling Irish morning" lights to achieve the look of "early evening," it will be necessary to select angles and colors that work to support the premise that the pub is actually lit by the oil lamps and the peat fire.

A wash of "night" colors (Roscolux 79, Bright Blue) could be used to flood the stage from the front-of-house positions, as shown in Figure 12.23A. By balancing the intensities of these night colors with those of the basic lighting key, we can ensure that the blue lights won't override the basic hues that were selected for the lighting key. They will, however, provide a blue wash over the whole acting area that will fill any shadow or underlit areas with a blue light to help create the illusion of nighttime.

FIGURE 12.23
Layering can be used to supplement the basic design key.

FIGURE 12.24
Light plot for a
proscenium
production of
*The Playboy of
the Western
World.*

FIGURE 12.25
Scenic design for a thrust produc-
tion of *The Playboy of the Western
World.*

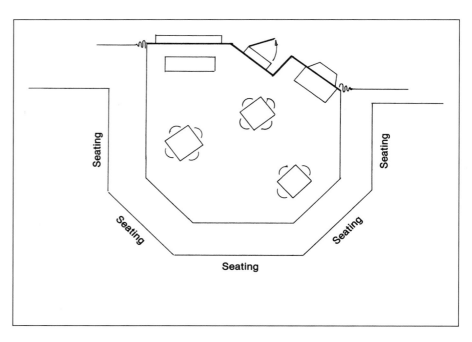

FIGURE 12.26
Lighting key for thrust production
of *The Playboy of the Western World.*

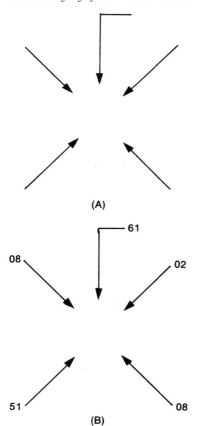

Additional instruments could be hung to augment the color selected to reinforce the source lights—the oil lamps and peat fire—in the first layer of the plot.
These instruments, as shown in Figure 12.23B, should be colored in more fully
saturated hues than their "first layer" counterparts, and they should be hung in
positions that will support the effects of the source lights.

Additional layers of light can be used for a variety of purposes. Figure 12.23C
shows the location of those instruments that are used to create the "daylight" and
"night light" that come through the window and door.

As indicated at the beginning of this discussion, layering is primarily an
organizational tool of the lighting designer. It isn't necessary to divide your
thinking about the design into segments, but many designers find that this com-
partmentalization of the design into specific segments, or layers, makes it easier
to concentrate on solving the challenges imposed by the individual elements of
the design. Figure 12.24 shows the finished light plot for *The Playboy of the Western
World.*

Designing Lights for Thrust and Arena Stages

Designing lights for an arena or thrust stage is not significantly different from
designing for a proscenium theatre. The only substantive difference is the location of the audience. In the thrust configuration, as you will recall, the audience
sits on three sides of the stage, and in an arena theatre it surrounds the stage. It
is the lighting designer's responsibility to light the stage so that all spectators,
regardless of where they are sitting, are able to see the production equally well.

We can use our hypothetical production of *The Playboy of the Western World* to
demonstrate the relative lack of difference between designing lighting for the
three modes of stages. Figure 12.25 shows a sketch of the modified scenic design
that would work for a thrust production of our play. Note that the side walls
have been removed so that the spectators sitting on the sides of the thrust stage
can see all of the action. Also notice that because the walls are gone, the ceiling
has been eliminated.

The image of light remains the same as before, simply because the concept of how we are going to produce the play hasn't changed. The distribution of the design key has been slightly modified because of the position of the audience relative to the stage. We are still surrounding the actors with light to recreate our "bright, twinkling Irish morning" as shown in Figure 12.26A. The color of the design key also remains relatively unchanged, although we will lower the saturation of the "warm" color because of the proximity of the audience, as shown in Figure 12.26B.

The second layer for our thrust production could concentrate on enhancing the source lights—oil lamps, fireplace, window, and door (Figure 12.27A). The third layer (Figure 12.27B) would concentrate on creating the "night" wash.

The lighting design for an arena production of our play would be very similar to the thrust design. The set for the arena production is shown in Figure 12.28. Notice how all of the walls that might in any way interfere with the spectators' sight lines have been removed. The scenic design has been essentially reduced to a furniture arrangement, with just enough set left to provide a hint of what the cottage or pub actually looks like. The set has been shifted to a diagonal angle so that the entrances are lined up with the auditorium entryways.

The distribution of the lighting key for the arena production is slightly different from the other two configurations (Figure 12.29A). The color portion of the design key is also different, but only because we want everyone looking at the play to get the same feeling. For the proscenium and thrust productions, we were able to have the light coming from the direction of the door and window gelled with colors that would support the "outdoors" look of the light coming through the window and door. Because we now have the audience surrounding the stage, however, we need to create the same feeling of "interior" lighting from all angles. These changes are shown in the color selection for the design key illustrated in Figure 12.29B.

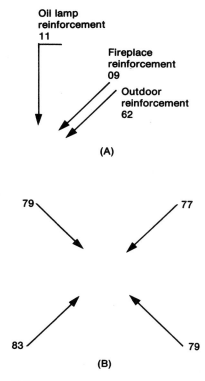

FIGURE 12.27
Additional layers for lighting key for thrust production of *The Playboy of the Western World.*

FIGURE 12.28
Scenic design for arena production of *The Playboy of the Western World.*

FIGURE 12.29
Lighting key for arena production
of *The Playboy of the Western World.*

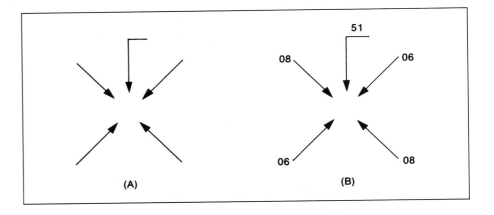

FIGURE 12.30
Additional layers for lighting key
for arena production of *The Playboy
of the Western World.*

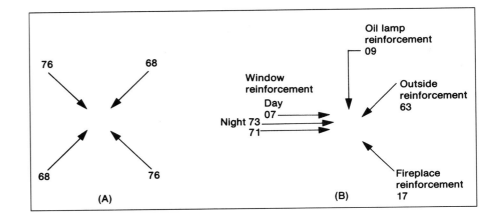

Similarly, the "night" layers must place lights in positions that will enhance the idea of "night" for all of the viewing audience, as shown in Figure 12.30A. In this particular design, the third layer of light is used to support both the internal and external source lights. These lights need to be reasonably directional, as shown in Figure 12.30B, because the apparent source lights that they are reinforcing (sunlight, moonlight, peat fire) are also directional. The instruments that are reinforcing the oil lamps are placed over the general area of the lamps, simply because the light from the oil lamps illuminates everything around it.

The only other type of design modification that needs to be made when working in an arena theatre is that the instruments are probably hung considerably closer to the actors than in either a thrust or proscenium configuration. Because of this you will want to use less-saturated color media, as the closer the instrument is to the actor, the stronger the effect of any color that is used with that instrument.

Other than these relatively minor adjustments required by the positioning and proximity of the audience, there really aren't any significant changes in philosophy, practice, or techniques when designing for thrust or arena theatres.

DRAWING THE LIGHT PLOT AND LIGHTING SECTION

The lighting designer needs to acquire several specific drawings or computer files from other members of the production design team before he or she can start to draw the light plot. In addition to sketches, models, or photos of the scenic models, the lighting designer will need

1. the ground plan(s) of the scenic design
2. the sectional(s) of the scenic design
3. a scale ground plan of the stage and auditorium
4. a sectional of the stage and auditorium
5. a layout of, and specifications for, the stage lighting system(s) of the theatre
6. an accurate inventory of the theatre's lighting equipment and/or a lighting rental budget.

The ground plans of the theatre and set are traced, using a thin line, onto the light plot. The layout of the stage lighting system provides information about the location of the various stage circuits (connecting strips, floor and wall sockets, and so on). The sectionals of the set and the stage and auditorium are traced to create the basic visual information necessary for the lighting section. See the box "Drafting for Lighting Design" on page 314 for specific drafting conventions and information.

Information regarding the lighting key, beam and field angles, and lighting areas was presented earlier in this chapter. However, some additional technical information may prove helpful when you start to draw the light plot.

Determining the Sectional Angle

The lighting key codifies the plan angle and color for each instrument, but it doesn't provide any information about the sectional angle for each instrument. Although the sectional angle should be determined from an analysis of the desired appearance of the light, in fact the sectional angles of most lighting instruments used in the theatre will usually be somewhere between thirty and sixty degrees. The reason for this apparently arbitrarily selected angle is that people living in temperate climates are used to seeing objects illuminated by the sun within this angle range, so we perceive of this angle range as being natural, normal, and appropriate.

Dance and other applications in which the revelation of form is more important than the visibility of the face are notable exceptions to this generalization about the sectional angle. Dance lighting normally makes very effective use of side lighting with an angle of approach parallel with the stage floor.

Figure 12.31A shows the plan view of a single lighting instrument. Figure 12.31B shows a sectional view taken at right angles to the axis of that same instrument. Since the lighting instruments are usually hidden from the spectators' view, the lighting designer will set a specific trim height (height above the stage floor) for the instrument. Since any point along the axial line will produce the "correct" sectional angle, the sectional line can be extended until it reaches the predetermined trim height (x). At that point, a vertical line can be dropped to the stage floor, and the distance from that point to the center of the lighting area can be measured (y). This information is recorded on the light plot by placing the symbol for the instrument at the measured floor distance from the center of the lighting area, as shown in Figure 12.31C. The trim height for the pipe is noted, at the end of the pipe, on the plot.

Selecting Instrument Size

At the same time that the sectional angle is being determined, the lighting designer can also determine the appropriate size of instrument to use. From the

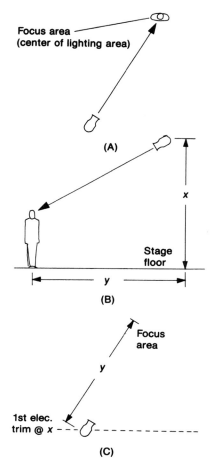

FIGURE 12.31
A sectional view of the hanging position of a lighting instrument provides an accurate picture of the angle from which the light will strike the actor.

Drafting for Lighting Design

As we have seen, the lighting designer uses two principal mechanical drawings to record the information that is needed to hang, circuit, and focus the lighting design: the light plot and the lighting section. The purpose of these drawings is to guide the master electrician and crew. The amount and kind of information shown on the paperwork associated with a lighting design vary greatly from production to production and designer to designer. But a set of basic criteria pertains to the drawings associated with any lighting design. The following information is based on the 1991 USITT "Revised Standard Graphic Language for Lighting Design," which is included in its entirety as an appendix.

1. The light plot and lighting section should be drawn to scale.

2. The light plot should show the location of the lighting instruments in relation to the set and the physical structure of the theatre. Instrument symbols should be scale representations of the size of the actual instruments they represent to precisely detail the amount of space they will occupy. They should also be drawn in the same scale as the rest of the drawing.

3. All drawings should adhere to the tenets of good mechanical-drafting techniques (see Chapter 20, *Mechanical Drafting*).

4. The darkest lines on the plot should represent instrument symbols and related information, architectural lines should be of medium dark-

ness, and set lines should be the lightest.

5. The instrument key or legend should be used to explain all symbols used on the plot. It should minimally contain
   - Symbol identification for all instruments and devices shown on the plot and controlled by the lighting console, including the instrument manufacturer and wattage.
   - A representation of the typical instrument notation method used.
   - A drawing of the technique used to represent "two-fers."

6. The instrument symbol should include
   - An instrument number as an aid to location.
   - A symbol for attached hardware (such as templates, irises, color scrollers, top hats, barn doors, and so forth).
   - The channel, the circuit and/or dimmer number, and the color notation.
   - A symbol for lamp axis alignment on PAR cans.
   - The method used to illustrate "two-fers."

7. The designation and numbering of hanging positions and instruments in proscenium configurations include the following conventions:
   - Onstage pipes should be numbered from downstage to upstage.

   - Onstage booms should be numbered from downstage to upstage.
   - Box-boom or torm positions should be numbered consistently within each plot.
   - All lighting positions should be designated by stage directions.
   - Front of house (FOH) ceiling positions should be numbered from the apron to the rear of the house as should FOH boom positions, side coves, ladders, or ports.
   - Balcony rails should be numbered from the floor to the ceiling.
   - Pipe grids in "black box" type theatres should be numbered on the x or y axis of the grid and lettered on the opposing axis.
   - Nonconventional black-box lighting positions should be identified by compass directions.
   - Trim heights should be indicated from the stage floor or the deck to the pipe with a note on the plot to verify that the measurement is from the "stage floor" or "deck."
   - Instruments on stage electric pipes should be numbered from stage left to stage right.
   - Instruments on booms should be numbered from top to bottom.
   - Strip lights should be labeled (using numbers or letters) from stage left to stage right.

8. Acceptable locations for titleblocks are in the lower right-hand or left-hand corners or centered on the bottom of the plate.

---

throw distance: How far light from an instrument travels from its hanging position to the center of its focus area.

working sectional: A drawing showing the sectional angle for a lighting instrument; used to determine its trim height; not to be confused with the lighting section.

beam and field angle information (see page 303), or from the manufacturer's specification sheets for specific lighting instruments, templates of the beam and field angles can be constructed for each instrument. These are simple triangular, scale, acetate, or cardboard templates that contain the **throw distance** and the beam and field angles of the light emitted by each instrument. The photometric data required to construct these templates is also available on computer programs such as Rosco Light Shop.

Figure 12.32 shows how to use the beam and field angle template. After the **working sectional** for the instrument has been drawn, the apex of the template is placed at the specified trim height for the instrument. The appropriately sized

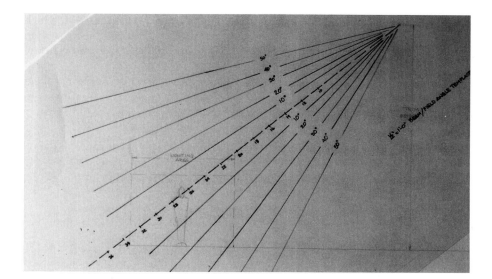

FIGURE 12.32
How to use a beam and field angle template.

instrument will have a field angle that slightly overlaps the lighting area and a maximum throw distance that is longer than the required throw distance.

This method of instrument selection is suggested only as a general guide. In the final analysis, the designer needs to make instrument selections based on what is aesthetically appropriate for the particular situation.

REHEARSAL AND PERFORMANCE PROCEDURES

It has been said that any lighting design is only as good as its paperwork. The light plot, lighting section, and instrument schedule are only about half of that paperwork. The rest of it is associated with the recording of the dimmer intensity levels and other data that are used when running the lights for a production.

This section will present a series of rehearsal and performance procedures, forms, and practices that can be used to assist in the running of the lighting for any production. Every action involving the adjustment of one or more lighting instruments needs to be recorded to ensure that the intensity settings for those dimmers and the timing of each **lighting cue** remain the same from rehearsal to rehearsal and performance to performance.

The forms and practices suggested in this section are not sacrosanct; they are just one of many methods that can be used to record the information that is needed to run the lighting for a production. Any well-organized system that works for the lighting designer and electrician can be used. The important point is the necessity of having a clearly written, systematic method of recording the necessary information.

Electrician's Cue Sheet

The electrician's cue sheet is the **board operator's** bible. It contains the primary operating instructions (cue number, what specific action the board operator takes, the timing of the cue, and so forth) for every lighting cue, as shown in Figure 12.33. It is also important to note what information the electrician's cue sheet does not contain. It doesn't give the specific dimmer intensity level settings (commonly referred to as dimmer settings) for major shifts in the lighting. That

lighting cue: A command to take some type of action involving lighting, usually, to raise or lower the intensity of one or more instruments.

board operator: An electrician who runs the lighting control console during rehearsals and performances.

information is stored in computer memory or written on the preset sheet, which will be discussed a little later in this section. But the electrician's cue sheet is often used to record the dimmer levels for minor shifts of intensity that involve only one or two dimmers.

If you carefully study the information written on the electrician's cue sheet shown in Figure 12.33, you will be able to follow the progress of the lighting from the lowering of the house lights through the end of the first scene of the play.

Lighting Instrument Specification Sheets

It is extremely useful for a lighting designer to assemble a collection of data sheets that specify the photometric data (beam, field angle, light output at specific throw distances, and the like) for the instruments of the various manufacturers (see example). The maximum throw distance is the far-thest distance at which the instrument can effectively be used. At this distance, the light emitted by the instrument measures fifty foot-candles, which is used as the industry standard and is considered to be the lowest effective illumination level for stage use.

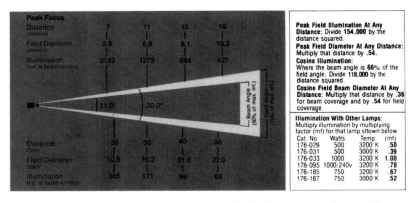

A portion of an instrument specification sheet for the Colortran 30-degree ellipsoidal reflector spotlight.

FIGURE 12.33
An electrician's cue sheet.

ELECTRICIAN'S CUE SHEET

Show_____   Script Page _1-25_

Cue	Preset	Count	Notations
1	1	—	House Preset @ 7:30
2	—	8	House to Half
3	—	4	House Out
4	2	6	Apartment (morning)
5	3	1	Kitchen when Hal hits switch
6	4	5	Fade to Black End of scene

PRESET SHEET	

Production:_____

Preset Bank:_____ Cue:_____

1		16	
2		17	
3		18	
4		19	
5		20	
6		21	
7		22	
8		23	
9		24	
10		25	
11		26	
12		27	
13		28	
14		29	
15		30	

FIGURE 12.34
A preset sheet.

Recording Dimmer Intensity Levels

There are actually two methods of recording lighting cues: electronically and in writing.

Electronic Cue Storage   Electronic cue storage is a significant advantage of the computer board. Although the capabilities of computer boards vary from manufacturer to manufacturer, they all provide a basic level of computer memory that allows them to electronically store the intensity levels of each dimmer that is used in each cue and the time associated with each cue. If a production company doesn't have a computer board to electronically record and store the data associated with each cue, that information will have to be recorded manually.

Preset Sheet   If a manual or preset control board is used, a preset sheet (Figure 12.34) is used to record the intensity levels for each dimmer during major shifts in lighting. The layout and content of the preset sheet are dependent on the type of control system used for the production. But regardless of the exact form of the sheet, it will have an open space adjacent to each dimmer or channel number for recording the intensity level of that particular dimmer for that particular cue.

FIGURE 12.35
A designer's cue sheet.

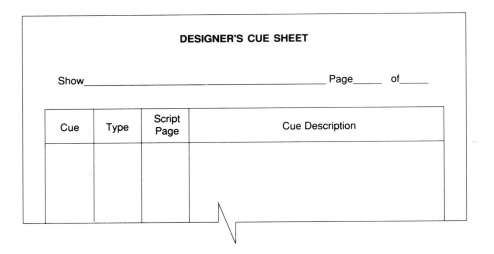

Each time a shift in the lighting involves more than two or three dimmers, a preset sheet is completed for that cue. The sheet provides the board operators with the information necessary to accurately adjust the dimmers.

Preset sheets are used in conjunction with electrician's cue sheets. The electrician's cue sheets tell the board operator what action is necessary for any particular cue, and the preset sheets are inserted between the cue sheets where they are needed. To keep everything tidy, the cue sheets and preset sheets are usually kept in a three-ring binder.

If the company has a computer board, it is advisable not only to make a backup disk of the show, but to make printout hard copies of each cue as well.

Designer's Cue Sheet

After the designer has a general idea of the intensity levels for each cue, the levels are recorded on a designer's cue sheet, also known as a tracking sheet, similar to the one illustrated in Figure 12.35. The designer's cue sheet, used by the designer during tech and dress rehearsals, allows the designer to record the rough intensity levels and timing of each cue in a systematic manner. Using one page per cue, the designer records the intensity level for each dimmer or channel that is used within the cue so that he or she will have a clear indication of what changes are being made to each dimmer or channel for every cue. Notations can be made on the sheets to indicate the purpose, function, or effect of that particular cue. Designer's cue sheets can also be kept in a loose-leaf binder so that cues can be easily added or deleted by inserting or removing sheets from the binder.

It is essential that the lighting designer and master electrician devise some type of organized system which will ensure that the lighting designer's concepts are accurately recorded and reproduced during each rehearsal and performance of the production. It is of the utmost importance that the various cue and preset sheets be clear and current; any changes in the timing, intensity, or location of any cue must be recorded so that they can be duplicated during the next rehearsal or performance.

Lighting Rehearsal

The lighting rehearsal is a period devoted to setting the intensity levels and timing for each lighting cue. The lighting designer, the electrician (board operator), the stage manager, an assistant lighting designer or assistant stage manager to **walk the cues,** a small crew to shift the scenery (if necessary), and the director are the only members of the production team who need be present for this rehearsal.

Before the lighting rehearsal, the lighting designer will have noted the position of any motivated or unmotivated lighting cues that he or she may want to use in the production. (Motivated cues are those prompted by an internal action of the play—for example, a sunset, a character's turning on a light, and the like. Unmotivated cues are prompted by an action external to the play—for example, changing the intensity of an instrument to shift the focus of action or changes the mood or tempo of the scene.) The designer will have discussed these cues with the director during one of the production conferences. The extent of this discussion varies greatly. Some directors want to know the exact location, purpose, and function of every cue, whereas other directors will leave the matter entirely up to the lighting designer. The lighting designer and board operator will have "roughed in" the intensity settings for each cue before the lighting rehearsal.

There are two primary reasons for holding a lighting rehearsal: (1) It provides the director and the lighting designer with a specific time to discuss the effect, purpose, and content of each cue when they are relatively unencumbered by other elements of the production. Additionally, it gives them an opportunity to discuss any additions, deletions, or other changes that they feel should be made in the location or duration of the cues or anything else affecting the lighting design. (2) It provides the designer, director, stage manager, and board operator with an opportunity to make sure that the paperwork affecting the lighting design is correct. Since the stage manager will be calling all of the cues, he or she can use the lighting rehearsal to make sure that the lighting cues have been noted in their appropriate positions in the prompt script. It also gives the board operator a chance to check the accuracy of the electrician's cue sheets and preset sheets.

Technical and Dress Rehearsals

Changes and adjustments to the timing, content, and positioning of lighting cues are normal during the technical and dress rehearsals. Although this can be a very frustrating time, it is essential that the lighting crew understand that the majority of the lighting cues will probably have to be adjusted; intensities and timing will be changed, entire cues will probably need to be added or deleted, instrument focus may need to be shifted, and the color in various instruments may also have to be changed. These adjustments should be considered as normal, rather than

walk the cues: To move about the stage as the cues are being run in order to show what the light looks like shining on a person rather than on the bare stage.

DIMMER/INSTRUMENT CHECK SHEET			
Dimmer	Number of Instruments	Instrument Location(s)/Color(s)	Area of Focus

FIGURE 12.36
A dimmer/instrument check sheet.

extraordinary, because it is part of the lighting designer's responsibility to develop the lighting design to work with the production concept that has evolved during the rehearsal period.

Instrument and Dimmer Check

Several routine equipment checks should be conducted before each technical or dress rehearsal and each performance. All dimmers and instruments need to be checked to determine that they are functioning properly. With the aid of a check sheet (Figure 12.36), two crew members can test all the instruments and dimmers in a short time. As the board operator turns on each dimmer, the other electrician checks to see that all of the instruments assigned to that dimmer are functioning properly. At the same time, the person checking the instruments can see if any of the color media are bleached out, torn, or otherwise in need of replacement. Each instrument should also be tested to determine if it is focused into its respective area.

The dimmer and instrument check is normally made about an hour and a half before curtain time to allow any necessary repairs, replacements, or adjustments to be made.

Chapter 13
Electrical Theory and Practice

As theatre (and everything else) enters the new millennium, it has become a pragmatic reality that students of technical theatre have to comprehend the function of electricity and electronics. The discussion that follows differentiates between the terms; electricity generally pertains to the use of the electromotive force to perform work—make lamps glow, motors run, and so on; electronics generally refers to the low-voltage circuits and devices used to control the flow of electricity.

ELECTRICITY—WHAT IS IT?

The study of electricity has to begin with a brief excursion into the not so mysterious realm of basic atomic theory. This is because some fundamental laws of electricity are based on the laws of atomic structure. For this reason we need to know a little bit about the **atom.**

The atom is the smallest complete building block in nature. But an atom is composed of even smaller particles: **protons, neutrons,** and **electrons.** These subatomic particles possess specific electrical properties. The proton has a positive charge, the neutron a neutral charge, and the electron a negative charge. The physical structure of any atom is similar to the configuration of our solar system. In the same manner that the earth rotates around the sun (Figure 13.1A), electrons follow a slightly elliptical orbit as they whirl around the **nucleus** of an atom (Figure 13.1B).

In a stable atom, the number of electrons in orbit around the nucleus is equaled by the number of protons in the nucleus. Hydrogen, the lightest and least complex atom, is a perfect example of this principle. Figure 13.2 shows the single electron of the hydrogen atom in orbit around the nucleus, which is composed of a single proton. Since the orbiting electron has a negative charge and the proton in the nucleus has a positive charge, an electrical attraction exists between them. The electron is prevented from being pulled into the nucleus by the **centrifugal force** of its orbital movement. At the same time, the electron is restrained from breaking out of orbit and flying away by the attraction. This attraction is an important underlying principle of electricity and is the basis for the first important law of electricity, the Law of Charges: *Like charges repel, and unlike charges attract.*

If it were physically possible to isolate two protons, they would defy all attempts to bring them together. The same results would occur if attempts were made to push two electrons together. But if an electron and a proton were placed

atom: The smallest particle of a chemical element that retains the structural properties of that element.

proton: A fundamental particle in the structure of the nucleus of an atom; possesses a positive charge.

neutron: A fundamental particle in the structure of the nucleus of an atom; possesses a neutral charge.

electron: A negatively charged fundamental particle that orbits around the nucleus of an atom.

nucleus: The central part of an atom; composed of protons and neutrons.

centrifugal force: Force that moves away from the center; for example, the circular motion of electrons spinning around a nucleus generates centrifugal force.

FIGURE 13.1
The structure of an atom is similar to the structure of the solar system.

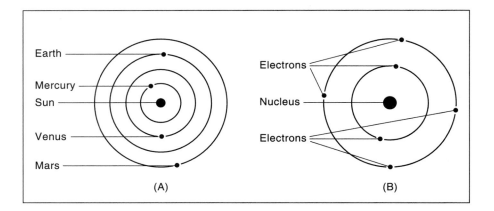

valence shell: The outermost plane of orbiting electrons in the structure of an atom.

free electron: An electron that has broken away from its "home" atom to float free.

electrical current: The flow or movement of electrons through a conductor.

ampere: The unit of measurement of electrical current.

FIGURE 13.2
A hydrogen atom.

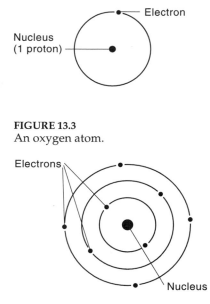

FIGURE 13.3
An oxygen atom.

in proximity, they would zip toward each other until they met. The Law of Charges is the "electrical glue" that holds the atom together.

In atoms that are more complex than hydrogen, such as oxygen (Figure 13.3), additional electrons orbit in several planes around the nucleus. These electrons are counterbalanced by an equal number of protons in the nucleus, so the atom remains in an electrically balanced, or stable, condition. These additional orbiting electrons occupy orderly spherical shells at specific distances from the nucleus. Each of these shells can hold only a certain number of electrons. When each shell is filled with its quota of electrons, a tight bonding takes place, and no additional electrons can be added. Although it is possible to dislodge an electron from one of these filled shells, it takes a relatively large amount of energy to do so.

As the structure and weight of the atom grow, the number of protons in the nucleus increases, as does the corresponding number of electrons orbiting around it. Since the electrons cannot force their way into the already filled shells, they must orbit at a greater distance. The increased distance between the orbiting electron and its counterbalancing proton in the nucleus decreases the attractive force that holds the electron in orbit.

An atom of copper has twenty-nine electrons in orbit around its nucleus. Because of copper's particular atomic structure, only a very weak force holds its outer electrons in orbit, and only a very weak force is needed to dislodge them from the outer shell, or **valence shell,** of the copper atom.

A strand of copper wire is composed of billions upon billions of copper atoms, all having the same characteristically weak valence electron. The atoms in the wire are in such close proximity to one another (most of them are intertwined with their neighbors) that the nuclei of adjacent atoms can actually exert the same or more attractive force on their neighbors' valence electrons than they do on their own. Consequently, many of the valence electrons break away from their "home" atoms, momentarily attach themselves to other atoms, or simply float freely within the confines of the wire.

If this cloud of **free electrons** meandering in the wire could be organized to move in the same direction, an **electrical current** would be generated, simply because an electrical current is defined as the flow of electrons from one point to another. The unit of measurement for this electron flow is the **ampere.**

How can free electrons be motivated to move from one point to another? The answer lies in a practical application of the Law of Charges (like charges repel, and unlike charges attract). Since the electrons have a negative charge, they are attracted to a body that has a positive charge. However, it isn't possible to create a positive charge by itself. A negative charge must be created simultaneously with the creation of a positive charge, because electrical charges are pro-

FIGURE 13.4
An electrical charge is created when electrons are transferred from one place to another.

duced by the transfer of electrons from one point to another. (In the process, electrons are neither created nor destroyed but simply transferred.) Figure 13.4 simplistically illustrates the principle that the positive charge is created by the removal of electrons and the negative charge is the result of an accumulation of electrons.

If two bodies of opposite charge are created, an electrical current could be generated if a conductor, such as a copper wire, were connected between them. Free electrons would flow from the negatively charged body to the positively charged body, as shown in Figure 13.5. The flow, or current, would continue as long as there was a difference in charge between the two bodies. This difference in the electrical charge between the bodies is called **potential** and is measured in **volts.**

The amount of voltage, or potential strength of the electrical system, is directly related to the difference in potential between the charged bodies. The greater the difference in potential between the charges, the greater that system's capacity to do work. A system with a rating of 220 volts has a greater potential capacity to do work than a 117-volt system.

potential: The difference in electrical charge between two bodies; measured in volts.

volt: The unit of measurement of electrical potential.

source: The origin of electrical potential, such as a battery or 120-volt wall outlet.

load: A device that converts electrical energy into another form of energy: A lamp converts electrical energy to light and heat; an electrical motor converts electricity to mechanical energy.

circuit: A conductive path through which electricity flows.

ELECTRICITY AT WORK

Every electrical system must have three parts: a **source,** a **load,** and a **circuit.** The source is a mechanism that provides a difference in potential, or voltage. The load is a device that uses the electricity to perform some function. The circuit is a pathway that the current follows as it flows from the negative to the positive

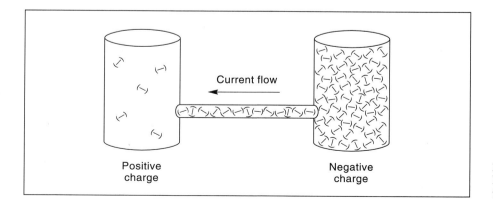

FIGURE 13.5
Electrical current flows from a negatively to a positively charged body.

FIGURE 13.6
A lamp will incandesce when current flows through it.

resistance: The opposition to electron flow within a conductor, measured in ohms; the amount of the resistance is dependent on the chemical makeup of the material through which the electricity is flowing.

FIGURE 13.7
As voltage increases, current increases.

FIGURE 13.8
As resistance increases, current decreases.

terminal of the source. (A negative terminal is created by an excess of electrons; a positive terminal, by a dearth of electrons. In batteries this electron transfer happens through a chemical reaction.)

A practical demonstration of the interrelationship between the three elements of any electrical system is provided by the example of a very simple battery and lamp, as shown in Figure 13.6. The source of this system is an ordinary flashlight battery. The load is a small incandescent lamp. The circuit is composed of copper wire. When the wires are attached to the lamp and the terminals of the battery, electrons flow from the negative to the positive terminal of the battery. As the electrons pass through the filament of the lamp, resistance to their flow causes the filament to heat up and incandesce, or give off light. The current will continue as long as the circuit is intact and there is enough voltage left in the battery to overcome the resistance within the circuit and lamp filament. When the voltage is reduced to the point that it cannot overcome the circuit resistance, the current will stop, and the lamp will no longer glow.

Ohm's Law

Although it's interesting to know that electrons flow within a circuit, unless there is some way of determining how the various parts of the circuit affect one another, there is no way to understand and predict what will happen in any electrical circuit. Fortunately, a German physicist, Georg Simon Ohm, discovered in the nineteenth century that some very basic rules apply to the functioning of electricity in a circuit. These relationships have been formalized as Ohm's Law, and they are the primary mathematical expressions used in determining electron action within a circuit. Ohm's Law states: *As voltage increases, current increases; as resistance increases, current decreases.*

The diagrams in Figures 13.7 and 13.8 will help illustrate these relationships. They show simple schematic diagrams or drawings that substitute symbols for the various parts of the circuit. The ⊣⊢ symbol represents a battery, and the -ʌʌʌ- symbol represents a **resistance,** or load, within the circuit. Figure 13.7 illustrates the first portion of Ohm's Law. The voltage of the battery in Figure 13.7A is ten volts. With this voltage, the one-ohm resistance allows a current flow of ten amperes. If the voltage is doubled to twenty volts, as shown in Figure 13.7B, and the resistance is not changed, the current will also double, to twenty amperes.

Figure 13.8 illustrates the second element of Ohm's Law. Figure 13.8A is a ten-volt system with a resistance, or load, of one ohm. This configuration allows a current flow of ten amperes. In Figure 13.8B, the voltage remains constant at ten volts, but the resistance has been doubled to two ohms, which results in a reduction of the current to five amperes.

In both cases, it is important to remember that the speed of the electron flow is constant. The increase or decrease in current flow is the result of an increase or decrease in the number of electrons flowing in the circuit.

Another way of looking at the relationships stated in Ohm's Law may help in understanding them. The voltage can be compared to the electrical pressure that causes the electrons to flow within the circuit. If more pressure (voltage) is applied, it would be logical for more electrons to flow. Since resistance is defined as opposition to the flow of electrons, any increase in the resistance would naturally cause the electron flow to decrease.

The relationships of Ohm's Law can be mathematically expressed as

$$I = \frac{E}{R}$$

Conductors, Insulators, Grounding, and Shorts

An electrical conductor is any material with an abundance of free electrons. Copper, aluminum, gold, and silver are excellent conductors. Water is also a very good conductor. Conversely, an insulator is a material with few free electrons. The lack of free electrons effectively prevents the flow of electricity through an insulator. Air, glass, paper, rubber, and most plastics are good insulators. In electrical wire, the conductor (usually copper) is surrounded with an insulator (normally rubber or plastic) to keep the electrical flow confined to the conductor and to prevent the conductor from making contact with anything else.

Safety dictates that all electrical equipment be grounded. This involves making a direct mechanical connection between the conductive housing of an electrical device and the earth. This connection is made through the ground pin on the electrical cord of the equipment. (The ground pin protrudes farther than the circuit connectors on all late-model plugs.) The ground pin makes contact with the ground wire, which, if you followed it back to the point where it enters the house or building, would be clamped to a metal rod driven five or more feet into the ground or to a metal water pipe. The purpose of the ground wire is to provide a low-resistance path for the electricity to follow in case of a short circuit between the power circuit and the device's metallic housing.

The difference between an overloaded circuit and a short circuit is really just a matter of degree. An overload occurs when the current flowing through a circuit is greater than the maximum current for which the system was designed. A short circuit is created when a very large surge of current in an overloaded circuit causes a portion of the wire, insulation, and anything else at the point of the short to melt very rapidly—basically explode.

An overload is created when a too heavy load is placed on a circuit—as when a 3,000-watt load is placed on a circuit that was designed to safely carry a load of only 2,400 watts. A short circuit, or short, happens when a very-low-resistance alternative to the primary circuit is created. These alternate paths form when a wire breaks or comes loose from its terminal or when the insulation is worn away from the conductor, allowing it to touch another conductor or come into contact with the unit's metal housing.

If a short occurs in a grounded circuit, the very-low-resistance path between the circuit and the earth invites the surge of current to follow the ground-circuit path. The high current flow activates a fuse or circuit breaker to shut off the electricity to the shorted equipment. If the circuit isn't grounded or the ground circuit doesn't function (perhaps because someone clipped off the ground pin from the plug), and you picked up the shorted device, you would be severely shocked, and possibly killed, because your body would act as the ground circuit to provide the path of least resistance between the shorted circuit and the earth.

You may find that some electrical hand tools do not have a grounding pin on the plug. The information plate attached to the tool's casing will probably carry the words *double insulated*. These tools don't need grounding, because the casing that you hold is actually a second, or outer, casing. These two layers of plastic insulators (casings) effectively isolate you from harm from any potential short.

where I = current in amperes, E = voltage in volts, and R = resistance in ohms. This basic formula can be rearranged into two other forms. Each of these can be used to find the value of the other components of the relationship:

$$E = IR$$

$$R = \frac{E}{I}$$

These mathematical expressions of Ohm's Law are extremely valuable when working with low-voltage electronic systems such as those found in microphone and low-power speaker hookups as well as the control portion of electronic dimmers.

The Power Formula

Another formula, which is a derivation of Ohm's Law, is much more useful when dealing with higher-voltage electricity. It is called the power formula. This formula is used when it is necessary to determine how much power will be consumed by an electrical circuit.

Household light bulbs, toasters, stage lamps, and electrical motors all convert electrical energy into mechanical energy, light, or heat in accomplishing their tasks. The amount of electrical energy converted, or consumed, is measured in watts. Usually the wattage figure is written on a label located somewhere on the device. Almost all household lamps have both the voltage and wattage printed on the top of the bulb. Toasters, electrical motors, and similar devices usually have a tag or label fixed on the bottom or back of the unit. The label states both the voltage and wattage of the unit. Stage-lighting lamps have this information printed on either the metal lamp base or the top of the lamp.

The power formula is usually referred to colloquially as either the "pie" or the "West Virginia" formula:

$$P = IE \qquad\qquad W = VA$$

where   where

P = power in watts W = power in watts

I = current in amperes V = voltage in volts

E = voltage in volts A = current in amperes

Both the power formula and Ohm's Law can be rearranged into the following expressions:

$$P = IE \qquad\qquad W = VA$$

$$E = \frac{P}{I} \qquad\qquad A = \frac{W}{V}$$

$$I = \frac{P}{E} \qquad\qquad V = \frac{W}{A}$$

With these three expressions of the power formula, it is possible to find the unknown quantity in an electrical circuit if the other two factors are known.

An everyday example will help illustrate the point. You want to put a desk lamp on a table, but the power cord connected to the lamp won't reach from the table to the wall outlet. You go to the hardware store to buy an extension cord, and the only information attached to the power cord indicates that it will safely carry 6 amperes of current. You know that the voltage in your apartment is 117 volts (standard household voltage in the United States). The lamp you plan to use is rated at 150 watts. To determine if the extension cord is safe to use, you will need to find out how many amperes of current the 150-watt lamp will create. To find the answer, just plug the known information ($V = 117$, $W = 150$) into the

Output and Input Voltage

Input voltage is the voltage that is fed into a device (amplifier, dimmer). The output voltage is the voltage that comes out of the same device. In stage-lighting systems, input voltage refers to the voltage that is fed to the dimmer pack (used with portable dimming systems) or rack (used with permanently installed systems). The input voltage (usually 208–240 volts) is broken down (reduced) inside the dimmer pack so that it can be used by the individual dimmers, which are designed to work at an output voltage of 117–120 VAC.

Electronic dimmers have two voltage systems: a low-voltage control circuit and a high-voltage load circuit. The low-voltage control circuit (which varies between 8 and 28 VAC depending on the manufacturer) is used to regulate the output of the high-voltage (117–120 VAC) load circuit. This means that the intensity of the lighting instruments, which are connected to the load circuit, is controlled by the low-voltage control circuit.

TABLE 13.1

American Wire Gauge Current-Capacity Chart

Gauge of wire	10	12	14	16	18
Capacity in amps	25	20	15	6	3

appropriate variation of the power formula—the variation that has the unknown variable (in this case, A) located on the left side of the equal sign:

$$A = \frac{W}{V}$$

$$A = \frac{150}{117}$$

$$A = 1.28 \text{ amps}$$

The lamp creates a current of 1.28 amperes, so the extension cord, which can carry 6 amperes, will be safe to use.

Practical Information   The output-load voltage of dimming systems in the United States is 117–120 volts alternating current (VAC). The input voltage for most portable dimming systems is 220 VAC. The input voltage for most permanently mounted dimming systems is either 220 or 440 VAC. (The figure 220 VAC is a generic term used to describe voltage in the 208–240 range. The specific voltage is important for calculating purposes and varies from community to community. The figure 440 VAC is a similarly generic term.) The voltage figure that you will use in calculating the safe loading capacity for dimmers is the output voltage—117–120 VAC.

Electrical wires and cables are designed to carry specific current loads, as shown in Table 13.1.

Any electrical system is designed to work within certain limits. If those safe limits are exceeded, the system will do one of two things: (1) If adequate protective devices (**fuses, circuit breakers**) have been placed in the circuit, those units will break the continuity of the circuit and stop the flow of electricity. (2) If there are no fuses or circuit breakers in the circuit, the various elements within the

fuse: A device to protect a circuit from an overload; has a soft metal strip that melts, breaking circuit continuity.

circuit breaker: A device to protect a circuit from an overload; has a magnetic device that trips open, breaking circuit continuity.

FIGURE 13.9
Problem number two.

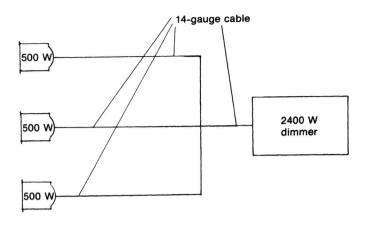

system will heat up. If the overload is sufficiently large, the elements within the system (dimmers, cables, plugs, and so on) will heat up to the point where they will either melt or burn up. If combustible material is in the immediate proximity of the overheated elements, it is very possible that a fire will be started.

The following problems illustrate how the power formula can be used to calculate the safe electrical-load limits of typical stage-lighting situations.

Problem No. 1   The output voltage of a dimmer is 120 VAC. The dimmer can handle 20 amperes of current. What is the maximum safe load that can be placed on this dimmer?

$$\text{watts} = \text{volts times amperes } (W = VA)$$
$$W = 120 \times 20$$
$$W = 2{,}400 \text{ watts}$$

The dimmer can safely carry any load up to, but not exceeding, 2,400 watts.

Problem No. 2   The system voltage is 120 VAC. The dimmer can carry 2,400 watts (2.4 kilowatts, or KW). The 14-gauge cable connecting the dimmer to the lighting instruments can carry 15 amperes (see Table 13.1). How many 500-watt lighting instruments can be safely loaded onto the dimmer (Figure 13.9)?

We already know that the dimmer can handle 2.4 KW, but we need to determine the load that can be safely carried by the cable.

$$W = VA$$
$$W = 120 \times 15$$
$$W = 1{,}800 \text{ watts}$$

The cable can carry a maximum load of 1,800 watts. To determine the number of 500-watt lighting instruments that can be carried by the cable, divide 500 into 1,800:

$$\begin{array}{r} 3.6 \\ 500\overline{)1{,}800} \end{array}$$

Theoretically, the cable can safely carry 3.6 instruments. Pragmatically, it can safely carry 3 instruments. Even though the dimmer can safely carry 4 instru-

FIGURE 13.10
A series circuit.

FIGURE 13.11
A parallel circuit.

FIGURE 13.12
A combination circuit.

ments, the single cable connecting the dimmer to the instruments can handle only the current flow generated by 3 500-watt stage lighting instruments.

Electrical Circuits

Two primary types of circuits, series and parallel, are used to distribute electricity. A third type, known as a combination circuit, combines the principles of the two.

Series Circuit In a series circuit, all of the electricity flows through every element of the circuit, as shown in Figure 13.10. In a series circuit, if any of the lamps burn out, the circuit will be broken, the electricity won't flow, and the remaining lamps will go out.

Parallel Circuit In a parallel circuit, only a portion of the electricity flows through each of the branches of the circuit. If one of the lamps shown in Figure 13.11 burns out, electricity will continue to flow in the rest of the circuit, and the other lamps will continue to glow.

Combination Circuit Any electrical circuit that uses a switch to control a light is a working example of a combination circuit. In a typical application of a combination circuit in stage lighting, a control device (switch, dimmer, fuse, circuit

Electrical Wiring

Before beginning this discussion of electric-power service, remember: These high-voltage distribution systems can kill; if you don't fully understand how the systems work, call a supervisor or licensed electrician.

A number of wiring configurations are used to distribute AC power. Figure A illustrates a typical 120-VAC service system. According to National Electrical Code (NEC) practice, in the United States the insulation of one wire is normally colored black; it is called the "hot" wire. The insulation on the other wire is white, and it is called the "neutral."

The ground wire is not included in any of these illustrations, because it should not be used as part of the electrical distribution system. However, it needs to be included in the wiring of the system, and according to code, its color should be green.

Figure B illustrates a three-wire single-phase 120/240-VAC system. The voltage between either of the two hot wires (normally black or red) and the neutral (white) will be 120 VAC. The voltage between the two hot wires will be 220–240 VAC. Electrical service is delivered to most houses with this three-wire system. At the main service box (fuse box or circuit-breaker panel),

the 120 VAC is distributed to the various lamp and wall outlets, and the 240 VAC service is usually routed only to the electric range and clothes dryer.

Figure C shows a four-wire three-phase 120/208-VAC service system. The voltage between the neutral (white) and any of the three hot lines (black) will be 120 VAC. Although the input voltage measured between any of the hot lines and ground will be 240 VAC, the voltage measured between any two of the hot lines (phases) will be 208 VAC.

High-voltage distribution systems.

Two-wire single-phase 120 VAC system

(A)

Three-wire single-phase 120/240 VAC system

(B)

Four-wire three-phase 120/208 VAC system

(C)

breaker) is used in series with the lamp load, and the lamps are wired in parallel, as shown in Figure 13.12. The series arrangement allows the switch or dimmer to exert control over the whole circuit, and the parallel wiring of the lamp outlets allows individual lamps to be inserted in or removed from the circuit without affecting its operation.

Safety Tips

Electrical Hazards

Electricity is extremely dangerous. It can burn, maim, and kill. Any piece of equipment that is connected to an electrical outlet should always be handled with caution and common sense. If you follow the safety procedures and work habits outlined below, your work with electricity can be safe and productive.

1. If you don't know what you're doing, don't do it. Ask your supervisor, or consult a trained electrician.

2. Use tools that are covered with plastic or rubber insulation when working with electricity.

3. Use wooden or fiberglass ladders when working on elevated electrical jobs. Electricity will always take the path of least resistance, and a metal ladder (and your body) provides a very-low-resistance path. If metal ladders must be used, insulate them with high-quality rubber foot pads. Movable metal scaffolds or adjustable ladders should have lockable rubber casters.

4. Disconnect any device (lighting instrument, motor, amplifier) from the circuit before you work on it. Unplug any lighting instrument before changing the lamp.

5. Use common sense: Don't touch any bare wires. Don't work in damp locations or put a drink where it could spill on an electrical or electronic component. Don't intentionally overload a circuit. Don't try to bypass fuses or circuit breakers.

6. Maintain the integrity of all ground circuits. Don't clip the ground plug off of any extension cord or power cord. When necessary, use ground-plug adapters.

7. Check cables and connectors periodically, and replace any items that show signs of cracking, chipping, or other deterioration. Cracks in the insulation of cables and connectors increase the chances of receiving a shock from the device.

8. Keep the cables and connectors clean. Remove any corrosion, paint, grease, dust, or other accumulations as soon as they become evident. These substances can act as insulation between the contacts of the connector, and if flammable they can pose a fire hazard.

9. When stage or microphone cables are not in use, coil them and hang them up. A cable will stay neatly coiled if the connectors are plugged together or if it is tied with light rope or fastened with a Velcro loop.

10. Always disconnect a plug by pulling on the body of the connector, not the cable. Pulling on the cable puts an unnecessary strain on the cable clamp and will eventually defeat the clamp. When the cable clamp no longer functions, pulling on the cable places the strain directly on the electrical connections.

11. Be sure that all elements of a cable are of the same electrical rating: twelve-gauge cable (capable of carrying twenty amperes of current) should have only twenty-ampere-rated connectors.

Electrical Current

There are two types of electrical current: direct and alternating.

Direct Current In direct current (DC), the electron flow is in one direction only. The battery demonstration discussed in a previous section is an example of direct current. The flow of the current is always from the negative terminal of

(A)

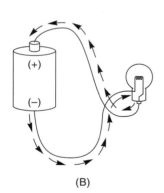

(B)

a battery to its positive terminal. All batteries are examples of direct-current sources.

Alternating Current   The overwhelming majority of electrical power generated by power stations throughout the world is alternating current (AC). The electron flow in AC is the same as in DC with one exception: The current flow periodically changes polarity, which causes the electron flow to change direction. In the United States, alternating current changes polarity at the rate of sixty cycles per second (60 Hz). This means that the electricity changes polarity (direction) every 1/120th of a second, as shown in Figure 13.13.

An example may help to explain this phenomenon. If the wires connected to the terminals of a battery, as shown in Figure 13.14A, were reversed (Figure 13.14B), the lamp would still emit light, but the current flow would have changed directions. Alternating current works like this example, except that the direction of current flow changes direction every 1/120th of a second.

The principal advantages of AC over DC are that AC is easier and cheaper to generate and that there is less voltage loss when the electricity is transmitted over a great distance.

This chapter has provided a brief glance at the nature and uses of electricity. Anyone who is thinking about a career in any area of theatrical design or production would be wise to take a course or two in practical electronics as well as making an intensive study of standard electrical-wiring practice.

Chapter 14
Lighting Production

You might dream up the most imaginative lighting design ever conceived, but unless you know how to execute that design, you won't get far as a lighting designer. In this chapter, we explore the tools and technology that lighting designers use.

It is very easy to become enamored of the various tools (some would call them toys) of lighting design. The lighting instruments and dimmers as well as the control and distribution systems are not ends in themselves, however; they are simply the metaphorical mallet and chisels that lighting designers use to create their sculptures in light.

Not so long ago it wasn't necessary for a practitioner of scenic or lighting design or technical production to have a thorough knowledge of electricity and electronics. Today that simply isn't true. Each of these technical areas uses a plethora of electronically controlled devices, and anyone who works in these areas needs to have a *thorough* working knowledge of both electricity and electronics. To help you prepare, the previous chapter presented a comprehensive discussion of the fundamentals of electricity and electronics.

LENSES

The angle of the beam of light emitted by the most frequently used stage lighting instruments is controlled by the optical properties of the lenses used with those instruments. Lenses refract light, which means that they redirect, or deflect, light from its normally straight path. The amount of deflection depends on the angle of intersection between the light ray and the surface of the lens, as well as the density of the medium through which the light is passing.

When a light ray passes from one medium into another of greater density—for example, from air into glass—it bends away from its original direction of travel. When the light ray passes out the other side of the glass and back into the air, it bends back toward its original line of travel. The angle or amount of this deflection depends on the angle of intersection between the light ray and the glass. If the glass has parallel sides, as illustrated in Figure 14.1, the light ray will be deflected in one direction when it enters the glass, then back the same amount in the opposite direction when it emerges from the glass on the other side. However, typical lenses do not have parallel sides. Figure 14.2 illustrates two plano-convex lenses. Unlike window glass, which redirects light passing through it in a direction parallel to its original line of travel, a curved-face lens causes light passing through it to be deflected away from its original direction of travel. The greater the curvature of the lens face, the greater the dispersion of any beam of light passing through it.

← NOT NECESSARILY TRUE

FIGURE 14.1
Light rays are deflected when they pass through a lens.

FIGURE 14.2
The greater the curvature of the convex face of a lens, the greater the angle of deflection, and vice versa.

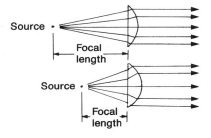

focal length: The distance from the lens at which the light rays converge into a point; for lenses used in stage lighting instruments the focal length is most frequently measured in even inches.

plano-convex lens: A lens with one flat and one outward-curving face.

diffuse: To soften the appearance of light by using a translucent filtering element to scatter the rays.

The distance between the convergence point of a plano-convex lens—labeled "Source" in Figure 14.2—and the plano, or flat, face of the lens is referred to as the **focal length** of the lens.

The focal length of a lens affects the angle of the beam of light emitted by that lens. When considered in relation to the diameter of the lens, the shorter the focal length, the wider the beam of light it produces. A standard stage lighting instrument—the ellipsoidal reflector spotlight (ERS)—can be used to demonstrate this principle. If it is equipped with a lens six inches in diameter that has a focal length of nine inches (known as a 6 × 9), it will produce a wider beam of light than an instrument equipped with a 6 × 12 lens. Similarly, a 6 × 12 ERS produces a wider beam of light than a 6 × 16 ERS.

The focal length of a **plano-convex lens** is determined by the curvature of the convex face of the lens. The greater the curvature, the shorter the focal length.

Three primary types of lens systems are used with theatrical lighting instruments: the double plano-convex lens train, the step lens, and the Fresnel lens.

Double Plano-Convex Lens Train

The double plano-convex lens train consists of two plano-convex lenses placed with their convex surfaces toward each other, as shown in Figure 14.3. This double configuration provides the same optical properties as a single lens of greater thickness and curvature, and the total thickness of the two lenses is less than the thickness of the optically comparable single lens. The single lens with short focal length is not used in lighting instruments, because its thickness makes it susceptible to heat fracture. The thicker single lens also transmits less light than its thinner optical equivalent in the double plano-convex lens system.

FIGURE 14.3
Double plano-convex lens train.

Step Lens

A step lens retains the optical characteristics and shape of a plano-convex lens, but the glass on the flat side is cut away in steps, as shown in Figure 14.4. The stepping process gives the lens the optical properties of a thick, short-focal-length, plano-convex lens while eliminating its negative characteristics.

An inherent property of step lenses is the prismatic effect caused by the steps themselves. Light passing through the steps at a shallow angle tends to create a spectral flare in the same manner that a prism breaks white light into a rainbow. Finishing the edges of the steps with a flat-black ceramic coating eliminates the spectral breakdown in most step lenses and does not interfere with the light passing through the rest of the lens (Figure 14.5).

FIGURE 14.4
A step lens.

FIGURE 14.5
A black ceramic coating prevents spectral breakdown.

FIGURE 14.6
A Fresnel lens.

Fresnel Lens

The Fresnel lens is a type of step lens with the glass cut away from the convex face of the lens instead of its plano side, as shown in Figure 14.6. The advantages of the Fresnel lens are the same as for the step lens; reduction of the thickness of the lens allows more light transmission and lessens the chances of heat fracture.

Fresnel lenses are primarily used in Fresnel spotlights. Occasionally you may encounter an older ERS with a Fresnel-type lens. You'll be able to identify it by the black ceramic coating applied to the vertical faces of the steps to eliminate spectral flare. Lenses for use in Fresnel spotlights don't have this coating, and the plano side of the lens is finished with a surface treatment to **diffuse** light. The diffusing treatment generally makes the plano side of the lens appear as though it has been sandblasted or dimpled, or it may be finished with a series of small rectangular indentations. Regardless of the appearance of the treatment, its purpose is to soften the light to create the characteristically soft, luminescent light of the Fresnel spotlight.

LAMPS

Each stage lighting instrument requires some type of lamp to produce light. The three primary sources used for stage lighting are the standard incandescent lamp, the tungsten-halogen lamp, and the encapsulated arc.

Incandescent Lamp

The standard incandescent lamp contains a tungsten **filament** that is placed in an inert gas environment inside the lamp **bulb,** as shown in Figure 14.7. The inert gas within the bulb is not pure and contains some oxygen. As an electrical current passes through the filament, heating it to incandescence, particles of tungsten are released. These particles are deposited to form the dark coating frequently found on the inside of older bulbs or envelopes. Eventually, the filament weakens sufficiently to cause it to break. The average life expectancy of a regular incandescent lamp designed for use in stage lighting instruments ranges anywhere from fifty to approximately two hundred hours. The life rating for a lamp does not mean that the light will burn out in the rated time. It means that the original output of the lamp will be reduced by 40 percent by the tungsten buildup on the inside of the bulb. Most lamps continue to burn long after their rated life, but at a significantly reduced output.

Tungsten-Halogen Lamp

Although it looks rather different than its cousin, the tungsten-halogen (T-H) lamp (Figure 14.8) is primarily the same as the standard incandescent lamp in all respects but one. That principal difference is that the atmosphere inside the bulb of the T-H lamp is a halogen, or chemically active, gas instead of an inert gas. As the particles of tungsten are released from the filament, they unite with the halogen gas to form a compound that is attracted back to the filament. The particles of tungsten reunite with the filament, and the halogen gas is released to repeat this chemical action. Because of the halogen cycle, the tungsten particles are not deposited on the inside of the bulb, and the filament of the T-H lamp is constantly being replenished. This results in a significantly longer life expectancy for the T-H lamp. Many T-H lamps designed for stage lighting instruments are rated from 150 to 2,000 hours, as shown in Figure 14.9.

The halogen cycle becomes active only in a high-temperature environment. To achieve this goal, the T-H filament is encased within a small, highly heat-resistant synthetic quartz envelope. The heat generated by the filament is confined within the small space, and the resultant temperatures are much higher than if a larger bulb were used.

Arc Sources

An electric arc that produces a brilliantly blue white light is created when an electric current jumps the air gap between two electrodes. An arc is used as the source on some followspots.

When an arc is struck in an oxygen-rich environment such as air, the electrodes are consumed in the same way that a welding rod deteriorates during arc welding. If the arc is encapsulated in a noncorrosive atmosphere, however, the

filament: The light-producing element of a lamp; usually made of tungsten wire.

bulb: The Pyrex glass or synthetic quartz container for a lamp filament and gaseous environment. Synonymous with envelope.

FIGURE 14.7
A standard incandescent lamp.

FIGURE 14.8
A tungsten-halogen incandescent lamp.

FIGURE 14.9
The rated life of tungsten-halogen lamps varies according to their color temperature and output. Generally, the higher the output, the higher the color temperature and the shorter the life (and conversely). (Courtesy of Sylvania Lighting Products.)

Sylvania Tungsten-Halogen Lamps

MEDIUM PREFOCUS – 3½" LCL – REPLACEMENT*

ANSI Code	Watts	Volts	Bulb	Fila-ment	Base	Lumens	Color Temp. (°K)	Avg. Rated Life (Hrs.)	LCL In.	LCL mm	MOL In.	MOL mm
EGC/EGD	500	120	T-4	CC8	Med. Pf.	13,000	3200	150	3½	88.9	5½	139.7
EGE	500	120	T-4	CC8	Med. Pf.	10,000	3000	2000	3½	88.9	5½	139.7
EGF	750	120	T-4	CC8	Med. Pf.	20,000	3200	250	3½	88.9	5½	139.7
EGG	750	120	T-5	CC8	Med. Pf.	15,000	3000	2000	3½	88.9	5½	139.7
DNT/FMD	750	120	—	—	Med. Pf.	17,000	3050	500	3½	88.9	6⅛	155.6
EGJ	1000	120	T-6	CC8	Med. Pf.	25,500	3200	400	3½	88.9	5¾	146.0
EGK	1000	120	T-6†	CC8	Med. Pf.	24,500	3200	400	—	—	5¾	146.0
DNV/FME	1000	120	—	—	Med. Pf.	27,500	3200	200	3½	88.9	6⅛	155.6

*Family of lamps which are replacements for existing incandescent T12 types primarily utilized in ellipsoidal reflector spotlights.
†Frosted

electrodes deteriorate extremely slowly. Encapsulated arcs such as the xenon and HMI (metal halide) lamps are frequently used in followspots and kinetic or moving light fixtures. Neither arc nor encapsulated arc sources can be dimmed, so they normally are not used in nonautomated stage lighting instruments.

Color Temperature

All the standard light sources appear to be white. They are actually a variety of colors, however, and these colors can be identified by using the color-temperature scale.

The color-temperature scale was originally determined by heating a device known as a blackbody radiator. As the blackbody was heated, its color was read at specific temperatures by a **spectrometer**. The color-temperature scale, measured in degrees Kelvin (K), was the result of this experiment. Table 14.1 shows the color temperatures of a number of standard sources.

There is a loose, but fairly constant, correlation among color temperature, light output, and lamp life. Generally speaking, the higher the light output of a lamp (which is measured in lumens), the higher its color temperature and the shorter its rated life. A comparison of the specifications for similar lamps such as the EGC/EGD and the EGE (the American National Standards Institute codes for two commonly used theatrical lamps) illustrates this relationship (Figure 14.9).

Although it isn't essential that the color temperatures of all lamps used to light a production be the same, the instruments that are going to be **gelled** with color media of a specific hue are generally equipped with lamps of the same color temperature so that the color of the resultant light will be uniform.

spectrometer: A device for measuring specific wavelengths of light.

gel: To put a color filter into a color frame and place it in the color-frame holder of a lighting instrument.

TABLE 14.1
Color Temperature of Some Common Sources

Color Temperature	Light Source
6,500	Xenon
6,000	
5,500	HMI (halide metal incandescent)
5,000	Sunshine
4,500	
4,000	Fluorescent (cool white)
3,500	
3,000	Theatrical Incandescent
2,500	(standard and tungsten-halogen)
2,000	

Lamp Structure

All lamps, regardless of shape or type, are composed of three basic parts: bulb, base, and filament, as shown in Figure 14.10.

Bulb   The bulb is the Pyrex or synthetic quartz envelope that encases the filament and acts as a container for the gas-filled atmosphere of the lamp. The shape and size of the bulb are determined by the position and shape of the filament, the burning position of the lamp within the lighting instrument, and the heat-dissipation requirements of the lamp. Figure 14.11 illustrates common incandescent bulb shapes. Bulb sizes vary depending on individual lamp requirements.

The diameter of the bulb is indicated by a figure representing eighths of an inch. Thus the T-4 bulbs listed under the "Bulb" heading in Figure 14.9 are T-shaped and have a diameter of ⅛—or ½—inch, and the MR16 lamp illustrated in Figure 14.14 has a diameter of roughly 2 inches.

Base   The lamp base secures the lamp in the socket and provides the electrical contact points between the socket and the filament. There are several styles of lamp bases, as illustrated in Figure 14.12. Generally, large, high-wattage incandescent lamps have the larger bases. Figure 14.12 shows not only the different bases but also the relative size relationship that each base has to the others. The candelabra base is approximately ½ inch in diameter, the medium-size bases are approximately 1 inch in diameter, and the mogul bases are about 1½ inches across.

The prefocus, bipost, and two-pin bases are used for instruments that need the filament in a specific location in relation to the reflector—such as the ERS or Fresnel spotlight.

Filament   Various lamp filaments are available, each designed to perform a particular function. All filaments for stage-lighting lamps are made of tungsten wire, usually tightly coiled, and strung in one of the general configurations shown in Figure 14.13.

MR16 Lamps

These small-diameter (approximately 2 inches), low-voltage, low-wattage lamps integrate a small, coiled-filament tungsten-halogen lamp into a focusing mirrored

FIGURE 14.10
Lamp structure.

Filament

Bulb or envelope

Base

FIGURE 14.11
Common incandescent lamp shapes.

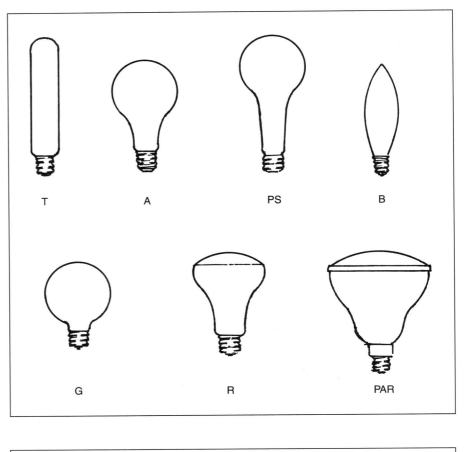

FIGURE 14.12
Typical lamp bases.

reflector (hence the designation MR16). The lamp, shown in Figure 14.14, is available in a variety of voltages and wattages as well as several beam-angle widths from very narrow to flood. The small size of the lamps allows fixtures to be created that are small in size and weight with light output characteristics similar, and in some cases superior, to the output of their larger-lamped counterparts. Each low-voltage fixture contains a transformer that reduces the input voltage from the dimmer to match the specific voltage of the lamp.

FIGURE 14.13
Filament styles.

Light Output of Lamps

The output of an incandescent lamp, while related to the lamp wattage, is primarily a function of the size and composition of the filament. This output is measured in lumens. Generally speaking, if two lamps have the same wattage but one has a smaller filament, the smaller-filament lamp will have a higher lumen output but a shorter life expectancy, as shown in Table 14.2.

Color Media

Three transparent color media are used to color the light output of stage lighting instruments. Each medium has its own particular characteristics and advantages.

Plastic   The majority of filters used in theatrical lighting are generally made of either Mylar or polyester because of the rugged, long-lasting, heat-resistant qualities of these plastics. They are available in a wide and ever-increasing variety of colors. Light, heat, and ultraviolet radiation from T-H lamps tend to bleach the color out of plastic **gels.** Low-saturation tints bleach out relatively slowly, while heavily saturated colors such as dark blues can bleach out within a few hours.

Glass   Glass filters are used infrequently because they are heavy and expensive, and they shatter if dropped. The most prominent use of glass is in **roundels,** the glass filters used with striplights. Roundels are generally available in red, blue, green, amber, and clear. Roundels normally have a slight diffusing treatment to help spread the light more evenly.

Dichroic   Dichroic filters are a relatively new addition to theatrical color media. Dichroic filters do not work in the same way as other color media. Plastic and glass filters allow their own color to pass through the filter while *absorbing* the undesired colors. Dichroic filters *reflect* the unwanted colors. To produce a particular color, you use a dichroic filter to remove its complementary. To illustrate, if you want to produce the color red from a beam of white light, you use a dichroic filter that reflects the complementary of red (cyan). Removing the cyan from white light produces red light.

FIGURE 14.14
An MR16 lamp.

gel: Generic term referring to flexible (gelatin or plastic) color media.

roundel: A glass color medium for use with striplights; frequently has diffusing properties.

TABLE 14.2
Comparison of Same Wattage / Different Output Lamps

Watts	Sylvania Ordering Abbreviation	Other Designation	NAED Code	Standard Case Quantity	Volts	Color Temperature (°K)	Nominal Lumens	Average Rated Life (hr)	Filament Class	Fused Silica Bulb Finish	Lighted Length (in.)
1,000	DXN	—	53993	12	120	3,400	33,500	30	CC-8	Clear	11/16
1,000	DXW	—	53997	12	120	3,200	28,000	150	CC-8	Clear	13/16
1,000	FBY	Frosted DXW	53996	12	120	3,200	26,000	150	CC-8	Frosted	—
1,000	FBZ	Frosted DXN	53999	12	120	3,400	31,500	30	CC-8	Frosted	—
1,000	BRH	—	54563	12	120	3,350	30,000	75	CC-8	Clear	—

Source: OSRAM SYLVANIA INC.

There are tangible advantages to this system of filtration. For one, the output of the resultant light is measurably greater (light input/light output) than that produced with traditional plastic and glass filters. Another advantage of dichroics is the property of reflecting rather than absorbing unwanted wavelengths of electromagnetic radiation (remember that light is just a small segment of the electromagnetic spectrum). Cold mirrors are dichroic filters that are coated to reflect the visible spectrum and allow infrared radiation (heat) to pass. A reflector made with a cold-mirror finish vents heat *through* the reflector, which makes the reflected light considerably cooler. Hot mirrors, as you would expect, are just the reverse. They reflect infrared radiation and allow the visible spectrum to pass. Hot mirrors are used as heat filters in projectors as well as several of the kinetic instruments discussed in another section of this chapter.

Further advantages of dichroic filters are that the filters, if made of glass, are extremely heat-resistant and that color fade is all but nonexistent. The range of colors currently available in dichroic filters for theatrical instruments is relatively limited, but it is anticipated that there will be more colors available as the use of these filters increases.

The primary disadvantage of dichroics is their cost. However, in professional situations where replacing the color in a lamp frequently requires bringing in a crew on a four-hour call, it may be cost-effective to use dichroic filters when you consider that heavily saturated plastic filters need to be replaced after two to three hours of use.

LIGHTING INSTRUMENTS

A variety of lighting instruments are used in the theatre, but the ellipsoidal reflector spotlight and the Fresnel spotlight are the real workhorses for the lighting designer.

Ellipsoidal Reflector Spotlight

The light produced by an ellipsoidal reflector spotlight (ERS) has a narrow beam width and is capable of traveling long distances. The quality of the light produced by this instrument, also generically known by the trade name Leko, can be characterized as generally hard edged with little diffusion. The shape of the beam is controlled by internally mounted shutters. The spill light from an ERS—that is, any light that escapes past the edge of the beam—is minimal. Because of

FIGURE 14.15
Ellipsoidal reflector spotlights. (A)
Source Four courtesy of Electronic
Theatre Controls (ETC); (B) Pacific
courtesy of Selecon Performance
Lighting; (C) Exploded view
courtesy of Lee Colortran.

all these characteristics, ERS's are the primary lighting tool of the designer. Several manufacturers' versions of the ERS, and an exploded view showing the main parts of the ellipsoidal reflector spotlight, are shown in Figure 14.15.

General Operating Principles   The reflector of an ERS is a truncated conical ellipse, which has properties that are uniquely suited to focusing light. The conical elliptical reflector shown in Figure 14.16A has two focal points, F1 and F2. Light emitted by a light source at F1 will reflect off the walls of the conical ellipse and pass through F2. If half of the elliptical reflector were removed (Figure 14.16B), light emitted from the source at F1 would again pass through F2, although some of the light would pass out of the open end of the reflector and be lost.

The ERS operates on this basic principle of gathering light from one focal point (F1) and focusing it on the second focal point (F2). Some ERS's have a kickback reflector placed at the open end of the conical ellipse to redirect any spill light back into the reflector, as shown in Figure 14.16C. The shutters, made of stainless steel or some other highly heat-resistant metal, are located in a plane close to the second focal point to shape the light.

Figure 14.17 shows a cross section of an axial-mount ERS, so called because the lamp is placed on the optical, or centerline, axis of the instrument. This configuration, now standard for almost all ERS's designed since approximately 1985, was made possible by the development of the tungsten-halogen lamp. Compare the position of the lamp in the axial-mount instrument (Figure 14.17) with the instrument shown in Figure 14.18, an ERS designed for the larger incandescent T-shaped lamp, which predates the T-H lamp. Note how the lamp filament is still located at the focal point of the ellipsoidal reflector even though the lamp is mounted in a different position.

FIGURE 14.16
Optical properties of a conical
ellipse reflector.

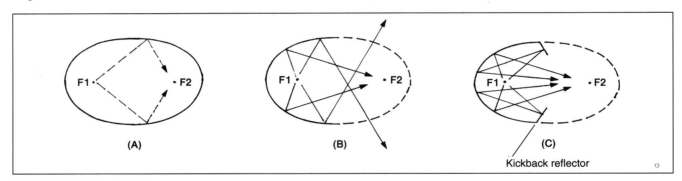

FIGURE 14.17
Cutaway view of an axial-mount
ellipsoidal reflector spotlight.

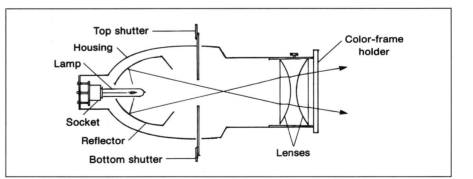

FIGURE 14.18
Cutaway view of an ellipsoidal
reflector spotlight designed for
a standard incandescent lamp.

The lens is placed at a point in front of the shutters to focus the light into the desired field angle, as shown in Figures 14.17 and 14.18. ERS's are equipped with one of three lens systems: a double plano-convex lens train, a step lens, or, on a few older models, a Fresnel lens without the diffusing treatment on the plano face. Although there may be slight differences in light output and quality, the three types generally work equally well.

The **zoom ellipse,** more officially known as the variable-focal-length ERS (Figure 14.19), is an extremely versatile instrument. This variation of the standard ERS has lenses that can slide forward or backward to change the focal length of the instrument. Changing the focal length affects the beam and field angles of the instrument, with those angles widening as the focal length becomes shorter. The field angle of most zoom ellipses can be varied between approximately twenty and forty-five degrees.

Recent additions to the ERS family, the ETC Source Four, the Source Four Jr., and the Altman Shakespeare 600 series, use an excellent innovation in theatrical instrument design—cold mirror reflectors. These reflectors, which are made of heavy Pyrex glass, have an applied dichroic coating that reflects visible light while transmitting infrared (heat) wavelengths. This means that the majority of the heat generated by the lamp *passes through* the reflector and is vented out the rear of the instrument rather than being reflected with the rest of the light. The result is less heat deterioration of the shutters, iris, and gobos, as well as longer color media life.

More innovative ERS design is evident in the Pacific family of fixtures by Selecon. This instrument has a unique shape because it is designed to reflect light off of a dichroic cold mirror before the light strikes the gate as shown in Figure 14.20. The cold mirror reflects visible light but passes infrared (heat) and ultraviolet light through the mirror. A heat sink vents the infrared heat outside of the housing. The net effect is a much cooler beam of light which, in turn, results in longer shutter and color media life. Additionally, the lens tube rotates 360 degrees, which allows the shutters to be positioned to make the most appropriate **shutter cut.**

Table 14.3 lists the beam and field angles in degrees of arc for several varieties of six-inch ERS's. As mentioned in Chapter 12, the beam angle (Figure 14.21) is that point where the intensity of the cone of light emitted by the instrument diminishes to 50 percent of its intensity as compared with the center of the beam. The field angle is that point where the light diminishes to 10 percent of the output of the center of the beam.

Accessories   The most basic accessory designed for use with an ERS is the **color frame** (Figure 14.22), a lightweight metal or heat-resistant fiber holder for plastic colored media. The color frame is inserted into the holder on the front of the ERS to color the light.

The **gobo** (Figure 14.23), also known as a pattern, template, or cookie, is a lightweight metal cutout that turns the ERS into a pattern projector. Most ERS's are equipped with a built-in pattern slot located adjacent to the shutter plane. A wide variety of commercially designed gobos, usually made of stainless steel, are available from scenic and lighting supply houses. Gobos can be constructed from metal offset printing sheets or from heavyweight disposable aluminum cookware (roasting pans, pie plates), as shown in Figure 14.24. Offset printing sheets are thin, flexible aluminum sheets, which can usually be obtained from local newspaper publishers at low cost. They can withstand the heat generated by an ERS, are stiff enough to prevent flexing or buckling, and can be worked easily with scissors, chisels, or a **Dremel tool.** The disposable aluminum pie plates are satisfactory for making cloud gobos and similar patterns that have little intricate

FIGURE 14.19
A continuously variable-focal-length ellipsoidal reflector spotlight. (Courtesy of Altman Stage Lighting.)

zoom ellipse: An ellipsoidal reflector spotlight with movable lenses that allow the focal length to be changed.

shutter cut: The shadow line created by the edge of the shutter when it is inserted into the beam of light emitted by an ERS.

color frame: A lightweight metal holder for color media that fits in a holder at the front of a lighting instrument.

gobo: A thin metal template inserted into an ellipsoidal reflector spotlight to project a shadow pattern of light.

Dremel tool: A hand-held router similar to a dentist's drill, which can be equipped with a number of bits for grinding, cutting, or carving of wood, plastic, and metal.

FIGURE 14.20
Light is bounced off a cold mirror reflector in the Selecon Pacific ERS. (Courtesy of Selecon.)

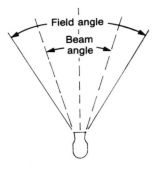

FIGURE 14.21
Beam and field angles.

TABLE 14.3
Beam / Field Angles for Typical ERS's*

Instrument Type	Beam Angle	Field Angle	Maximum Effective Range†
6 × 9	16°	37°	35 feet
6 × 12	11°	26°	50 feet
6 × 16	9°	18°	60 feet
20°	10°	20°	70 feet
30°	12°	30°	60 feet
40°	15°	40°	55 feet

*All data are approximate but typical. Specific data varies with manufacturer.
†Determined by point at which output diminishes to 50 footcandles.

detail. The aluminum used in these products is about one-third as thick as the offset printing sheets and will vaporize under the high heat generated by the instrument lamp if the pattern is too detailed. It is much better to make intricately designed gobos from offset printing sheets or from stainless steel.

Colored glass gobos—using dichroic filters to create the color—are commercially available from manufacturers such as American Market and Rosco. Additionally, custom gobos can be designed with a software program such as Photoshop and manufactured by the custom divisions of American Market and Rosco, among others.

Another useful accessory for an ERS is the **iris** (Figure 14.25). The iris varies the size of the circular pattern produced by an ERS. It is mounted in the shutter plane, and the size of the aperture is controlled by an external handle.

iris: A device with movable overlapping metal plates, used with an ellipsoidal reflector spotlight to change the size of the circular pattern of light.

Fresnel Spotlight

The Fresnel spotlight produces a soft, diffused, luminescent light. Some Fresnel spotlights are shown in Figure 14.26. When the instrument is focused on narrow beam, or spot, as shown in Figure 14.27A, it produces a beam with a central hot spot that rapidly loses intensity toward the edge. When the instrument is focused on wide beam, or flood (Figure 14.27B), it produces a smooth wash of light.

The standard Fresnel spotlight is equipped with a Fresnel lens producing a circular beam of light. The oval-beam Fresnel lens (Figure 14.28) has the same luminescent and optical qualities as its round-beam counterpart but produces an oval, instead of round, beam of light.

Lamp Comparison Chart

Although the specific lamp that is used with any instrument depends on the design of the instrument, some fairly standard wattages are used with various families of instruments.

Instrument	Standard Lamp-Wattage Range
4-inch ERS	250–600
6-inch ERS	500–1,000
8-inch ERS	1,000–2,000
6-inch Fresnel	250–750
8-inch Fresnel	750–1,000
Scoop	350–1,500
Striplight	150–500
Followspot (incandescent)	1,000–2,000

FIGURE 14.22
A color frame.

(A)

(B)

FIGURE 14.23
(A) A gobo and (B) the pattern that the gobo projects.

FIGURE 14.24
Gobos can be built in the shop by cutting the pattern out of disposable aluminum cookware.

FIGURE 14.25
An ellipsoidal reflector spotlight equipped with an iris.

(A)　　　　　　　　(B)

FIGURE 14.26
Fresnel spotlights. (Courtesy of Strand Lighting and Colortran.)

General Operating Principles　The Fresnel spotlight is simple. The instrument housing holds the lens and provides a mounting platform for the socket, lamp, and reflector assembly, which are mounted on a small sled that moves closer to or farther from the lens during focusing, as shown in Figure 14.29. Figure 14.30A shows the instrument on spot focus with the socket and reflector assembly moved toward the back of the instrument housing. In this position, most of the light is concentrated into a hot spot in the center of the beam. Fig-

FIGURE 14.27
The Fresnel spotlight can be focused on spot (A) or flood (B).

(A)　　　　　　　　(B)

FIGURE 14.28
An oval-beam lens for a Fresnel spotlight.

FIGURE 14.29
A cutaway view of a Fresnel spotlight.

ure 14.30B shows the instrument on flood focus, with the socket and reflector assembly moved all the way forward. This creates a smooth wash of light from edge to edge, with only a small, almost undetectable, hot spot in the center of the beam.

Accessories The primary, and almost indispensable, accessory for the Fresnel spotlight is the **barn door** (Figure 14.31). Its flippers are movable and can be swung into the beam of light until they cut off as much light as desired.

Another accessory is the **funnel** (Figure 14.32). The funnel, like the barn door, fits into the color-frame slot on the front of the instrument. The circular pattern of light that it creates is dependent on the diameter of the funnel's cone.

barn door: An accessory for a Fresnel spotlight whose movable flippers are swung into the beam to control it.

funnel: An accessory for a Fresnel spotlight that masks the beam to create a circular pattern; also called a snoot or a top hat.

Striplight

The striplight is used to create a smooth wash of light. It resembles a long trough with a series of lamps inside, as shown in Figure 14.33. Striplights are available in a variety of lengths and configurations, but they are most often between four and ten feet in length.

The individual lights within the instrument are wired in parallel to form three or four circuits, as shown in the block diagram of Figure 14.34. This type of

FIGURE 14.30
The sled holding the lamp/reflector assembly is (A) moved backward to produce a hot spot in the middle of the beam or (B) moved forward to produce a smooth wash of light.

FIGURE 14.31
A four-flipper barn door.

FIGURE 14.32
Funnels are used to create small circular patterns of light with a Fresnel spotlight.

configuration provides designers with the opportunity to mix and blend color if they gel all the lamps of each circuit with a separate color. By placing each circuit of the striplight on a separate dimmer, designers can manipulate the intensities of the individual colors to mix the desired resultant hue. To create the maximum potential for color mixing, designers frequently color the individual circuits of a three-circuit striplight with the primary colors in light (red, blue, and green). If a four-circuit striplight is used, the fourth circuit is frequently gelled with amber. It is not mandatory that striplights be colored with red, blue, and green; if the designer knows that he or she will be working in a narrow color spectrum, it is usually preferable to color the individual circuits in the appropriate hues.

Striplights are primarily used to light background drops and cycloramas, although they can be used in any position wherever a diffused, general wash of light is desired. Striplights are equipped to hold plastic color media as well as roundels (Figure 14.35), which are glass color media that have diffusing properties to help blend the light. Roundels are available in the primary colors as well as amber, frosted, and clear.

FIGURE 14.33
Striplights. (A) A standard striplight. (Courtesy of Colortran.) (B) A "mini" striplight. The lamps are low-voltage MR16 lamps allowing the fixture to be relatively small—6 feet long, 3½ inches wide, and 7 inches deep. (Courtesy of Strand Lighting.)

(A)

(B)

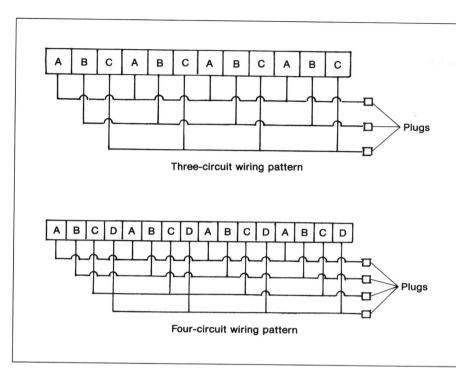

Three-circuit wiring pattern

Four-circuit wiring pattern

Plugs

Plugs

FIGURE 14.34
Circuiting pattern for striplights.

FIGURE 14.35
Roundels are glass filters used with striplights.

Cyc Light

The cyc light (Figure 14.36) is superior to the striplight for creating a smooth wash of light over the expanse of a cyc or drop. This fairly new type of fixture uses an eccentric reflector to create such a wash from only seven or eight feet away. The cyc light emits a much smoother light than does the striplight, and it is equipped with a color-frame holder so that the light can be colored as desired.

FIGURE 14.36
A four-circuit cyc light. (Far Cyc courtesy of Colortran.)

Ellipsoidal Reflector Floodlight

The ellipsoidal reflector floodlight (Figure 14.37), also known as the scoop, is primarily used to light drops and cycloramas. It is a lensless instrument that has the light-focusing characteristics of a conical ellipsoidal reflector, which provides a wide, smooth wash of light. It is equipped with a large color-frame holder that, in many cases, has wire restraining lines crisscrossed over the circular opening to prevent the color medium from falling out. The scoop is available in a variety of sizes, but in the theatre the fourteen-, sixteen-, and eighteen-inch diameters are most commonly used.

FIGURE 14.37
An ellipsoidal reflector floodlight. (Courtesy of Kliegl Bros.)

Beam Projector

The beam projector (Figure 14.38) is a lensless instrument with a parabolic primary reflector and a spherical secondary reflector. This now obsolete instrument produces a very intense shaft of light that has little diffusion and cannot be easily controlled or modified.

The parabolic reflector focuses the light into parallel rays, and the spherical reflector redirects the light emitted from the front of the lamp back through the filament to the parabolic reflector. The beam projector's characteristically hard-

FIGURE 14.38
A beam projector. (Courtesy of Kliegl Bros.)

(A)   (B)

FIGURE 14.39
(A) A PAR 64 can. (Courtesy of Altman Stage Lighting.) (B) A Source Four PAR. (Courtesy of ETC.)

edged, intense beam of light makes it desirable for creating shafts of sunlight and in similar situations. The beam projector effectively has been replaced by the PAR can.

PAR Can

The parabolic aluminized reflector, or PAR, is a sealed-beam lamp similar to the headlight of an automobile. The lamp housing, known as a PAR can (Figure 14.39), performs no function other than safely holding the lamp and its color media.

The most widely used size of PAR can is designed to hold the PAR 64, a 1000-watt lamp about eight inches in diameter. The PAR 64 lamp is available in a variety of beam and field angles, as shown in Table 14.4. The PAR 64 produces a powerfully intense oval punch of light, yet it has a soft edge. It is used extensively in dance and concert lighting and is finding increased usage in theatre lighting because of its relatively low cost, portability, durability, and light weight.

Followspot

The followspot is used when a high-intensity, hard-edged beam of light is required to follow a moving performer. Followspots are manufactured in a variety

TABLE 14.4
Beam and Field Angles for Various PAR 64 Configurations

PAR 64 Lamp	Beam Angle (in degrees) (height × width)	Field Angle (in degrees) (height × width)
Very narrow	6 × 12	10 × 24
Narrow	7 × 14	14 × 26
Medium	12 × 28	21 × 44
Wide	24 × 48	45 × 71

(A)   (B)   (C)

FIGURE 14.40
Followspots. (Courtesy of Strong
International.)

of sizes and styles (see Figure 14.40). The smallest followspot is an incandescent model capable of a useful light throw of about thirty-five feet. The larger models use high-intensity xenon, HMI, or unencapsulated arc-lamp sources and have a useful light throw of up to three hundred to four hundred feet.

All followspots function on the same general principles, illustrated in Figure 14.41. They have an illumination source—incandescent, tungsten-halogen, HMI, xenon, or arc. Many have a forced-air cooling system that helps to dissipate the heat generated by the light source.

The iris and **shutter** are internal control devices used to shape the beam of light. By manipulating them simultaneously, the operator can create a variety of beam-edge patterns.

All followspots have some type of lens or reflecting system to gather and shape the light. Portions of the system can be adjusted to focus the light and adjust the crispness of the edge of the beam.

Some followspots are equipped with a mechanical dimming device called a **douser.** Since the intensity of some of the light sources used in followspots (arc,

shutter: A lever-actuated device used to control the height of the top and bottom edges of a followspot beam; also called a chopper.

douser: A mechanical dimming device used in followspots.

Rear
condensing
lens

Shutter/iris
assembly

Focusing
lens

Spherical
reflector

Source

Front
condensing
lens

Shutter/iris
operating
control

Focus control

Fan

FIGURE 14.41
Cutaway drawing of a followspot.

FIGURE 14.42
A low-voltage lamp and
transformer.

encapsulated arc, xenon, HMI) cannot be adjusted, the douser provides the only way of smoothly dimming those sources. The douser can also be used to achieve a slow fade-in or fade-out of the light. Followspots are also equipped with a color boomerang, which holds five or six color filters that can be easily inserted into the beam of light to control its color.

Specialty Instruments

Several lighting instruments do not fall conveniently into other categories.

Low-Voltage Sources   A number of specialty lamps use a voltage lower than the 120 output volts of most stage dimmers. The output of these low-voltage lamps is frequently as high as that of their 120-volt cousins. Aircraft landing lights (ACL's) have a very high output and high color temperature, and the parabolic reflector provides a very narrow beam spread. Automobile headlights provide another narrow-beam, low-voltage source.

A primary advantage of lower-voltage lamps is that their filaments can be much smaller than their higher-voltage counterparts. The smaller filament can be used effectively in some types of scenic projectors discussed in Chapter 15, *Projections.*

These low-voltage lamps require a **transformer** to decrease the 120-volt source voltage before it reaches the lamp, as shown in Figure 14.42. A step-down transformer of appropriate voltage and capacity to match almost any lamp can be purchased at any electrical supply store. For 12-volt lamps, a heavy-duty automotive battery charger can be used as long as the current created by the wattage of the lamp does not exceed the rated capacity of the battery charger or its leads.

A number of lighting instruments and projectors have been designed to take advantage of the properties (small filament size, low heat output) of low-voltage lamps. These instruments normally have the required step-down transformer mounted inside of the instrument housing.

Intelligent or Kinetic Instruments   One of the primary functions of an effective lighting design is the establishment of a mood that supports the production concept. To creatively, and effectively, light a **legitimate theatre** production, the lighting designer generally uses the basic tools just discussed—ERS's, Fresnels, PAR's, cyc lights, and so forth. With this equipment he or she can create the normally subtle lighting that supports the production concept and covertly affects the audience's understanding of the play.

In the application of its basic principles, lighting design for **concerts** and **clubs** is no different than lighting design for legitimate theatre. However, there are two substantial differences: the nature of the production concept and the impact of the lighting on the audience. Production concepts for legitimate theatre productions are almost always intellectual, cerebral, and metaphorically introspective. The production concept for rock concerts and clubs is almost always visceral, bold, and extroverted. The atmosphere at a rock concert or club is about as far removed as you can get from a production of Shakespeare, Williams, or Stoppard. The music is fast, hard, and loud. The atmosphere is high energy. So is the lighting. It is overt and spectacular, and the way it affects meaning and mood is anything but subtle. Basic area lighting is normally done with multiple washes of heavily saturated color from PAR 64s. Moving light fixtures provide punch, emphasis, and focus.

The kinetic fixtures and associated digital control equipment that constitute this exciting class of instruments provide the lighting designer with the capability

transformer: A device that changes the voltage in an electrical system; the output voltage of a step-down transformer is less than its source; a step-up transformer increases it.

legitimate theatre: Refers to plays that rely on the spoken word to convey the message. Does not include musicals, reviews, dance, opera, or concerts.

concert: In this context, primarily refers to touring rock and country western shows.

club: In this context, refers to night clubs in which high-energy music (live or recorded) is the prime attraction.

FIGURE 14.43
Types of moving light fixtures.
(Courtesy of Light Quest, High End,
Martin, Elation.)

to create the in-your-face lighting (both literally and figuratively) that supports the production concept and mood of many concert productions.

The common feature of kinetic fixtures is movement: Light beams **pan** the stage, zoom in and out, change shape, change color, diffuse, and sharpen; gobos materialize, spin around, change pattern, then disappear. This is an exciting and active class of instrument.

There are a plethora of moving light fixtures available, as shown in Figure 14.43. Obviously, they don't all function in the same way, nor do they all have the same features. But generally they all use the same principles of operation. Almost all functions—pan, **tilt,** mechanical dimming, color changing, gobo movement and changing, beam spread, beam diffusion, and so forth—of these instruments are controlled by very precise electric **step motors.** Some of these instruments contain up to twenty separate motors to control the various functions.

Control of these step motors would be almost impossible without the development of USITT DMX512, a digital control protocol employed by a majority of the kinetic lighting and control manufacturers, as well as the manufacturers of "regular" stage lighting systems. (See the box "USITT DMX512" on page 359.) Digital control allows control signals for all functions of these instruments to be fed to the fixture through one low-voltage control cable. A separate 120 or 208/220 VAC power line is required to power the lamp and control motors.

Tungsten-halogen and encapsulated arc lamps are most commonly used with these instruments. T-H lamps can be dimmed, but encapsulated arc lamps, which are used because of their very high output, cannot be dimmed. They require mechanical dimming or dousers. The dousers are very precisely regulated with digitally controlled step motors.

Many kinetic instruments have internally mounted gobos and gobo changers. In some fixtures the gobos can be made to spin either forward or backward.

pan: To rotate an object, such as an ERS, about its vertical axis.

tilt: To rotate an object about its horizontal axis; to pan vertically.

step motor: An electric motor whose movement consists of discrete, angular steps rather than continuous rotation. Precise movement is achieved by programming the motor to run, in either direction, for a specific number of steps.

Safety Tip ⚠

Instrument Maintenance

To function effectively, the various instruments discussed in this chapter must be maintained in good working order, and as with any delicate piece of equipment, they must be handled with care.

The position of the lamp filament and the reflector must be kept in alignment, particularly in an ellipsoidal reflector spotlight. If this relationship is disturbed, the light output from the instrument will be greatly reduced, and the hot spot will be moved from the center of the beam. One of the significant advantages of the PAR 64 is that the filament and reflector are permanently aligned during the manufacturing process, so when the lamp in a PAR can is changed, there is no need to check the relationship.

The lenses and reflectors need to be kept clean and free from dust and fingerprints, and all nuts and bolts on the housing, yoke, and pipe clamp should be maintained so that the instrument can be locked securely into place.

When not in use, instruments should be hung on pipes or on rolling racks so that they won't be knocked over. If the theatre does not have an instrument storage cage, the instruments can be stored on a counterweight batten above the stage.

Ellipsoidal reflector spotlights should be stored with the shutters pushed all the way in to prevent them from being accidentally bent. When the instruments are in storage, care should be taken that the electrical pigtails are not pinched between the yoke and the instrument housing. The electrical plug and pigtail must be kept in good working order.

Followspots are mounted on a yoke and swivel-stand base that must move smoothly to follow the action of a performer. The base and yoke need to be properly lubricated, usually with graphite rather than oil or grease, and all nuts and bolts must be properly tightened.

Again, the functions of inserting, changing, and spinning the gobos are controlled by step motors.

Almost all of these instruments move the beam of light around the stage. Generally this is done in one of two ways: (1) moving the instrument; or (2) directing the beam of light at a mirror located on the instrument, then moving the mirror. These movements are again controlled with step motors. Generally, the "whole instrument" approach is employed with small, relatively light instruments, while the larger, more complex fixtures utilize the "moving mirror" technique.

The technological wizardry and aesthetic uses of this class of instrument are just beginning to be explored. While their use in most plays is generally limited by both budgets and aesthetic need, kinetic fixtures have already become a staple fixture in the equipment inventory of big-budget Broadway musicals. Their use in dance and concert lighting as well as in clubs is very exciting and will continue to evolve.

Color Changers   Color changing is accomplished with either a color scroller or a dichroic color changer. The color scroller, Figure 14.44, normally is used with an ERS, a Fresnel, a PAR, or any other instrument that doesn't have internal color-changing capability. It fits in the color-media holder on the front of the instrument and contains a roll of plastic color media that, if stretched out, would look like a series of different-colored gels taped together. A dichroic color changer generally uses three dichroic filters—normally the secondary colors—to change the color

(A)   (B)

FIGURE 14.44
Color changers utilize two different types of systems to change the color of the light output. Color scrollers, such as the Chroma-Q by A.C. Lighting, Inc. (A), use a scroll of colored plastic media. The ColorFader by Morpheus Lights, Inc. (B) utilizes dichroic filters. (Photos courtesy of manufacturers.)

of the light. The individual filters can be partially or fully inserted into the fixture's beam of light. The degree of insertion determines the color and level of saturation of the resulting hue. The three filters are used in combination to produce virtually any possible hue.

DIMMERS

In the relatively brief history of electrical stage lighting, many different kinds of dimmers have been used to control the intensity of instruments. Some of the older dimmers, such as the salt water, saturable core, thyratron tube, and resistance dimmer, have dropped by the wayside. Other older dimmers, such as the autotransformer, have continued in use.

Dimmer-Control Techniques

Dimmers can be divided into two groups based on the type of control used to regulate the current flow through them, mechanical or electronic.

Mechanical Dimmer Control   Older types such as the resistance and autotransformer dimmers require direct mechanical manipulation of an axle running through the central core of the dimmer to adjust the intensity of a lamp, as shown in Figure 14.45. This method of dimmer control is awkward. When a number of dimmers are linked, as shown in the illustration of an archaic resistance board (Figure 14.46), the resultant dimmer board is noisy, is difficult to operate, and requires at least several muscular electricians to run even a moderately complex production. You can imagine that a certain delicacy of touch and smoothness of operation are lost when you have to control one dimmer with each hand and try to operate another one with your foot.

Electronic Dimmer Control   When you move a controller to increase or decrease the intensity of lights connected to an electronic dimmer, you are using a low-voltage control circuit to manipulate the high-voltage output of that dimmer. Until recently, analog control systems were the only method available for controlling SCR dimmers. Now digital control has become the new standard.

To appreciate why "digital is better," you first need to understand how both analog and digital systems work and the basic differences between them.

Archaic Dimmers

Although the dimmers described in this box are no longer installed in theatres, they do have historical significance in the progress of stage lighting.

Saltwater Dimmer

The oldest type of dimmer was a frightening contraption. The primary component of this death trap was a bucket of salt water. Metal plates were attached to one leg of the circuit, and one of these plates was completely immersed in the bucket. The current passing through the circuit varied with the depth of immersion of the second plate.

Saturable-Core Dimmer

Another old dimmer worked by using a small DC current to magnetize an iron core. The AC load current passed through this iron core. As the level of magnetism was increased, the conductivity of the core also increased, and the lights connected to the dimmer came on.

Magnetic-Amplifier Dimmer

A more efficient version of the saturable-core dimmer, the magnetic amplifier was introduced in the 1950s but was soon relegated to obscurity by the development of the silicon-controlled rectifier dimmer.

Thyratron-Tube Dimmer

The thyratron-tube dimmer was the first dimmer to use the gating principle —a rapid switching on and off of the load current. However, thyratron vacuum tubes were large, had to warm up before they worked, didn't last very long, and were somewhat expensive.

Resistance Dimmer

The resistance dimmer functioned as a large variable-capacity resistor. When lights connected to it were turned off, it converted all the electrical energy flowing to it into heat. As it was turned on, its resistance decreased and current reached the lamps.

line: The wires in low-voltage control systems are frequently called "lines" rather than "wires."

Analog systems work on the following principle: Output varies as a continuous function of input. For example, increasing or decreasing the output of the control circuit causes a corresponding increase or decrease in the output of the dimmer. This control signal is sent from the light board over a control **line** to

FIGURE 14.45
Some archaic dimmers require a mechanical control technique.

FIGURE 14.46
A resistance board.

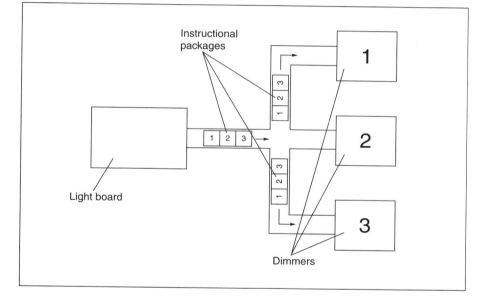

FIGURE 14.47
Digital instructional packages are continuously sent to all dimmers. The dimmers read only those instructions addressed to them.

the dimmer. Because the analog system requires a continuous signal, every dimmer in the system must be connected to the light board by its own control line.

Digital systems work on a different principle: Output varies in discrete steps. At first glance the difference in operating principles between analog and digital systems appears relatively inconsequential. But the differences are significant. To understand why, we first need to understand how digital information differs from analog. As stated earlier, analog information is continuous. Digital information isn't. Digital information is **discrete.** It is neither continuous nor variable. Digital information exists as binary code—a series of on-off pulses.

The finite nature of the digital signal is very important. It enables digital information to be made up into discrete information or instructional packages. These "packages" can contain any information that we want them to. Further, they can be sent to specific locations. Figure 14.47 shows a light board and three dimmers using digital control. The light board continuously sends information—instructional packages—to all three dimmers. However, the dimmers "read" only those instructions that are addressed to them. For example, dimmer 1 reads only instructional packages addressed to itself. It pays no attention to the

discrete: Separate and complete; in this case, pertaining to information represented by binary code.

FIGURE 14.48
Schematic drawing of lighting control systems: (A) analog and (B) digital.

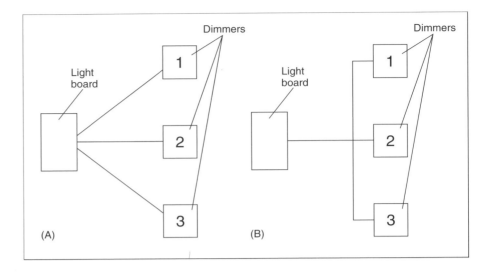

multiplex: (1) To transmit two or more messages simultaneously on a single channel. (2) To carry out several functions simultaneously in an independent but related manner.

instructions for any other dimmer. Dimmers 2 and 3 react the same way, reading only that information addressed to them. Because each instructional package is read only by the dimmer to which it is addressed, different information can be sent to each dimmer.

The process of sending two or more messages simultaneously on the same channel is called **multiplexing** and is the primary advantage of digital over analog control systems.[1] Figure 14.48 shows the two types of control systems. Figure 14.48A is an analog system. It requires that each dimmer be connected to the light board by its own control line. Figure 14.48B is a digital system. Notice that there is only one control line connecting all three dimmers to the light board. This is because the multiplexed instructional packages are sent to all dimmers but are read by only those dimmers to which they are addressed.

Saving on costs in the wiring of control circuits isn't the only advantage that digital control offers. Multiplexing offers another distinct advantage with digital control. Some of the intelligent or moving light fixtures require up to twenty control channels to function as designed. Digital control requires only one control line to provide instructions to all twenty functions. An analog system would require that twenty separate control lines be connected to the instrument. The final advantage that digital offers over analog is precision of control. Digital instructional packages are finite. Once encoded, they don't change. While analog signals can be remarkably accurate, they aren't as accurate as the unchanging digital code. For all of these reasons, digital is now the mode of choice in almost all dimmer control applications.

Autotransformer Dimmer

Autotransformer dimmers increase or decrease lamp intensity by varying the voltage within the circuit. Although this type of dimmer is only rarely used to control stage lights, houselights in some theatres are controlled by a motorized autotransformer dimmer, as shown in Figure 14.49. A control switch, usually located in the light booth, is used to activate a motor, which runs a mechanical linkage that controls the dimmer and enables it to raise or lower the intensity of the houselights. The only drawback to the motorized autotransformer dimmer

FIGURE 14.49
A motorized autotransformer dimmer.

[1] Analog signals can also be multiplexed, but the quantity of signals that can be multiplexed and the quality of the individual signals are lower than with digital.

USITT DMX512

USITT DMX512 is not the title of a bad science fiction movie. It is a standard created by the United States Institute for Theatre Technology (USITT) ". . . as a means to control dimmers from lighting consoles via a standard interface."[1] Basically, DMX512 is a recommended practice that allows the various pieces of a digitally controlled lighting system—computer boards, dimmers, and peripherals—to "talk" to each other. Prior to the adoption of this standard in 1990, each manufacturer had its own proprietary method of control, which made it difficult, if not impossible, for the customer to use a light board from one manufacturer to control dimmers, or any other equipment, made by another manufacturer. DMX512 resolved that issue. Now almost all digitally controlled equipment manufactured for the entertainment industry uses the DMX512 protocol.

To understand DMX512, you first need to understand how digital control works. (In the example explaining the process, dimmers are used as the controlled device. However, it is important to understand that digital control isn't used solely to control dimmer output. It also can be used to manipulate the functions of any type of electrical equipment, such as the stop/start functions and speed of the electrical motors found in moving light fixtures.)

The signal of most controllers—for example, the slide pots on a light board —is analog. When a controller is set to a specific level, it generates a signal that is an electronic indication of that setting. An analog-to-digital converter reads the controller's signal. Each time the converter reads the signal, it translates that information into binary code, adds the address of the dimmer or equipment associated with that particular command, and sends this "instructional package" to all the dimmers and equipment in the system. Each dimmer and piece of equipment receives all the instructional packages, but responds only to those addressed to it. This send/receive process occurs 44,000 times per second—the rate at which the analog-to-digital converter reads the original signal.[2]

DMX512 is simply a technical standard that specifies how much information is sent out on each of the 44,000 cycles that occur every second. DMX512 specifies that the signal shall contain 512 instructional packages and each package will have 256 discrete steps. This protocol has been adopted by the majority of equipment manufacturers and has significantly increased the compatibility of equipment used in the entertainment industry.

[1] Bennette, Adam, "Recommended Practice for DMX512: A Guide for Users and Installers," PLASA/USITT, 1994, p. 7.

[2] Some systems create the control signal digitally, which eliminates the need for the analog to digital conversion. These signals also are scanned and distributed 44,000 times a second.

occurs when the motor runs at a single speed so that the fade time for the houselights cannot be varied.

Silicon-Controlled Rectifier Dimmer

The silicon-controlled rectifier (SCR) dimmer (Figure 14.50) is the most reliable and efficient unit that has been developed for stage lighting. The SCR dimmer operates on a gating principle, which is simply a rapid switching on and off of the power. That principle is explained in the box "Gating Principle" on page 362.

The SCR is a solid-state power transistor, which means that it has no moving parts and no filaments to burn out. The electronic circuitry necessary to switch

FIGURE 14.50
(A) An SCR dimmer. (Courtesy of Strand Lighting.) (B) A portable dimmer pack containing six SCR dimmers. (Courtesy of Electronics Diversified.)

the SCR to a conducting state is also fairly simple. These properties result in a dimmer that is rugged, long lived, compact, relatively lightweight, moderate in cost, and reasonably quiet in operation.

With the rapid advancements being made in the electronics industry, discoveries will undoubtedly lead to even more efficient dimmers. At present, however, the SCR dimmer is recognized as the best solution.

Safety Tip

Dimmer Maintenance

The greatest enemy of an electronic dimmer such as the SCR is heat. To dissipate the heat, some dimmers are equipped with large heat sinks. Heat sinks are metal—usually aluminum—structures that absorb the heat generated by an SCR and radiate it to the atmosphere. Other dimmer packs are equipped with fans.

It is vital for the longevity of dimmers that they have plenty of air circulating around them. Don't pile anything on top of a dimmer. If you are working with portable dimmers, be sure that the dimmer pack is raised off the ground so that air can circulate under, as well as over, the case.

If your dimmer system is equipped with fans, be sure that they are running smoothly. The dimmers will frequently function for several hours even if the fan isn't working, but the heat buildup will cause a rapid deterioration of the electronic equipment that will usually lead to premature dimmer failure.

Almost all SCR dimmers need to be adjusted periodically so that they will smoothly increase or decrease their lamp loads. The specific methods vary from manufacturer to manufacturer, but they all involve an adjustment of the low, midpoint, and high-output voltage of the dimmer. These adjustments should be made by a qualified electrician at least annually.

FIGURE 14.51
Dimmers 1 through 6 are controlled by submaster A; dimmers 7 through 12 by submaster B; dimmers 13 through 18 by submaster C. The grand master acts as a master control for all submasters.

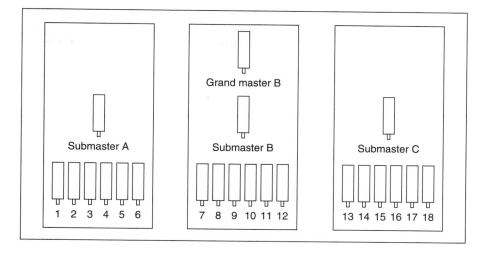

Control Consoles

The design and style of any control console is dictated by the type of dimmer that will be used with the system. Because the mechanically controlled dimmers are for the most part outdated, their control consoles will not be discussed here. However, the types and designs of the electronic control consoles are predicated on the principles that were developed and refined with mechanically controlled dimmers. Electronic control consoles are divided into four main categories: (1) group master, (2) preset, (3) combination, and (4) computer-assisted memory.

Group Master   The group-master console design is a direct carry-over from the control-board configurations used with mechanically controlled dimmers. Individual dimmers are controlled by a submaster, which is subsequently controlled by a grand master, as shown in Figure 14.51.

Two general operating techniques are used with group-master consoles. The first is to set individual dimmer intensity levels on a group of dimmers that are assigned to one particular submaster, as shown in Figure 14.52A. When the submaster is activated, the dimmers will fade up to the previously set levels. This technique is particularly useful when a designer wants to change the color blend of the lighting. For example, group A could be assigned all of the lights that are colored red; group B, blue; and group C, green. The color of the onstage light can be changed by varying the intensity of the submaster control for each color group.

The second operating technique involves using the dimmers of one group to control the lighting instruments from a particular direction or location, as shown in Figure 14.52B. For example, group A might control all **front-of-house** instruments; group B, side lights; and group C, the top lights.

front-of-house: Describing lights that are hung on the audience side of the proscenium arch.

Preset   The primary advantage of a preset control console is that it allows you to keep ahead of the onstage action by presetting the intensity levels for each dimmer before it will be needed. Figure 14.53 is an example of a three-scene lighting control console. Although there may not actually be a control console that works like this one, all preset lighting boards work on the same basic principles being discussed for this hypothetical board.

The controls for dimmers 1 through 6 are repeated three times in the blocks of dimmer controls labeled Preset Scenes I, II, and III. In this simplistic example,

Gating Principle

If, in a given period of time, you turn a lamp on, then off, then on, off, on, and off, you effectively control the amount of light it puts out for that specific amount of time. If the lamp is turned on, and left on, for one second, it burns at full intensity for that one-second period. If you turn the lamp on for half a second and turn it off for half a second, it burns at half intensity for the one-second span. If you turn the lamp on for three-quarters of a second and off for one-quarter of a second, it burns at three-quarters intensity for the one-second span. In each of these cases, you will obviously see the lamp being switched on and off. But if the time span for the on-off cycle is reduced to 1/120th of a second, you perceive the on-off sequence as being a continuous level of illumination—an average of the on-off cycle ratio.

The SCR dimmer operates on this principle. The SCR is actually an electronic switch. The switch, or gate, opens and allows current to pass through the SCR when it receives the proper electronic command. The gate stays open until the power to the SCR is turned off. Sixty-cycle alternating current (AC), the standard current in the United States, alternates its polarity 120 times a second, or twice in each cycle, as illustrated in Figure A. Each time that it alternates its polarity, or crosses the zero point on the graph, there is no voltage. The effective result of this "no voltage" situation is that the electricity is turned off. If a command is fed to the SCR to start conduction at the beginning of the cycle, point A in Figure B, the SCR will conduct for the full half cycle, or until the electricity is shut off when it

changes polarity at point B. Similarly, if the command specifies that the SCR is to begin conducting halfway through the cycle (Figure C), the transistor conducts for only half the cycle, or half as long.

By varying the time that the SCR is able to conduct electricity, you vary the intensity of any lamp load connected to it. This means that if the SCR conducts for a full half cycle, the lamp will glow at full intensity for the duration of that half cycle. If it conducts for only half of the half cycle, the lamp will be perceived to be glowing at half intensity. Similarly, a quarter-cycle electrical conduction means the lamp will appear to be glowing only one-fourth as brightly. Since each SCR conducts for only half a cycle, two SCR's, one for each half cycle, are necessary to make an effective dimmer.

The gating principle.

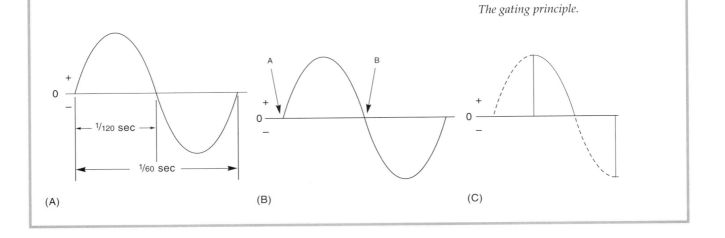

(A)   (B)   (C)

fader: A device, usually electronic, that effects a gradual changeover from one circuit to another; in lighting it gradually changes the intensity of one or more dimmer circuits; in sound it changes audio circuits or channels.

we will assume that the intensity levels of the lighting for the first cue will be preset on Preset Scene I, the second cue will be assigned to Preset Scene II, and the third cue will be set on Preset Scene III. After the board operator sets the appropriate intensity levels for each dimmer on the three preset scenes, he or she assigns control of Preset Scene I to **fader** A by pushing the button marked I next to fader A. When the cue is called by the stage manager, the operator brings up fader A, which automatically raises the intensity of the lights to the levels that had been preset on the dimmer controls of Preset Scene I. The second cue, preset on Scene II, is assigned to fader B. When the cue is called, the operator simultaneously moves fader B up and fader A down, which results in a cross-fade between the lights preset on Preset Scenes I and II. Similarly, before the third cue

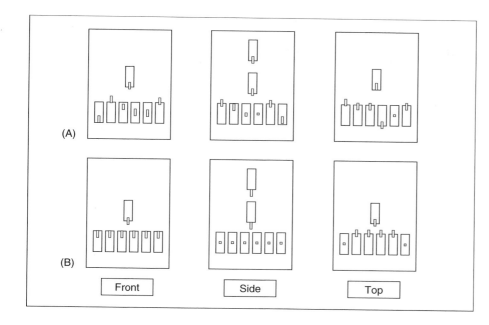

FIGURE 14.52
Group-master operating principles.
See text for details.

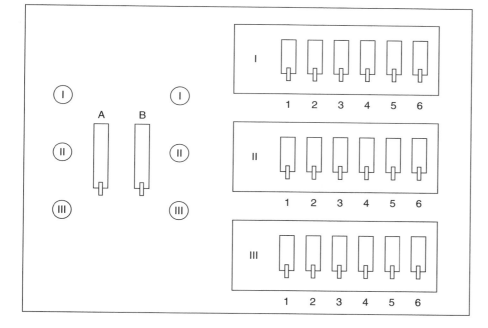

FIGURE 14.53
Preset board operating principles.

being called, the operator assigns control of Preset Scene III to fader A. When the cue is called, the operator cross-fades between faders B and A, which results in activation of the dimmer intensity levels associated with Preset Scene III.

To preset the intensity levels for the fourth cue, the operator presets the appropriate intensity levels on Preset Scene I as soon as he or she has cross-faded into the second cue. To run the remaining cues in the show, the operator repeats the process of presetting intensity levels on open, or nonactive, preset scenes as often as necessary. Many preset control consoles have mechanically or electronically interlocked faders, so when either fader A or B fades up, the other fader automatically dims down.

FIGURE 14.54
Combination boards. (Courtesy of
Colortran and Strand Lighting.)

Combination   A fusion of the principles of preset and group-master control
provides an extremely flexible lighting-control system. In the combination console (Figure 14.54), each dimmer channel has an associated switch capable of
assigning the dimmer to preset, group-master, or independent control. The combination control console provides an operator with more creative choices in
controlling dimmer intensities, because it enables him or her to choose the control best suited to each individual production situation.

Computer-Assisted Memory   Computer boards—computer-assisted memory
control for stage lighting—have become the standard for the industry. These
systems offer much greater control flexibility than any other method of lighting
control, and are less expensive to manufacture.

All computer boards (Figure 14.55) function in fundamentally the same way:
A computer electronically stores the intensity levels of all dimmers for each cue.
The computer memory replaces the cumbersome preset board and eliminates the

FIGURE 14.55
Computer boards. (Courtesy of
Electronics Diversified, Strand
Lighting, and Colortran.)

Computer Boards: A Comparison of Features

Smaller Systems

1. memory for up to several hundred cues

2. capability of controlling 100–150 dimmers

3. maximum of one video screen for displaying various system functions

4. a timed fader

5. some type of group or submaster control

6. control of dimmer intensity by individual sliders

7. keypad for addressing memory and functions

8. limited backup system in case of main-computer malfunction

   These smaller, less expensive systems work well in theatres that have modest production demands.

Larger Systems

1. memory for approximately 1,000 cues

2. control of 1,000 or more dimmers

3. expanded functions

   A. two or more video screens to display more functions simultaneously

   B. advanced backup systems

   C. sophisticated group or submastering

   D. more control functions to permit simultaneous cues at different fade rates

4. dimmer and other functions addressed through a keypad

5. remote keypad

6. hard-copy printer for printing data about the lighting design

7. self-diagnostic program to identify malfunctioning component in case of breakdown

   These larger and more expensive systems work well in facilities that have extensive production programs.

---

chance of human error in the setting of intensity levels during a show. Even the most basic computer boards have a minimum of about 100 memories for cue storage. More expensive boards have sufficient storage capacity for over 1,000 cues.

Computer boards have functions in addition to cue or preset memory capability. Almost all systems memorize the timed duration for each cue or preset. Most systems have a minimum of two or more faders, so a cue can be assigned to each fader to allow two or more lighting actions to occur at the same time.

Whenever a system has an automatic, or timed, fader, it usually has a manual override feature that enables the electrician to interrupt the timed fade to increase, decrease, stop, or reverse the rate of fade. Almost all computer boards except the lowest-priced ones have one or more video screens to display information about the various memory functions.

Since any computer will lose its memory when the power is turned off, most systems have some type of battery backup that provides enough power so that the system can retain its memory for a reasonable length of time. This period varies from several hours to several days, depending on the manufacturer.

Because of the **volatility** and limited storage capacity of the memories used in most systems, almost all but the lowest-priced computer boards have some method of storing the cuing and programming information. This additional storage capability is generally referred to as library storage. The most common methods used for library storage are the **floppy disk** and the **cassette tape**.

volatility: Nonpermanence; in computers, a volatile memory will be lost if the computer loses its power supply.

floppy disk: A thin plastic disk coated with metal oxide, used to record the information stored in a computer's memory.

cassette tape: Audio recorder tape, used in computer storage.

FIGURE 14.56
An electrical wire.

CABLES AND CONNECTORS

A flexible system of distributing electricity to lighting instruments is necessary, because the hanging position of the lights will be changed for each production. This section discusses the types of cables and connectors that make up this flexible distribution system, as well as several methods of circuiting, or connecting, the lighting instruments to the dimmers.

Electrical Cable for Stage Use

The National Electrical Code (NEC) stipulates that the only electrical cables approved for temporary stage wiring are types S, SO, ST, and STO. These cables have stranded copper conductors and are insulated with rubber (S and SO, shown in Figure 14.56) or thermoplastic (ST and STO). S and SO cables are more commonly used than ST and STO, because their thick rubber jacket can withstand more physical abuse than the thin, heat-resistant thermoplastic insulation of the ST and STO cable. Type S cable is generally used for stage lighting, because SO costs more and its only advantage is that it is impervious to oil and gasoline.

Wire Gauge

The American Wire Gauge (AWG) system rates wire according to the amount of current that a conductor of a particular size and composition can safely carry. The rated current capacity for any given gauge should never be exceeded. Most cables have the gauge and wire type imprinted every foot or so on the insulating jacket.

The amount of current that can be safely carried varies greatly, as we saw in Table 13.1. There is no standard size of cable for theatre use, because load requirements differ from one theatre to another. However, the NEC stipulates that receptacles used to supply incandescent lamps on stage must be rated at not less than twenty amperes and must be supplied by wires of not less than twelve gauge. Practical or decorative lamps are the only exception to this rule. These lamps may be wired with cable of smaller capacity as long as the lamp load doesn't exceed the rated capacity of the cable. This means that you can use eighteen-gauge wire (also known as lamp or zip cord) as long as the lamp load doesn't exceed 360 watts (assuming the system voltage is 120 volts: $W = VA$; $360 = 120 \times 3$).

Connecting Devices

Several different styles of connectors are used in stage lighting, as shown in Figure 14.57. Twist-lock connectors (Figure 14.57A) are considered by many people to be the best type of stage connector. The male portion, or plug, fits into the female portion, or receptacle, and is twisted to lock the two halves together. This locking action prevents most accidental disconnections of the circuit.

Pin connectors are probably more widely used than twist-lock connectors, primarily because they have been in existence longer. Older models of pin connectors (Figure 14.57B) have three distinct disadvantages: (1) They can be easily disconnected by accident; (2) the pins of the plug do not always make a good electrical connection with the receptacle; and (3) if the cable is connected to a live power source, it is very easy to be shocked, because the metal conductors in the receptacle are not deeply recessed.

Newer models of the grounded pin connector (Figure 14.57C) overcome the previously mentioned disadvantages. The new designs, which also meet the

(A)   (B)   (C)   (D)

FIGURE 14.57
(A) A twist-lock; (B) grounded pin connector; (C) locking grounded pin connector; (D) grounded parallel blade (Edison) connector. ([B] and [C] Courtesy of Union Connector Co.)

NEC guidelines, have an excellent locking device that prevents accidental disconnections, and the metal contacts within the receptacle are recessed quite deeply into the insulating body of the connector.

The Edison, or parallel blade, plug (Figure 14.57D), should be used only on decorative lamps or devices that carry a similarly small load.

All connectors, regardless of style, are designed to carry a specific amount of current. The maximum load is usually printed somewhere on the plug, and that limit should be strictly obeyed.

The NEC stipulates that each plug should be equipped with an effective cable-clamping device (see Figure 14.58). The purpose of the cable clamp is to secure the connector to the jacket of the cable. This clamping action transfers any physical strain from the plug casing directly to the cable jacket, which effectively eliminates any strain on the electrical connections inside of the plug.

Extension Cables

Extension cables can be purchased, or made in the theatre's electrical shop, in any reasonable length. As previously noted, they are generally made of type S cable, although types SO, ST, or STO can also be used. Different theatres present differing requirements, but in general, if a theatre has a permanent lighting system, an inventory of cables five, ten, and twenty feet long should meet the needs of most operations.

(A)   (B)

FIGURE 14.58
(A) Internal and (B) external cable clamps.

Safety Tip

Control-System Maintenance

The operating voltage for most electronic lighting-control systems is relatively low—normally, between eight and twenty-four volts. Because of the low voltage and the miniaturization of the electronic components, the systems need to be kept scrupulously clean and free from dust, dirt, and grease. For this reason, smoking and eating should not be permitted in the lighting control booth. The tar from tobacco smoke can settle on the printed circuit boards and actually change the resistance within the electronic circuits. Even a small change in resistance can cause some elements of the system to malfunction. The obviously disastrous results of spilling a soft drink on a computer or control board don't need further elaboration.

The floppy disks that are used for library storage in many computer systems need to be handled carefully. They should be stored vertically in a dust-free environment away from power lines and electric motors. (The power lines and motors generate magnetic fields that can scramble or erase the information stored on a disk.) Use only a soft-tip marker to write on the floppy-disk label. Pencils and ballpoint pens can dent the recording surface of the disk, and the graphite and ink can interfere with the reading head.

FIGURE 14.59
A "Y," or two-fer.

A **two-fer** is used to connect two instruments to the same circuit. When using two-fers (Figure 14.59) or any other device that can increase the electrical load on a circuit, take particular care not to exceed the maximum current rating of any element (cable, plug, dimmer, and so on) in that circuit.

two-fer: An electrical Y that has female receptacles at the top of the Y and a male plug at the bottom leg of the Y; used to connect two instruments to the same circuit.

CIRCUITING

The distribution of electricity from dimmers to lighting instruments creates a complex system. Any complex system is built on compromise, simply because the maximum amount of efficiency that can be built into any system is finite. The compromises on which stage lighting systems are predicated are speed and ease of hanging and circuiting versus flexibility of hanging position. The following methods of stage circuiting demonstrate the effects of tinkering with the variables of this complex equation.

work light: A lighting fixture, frequently a scoop, PAR, or other wide-field-angle instrument, hung over the stage to facilitate work; generally not used to light a production.

Permanent Wiring

The simplest method of circuiting is to permanently wire the instruments to the dimmers. In this system, a few ellipsoidal reflector spotlights are usually hung somewhere on the ceiling of the auditorium, and some striplights or **work lights** over the stage. These instruments are permanently wired to specific dimmers. To operate the system, you just turn on the dimmers. The only possible changes or adjustments within the system are changing the color or area of focus for each instrument.

Although this method is certainly the easiest to operate, it provides little flexibility and just about eliminates any chance for creatively designing with light. Permanently wired lighting systems appear with great frequency in high school auditoriums, music halls, and other facilities where the lighting installation has been guided by criteria other than the needs and requirements of the creative use of designed light.

Spidering

Spidering, also known as direct cabling, involves running a cable from each lighting instrument directly to the dimmer to which it is assigned. It gets its name from the tangled web of cables created by circuiting a production in this manner.

Spidering is used extensively in Broadway theatres and on touring shows. It provides the greatest flexibility, because it allows the designer to put an instrument wherever it is needed. On the negative side, spidering requires an extensive inventory of electrical cable, and this method takes a long time to hang unless the hanging crew is very experienced and the designer or master electrician has carefully planned the cabling requirements for the production.

Connecting Strips and Patch Panels

An electrical distribution system that utilizes connecting strips and a patch panel provides two advantages in a theatre that has an extensive production program: (1) The light plot can be hung and circuited quite rapidly, and (2) the system provides a great deal of flexibility by enabling you to patch any circuit into any dimmer.

FIGURE 14.60
A connecting strip.

(A)

(B)

(C)

FIGURE 14.61
(A) Drop box; (B) floor pocket;
(C) wall pocket.

Two principal parts make up this system: the stage circuits and a patch panel. Most of the stage circuits are contained in connecting strips, which are sections of wireway, or electrical gutter, that contain a number of circuits (Figure 14.60).

The connecting strips are hung in a variety of positions about the stage and auditorium—counterweighted battens over the stage; various front-of-house positions (ante-proscenium cuts or slots, beamports, coves, boxes); and various locations on the walls of the stage house. Each circuit terminates in a receptacle that is usually mounted at the end of a two- to three-foot pigtail, although the receptacles are sometimes mounted flush on the gutter itself.

Additional stage circuit outlets are often contained in **drop boxes, floor pockets,** and **wall pockets** (Figure 14.61). Drop boxes are small connecting strips fed by cables that are attached to the grid above the stage. They usually contain four to eight circuits and are equipped with one or two pipe clamps so that they can be easily attached to pipes or booms. Floor and wall pockets are recessed into the floor or wall and usually contain three to six circuits.

All of the circuits contained in connecting strips, drop boxes, and floor or wall pockets have certain properties in common. Each circuit is a rather long extension cable that, at the stage end, terminates in a female receptacle. Some connecting strips are designed to provide two receptacles for each circuit. In the patch-panel system, the other end of the circuit terminates at the patch panel in a male plug, as shown in Figure 14.62.

drop box: A small connecting strip, containing four to eight circuits, that can be clamped to a pipe or boom.

floor pocket: A connecting box, usually containing three to six circuits, the top of which is mounted flush with the stage floor.

wall pocket: A connecting box similar to a floor pocket but mounted on the wall.

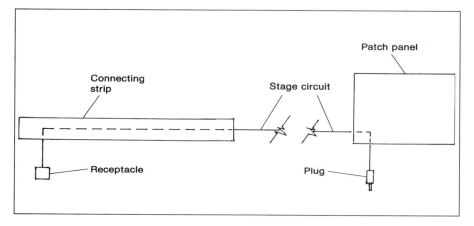

FIGURE 14.62
In a patch-panel system, the stage circuit runs from the female receptacle on the stage outlet to a male plug at the patch panel.

FIGURE 14.63
Patch panel. (Courtesy of Colortran.)

Safety Tip

Cable storage.

Cable and Connector Maintenance

The following steps are suggested to keep cables and connectors in good operating condition and in compliance with NEC and federal regulations.

1. When a cable is not in use, coil it and hang it on the wall of the lighting storage room. The cable will stay neatly coiled if the connectors are plugged together or if it is tied with heavy twine or narrow rope.

2. Check cables and connectors periodically, and replace any items that show signs of cracking, chipping, or other deterioration. Cracks in the insulation of cables and connectors increase the chances of someone's receiving a shock from the device. Also, dust can accumulate in the crack and may cause an electrical fire.

3. Always disconnect a plug by pulling on the body of the connector, not the cable. Pulling on the cable puts an unnecessary strain on the cable clamp and will eventually defeat the clamp. When the cable clamp no longer functions, pulling on the cable places the strain directly on the electrical connections.

4. Keep the connectors clean. Remove any corrosion, paint, grease, or other accumulations as soon as they become evident. These substances can act as insulation between the contacts of the connector and, if flammable, pose a fire hazard.

5. All elements of a cable should be of the same electrical rating; for example, twelve-gauge (AWG) cable (capable of carrying twenty amperes of current) should have only twenty-ampere-rated connectors, and so forth.

The second part of the distribution system is the patch panel, or patch bay. It is an interconnecting device that provides the system with the capability of connecting, or patching, any stage circuit into any dimmer. Patch panels (Figure 14.63) are manufactured in a variety of styles and configurations.

Figure 14.64 illustrates the basic operational design of a patch panel. The lighting instrument is connected into a stage circuit, which terminates at the patch panel in a male plug. The dimmer, which is usually located in another part of the theatre, is permanently wired to a receptacle on the face of the patch panel. To enable the electricity to flow from the dimmer to the lighting instrument, it will be necessary to complete the circuit. This is done by patching the circuit into the appropriate receptacle for the dimmer.

FIGURE 14.64
The patch panel allows you to plug more than one circuit into a single dimmer.

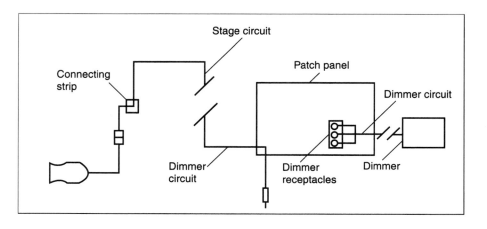

The patch panel is actually very simple to operate. What makes it seem so complex is that it contains many more than the one circuit and one dimmer cited in this example. In fact, a patch panel usually contains between sixty and several hundred stage circuits and from forty to several hundred dimmers. In addition, each dimmer is usually provided with several receptacles on the face of the patch panel so that more than one circuit can be patched into each dimmer.

Patch panels usually have some type of electrical-overload protection for both the stage circuit and the dimmer circuit. The circuit breaker automatically breaks the continuity of the circuit when an unsafe amount of current is passed through the line. Each stage circuit has a circuit breaker, as shown in Figure 14.65, that provides overload protection. Another circuit breaker is usually located either in the line connecting the patch panel to the dimmer or in the dimmer itself. This circuit breaker protects the dimmer circuit and dimmer from an overload.

FIGURE 14.65
Circuit breakers provide overload protection for both the stage circuits and the dimmer circuits.

Dimmer Per Circuit

The dimmer-per-circuit configuration combines the efficiency in hanging and circuiting of the connecting strip with the ease of operation of the permanently wired system.

As in the connecting strip and patch-panel system, the onstage end of each circuit terminates in an outlet on a connecting strip, floor pocket, or similar location. The other end of the circuit is directly wired to a dimmer instead of terminating in a male plug at the patch panel.

Before the introduction of computer boards, it required a very large and unwieldy control system and three to six—or more—electricians to run all the dimmers required by this type of system. But the computer board makes control of the large number of dimmers associated with this type of system a fairly simple task for one person. The dimmer-per-circuit configuration, when combined with a computer board, provides what is possibly the most flexible system available at this time.

Chapter 15
Projections

Projections enhance the visual texture of a design immeasurably. They can provide the stage with seemingly unlimited depth or create an aura of surrealism as one image dissolves into another. They can be used to replace or complement other visual elements of the setting, or as an accent.

However, projections aren't a universal panacea. They are simply another tool for the designer to use in the never-ending quest for an evocative visual expression of the production concept.

Two basic systems of projections are used in the theatre: lens and lensless.

LENSLESS PROJECTORS

If you've ever made shadow pictures by holding your hands in the beam of a slide or movie projector, you understand the principle of lensless projection. As shown in Figure 15.1, a shadow image can be projected when an opaque object is placed in the path of a light source. If the object casting the shadow is colored and transparent rather than opaque, a colored image is projected instead of a shadow.

Several factors determine the sharpness of the projected image, but the primary one is the size of the projection source. Although an arc or encapsulated arc provides a very small point source, it isn't particularly practical in this application because its intensity can't be varied through the use of a dimmer. There are two practical lamp sources for lensless projectors:

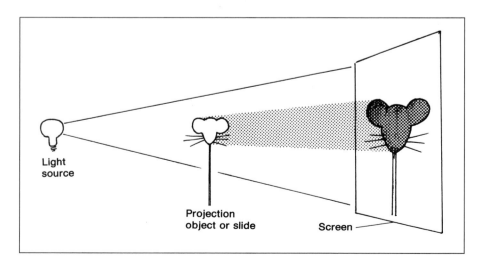

FIGURE 15.1
Principles of lensless projection.

1. For large-scale projections, a 500-, 750-, or 1,000-watt, 120-volt, tungsten-halogen lamp normally used in an ellipsoidal reflector spotlight works well. When selecting a specific lamp, remember that the smaller the filament, the sharper the image.

2. For small-scale projections—under six feet wide—a single-filament, twelve-volt lamp (used for automotive brake and turning lights) can provide a high-intensity, small-filament source. For the lamp to provide enough output, it must be run at about fifteen volts. This voltage is supplied to the lamp through a fifteen-volt step-down transformer, as shown in Figure 15.2. The transformer may not work properly, however, and the intensity of the twelve-volt lamp will probably flutter if you try to dim the unit with an SCR dimmer. The flicker occurs because the filaments of these twelve-volt lamps usually don't have sufficient mass to retain the heat necessary to give off light during the SCR's "off" cycles, particularly at low-intensity readings. (The operational principles of an SCR dimmer were discussed in the previous chapter.) A smooth fade can be achieved only if the transformer is dimmed with an autotransformer or a resistance dimmer.

FIGURE 15.2
A low-voltage lamp can provide a high-intensity, small-sized source for a lensless projector.

Another important factor in determining image sharpness with a lensless projector is the distance between the slide and the projection surface. The closer the slide is to the screen, the sharper the image. Having the slide closer to the screen does not necessarily mean that the projector is closer to the screen. A fairly long, somewhat skinny projector, as shown in Figure 15.3A, can be built in the shop. If the ratio of the distance between the projection surface and the slide and the distance between the slide and the lamp of this somewhat bizarre projector can be kept at approximately 1:1, an acceptably sharp image can be produced. The multiplane lensless projector (Figure 15.3B) is a natural adaptation of this development. As slides are placed closer to the lamp, the image they project becomes less focused. This phenomenon can be used to good advantage to create **aerial perspective.** In the projection of a landscape, the clouds and distant objects could be painted on one slide and placed relatively close to the lamp to create a soft-edged image. Middle-distance objects, such as hills and a forest, might be painted on a second slide and placed farther from the lamp, so the image they project is more clearly defined. A third slide, with perhaps a fence row and the

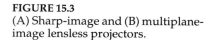

aerial perspective: An optical phenomenon in which objects that are farther away appear less sharply in focus and less fully saturated in color.

FIGURE 15.3
(A) Sharp-image and (B) multiplane-image lensless projectors.

FIGURE 15.4
Principles of operation of a Linnebach projector.

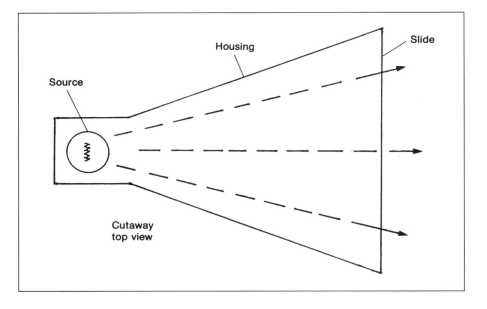

branch from an overhanging tree, could be painted on a third slide and placed
farther away from the lamp, so its image is the sharpest of the three.

Although the multiplane projector might seem to be an ideal solution, there
is one very basic problem: slide size. You will remember that for a slide to project
a sharp image it needs to be approximately the same distance from the screen as
it is from the lamp. If you wanted to project an image twenty feet wide, the sharp-
image slide would have to be ten feet wide! However, if you are only trying to
project on a small area (five feet wide or less), the multiplane projector can provide you with a realistic aerial perspective effect.

A multiplane projector can be built in the shop using the techniques described in the next section for making Linnebach projectors. A 750- or 1,000-watt
tungsten-halogen lamp from an ellipsoidal reflector spotlight will usually provide a more than adequate light for projections less than five feet wide, and the
slides can be painted on one-eighth-inch Plexiglas with transparent acetate inks.

Linnebach Projector

The primary lensless projector used in the theatre was developed by Adolph
Linnebach. All lensless projectors are based on its principles of operation, which
are illustrated in Figure 15.4. The metal housing holds the lamp at a fixed distance
from the open front of the projector, which is designed to securely hold a removable glass slide. The design is painted on the slide with transparent acetate inks.

Projectors that work on the Linnebach principles can easily be made in the
theatre shop using galvanized tin and a **pop riveter.** They can also be fabricated
using plywood (Figure 15.5), but the inside of the back and top sides of the
plywood box must be lined with tin or some other heat-reflecting or -absorbing
material.

Linnebach projectors for use with curved cycs can also be shop-built, as
shown in Figure 15.6. These projectors, while using only a 1,000-watt **FEL lamp,**
can project a patterned wash of pastel color over a full semicircular cyc. Slides
for the curved-front Linnebach are made from twenty-mil acetate. These slides
are fitted to the curved edge of the projector, and the image is painted on the
slide using transparent acetate inks. Dr. Martin's Watercolors, when supple-

pop riveter: A tool used to secure
rivets in thin metal.

Fel lamp: Lamps made in the United
States are designated with a three-
letter code that specifies all design
criteria such as wattage, voltage,
filament and base type, color-
temperature-rated life, and so forth.
FEL specifies a very specific 1,000-
watt lamp.

FIGURE 15.5
Shop-built Linnebach projector.

mented with a commercial additive that allows the paint to adhere to plastic, work extremely well for this purpose.

Other Lensless Projectors

Small lensless projectors can be made by removing the lens from Fresnel or plano-convex spotlights and inserting a slide (painted or photographic transparency) in the instrument's color-frame holder. Although these makeshift projectors won't cover a large surface, they are handy for making soft projections on small surfaces.

LENS PROJECTORS

The second basic type of projector uses a lens to control the focus and size of the image on the projection surface. Two primary types of lens projectors are used in the theatre: the **scenic projector** and the **slide projector.**

Scenic Projector

The scenic projector is composed of three basic parts: the lamp housing, the optical train, and the slide, as shown in Figure 15.7A.

Lamp Housing   A lamp of high intensity is a prime requisite of a good scenic projector. Incandescent lamps of 1,000 to 2,000 watts are fairly typical, and some top-of-the-line scenic projectors use xenon or HMI lamps and mechanical dimming systems. The housings are frequently equipped with blowers that help dissipate the rather substantial heat that these powerful sources generate. Unfortunately, the fans on many scenic projectors are less than whisper quiet, so the scenic projector should be placed in a location that will mask the fan noise.

Optical Train   The optical train, shown in Figure 15.8, is composed of several parts that perform specific functions. The reflector (usually ellipsoidal or spherical) and collector lens gather and concentrate the light. Some scenic projectors utilize a **hot mirror,** which is a clear dichroic filter that reflects a substantial

scenic projector: A high-wattage instrument used for projecting large-format slides or moving images.

slide projector: A reasonably high-output instrument capable of projecting standard 35mm slides.

hot mirror: A glass dichroic filter that reflects the infrared spectrum while allowing visible light to pass.

FIGURE 15.6
Curved-image Linnebach projector.

condensing lens: A device that condenses the direct and reflected light from a source and concentrates it on the slide-plane aperture of a projector.

slide-plane aperture: The point in a projection system where a slide or other effect is placed.

portion of the infrared (heat) segment of the electromagnetic spectrum emitted by the lamp. The **condensing lenses** focus the light onto the **slide-plane aperture**, which is the point where the slide or moving projection effect is placed. The

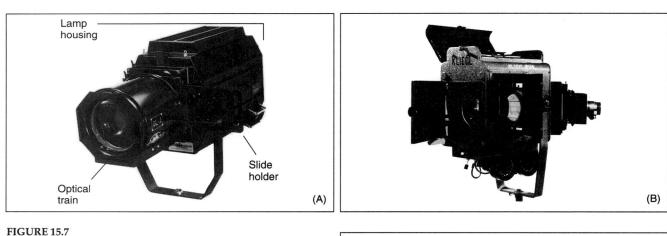

FIGURE 15.7
(A) A scenic projector is composed of the lamp housing, the optical train, and the slide. (Courtesy The Great American Market.) (B) Scenic projector. (Courtesy Kliegl Bros.) (C) Slide projector. (Courtesy George R. Snell Associates.)

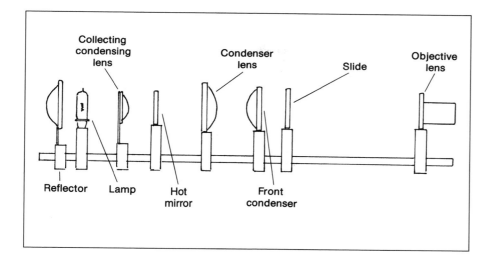

FIGURE 15.8
A typical scenic-projector optical train.

objective lens is used to focus the material in the aperture onto the projection surface.

The reflector, lamp, collector lens, and aperture are normally mounted in fixed positions within the lamp housing unit. In contrast, the relative positions of the condensing lens and objective lens are variable on some models of scenic projectors to allow the size of the projected image to be changed. Other scenic projectors are available with several **heads,** which hold the condensing and objective lenses in fixed positions to control the image size.

Slide   Glass slides are frequently used with scenic projectors to project still images. The image can be painted, with transparent inks, on a single glass slide, or a photographic transparency can be sandwiched between two glass slides. The longevity of a painted or photographic image on the slide can be increased if a dichroic hot mirror is placed between the collector lens and the slide.

A variety of moving effects can be created through the use of **effects heads.** These motorized devices are attached to the lamp housing in place of the slide holder. Effects heads move images in front of the aperture gate to create abstract or relatively realistic moving images, such as the lighted windows of a passing train, on the projection surface. The speed of the control motor is usually variable, so the speed of the projected effect can be adjusted to suit the design need. Depending on the specific model, effects heads use either rotating disks or bands to create the specific effect desired. Most scenic-effects projectors are equipped to use either Plexiglas or metal disks or plastic bands.

objective lens: A device to focus a projected image on a screen or other surface.

head: A housing that holds scenic-projector lenses in fixed positions to project images of a specific size.

effects head: A motor-driven unit capable of producing crude moving images with a scenic projector.

Slide Techniques for Lensless Projectors

A number of systems based on mathematical principles can be used to lay out the slides for lensless, or Linnebach, projectors. However, the fastest and most accurate method is also the easiest. Put a slide into the projector, and place it and the projection screen (usually a cyc or sky tab) in the onstage positions that they will occupy during the production. Turn the projector on, and draw or paint the projection on the slide while watching the projection grow across the screen.

Keystoning

Unless the projector is placed on a perpendicular axis to the projection screen, some linear distortion will be introduced to the projected image. This phenomenon is known as keystoning, because the distortion generally resembles the shape of a keystone.

Keystoning results when the light from one side of the projected image (slide) has to travel farther than the light from the other side of the slide, as illustrated in the figure (A).

Keystoning can be corrected in one of two ways: (1) The screen can be tilted so that the projection axis is perpendicular to the screen (C), or (2) a distortion can be introduced to the slide that counteracts the effects of the projection distortion. To do this, determine the angle of intersection between the projection axis and the screen. To introduce the counterdistortion to the slide, place the camera at the same angle, but on the opposite side, when you are taking the picture of the slide material (D).

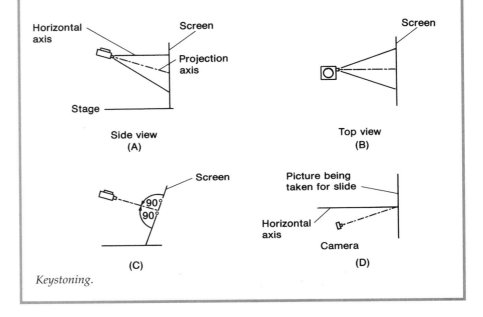

Keystoning.

Carousel Projector Tips

1. Use the slide tray that holds 80 slides rather than its larger-capacity (140-slide) cousin, because the greater space allocated to each slide in the 80-count tray significantly reduces the chances of the slides becoming stuck in the tray.

2. Mount the slides in plastic, rather than pasteboard, slide holders. The plastic holders are slicker and slightly heavier, which makes it easier for them to be fed into the projector.

3. For the best image, use the highest-wattage lamp designed for the specific model with which you are working.

4. Select a lens that will permit you to place the projector as close to the projection surface as possible.

Slide Projector

Projectors using 35mm (two-by-two-inch) slides provide another excellent system for producing scenic projections. The challenge of using these projectors, which are designed for audiovisual, not theatrical, purposes, is that the lamp output is frequently not as bright as that of a scenic projector. If you work within the limitations that the lower lamp output imposes, however, the slide projector can be an extremely useful tool.

The Kodak Carousel equipped with a 300-watt lamp provides sufficient light to create a readable image if the slide is of normal contrast and the maximum dimension of the projected image is kept at about six to eight feet.

Adaptations of the basic audiovisual (Ektagraphic) line of Kodak Carousel projectors, Figure 15.7C, provide higher-wattage lamps and a number of other interesting features. Although the 300-watt lamp available on the basic models will work adequately, by all means acquire the higher-output models if your budget can afford them. The image can be significantly brighter.

Other types of 35mm slide projectors can be used, but the carousel types generally offer specific qualities that make them preferable for theatrical projection work: dependable and versatile slide-feeding capabilities, adequate light output, and interchangeable lenses.

Gobo

An ellipsoidal reflector spotlight can be converted into a pattern projector through the use of a gobo. A full discussion of gobos and how to make them can be found in Chapter 14.

PROJECTION SCREENS

Actors' bodies, painted scenery, dust motes, smoke, and fog have all been used as projection surfaces. However, they don't work nearly so well as scenic elements that have been specifically designed as projection screens. There are two basic types of screen materials: front and rear.

Front-Screen Material

Front-screen projection materials are those surfaces that are designed to reflect light. The best front-projection materials are slide or movie screens. They are white and highly reflective, and the surface is often designed to focus the reflected light in a specific angular pattern. Unless you want a large, glaringly white screen sitting in the middle of the stage, however, it is essential that the screen be lit with either a projection or color wash at all times.

A smooth, white, painted surface (muslin, Masonite, and the like) provides a low-cost alternative to the commercial projection screen. Although the reflected image won't be so crisp as that from the projection screen, it will be more than adequate for most theatrical purposes. When the projections or color washes are turned off, however, the challenge of what to do with the "great white blob" continues.

Unless you are planning on using continuous projections or removing the screen from the set, it is frequently desirable to have the projection screen blend into the surrounding scenic elements until it is time to use it. In these cases, the vertical or horizontal surfaces of the set itself can be used instead of a projection screen. When you are projecting on scenery, the sharpness and brightness of the

FIGURE 15.9
A typical rear-screen projection setup.

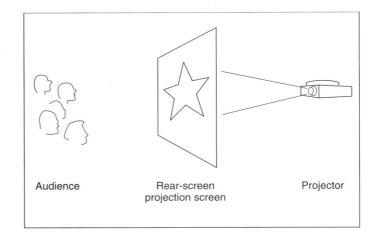

Audience   Rear-screen   Projector
                projection screen

reflected image will be directly related to the hue, value, and texture of the paint job used on the scenery. Surfaces with low saturation, high value, and little texture provide the best reflective surfaces for projected images.

Rear-Screen Material

A major challenge of front-screen projection—actor shadows on the projection surface—is eliminated through the use of rear-screen projection. In this technique, illustrated in Figure 15.9, the projector is placed behind the screen, and the image is transmitted through the screen to the audience.

A significant challenge of rear-screen projection is created by the **hot spot.** If the projector is located within the audience's sight line, as illustrated in Figure 15.10, a small, intensely bright circle of light will appear on the screen. This bright circle is caused by seeing the actual lens of the projector through the screen material. The hot spot can be eliminated in one of two ways. You can position the projector so that the hot spot is out of the audience's sight line, or you can use a screen material that eliminates the hot spot.

Commercial rear-screen materials transmit clear, crisp images while diffusing or eliminating the hot spot. Rosco Labs produces several types of reasonably priced flexible plastic rear-screen materials in rolls fifty-five inches wide. Wider

hot spot: *An intense circle of light created when a projector lens is seen through a rear screen.*

FIGURE 15.10
A hot spot, caused by seeing the lens of the projector through the screen, will result unless special rear-screen projection material is used.

screens, with invisible seams, can be made by butting strips of the material edge to edge and taping the joints with No. 200 Scotch transparent plastic tape. Unless the atmosphere is of low humidity, however, the tape seams are only a temporary solution. **Heat welding** of the seams will provide a permanent bond.

If the projector can be placed in a position that will eliminate the hot spot, a variety of translucent materials can be used to receive the projected image. Scenic muslin and other fabrics of similar weight and weave transmit light quite well. The muslin (which will present a crisper image if it is primed with a starch solution—one cup of starch per gallon of hot water) can be painted with dye if it is necessary or desirable for the screen to blend into the set. When using this technique, be sure to use dye, not paint. Dye is transparent and won't interrupt the transmission of the image.

Plain white shower curtains provide another effective, low-cost rear-screen material. The plastic transmits light well, the larger-sized shower curtains are big enough for many scenic uses, and some of the plastics diffuse the hot spot.

White (not clear) polyethylene plastic sheeting, sold as plastic drop cloths in paint stores, is also an effective rear-screen material.

heat welding: The use of a heat gun (a high-temperature air gun, visually similar to a hand-held hair dryer) to fuse two pieces of plastic.

SLIDE PREPARATION

Slides for the various types of commercial and shop-built Linnebachs are generally made from one-eighth-inch clear Plexiglas. Slides for the curved-image Linnebach can be made from .020-inch acetate. Although still quite flexible, the .020 thickness provides enough stiffness so that these slides don't bend or flop when secured to the projector.

The slide image can be painted on the acetate with a variety of materials. Transparent acetate inks, which are available in a wide range of colors, are a standard type of slide paint. If an additive, which makes the water-base dyes adhere to the plastic, is used, Dr. Martin's Watercolors are an excellent choice. As a last resort, the bottles of Magic Marker refill inks can also be used. Although the Magic Marker inks remain slightly tacky, they don't smear easily, but they do attract a great deal of dust.

Scenic projectors can use both photographic and painted slides. To be used in a scenic projector, photographic transparencies should be sandwiched between sheets of projection-grade glass. This type of glass is usually available from photography stores. This "sandwich" accomplishes two things: It keeps the heat of the lamp from crinkling or melting the slide, and it keeps the slide in a vertical plane. Painted scenic-projector slides are also usually sandwiched for heat protection. The image is painted on a glass slide, and either that slide is sandwiched between two other clear slides or the painted surface is simply covered with a second slide. The transparent inks mentioned previously will also work on glass. Additionally, silhouettes can be created by using opaque acetate inks. However, you must take care when using opaque inks, simply because they absorb more heat than do transparent ones. The additional heat may crack the glass or cause a deterioration of the other inks.

Thirty-five-millimeter slides shouldn't be used in the cardboard mounts in which they are placed by the film processors. These mounts don't really have enough weight to drop the slide into the projector if the projector is mounted at anything other than a perfectly horizontal angle. At a minimum, the slides should be remounted in plastic slide mounts, and ideally you will sandwich them between two layers of slide glass. (The plastic mounts and 35mm glass mounts are available at photography stores.)

FIGURE 15.11
An overhead projector. (Courtesy of George R. Snell Associates.)

OTHER PROJECTORS

A wide variety of other projectors can be used for special situations in the theatre. However, two of them, the overhead projector (Figure 15.11) and the opaque projector, are arguably the most useful.

A large transparent slide (most overhead projectors will accept slides up to eleven by fourteen inches) is placed on the light table of the overhead projector. A high-output lamp shines through the slide, and the image is redirected and focused on the screen by a mirror mounted in an optical head located a short distance above the light table. The luminance level of this projector is fairly low, but it can work well in short-throw, low-light situations.

The opaque projector works in generally the same fashion, except that the slide is opaque and the lamp is located above the slide so that the light can be reflected, rather than directly transmitted, to the mirror and optical head. The output of the opaque projector is generally less than that of the overhead projector, because some of the lamp output is lost to absorption and scattering during the reflection process. Although this projector is effective on stage only for specific low-light applications, it is very helpful in the scene shop, where it can be used to project detail from painters' elevations and other drawings or photos onto scenic elements during the scene-painting process.

GENERAL PROJECTION TECHNIQUES AND HINTS

It is prudent to test the characteristics of any projection system, technique, or material (commercial or noncommercial) under actual stage conditions before you launch into a design concept that depends on projections. You will frequently discover that your vision of how the projections should look is at odds with the physical reality of how they actually appear on stage. Some general hints and guidelines may help you in working with projections:

1. To prevent the projected images from being washed out, keep ambient light off of the screen. Be sure that the stage lights for the acting areas in the vicinity of the screen(s) are placed at angles that minimize their effect (direct and reflected) on the screen.

2. To reduce the effects of ambient light and to keep the actors from blocking the spectators' view of the projected image, try to place the screen so that its bottom edge will be no lower than five to seven feet above the stage floor.

3. To maximize the brightness of the image when working with an audio-visual slide projector:
   A. Keep the size of the projection as small as possible.
   B. Use a lens with a low f-stop (3.5 or less).
   C. Use a short-focal-length lens, and place the projector as close to the screen as possible.

4. Rear-screen projection is affected by ambient light less than front-screen projection is, so whenever possible try to work with rear-screen techniques.

5. Become thoroughly familiar with the equipment that you will be using well before technical rehearsals begin. Shoot your slides early so that you will have time to shoot and process additional slides if it becomes necessary.

Chapter 16
Costume Design

There may be some truth to the adage that "clothes make the man." A study, summarized in the book *The Four Minute Sell,* by Janet Elsea, indicates that during the first four minutes of contact with a stranger our understanding of that person's nature and personality will be based on three primary, but unequal, factors: appearance, 55 percent; tone of voice, 38 percent; and what the person is saying, 7 percent.

Costume designers are aware of these factors, either intuitively or from training. They know that when an actor walks onto the stage for the first time, the audience's feelings about the character will be based, to a great extent, on the information that guides all first impressions.

What is a costume? According to Barbara and Cletus Anderson in their text *Costume Design,* "Anything worn onstage is a costume, whether it be layers of clothing or nothing at all."[1] More specifically, this definition includes all clothing, underclothing, hairdressing, makeup, and accessories such as hats, scarves, fans, canes, umbrellas, and jewelry, worn or carried by each character in a production. The design and appearance of all these costume elements is the province of the costume designer.

Most people agree that the costume worn by an actor profoundly affects the audience's perceptions of the character being created by that actor. If that assumption is correct, then it would logically follow that the costume designer's job entails the manipulation of the design of each character's clothing to project some specific personal information about that character. How can the costume designer shape that information? That and other questions are the subject of this chapter.

THE NATURE OF COSTUME DESIGN

In fashion design, primary attention is given to creating a striking visual design that gives little, if any, thought to the personality or character of the person who ultimately will wear the clothes. The fashion designer may follow the fashion currently in vogue, may look to historical antecedents, or may strike out in a new stylistic direction. In a fashion collection there may be little, if any, stylistic consistency from one design to the next. Costume design is different. To be effective, the costume designs for a production need to (1) reflect the production design team's agreed upon interpretation of the production concept (discussed in Chapter 1); (2) exhibit a unity of style among all the costume designs for that production; (3) provide a visual reflection of the personality and nature of each character at a given time in the play; and (4) provide visual information about the world of

[1] Barbara and Cletus Anderson, *Costume Design* (New York: Holt, Rinehart, Winston, 1984), p. 20.

The Design Process in Costuming

This discussion is a capsulization of the specific applications of the design process to costume design. A review of Chapter 2 may be appropriate if you are hazy on the fundamentals of this problem-solving technique.

Commitment

In order to accomplish your best work, you have to promise yourself that you will perform the task to the best of your ability.

Analysis

The type of information that is needed to clarify and refine the challenge can be gathered by reading the script and asking questions of the other members of the production design team. Typical questions that relate specifically to costume design include:

1. What is the costume budget?
2. What is the production concept?
3. Are we going to be producing the play in the period in which it is written? What is that period?
4. When is the first dress rehearsal?
5. Does the director want a costume parade?
6. What does the set design look like? What is its color palette?
7. What is the lighting designer's color palette?

Some questions will be answered when you study the script. Others will be discussed and answered during the production conferences, in which the director and all designers freely exchange ideas and information.

The second phase of analysis involves discovering areas and subjects that will require further research. Note these areas so that you can investigate them during the next phase of the design process.

Research

Research is divided into two separate areas: background research and conceptual research. The primary function of background research is to answer the questions generated during the analysis phase. The vast majority of costume designs are based on a fairly realistic interpretation of the style of clothing worn during some particular period of history. For this reason it is particularly important in costume design to consult primary research materials whenever possible.

Primary research items include clothing and accessories actually made during the period under investigation. The reason for primary research is to obtain the most accurate information about the period silhouette, the type and nature of the fabrics used, and construction techniques. Nothing tells you more about the design and construction of a dress of the 1890s than examining a dress made in the 1890s.

If primary resources are not available for examination, then the costume designer's research naturally expands to include examining photographs of actual garments of the period, museum displays of actual clothing and accessories, paintings appropriate to the time and locale of the intended production, and texts on the history of clothing and costumes.

The further back one goes in history, the greater will be the variations in the style of clothing from region to region and country to country. Before 1800 land transportation was by foot, horse, carriage, or cart. Travel between continents was by sailing ship. With the development of steamships, railroads, and the telegraph, the time that it took for information to travel from one place to another shrank from months and years to merely minutes and days. Consequently, the readily identifiable regional variations in the style of clothing began to diminish as the interchange of ideas, goods, and services became easier.

Even in our own age of information, regional differences in dress are still alive and well. But the current variations in clothing between regions and countries are generally more subtle today than they were even one hundred years ago.

During conceptual research, you need to visualize as many potential solutions to the design challenge as possible. Sketch a lot of ideas. Gather fabric samples that might be appropriate for material from which to construct the various costumes, and attach them to the sketches.

Incubation

Rest. Relax. Get away from the project. Work on something else. Go for a walk. Go to the library. Go see a play or movie. Do anything but work on or think about the project.

Selection

After you have selected the appropriate overall costume concept for the production, you will also need to select the appropriate design idea that will be used for each individual costume in the production.

Implementation

The implementation phase in costume design involves the drawing and painting of costume renderings, the selection of the appropriate fabrics for each design, and sometimes the supervision of the construction of each garment. (To be technically correct, the costume designer is responsible for the appearance, not the construction, of the finished costume. It is the costumer, not the costume designer, who is responsible for the supervision of the actual making of the costumes. In some production companies, these lines of responsibility become fuzzy.)

Evaluation

Finally, take an objective look at the communication process that has taken place between you and the other members of the production design team and your own use of the design process. The purpose of this evaluation is to discern ways in which you could improve your communication with other members of the production design team as well as your use of the design process.

the play including locale, period, season, time of day, culture, as well as the play's socioeconomic, religious, and political environment.

After the production design team agrees on the style of the production concept—the compositional characteristics that will be used as the unifying elements in each designer's work—the costume designer uses those compositional principles as guides in creating the costume designs for the production. The particular style selected might mimic the line and color palette used in a specific painting by a particular artist. Or it might be synthesized from the works of several artists, filmmakers, or composers. It could even be a subjective reaction to seemingly random thoughts, textures, and colors. The actual elements used in its creation aren't important. What is important is that the production design team agrees on, and understands the meaning of, the stylistic guide called the production concept.

Types of Costume Designs

In a manner similar to opposite ends of the continuum separating representational and nonrepresentational style, there are two opposing categories of costume designs: character and decorative.

Character costume designs (Figure 16.1) are those designs that are dictated by specific information contained in the script. Such facts as the historical period, socioeconomic status and occupations of the characters, and the season and climate can be gleaned from general information in the script, whereas personality traits and other information are frequently revealed by what the characters say about themselves and others say about them.

Decorative costume designs (Figure 16.2), while still subscribing to the tenets of the production concept and the visual world of the play, are simply those costumes that appear to be no more than decorative elements in the general stage picture—extras in a crowd scene or statuesque showgirls in spectacular head-dresses in a Las Vegas revue.

Every costume in a production could be placed somewhere on this character/decorative continuum. Costumes for the principal parts will be strongly influenced by the character traits of that role, but they will undoubtedly have some decorative touches. Even purely decorative costumes—those worn in revues such as The Ice Capades, for example—have some "character" elements because they need to conform to the stylistic principles dictated by the production concept.

The Psychological Meaning of Clothes

What a person wears, and how it is worn, says a great deal about that person and the society in which he or she lives. In contemporary Western countries, corporate businesspersons traditionally wear conservatively cut, somber-colored suits and ties. A man or a woman who wants to fit into that environment would buy only those clothes appropriate to the fashion and wear them as prescribed by the style. Don Johnson's character in the TV series "Miami Vice" visibly demonstrated his individualism and rebellion against the bureaucratic norm of the Miami Police Department by rolling up his jacket sleeves and wearing T-shirts instead of dress shirts and ties. In "Nash Bridges," Johnson's current series, his character is still wearing linen jackets and colored T-shirts to show his disdain for bureaucratic expectation. But now his sleeves are rarely rolled up. Whether this is an indication of some subtle psychological character shift or the temperature difference between Miami and San Francisco could be, I imagine, the subject of some discussion.

FIGURE 16.1
Character costume design by Peggy
Kellner for *Carousel*.

A certain type of clothing can be worn to conform to or rebel against a certain segment of society. During World War II, American pilots demonstrated their collective individualism by wearing their hats at jaunty angles rather than the "hat bill level and two fingers above the bridge of the nose" prescribed by the military dress-code manual. A visit to a contemporary American high school would reveal numerous distinctive styles of dress—"mod," "preppie," "stoners," "skaters," and "jocks"—that visibly demonstrate the peer groups to which the various students belong.

Clothes can also be visible clues to the wearer's emotional state. An introvert would probably wear something that would make him blend into the crowd, whereas an extrovert might wear something that would make her stand out and be noticed. Similarly, someone who is gloomy might wear something dark and dreary to reinforce and visually announce their mood, whereas a cheerful, happy individual might dress in bright and cheerful colors.

FIGURE 16.2
Decorative costume design by
Peggy Kellner for *Carousel*.

Objective Information Provided by Clothes

In addition to providing psychological clues, clothing can provide a variety of
objective information about a person.

Historical Period   The shape or silhouette of garments can provide clear indications of their historical period. Theatrical costumes may be faithful to their
historical period, or the costume designer may choose to use history as a reference point from which to create a design that is more meaningful to the production concept for a particular play. Either way, the historical silhouette can be a
primary indicator of the historical period of the play, as shown in Figure 16.3.

Age   In any period the color, style, and fit of clothes provide a great deal of
information about the age of the wearer. While the clothing of each period has its

Design Inspiration: Costume Design

The following discussion is based on "Designing Woman," by Ginia Bellafante (Time, February 22, 1999, pp. 82–83).

How often can articles of clothing be credited with having performance-enhancing power? It happened, it seems, during the shooting of Todd Hanes' *Velvet Goldmine,* an homage to the David Bowie '70s and the world of men in makeup. According to Toni Collette, who played a rock-star's wife, all the leopard print and lamé she wore in the film coaxed the hidden extrovert right out of her. "The clothes made me want to show off," she said, "which is just what the character had to do."

The pen—and mind—behind that transformative wear is Sandy Powell, [winner of the 1999 Oscar for costume design for *Shakespeare in Love* and] perhaps the movies' most celebrated costume designer since the heyday of Edith Head, a 35-time Oscar winner.

Powell briefly attended London's venerable Central Saint Martin's College of Art and Design before dropping out to work as an assistant designer in the theatre. Her movie career was launched in the mid '80s when she met director Derek Jarman, with whom she collaborated on *Caravaggio.*

She has since developed a working method that involves little initial sketching. Powell first researches the era she's dealing with by visiting museums and galleries and studying paintings and photographs. "Unless of course the film requires it, I'm not interested in an exact replica of the period. I look at the period, how it should be, how it *could* be, and then I do my own version," she says. Next, she scours London for splendid fabrics. "I rarely start with a drawing," says Powell. "I start with a fabric I like and base the design on how that fabric behaves. . . ."

"Sandy comes with strong responses to the material," noted John Madden, director of *Shakespeare in Love,* which speculates fancifully about the Bard's inspiration for *Romeo and Juliet.* "She comes armed with instinct." Among Madden's favorite creations for the film were the costumes she made for the staged production of *Romeo and Juliet.* He loved the way in which the lavishness of the players' dress contrasted with the shabby browns worn by the commoners in the audience. "At first we thought it looked bizarre," said Madden, "but what was so brilliant was how she captured in costume how extraordinarily intoxicating that play must have

been to the grubby creatures down in the pit watching."

Shakespeare [in Love] also showcased Powell's obsession with detail. In the film, the dressing gown worn by Gwyneth Paltrow appears to be festooned with iridescent jewels—but they are actually dried beetle wings, intended to replicate Elizabethan materials. When Paltrow's character pretends to be a boy, she wears a top with embroidery delicate enough to remind us that she is female. But Powell also put birdseed pouches in the crotch of Paltrow's breeches so the actress would remember to walk like a boy . . .

Despite her obvious talent for the splashy, one could argue that Powell's gift best manifests itself in smaller, brocade-free dramas such as the film *Hilary and Jackie.* Powell's mod clothes never overwhelm the tale of the relationship between the impassioned cellist Jacqueline Du Pré and her sister, but instead lend a keen visual intensity to the women's profound differences. As Jackie becomes increasingly famous—and depressed—her knits seem to get more blindingly pink and blue; Hilary, meanwhile, recedes into neutrals. The look stays with you. Powell's work, it seems, never fades to black.

own characteristics that differentiate between youth and age, one generalization holds true for almost all periods: Young people tend to reveal more of their bodies than do their elders. Two theories suggest the reasons: Young people generally are more interested in attracting romantic partners than are their elders, and exposed skin attracts notice; young bodies with smooth skin and superior muscle tone are generally more attractive to look at than the skin and muscles of their elders, on whom time and gravity have taken their toll. For example, miniskirts, short-shorts, halter tops, and muscle shirts are all clothes of youth. Put these clothes on an out-of-shape middle-aged body and the almost universal viewer response will be that that person is trying to recapture, or doesn't want to let go of, his or her youth.

Gender   Throughout history, with a few exceptions, clothes have almost always clearly indicated the gender of the wearer. When specifying gender differentiation, fashion design has almost always provided a visual reflection of the society from which it sprang. For example, during the Victorian and Edwardian periods,

(A)

(B)

(C)

(D)

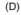

FIGURE 16.3
The silhouette of a costume can provide visual clues about character and historical period. Costume designs by Kathi Perkowski Mills for (A) the Madame in the Lincoln Boyhood Drama Association's production of *Young Abe Lincoln* and (B) Sahtin in *The Lower Depths.*
(C) Asolo State Theatre's (Sarasota, Florida) production of *Charley's Aunt.* Costume design by Catherine King, scene design by Gordon Miconis; photo by Gary W. Sweetman. (D) Jeri Leer, Candy Buckley, Linda Gehringer (left to right) and Michael O'Hara (background) in Dallas Theatre Center's production of *The Three Sisters.* Designed by Leo Akira Yoshimura; photo by Linda Blase.

women were fully covered from neck to foot, but there was visual emphasis on the hair, bust, and bustle, providing a visual reflection of the Victorian ideal of woman as wife and mother. The 1920s saw a revolt against the strict Victorian codes and the bold (for the time) assertion that women were individuals who could possibly have a life outside the traditional roles of wife and mother. A primary fashion statement of the 1920s, the flapper style, reflected the societal reevaluation of the role of women with its boyish look of short hair, flat bosom, and slender hips.

Socioeconomic Status   Social status has always been indicated with clothes. Someone dressed in shabby, ill-kempt clothes of rough homespun materials would rarely be mistaken for a member of the upper class. A woman dressed in beautifully fashioned linens, silks, and satins would rarely be mistaken for a servant. Prior to about 1930, the cut and fit of many upper-class clothing styles actually precluded the possibility of manual labor. The upper classes didn't work, so their clothes were designed to reflect and enforce their lives of leisure. Generally, servants' clothes have always been similar to those of their masters, but the designs have been simpler, the cloth plainer, and the colors more drab.

Occupation   Similar to the clues that clothing provides about a character's socioeconomic status, clothes can also tell us about a person's job. Uniforms are obvious indicators of occupation. Police officers, military personnel, chefs, maids, workers in franchised businesses such as McDonald's and Pizza Hut, and the gold-jacketed realtors with Century 21, are all readily identifiable. Sometimes the identification is not so clear. But we would probably identify a man in a flannel shirt, jeans, and heavy boots, with a tool pouch hanging from his belt, as some kind of workman, not a corporate lawyer. If he *were* a corporate lawyer, then we probably would instantly label him as eccentric.

Climate and Season   If we see someone bundled up in a heavy fur coat, we assume that the weather is cold. Dark hues, heavy fabrics, and multiple layers are also strong indicators of cold climate. Light colors, lightweight fabrics, and fewer clothes provide good indications that the weather is warm. Interesting inferences can be made about the personality of a character who dresses "out of season," such as the Reverend Hale, who, in James Michener's novel *Hawaii*, wears long underwear and a woolen frock coat while living in the tropical heat and humidity of the Hawaiian islands.

GENERAL CONSIDERATIONS FOR COSTUME DESIGN

A variety of diverse considerations and sources of information affect the work of the costume designer.

Analyzing the Script

The costume designer reads the script to gather various kinds of information about the play and the characters in it.

The script provides specific factual information about the historical period in which the play is set: the time of day, season, climate, and time span covered by the play; the sex, age, socioeconomic status, occupation of each character; and so forth. In addition to discovering this historical data, the costume designer gleans the emotional quality of the play and learns about the interrelationships existing between the various characters in the play from reading the script.

The analysis of the script expands beyond the printed page to include the views and interpretations of the producer, the director, and the other designers. Any or all of these other members of the production design team may see the relationships between the characters differently than you do. Their opinions must be acknowledged and evaluated.

All of this information provides the essential background material that the costume designer uses to create designs which effectively reflect the personality and characteristics of each role in the play.

Chapter 2, *The Design Process*, contains a specific script-analysis discussion and suggests a procedure that can be used to create effective costume designs.

Other Conceptual Considerations

While an analysis of the script provides a substantial beginning point in the conceptualization of each costume design, several other considerations must be addressed by the costume designer during the design process.

Stereotypical Costuming   The actor, not the costume, is the primary vehicle for conveying a character's nature and personality. For this reason, costume designers normally avoid stereotypical designs that clearly proclaim who or what a character is—a gangster in dark pinstripe suit, black shirt, and white tie or a prostitute in a tight, bust- and thigh-revealing red dress. The obvious exception to this principle involves those vehicles or production concepts which are based on flat, two-dimensional cartoonish characters, as in musicals such as *Li'l Abner* or *Guys and Dolls*. The use of design features that hint, rather than scream, at the true nature of the character allows the actor to develop the character with the aid of the costume, rather than being upstaged by it.

Character Evolution   Costumes need to match the growth and change that characters experience during the course of the production. In Carson McCullers' *The Member of the Wedding*, the character of Frankie matures and changes from a child into a young adult in the course of the play. The costumes that she wears should reflect this maturation process. Similarly, costumes worn by characters who experience emotional or intellectual growth should reflect those changes. A young woman who evolves from a flirt into a serious businesswoman might start out dressed in light-colored, ruffled tea dresses and finish the play costumed in dark-hued business suits.

Costume Stylization   The degree of stylization dictated by the script and production concept must be recognized by the costume designer. Some plays set in contemporary America are populated by ordinary characters using vernacular language. These slice-of-life dramas may be appropriately costumed with clothes purchased or faithfully copied from fashions available at JCPenney, Saks Fifth Avenue, or a local Salvation Army store. These costumes should reflect the everyday world of the play. Verse dramas, on the other hand, are populated by people who speak in heightened language. The thoughts, speech, and actions of Shakespearean characters, for example, are frequently more lofty, or at least more exaggerated, than ours. Their costumes should mirror their eloquence and grand thoughts. Similarly, plays in which the protagonist struggles against the gods or the cosmos are not "ordinary" or "normal" in their scope. The costume design for such a production should reflect the "supernormal" world of the play.

Interpretation of Period   Costumes make a statement that visually unifies the historical period, the style of the script, and the production concept. However, any historical period, regardless of whether it is one or forty years long, has a plethora of design styles, and each of those styles has an overwhelming number of subtle variations. If the costume designer were to randomly select costume

Design Inspiration: Costume Design

The following discussion is based on "Designing Women," by Amy Reiter (Entertainment Design, May 1999). Photo by Stan Barouh.

Claire Booth Luce's *The Women* may not be 100% politically correct—its portrayal of the so-called gentle gender is far more tart than sweet—but the early 1999 production of the 1936 play, which took place in the Fichandler Theatre of Washington D.C.'s Arena Stage, seduced even the most PC audiences, like a dazzlingly beautiful, tough-talking, wisecracking femme fatale.

In many ways the production was as much about clothes as it was about

power: the power of clothes, clothing as power. "How glamorous these women look is of paramount importance," director Kyle Donnelly said. Costume designer Paul Tazewell's costumes didn't just suit the characters; the costumes helped to define the characters and traced their trajectories through the play.

Although director Donnelly cast all women, "there was an element of the drag idea that interested her," Tazewell recalled. "It was this idea of facade, which synthesized itself down to being kind of a Hollywood facade, where many American women got their sense of glamour and style in that period." The world of *The Women* mirrored that Hollywood facade in that the characters in the play are beautiful but backstabbing, outwardly friendly but inwardly false.

Once the Hollywood concept was established, said Tazewell, "the door was open for it to be as out there as possible and not feel that I had to stick to a natural or realistic scale in either choices of color or silhouette."

Tazewell and scenic designer Thomas Lynch decided to art direct the play as they might have a film. Because capturing the black-and-white look of the films of the period in which the play takes place was not feasible— "You can't really get to the subtlety of everything, even the skin tones being some shade of gray," Tazewell pointed out—the designers decided to color-coordinate each scene. They found inspiration in the vivid Technicolor movies of the 1950s.

"We identified the pervading color that spoke of each scene," Tazewell said. They then integrated that color into all the design elements. For the play's opening scene, which takes place in the living room of the lead character, Mary, the designers chose Wedgwood blue, which evokes upper-crust coolness and polish, but also has a warm undercurrent. Tazewell dressed the women in chic, somewhat true-to-period suits in blues and grays. Black and yellow accents—in hats and other accessories—provided highlights and shading.

Other scenes were similarly constructed around color themes. The final scene centers around an evening gown–clad cat fight in a casino. The dresses in this scene were sumptuous—beaded bodices, feathers, and shimmering metallic fabrics.

The play "is structured that way," Tazewell said. "You start off in day clothes and go into evening. Once you're in Mary's boudoir (the penultimate scene), you think the story is done. She's in her nightgown. She's in bed. And then she gets more information—and here we go into this casino room, with all these women in glamorous dresses, and then Mary comes in in her red dress. It really hits the height you hope it will. You feel like it's never-ending, like there's all this abundance. That feels good for me."

Costume designer Paul Tazewell concluded, "I didn't worry so much about trying to make it the late '30s. It has the flavor of the '30s and then a lot of Paul in it."

detailing: Trim, appliqués, buttons, ribbons, braid, and so forth attached to a garment to enhance its appearance.

elements from the entirety of the period, the result would be a visual hodgepodge. Therefore, the costume designer needs to distill that mound of information into a few typical lines, colors, textures, and details that represent the essence of the period. Once that visual theme is established, then variations can be created within it to reflect the traits of the individual characters in the play. This distilled line is frequently an interpretation of the historical data. Character traits, or merely the importance of a character within a scene, sometimes require a departure from historical accuracy of the costume. Sometimes historical accuracy itself can cause visual problems. The **detailing** on gowns of Elizabethan nobility was incredibly ornate. If accurately reproduced for the stage, it could result in a visual "war" between the various trim designs. Simplification of the trim could increase the significance of what is selected and, depending on the production concept, perhaps create a design more appropriate to the production.

Interpretation of Color and Fabric   Part of his or her historical research will acquaint the costume designer with the color and types of fabrics used in a particular historical period. This information needs to be manipulated in the design process. While historically accurate data may form the root of the design, the colors and fabrics selected must be appropriate to the production concept and the individual characterizations. Typically, the designer will select a range of colors, textures, and fabrics appropriate to the period and production concept and then develop variations within those themes for individual characters.

Practical Considerations

In addition to historical, analytical, and conceptual considerations, the costume designer must be aware of a number of practical matters before the designs can be finalized.

Needs of the Actor   The actor's needs can be divided into two categories—physical and psychological. The physical needs are fairly simple: The costume should fit, it should be reasonably comfortable, and it shouldn't inhibit any necessary and appropriate motion. Because people today are not used to the physical constraints imposed by many fashion modes of the past, the costume designer needs to adapt the costume design to accommodate the actors, while still retaining the historical silhouette and line of the costume. The circumference of the hem of the hobble skirt (shown in Figure 16.4) was so small that women wearing them could take only very tiny steps; it was all but impossible to move up or down stairs. For stage use hobble skirts, and similar movement-inhibiting clothes, are usually designed with authentic lines but with slight modifications to allow for a little more freedom of movement.

Production Venue   Costume design is also influenced by the production venue. The small, delicately tinted pastel embroidered flowers on a peasant blouse, detail totally appropriate to the character and clearly visible in a production staged in an intimate arena theatre seating 125 people, would be completely lost in a large proscenium theatre seating 3,000 or 4,000.

Budget   Obviously, the amount of money in the costume budget, and the time and staff available to design and construct the costumes, have a direct effect on design choices.

Construction Demands of the Design   Construction demands in costume design are generally predicated on the number of costumes in the production, the complexity of the individual designs, the budget, and the expertise of available personnel. Costumes for professional productions are constructed under contract by a costume production house or the resident costume crew, although contemporary tailored clothes such as men's suits are frequently purchased. Because of time, fiscal, or other constraints, some of the costumes for educational and regional professional company productions may be rented or **pulled** from stock and modified. When a production uses a combination of rented, pulled, and constructed costumes, the designer needs to pay extra attention to creating a

FIGURE 16.4
A hobble skirt. Costume design by Peggy Kellner for *Hotel Paradiso*, Old Globe Theatre, San Diego, California.

pull: To remove a costume from storage for use in a production.

unified overall design and a visual blending of the costumes acquired from these disparate sources.

Renting Costumes   Carefully tailored, period-specific items such as military uniforms and expensive men's suits are frequently rented. An advantage of renting uniforms is that the costume houses often have the appropriate accessories, such as swords, decorations, headgear, and footwear.

Buying Costumes   When producing a contemporary production, costume designers frequently buy clothes "off the rack" and modify them as necessary to fit the production concept and the specific actor. For productions that are set in the past twenty to thirty years, costume designers can browse through used-clothing stores and pick up many appropriate garments.

Modifying Stock Costumes   Educational and regional professional companies frequently have a stock of costumes that have been used in previous productions. Costumes can be pulled from stock and modified by dyeing and/or the addition or deletion of trim and accessories. Significant variations in the appearance, and apparent period, of a costume can be made by something as simple as creating a lace **overlay** for the **bodice** of a gown. Similar changes can be effected by changing from lace to fur trim or vice versa.

overlay: A garment, usually made of lace or a similar lightweight, semitransparent fabric, designed to lie on top of another garment.

bodice: The upper part of a woman's dress.

ORGANIZATIONAL PAPERWORK

Since there are frequently between twenty and one hundred costumes per production, the costume designer must use a variety of organizational paperwork to keep track of the myriad details during all phases of production.

The costume designer must keep track of amazing amounts of detail regarding every costume in the production, so it is essential that he or she make copious and complete notes. There are an ever-increasing number of software programs that greatly aid the costume designer and the costume shop personnel in keeping track of all these details. Reviews and contents of some of these products may be found by accessing appropriate listservs found in the Appendix, "Listservs for Theatre Production," and through the Website of the USITT—www.usitt.org.

In Chapter 2, it was suggested that designers carry a notebook for jotting down ideas. In addition to using a notebook, costume designers often jot notes in the margins of the script because of the frequent references to specific items worn by the characters.

Most costume shops have an organizational tool that is frequently referred to as the "costume bible."[2] This book holds all the information regarding the planning and construction of a particular show. If the production company or construction shop is working on more than one show at a time, each show normally will have its own "bible." While the specific information contained in the "costume bible" obviously varies from company to company, it will normally include the following:

cast list and production contact sheets;

measurement sheets;

calendars and deadlines;

costume plots and lists;

budget sheets, including an area to keep a running total of costs;

[2] Information extracted from Ingham, Rosemary, and Liz Covey, *The Costume Designer's Handbook,* 2nd edition (Portsmouth, N.H.: Heinemann, 1992), p. 157; Cunningham, Rebecca, *The Magic Garment: Principles of Costume Design* (Prospect Heights, Ill.: Waveland Press, 1994), p. 229.

Romeo & Juliet	I:1	I:2	I:3	I:4	I:5	II:1	II:2	II:3	II
Romeo	Cream sweater Beige silk slacks Beige shoes, socks & belt	Same		White linen suit Black knit shirt Black belt & shoes	Add mask and cape	Same	Same	Same	S
Juliet			Peach kimono Beige slip		White dress White petticoat White shoes Nylons Mask		Kimono Slip		
Nurse			Day dress Nylons Shoes Necklace		Eve. dress Shoes same Jewelry Mask?		Voice only		
Capulet	2 pc. gray silk suit Gray striped shirt Rose tie & handkerchief Black shoes	Same			D. breasted tux Cummerbund Tux shirt Black bow tie, socks, & shoes Wht. handkerchief Cufflinks, studs				
Lady Capulet	Blue knit dress, belt & shoes Slip, nylons Necklace Earrings, purse Bracelet, fur		Same		Black velvet gown Earrings Bracelet Black shoes Mask				
Mercutio	White tux shirt Black leather pants Black boots			Same Add blue cape Baldric sword	Same Add mask	Same			
Time of Day	Sunday about noon	Sunday, minutes later	Sunday late afternoon, early evening	Sunday late afternoon, pre-party	Sunday night, party, visual climax	Sunday night, late post-party			

FIGURE 16.5
A sample costume chart. (Courtesy of Dianne J. Holly.)

rental contracts and pull lists;

copies of renderings;

swatches and dyeing instructions;

production notes from the stage manager.

Many of the items mentioned above will be discussed a little later in this chapter.

Costume Chart

The costume chart (Figure 16.5), also known as the actor's scene chart, is used to visually plot what each character (or actor if he or she is playing multiple roles) wears in each scene in the play. Reasonably large squares are gridded off on a large sheet of paper. The characters' names are listed down the left side, and each act (or each scene if the acts are subdivided into scenes) is noted across the top of the page. A check is placed in each scene in which the character appears. All costume items, including accessories, are noted in the scene in which they are first worn. Subsequent costume changes are noted in the appropriate scene.

As an organizational device, some costume designers attach color samples to each listing so that they can see the development of the overall color scheme of the production, as well as be able to trace the color progression of individual characters at a glance. Wardrobe personnel use the costume chart as a guide when dressing the actors, and directors and actors use it to help keep the costumes organized in their minds.

FIGURE 16.6
A sample costume list.

PRINCIPAL MEN

Romeo

1. Cream sweater, beige silk slacks, beige shoes, beige socks, beige belt
2. White linen suit, black knit shirt, black belt, black socks and shoes
3. Mask, cape MEDIUM QUICK CHANGE

Capulet

4. Two-piece gray silk suit, gray/white striped shirt, rose tie and handkerchief, black socks/shoes
5. Double breasted tux, cummerbund, tux shirt, black bow tie, black socks/shoes, white handkerchief, cufflinks and studs (gold)
6. Pajamas, robe, slippers

Mercutio

7. White tux shirt, black tux trousers, dinner jacket, black boots
8. Blue cape, baldric sword

Extra Men

18. Guard I — dark gray suit, black shoes, black shirt, black tie
19. Guard II — dark gray suit, black shoes, black shirt, black tie
20. Servant I — black dress pants, white shirt, black bow tie

PRINCIPAL WOMEN

Juliet

9. Pink kimono, beige slip
10. White dress, white petticoat, white shoes, nylons mask
11. Cream skirt, yellow sweater, cream nylons/shoes, straw hat

Nurse

12. Day dress, nylons, shoes, necklace
13. Evening dress, matching shoes, jewelry, mask
14. Shawl

Lady Capulet

15. Blue silk dress, matching belt, slip, nylons, blue shoes, necklace, earrings, bracelet, fur
16. Black velvet gown, earrings, bracelet, black shoes, mask
17. Pink nightgown, blue robe, blue slippers

Extra Women

21. Servant I — black maid's uniform, black shoes, nylons
22. Servant II — black maid's uniform, black shoes, nylons

Costume List

Frequently created simultaneously with the costume chart, the costume list (Figure 16.6) specifies every element, including accessories, of each costume worn by every actor. Broken into two sections, men and women, in larger productions it is further subdivided into Principal Men, Chorus Men, Extra Men, Principal Women, Chorus Women, and Extra Women as necessary. Each costume is numbered so that the total number of costumes in the production is readily apparent. Other information, such as any necessary quick changes, is also noted.

This list is extremely useful to the designer when estimating costs or when dealing with a costume house that may build the costumes or with a business from which certain costumes may be rented. The costume list is also used by the dressers/wardrobe maintenance crew as a checklist to verify that all elements of each costume are together and that each costume is placed in its proper location prior to each performance.

Character–Actor Dressing List

This list is used by the actors and **dressers** during dress rehearsals and performances. Primarily posted in the actor's dressing room, it can also be located wherever the actor makes a costume change (dressing-room locker, makeup mirror, offstage costume-change enclosure). It details everything, including accessories, that the actor wears in each scene, as shown in Figure 16.7.

dressers: Costume-crew personnel who assist actors in putting on their costumes.

Costume Calendar

The costume calendar (Figure 16.8) helps the costume designer budget time and provides a visualization of how much time is to be devoted to each phase of the costume design and construction process. To be effective it must include all facets of the process: readings/conferences, research, design, fabric shopping, construction, and rehearsals leading up to the opening performance.

The above listed forms are almost indispensable to the costume designer, but they can also trap the unwary. It is sometimes easy to lose sight of the fact that any theatrical production is always a work in progress. In even the best-planned production, designs are rarely finalized in the preliminary stages. Adjustments to the costume chart and costume list are frequently made during dress rehearsals. Accessories that were agreed on by both the director and costume designer during the design phase may need to be changed once they're seen onstage during dress rehearsals. Whole costumes may need to be replaced. If the director is truly prepared, and if the agreed on production concept is fully understood by all concerned, then these adjustments should be minimal and not overly disruptive. Experienced costume designers know and understand these needs, plan for them, and adapt as necessary.

VISUAL PRESENTATION OF THE COSTUME DESIGN

At some point, costume designers need to begin to codify their thoughts about the costume designs. This is when they need to start drawing. There are several types of drawings that costume designers create: preliminary sketches, the costume layout, and the final costume sketch or rendering.

A vital element in all costume drawings is that the sketches should do two things: show the nature and personality of the character at the time in the play

FIGURE 16.7
A sample character–actor dressing list.

DRESSING LIST

PLAY: ___Romeo & Juliet___

ROLE: ___Capulet___

ACTOR: ___Carl Douglas___

DRESSER: ___Ted Freeman___

I: i — 2-piece gray suit, gray/white striped shirt, rose tie
& handkerchief, black shoes & socks

I: ii— Same

I: iv — Double-breasted tux, cummerbund, tux shirt,
black bow tie, black shoes/socks, white handkerchief,
gold cufflinks and studs

III: i — Same as Ii

III: iv — Same as Ii

III: v — Pajamas, robe, slippers

when the illustrated costume is being worn; evoke the mood and spirit of the play. Obviously, these demands require that costume designers be able to draw the human body and clothes with ease and confidence. Chapter 22, *Drawing and Rendering*, provides an introduction to the subject of figure drawing, but students who are truly interested in pursuing costume design are strongly encouraged to take courses in figure drawing and painting in the appropriate departments of their colleges or universities.

Preliminary Sketches

Frequently the most exciting time in the creation of costume designs, the preliminary-sketch phase, is that time when the first visible results of the creative process appear on paper. These sketches, often rapidly drawn in pen or pencil on the pages of a sketch pad or notebook, are the first tangible results of the synthesis of the costume designer's thoughts, ideas, impressions, and research. Normally not fully completed drawings, they are rough sketches, equivalent to the thumbnail sketches of the scenic designer, showing the silhouette and perhaps a little detail of the costume, as shown in Figure 16.9. Frequently, costume designers will

	Sunday	Monday	Tuesday	Wednesday	Thursday	Friday	Saturday
August	18	19	20	21	22	23 Production Meeting 9 AM	24
	← CONCEPT MEETINGS →						
	25	26	27	28	29	30 Prod. Meeting 9 AM	31
	← RESEARCH/DESIGN →						
September	1	2	3	4	5	6 Prod. Meeting 9 AM	7
	← DESIGN →						
	8	9	10	11	12	13 Prod. Meeting 9 AM	14
	← SHOPPING →						
	15	16	17	18	19	20 Prod. Meeting 9 AM	21
	← SHOP CONSTRUCTION →						
	22	23	24	25	26	27 Prod. Meeting 9 AM	28
	← SHOP CONSTRUCTION →						
October	29	30	1	2	3 1st Tech	4	5 Dress Parade
	← SHOP CONSTRUCTION →						
	6	7 1st Dress	8 2nd Dress	9 3rd Dress Preview	10 Opening Performances →	11	12
	13	14	15	16	17	18	19
	← PERFORMANCES →						

FIGURE 16.8
A sample costume calendar.

cover one or more pages of the sketch pad with numerous variations of the same design as they try out different ideas and concepts in search of an appropriate and meaningful design.

As these first sketches are distilled toward their final form, the costume designer will show them to the director and other members of the production design team so that they all can be assured that their work is progressing toward the same goal. During these production conferences, it is typical for adjustments to be made to the design concepts and also quite normal for the sketches to be revised. Some designers make multiple photocopies of the pencil sketches so that they can present a variety of color schemes by coloring the photocopies with markers or watercolor pens. The sketch can be scanned into a computer and modified in line, color, or texture as was discussed in Chapter 7. Sometimes a solution is not readily apparent, in which case the designer goes "back to the drawing board" and continues making new design choices and sketches based on the input from the production design team.

Computer drawing and painting programs, as described in Chapter 22, *Drawing and Rendering,* can also be used for making costume sketches.

(A)

(B)

FIGURE 16.9
Preliminary costume sketches for (A) extras in *Carousel*, designed by Peggy Kellner,
(B) the Tinker in *Young Abe Lincoln*, designed by Kathi Perkowski Mills.

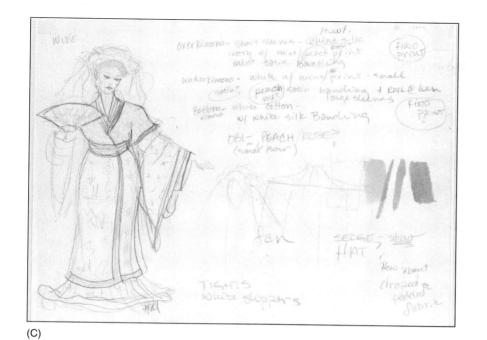

(C)

FIGURE 16.9 *(continued)*
(C) The Wife in *Rashomon,* designed
by Kathi Perkowski Mills.

FIGURE 16.10
(A) Costume layouts for the finale
in the American Southwest Theatre
Company's production of *Barnum,*
designed by Kathi Perkowski Mills.

(A)

FIGURE 16.10 *(continued)*
(B) Costume layouts for the family in the Lincoln Boyhood Drama Association's production of *Young Abe Lincoln,* designed by Kathi Perkowski Mills.

(B)

Costume Layout

The costume layout (Figure 16.10) is a group of small figures, simply and clearly drawn, that illustrate the costume designs for a number of characters. Normally sketched in pencil or ink, the costumes may be fully or partially colored with pencils, markers, dyes, or pigment (see Figures 6.24 and 6.25, p. 103, for costume layouts in color). Their purpose is to provide an overall view of the costume concept for the entire production. If the cast for the play is small and the costume changes are few, one layout may suffice, but more frequently several layouts will be necessary. Characters are normally grouped in some logical sequence. For a musical, all dancers might be on one layout, while the leads may be grouped on another, and the secondary characters and extras are on yet another.

Costume layouts are primarily used to provide the director and costume designer with an overview of how the costumes will look, or work, together.

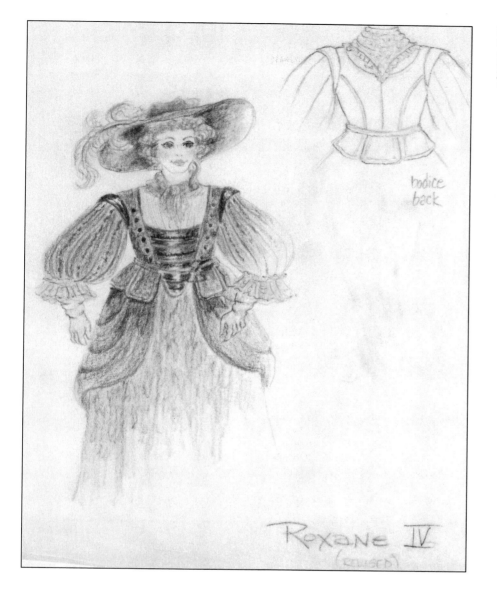

FIGURE 16.11
Costume sketch. Roxane from *Cyrano de Bergerac,* designed by Kathi Perkowski Mills for the Southwest Theatre Company's production.

Costume Sketch

Created by the costume designer, the costume sketch or plate is a full-color drawing that should give a strong indication of character, and the costume should look like it is being worn by the specific character for whom it was designed. Drawn with a single character per plate, as shown in Figure 16.11, the sketch should be large and clear enough to provide accurate information about the line and detail of the garment, yet not look cramped on the plate. Generally, a figure between ten and fifteen inches tall will satisfy those demands, although larger or smaller figures can be used as necessary. Swatches of the fabrics to be used in the construction of the costume frequently will be attached to the drawing. Notes about the costume are often penciled into the margins of the plate. If the design is complex, pencil sketches showing other views of the garment may be drawn

Design Inspiration: Costume Design

The following discussion is adapted from "I Want My Mummy," by David Barbour (Entertainment Design, February 1999, pp. 5–6). Photo by Anita and Steve Shevett.

The Mystery of Irma Vep is a wonderful little mystery in which the entire cast—the tormented heroine Lady Enid Hillcrest, her equally tormented husband Lord Edgar Hillcrest, the manservant (and sometimes werewolf) Nicodemus Underwood, the sinister Cockney maid Jane Twisden, the shadowy Egyptian guide Alcazar, the mummy Pev Amri, and the mysterious Intruder—are all played by two male actors.

The late Charles Ludlam's so-called "penny dreadful" is made up of bits and pieces of *Jane Eyre, Rebecca,* the novels of Wilkie Collins, and the entire output of Universal Studios from 1930–45. The revival opened off-Broadway in 1998 at the Westside Theatre in New York City.

As the convoluted plot of this over-the-top melodrama unfolds, both actors constantly switch characters, costumes, and genders at a moment's notice. Every costume change was a quick change—some of them ultra-quick.

There was another no less daunting challenge for the costume designer, William Ivey Long. Designing the costumes ". . . was a humbling experience," Long said, "because my director (Everett Quinton) was the original costume designer—and he won the coveted Maharam Award for it."

Costume designer Long indicated, "Our intention was to make very beautiful 1895 dresses for rather stocky ladies. The proportions change, but you fit them beautifully."

The period of the show is "1895," Long said, "because that's the most exaggerated moment—the huge leg-of-mutton sleeves and the tiny, tiny little waist—absolutely ignoring the

---

on the plate or provided on additional sheets. Research materials that indicate construction details frequently provide more accurate information for the cutter/draper than any pencil sketches. If available, photocopies of these research materials are frequently provided with the costume rendering. Basically, any information that will help construct the costume as the designer envisions it can, and should, be provided with the costume sketch or rendering. Finally, each plate should identify the play, the name of the character, and the scene(s) in which the costume is worn.

The costume sketch or plate is a working drawing that must communicate in a variety of ways with a number of production staff. The costume sketch conveys the designer's design concepts to the director and producer for approval of the design. It is used by the scenic and lighting designers to provide information about the costume color palette and fabrics, and by the costumer and shop staff as the master construction guide.

Specific information on the pragmatic aspects of designing, drawing, and coloring costume designs is given in other chapters. Figure drawing and render-body underneath. It's a very clever choice, because you can disguise masculine shoulders. I got out books of late 19th-century fashion, and Everett and I went through them, page by page. Every time he oohed over a picture, I put a yellow Post-It note on it. When he did an extra ooh-ooh, I put two Post-Its on it. Then I noticed that every double Post-It was a striped dress; Everett adores vertical stripes."

But where to find the suitably lavish materials on a budget? Fortunately, Long had a binful of drapery and upholstery fabrics from Scalamandre (the Manhattan fabric house) saved up for the ongoing decoration of his Chelsea home, which became the basic stuff of the *Irma Vep* design. For Lady Enid's striped dressing gown, the designer had a moment of invention worthy of Scarlett O'Hara: "There was this curtain in my garden room in my country house in the Berkshires. It's the widest stripe ever known to God and man—I think it's 10 inches wide. I took it down, dusted it off, and there was just enough material for two costumes—we have doubles."

Other costumes required other flights of invention. Jane's maid uniform is, says Long, "a Chanel suit fabric. It's 100% silk, because Stephen DeRosa (one of the actors) is allergic to wool. For Jane, plaid and checks were the words—even the fabric for her apron, which actually was an old curtain that I got at the Haddassah Thrift Store in New Haven. I've had it for 18 years. I thought I was going to make a curtain out of it, but it was just too fabulous."

One of the costumes is "based on three of Charles James' dresses, from the book, *The Genius of Charles James*," says Long, invoking the name of the famous couture designer.

In the construction of the costumes, Long said, "Everything is flatlined; before you make the pattern, you lay down a layer of cotton twill and then stitch them together. It stiffens it and makes it sturdier. The sleeves are extra wide, for stuffing your hands through. The peignoirs, made out of nice linen curtains, are unlined, because I wanted them to flow—so they're beautifully finished off on the inside. The costumes were made by Werner Kulovitz at EuroCo, with his associate, Janet Bloor. Jennifer Love made Jane's costumes

and Lord Edgar's fabulous herringbone suit."

Topping off Long's costumes are the wigs designed by Zsamira Sol Ronquillo, who also designed the show's makeup. Ronquillo says her biggest challenge is creating wigs that go on and off in seconds. Thus, "They're not secured," she says. "They're made to fit the actors' heads. They have elastic inside and, after a while, they mold themselves. I make my wigs on a 24" head block, which is the biggest available, and, once I'm through with them, they stretch themselves. When they come off the block, they're already molded, so it's much easier to put one on a head. Each one fits like a skullcap underneath the wig."

Ronquillo adds that the wigs are "all nylon. I don't use hairsprays made for human hair." The spray that was used is ". . . made to bond with the nylon fibers, so each wig keeps. Normally, a wig takes one to two days, because of the mixture of hairsprays that I use, to keep the wig rubbery and bouncy. The hairspray takes two hours to dry. After it sets, I add another coat. I build it up in layers, like lasagna."

ing techniques are covered in Chapter 22, *Drawing and Rendering,* while design elements and color are discussed in Chapter 5, *Style, Composition, and Design,* and Chapter 6, *Color.*

Costume design is a challenging and rewarding craft. To be able to design effectively, you must be imaginative, be able to draw and paint with ease and authority, and have a thorough understanding of fabrics and their characteristics, as well as an encyclopedic knowledge of the history of clothing. While the acquisition of this required body of knowledge may seem daunting, your reward comes from watching the costumes you've designed help actors create beautifully drawn characters in a well-produced production.

Chapter 17
Costume Construction

Costume construction is a broad field concerned with the processes, materials, and techniques used in making costumes and costume accessories. Specifically, the field requires knowledge of the **hand** of fabrics used in theatrical costumes; techniques of making and adjusting patterns; sewing; fabric painting, dyeing, and distressing; as well as such specialty skills as jewelry-, shoe/boot-, wig-, and armor-making techniques.

ORGANIZATION OF COSTUME SHOPS

In the Broadway theatre, all of the technical personnel are hired for a single production. After the producer has approved the designs and the costume construction bids, the costumes are built by a professional costume house. During construction the costume designer is in frequent contact with the shop supervisor to answer any artistic and practical questions about the costumes. When dress rehearsals begin, the costumes are moved into the theatre dressing rooms or costume storage area; their use and maintenance is coordinated by the wardrobe supervisor (also known as the wardrobe master or mistress) and the dressers or **wardrobe crew or staff.** In the professional theatre, the costume running crew personnel belong to a different union than do the construction crew personnel.

The organization of the costume shops of regional professional theatres, university theatre arts departments, and community theatre groups is not significantly different from the organization of a professional costume house because both are frequently working on more than one production at the same time. The job descriptions of the various costume shop personnel were discussed in Chapter 1, *Production Organization and Management.*

COSTUME SHOP TOOLS

Because of the wide variety of materials used in the construction of costumes, many types of tools and basic equipment are necessary in any well-equipped costume shop.

Basic Shop Equipment

While costume shops come in a variety of shapes and sizes, all must be equipped with certain basic equipment.

Cutting Tables   Used for laying out patterns and fabrics, cutting tables should be forty-two to fifty inches wide (to accommodate all but the widest fabrics), about thirty-six inches high (so people of average height won't have to bend over while working on the table), and six to eight feet long. A cork or Upson-board table top is skid-resistant (so slick material won't slide off), and fabric can be pinned directly to it. The considerable area under the table can be used for storage.

Dress Forms   Dress forms, also known as dressmaker's dummies, are extremely useful in the costume shop. These rigid forms, which are padded so that material can be pinned directly to them, are used for draping as well as pinning and adjusting cut pattern pieces. Available in standard men's and women's sizes, a well-equipped shop will have a variety of sizes (Figure 17.1). Foam mannequins should be used only if commercial dress forms cannot be afforded. Adjustable home sewing dummies are more trouble than they are worth.

Fabric Storage   Large pieces of scrap fabric should be stored for future use in bins or drawers identified as to fabric type and color. Additional bin/drawer storage should also be available for such accessories as jewelry, millinery, parasols, and so forth. Shelf storage should be available for bolts of fabric such as muslin and rolls of brown paper (both regularly used in pattern-making) and for special-purchase items such as close-out specials and remnants.

Washing Machine and Dryer   Used for cleaning washable costume elements during dress rehearsals and performances, and for dyeing fabrics, large-capacity, heavy-duty machines with a variety of settings are best. It is preferable to have one set for washing and one for dyeing. However, if one set is used for both dyeing and cleaning, both the washer and the dryer must be kept scrupulously clean, including the drain hoses, so that leftover dye won't spot, stain, or discolor clothes that are being washed and dried. Again, it is infinitely preferable to have two sets of machines: one for dyeing and one for washing.

Dye Vat   Commercial dye vats are expensive, but commercial soup kettles, shown in Figure 17.2, cost less and work equally well. The dye vat should be able to heat twenty to forty gallons of water to boiling.

FIGURE 17.3
A heavy-duty steam iron. (Courtesy of Sussman.)

FIGURE 17.4
Portable steamer. (Courtesy of Sussman.)

FIGURE 17.5
A movable clothes rack.

Safety Tip ⚠

Most of the dyes used in the costume shop recommend heating the dye anywhere from 100°F to boiling. Heated dye solutions give off vapors that are hazardous to some degree. In addition to reading the directions of the dye containers, also order, and read, the MSDS's for the specific dyes that are being used in your costume shop. Be sure to follow their recommendations for safe handling of wet and dry dyes, protective clothing and eyewear, respirators, ventilation, and related safety issues.

Hot Plate   A hot plate useful for boiling water for dyeing when the amount of fabric to be dyed does not warrant the use of the dye vat.

Stove   A residential-type stove can be used in place of a hot plate for boiling water. Additionally, the oven can be used for heating certain types of plastics and craft materials frequently used in the construction of costume ornamentation and accessories.

Irons   Heavy-duty steam and dry irons with a multigallon water capacity, such as the Sussman model in Figure 17.3, are preferred because the steam is more concentrated and the irons last longer than those designed for home use. Each iron should be equipped with a metallic or heat-resistant iron rest on which the iron can be placed when heated but not in use. Distilled water should always be used to avoid mineral buildup in the iron and the possibility of inadvertently staining the costumes.

Ironing Boards   Large, heavy-duty ironing boards with sturdy tip-resistant bases are desired. Smaller specialty boards, such as sleeve boards, and needle boards for pressing velours and velvets are highly desirable.

Steamer   Portable steamers (Figure 17.4) generate a stream of steam that is useful for taking wrinkles out of materials that cannot be ironed easily such as velvets, velours, and corduroys. Portable steamers are also useful in millinery for shaping felt.

Sink   A sink with cold and hot water is essential for cleaning equipment and providing water for a variety of costume shop activities.

Mirror   A full-length three-way mirror is extremely useful during fittings. It allows the costume designer, crew members, and the actor to see the costume from all directions and aids checking fit and finish while the costume is being worn.

Racks   Large castered, sturdy, movable clothes racks (Figure 17.5) can be moved to convenient locations and used to hang clothes under construction, in storage, or in production.

Tables and Chairs   These are extremely useful for doing hand sewing and other detail work.

Sewing Machines A variety of sewing machines are used in the costume shop. Every shop will need at least three or four straight-stitch machines and one zigzag machine. Commercial-grade zigzag machines are normally capable of straight stitching as well, so they can be used for both purposes. The more exotic specialized machines can be added to the shop's inventory as finances permit.

Straight-Stitch Sewing Machines Heavy-duty, commercial grade (not light-duty homemaker models) straight-stitch machines are used for the majority of the machine sewing in the costume shop.

Zigzag Sewing Machines There is also a need for one or more heavy-duty machines capable of making zigzag, buttonhole, and similar specialty stitches. These machines, shown in Figure 17.6A, can be used for straight stitching as well.

Walking-Foot Machine Also called power machines (Figure 17.6B), these high-speed, straight-stitch machines have the power to stitch any fabric from chiffon to leather with equal ease.

Serger The serger, also called a merrow machine, or overlock (Figure 17.7), sews a seam, cuts both pieces of fabric about one-quarter inch from the seam, and makes an overcast stitch on the edge of both pieces of fabric to prevent it from raveling—all in one operation. Again, as with all shop machines, the heavy-duty, industrial grade models are preferred.

Blind-Stitch Machine This is a specialty sewing machine used to make hems quickly with an easily removable stitch. The blind stitch is now available on most straight-stitch and zigzag machines.

Sewing Equipment

The following is a nonexhaustive list of basic sewing supplies commonly used in costume construction. Many of these items are illustrated in Figures 17.8 and 17.9. To save money, staple items such as needles, pins, and fasteners should be bought in bulk.

Measuring Devices Accurately inscribed sixty-inch, plastic tape measures are used for the majority of measuring in the costume shop. Aluminum rules, forty-eight to seventy-two inches long, are helpful for laying out large garments such as skirts and capes.

Hand Needles Long-eyed needles are used because they are the easiest to thread. Sizes 5 to 10 are the most commonly used. Heavy materials require heavy-duty needle types such as carpet and darning, as well as straight and curved upholstery needles.

Machine Needles Medium-sized needles are used for the bulk of the sewing in the costume shop, although lightweight and heavy needles are used for sheer and heavyweight fabrics. Ball-pointed needles are used on knit and polyester fabrics, while sharp-pointed needles are used on the rest.

Thread To save money, many costume shops prefer to match the value of thread to costume rather than match color. These shops use only black, white, and gray thread. However, if the audience is particularly close to the stage, they may match the color of the topstitch thread to the fabric. Heavy-duty carpet and button threads are also used for special applications.

(A)

(B)

FIGURE 17.6
Sewing machines: (A) heavy-duty machine (courtesy of Husqvarna Sewing Machine Co.), (B) power machine (courtesy of Chandler Sewing Machine Co.).

FIGURE 17.7
A merrow machine.

FIGURE 17.8
Hand tools commonly used in costuming.

Thimbles   A plastic or metal cap for the end of the finger, thimbles are used to protect the finger when pushing a needle through the fabric. Thimbles in a variety of sizes are normally stocked in the costume shop.

Straight Pins   Rustproof pins of medium size are used to pin fabric together and pin patterns to most fabrics. Silk pins are available for use with sheer fabrics. Larger pins are useful when working with heavier fabrics.

Safety Pins   Large sizes are most frequently used, although there is a need for all sizes.

Tracing Wheels   These are toothed wheels used with tracing paper for transferring markings from a pattern to fabric. Available with several "tooth" designs, the regular V-toothed wheel works well in most applications, although the very sharp stiletto-toothed wheel works better with heavy fabrics.

Tracing Paper   A heavy paper with transferable color, it is used with the tracing wheel to transfer markings from patterns to fabric. Several colors are normally stocked so a hue that contrasts with the color of the fabric on which the markings are going to be made can be used.

Tailor's Chalk   Manufactured in chalk and wax bases, it is available in white and colors. It is used for transferring pattern lines and for marking fabric during fittings.

Shears and Scissors   The cost of fabric-cutting shears is directly related to their quality. Buy the best you can afford—as the more expensive ones generally stay sharp longer—and use them for fabric cutting only, as cutting other materials dulls the blades. Bent-handle shears with eight-, ten-, or twelve-inch blades are

FIGURE 17.9
Fasteners used in costuming.

best for fabric cutting. Less expensive shears and scissors in a variety of sizes should be kept on hand for cutting other things.

Seam Rippers   The small ones seem easiest to use, although this is usually a matter of personal preference.

Single-Edged Razor Blades   These are sometimes unadvisedly used as a substitute for a seam ripper. Murphy's Law would indicate that when so used, the fabric will be cut more often than the thread.

Tables and Chairs   A table with a couple of reasonably comfortable chairs can make the life of someone doing hand or detail work much more pleasant.

Snaps   All sizes from tiny to huge, in both black and silver, should be kept in stock in the costume shop.

Hooks and Eyes   Again, all sizes from small to large, in both black and silver, should be kept on hand, although the larger sizes—3 through 5—seem to be used most often.

Zippers   Although zippers will frequently be bought for a specific costume, a stock of metal dress zippers in both black and white, from seven to twenty-two inches long, should be kept on hand. White zippers can be dyed to match the color of the costume.

Velcro   This is used as a substitute for snaps, hooks and eyes, zippers, and buttons, particularly when a very quick change is called for in the play. It is manufactured in twelve-yard rolls, and many shops maintain a supply of both black and white Velcro. Although the white doesn't dye particularly well, it can be tinted to approximate the hue of the costume fabric.

Hot Glue Gun This electrically heated pistol-shaped device melts sticks of glue and dispenses the glue in a narrow line. Arguably the most versatile tool in the costume shop, it can be used as a substitute for sewing in some projects and is almost indispensable in jewelry and ornamentation making, parasol repair, and so forth.

Seam-Binding Tape This includes any of the twill and/or bias tapes that are sewn to the cut edges of fabric to prevent seams from raveling. It is useful in ¼-, ½-, and 1-inch widths. Finishing seams with seam-binding tape is not necessary if a serger is used.

FABRICS

Fabric is the basic material from which costumes are made, so it is imperative that the costume designer understand fabric materials. Each type and weight of fabric has its own intrinsic characteristics. Some fabrics are crisp and stiff, and when draped they fall in stiff, angular lines. Other fabrics are soft and limp, and when draped they flow into smooth, sensuous curves. The costume designer must select the specific fabric or material that will most appropriately recreate the visual impression conveyed by the costume sketch.

The hand of a fabric—its characteristics that can be determined by a sense of touch—is of prime importance in determining the suitability of a fabric for a particular costume. The hand of any fabric is determined by the type of fiber used in its construction; the weave or structure of the fabric; how, and with what, the fabric is treated; and how it is finished.

Fabric Fibers

Two general types of textile fibers are used in the manufacture of cloth: natural and synthetic. Each type of fiber has its own distinctive characteristics.

Natural Fibers

Cotton Cotton—the white fiber contained in the seed pod, or boll, of the cotton plant—has been used in making cloth for more than 3,000 years. Cotton **breathes** well, readily accepts dyes, and wrinkles easily unless treated. Cotton thread is characterized by ribbonlike twists. Available in a huge number of weaves and **blends,** the varieties of weights, textures, and finishes of cotton fabrics are truly amazing. Mercerization is a caustic soda treatment applied to cotton that causes the fibers to swell and straighten out slightly. Mercerized cotton is more lustrous and dyes better than unmercerized cotton.

Linen The oldest textile fiber known, linen, derived from the flax plant, is stronger than cotton, has a silky luster, is a good conductor of heat, is lint-free, but does not dye well because of the hardness of the fiber. It washes easily, is hard to stain; shrinks and creases easily.

Silk Silk is the natural substance from which silkworms spin their cocoons. Silk is expensive, strong, lightweight, pliable; has good elasticity; is lustrous; holds heat; and takes dye extremely well. There are two basic forms of silk filament: cultivated and wild. Wild silk filament is brown and has a rough texture. Cultivated silk filament is smoother, more lustrous, and grayish-yellow. There are two ways of collecting the filament from the cocoon—reeling and spinning—and each method affects the appearance of the silk. Reeling yields longer filaments

breathes: A term that defines a material's ability to transmit heat, air, and water vapor.

blend: A combination of more than one type of fiber, blends are created to take advantage of the best properties of all fibers in the blend.

with little twisting than spinning does. These longer, less twisted filaments result in a stronger, more lustrous filament.

Wool   One of the oldest fibers used in textiles, wool is made from the fleece of sheep. There are two primary types of woolen yarns: woolen and worsted. Woolen yarns are loosely twisted, soft, and weak with a fuzzy, textured surface. Worsteds are more tightly twisted and stronger and have a smoother surface. Worsteds tend to breathe well, whereas the softer surface of woolen yarn traps air, making it a good insulator. Wool readily absorbs moisture and dyes. However, the boiling water used with most dyes can cause substantial shrinkage as well as texture changes. Woolen and worsted fabrics don't readily wrinkle, and most wrinkles **hang out** easily. Wool fabrics can be shaped with steam, which makes them ideal for making form-tailored garments.

Synthetic Fibers   Synthetic fibers are chemical compounds that are changed into hardened filaments by a variety of patented processes. Unless treated further, these fibers have a tendency to be slick, smooth, and dense. In general, synthetic fibers do not absorb moisture or breathe as well as natural fibers, so they tend to trap body heat inside the costume. On the positive side, most synthetic fabrics have an inherent resistance to wrinkling and are quite durable.

Two or more synthetic and/or natural fibers are often blended to form a fabric that will take advantage of the best attributes of each while deemphasizing their negative aspects. These blended fabrics are usually wrinkle-resistant and durable.

The care of any fabric, as well as its fiber content, must by law be indicated on the **hang tag** of the bolt of fabric. Synthetic fabrics that have approximately 40 to 50 percent natural-fiber content (cotton, linen, wool, and so forth) generally breathe well. Fabrics that are 100 percent synthetic generally do not breathe well. The costume designer and the costumer should be acquainted with the care of any fabric used in a stage costume, since those garments will normally need to be cleaned or washed and pressed frequently during the run of the production.

Acrylic   Acrylics are made from compounds based on coal, petroleum, and other materials. The acrylic fiber is soft and lightweight. Commercially, acrylics are frequently made into sweaters, blankets, and socks. Factory dyes are colorfast, but the material does not dye well in the costume shop. It is wrinkle-resistant, holds its shape well, and needs little if any ironing. Common trade names include Acrilan, Orlon, and Creslan.

Nylon   A slurry of air, water, and coal is heated and extruded through spinnerettes to produce the continuous-filament fiber known as nylon. Nylon is light, strong, extremely elastic, and resistant to abrasion. Wrinkles easily fall out of fabrics made from nylon. Nylon fiber doesn't conduct heat well or absorb moisture, so the fabric's heat-transmission characteristics depend on the weave: Smooth, tight weaves trap heat; loose, open weaves do not. Some nylon fabrics dye well, others do not. Common trade names include Antron, Capriolan, and Qiana.

Polyester   Another petroleum-based product, polyester fibers are highly resistant to wrinkling, are very strong, are commercially colorfast and reasonably stain-resistant, but they do not dye well in the costume shop. Polyester fibers are made into many types of light-, medium-, and heavyweight fabrics and, blended with cotton, create a fabric with excellent wash and wear characteristics and breathability. Trade names include Dacron, Kodel, and Quintess.

Rayon   Rayon was one of the first synthetic fabrics. It is made from regenerated cellulose, a viscous solution of **cotton linters** and wood pulp that is extruded

hang out: In this instance, hang out means that most wrinkles will disappear from the fabric if it is hung up.

hang tag: The small label usually attached to the cardboard core of a bolt of fabric that indicates the percentages of various component fibers.

cotton linters: The short hairs covering the cotton seed.

FIGURE 17.10
Types of weave patterns: (A) plain weave, (B) basket weave, (C) twill weave, (D) satin weave, and (E) plain knit.

wale: Visible, usually narrow, ridges in the surface of a fabric caused by a variation in the weaving pattern.

through spinnerettes to form a continuous fiber. Rayon dyes easily, has excellent colorfastness, works well when blended with other fibers, and is very absorbent. Similar in many characteristics and weaves to silk, rayon can frequently be used as a low-cost alternative to silk. Common trade names include Avril, Celanese, Fibro, and Zantrel.

Acetate   Similarly to rayon, chemicals are added to the regenerated cellulose solution to create cellulose acetate before the fibers are extruded. Acetates have little strength, must be ironed with low heat, don't hold a crease well, but have good draping characteristics and wrinkle resistance. Triacetates solve the heat-toleration and crease-retention problems associated with acetates while retaining their better qualities.

Weaves

Numerous types of weaves are used in making fabrics, and each type produces specific textural and visual effects. The fiber content of the threads woven into the fabric greatly affect the appearance and hand of the resultant material.

The threads running the length of the fabric are called the warp, and the threads running the width of the fabric are called the woof, fill, or weft. Some common ways that those threads are configured are shown in the weave patterns illustrated in Figure 17.10. Each pattern produces fabric with specific characteristics.

Plain Weave   In the plain weave, the fill passes over one warp thread and under the next. In the next row this pattern is alternated, as illustrated in Figure 17.10A. The visual effect of a plain weave is a simple, uncomplicated fabric. Variations of the plain weave include the ribbed weave, in which the fill yarn is much bulkier than the warp.

Basket Weave   In the basket weave, a variation of the plain weave, two or more fill yarns are passed over an equal number of warp yarns, as shown in Figure 17.10B. Oxford cloth is an example of a basket weave. Variations of the basket weave are numerous.

Twill Weave   The most durable of all weaves, twill is created when the fill yarn is interlaced with the warp to create diagonal ridges in the fabric, as shown in Figure 17.10C. Depending on the design of the weave, the **wales** may run diagonally from left to right, right to left, or both ways. Herringbone, in which the direction of the diagonal wales changes directions every few rows, is a common variation of the twill weave.

Satin Weave   The satin weave produces a smooth, very rich-looking fabric. This lustrous look is achieved by passing warp threads over a specific number of fill yarns, passing under one, then repeating the pattern (Figure 17.10D). The number of skipped threads, or floats, varies between four and twelve but remains constant for any particular piece of fabric. The lustrous sheen of satin has a definite direction, and patterns need to be cut keeping the direction of the fabric in mind.

Pile Weave   Lustrous velvets and velours have a plush texture and appearance that is extremely rich. The fabric is created by weaving an extra warp or fill yarn between the warp or fill of the base material. This extra yarn is looped higher than the base material and may, or may not, be cut. Velvets, velours, terrys, plush, velveteens, and corduroys are all variations of the pile weave, and they all have directional characteristics (like satin), so care must be taken to match the direction when cutting the fabric.

Plain Knit   Technically not a woven fabric, knits are constructed from a series of interlocking loops, and each row of loops is dependent for its support on the rows of loops below and above it, as shown in Figure 17.10E. There are many types of knits, and they are all very elastic and porous.

FABRICS AND NONFABRIC MATERIALS USED IN COSTUME CONSTRUCTION

Fabrics

A number of fabrics are used in the construction of stage costumes (and street clothes, for that matter). This list is not exhaustive, but it does provide examples of the types of fabrics typically used in costume construction.

Brocade   Available in light, medium, and heavy weights, brocade has a slightly raised pattern and is made from high-luster yarn that is woven into the matte finish of the background cloth. These patterns are reversed on the back side of the fabric. Usually made from rayon or silk, the fabric normally has a rich, reflective, multitextured surface.

Buckram   An open-weave material, buckram is a stiff fabric that has been sized with a heavy glue. Available in light, medium, and heavy weights, buckram is used as a foundation for millinery and other costume elements needing stiffness.

Fabric Finishes

Irrespective of the type or fiber content of a fabric, most textiles are treated with either a functional or a decorative finish or with both.

Functional Finishes

Functional finishes are normally applied to the fabrics before they leave the mill:

1. Permanent-press processes enable permanent creases to be put into trousers and other garments while all but eliminating wrinkles from the finished fabric and clothes.
2. Mercerization is a chemical process that adds strength and shine to cotton thread.
3. Flameproofing is a chemical treatment of cloth that prevents it from supporting flames. It does not, however, prevent the cloth from charring and smoldering.
4. Preshrunken cloth, particularly cotton, has been bathed in water.
5. Cloth can be impregnated with antibacterial agents to reduce the severity of stains from perspiration and other natural substances.

Decorative Finishes

Decorative finishes alter the appearance of the fabric. These treatments include bleaching, dyeing, printing, and texturing. Although the vast majority of these treatments are applied to fabrics before they leave the mill, some decorative treatments, such as dyeing and fabric painting, are frequently performed in the costume shop.

Buckram can be shaped and molded because it becomes limp when dampened but regains its stiffness when dry.

Canvas   Normally a cotton or cotton–synthetic blend, canvas is a heavy, plain-weave fabric used as lining material or other applications where its semistiff, extremely durable characteristics might prove helpful. Duck and sailcloth are lighter-weight versions.

Chiffon   Chiffon is a sheer, usually translucent, cloth frequently made from rayon or silk with soft, diaphanous draping qualities.

Corduroy   A medium to heavy material, most frequently made from cotton or cotton–synthetic blends, corduroy has raised ridges (wales). The material is fairly stiff and doesn't drape well. Waleless and pinwale (very narrow) corduroy can be used as low-cost substitutes for velvet and velour although they don't have the softer draping qualities of those fabrics.

Crepe   This is a thin, crinkle-finished fabric with a low luster and soft draping qualities. Rayon, silk, and fine cotton crepes are most frequently used for lingerie, blouses, and flowing gowns.

Crinoline   This tight-weave material has permanent sizing to provide stiffness.

Denim   A fairly course twill weave of cotton or cotton–synthetic blend, this slightly stiff fabric is primarily used for blue jeans and similar working-class clothes.

Drill   Similar to denim but of smoother surface and more luster, drill is a twill weave of cotton or cotton–synthetic blends.

Felt   Felt is a woolen, cotton, or rayon material made from fibers that have been matted or pressed together under pressure. Shaping is best accomplished with wool felt. When steamed it becomes limp and can be shaped and formed. It will retain the molded shape when dry. Felt is primarily used for hats and trimmings.

Flannel   A lightweight material woven with soft-finish threads of wool, wool blend, or cotton, flannel is normally used for men's and women's suits, trousers, and shirts.

Gabardine   This is a light-, medium-, or heavyweight, hard-surfaced twill-weave material made from wool, cotton, synthetics, or blends. It is used for inexpensive suits and outerwear.

Jersey   A knit fabric with excellent draping qualities, jersey is manufactured in a variety of fibers—wool, cotton, rayon, and blends—in a full range of weights.

Linen   Its irregular yarns of linen and linen–synthetic blends give the fabric a nubby, soft-luster surface. It is primarily used for tropical suits and sportswear.

Muslin   A plain-weave durable cotton with moderate sizing, unbleached muslin is commonly used as a lining material. It is also used for making patterns.

Net   Net is a stiff, very open-weave material commonly made from cotton, rayon, or nylon. Nylon net is the most stiff and is used where light, airy stiffening—ballet skirts, stiff veils—is desired.

Pellon   This is the brand name of a nonwoven stiffening material. Similar to felt in manufacturing method, Pellon is used as a stiffening interfacing material and in petticoats. Pellon does not soften when dampened and will retain its stiffness through many cleanings.

Sateen   A satin-weave cotton fabric of low luster, sateen is primarily used as a lining material.

Satin   This high-luster, satin-weave fabric is made from silk, rayon, and other synthetics. Available in a variety of weights and subcategories, satin is used for a variety of purposes from evening wear to draperies.

Taffeta   This plain-weave, smooth-surfaced, high-luster fabric is normally made of rayon but is occasionally available in silk. *Moire taffeta* has a nonrepetitive pattern pressed into the surface of the cloth that creates an interesting surface treatment. It is used extensively in eighteenth- and nineteenth-century clothes.

Velour   A pile-weave fabric normally made of cotton or cotton–nylon blends, velour has a soft, reflective quality. Heavyweight velour is normally used for upholstery and drapes, while lightweight velour is used for sportswear.

Velvet   Velvet is a pile-weave fabric normally made of rayon or nylon, also available in silk. It drapes sensuously and has rich, light-reflective characteristics. Available in a variety of weights, the heavier are used for capes, drapes, and upholstery, while the lighter weights are typically used for evening wear.

Nonfabric Materials

A variety of materials other than cloth are used in costume construction. Some of these materials are substituted for fabric, and others are used to bind various costume materials together. This list is neither exhaustive nor exclusive. Almost any material can be, and has been, used to make costumes. In addition to the cloth and fabric materials that form the basis of most costumes, any number of decorative materials can be appliquéd to the fabric to enhance its appearance. The only limitations on appropriateness are commonsense rules of safety for the actors and those around them, and the suitability of the material to the design concept for that particular costume.

Leather   Leather is often used for hats, shoes, and certain period pieces such as vests, armor, and belts. In the United States most leather is treated cowhide, although leather can be made from the hide of almost any animal. Leather has a smooth side and a rough side. The side that is used by the costumer is solely dependent on the particular look that is wanted. Most leather can be dyed with special leather dyes and sprays. It can be machine-stitched using a heavy-duty sewing machine equipped with a leather needle. It can also be hand-stitched. The surface of the leather can be tooled, and a variety of tools (awls, leather punches) can be used to punch holes in the material.

Leather can be formed into curves for such items as helmets and breastplates by steaming it and forming it to an appropriately shaped mold. Leather can be

FIGURE 17.11
Uses of Sculpt or Coat. (A) Helmet construction. See text for details. (B) Sculpt or Coat was used as an adhesive to glue the elements of this hat together.

(A)

(B)

rather heavy, is extremely durable, and holds heat well. Complete costumes constructed of leather can become very warm and uncomfortable.

Sculptural Arts Coatings   Sculptural Arts Coatings of Greensboro, North Carolina, has recently developed a line of water-base, low-emissivity craft products, paints, and finishes that can be used for myriad projects in the costume as well as scenic and prop shops.

Helmets can be made with Sculpt or Coat by coating a head form with a release agent (Vaseline), then forming a felt foundation over the head form. The felt is coated with a mixture of Sculpt or Coat, plaster, and water. When the surface is dry, it can be sanded or worked with power tools (angle grinder, sander) and finished to a high metallic sheen using acrylic paint and plastic varnish as shown in Figure 17.11A. Figure 17.11B shows millinery that has been glued together using Sculpt or Coat. Forms for other objects can be made from just about anything—Styrofoam, Ethafoam, foam rubber, metal, wood, hard plastics. A cheesecloth covering, applied with a layer of Sculpt or Coat, will increase the strength of the form. Filling the texture of the underlying fabric will probably take an additional coating or two of Sculpt or Coat. Textural additives such as white paper towels, sand, dirt—anything that will help you achieve the surface look you envision—can be built up on the form by applying the material after wetting it with Sculpt or Coat, by working it into the still-wet surface, or by mixing it with the Sculpt or Coat before applying it. Basically, any type of material—rigid or flexible—can be bonded together and finished with the products in this line and still retain the structural qualities of the original material.

Plaster Bandage   Plaster-impregnated gauze can be used to make built-up forms such as masks and small armor pieces. Available from surgical supply houses and some drugstores, it is the material that doctors use to make casts. It is water-soluble, creates no toxic or noxious fumes, and can be formed easily. After the material has dried, it can be sanded and painted with both water- and oil- or lacquer-base paints.

Thermoplastics   These are stiff plastics that soften in hot water and can be molded before they cool and stiffen. They are available in pellet, mesh, and fabric forms. They can be molded on the face and body for masks and armor, and finished with most paints.

Fiberglass   As we have seen, fiberglass is an extremely strong material formed of two parts: glass fibers in the form of mat or woven cloth and a resin coat that cures into a hard plastic. It is used for constructing armor and helmets, while the resin can be used by itself in the production of jewelry. More information about fiberglass can be found in Chapter 11. Rose Brand Fabric has introduced Aqua-Resin, a water-base, two-part resin that can be substituted for the polyester or epoxy resin normally used in fiberglass construction.

Metal   Aluminum, copper, and brass appliqués and jewelry are often used in the construction of various accessories for gowns, armor, buckles, and similar applications. Metal appliqués (Figure 17.12) can usually be found in fabric stores, while thin sheet metal can be found in craft shops. The sheet metal can be formed using standard woodworking tools, and the copper and brass sheets can be soldered. All three metals can be fastened with pop rivets or glued with appropriate cyanoacrylate cements such as Super Glue or Krazy Glue. (See Chapter 8 for more information on adhesives.)

FIGURE 17.12
Metal is frequently used in the fabrication of decorative items such as appliqués and buckles.

SPECIAL-EFFECTS TREATMENT OF FABRICS

Fabric Dyeing

Fabric must be washed and rinsed before it is dyed. If the material was heavily sized, it should be soaked in a light soda–ash solution before it is washed. Dyes go into solution best when initially mixed with boiling water. The working temperature of the dye solution depends on the type of dye and material being dyed. Tightly woven fabrics do not dye as well as those with looser weaves. The colorfast characteristics of any dyed fabric are enhanced if the material is thoroughly rinsed after it has been dyed. (Please review the Safety Tip on page 410.)

Types of Dyes   There are a large number of fabric dyes that can be used in the costume shop. Since no single dye works equally well on all types of fabrics, this section will discuss the characteristics of several common dyes. The description of the effects and characteristics of these dyes is necessarily vague simply because the exact impact that a particular dye will have on a specific fabric depends on many variables—the saturation and heat of the dye solution; the amount of time the material is left in the dye vat; the type and amount of **setting** agent in the dye; the type, blend, and finish of the fabric; and so forth.

Union Dyes   Union dyes contain several types of dyes and are designed to be moderately effective on many fabric types. Union dyes are exemplified by household dyes such as Rit or Tintex that are available in most fabric stores. If used with boiling water, union dyes will work well on most natural-fiber fabrics and rayon if you are trying to achieve a tint or medium shade. Slightly more intense

setting: To help lock the dye into the fiber of the fabric; to reduce or prevent the dye from being rubbed off the fabric.

unified aniline dye: A coal-tar-derivative dye formulated to work on both animal- and plant-derivative fibers.

French enamel varnish (FEV): Made by dissolving aniline dye in alcohol and mixing that (one part to one part) with white shellac which has been reduced somewhat with alcohol.

colors can be achieved by using more dye than is called for in the instructions, but it is almost impossible to achieve a deep shade of full saturation using union dyes. When dyeing cotton or linen, you can enhance the setting of the dye by adding salt to the solution. When dyeing wool or silk, add vinegar to the dye. Union dyes are not particularly effective on synthetic materials other than rayon. To maintain color intensity, wash union-dyed materials in cold water or have them dry cleaned.

Aniline Dyes All-purpose or **unified aniline dyes,** also known as acid dyes, create strong colors of light to full saturation on natural-fiber fabrics and a few synthetics. Either salt or vinegar (one-half cup per teaspoon of dry dye) is used in the dye solution as a setting agent. A little alcohol is added to the dry dye to form a paste, then boiling water is added to the paste. In general, one teaspoon of dry dye will make one quart of full-strength dye, although the ratio of the mixture can be varied.

Disperse Dyes Designed for use with synthetics like acetate, nylon, and polyester, disperse dyes have intense color and are quite colorfast if the dye solution is almost boiling when the fabric is dyed. A little liquid detergent in the dye solution helps the dye penetrate the fabric fibers.

Fiber-Reactive Dyes These dyes are arguably the most useful for fabric painting of natural-fiber fabrics because they produce intense, colorfast colors when the temperature of the dye bath is lukewarm or cool. Salt is used as the setting agent.

Fabric Painting

Fabric can be painted for a variety of reasons, but it is normally painted to create added texture, enhance the fabric's three-dimensional qualities, age the fabric, and create or reinforce a pattern.

Fabric can be painted with almost anything that will adhere to or penetrate the fabric fibers. Union dyes, aniline dyes, acrylic fabric paints from craft stores, leather and vinyl spray paints, spray enamels, textile inks, **French enamel varnish,** permanent markers, shellac and bronzing powders can all be used effectively in fabric painting.

Fabric dyes and paints are applied with a variety of applicators. Brushes are frequently used with both wet and dry brush techniques. Larger brushes can also be used for spattering when texturing or aging costumes. Sponges and rag rolls can be used to apply texture. (See Chapter 10, *Scene Painting,* for information on these painting techniques.) Automotive-paint stores sell compressed-air touch-up spray guns that have small, removable glass paint canisters. These spray paint and dyes effectively. Air brushes, when equipped with a variety of nozzles, can spray any of the liquid media in patterns from a sharp line to a fan-shaped mist. Stencils can be cut and the pattern sprayed, brushed, or sponged onto the fabric. Stamp stencils, made from sponges or hard foam, can be used to apply a repetitive pattern. Hot glue guns can be used to apply ornamentation or decorative patterns to the fabric. These patterns can be painted after they've cooled.

The actual effects that each of these processes will have on fabric can be learned only through experimentation. However, some general guidelines may be helpful. Almost everything but dye will stiffen the fabric to some degree. When brushed or sprayed, the color of most dyes will not be as intense because the water is not boiling. After brushing or spraying, most dyes can be set if they are steamed in a steam cabinet. Alternatively, pressing the garment with a steam iron also works but exposes the presser to any gasses released in the process. Be sure to read the MSDS's for any types of dyes you're using and follow their safety

Safety Tip

The Costume Shop Can Be Hazardous to Your Health

There are a wide variety of safety hazards in the costume shop. Some of them are readily apparent—sharp scissors and needles, sewing machines, hot irons, and boiling water. Others, such as fabric lint and chemical fumes, are a lot less apparent and potentially much more dangerous.

A variety of noxious and toxic chemicals are used in finishing textiles. Every time you work with fabric—unroll it, smooth it out, cut it, and sew it—small amounts of lint are released into the air. That lint continues to float until it settles to the ground or you and your co-workers inhale it. Potentially hazardous chemical vapors are released from paints, dyes, glues, and adhesives. Neither the chemically coated lint nor the chemical vapors are good for your health, and the long-term effects of continuous exposure to some of them could be harmful.

To reduce these hazards, the costume-shop area needs to be well ventilated. Frequently, the shop is in the basement, and many of those buildings were constructed before OSHA's safety guidelines became law, so little or no thought was given to proper ventilation. If the air is not constantly changing and/or being filtered, make sure that there are fans to do so. Move fresh air into the workplace, and move stale, contaminated air out.

Frequently, the dye vat will be set up in a small room separate from the rest of the costume shop. It should be well ventilated, but if that's not possible, be sure to wear a proper respirator while working with the heated dye water.

When working with sprays of any type, work outdoors or in a space in which the air flow ensures that the air changes several times a minute. Even if the area is well ventilated, wear a respirator designed to filter the specific chemical vapors emitted from the materials with which you're working.

Following these safety tips, plus using your common sense and becoming familiar with the safety tips listed in Chapters 8, 9, 10, 13, and 14, should help make the costume shop a safe and enjoyable place in which to work. If you see something that doesn't look, sound, feel, or smell safe, it probably isn't. Report it to your supervisor. Remember that safety is everybody's business.

---

recommendations. Be sure to use a **pressing cloth** between the iron and the fabric to prevent the fresh dye from adhering to the sole of the iron. French enamel varnish produces brilliant color, but the shellac stiffens the fabric. Increased flexibility with no significant loss of brilliance can be achieved if you substitute flexible clear-acrylic textile medium—found in the fabric-painting supplies at most craft stores—for the shellac. Most of the pigments applied in fabric painting will lose their saturation and brilliance with washing or dry cleaning.

pressing cloth: A cloth placed between the iron and the fabric being pressed.

Costume Aging

While the techniques discussed under fabric painting can, and frequently are, used to make costumes look old, abused, and worn, there are times when it may be necessary to severely distress the costume. Garments generally show their age at those points where the fabric receives the greatest stress—seats, knees, elbows, cuffs, hems, collars. The fibers in these places can be roughed up with sandpaper or a wood file. Old sweaters, coats, and pockets also show their age by stretching out of shape. This type of aging can be simulated by wetting the fabric (after the garment has been constructed) and pulling and stretching it out of shape until it is dry. Dirt-colored paints or dyes—primarily shades of brown for light fabrics and off-white for darker fabrics—can be rubbed into worn areas. Many painter/

sloper: A paper pattern for a costume.

baste: To temporarily sew together with long, easily removable stitches.

shell: The basic form of a costume, basted or pinned together, which covers the torso, arms, and legs.

darts: A short, tapered seam resembling a very narrow "V"; used to make clothes fit more closely.

dyers assemble a "morgue" of photos of old clothing and use these examples as they distress costumes.

Again, experience is the best teacher. Get into the costume shop and learn by doing. Besides, it's fun.

GARMENT AND ACCESSORY CONSTRUCTION

Patterns

Two general methods are used in pattern engineering or pattern development: flat patterning and draping. In flat-pattern development, the pattern is created in two-dimensional form through a process of drafting from body measurements. Once the paper pattern—also called a basic or **sloper**—has been developed, it is cut out of muslin. The cut pieces are **basted** together, and any necessary adjustments are made after the costume has been fit on the actor. In draping for pattern development, the uncut fabric is pinned onto a dress dummy and the fabric is cut away to achieve the final form. The pin lines show where the garment needs to be sewn. Again, adjustments are made after the garment has been fit on the actor.

Neither flat patterning nor draping should be considered as a preferred system. Both have advantages, and both should be learned. Some shapes, such as bustles, are more easily constructed by draping rather than flat patterning. Tailored or form-fitting garments, such as men's suits and uniforms, are generally better suited to flat-pattern methods.

A variety of sources of flat patterns for historical costumes are listed in the Selected References section at the back of this book. These publications provide scaled patterns for many historical periods. These patterns normally have to be altered, because it is rare that a stock pattern will exactly match the costume designer's sketch. Additionally, they need to be adjusted to fit the measurements of the actors. These measurements are recorded on costume-measurement charts (Figure 17.13) and provide all the information necessary to alter a stock pattern to fit a particular actor.

Enlarged onto brown butcher paper or gridded pattern-making paper from the scaled pattern, the pattern is often cut out of muslin, basted together, fit to the actor, and adjusted as necessary. This muslin mock-up is then used as the pattern to cut the more expensive costume fabric.

After the basic **shell** of the costume has been completed, the actor will need to come to the costume shop for a fitting, as shown in Figure 17.14. The shell of the costume is placed on the actor, and all the seams, **darts,** and measurements are checked for accuracy, fit, and comfort. After any necessary adjustments are made, the costume is again stitched, normally with standard stitch length, and the actor returns to the shop for a second fitting. The actor tries out the costume for fit and to make sure that none of his or her stage business, or movements, is impeded by the garment. At this time the correct length of the hem is marked, and the fit of the garment is again checked and adjusted if necessary.

There is frequently a final fitting once the garment has been completed. The purpose is to check not only the fit and comfort of the garment but also the appearance and appropriateness of the accessories that will be carried or worn with the costume.

Costume Software

Several software programs facilitate the work of the costumer. Pattern layout programs, such as Patternmaker by Patternmaker Software, allow the costumer

MEASUREMENT CHART

Name: _____ Height: _____ Weight: _____

Bra Size: _____ Dress Size: _____ Tights/Pantyhose: _____ Leotard: _____

Men's Shirt: _____ Trousers: _____ Men's Suit: _____ Shoe: _____

Chest/Bust	Ribcage (Underbust)	Head (Circ)	Head (Temple to temple, around back of head)	Head (Forehead to nape)	Head (Ear to ear; over head)
CF Neck to waist	F Shoulder to waist	Center of shoulder to bust point	Bust point to bust point	Underbust to waist	Neck at base Neck at midpoint
F Chest width (armseye to armseye)	X Both shoulders (Front)	CB Neck to waist	B Shoulder to waist	B Chest width (X shoulder blades)	X Both shoulders (Back)
Arm length to wrist	Arm length to elbow	Men's sleeve (CB neck to wrist)	Left shoulder	Right shoulder	
Armseye	Bicep	Elbow	Wrist	Overhand	
Waist	Hips	Thigh	Knee	Below knee	Calf
Waist to hip (on side)	Waist to above knee	Waist to below knee	Waist to ankle	Waist to floor	Outseam
CB Neck to floor	CF Neck to floor	Side neck to floor	CB Waist to floor	CF Waist to floor	Inseam
Crotch depth (Seated)	Crotch or 1/2 girth	Full girth (for leotards)			
Glasses?	Contacts?	Pierced ears?	Tattoos?	Other Notes	

FIGURE 17.13
Costume-measurement chart.

FIGURE 17.14
A costume fitting.

to create patterns and alter any of the measurements of existing patterns to tailor those patterns to specific actors. These patterns are then printed out on a plotter and can be used by the cutter.

Costumers can create their own wardrobe maintenance programs using database programs or purchase specialized programs. *The 5th Biennial USITT Theatre Technology Exhibit Catalog* (1995) describes a program, Wardrobe Wizard, that is being developed by Robert W. Haven of the University of Michigan. This program was "designed primarily as a production tool and has a variety of uses during the construction phase and for technical and dress rehearsals."[1] Haven indicates that he intends to make the program available via the Internet when field testing is completed.

Wigs

A wig is an important element of the costume. It is frequently necessary to use a wig to achieve the correct hair style, either male or female, for a particular histor-

[1] Robert W. Haven, "Wardrobe Wizard: Computers in the Costume Shop," *The 5th Biennial Theatre Technology Exhibit Catalog* (New York: USITT, 1995), pp. 14–17.

Sumerian 2900–2685 B.C.

Egyptian wig 1555–7330 B.C.

Second-century Greek

French c. 1150

Italian c. 1488

Spanish c. 1613

French c. 1660

French c. 1778

English c. 1831

American Gibson style c. 1895

American c. 1926

American bubble c. 1963

Assyrian

Roman

French c. 1150

Burgundy c. 1448

Elizabethan Van Dyke beard

English c. 1670

American c. 1776

English c. 1831

American mutton chops and handlebar moustache c. 1884

American Valentino look c. 1930

American crew cut c. 1942

American flower child c. 1960s

FIGURE 17.15
A progression of hair styles. Drawings by Peggy Kellner.

ical period. A well-**dressed** wig can be used to enhance the appearance of contemporary costumes as well.

Period wigs can be rented from many theatrical-costume supply houses, or they can be made in the shop using synthetic hair such as horsehair rayon or dynel. Wigmaking is a difficult craft that requires a great deal of patience and experience. However, excellent results frequently can be achieved by restyling contemporary wigs. Long-haired wigs of either synthetic or (preferably) human hair can be purchased at local wig shops, and they can be styled to achieve most of the period looks shown in Figure 17.15. Frequently, these wigs are manufactured with an overabundance of hair. If a natural rather than "wiggy" look is desired, the wig stylist removes about one-third of the hair from the commercial wig. This hair is used to **ventilate** a piece of netting attached to the front of the wig foundation. (The ventilating process is explained and illustrated in Chapter

dress: To work with hair or a wig to create a specific style or look.

ventilate: A method of tying hair to the net foundation of a wig. The technique is similar to that used in hooking rugs.

18, *Makeup.*) The modified commercial wig looks quite natural, and the ventilated portion creates a realistic hairline.

The wig stylist, who works under the supervision of the costume designer, consults the costume designer's sketch to determine the designer's concept for the hair style. He or she will also need to consult primary source materials (paintings, photos, and so on) for additional information on the look and style of hair in the period being used.

Hair pieces or extensions provide another way of creating a period hair style that uses the actor's natural hair, and hairline, as the basis of the design.

Human-hair wigs can be coiffed with conventional curlers, electric rollers, or curling irons. Synthetic wigs can be dressed by rolling the hair on a cold curling iron or cold rollers and gently heating the hair with the warm air from either a hand-held or cap-style hair dryer. Wig dressing is an exacting craft and should be attempted only under the supervision of someone with experience in the field.

Millinery

In the same manner as wigs, hats are frequently a requirement for completing the costume in many periods of history (see Figure 17.16).

Hat styles from many periods can be created with a basic broad-brimmed, deep-crowned felt hat. Steaming makes the felt soft and pliable, and while the felt is limp it can be stretched, molded, and shaped. The drying/shaping process is aided by using an electrically heated hat block or hat mold (Figure 17.17).

Many elaborate hat foundations can be formed from buckram. When dampened, the glue sizing in the fabric becomes soft and pliable, and like felt the buckram can be formed over a heated hat form. When dry the buckram regains its stiffness. This armature can then be painted or covered with fabric and decorated. Heavyweight theatrical buckram will probably have to be mail ordered from a millinery supplier.

A number of excellent source books, including books that provide patterns for various period headdresses, are listed in the Selected References. Almost any period hat can be constructed using these patterns and the materials available from a well-supplied fabric store or mail-order millinery supplier.

Footwear

Just as many costumes would not be complete without a wig or a hat, no costume is complete without the appropriate footwear. Examples of shoes from various periods are shown in Figure 17.18.

Although the ideal solution to this challenge is to contract with a cobbler or a shoe company to custom-build footwear of an appropriate style and design, this prohibitively expensive solution is beyond the fiscal means of the vast majority of production companies. Instead, many producing organizations adapt modern shoes by adding elements more appropriate to the desired period. When adapting a modern shoe to a period look, select one in which the toe and heel shape most closely resemble the appearance of the intended style.

Soft- and hard-soled house slippers, in both cloth and leather, with and without heels, are standard items in many costume shops. By dyeing the leather or fabric and adding appropriate accessories such as buckles or bows, you can turn the ubiquitous house slipper into footwear appropriate for many male and female fashion periods. Period-specific boots can frequently be made by sewing a leather boot top to a leather slipper.

Egyptian c. 500 B.C.   Byzantine c. 565 A.D.   French c. 950 A.D.   German c. 1275 A.D.   English c. 1476   German gable headdress c. 1563

French/English fontage c. 1695   French mobcap c. 1780   American bonnet c. 1830   American Lillian Russell hat c. 1910   American felt clóche hat c. 1927   English Princess Diana c. 1983

Egyptian—crown of Upper and Lower Egypt   Greek helmet c. fifth century   Viking helmet c. 1000 A.D.   English hood and liripipe c. 1325   German c. 1525

French tricorne c. 1650   French bicorne c. 1795   English top hat c. 1822   American Panama hat c. 1902

Early twentieth century   Later twentieth century   Twentieth-century American

Homberg   Fedora   Golf cap   Sport cap   Plastic visor   1980s cowboy hat   Baseball cap
Derby   Straw boater   Sweat band

FIGURE 17.16
A progression of styles in hats, headdresses, and crowns. Drawings by Peggy Kellner.

FIGURE 17.17
A hat mold.

Jewelry

A variety of techniques can be used to create jewelry and ornamentation such as buckles, crowns, brooches, and so forth. When making these objects, it is important to adhere to the shape, size, and materials of historical antecedents, but how it will look from the back of the house is more important. "Simplicity and the right amount of exaggeration are the key to good stage jewelry and ornament."[2]

[2]Douglas A. Russell, *Stage Costume Design,* 2nd edition (Englewood Cliffs, N.J.: Prentice-Hall, 1985), p. 157.

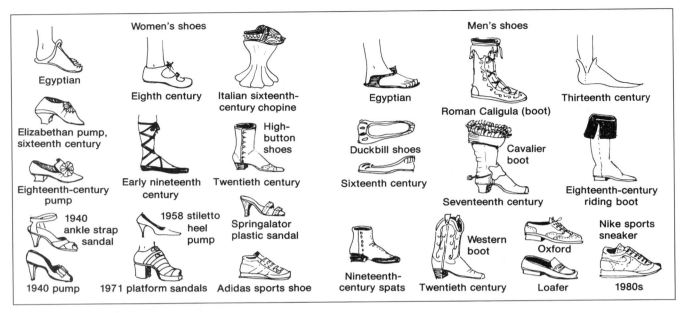

FIGURE 17.18
A progression of period shoe styles.
Drawings by Peggy Kellner.

The basic shape of the object to be created can be formed out of wood, metal, Celastic, thermoplastic, or any other material appropriate to the object being built. Bits of cording, lace, or other objects can be glued on to add texture. The object is painted flat black, brown, or deep blue, and the raised areas dry-brushed with metallic paints such as silver or gold to add luster and highlights. If a deep, high-sheen surface is required, catalyzed fiberglass resin can be used for the dark base coat. The resin can be colored with dry scenic pigments, aniline dyes, and bronzing powders. Rhinestones or colored glass "jewels" can be hot-glued onto the finished form. (Chapter 11, *Stage Properties,* discusses a number of craft processes that are useful in the construction of jewelry and other costume accessories.)

Every costume shop should have a collection of "junk jewelry." These rings, brooches, necklaces, and similar pieces, which almost always look fake and gaudy up close, project a rich, elegant look from the stage.

Armor

Body armor such as breastplates and helmets are frequently made from Fabric Form, fiberglass, or several types of thermoplastics. (See Chapters 8 and 11 for discussions of fiberglass, thermoplastics, and vacuum-forming techniques.)

Fiberglass armor is frequently formed by building up the basic shape on a clay-covered armature, covering the mold with aluminum foil, and applying the material to the form to create the basic rigid shell. Decoration is then applied by hand. When casting items that are fairly detailed and need to be uniform in appearance—military helmets, breastplates, leg shields, and so on—a rigid plaster-of-paris mold of the clay-covered armature is frequently cast. The mold will reveal all the detail on the clay original, particularly if fiberglass construction is used to create the object. After the release agent is applied to the mold, a gel coat of appropriately colored, catalyzed fiberglass resin is applied to capture the detail. After the gel resin has set, glass mat or cloth is applied to the gel coat, while it is still in the mold, to build up the strength of the piece.

Armor can also be formed from thermoplastic materials such as those illustrated in Figure 17.19. These thermoplastics, available from medical supply

FIGURE 17.19
Low-temperature thermoplastics used in mask and costume construction.

(A)

(B)

(C)

(D)

FIGURE 17.20
Papier-mâché mask construction
technique. Cover the armature, a
life mask (A), with aluminum foil.
Apply several layers of glue-soaked
strips of newspaper to the armature
(B). Allow the finished mask to dry
(24–48 hours) on the armature, and
finish it as desired (D).

houses under such trade names as Vara-form, Polyfoam, and Hexcelite, become
limp and formable when heated in 160-degree water for approximately thirty
seconds. They can also be heated with hand-held hair dryers. The nontoxic (unless burned) material can be worked, formed, and fused for approximately two
to four minutes before it must be reheated. Although expensive, these materials
are very durable and cost-effective, as any waste scraps can be heated and fused
together to form workable-sized pieces. As with Fabric Form fiberglass, these
thermoplastics can be formed on or in a mold. If care is taken to insulate the
actor—a sweatshirt or cloth of similar thickness is usually enough—the warm
thermoplastic can be formed directly on the actor's body.

Masks

Masks are made from a wide range of materials and fabrics, but like armor the
base layer of most masks is constructed on a clay or plaster mold. Masks used to
be built on a mold using papier-mâché, as shown in Figure 17.20, but now plaster
bandage, Fabric Form, fiberglass, and thermoplastics are more commonly used
to form rigid shells, while synthetic latex, netting, and various foams are used to
create flexible elements, as shown in Figure 17.21. Rather than using a generic
face mold, you can make an exact fit for a specific actor if the thermoplastic or
plaster-bandage material is formed directly on the actor's face or from a life
mask. Again, the painting, texturing, aging, and appliqué techniques discussed
in the jewelry- and armor-making sections, and elsewhere in this and other chapters of the text, are equally applicable to the construction of masks.

FIGURE 17.21
A mask made from plastic furnace
filter foam hot glued onto a latex/
gauze/Celastic base.

Chapter 18
Makeup

Makeup is a vital element in creating the total appearance of the actor. To a great extent, the makeup design gives the audience its primary clue to the age, health, and vitality of the character. Although the overall appearance of the actor is the costume designer's domain, the makeup designer, working under the artistic supervision of the costume designer, is frequently responsible for the design and execution of the makeup.

Stage makeup enhances the illusion that the actor has become the character. In almost every production some of the actors, for one reason or another, do not facially resemble the characters they are playing. Makeup can help solve this challenge by providing actors with the means to change their appearance. Through the skillful application of the various techniques of makeup, young faces can be made to look older, older faces younger, pretty faces less attractive, blemished skin clear, and rather plain faces ravishingly attractive. On a more mundane level, bright stage lights tend to lighten skin tones, so makeup is also used to put color back in the cheeks of the actor. By thoughtful design, that color can be made more appropriate to the character than are the actor's natural skin tones.

A great deal of the communication process that transfers information from the actor to the audience takes place visually. To fully understand what the actors are saying (actually, what they are meaning), the audience must be able to read the actors' facial expressions. But makeup does more than simply exaggerate the facial features of the actor. Effective makeup will project the character (not the actor) to the audience.

DESIGNING THE MAKEUP

It is the responsibility of the makeup designer to create a design that will help transform the actor into the character. In order to accomplish this goal, the makeup designer must understand what the character should look like. As well as looking at the costume sketches and analyzing the script for information about the appearance of the character, the makeup designer uses additional information to help determine the physical appearance of the character. Richard Corson, in his excellent text, *Stage Makeup*, suggests that *genetics, environment, health, disfigurements, fashion, age,* and *personality*[1] are the main influences that affect physical appearance. Genetics is the prime determinant of anyone's physical appearance. Genetics determines height, skeletal structure, hair and eye color, and so forth. While genetics also determines basic skin color, environment shapes that as well.

[1] Richard Corson, *Stage Makeup*, 8th edition (Englewood Cliffs, N.J.: Prentice-Hall, 1989), p. 19.

The Design Process in Makeup Design

This discussion applies the features of the design process to makeup design. Another tour of Chapter 2 would be appropriate if you think that you don't fully understand the fundamentals of this problem-solving technique.

Commitment

To do your best work, you must promise yourself that you will perform the work to the best of your ability.

Analysis

The first phase of the analysis step involves clarifying and refining the challenge, "What should the makeup look like for this show?" Answers to this question are found by reading the script and asking questions about the characters, costume designs, budgets, schedules, and so forth. Some of these questions will be answered when you study the script. Others will be answered during the production conferences, in which the director and designers freely exchange ideas and information.

The second phase of analysis involves discovering areas and subjects about the appearance of the character(s) that will require further research. You will investigate these areas during the research phase of the design process.

Research

Research is divided into two areas: background research and conceptual research. Background research involves finding answers to the questions raised during your analysis of the challenge. In makeup design, the primary research sources are the designer's analysis of the script and conversations with the costume designer. During the background-research phase, you need to analyze each character in terms of those elements that affect their appearance.

Conceptual research is the process of putting together as many potential solutions to the design challenge as possible. This is the time that the makeup designer begins to draw the preliminary makeup sketches. The best designs are normally achieved when the designer creates several variations of each design during this preliminary design stage.

Incubation

After doing the preliminary sketches, you should move on to some other project or activity. This will give your subconscious mind a chance to sort through the material and synthesize the best design choice.

Selection

After a period of incubation, focus on the project again and consciously make your final design choices.

Implementation

Since the implementation phase of the design process involves the actual production of the design, you are implementing the design when you are producing the sketches for the makeup design *and* when you are creating the makeup design on the actor.

Evaluation

Evaluation involves objectively studying your application of the design process to the creation of the makeup design. Honestly analyze your work. Did you do enough background research? Did you spend enough time analyzing the challenge? The answer to these and similar questions should tell you ways in which you could improve your communication with other members of the design team as well as your own use of the design process.

Exposure to the elements—sun, wind, water, temperature—affects the color and texture of skin, so whether a character spends the majority of his time indoors or outdoors, and the climate in which he lives, will definitely help shape his appearance.

Disfigurements may be genetically or accidentally caused. Richard III's disfigurements are noted in the script of *Richard III* by Shakespeare. Obviously, those deformities must be created in the costume and makeup. But a broken nose or a scar, uncalled for in the script, may aid in projecting the nature of a particular character to the audience.

Research will tell the makeup designer the particular makeup fashions of the period in which the play is set. Unless it is desired to have the character seem eccentric, out of fashion, or weird, the makeup should generally adhere to the fashion of that period.

A character's appearance also reveals something about his or her age and general health. Young, healthy skin usually has good color and a firm, smooth texture, whereas older skin or that of an ill person tends to be pallid, wrinkled, and less firm.

Personality is also revealed by facial appearance. Although we may do it subconsciously, almost everyone monitors the faces of people with whom they're talking to determine that person's mood. An arched eyebrow, eyes that suddenly narrow, a smile that turns into a frown communicate specific meanings. In the same manner, the shape of the face at rest communicates information about the personality of the character. If the mouth is set in a perpetual frown, we tend to assume that the person is serious and/or grumpy. If there are "smile lines" at the edges of the eyes and mouth, we tend to think of the person as happy. Makeup designers use these visual clues to help the actor reveal the character of the roles he or she is playing.

The process of creating makeup designs is similar to that followed by other designers. The script is read; production meetings are attended; individual conferences are held with the director, costume designer, and actors; research is done; sketches of the designs are created; and finally, the makeup is applied to the actors. The specific steps that the makeup designer follows are outlined in the box "The Design Process in Makeup Design."

Makeup Drawings

There are several types of drawings that the makeup designer uses. Preliminary sketches are quick sketches (Figure 18.1) drawn in any medium, that show what

FIGURE 18.1
Preliminary makeup sketches show the idealized design of what the makeup should look like.

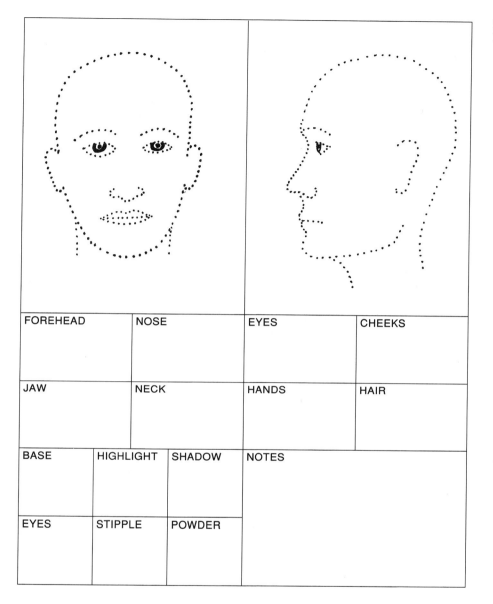

FIGURE 18.2
Predrawn makeup worksheet.

the makeup should look like. If the makeup artist is inexperienced in sketching, worksheets with predrawn frontal and profile views are used, as shown in Figure 18.2.

When the design is finalized, it should be adapted to the actor. This can be accomplished by placing tracing paper over a photo of the actor, tracing his or her natural features onto the paper, and then adapting the makeup to the actor's face, as shown in Figure 18.3. This process can also be accomplished by scanning the two images into a software program such as PhotoShop and printing a composite image.

Working drawings in makeup are similar to working drawings in other design areas. They detail information that shows the actor or makeup artist how to apply the makeup. The working drawing in Figure 18.4 shows frontal and profile views of the makeup design and contains written notes specifying techniques and materials to be used to recreate the design on the actor's face. Whether drawn

(A)

(B)

(C)

(D)

FIGURE 18.3
The makeup design is adapted to the actor's face by (A) transferring the outline of the actor's face to tracing paper from a photo and (B–D) redrawing the idealized design on the representation of the actor's face.

in black and white or color, the most important point is that these drawings fully explain how and what makeup should be applied.

TYPES OF MAKEUP

Various materials are used for makeup base, liners, beards, mustaches, and prosthetic devices, as shown in Figure 18.5.

Cake Makeup

Cake makeup is the most common type of makeup used in the theatre today. Cake makeup—both dry and moist—is pigmented material compressed into cake form. A variety of bases as well as highlight and shadow colors are available. Natural silk sponges are normally used to apply cake-foundation colors, whereas flat, pointed, and eyeliner brushes are used for detail work.

To apply cake makeup, you dampen the applicator and draw it across the cake, as shown in Figure 18.6. If the applicator is too dry, the makeup won't easily transfer to the face. If it is too wet, the makeup will seem thin and may streak. Best results are achieved if the face is cleaned of any other makeup and moisturizers before application of the cake makeup. Normally, the entire face is covered

FIGURE 18.4
Makeup working drawing.

FOREHEAD	NOSE *putty—*		EYES	CHEEKS
Light wrinkles	*hooked & broken (see sketch)*		*- Prominent crows feet* *- Sunken, dark, brooding*	*- hollow* *- scar on right cheek* *- Deep wrinkles*
JAW - *Emphasize* *- Highlight* <u>*on*</u> <u>*top*</u> *of bone* *- shadow under bone*	NECK *- Latex for wrinkles*		HANDS *- Latex for wrinkles*	HAIR *- Highlight silver at temples* *- Comb back & spray*

BASE	HIGHLIGHT	SHADOW	NOTES
SF-2-d	*0-4-b plus white*	*F-11-9*	*- Crepe beard / mustache* *= ⅔ Grey, ⅙ silver, ⅙ black for beard* *= Mustache ⅓ black ⅔ grey* <u>*Coarse stipple (for bad acne)*</u>
EYES *Grey liner on lower lid* <u>*only*</u>	STIPPLE *SF-7-9 and 0-4-b*	POWDER *Neutral*	

FIGURE 18.5
A well-equipped makeup table. All makeup shown here and in the following illustrations was generously provided courtesy of Kryolan Corporation.

with a smooth, translucent foundation color and highlights and shadows are applied over the foundation. However, highlights and shadows can be applied *under* the foundation to achieve muted effects or to cover a heavy beard or pigmentation abnormality. If a heavy, opaque quality is desired, it is normally built up with several light applications rather than a single heavy one. Blending between colors once they're on the face is normally achieved by brushing lightly with a clean, slightly dampened brush. Cake makeup does not require powdering. Kryolan Aquacolor is a brand of cake makeup in common use today. It is heavily pigmented, so not much has to be used, and it blends easily, is available in a wide variety of colors, and doesn't **sweat off.**

Creme Makeup

This moist, nongreasy foundation makeup is applied with a sponge, a brush, or the fingers, as shown in Figure 18.7. It is compatible with cake makeup but does

sweat off: When an actor's face perspires, some makeups will run. These makeups are said to "sweat off."

(A)

(B)

(C)

FIGURE 18.6
Application of cake makeup. (A) A damp sponge is drawn across the cake. (B and C) A smooth translucent foundation color is applied to the face and neck. Makeup by Amy Lederman, professional makeup artist.

(A)

(B)

(C)

FIGURE 18.7
Application of creme makeup. The creme (A) is softened and blended before application (B) with a sponge or fingers. Various color powders are blended (C and D) to match the foundation before it is patted or rolled onto the face (E) with a powder puff. Makeup by Amy Lederman, professional makeup artist.

(D)

(E)

require powdering to be **set**. Creme makeup is also available in stick form that is generally referred to as crayons.

Liquid Makeup

Liquid makeup manufactured for theatrical purposes is pretty much limited to body makeup. However, a variety of liquid bases formulated for street wear work perfectly well for the stage. The only problem with the use of liquid bases is that they dry quickly, which makes them difficult to blend if more than one color of base is being used.

Dry Makeup

This category includes all makeup that is dry when applied to the skin. Dry makeups, such as face powders and pressed powder rouge, are normally used to supplement other types of makeup such as cake and greasepaint.

Face powder is primarily used to set creme and greasepaint makeup or to reduce shine, although it can be used by itself as a "quick" foundation. It is applied by pressing on the face with a powder puff. Any excess powder is removed by gently brushing with a soft powder brush or clean rouge sponge.

Dry rouge is a pressed cake form of face powder. It is normally applied with a rouge brush, cotton ball, or powder puff.

Greasepaint

Until the development of quality creme and cake makeup, greasepaint was the most commonly used type of theatrical makeup. Opaque and cream based, it is available in jars, tubes, and tins in a wide variety of colors. Hardened greasepaint is available in stick form but isn't used very much.

After the skin has been cleansed, soft greasepaint from tubes or jars is applied to the face and neck in little dots, then blended with the finger tips to create a smooth translucent foundation, as shown in Figure 18.8. Greasepaint creates a greasy, shiny base that does not take highlights and shadows well and requires a coating of powder to set the makeup. If successive layers are to be built up, as

set: To prevent smearing or smudging. Once a greasepaint makeup design is finished, it is locked in place with a coating of powder.

FIGURE 18.8
Application of greasepaint. The greasepaint is applied in dots (A) then blended to form a smooth foundation (B) and set with powder (C). Makeup by Amy Lederman, professional makeup artist.

(A)

(B) (C)

stippling: A texturing technique in which makeup is applied by touching the skin with a textured surface, usually a stippling sponge. Similar to stippling in scenic painting.

when **stippling,** each layer needs to be set with powder. Another drawback to greasepaint is that it clogs the pores, which promotes facial perspiration.

Rubber-Mask Greasepaint

This specialty greasepaint, made with a castor-oil base, is primarily used to cover latex. Unlike regular greasepaint, it is applied by gently patting or stippling with a sponge, and it must be thoroughly powdered before any additional makeup can be applied.

Makeup Removers

Makeup removers such as Kryolan's Makeup Remover and Mehron's Liquefying Cream are sold by the individual manufacturers for use with their products. All-purpose makeup removers such as Ben Nye's Quick 'n Clean Makeup Remover take off both makeup and spirit gum. Spirit gum can also be removed with spirit-gum remover. Cleansing creams, cold cream, and baby oils sold in drugstores remove most makeups but may be slightly harsher on the skin than are the more specific commercial products.

APPLICATION TECHNIQUES

Several application techniques can be used with all types of makeup.

Highlights and Shadows

To a great extent, humans perceive the three-dimensional quality of objects by "reading" the patterns of highlight and shadow created by light falling on the object. Ever since birth we've subconsciously studied the patterns that light creates on faces. We've all learned experientially that highlights are reflected from protruding structures such as the bridge of the nose, cheekbones, and the eyebrow ridge. Therefore, when looking at a face we *expect* to see highlights in those areas. Similarly, we *expect* to see shadows in areas shaded from the light such as eye sockets and under the jaw.

Makeup artists, by painting artificial, two-dimensional highlights and shadows on an actor's face, manipulate the audience's perception of that face. For example, the eye socket is a natural shadow area. By painting the eye socket with a color that is lighter than the foundation color, the makeup artist decreases the apparent depth of that eye socket, as shown in Figure 18.9A and B. Darkening the eye-socket color and the use of eye liner will increase its apparent depth. Darkening the eye-socket color also increases its contrast with the white of the eye, which focuses more attention on the eye, as shown in Figure 18.9C and D. A straight nose can be made to appear crooked by painting the bridge with a crooked highlight, and a crooked nose can be made to appear straight by painting a straight highlight line.

Because there are few harsh angles, such as creases or deep wrinkles, on most faces, almost all junctures between highlight, base, and shadow are soft edged. A soft edge is created by blending—stroking with a brush from the lighter color to the darker, as shown in Figure 18.10. If a hard-edged line is needed, simply brush the shadow color into place with the edge of a small flat brush and don't blend it, as illustrated in Figure 18.11.

(A)

(B)

(C)

(D)

FIGURE 18.9
Application of highlight and shadow. (A and B) Use of highlight to decrease natural shadows. (C and D) Use of shadow and liner to emphasize eyes. Makeup by Amy Lederman, professional makeup artist.

Highlight and Shadow Colors

Facial highlights are simply those areas that reflect more light than the surrounding skin reflects, whereas shadows are those areas that reflect less. Therefore, the highlight color is simply a lighter version of the foundation, whereas shadow color is darker. The amount of difference between the foundation color and its highlight and shadow hues is dependent on a number of variables—principally whether the foundation color is light or dark, skin condition, and age. For normal effects on Caucasian skin, highlights and shadows will be just a bit lighter and darker, respectively, than the foundation. As the value—relative lightness or darkness—of the skin tone decreases—becomes darker—the contrast between the highlight/shadow colors needs to increase in order to project a realistic effect. Increasing the contrast between the highlight/shadow colors and the foundation will increase the apparent age of the skin.

Stippling

Stippling is a method of applying makeup by daubing or patting rather than stroking. Normally accomplished with a sponge, and occasionally with a brush, stippling roughens the apparent skin texture, as shown in Figure 18.12. The roughness of that texture depends on two elements: the surface texture of the applicator and the contrast between the stipple color and the foundation. Generally, the larger the pores of the applicator, and the more contrast between the stipple color and the base, the rougher the apparent texture.

Black stipple sponges, red rubber sponges, natural sponges, and household sponges can be used for stippling. The stipple color is applied to the sponge, then pressed onto the face. The use of two or more stipple colors (rather than one) will create a more natural look. Large textural elements such as freckles are normally applied with a small, flat makeup brush.

FIGURE 18.11
A hard edge is created by not blending the highlight color. Makeup by Amy Lederman, professional makeup artist.

Shadow or highlight areas that are too dark, bright, or intense can be toned down by stippling them with the base color.

Corrective Makeup

Corrective makeup is similar in purpose and design to everyday, or street, makeup. Its purpose is to enhance the natural appearance of the actor. Corrective makeup normally begins with a foundation color of one or more colors that are specified on the makeup worksheet.

After the foundation has been applied, the face's natural structure is either emphasized or de-emphasized through the application of highlights and shadows. The highlights are normally applied where highlights would naturally occur, such as the bridge of the nose, the cheekbones, and the top of the eyebrows. Shadow colors are applied to natural shadow areas, such as wrinkle lines, eye sockets, and cheeks.

THREE-DIMENSIONAL MAKEUP

Three-dimensional makeup involves the use of various materials to alter the shape of the actor's face, neck, or hands. A variety of materials and processes can be used to achieve these effects.

Nose Putty

Nose putty can be used to alter the shape of the nose, chin, and other nonflexible areas of skin, as illustrated in Figure 18.13. When working with nose putty, be sure the application site is free from all makeup and grease. Apply just enough K-Y jelly or cleansing cream (not petroleum jelly) to your fingers to prevent the putty from sticking to them, and knead the putty until it is soft. Press the putty onto the skin to firmly attach it, then shape it and smooth it into the surrounding skin. Adhesion will be increased if a coat of spirit gum is applied to the skin and allowed to dry until it is very tacky before the nose putty is applied. When it is properly shaped, stipple the putty to give it skin texture, then apply makeup to match the actor's natural skin tone, powder if necessary, *then* apply the foundation color and any appropriate highlight or shadow colors.

To remove nose putty, pull or scrape it off and gently massage makeup remover onto the area until the remaining putty is softened enough to be removed with tissues.

Derma Wax

Derma wax is softer than, but does not adhere as well as, nose putty. It is used for similar modifications of hard structures such as noses and chins. The application of derma wax follows the same procedure as nose putty except that the coating of spirit gum is required to firmly attach the derma wax. Increased adhesion will result if cotton fibers are embedded in the spirit-gum layer. When the spirit gum is very tacky, press a cotton ball into it. When the spirit gum is dry, pull the ball off. Some cotton fibers will remain. Work a small amount of derma wax into the cotton fibers, then apply the remaining wax and build up the desired shape.

Derma-wax structures can be pulled off and the residue removed with an all-purpose makeup remover or with spirit-gum remover and makeup remover.

FIGURE 18.12
Stippling made with contrasting highlight and shadow colors gives the appearance of rough skin texture. Makeup by Amy Lederman, professional makeup artist.

(A)

FIGURE 18.13
Application of nose putty. (A) The
nose putty is kneaded until soft and
pliable. (B) Spirit gum is applied to
the nose and allowed to dry until
tacky. (C) The nose putty is applied
and shaped. (D) The nose putty is
patted with a black stipple sponge
to give it texture. (E) Foundation
makeup is applied. Makeup by
Amy Lederman, professional
makeup artist.

(B)

(C)

(D)

(E)

Gelatin

Gelatin, such as unflavored Knox gelatin available in grocery stores, when mixed
with hot water to form a thick paste that solidifies when cool, can be used to form
three-dimensional shapes such as warts, moles, and scars. If mixed with cool
water, the gelatin will have a more grainy texture. Gelatin adheres to thoroughly
grease-free skin and is more flexible than either nose putty or derma wax, so it
can be used on fleshy, flexible skin such as cheeks.

A working paste is formed by mixing the gelatin one to one with very hot
tap water. The paste must be applied when warm and shaped quickly with an
orange stick, modeling tool, or similar applicator before it cools. Successive layers
can be built up until the desired shape is achieved, as shown in Figure 18.14. If
the edges start to peel, they can be glued down with spirit gum. Shapes can also

(A)

FIGURE 18.14
Application of gelatin. (A) Gelatin is mixed with water and (B) applied to grease-free skin. (C) The gelatin mole is colored and stippled with a brush. Makeup by Amy Lederman, professional makeup artist.

(B)

(C)

be preformed either in a mold or on a flat glass surface and attached to the skin with spirit gum, which improves adhesion. The gelatin forms can be covered with any type of makeup.

The disadvantages of gelatin forms are that they can melt when heated and perspiration loosens them, although the perspiration problem can be overcome with spirit gum.

Latex

Several types of latex systems are used for a variety of purposes such as forming prosthetic pieces, creating wrinkles, and applying crepe hair. Liquid latex is available in clear and flesh-colored formulations. Foam latex is a soft, flexible expanding foam that is poured into molds to form prosthetic pieces. It is made by mixing liquid latex with foaming, gelling, and curing agents. The mixture is poured into a cast and baked in a low-temperature oven. Specific instructions come with foam-latex kits, which are available from theatrical supply houses that handle makeup.

Liquid latexes specifically designed for forming in molds should not be applied directly to the skin as they may cause irritation or burning. Liquid Plastic Film, manufactured by Kryolan, is a clear liquid plastic, available in two formulations, that is used in the same way as liquid latex. Glatzan L is used for making **bald caps, eyebrow masks,** eye pouches, and so forth. It should not be applied directly to the skin. A variety of manufactured latex pieces (noses, chins, pouches, warts, and so forth) are available from makeup manufacturers or distributors such as Paramount, Bob Kelly, and Kryolan.

Liquid latex is frequently used to create wrinkles. The skin to be aged is pulled tight, and clear latex (white when liquid, clear when dry) is stippled onto the skin with a sponge or fingers, as shown in Figure 18.15. When the stretched skin is released, wrinkles magically appear. Additional coats of latex on the stretched skin will deepen the wrinkles. Kryolan's Old Skin Plast can be used as a substitute for liquid latex. An age makeup can be applied either under or over the latex. If the makeup is under the latex, apply the latex carefully to avoid

bald cap: A latex cap that covers a person's hair.

eyebrow mask: A thin piece of plastic film or latex glued over the eyebrow. Also known as an eyebrow block.

FIGURE 18.15
Making wrinkles with liquid latex.
(A) The skin is stretched tight and
(B) painted with latex. (C) The moist
latex is stippled to give it texture.
(D) The dried latex causes wrinkles.
Makeup by Amy Lederman, profes-
sional makeup artist.

(A)

(B)

(C)

(D)

smearing. If makeup is being applied over the latex, you can tint the latex with appropriate hues of food coloring to approximate the actor's natural skin tone.

A cautionary note when using liquid latex: Before you apply latex to any hairy parts such as the backs of hands, beards, stubble, eyebrows, or soft, downy facial hair, you need to understand that when you pull off the latex, most of the hair will come with it. To avoid this problem, either **block out** or shave off the hair before applying the latex.

If deep wrinkles are desired, torn (not cut) facial tissue can be applied to the stretched skin of the face with either latex or spirit gum. When the tissue has dried on the stretched skin, a coat of latex is applied over the tissue. The use of a hair dryer will speed the drying process. Work a small area at a time, and be sure that the skin is stretched until the latex is dry. If even deeper wrinkles are desired, soft paper toweling can be substituted for the tissue. After the whole face is

block out: To cover with soap, spirit gum, wax, material, or preformed plastic film so that no hair is evident.

Safety Tip ⚠

Using Liquid Latex

If any burning, itching, or irritation is felt when applying liquid latex directly to the skin, don't apply any more. Each company (Bob Kelly, Kryolan, Mehron, Ben Nye, Joe Blasco, among others) manufactures their liquid latex with slightly different formulations. The chances are good that if one type irritates your skin another won't. Try a different product until you find one that doesn't irritate your skin. Also, remember that some liquid latexes are not designed to be applied directly to the skin. Be sure to read the instructions on the bottle or can before applying the liquid latex to your skin.

(A)

(B)

(C)

(D)

(E)

FIGURE 18.16
Casting a life mask mold with dental alginate. (A–C) The face is coated with K-Y jelly and covered with alginate. The straws allow the subject to breathe. (D–E) The alginate is covered with plaster bandages to provide rigidity and strength. Casting by Shelly Neal.

covered with the tissue (or paper towels) and latex, a rubber-mask greasepaint or greasepaint foundation with appropriate highlights and shadows is applied over the latex. Additional skin texture can be created by stippling with latex or a honey-thick mixture of latex and gelatin.

Prosthetics

Prosthetic devices—latex noses, chins, bald caps, eyebrow blocks, and so forth—can be purchased or made in the shop. If purchased, generic shapes such as bald caps and eyebrow blocks normally can be made to fit well. However, items such as noses and chins that must fit well because of the movement of the fleshy parts of the actor's face are frequently better created on the actor's face or cast from a **life mask** of the actor.

The process of creating a life mask using dental alginate, or *moulage* (a rubbery casting material that can be purchased from makeup suppliers or dental supply stores), is shown in Figure 18.16. After the negative mold is removed from the subject's face, you'll want to make a positive mold immediately because

life mask: A plaster mask of a person's face. A negative mold is made by covering the person's face with plaster of paris. The negative mold is used to make a positive cast that is the life mask.

FIGURE 18.17
A life mask. Casting by Shelly Neal.

the alginate mold shrinks quickly. The positive mold, which is the life mask, is normally made from dental stone or plaster and is illustrated in Figure 18.17. When the life mask is fully cured—two to five days, depending on temperature and humidity—it should be sealed with several coats of shellac. After the life mask has been sealed, clay can be used to sculpt such features as noses, eye pouches, eyebrow blocks, or anything else. Small plaster or moulage casts can then be made of these features, as shown in Figure 18.18, and these molds used to cast the features in latex. When making these small prosthetic molds, be sure to thoroughly apply a thin layer of K-Y or petroleum jelly to the life mask to prevent the new mold material from sticking to it.

Two forms of latex are used for creating prosthetics—the previously described liquid latex and foam latex. Probably the easiest method of casting prosthetics is the slush method, illustrated in Figure 18.19. While holding the negative plaster mold in your hand, pour in a little liquid latex and rotate the mold to coat the inside. Pour in a little more and repeat the process. Be sure that the edges are the thinnest part and that enough thickness has been built up so that the object will retain its shape when you remove it from the mold. The mold should be dusted with baby powder to prevent the latex from sticking to the mold. Because dried latex will also stick to itself, you'll also need to thoroughly powder the cast

(A)

(B)

FIGURE 18.18
Casting a nose from a life mask. (A) A clay dam is built around the area to be cast and coated with K-Y jelly. (B) The dam is filled with plaster (if there are no undercuts in the form), alginate, or moulage. (C) The dam is peeled away and (D) the casting removed. Casting by Shelly Neal.

(C)

(D)

(A)

(B)

(C)

FIGURE 18.19
Slush casting. (A–B) The area to be
cast is dusted with powder. (C) Liquid latex is poured into the mold
and (D) rolled around to cover the
entire area to be cast. The prosthetic
is built up by applying several thin
layers, allowing the latex to dry between applications. (E) A latex, also
known as a rubber, nose.

(D)

(E)

object and continue to dust both sides of it as you work it loose from the mold.
Additional techniques for casting with molds are discussed in Chapter 11, *Stage
Properties.*

Latex prosthetics can be attached to the skin with either latex or, preferably,
spirit gum. Latex can be used if you don't intend to reuse the piece and the skin
you're attaching it to doesn't perspire much. (Perspiration weakens the adhesive
power of the latex.) If you are planning to reuse the piece, attach it with spirit
gum. Spirit gum is applied to the inside edges of the piece (Figure 18.20), allowed
to dry until very tacky, then firmly pressed into place with the fingers. An orange
stick can also be used to press down the edges.

Latex prosthetics require special treatment during makeup. Rubber-mask
greasepaint is blended into the other makeup used on the skin, or if several pieces
are being used, it might be easier to cover the whole face with rubber-mask
greasepaint rather than try to blend several types of makeup together. Regular
greasepaint and creme makeup can also be used to cover latex prosthetics, but
because they are a little more viscous they are harder to apply and blend

(A)

(B)

(C)

(D)

(E)

FIGURE 18.20
Application of latex nose. (A) Spirit gum is applied and allowed to dry until tacky. (B) The nose is pressed into place. (C) Hard-to-stick areas are reglued and held in place. (D) Liquid latex covers the juncture between skin and prosthetic. (E) Covered with foundation, the nose is a thing of beauty.

smoothly. Stippling with several colors can help blend between the prosthetic device and the actor's skin.

If you're planning to reuse the piece, remove it by loosening the adhesive with spirit-gum remover, peel back the edges, and apply more remover. Repeat this process until the piece can be lifted off, then clean off any residual spirit gum with additional remover.

Beards and Mustaches

False beards and mustaches are usually made from crepe hair, animal hair, or human hair. Crepe hair is the least expensive and is commonly used. Crepe hair is sold in tightly braided strands that can be straightened by unbraiding and pressing with a steam iron. It, like animal and human hair, is available in a wide variety of colors.

Real beards and mustaches contain whiskers of numerous tones, shades, and colors. To appear real, constructed beards and mustaches need to mimic this

(A)

(B)

(C)

(D)

(E)

(F)

FIGURE 18.21
Application of a crepe-hair beard.
(A) The crepe hair is straightened,
colors blended, and cut to a length
about twice as long as its final form.
(B–D) The crepe hair is attached
with spirit gum and (E–F) trimmed
to the desired shape.

variety. Be sure to use at least three or four different tones or colors. Mix the
strands before you apply them.

Figure 18.21 illustrates a standard method of applying crepe hair with spirit
gum. Before application the crepe hair is cut to a length about twice as long as its
final form, which will allow plenty of hair for trimming to the proper shape. The
spirit gum is applied to a small area and allowed to dry until it becomes very
tacky; then crepe hair is pressed into the spirit gum. This process is repeated until
the mustache or beard is fully applied. After the beard or mustache is in place on
the actor, it is trimmed to the desired shape.

If the beard is to be reused, it can be built on a latex base. The latex can be
applied either to the actor's face or to a life mask of the actor, and the beard built
up as previously described. The latex-based beard can be applied to the actor
with spirit gum.

Ventilated beards and mustaches take more time to construct, but they look
much more realistic. They are generally made from synthetic or relatively coarse

FIGURE 18.22
A ventilated mustache from Kry-olan. (A) Front view and (B) rear view showing the lace backing.

(A)

(B)

FIGURE 18.23
The ventilating process. A few hairs are caught with the tip of the venti-lating hook (A) and pulled through the lace backing (B) to form a loop (C). The hook is then rotated around the strands (D–F) and pulled through the loop (G–H) to form a knot (I). This process is re-peated with additional strands to tie the hair to the lace backing. While tedious and time consuming, venti-lating does create the most realistic beards, mustaches, and wigs.

human hair, as opposed to crepe hair, and are constructed on lace or gauze back-ing, as shown in Figure 18.22. Figure 18.23 illustrates the ventilating process.

Ventilated pieces are normally attached with spirit gum. Generally the spirit gum is applied to clean skin and allowed to dry until tacky, and the gauze or lace netting is pressed into it using a clean, slightly moistened cloth. Any hairs that are glued down can be lifted using a pointed, stiff object such as an orange stick or eyebrow brush. As the netting is delicate and can easily tear, removal of the piece requires the copious use of spirit-gum remover and patience.

(A)

(B)

(C)

(D)

(E)

(F)

(G)

(H)

(I)

Chapter 19
Sound Design and Technology

Not so many years ago, sound in the theatre was fairly simple. If the director wanted some preshow music, you got some records that approximated the mood and spirit of the play and played them over the auditorium public-address system for about ten minutes before the curtain went up. You might get daring and play them again during the intermission.

If the script called for specific sound effects such as a doorbell or a telephone ringing, you either made the sounds live or consulted your sound-effects library, composed of low-fidelity 78-RPM records. If you used library effects, you either recorded them on your wire or tape recorder, or you cued the records up and played them just the way a disc jockey would.

Sound in the theatre has changed substantially since the bad old days. Instead of being an afterthought, sound is now frequently an integral part of the production concept. Increasing numbers of productions are giving credit to sound design as well as to the more traditional scenic, costume, and lighting design.

Arguably the most important reason for the increased use of sound is the improvement in sound equipment. A second reason stems from the tastes and expectations of the audience and of theatre craftspeople. Almost every member of the contemporary theatregoing public, as well as those of us who work in the theatre, have seen a lot more television and motion pictures than theatre. Our aesthetic expectations have been strongly influenced by what we have seen and heard in these media. For years both television and motion pictures have made very effective use of music and sound effects to focus the audience's attention and reinforce the dominant emotional theme of the material being presented. Higher-quality home and auto stereo systems have raised our sound expectations, too. It seems only natural, then, that carefully designed sound and music should come to be expected in the theatre.

FUNCTIONS OF SOUND IN THE THEATRE

Theatre sound can be subdivided into three categories: music, effects, and reinforcement.

Music

The use of music in a nonmusical production has historically been limited to preshow, intermission, and postshow instrumentals that create an aural

constructed sound: Any sound effects created by editing, manipulating, or changing previously recorded sounds.

synthesizer: A musical instrument that creates sounds electronically; can be used to create a close facsimile of instrumental, natural, or vocal tones.

atmosphere selected to put the audience in the proper mood for the play. Comedies have been, and frequently continue to be, accompanied by light and sprightly music, while full orchestrations of somber or ominous music have traditionally been associated with Shakespearean tragedies and plays of equally heavy subject matter. Plays that fall between these dramatic extremes are accompanied by music appropriate to their particular mood and subject matter.

Although this musical accompaniment has certainly been functional and effective, the contemporary use of music in the theatre has expanded in a variety of directions. Nonspecific musical effects, such as musical themes for specific characters or scenes, are now used to create or reinforce a particular psychological mood or feeling. Preshow selections have expanded to include almost any type of music or **constructed sound.** Lyrics, which used to be taboo, are now used whenever the production design team decides that their use would be appropriate. Furthermore, sections of many productions are now scored with music, the way motion pictures are, to reinforce the psychological content of particular moments in the script.

Effects

The creation of specific sound effects such as barking dogs, telephones, doorbells, and train whistles is still an important element of the sound designer's work, but it is no longer the sole element. Many production concepts now call for the creation of an effects track to provide an aural backdrop of appropriate sound for the environment of the play. For example, in the University of Arizona's production of Ted Tally's *Terra Nova*, which is set in Antarctica, the director wanted to create an effect that would emphasize the bitter cold and lonely emptiness of that hostile environment. Sound designers Mark Ruch and David Coffman, using a **synthesizer** (Figure 19.1), created a very effective sound effect of wind sweeping across the empty frozen wastes. This sound effect, together with original music composed by Mark Ruch, was played, at varying levels of loudness, throughout all of the Antarctic scenes. When the sound was combined with the impact of an all-white set, the "cold" colors of the lights, and the cold-weather gear worn by the actors, the audience felt so chilly that it was necessary to turn the air conditioning to an above-average setting during the run of the production.

This type of fully scored effects design, which was extremely rare prior to 1980, is not that unusual anymore. Arena, thrust, and black-box productions frequently use specific sound effects, such as waves lapping a beach or "jungle noises," to provide aural images of specific locations.

FIGURE 19.1
A synthesizer. (Courtesy of Yamaha.)

Reinforcement

Reinforcement is used whenever there is a need to boost the loudness level of the actors' voices, as when the **acoustics** of the auditorium are not good or during musicals when the singers can't be heard over the orchestra. In the not-too-distant past, actors projected loudly enough to be heard by every member of the audience in all but the largest theatres without the need for electronic reinforcement. Today most actors can still project loudly enough to be heard, but the growth in the use of background and effects sound has introduced a new challenge to theatrical production.

The audience wants and deserves to hear balanced sound. It shouldn't have to strain to hear the actors, nor should it be overwhelmed by the music or noise of a sound effect. The answer to these specific challenges has been to mike the actors' voices, then mix and **balance** the sound with the effects and background music before all three sources are amplified and sent into the auditorium.

Reinforced sound needs to be balanced. The various elements of the sound design, with obvious exceptions, should not call attention to themselves. The loudness level of any music or sound effect should not overwhelm the voices of the actors, nor should the content of the sound, either music or effects, be so vibrant or strident as to draw attention from the central focus of the scene.

acoustics: The sound-transmission characteristics of a room, space, or material; also, the science that studies these qualities.

balance: To adjust the loudness and equalization levels of individual signals while mixing, to achieve an appropriate blend.

pitch: The characteristic tone produced by a vibrating body; the higher the frequency of vibration, the higher the pitch.

THE NATURE OF SOUND

To develop a working knowledge of how sound systems operate, you'll need to understand the nature of sound. Sound is a pressure wave that moves, in air and at sea level, at about 1,130 feet per second. The pressure wave is instigated by a source such as the drum in Figure 19.2. The drum compresses the air immediately adjacent to the drumhead when the head is struck with the drumstick. This compression wave travels through the air until it strikes a receptor, in this case the ear. The ear converts the mechanical force of the pressure wave into a neurological impulse that is sent to the brain, where the stimulus is interpreted as a drum beat of a particular tone and quality.

Frequency

Frequency is the rate, measured in cycles per second (hertz, or Hz), at which an object vibrates. At one time or another, most of us have strung a rubber band between our fingers and strummed it. The rubber band vibrated and made a sound. As we stretched the rubber band tighter, the vibrations of the rubber band seemed to get smaller, and the **pitch** of the sound increased. This was a demonstration of the direct relationship between frequency and pitch; as frequency increases, pitch increases.

To better understand the concept of frequency and its effect on pitch, let's assume that when the drumhead discussed above was struck with the drumstick, it took one second to complete twenty full vibrations, or cycles, as shown in Figure 19.3. We would hear this twenty-cycle vibration as a very low sound. If we were able to tighten the drumhead so that it vibrated at a frequency of 200 cycles per second (200 Hz), we would hear this sound as a much higher pitched sound. Figure 19.4 illustrates the relationship between the frequency of a sound and its pitch.

The average human being can hear sounds that have a frequency range from 20 to 17,000 Hz, although people with very acute hearing can discern sounds

FIGURE 19.2
The transmission of sound in the air.

FIGURE 19.3
The higher the frequency, the higher the pitch. (A) A 20-cycle (Hz) sound; (B) a 200-cycle (Hz) sound.

(A)

FIGURE 19.4
As frequency increases, pitch increases.

(B)

from approximately 15 to 22,000 Hz. Figure 19.5 may help to clarify the relationship that exists between frequency and some readily identifiable sound sources.

Intensity

The intensity of a sound is synonymous with its loudness. Figure 19.6 is a demonstration of the fact that the intensity of a sound can change without affecting the pitch.

The intensity, or loudness, of sound is measured in **decibels** (dB). Figure 19.7 illustrates the relative loudness levels of a variety of sounds.

Timbre

Timbre refers to the distinctive quality of a sound that makes one voice sound different from another or a trumpet sound different from a violin. This qualitative difference is based on the **harmonics** of the sound-producing body.

Pure sounds, as shown in Figure 19.8A, rarely occur in nature. Most natural sound sources (voices, violins, pianos, surf noises) produce a variety of overtones, or harmonics, as shown in Figure 19.8B. These harmonic frequencies are based on the pitch of the fundamental, or base, frequency (Figure 19.9).

decibel: A unit for expressing the intensity of sounds; an increase or decrease of one decibel is just about the smallest change in loudness that the human ear can detect.

harmonics: Frequencies that are exact multiples of a fundamental pitch or frequency.

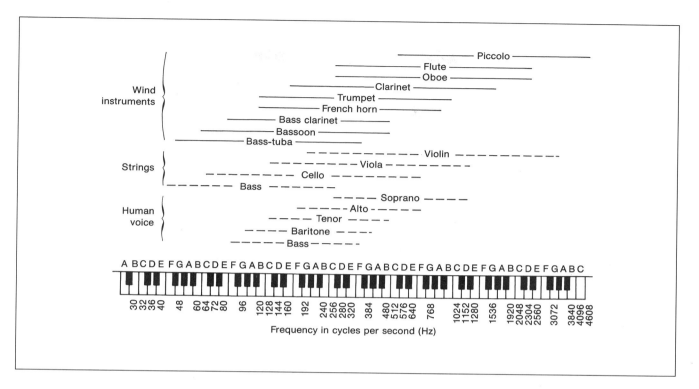

FIGURE 19.5
A sound-spectrum comparison chart.

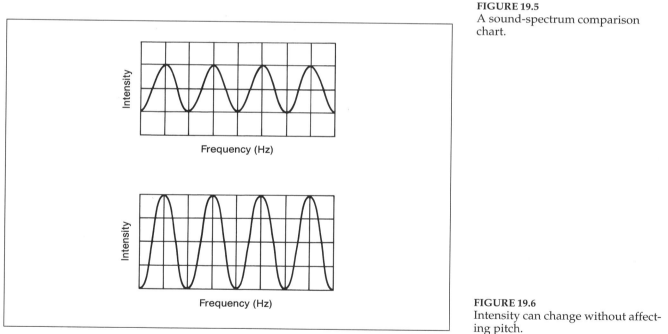

FIGURE 19.6
Intensity can change without affecting pitch.

The amplitude, or loudness, of each harmonic will be less than the loudness of the fundamental frequency, and the amount of each harmonic in the final tone will be determined by the physical structure of the source. The reason that no two voices or instruments sound exactly alike is that each voice or instrument structure has minor, but significant, physical variations that affect the amplitude of the various harmonics it produces.

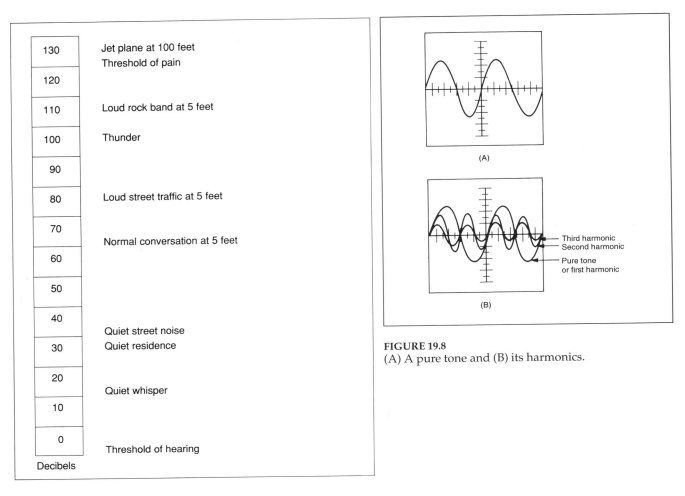

Decibels	
130	Jet plane at 100 feet Threshold of pain
120	
110	Loud rock band at 5 feet
100	Thunder
90	
80	Loud street traffic at 5 feet
70	Normal conversation at 5 feet
60	
50	
40	Quiet street noise
30	Quiet residence
20	Quiet whisper
10	
0	Threshold of hearing

FIGURE 19.8
(A) A pure tone and (B) its harmonics.

FIGURE 19.7
Relative loudness of some common sounds.

reverberate: To reflect in a series of echos.

FIGURE 19.9
The loudness of a harmonic will be less than its fundamental frequency.

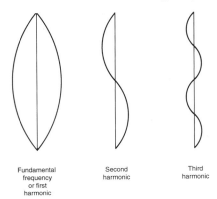

Fundamental frequency or first harmonic   Second harmonic   Third harmonic

BASIC ACOUSTICS

Acoustics is the science that studies the absorption and reflection of sound. In the theatre, acoustics is concerned with the study of those qualities of the stage and auditorium space that affect the audience's hearing and understanding of the sound (language and music) of the play.

A theatre with good acoustics will allow every member of the audience to hear, and understand, the words being spoken by an actor standing anywhere on the stage. An almost limitless number of factors determine the acoustics of an auditorium. The room's shape vitally affects the reflection of sound. If the walls are parallel, the sound will **reverberate,** or bounce back and forth between them, reducing the intelligibility of the spoken word. Severe reverberation in an auditorium can so garble the sound that the audience cannot understand anything that the actor is saying. To reduce the reflection of sound waves, many architects slightly curve the auditorium walls so that no wall will be parallel with any other.

The materials used to finish the walls, ceiling, and floor of the auditorium also have a great impact on the reflection of the sound. In general, hard-surface materials (wood, metal, plaster, and the like) reflect sound, and soft- or open-surface materials (cloth, foamed or loosely spun insulation, and the like) absorb sound, as shown in Figure 19.10.

Acoustically balancing a theatre for music creates a problem. Music sounds better when the sounds of the various instruments blend. Sound blending is

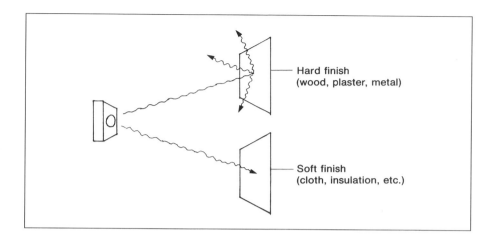

FIGURE 19.10
Sound reflection and absorption are dependent on the type and finish of the reflecting/absorbing surface.

Acoustic Balancing

An auditorium that is well balanced for understanding the spoken word will have a decay time (the period it takes a sound to quit reverberating and become inaudible) of ¼ to ¾ of a second. An auditorium with a good balance for music will have a decay time between ¾ second and 1½ seconds.

Since it is not possible to create a theatre that can be equally effective for both speech and music, some type of compromise needs to be made. In any situation where nonmusical plays are going to be presented, the compromise should lean toward balancing the auditorium for the spoken word. This rationale is based on the premise that the audience needs to discern the spoken language in order to understand what is being said, while the music can be heard with the shorter reverberation time even though it won't sound as good to a trained musician.

A reasonable solution to this very realistic problem has been the development of acoustically adjustable auditoriums and stages. These multipurpose theatres are frequently equipped with adjustable acoustical baffles mounted in various positions on and over the stage as well as in the walls and on the ceiling of the auditorium. These panels can be adjusted to "tune" the auditorium for the appropriate degree of reverberation for the type of group (nonmusical theatre, musical theatre, opera, orchestra) performing on the stage.

The carpeting on the wall and the alternating vertical wood strips and cloth effectively reduce reverberation in the Constans Theatre, University of Florida.

The Design Process in Sound Design

Commitment

If you don't fully accept the challenge and promise yourself that you will do your best work, you will end up with a mediocre product.

Analysis

In defining and refining the challenge of sound design, you will need to read and analyze the script according to the guidelines suggested in Chapter 2. You will also need to ask questions of the other members of the production design team, such as:

1. What is the budget for sound?

2. What equipment does the theatre own? What is its status?

3. Are there any local shops where I can rent equipment?

4. Will the actors' voices need to be reinforced?

5. What are the director's thoughts regarding the use of nonspecific background sound?

6. What is the rehearsal schedule for sound? When will the director want the effects tape? When will he or she want the microphones working for the reinforced sound?

Questions regarding the design, use, and scheduling of any live or recorded sound must be asked so that the sound designer will have a thorough understanding of the nature and scope of the design challenge.

Research

Background research for sound design needs to be conducted into both the music and the sound effects for the production. It normally requires that the sound designer become familiar with the music of the particular period in which the production concept is set. Whether the music comes from a specific period is secondary to the dictum that any music used must reflect the mood and spirit of the production. Any preshow, intermission, and post-show music should support the psychological mood dictated by the script and the production concept. Any incidental music that is selected for use during the production should enhance the audience's feelings and understanding about that particular moment in the play.

Research into sound effects is a little more arcane than research in music, because recorded sound doesn't always sound as you would expect. The recorded sound of water rushing down the rocky course of a mountain stream, when played back, may sound exactly like someone crumpling up a piece of cellophane, water running from a spigot, or a flushing toilet. The sound designer needs to be aware of this phenomenon and prepared to deal with it.

It is vital that the sound designer understand the psychological purpose and desired impact of each sound effect as well as the nature of that particular effect. Specifically, if the script calls for a horn honking, the sound designer needs to create a whole little scenario about that effect. He or she needs to know a great deal of specific information about the horn. Is it attached to a vehicle? What kind, type, and year of vehicle is it? Is the driver casually honking, or is he (or she) really mad and insistent? Is the vehicle nearby or far away? Is it moving or standing still? These and similar questions need to be answered by the director before the sound designer can begin to produce a genuinely useful and original sound effect.

The sound designer will need to have access to a good library of sound effects. There are several commercially available collections of effects that should be part of any production company's sound equipment. The *BBC Sound Effects Library* and the *CBS Sound Effects Library* are two excellent collections. Other effects CDs are generally available through any well-stocked music store.

It is rare that any of these prerecorded effects can be used without editing. A usual practice involves the editing and mixing of two or three separate effects to create a new effect that is appropriate for a specific cue.

Conceptual research in sound design means creating, either mentally or by recording, as many potential solutions to each sound cue as possible. For the preshow music, select from the work of a number of composers. With sound effects, let your ideas flow, even if some of them seem to be strange, bizarre, and nonworkable. Do not judge them at this point.

Incubation

Let the ideas sit unattended for a while. Do something else.

Selection

Choose the specific music and sound effects that you intend to use for each particular cue.

Implementation

Stop talking and start recording. Since all sound cues (except those that are going to be produced live such as doorbells, telephones, and similar sounds that demand specific location and presence) need to be stored on tape or disk, you will have to record and edit any and all music and sound effects that you intend to use. Specific instructions on making edited show tapes or disks are provided later in this chapter.

Evaluation

Review your use of the design process on this particular project as well as your communication with the other members of the design team. This review will provide you with a mechanism to improve your use of the process as well as your communication on your next production assignment.

dependent on the reverberation, or multiple reflection, of the sound among several of the reflecting surfaces in the auditorium.

Designing a theatre that is acoustically balanced for both speech and music is a very great, if not impossible, challenge. Speech requires a short reverberation time, whereas music sounds better with a longer period of reverberation. No totally satisfactory solution to this problem exists, but many modern architects and acousticians have tried to solve it by designing acoustically adjustable auditoriums and stages (see the box "Acoustic Balancing").

Another not overly satisfactory solution that is frequently tried in an attempt to overcome the challenges posed by poor acoustic design of an auditorium is the use of a complicated and sophisticated sound system. Although the installation of very carefully engineered sound systems may alleviate the problems associated with poor acoustical design, a sound system has not been invented that will completely eliminate the need to have the shape and finish of an auditorium designed with extreme care and expertise.

SOUND PRODUCTION

As with every other area of theatre production, computers are facilitating significant improvements in the field of sound production. Recording tape was the technology of choice for recording and playback of music and sound effects from approximately 1960 to the early 1990s. The development of CD technology in the early 1980s, with its digital signal, offered significantly improved sound quality. The advent, and continuing evolution, of inexpensive and highly effective computer-based sound editing programs provided sound designers with digital recording, editing, and playback capabilities. Together they signaled the end of the **tape deck's** reign. However, not everyone has jumped on the digital bandwagon. Tape is still a viable technology for theatrical sound production. Some sound designers prefer what they refer to as the "softer" sound produced by tape. Some like the "hands on" editing style that is required by recording tape. Some producing organizations simply haven't had the money required to "make the switch." For whatever reasons, tape is still used in many theatres.

In spite of what seems to be a bewildering array of equipment used to record and play back sound in the theatre (Figure 19.11), a logical, fairly straightforward set of principles guides the design of any sound system.

Basic Sound-System Configuration

Every sound system works on the principles illustrated in Figure 19.12. Sound is picked up by a **transducer** such as a **microphone** which converts the sound from mechanical energy (the pressure waves generated by the sound source) into electrical energy (a very small electrical signal), as shown in Figure 19.12A. The transducer sends the signal to a storage device (tape recorder, recordable CD, or computer) where it is recorded and stored.

To produce an audible recorded sound, the electrical signal is sent from the tape deck or computer to an **amplifier,** as illustrated in Figure 19.12B. The amplifier increases (amplifies) the power of the electrical signal so that it can drive the **loudspeaker.** From the amplifier the electrical signal is sent to the loudspeaker, which converts the electrical energy back into mechanical energy. The mechanical energy (sound-pressure waves) reaches our ear.

Every sound system works on these principles, but the electrical signal needs to be manipulated to control the **tone** (bass through treble frequencies) of the sound. To accomplish this function, an **equalizer** (a device that manipulates and modifies the signal) is placed in the system, as shown in Figure 19.13.

tape deck: A magnetic-tape transport mechanism used to record an electrical signal on magnetic tape; also used to play back that signal; does not contain a playback amplifier and speaker.

transducer: A device that converts energy from one state into another, for example, a microphone or loudspeaker.

microphone: A transducer used to convert sound waves into electrical energy.

amplifier: A device used to boost the signal received from a transducer to a level that will drive a loudspeaker.

loudspeaker: A transducer used to convert an electrical signal into mechanical energy (the movement of a vibrating membrane); converts a signal from an amplifier into audible sound.

tone: A generic term referring to the intensity of the component frequencies contained in any particular sound.

equalizer: An electronic device that selectively boosts or attenuates specific frequencies or ranges of frequencies.

(A)

(B)

FIGURE 19.11
An open theatrical sound booth located in the house (A) and an enclosed booth (B).
The open booth is preferred because the operator can hear the sound balance coming
from the stage and adjust it as necessary.

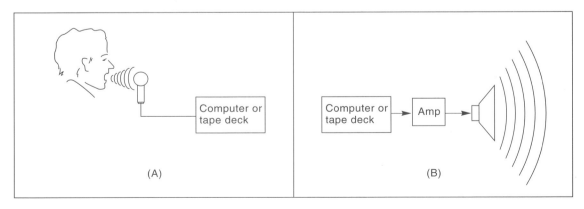

FIGURE 19.12
Block diagram of a monaural sound system.

Figure 19.13A shows the placement of an equalizer between the microphone and the computer or tape recorder. The purpose of this equalizer is to modify the signal coming from the microphone to enhance the tonal quality of the sound before it is recorded.

Figure 19.13B shows another equalizer inserted into the **playback system** between the computer or tape deck and the amplifier. The purpose of this equalizer is to modify the signal being fed to the amplifier, which will ultimately change the tonal quality of the sound being produced by the loudspeaker.

The basic sound systems illustrated in Figures 19.12 and 19.13 are monaural, or single-channel, systems. They mix all of the sound produced by the various sources (voices, noise, music, synthesizers, and so on) into one channel. Figure 19.14 illustrates a stereo, or two-channel, sound system. A stereo sound system is actually a paired monaural system. There are two electronically discrete (separated) sources, **preamplifiers,** tape decks or computers, amplifiers, and speakers. What makes this rather confusing is that in home systems, where we first learned about "stereos," these separate elements are usually contained in the same housing. Figure 19.15 shows a stereo tape deck and a **graphic equalizer.** Notice that each unit has a complete set of controls for the two separate channels.

Most theatrical sound systems are stereophonic or multichannel (more than two channels), simply because such systems can produce a more lifelike quality of sound than a monaural system can produce.

Sound-System Equipment

Each piece of equipment in a sound system has a specific function, as we have seen. The functions of those elements of a sound system are described in more detail in this section.

FIGURE 19.13
Block diagrams of (A) equalizers in a recording system and (B) a playback system.

playback system: Devices used to play recorded sound; usually composed of some combination of a turntable, a tape deck, a CD player, or a computer; an equalizer; an amplifier; and a speaker.

preamplifier: A device that boosts the level of a signal, without alteration or reshaping, to the requisite input signal level of the next piece of equipment in a sound system.

graphic equalizer: An equalizer with individual slide controls affecting specific, usually narrow, segments of the sound spectrum; so called because the position of the individual controls graphically displays a picture of the equalization of the full sound spectrum.

FIGURE 19.14
Block diagram of a stereo system.

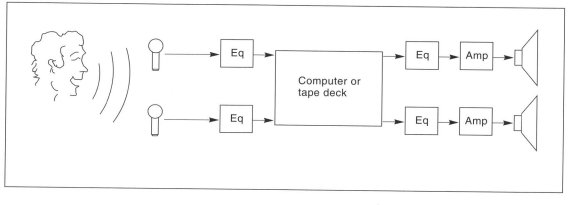

FIGURE 19.15
Stereo equipment has separate controls for each channel. A stereo tape deck (A) and a graphic equalizer and amplifier (B).

(A)

(B)

Loudspeakers and Speaker Systems   The loudspeaker is a transducer that converts the electrical energy of the signal to a mechanical energy that we can hear. Figure 19.16 illustrates this principle and shows the primary parts of the speaker. The signal activates an electromagnet attached to the loudspeaker frame. The electromagnet generates a magnetic field that corresponds in intensity to the frequency and loudness of the electrical signal emitted by the amplifier. The variation in this magnetic field causes a voice coil, which is attached to the rear of a flexible cone, to move the cone forward and backward in a pattern that mimics the frequency and loudness dictated by the electrical signal.

Generally speaking, the quality of a cone-type loudspeaker is directly related to the power of its electromagnet, the rigidity of the speaker frame, and the flexibility of its cone. The power of an electromagnet is roughly determined by its weight—the heavier the magnet, the greater the power.

Speakers work most effectively and efficiently when they are designed for a relatively narrow frequency range. Speakers are generally classified as low-frequency (**woofers**), middle-frequency (**mid-range**), and high-frequency (**tweeters**).

Almost all woofers are cone-type loudspeakers. Mid-range speakers and tweeters are also made using cones, but they are also manufactured using a

woofer: A low-frequency speaker, with a frequency range from 20 to approximately 150–250 Hz.

mid-range speaker: A speaker designed to reproduce the middle range of audible frequencies—roughly 200–1,000 Hz.

tweeter: A high-frequency speaker, generally designed to reproduce from approximately 1,000–20,000 Hz.

Planning a Theatre Sound System

The end product of any theatrical sound system is to produce sound that will support and enhance the mood and feeling of the production. Although it might seem appropriate to begin the planning of such a system from the point of origin of the sound (the microphone, CD player, or tape deck, and so forth), actually the opposite is true. You should begin planning your system with the selection of a speaker system capable of producing the best-quality sound for the money.

Once an appropriate speaker system is selected, you will need to choose an amplifier that can drive those speakers efficiently and effec-tively. Working backward, you will next need to select equalizers and a mixer that can modify the tonal qual-ity of the separate channels of the playback sources and can route the signal from any source to any of the amplifiers.

For planning purposes, the record-ing system can be thought of as being separate from the playback system. In actual practice, the average production company or theatre usually doesn't have the budget to purchase two sepa-rate systems, so the same equipment is usually used for both purposes.

The heart of the recording system is the recording device—a computer or tape deck. A computer needs to have a multichannel sound recording/editing program. If tape decks are be-ing used, the deck (preferably two or more decks so that you can dub, or transfer, sound from one deck to the other) should be stereophonic and commercial quality—the best deck that you can afford. A quality equal-izer will provide the capability of modifying the tonal qualities of the signals before they are recorded. You will also need a CD player for trans-ferring sound effects and music to computer or tape, and you will need at least two microphones to record live sounds and music.

Sound reinforcement is also an ac-tive part of many theatrical sound systems. In this case, the source for the system is a microphone. Regardless of the number and type of microphones used on the production, the signal from each microphone is fed to a sound-mixing console or mixer, where the signals are equalized, balanced, and distributed to the proper amplifi-ers and speakers.

Block diagram of typical theatre sound systems:
(A) record,
(B) playback,
(C) reinforcement.

FIGURE 19.16
How a loudspeaker converts electrical energy to mechanical energy. (A) The structure of a typical loudspeaker. (B) The cone is moved forward and backward by the magnet to produce sound.

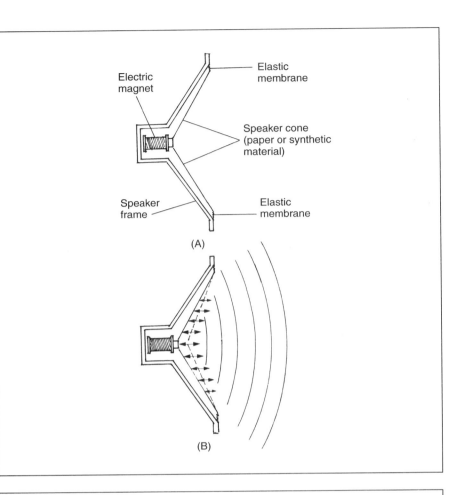

FIGURE 19.17
How a pressure driver works. (See text for details.)

pressure driver and **horn.** The pressure driver (also known simply as a driver), illustrated in Figure 19.17, creates sound in the same way as a cone speaker (a signal drives an electromagnetic voice coil, which is attached to a diaphragm that compresses air to create sound waves). The primary difference between the two is that the diaphragm in the pressure driver is made from very thin metal instead of paper or synthetic material. The metal is stiffer and more resilient and is capable of producing mid- and high-frequency sounds with greater intensity and clarity than a cone.

The pressure-driver unit is used in conjunction with a horn. The horn is used to direct the sound from the driver in a particular direction and pattern. As shown in Figure 19.18, there are a number of different models of acoustical horns. The differing shapes cause the sound to be focused in specific horizontal patterns. The 60-, 90-, and 120-degree horizontal dispersion patterns are fairly standard.

Speaker Cabinets Speaker cabinets do more than protect the delicate speaker cones from damage. They form an inextricable part of the speaker mechanism, because the sound produced by any cone-type speaker is greatly affected by the shape and volume of the enclosure in which it is housed.

The design of speaker enclosures is very complex, depending on the number of interrelated variables such as the frequency range of the speaker and the volume of the cabinet. However, the operation of all speaker cabinets is based on certain common properties.

Low-, middle-, and high-frequency sounds have differing characteristics. Low-frequency sounds are fairly nondirectional and require more power to produce than do mid- or high-frequency sounds. The mid-range and high-frequency sounds are more directional. Because of these characteristics, most speaker cabinets are designed to enhance the reproduction of the low-frequency sound spectrum.

When the cone of a woofer moves forward, as shown in Figure 19.19A, it compresses air, which produces sound waves. When the cone moves backward, as shown in Figure 19.19B, it compresses the same amount of air and produces the same amount of sound waves. If the woofer were mounted in a hole in a wall between two rooms, it would produce the same frequency, quality, and intensity of sound in both rooms. Any speaker cabinet is designed to do one of two things: either absorb the sound radiating from the back of the speaker into the "room" in back of the woofer or redirect the sound radiating from the back of the woofer to reinforce the sound coming from the front of the speaker.

Finite Baffle The cabinet design that absorbs sound waves produced by the rearward excursion of the speaker cone is called a finite baffle. It is basically an airtight box heavily lined with sound-absorbing fiberglass batts, as shown in Figure 19.20. The fiberglass helps reduce sound reflections inside the cabinet. In practical terms, it is rather inefficient, because it doesn't let the speaker work freely, and it requires a high-powered amplifier to achieve a satisfactory level of sound.

Bass-Reflex Enclosure A bass-reflex enclosure is a cabinet with a carefully designed hole or port in the front. This port, shown in Figure 19.21A, is designed so that the sound produced by the rearward excursion of the speaker cone comes out synchronized, or in phase, with the sound being produced by the forward excursion of the cone.

The bass-reflex enclosure is also lined with sound-absorbing material to help reduce sound reflections inside the cabinet. Otherwise, it is distinctly possible that the bass frequencies could overwhelm the mid-range and high-frequency sounds being produced by the other elements of the speaker system.

pressure driver: A unit housing a large magnet that vibrates a very thin metallic diaphragm to create mid-range and high-frequency sounds.

horn: A dispersion device attached to the front of a pressure driver to direct the sound emitted by the driver into a specific pattern.

FIGURE 19.18
Acoustical horns. (Courtesy of Peavey Electronics Corp.)

FIGURE 19.19 ▶
A loudspeaker compresses air on (A) its forward excursion and (B) its rearward excursion.

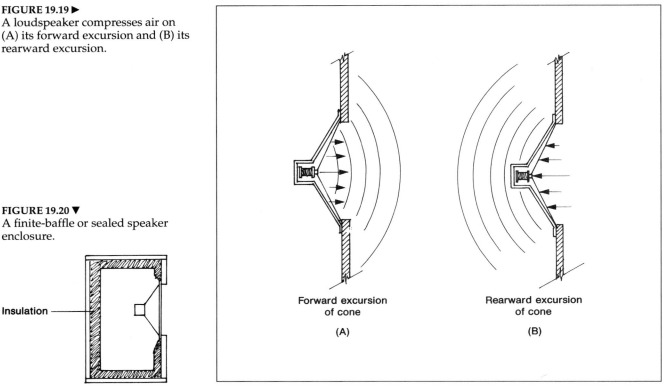

Forward excursion of cone

(A)

Rearward excursion of cone

(B)

FIGURE 19.20 ▼
A finite-baffle or sealed speaker enclosure.

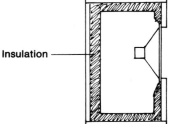

Insulation

FIGURE 19.21
(A) A bass-reflex speaker enclosure. (B) A ducted-port speaker enclosure.

Port

(A)

Tuned port

(B)

Ducted Port   Ducted-port speaker cabinets are variations of the bass-reflex design. Instead of an open port, as in the bass-reflex design, they have a tube of a specific length and diameter that projects into the cabinet from the face of the speaker board (the board on which the speaker is mounted). The length of this tube is "tuned" to a specific frequency range to reinforce a particular portion of the bass spectrum (Figure 19.21B).

Speaker cabinets tend to help reinforce the low frequencies of the woofers and generally smooth out the quality of the bass response. Low-frequency sounds are omnidirectional, and unless they are focused, they spread in every direction from their source, as shown in Figure 19.22. Even though speaker cabinets are relatively transparent to low-frequency sounds, they do provide some help in focusing the direction of the bass response. Greater focusing help is provided by solid reflecting surfaces such as floors, ceilings, and walls. Mid-range and high-frequency sound waves tend to radiate more directionally from the front of the speaker. In general, mid-range sound waves radiate approximately 180 degrees from the face of the speaker, and the angle of radiation for high-frequency sound waves becomes narrower as the frequency increases.

The backs of most high-quality, cone-type, mid-range speakers and tweeters are sealed with a thin covering of metal to avoid any possibility of resonant interference from the vibrations of the woofer(s) when the smaller speakers are mounted in the cabinet.

Crossover Network   Optimum sound is achieved from a speaker when it is designed for a narrow frequency range. For those speakers to work most efficiently, however, they must receive only the specific frequency range for which they were designed. A crossover network, an electronic device normally mounted inside the speaker cabinet, splits the signal from the amplifier into the

FIGURE 19.22
Radiation characteristics of woofers, mid-range speakers, and tweeters.

frequency ranges most appropriate for use by the speakers being used in the system. The woofer receives the low frequencies (approximately 20–300 Hz), the mid-range speaker is sent the middle frequencies (roughly 200–1,000 Hz), and the high frequencies (approximately 800 Hz up to inaudibility) are sent to the tweeter. There is a little overlap between the branches of the crossover network to smooth the transition of the sound as it moves from one speaker to the next within the system.

Crossovers are also designed for two-speaker systems (with a woofer and a combination mid-range and tweeter) as well as speaker systems that use more than three speakers.

Power Amplifier   The power amplifier is a relatively simple beast. Its sole reason for existence is to boost the low-voltage input signal that it receives from the tape deck or computer to a higher-voltage output signal capable of efficiently driving the loudspeakers.

There are usually only two controls associated with an amplifier: an on-off power switch and a loudness control. The amplifier pictured in Figure 19.23 has two loudness controls because there are two separate amplifiers mounted on the same chassis.

FIGURE 19.23
A power amplifier. (Courtesy of Crown International.)

More On Amplifiers

A power amplifier does not have the capability of shaping or modifying sound. This is confusing to many people who have home stereo units. Their "amplifiers" almost always have controls that can boost or attenuate the bass and treble spectrum in addition to controls that adjust the volume or loudness of the music.

These home stereo units are more properly called "integrated amplifiers," because they integrate the functions of the preamplifier and equalizer (the shaping of the sound spectrum—bass and treble control) and those of the power amplifier (volume or loudness) into the same piece of equipment.

In professional-quality sound systems, such as those used for theatre sound, it is more usual to provide separate pieces of equipment (preamplifiers, equalizers, and amplifiers) rather than integrated amplifiers in order to increase quality, flexibility, and usefulness.

RMS wattage rating: A system (root-mean-square) providing an accurate picture of the energy-dissipation characteristics of sound equipment.

line level: A signal voltage range of approximately .75 to 1 volt; specified as a range rather than one particular voltage because the voltage and current of the signal vary with the intensity and frequency of the sound.

attenuate: To decrease or lessen.

Appropriately, the power rating of the power amplifier is its most important statistic. The **RMS wattage rating** of the amplifier should match the power-loading capabilities of the speaker with which it will be used. If the speaker system can handle fifty watts of steady power, the amplifier should be rated at no more than fifty watts RMS.

It isn't uncommon to find amplifiers rated at 100 or 200 watts RMS in the theatre. Rock bands routinely use 400- or higher-watt amplifiers to amplify each instrument and microphone in the group.

People frequently wonder why it is necessary to use amplifiers capable of generating so much power. The answer is clarity and quality of sound. A hypothetical, but realistic, example will illustrate the point. An average-sized auditorium may require twenty watts of power to play a musical selection at a reasonable listening level. If there is a momentary peak in the music that is twice as loud, it will take ten times the power from the amplifier to accomplish the task. The amplifier must be capable of putting out 200 watts of power to make the music seem twice as loud. If the amplifier cannot achieve this peak, the music will become distorted and will sound fuzzy and muddy rather than clear and crisp.

Preamplifier   A preamplifier, or preamp, is an electronic device that raises the output of a low-level signal so that it can be read and processed, without distortion, by the next piece of equipment in the sound system. If a preamplifier uniformly boosts the full spectrum of a low-level signal to **line level,** which is the standard input voltage for mixers and equalizers—if it doesn't have the capability to boost or **attenuate** selected portions of the spectrum—it is generally referred to as a black-box preamp, as illustrated in Figure 19.24. A black-box preamp is typically used to boost the very weak signal from the magnetic cartridge of a turntable to line level (Figure 19.25).

Equalizer   An equalizer, as we have seen, boosts or attenuates portions of the signal to affect the loudness of specific segments of the sound spectrum. The tone controls for bass and treble on a home stereo integrated amplifier are "broad-band" equalizers that affect a wide range of the bass and treble spectrums.

The equalizer pictured in Figure 19.26 has controls for boosting or attenuating a wide range of the bass and treble portions of the sound spectrum. It also has progressive filtering controls. These two controls, which can be used as a rumble filter (bass) and a scratch filter (treble), progressively filter out more and more of the bass and treble spectrums. Although this style of equalizer is still

FIGURE 19.24
A black-box preamplifier is used to boost a weak signal to line level.

FIGURE 19.25
A block diagram of the use of a black-box preamp.

Turntable   Black-box   Equalizer
                      preamp

FIGURE 19.26
An equalizer.

FIGURE 19.27
A graphic equalizer. (Courtesy of
Ashly.)

used in both recording and playback, it has, to a great extent, been replaced by the graphic and parametric equalizers.

Graphic Equalizer   The equalizer pictured in Figure 19.27 is called a graphic equalizer because it graphically displays the equalization of the full sound spectrum. A specific portion of the sound spectrum is assigned to each slide control. When these controls are raised above the center position, they are boosting the specific portion of the sound spectrum that they control. When they are placed below the central position, they are attenuating the same element of the sound spectrum. When they are placed in the center of their movement range, they are not affecting the sound at all.

The graphic equalizer can be used during recording to help mask any scratch, rumble, or unwanted frequencies as well as enhance or shape the sound as envisioned by the sound designer. It is also used during playback of the sound into the auditorium to help balance the sound to the acoustics of the auditorium.

Parametric Equalizer   The parametric equalizer (Figure 19.28) is similar in function to the graphic equalizer in that it boosts or attenuates specific frequencies within the sound spectrum. The primary difference is that individual frequencies or very selective custom-designed bands of frequencies can be programmed for enhancing or attenuation with this equalizer. Although it can be used very

FIGURE 19.28
A parametric equalizer. (Courtesy
of Orban Associates.)

FIGURE 19.29
A sound mixer.

effectively during recording, the parametric equalizer is primarily used for balancing the sound during playback into the auditorium.

Mixers   The mixer (see Figure 19.29) is aptly named. It is a device that is used to mix the output from a variety of sources and route the blended signal on to other devices. With the increased use of complex sound designs, a mixer has become an almost indispensable part of the permanent sound-equipment inventory of a producing theatre group.

Almost all mixers have inputs for microphones as well as line-level equipment (preamps, computers, tape decks, and so on). These inputs are usually permanently wired into a specific control channel. In most mixers, each of these channels has the capability to control not only the loudness but also the equalization of that signal. Either the output from each control channel is hard-wired to a specific master control, or it can be assigned to any one of a number of master output controls through the use of buttons, as shown in Figure 19.30.

In operation, the equalized signal from any number of individual control channels is sent to a master control that reroutes the signal to whatever equipment is connected to the output for that master. This electronic capability allows

FIGURE 19.30
A block diagram of mixer operation.

the operator to create a designed mix, or blend, of almost any number of sources (including voices, instruments, tape decks, CDs, turntables). The latest generation of mixers have internal computers that allow the operator to record, recall, and play multichannel settings in exactly the same way that a light board operator recalls and plays the settings for hundreds of dimmers when he or she calls up one specific cue. This feature allows the sound operator to create sound presets for individual scenes or moments within scenes and dispenses with most of the "on the fly" mixing that used to be required during musicals and other multisource presentations.

In practice, the mixer is used for both recording sound and playing it back. To illustrate how the mixer can be used in recording, let's assume that the production requires a recording of a small band. The sound designer mikes the singer and the individual instruments in the band, as shown in Figure 19.31. Each microphone is connected to an input on the mixer. During rehearsal the sound designer sets the loudness and equalization for each of the input sources. Appropriate loudness levels of these individual sources are then sent to two master controls (so that the song can be recorded in stereo), where those signals are blended. The outputs of these two masters are connected to the inputs of a stereo tape deck for recording.

The mixer can also be very useful when you need to blend a number of sources during playback. Musical comedies present interesting challenges to the sound designer, who may be asked to blend the voice of one or more lead singers, the chorus, the band or orchestra, and perhaps one or more sound effects. This type of balancing act would be all but impossible without the aid of a mixer.

The lead singers are usually fitted with wireless (radio transmitter) microphones, the chorus voices are picked up with some general area microphones, the band is either miked or perhaps prerecorded, and the effects are on computer or tape. Each one of these sources is assigned to a control channel of the mixer, as shown in Figure 19.32. As in the previous example, the sound designer determines appropriate levels for each of these sources, and they are blended on the

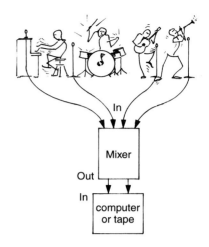

FIGURE 19.31
A block diagram of how a mixer is used in recording.

FIGURE 19.32
A block diagram of a mixer used in playback and reinforcement.

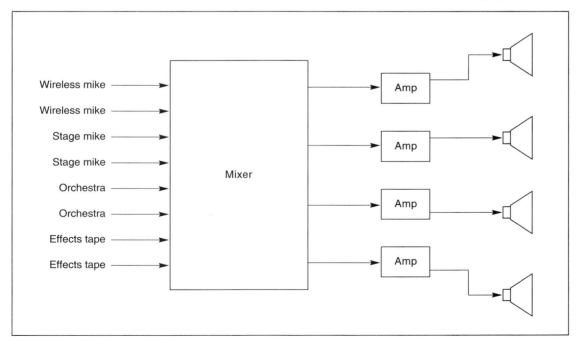

Digital Recording

Digital recording is an important advance in the recording industry. The principle behind it is fairly simple. In a nondigital, or analog, recorder, the continuously varying voltage of the signal is converted into a magnetic field by the recorder head. The strength of that field varies according to the frequency, intensity, and timbre of the sound. This continuous signal is recorded onto the tape or disk.

In a digital recorder, the signal is converted into a series of individual, or discrete, numbers rather than a continuously varying magnetic field. The signal is read by an analog-to-digital converter 44,000 times a second. Each time the converter analyzes the signal, it translates that information into a binary number—a series of on-off pulses. It is this binary information that is stored on the tape or disk.

When a digital recording is played back, the process is simply reversed. The playback head reads the stored binary information. A digital-to-analog converter translates each binary number into a signal of a specific voltage and amplitude. The resulting output signal is essentially continuous, because the digital-to-analog conversion happens so frequently.

The advantages of digital recording are a significant increase in the accuracy or fidelity of the recording and a reduction in background noise—tape hiss. The price of professional-quality digital tape and disk recorders is now within the range of most production companies, and they are being used with increasing frequency.

master control(s). In this situation, the output signal of the master control(s) is sent to one or more amplifiers and loudspeakers. It is the sound designer's responsibility to ensure that the final mix of these various sources is what is needed to support the mood and feeling of the production.

Patch Bay   A sound patch bay (Figure 19.33) is similar in purpose and construction to the patch panel used in lighting. The sound patch bay is used to cross-connect between the various pieces of equipment (CD player, tape deck, computer, equalizers, amplifiers, speakers, and so on). The outputs and inputs for each piece of equipment are connected to corresponding receptacles on the patch panel. A patch cord is used to connect the output of one piece of equipment to the input of another.

Tape Deck   A tape deck transports the magnetic tape on which music and sound effects are recorded. There is a subtle distinction between a tape deck and a tape recorder. A tape deck is simply a transport mechanism for the tape; a tape recorder is a self-contained unit with a built-in amplifier and speaker so that it

FIGURE 19.33
A sound patch bay. (Courtesy of Audiovisual Systems.)

can be used to play back the sound without the need for an external amplifier and speaker.

The tape deck has several functions, which are illustrated in Figure 19.34. The **heads,** which implant electrical data on the recording tape, are vital to the functioning of the tape deck. Top-quality decks appropriate for use in theatre sound have three or four heads. Less expensive models normally have only two heads.

Regardless of the number of heads on the tape deck, they all work in the same way. The head is basically an electromagnet made of a ring of iron, as shown in Figure 19.35. There is a small gap in the ring at the point where the recording tape contacts the tape head. (The gap isn't open; it is filled with a nonconductive metal to prevent it from snagging the tape or filling with dust.)

When an electronic signal from a microphone or other source is fed to the wire wound around the bottom of the iron ring, it creates a magnetic field across the gap at the top of the ring. When the tape deck is recording, the strength of the magnetic field across the gap in the head will vary in a pattern that mimics the voltage variations of the electronic signal.

The configuration of a three-head deck is always the same. The erase head is located on the left, the record head is in the middle, and the playback head is on the right. The erase head feeds an ultrasonic (a sound frequency above the range of human hearing) signal to the tape. This effectively scrambles any previously recorded information. The record head encodes magnetic information on the tape in a pattern that mimics the electronic signal generated by the microphone or other source. The playback head is actually a reverse of the record head. The varying density of the magnetic field recorded on the tape creates a corresponding signal of varying voltage within the playback head. This signal, which is theoretically identical to the signal that was fed to the record head, is then sent on to the various equalizers and amplifiers to be turned into sound waves.

If a tape deck has a fourth head (which is somewhat rare), it is dedicated to monitoring the tape.

Aside from providing the capability to erase, record, and play back the magnetically stored data, the tape deck must be capable of smoothly transporting the tape at a constant speed. Although a wide variety of tape speeds are available—$^{15}/_{16}$, $1^{7}/_{8}$, $3^{3}/_{4}$, $7^{1}/_{2}$, and 15 inches per second (IPS)—most theatrical second designers prefer to use $7^{1}/_{2}$ IPS. This speed provides a high quality of sound reproduction (approximately 20–20,000 Hz) with an acceptable level of tape consumption. A speed of $3^{3}/_{4}$ IPS can be used for background effects and low-level preshow "Muzak" tracks on which its lower-frequency range (approximately 50–12,000 Hz) won't adversely affect the production. If the sound equipment is of extremely high quality and tape consumption isn't a budgetary consideration, 15 IPS is often used, because it does provide the highest level of frequency response.

Anywhere from one to three or more motors are used in various models of tape decks to transport the tape. Generally speaking, the more motors the better, simply because the individual motors can be devoted to specific functions (the various playing speeds, fast forward, rewind) rather than having one motor provide all functions through some type of gearing mechanism.

A variety of track configurations are used on tape decks, as shown in Figure 19.36. Generally speaking, the more tape that comes into contact with the head, the better the sound. Most professional-quality theatre sound is recorded on full track (for monaural recording), or half-track stereo (for stereo), or four-track (for quadraphonic sound).

Almost all theatre sound that is not recorded as a computer file is recorded on one-quarter-inch reel-to-reel tape decks, because these commercial- or studio-

head: A very high quality electromagnet on a tape deck or tape recorder that is used to implant, retrieve, or erase electrical data from audio tapes.

FIGURE 19.34
Tape-deck heads.

FIGURE 19.35
How a tape head works (see text for details).

FIGURE 19.36
Monophonic, stereophonic, and quadraphonic tape tracks.

FIGURE 19.37
Tape deck. (Courtesy of Nakamichi and Otari.)

burn: To record on a CD.

quality decks (Figure 19.37) are readily available and the tape is fairly easy to handle and edit.

Compact Disk Player   The compact disk (CD) is the standard storage device in the recording industry. The process of digitization is explained in the box "Digital Recording," found on page 474. Like digital tapes, CDs have audio information stored on them in binary code. But instead of the code being stored as magnetic pulses on the recording tape, the information is stored on the disk as a series of reflective and nonreflective surfaces. To read the information, the CD player directs a laser on the surface of the spinning disk. The light from the laser is reflected from the shiny surface and absorbed by the nonreflective (black) surface. A light-sensitive reader interprets this information as binary code—a series of on/off pulses—which is then sent to the equalizer and on to the tape deck, computer, or amplifier.

Because the equipment required to **burn** CDs is quite inexpensive, and the resultant sound quality is amazingly high, many production companies are choosing this recording medium over tape for their production sound designs. The equipment to record erasable CDs—CDs which can be recorded on more than once—is, at this writing, only slightly more expensive and will likely find many uses in theatre sound in the near future.

Microphones   As noted, microphones convert mechanical sound waves into an electrical signal. Although the ideal microphone would make this conversion without altering the frequency, timbre, or dynamic range (loudness variations) of the mechanically produced sound, such a microphone, unfortunately, does not exist. There are five basic types of microphones, each making the conversion of sound waves into electrical signals with slightly different techniques and with considerable differences in quality.

Carbon Microphone   When the vibrations of sound waves strike the diaphragm of a carbon microphone, as shown in Figure 19.38, they exert minute pressure changes on the granules of carbon. These pressure changes cause a change in the electrical resistance of the granules. The change in resistance causes corresponding changes in a low-voltage current that is applied to the variable resistance of the carbon granules.

FIGURE 19.38
A carbon microphone.

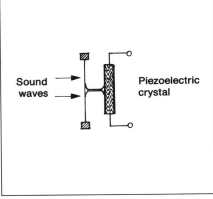

FIGURE 19.39
A crystal microphone.

The carbon microphone is widely used in the mouthpiece of telephones. It is extremely rugged and has a very narrow frequency response. Carbon mikes are not really suitable for recording theatre sound unless you are trying to duplicate the sound of someone talking over a telephone.

Crystal Microphone   Crystal microphones take advantage of the **piezoelectric** properties of certain crystalline minerals. In a crystal microphone, piezoelectric crystals are sandwiched between two pieces of metal, as shown in Figure 19.39. Sound waves striking the diaphragm exert pressure on the crystals, and they produce a signal whose voltage variations mimic the pressure changes caused by the sound source.

Crystal mikes have a little better frequency response than carbon ones have, and they are also extremely rugged. They are often sold with less expensive tape recorders. They are not of high enough quality to be used for recording sound that will be used in the theatre.

Ribbon Microphone   Ribbon microphones are made of a corrugated strip of very thin metal that is suspended between the poles of a magnet, as shown in Figure 19.40. When someone speaks into the microphone, the sound waves strike the ribbon of metal, moving it back and forth within the field of the magnet. This movement induces a small voltage between the two ends of the ribbon. The pattern of this varying voltage is an electrical duplication of mechanical pressure changes produced by the voice of the person speaking into the mike.

The ribbon microphone has a very good frequency response, but it is quite delicate. The ribbon can be easily broken just by blowing on it. High-quality ribbon mikes are frequently used in radio broadcasting, but their delicacy makes them a little too fragile to stand up to the sometimes abusive treatment they receive in the theatre.

Dynamic Microphone   Dynamic microphones create their signals by inducing a small current in a coil that is firmly attached to the diaphragm of the microphone. The coil is surrounded by a magnetic yoke, as illustrated in Figure 19.41. Pressure changes caused by the sound waves striking the diaphragm move the coil up and down within the magnetic field generated by the yoke, with the result that a current is induced in the coil. The strength of the induced current mimics the frequency and intensity of the sound source. Dynamic microphones have very good frequency response, are rugged, and are suitable for recording of theatre sound.

Condenser Microphone   The condenser mike is the most electrically complex type of microphone. The diaphragm, which is made of thin conductive material, forms one plate of a condenser, or capacitor. The other plate is placed very close to it, as shown in Figure 19.42. A constant voltage is applied across these plates. When a sound wave strikes the diaphragm, the pressure changes the space between the two plates. This causes a change in the **capacitance** of the condenser, which results in a change in the voltage applied between the two plates. The resultant variations in the voltage are an electrical reproduction of the mechanical pressure changes originated by the sound source.

The condenser microphone is probably the highest-quality one used for recording sound in the theatre. It has excellent frequency response and dynamic range (sensitivity to changes in loudness). It needs a power supply, but in most cases a small battery supplies the necessary power. As with any precision instrument, the condenser microphone needs to be handled with care, but it is reasonably rugged and can stand up to the type of abuse that it will receive in theatrical work.

piezoelectricity: Voltage produced when pressure is placed on certain crystals.

capacitance: The electrical capacity of a condenser, or capacitor.

FIGURE 19.40
A ribbon microphone.

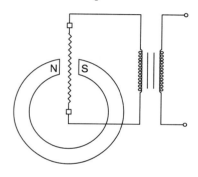

FIGURE 19.41
A dynamic microphone.

FIGURE 19.42
A condenser microphone.

How a Condenser, or Capacitor, Works

Condenser is actually an obsolete word for a capacitor. A capacitor is a device that has two conductive surfaces separated by some type of insulating material, such as air. The capacitor acts as an electrical reservoir and floodgate. It will store a certain amount of electrical energy. When it reaches its capacity, it allows an alternating current to pass through it as long as the current does not reduce its "full" state. If the distance between the two conducting plates is changed, the "capacity" (more properly known as capacitance) of the capacitor is similarly changed. A greater distance between the plates increases the capacitance; less distance decreases it.

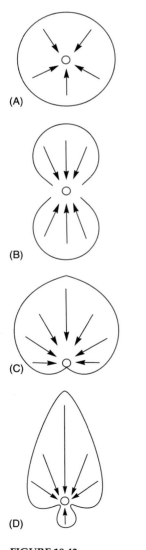

FIGURE 19.43
Microphone pickup patterns.

Microphone Pickup Patterns   Microphones do not discriminate in what they hear. They will pick up, and convert into an electrical signal, any sound within their pickup range. Several distinct pickup patterns have been developed to assist in making microphones somewhat discriminating.

An *omnidirectional* microphone pattern extends in a spherical pattern around the mike head, as shown in Figure 19.43A. Wireless microphones (see box) frequently have omnidirectional patterns. For stage use, the microphone is usually small enough to be hidden somewhere in the actor's costume. The microphone is connected to a small battery-powered transmitter that is also hidden within the costume.

Stage monitor systems, which pick up the actors' voices and send them to various remote locations around the theatre (lighting and sound booths, dressing rooms, and so on) generally use a microphone with an omnidirectional pattern so that the voices and noises of the production can be picked up regardless of their location on stage.

The *bidirectional* configuration, commonly referred to as the figure 8 pattern (Figure 19.43B), easily picks up sounds in front of and behind the microphone but does not readily "hear" sounds to its side. Because of their structure, ribbon microphones, which were described in the previous section, inherently possess this bidirectional property. They can, however, be designed to have other pickup patterns. This type of microphone pattern is very good for conducting interviews, for recording two instruments when the musicians are facing each other, and for similar situations.

Directional microphone patterns use two primary configurations, cardioid and hypercardioid. The *cardioid* pattern, shown in Figure 19.43C, is somewhat heart shaped. It has excellent pickup characteristics directly to the front of the microphone, and the sensitivity falls off as you move to the sides. Once you move past the sides of the microphone, there is almost no pickup from the rear. The cardioid pattern is probably most useful for general theatrical applications. It is very good for recording and reinforcement, because of its characteristic rejection of noise from the side and back.

The *hypercardioid*, or supercardioid, pattern is simply a more directional adaptation of the cardioid pattern, as shown in Figure 19.43D. Although it has a stronger rejection of lateral sounds, it does have an increased sensitivity to the rear.

Any type of microphone (carbon, crystal, ribbon, dynamic, or condenser) can be designed with any pickup pattern. For theatrical purposes, high-quality dynamic or condenser microphones with cardioid pickup patterns are the most useful.

Wireless Microphones

A wireless microphone has a significant advantage over its wired counterpart. It does not need a mike cable to connect it to the mixer. Instead, the signal is broadcast by a low-power FM radio transmitter to a receiver and subsequently fed into the mixer.

At first glance, the wireless microphone may seem the answer to the sound designer's dreams. However, it does have some significant drawbacks. The batteries that power the microphone transmitter must be checked, and usually changed, for every performance. Since the signal is broadcast, the receiver is also subject to receiving other broadcast signals, as well as other types of interference. In moderate to large cities, it is not unusual for wireless microphone receivers to pick up local radio stations as well as the microphones. If more than one wireless microphone is to be used, they need to transmit on different frequencies so that the sound operator can monitor the individual performers. Typically, a production requires three to five leading characters to be equipped with wireless microphones. Finally, the systems are expensive. A good-quality wireless microphone, which will transmit and receive within a very narrow frequency range, costs between $1,000 and $3,000.

But even with all of these drawbacks, the wireless microphone provides an excellent method of miking a show. If the challenges outlined above can be surmounted (and they can), the wireless microphone provides probably the finest method of reinforcing the voice in the theatre. The presence attained by having the microphone placed close to the actor's mouth can be matched only with a hand-held microphone; no other theatrical reinforcement system comes close.

As with almost every other type of equipment, a wide variety of microphones are available. A few of the more common types used in the theatre are illustrated in Figure 19.44.

It is all but impossible to determine the pickup pattern of a microphone simply by looking at it. However, every quality microphone will have the manufacturer's name and the model number indicated somewhere on the case of the microphone. When this information is known, the type and pattern of the microphone can be found by referring to the appropriate manufacturer's catalog.

The Sound Booth

The sound booth is designed to facilitate both the recording of cues and the playback of sound effects during the production. The specific layout, or placement, of the equipment in the booth is a matter of individual taste, but the operator should have a view of the stage when playing the sound during the production. The layout should be both logical and efficient (Figure 19.45).

If extensive reinforcement or balancing of a variety of sources has been dictated by the sound design, the sound operator needs to be located in the auditorium rather than the sound booth (see Figure 19.11 on page 462). This configuration is required because the operator needs to hear what the audience is hearing to create a properly balanced mix of the various sources. Although this arrangement may annoy some theatre patrons, the improvement in the balance and focus of the sound mix more than compensates for the slight aesthetic annoyance of having the sound operator and his or her equipment perched in the middle of the audience space.

FIGURE 19.44
Microphones. (A) Hand-held micro-phones can be held by performers or mounted on stands. (Courtesy of Electro-Voice.) (B) Wireless microphones use a small radio transmitter and receiver to send the signal to the mixer. (Courtesy of Cetec Vega.) (C) Pressure-zone microphones (PZM) are very small omnidirectional condenser micro-phones that pick up, with great clarity and presence, sounds up to ten or fifteen feet away. (Courtesy of Crown International.)

(A)

(B)

(C)

FIGURE 19.45
A typical sound booth layout.

Rehearsal and Performance Procedures

For a very good reason, the rehearsal and performance procedures for sound are almost identical to those for lights. Both media are intangible, so you must have clear, concise instructions that tell you at what level to set each piece of equipment (preamps, mixers, equalizers, and amplifiers) for every cue in the production. In this way, the loudness level of the sound will be the same from each rehearsal or performance to the next. A sample cue sheet is shown in Figure 19.46.

The sound cue sheet provides the sound operator with an organized method of recording not only the level of each piece of equipment but also notations on

---

Sound Equipment Maintenance

Despite the rugged appearance of some pieces, all sound equipment is delicate. The proper functioning of speakers, microphones, and tape decks relies on the maintenance of physical tolerances measured in thousandths of an inch. All electronic equipment is adversely affected by dust, moisture, and smoke. For these reasons, the following procedures should be followed:

1. Never smoke, eat, or drink in the sound booth or around sound (or other electronic) equipment.

2. Cover all tape decks, amplifiers, and other equipment with cloth dustcovers when they are not in use. While plastic dustcovers will protect the equipment from dust, the static electricity charges that can be generated with some types of plastics can adversely affect the equipment.

3. Store microphones on some type of padded surface in a cabinet.

4. Coil all microphone and speaker cable and hang on a peg board when not in use.

5. Inspect the connectors for all microphone and speaker cables before and after each use. Make sure that there are no loose or frayed wires and that the strain reliefs (where applicable) are in place.

6. Never blow into a microphone when trying to determine if it is "on" or "live." Blowing can damage or get moisture on the internal parts. Don't thump the mike. Speak into the microphone in a normal voice, or gently snap your fingers.

FIGURE 19.46
A sample sound cue sheet.

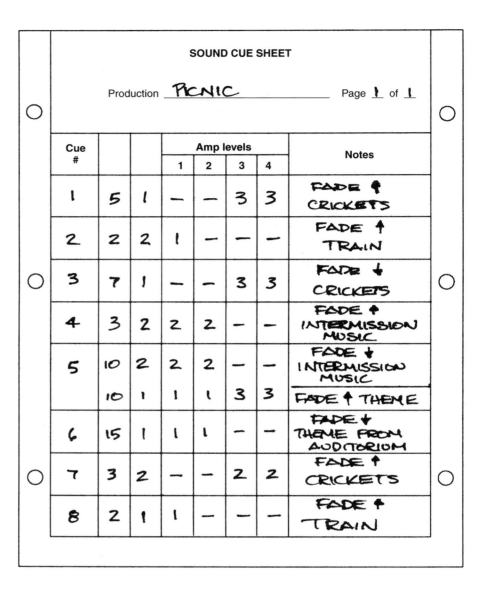

Cue #			Amp levels				Notes
			1	2	3	4	
1	5	1	—	—	3	3	FADE ↑ CRICKETS
2	2	2	1	—	—	—	FADE ↑ TRAIN
3	7	1	—	—	3	3	FADE ↓ CRICKETS
4	3	2	2	2	—	—	FADE ↑ INTERMISSION MUSIC
5	10	2	2	2	—	—	FADE ↓ INTERMISSION MUSIC
	10	1	1	1	3	3	FADE ↑ THEME
6	15	1	1	1	—	—	FADE ↓ THEME FROM AUDITORIUM
7	3	2	—	—	2	2	FADE ↑ CRICKETS
8	2	1	1	—	—	—	FADE ↓ TRAIN

whether the cue is to fade in or start at a specific level. There is also space to make notes regarding anything of importance pertaining to the cue.

Playback Layout Pattern

Sound cues are similar in many ways to lighting cues. They are most noticeable when a mistake is made. Comedians have developed entire comedy routines around sound cues that either don't happen or happen too early or too late—gunshots that come three seconds after the trigger is pulled, explosions that don't go off, clocks tolling the wrong time, and so on. Many of these glitches can be prevented by careful preparation of the playback tape or files.

Sound cues can be played back from computer files or tape. Computer-recorded cues are relatively straightforward and dependent on the capabilities and requirements of the computer program used. Each cue is recorded as a separate file and the filename correlated with a specific cue: for example, "Sound Q3—Distant Dog Howl." The cues are stored in sequential order—the order in

FIGURE 19.47
A typical production tape layout.

which they will be played in the production—in a show directory. If a cue is added, it is a relatively simple matter to insert the cue in its appropriate location in the show directory. Cues that are dropped from the production are easily deleted from the show directory. (Note: *Always* run a backup disk after *any* change to the sound cues. It's better to be safe than sorry.)

Tape—whether analog or digital—is still a viable and effective method of production sound playback. Figure 19.47 illustrates the layout pattern for a typical production sound tape. A four- to five-foot-long piece of white or colored leader tape clearly marked with the word *head* and the name of the production is located at the beginning, or head, of the tape. The first sound cue is spliced to this piece of leader. The point on the magnetic tape at which the sound begins is placed one-half inch from the splice. The tape containing the first cue is cut about

Magnetic Fields and Inductance

A magnetic field is generated around any electrical wire that has current flowing through it. This includes the permanent wiring running through the walls of a theatre, an electric motor, a table lamp, or an extension cord. To minimize the effects of interference caused by these magnetic fields, you need to understand how they are generated. The field takes the form of a cylinder of varying density and size around the current-carrying wire. The size and strength of the field are dependent on the amount of current passing through the wire: the more current, the stronger and bigger it is.

If a cable carrying a sound signal is placed parallel with the offending electrical wire, a strong signal is induced in the cable. This induced signal is heard as a hum or hiss. If the cable is placed perpendicular to the wire that is generating the field, however, almost no signal is induced in the cable.

The effects of induced interference (known as inductance) can also be lessened by removing the sound cable from the vicinity of the power wire. This solution doesn't always work, because when you move the cable away from one power line, you are probably moving it closer to another.

If you have ever been in a recording studio, you may have noticed that the microphone cables look rather messy, zig-zagging across the floor. This frequently changing, apparently random pattern is created to reduce the effects of inductance from nearby power lines.

FIGURE 19.48
Audio tape splicing techniques. (A) Place uncut tape in a splicing block (magnetic face down). (B) Cut the tape with a single-edge razor blade. Be sure the blade isn't magnetized. (C) Tape the splice with mylar splicing tape. (D) A finished splice.

(A)

(B)

(C)

(D)

one foot after the sound of the first cue has ended. The end of the first cue is spliced to a two-foot piece of white or colored leader tape. *Cue 2* is marked toward the end of this leader tape near the splice for the second cue. The point at which the sound for the second cue begins is again located one-half inch from the splice. The pattern of leader, cue, leader, cue is repeated until either the reel is full or the cues for the show are completed. After the last cue on the tape, attach another six- to eight-foot piece of leader marked with the name of the production and the word *end* in several places. Be sure that this "tail" is long enough to allow the machine to be stopped after the last cue has ended and before the leader comes off the reel. It will make the job of rewinding the tape considerably less frustrating if you don't have to rethread the machine. Figure 19.48 provides instructions on how to splice one-quarter-inch audio tape.

Every reel of tape that is used on a production should be clearly marked with the name of the production and the tape deck on which it will be played. If more than one reel is to be used on any deck during the show, the sequence (*1 of 2, 2 of 3*, and so forth) should also be marked on those reels.

PRACTICAL CONSIDERATIONS

Every time you hook up a modular sound system (one in which each component of the system is a separate unit), you need to be aware of the input and output levels of the various elements. Otherwise, you could damage or destroy one or more of the pieces of equipment.

Preamp and Power-Amp Output

The electronic signal that is created by a sound source (microphone, turntable, synthesizer, and the like) is a low-voltage AC signal. Generally, this signal ranges from about 1 to 750 millivolts, depending on the intensity and frequency of the

(A)   (B)

FIGURE 19.49
(A) Output terminal board; (B) eight-ohm speaker hookup.

sound. This very small signal is susceptible to interference from almost any device in the vicinity that generates a magnetic field around it. The interference creates noises that range from clicks and hisses to a steady hum, depending on its strength and nature. If the voltage of the signal were greater, however, the effects of the interference would be lessened. Consequently, as soon as the signal is generated by the source, it is usually boosted to line level by a preamp.

Line level is the dynamic voltage range of the signal that is used between the various pieces of equipment of a typical sound system. Because the input and output signal is the same strength (line level) for the various pieces of equipment that make up the major part of any theatrical sound system, it is possible to configure the equipment in any way that suits your needs (mike to preamp to equalizer to tape deck; tape deck to mixer to equalizer to power amp; and so on).

The output of a power amplifier has a much higher voltage so that it will be capable of driving its associated speaker system. Depending on the loudness of the sound, a typical power amp output signal can range between one and thirty-five volts. Because of the power amp's relatively high voltage output, its output terminal should never be patched into the input of anything other than a speaker. If you were to do so, you would probably destroy the equipment that the power amp was patched into and severely damage the amplifier as well.

Speaker Hookup Methods

A wide variety of wiring practices can be used to connect a speaker to a power amplifier. Most of these methods can be conveniently categorized as either low- or high-voltage systems.

Low-Voltage Systems Most power amps have a variety of output options, as shown in Figure 19.49A. To ensure the best quality sound from the system (and to avoid damaging the amplifier), you should always match the **impedance** of the speaker (normally four, eight, or sixteen ohms) with the output impedance of the amplifier. The most expedient method of matching impedances is to connect a speaker system of a specific impedance to the power-amp speaker output of the same impedance, as shown in Figure 19.49B. However, it is frequently necessary or desirable to drive more than one speaker with a single amplifier. This can be accomplished by wiring the speakers in a series, a parallel, or a combination circuit before attaching them to the output terminal of the amplifier.

Figure 19.50 illustrates how to wire speakers in series. To determine the total load for a series circuit, you simply add the impedances of all speakers in the

impedance: Resistance in an AC circuit; the only difference between impedance and resistance is that impedance is defined as resistance to the flow of an *alternating* current.

FIGURE 19.50
Series wiring of speakers.

FIGURE 19.51
Parallel wiring of speakers.

circuit. In the illustrated example, the two speakers each have an impedance of eight ohms. Adding them yields sixteen ohms, which is the total load for the speaker circuit. To achieve distortion-free sound, you would connect this circuit to the sixteen-ohm connection on the speaker terminal board of the amplifier.

Loudspeakers or speaker systems can also be wired in parallel, as shown in Figure 19.51. The load for a parallel circuit is determined by the formula

$$\text{Circuit impedance} = \frac{\dfrac{S + S + S}{N}}{N}$$

where S equals the impedance of each speaker in the circuit and N equals the number of speakers in the circuit. In Figure 19.51, each of the two speakers in the circuit has an impedance of eight ohms. Inserting those figures in the formula provides the answer to the circuit impedance:

$$\frac{\dfrac{S + S}{N}}{N} = \frac{\dfrac{8 + 8}{2}}{2} = \frac{\dfrac{16}{2}}{2} = \frac{8}{2} = 4 \text{ ohms}$$

This circuit should be connected to the four-ohm outlet by attaching one wire to the four-ohm and the other to the ground or neutral outlet on the speaker terminal board of the amplifier.

Unbalanced and Balanced Lines

Two systems are used for distributing the electronic signal between the various pieces of a modular sound system: unbalanced line and balanced line.

Unbalanced Line

The unbalanced-line method of circuiting, shown in Figure A, utilizes one insulated conductor wrapped in a braided or foil shield. This shield is protected by an outer covering of insulation. The single conductor carries the signal, and the shield is used as a combined neutral and ground connection.

Balanced Line

The balanced line is identical to the unbalanced line, except that it has two conductors wrapped in the shield. One of the conductors carries the signal, and the other acts as the neutral. The shield is used as a ground connection. The balanced line requires the use of two small line transformers, so called because they are connected into the line or cable. One, a step-up transformer, is used at the source; a step-

down transformer is attached at the other end of the cable. The balanced line creates a circuit that is immune to the effects of magnetically induced interference.

There are two primary differences between the two types of lines. The balanced line (two conductors) costs more and greatly reduces magnetically induced interference.

Balanced lines are frequently employed with microphones used to reinforce actors' voices during a production. In these cases, it is almost always necessary to run the microphone cables for a long distance before they are fed into a mixer. Using a balanced line for these long cable runs keeps induced interference to a minimum.

Unbalanced lines are normally used to hook up the various pieces of equipment in the sound booth. In this type of situation, the cable runs are usually short, which keeps the effects of magnetically induced interference to a minimal level.

(A)
Unbalanced line

(B)
Balanced line

In order to balance the impedance of the speakers to the impedance of the amplifier output, it may become necessary to use a combination circuit, as illustrated in Figure 19.52. The combination circuit combines the effects of both series and parallel circuitry. To calculate the total impedance of the circuit, first calculate the impedance of the parallel portions of the circuit. Then, treating each parallel

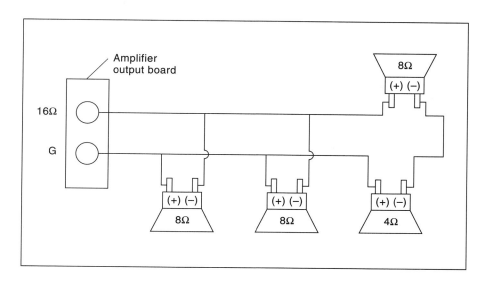

FIGURE 19.52
Combination wiring in a speaker circuit.

portion of the circuit as though it were just one speaker in a series circuit, add the impedances of the individual speakers to determine the impedance of the whole circuit.

In general, speakers wired in parallel have a cleaner sound than speakers wired in series. Series-wired speakers suffer a slight loss of quality, and the sound may seem somewhat muddy.

Most quality amplifiers are capable of driving speakers or speaker systems whose impedance is from one-half to double the rated output impedance of the amplifier. There will be some loss of quality, but most amplifiers are capable of driving these mismatched loads without suffering major damage. However, it is infinitely preferable to exactly match the impedance of the load with the impedance of the speaker. This solution will produce the best possible sound and will also minimize the chances of damaging the amplifier. The ideal solution to all of these challenges is to have each speaker driven by its own matched amplifier.

To avoid any loss of signal due to resistance in the wire that is used to connect the speaker to the amplifier, all connections where the speaker is less than 50 feet from the amplifier (or wall-mounted speaker outlet terminal) can usually be made with eighteen-gauge electrical wire. When the speaker is between 50 and 150 feet away from the amplifier (or wall-mounted speaker outlet), sixteen-gauge electrical wire can be used. Lamp cord (also known as zip cord) provides a perfectly adequate, reasonably low-cost alternative to the more expensive speaker hookup wire sold in sound shops.

High-Voltage Speaker Systems   As previously shown in Figure 19.49A, there are often additional speaker-output terminals besides the traditional low-voltage four-, eight-, and sixteen-ohm outputs. In the United States, these high-voltage outputs have been standardized at twenty-five and seventy volts.

High-voltage outputs have three primary advantages: (1) They provide an effective alternative solution when it is necessary to have a number of speakers on the same system, (2) they transmit the signal over a long cable run with less loss of quality than a low-voltage system, and (3) they reduce the effects of inductive interference.

The high-voltage transmission system steps up the voltage of the output signal at the amplifier. When the high-voltage signal reaches the speaker cabinet, it is first passed through a step-down transformer, which decreases the voltage to a level that will not burn out the speaker (nominally 3.2 volts), as shown in Figure 19.53. If the step-down transformer is not used, the voice coil of the speaker will probably be destroyed.

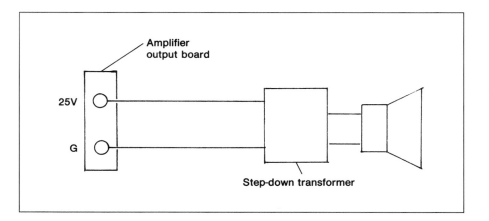

FIGURE 19.53
High-voltage speaker system.

Determining the proper loading of the amplifier and speakers in a high-voltage system isn't difficult. The relatively high voltage of the signal pragmatically nullifies the effects of the impedance in the system. When connecting a speaker or speakers to the system, simply make sure that you do not exceed the output wattage of the amplifier with the total wattage of the transformer and speakers attached to the system. Since, in any system, the low-wattage speakers will not be as loud as the high-wattage speakers, the system can be designed to take advantage of this phenomenon. Figure 19.54 shows a typical stage monitor system. The dialogue is picked up by an omnidirectional mike and sent to various locations around the theatre. The higher-wattage speakers are normally located in the makeup and dressing rooms, where the ambient noise level is fairly high. The lower-wattage speakers are used in the quieter offices and box office. A multispeaker high-voltage system can also be used to distribute sound throughout an auditorium. The higher-wattage (louder) speakers are placed on stage, and the lower-wattage (quieter) speakers are distributed in various locations about the auditorium. While this configuration does blanket the auditorium with sound, it has its challenges. Unless some type of time delay is added to the speakers farthest from the stage, it may appear to audience members sitting nearby that the sound is emanating from those speakers rather than from the stage. Also, this system does not allow the loudness levels of the individual speakers to be adjusted during the run. To have effective loudness control, each speaker must be driven by its own amplifier.

The step-down transformers used with high-voltage speaker systems normally have several different input taps (terminals) that can be used to vary the wattage associated with the speakers. They also have additional taps that are used to match the impedance of the transformer to the impedance of the speaker.

The contemporary theatre is truly an exciting place to be for someone interested in sound design, simply because what were formerly regarded as "rules" for the "proper" use of sound and music in the theatre have been thrown out, to be replaced with an exciting atmosphere of experimentation and dynamic growth.

FIGURE 19.54
Typical application of a high-voltage speaker system.

Chapter 20
Mechanical Drafting

Diagrams, freehand drawings, and perspective sketches give a clear, general picture of what a proposed design or prop is supposed to look like, but they don't tell you how to build it. Similarly, sketches, notes, and verbal explanations describing the hanging location of the various instruments used to light a production are frequently more confusing than helpful. Fortunately, mechanical drawing provides a convenient, and efficient, solution to these challenges.

Mechanical drafting can be done by hand or with a computer. Hand drafting involves the use of a drafting instrument, such as a T square, triangle, compass, or template, to draw each line. Computer drafting requires a computer equipped with an appropriate drafting program. Computer drafting will be discussed a little later in this chapter. Regardless of which method is used, the object being illustrated is **drawn to scale** and is shown from as many views as necessary to provide a clear understanding of the shape of the finished object. Mechanical drawings, when accompanied by **specifications,** provide a complete visual and verbal description of the object.

In theatrical drafting, the scale used for the mechanical drawings needed for most scenic construction is ½ inch to 1 foot. This means that each ½ inch measured on a drawing represents 1 foot on the corresponding full-scale object. The width of the flat drawn to scale in Figure 20.1 is indicated to be 3 feet, but if you measured the drawing, you would find that the flat was only 1½ inches wide.

Mechanical drawings, and the ability to produce them, are extremely important in technical theatre. The scenic designer uses them to accurately describe every element of the setting(s) so that those elements can be built as he or she envisioned them. The technical director uses them to show how each object is to be constructed. For the lighting designer, mechanical drafting provides the accurate scale "road map" that the electricians will use as a guide for hanging the lighting instruments. The sound designer uses mechanical drafting to show, in exact scale representation, the location of the equipment that will be used in support of the production. The scenic technicians, electricians, and sound technicians must be able to read and understand the information contained on the mechanical-drafting sheets, or plates.

draw to scale: To produce a likeness that is a proportional reduction of an object.

specifications: Clarifying notes that explain the building materials, textures, or special effects to be used in a design or other project.

DRAFTING MATERIALS AND INSTRUMENTS

The list of equipment used in hand-drawn mechanical drawing isn't extensive. It includes a drafting board minimally twenty-four inches high by thirty-six inches wide (a larger board of approximately thirty by forty-two inches will be better if you are also going to be drawing light plots); a good T square with a shaft long enough to reach across the width of the drafting board; one eight-inch 45-45-90-degree triangle and one twelve-inch 30-60-90-degree triangle; a pencil compass; an architect's scale rule; an eraser; 2H, 3H, and 4H drafting pencils; and drafting tape.

All hand drafting should be done on good-quality, translucent drafting paper such as Clearprint or a brand of similar quality. Drawings made on this type of paper can be easily **bluelined** for use by other members of the production design team and the various construction shops. Cheap tracing paper tears easily when an erasure is attempted, and becomes brittle and unusable with age. Tracing paper with grids shouldn't be used, as the lines will interfere with the drawings that you will be making on the paper.

Drafting Board

The size of the drafting board is not too important provided that the board is large enough to accept the dimensions of the stage for which you will be designing drawn to a scale of ½ inch to 1 foot. The board is usually made of white pine and may be covered with a plastic laminate. The ends of the board should be finished smoothly or, preferably, covered with a metal or plastic cap strip. The edges of the board must be absolutely straight so that the head of the T square will ride evenly on them. (See Figure 20.2.)

If the face of the drafting board is not covered with a plastic laminate, it should be padded with either a sheet of heavy white paper or drafting board padding material. The padding not only makes the drawing easier to see but also prevents sharp pencil points from scoring the wooden surface of the board.

T Square

The accuracy of any hand-produced mechanical drawing depends, to a great extent, on the condition of the T square. All horizontal lines are made by placing the head of the T square snuggly against the edge of the drawing board and guiding a pencil along the upper edge of the leg of the T square, as shown in Figure 20.3A. Vertical lines are drawn by placing the base of the triangle against the leg or shaft of the T square and guiding a pencil along the vertical edge of the triangle, as shown in Figure 20.3B. If the head of the T square is not firmly attached to the shaft at a true right angle, neither vertical nor horizontal lines will

blueline: To copy drawings made on tracing vellum; the lines on the vellum are printed in blue or, sometimes, in black; also known as the diazo process.

FIGURE 20.1
A flat drawn to scale.

FIGURE 20.2
Drafting equipment.

(A)

(B)

(C)

FIGURE 20.3
How to use a T square. (A) Pull on the leg to keep the head of the T square flush with the edge of the board when drawing horizontal lines. (B) Hold the triangle snuggly to the leg of the T square when drawing vertical lines. (C) A Mayline drawing machine.

be accurate. Other types of equipment, such as the Mayline (Figure 20.3C), perform the same function as the T square but are considerably more expensive.

Triangles

Triangles can be purchased in many different sizes, but the eight-inch 45-45-90-degree and the twelve-inch 30-60-90-degree triangles are ideally suited for most drafting purposes. Triangles any smaller than these necessitate shifting both the T square and triangles to a new position to draw a long vertical line. By placing one triangle against another, as shown in Figure 20.4, and guiding both with the T square, angles of 15 and 75 degrees can be drawn.

The set square, shown in Figure 20.5, is an adjustable triangle with two parts joined by a plastic protractor reading from 0 to 45 degrees. A threaded bolt and thumbscrew allow the two halves of the triangle to be locked in any desired position.

Compass and Circle Template

A medium-quality compass (Figure 20.6A) is needed for drawing circles and arcs. A substitute preferred by many drafters is a circle template, shown in Figure 20.6B. When purchasing a circle template, select one with a large number of circle diameters, because a template will almost invariably have every size except the one you want to use.

Architect's Scale Rule

The key to making all scaled mechanical drawings is the use of an architect's scale rule. The scales found on the rule make the process of allowing a fraction of a foot to represent a full foot practically painless.

FIGURE 20.4
How to draw 15- and 75-degree angles.

The architect's rule (Figure 20.7) is made in two shapes, triangular and flat. The triangular rule (which is less expensive) has a standard foot measure on one edge and ten different scales, two on each of the remaining five edges: 1 foot to ³⁄₃₂, ⅛, ³⁄₁₆, ¼, ⅜, ½, ¾, 1, 1½, and 3 inches. The flat rule may be a little more convenient to use, but it has only eight scales and is more expensive.

The one-half-inch scale, as noted, is the most frequently used in theatrical drafting. This scale reads from right to left on the architect's scale shown in Figure 20.8A. At the extreme right of the rule is a one-half-inch space that has been divided into twelve spaces representing inches, with each scale inch subdivided into halves by shorter lines. Foot measurements are indicated in multiples of two; they read zero, two, four, six, and so on. Odd-numbered foot measurements, not indicated by a numeral, are found by using the marks for the one-inch scale. These marks fall midway between the numerals of the one-half-inch scale. On the one-half-inch scale the foot measurements are read to the left of the zero, and the inches are read to the right.

Figure 20.8B shows how the architect's scale rule is used to measure a line. One end of the line is placed on a full-foot mark, and the other end of the line projects into the inch breakdown of the scale foot. The length of the line is read by counting the number of feet to the right of the zero point on the scale and the number of inches to the left.

Drawing Pencils

Most drafting for theatrical work is done with drafting pencils marked 2H (soft), 3H (medium), and 4H (hard). Drawing pencils (those designated by the letter *B*) leave a blacker line, but they smudge easily and quickly leave both the drafter's hands and drawing instruments covered with graphite. It is much easier to handle and manipulate a long drafting pencil than one that has been worn down to a stub. A sharp pencil is essential for accurate drafting, because only a sharp point can draw a clean, crisp line of unvarying width. The mechanical push-point drafting pencils, which use leads of diameters that correspond to the widths of the various drafting lines—approximately 0.3 mm for thin lines and 0.5 mm for thick lines—solve a lot of the problems with dull points that seem to plague neophyte drafters. However, whether you choose mechanical or wood pencils is strictly up to you; the two work equally well.

Eraser

A soft, pliable, pink eraser or a kneadable eraser (Figure 20.9) is the best choice for correcting penciled mistakes. Each removes the graphite without discoloring or damaging the paper.

Powdered eraser, contained in either a shaker can or a bag called a **pig**, can be sprinkled on the drafting paper while the drawing is being made. The movement of the T square and triangles over these particles keeps the underside of the instruments clean and prevents a graphite "shadow" from forming on the paper.

Drafting Tape

Drafting tape is used for holding the paper in place on the drafting board. Drafting tape and masking tape look alike. However, drafting tape will not leave a sticky residue on your drawings, whereas masking tape will.

To tape the paper to the board, you will need to adjust it until the upper or lower edge of the paper is parallel with the T square shaft. Use two- to three-inch strips of drafting tape to hold down the four corners of the paper, as shown in

FIGURE 20.5
A set square.

(A)

(B)

FIGURE 20.6
(A) A compass and (B) a circle template.

pig: A bag of loosely woven fabric containing powdered eraser material.

FIGURE 20.7
Architect's rules.

Figure 20.10. Commercially available small circular taping tabs can also be used to tape the paper to the drawing board.

Computer Drafting

Probably the most common use of computers in theatrical production is in the area of drafting. There are numerous excellent two- and three-dimensional drafting programs. Two of the more commonly used are MiniCad by Graphsoft (for MACs and PCs) (Figure 20.11) and AutoCad by Autodesk (for PCs).

An additional piece of hardware that is necessary for use when computer drafting is a **plotter** that will print on sheets of paper up to approximately 24 × 36 inches. These machines are relatively expensive, but access to them is frequently available through local quick-copy centers, blueprint shops, or university computing labs or centers. You simply take the disk containing your drafting file(s) to the shop and it prints the file(s) at a nominal fee.

plotter: A printer used to produce computer-generated drafting sheets and drawings on large paper.

Scenic Drawings   Software drafting programs facilitate the rapid production of scale ground plans, sections, elevations, and other drawings used to describe scenery and properties. Depending on the skill and experience of the draftsperson and the complexity of the object being drawn, it may take longer to draft an object on the computer than by hand (or vice versa). For most draftspersons, once you have mastered the basic principles of computer drafting, use of these programs reduces the overall time spent drafting. Computer drafting certainly re-

FIGURE 20.8
(A) A half-inch rule. (B) How to measure the scale length of a line.

The line measures 6' 8"

You Still Need to Know Both

While many of the computer drafting software programs contain excellent features, computer drafting does not negate the need to know the craft of drafting by hand. Although it is certainly debatable that learning to draft by hand is a "better" way to learn the basic principles of drafting, it is irrefutable that at some time you may be caught in a situation where you have to draft something and either you don't have access to a computer or you don't know how to operate the drafting program on the computer. Therefore, you still need to be able to read an architect's rule, operate a T square and triangle, draw a straight line, and perform the other drafting skills. However, computer drafting is also an indispensable skill to possess.

FIGURE 20.9
Auxiliary drafting equipment.

duces the time required to make corrections or changes on previously drafted plates. When making a change you simply recall the file, redraft only those sections of the plate that need to be altered, and print out a new copy of the full plate. Figure 20.12 is an example of computer drafting for scenery.

Drafting programs also are ideal for those situations in which you want or need to change the scale of a particular drawing. All you need to do is select the new scale. The computer recalculates the data and prints out a copy of the re-scaled drawing.

Light Plots There are a number of programs available to assist the designer in drafting the light plot and creating associated paperwork such as the instrument schedule/hook-up sheet, gel **cut list,** circuit to dimmer patch reports, and so forth.

Although programs that create light plots and lighting drawings are useful, and programs that generate the associated paperwork are also quite helpful, the most effective programs are those that integrate the functions of drafting the light

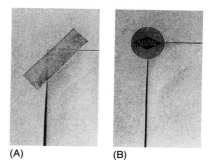

FIGURE 20.10
(A) Use of drafting tape. (B) Taping tabs.

cut list: A list of the color media required for the lighting design for a particular production categorized by hue and size; used to assist in ordering and cutting the color media for a lighting design.

FIGURE 20.11
On-screen view of ground plan for *School for Scandal,* scenic design by Peter Beudert. Software: MiniCad by Diehl Graphsoft, Inc.

FIGURE 20.12
On-screen view of elevation for *School for Scandal,* scenic design by Peter Beudert. Software: MiniCad by Diehl Graphsoft, Inc.

plot and lighting sectional with the creation of the associated paperwork. As indicated elsewhere in this book, the functionality of a lighting design is only as good as its paperwork. Integrated lighting design programs automatically update all the paperwork associated with the light plot. If, for example, on the light plot you add a six-inch Fresnel to one of the on-stage pipes, that information is automatically transferred to the instrument schedule and other paperwork. When you select a specific gel color or dimmer/circuit number for that instrument, that information is incorporated on the plot *and* on the instrument schedule, gel cut list, and any other paperwork that you are generating for the design. This integrated software keeps all the paperwork up-to-date. All you will need to remember is to put any changes on the plot and print out the new information. Examples of computer-generated drafting for lighting are shown in Figure 20.13.

There are other useful tools for the lighting designer and master electrician that are not directly associated with drafting a plot or producing the associated paperwork. One of those tools is the Rosco Light Shop. This program provides photometric data for an extensive library of lighting instruments. For example, students can use this program to learn about the beam/field spread and illumination capabilities of various types of instruments; lighting designers can use this information to select specific brands and types of instruments that they want to use in their designs; electricians can use the data during instrument maintenance.

DRAFTING SYMBOLS AND CONVENTIONS

The information in this section has been extracted from the United States Institute for Theatre Technology's (USITT) recommendations for standard graphic language in scenic design and technical production. The concept of a standard must evolve from some logical base. In this case, that base is the only inflexible rule of technical drawing—that any graphic communication must be clear, consistent, and efficient. Although the USITT recommendations do not contain specific guidelines for the spacing of objects on a plate, any graphic presentation needs

SoftPlot Report for file: C:\LITDES\USERINFO\SHOWS\GUYS\GUYSPLOT.LDP

Venue: Meadowvale Theatre
Production: Guys & Dolls
Director: Bob Ridell
Lighting Designer: Glen Miller
Date: 06-02-1996

Instrument Inventory Listing

Stock	Used	Hire	Type	Watts	Notes
44	44		STRAND ZOOM Lekolite 2206	1000	
18	18		STRAND 6 x 9 Lekolite 2209	1000	
15	15		STRAND 6 x 9 LEKO 40 - 12240	1000	
8	8		STRAND 6 x 16 LEKO 20 - 12220	1000	
2	2		STRAND 6 x 22 LEKO 15 - 12215	1000	
6	6		STRAND 6 x 12 Lekolite 2212	1000	
4	4		ALTMAN 6 x 12 360Q 6x12	750	
24	25	1	STRAND 8" Fresnel 3480	1000	
15	14		STRAND 6" Fresnel 3380	1000	
6	0		STRAND CODA 500/1 MkII - 5801	500	
6	0		STRAND Iris 1- 5911	1500	
4	2		STRAND 14" 4271	1000	
38	35		PAR-64 Q1000		
2	4	2	STRAND FLOODLIGHT	2000	

End of Report

(A)

(B)

FIGURE 20.13
(A) Example of paperwork, in this case an Instrument Inventory Listing, produced with Soft Plot by Crescit Software. Lighting design by Glen Miller. (B) On-screen view of a portion of a light plot on the MacLux Pro demo disk. Software: MacLux Pro v. 1.5 by Aladdin Systems, Inc., and Raymond Lau.

to adhere to the general recommendation of clarity: Do not crowd or unevenly space individual items on a plate. Equally important, all line weights, line types, symbols, conventions, and lettering should be consistent from plate to plate in a given set of drawings. This does not mean that everyone will be expected to letter in the same manner or draw arrowheads in precisely the same way. It means that

FIGURE 20.14
A ground plan for Arizona Summer Arts Festival, production of *K2*, designed by K. Pistor.

each drafter should be able to establish his or her style within the guidelines of the recommended standards and conform to that style throughout the drawings for a particular project or production. Finally, the standards and symbols used in any recommended guide should be efficient, both in ease of drawing and in ease of comprehension for the reader.

A great deal of technical theatre drafting is directly related to the ground plan. A modification of the USITT-recommended definition of a light plot provides a good working definition for a ground plan: A ground plan is a **horizontal offset section** in which the cutting plane intersects the theatre at whatever level gives the most descriptive view of the set and stage configuration (Figure 20.14).

Line Weights

The USITT's adopted line weight standards for light plot drafting, which, in lieu of a specific standard for general theatrical drafting can be used as a guide for scenic drafting, are as follows: Line widths for pencil are 0.3 mm for a thin line and 0.5 mm for a thick line. For ink, the line weights are 0.010 inch to 0.0125 inch for a thin line and 0.020 inch to 0.025 inch for a thick line.[1] The standards for ink are broad enough to be inclusive of the parameters for both DM/PL and HPGL plotters. For scenic drafting, an extra-thick line (0.9 mm in pencil) may also be used to provide additional emphasis, as for a plate border, suitable section cutting plane line, and so on.

Drafting Conventions

horizontal offset section: A section drawing with a horizontal cutting plane, which does not remain fixed but varies to provide a view of important details.

The drawing on the ground plan of standard theatrical units such as chandeliers, shelves, fireplaces, and the like should be made using a sectional cutting plan at

[1] Patrick Gill, Chair of USITT Lighting Graphic Standards Committee, "A Revised Standard Graphic for Lighting Design," *Theatrical Design and Technology*, Fall 1991, p. 61.

whatever height is appropriate to provide the most descriptive view of the object. Using this guideline, an item such as a chandelier would be indicated by a circle utilizing a hidden line style (see Table 20.1), because it is not in contact with the stage floor. The circle should be drawn, in scale, as the actual diameter of the chandelier at its widest point. This graphic would be placed in its appropriate location on the floor plan.

Other suspended objects such as ceiling beams or drops not in contact with the stage floor (for example, an Act II drop on an Act I floor plan) would be drawn in the appropriate outline using the hidden line type.

The USITT's guidelines for object emphasis—using the darkness or lightness of a line to direct attention to objects on the plate—for light plot drafting (see the box "Light Plot Drafting" in Chapter 12) provides an effective basis for similar standards in scenic drafting. In scenic drafting, the object definition lines—those lines used to define the shape of an object—and any notes/dimensions associated with them should be the darkest or most prominent, architectural lines should be of relatively medium darkness, and dimension lines should be the lightest.

Another recommended convention involves the drafting of flats on the ground plan. They should be drawn in scale thickness and should have the space darkened between the two visible lines that outline the thickness of the flat.

Lettering

Hand lettering should be legible, and the style should allow for easy and rapid execution. Characters that generally conform to the single-stroke Gothic style shown in Figure 20.15 meet these requirements. The criteria for computerized drafting are the same as for hand-drawn lettering. Fonts which are clearly legible and consistent within a set of drawings meet the USITT guidelines. As font names and their appearances vary, often quite a bit, from manufacturer to manufacturer, it is advisable to look through the available fonts on your computer and find one that generally looks like the aforementioned single-stroke Gothic and that pleases your aesthetic taste. Then use it.

Title Block

The title block should be in the same location on all drawings of a single project. It should be located in either the lower left- or right-hand corner of the drawing or in a strip along the bottom of the drawing. In either case, the block should include the following information:

1. name of producing organization or theatre
2. name of production, act, and scene, if appropriate
3. drawing title
4. drawing number of drawings in the set: for example, 2/10
5. predominant scale of the drawing
6. date the drawing was drafted
7. designer of the production
8. drafter, if different from the designer
9. approval of drawing, if applicable

Dimensions

Use of the following guidelines will help to ensure that your drawings are easily understood by everyone who must read them.

TABLE 20.1
Drafting Conventions

Type	Style	Notes and Line Weights
Plate border		Extra thick Thick two lines
Cutting plane		Thick
Section outline		Thick
Visible outline		Thick
Hidden construction		Thin
Plaster ceiling and set line	Plaster line	Thin—note indicates type
Center line (all applications)		Thin—label Ⅽ̶L on axis
Leader line	To dimension Within outline To outline	Thin
Extension and dimension lines		Thin—full arrowhead preferred
Section interior		Thin—evenly spaced at 45° angle to edge of paper or as clarity requires
Break line	Short Long	Thin—both applications
Phantom line		Thin—used when an object repeats between points. Used as alternate position line. Also used to designate location of adjacent parts

Any special lines not listed above should be noted in the legend of each sheet.

FIGURE 20.15
Single-stroke Gothic lettering.

1. Dimensions must be clear, consistent, and easily understood.

2. Dimensions should be oriented to read from the bottom or the right-hand side of the plate.

3. Dimensions less than one foot are given in inches without a foot notation (for example, 6″, 9½″).

4. Dimensions one foot and greater include the whole foot with a single apostrophe followed by a dash and then inches followed by a double apostrophe (for example, 7′-0½″, 18′-5¼″, 1′-3′).

5. Metric dimensions less than one meter should be noted as zero, decimal point, and portion of meter in numerals (for example, 0.25 m, 0.90 m). All measurements one meter and greater should be given as a whole meter number, decimal point, and portion of meter (for example, 1.5 m, 2.35 m).

6. Dimensions that require more space than available between extension lines are placed in proximity to the area measured, parallel with the bottom edge of the sheet, and directed to the point of reference by means of a leader line (see Table 20.1), as shown in Figure 20.16A.

7. Platform and tread heights are given in inches above the stage floor. Such heights are placed in circles at or near the centers of the platform or tread, as shown in Figure 20.16B.

FIGURE 20.16
(A) Methods of indicating dimension. (B) Heights above or below the stage level are placed in circles near the center of the tread or platform. (C) Arrows are used to indicate change of elevation point away from the primary level of the drawing.

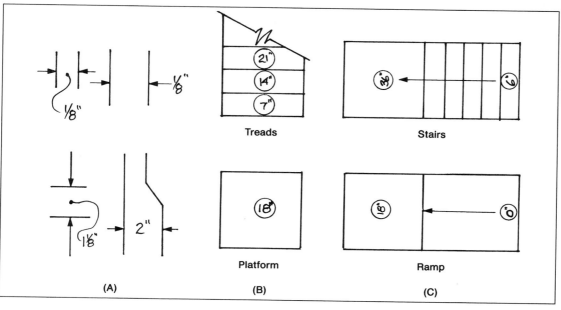

Treads Stairs

Platform Ramp

(A) (B) (C)

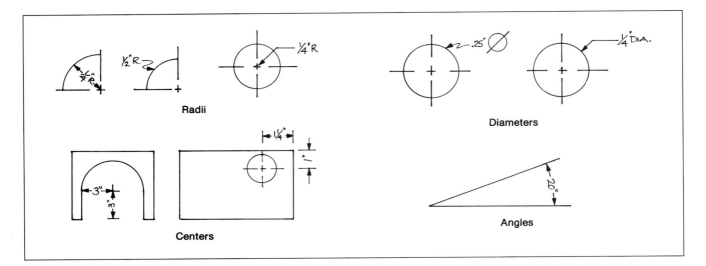

FIGURE 20.17
Methods of indicating radii, diameters, centers, and angles.

8. Directions of arrows (when used to indicate elevation change on stairs, ramps, and the like) point away from the primary level of the drawing, as shown in Figure 20.16C.

9. A number of acceptable ways to indicate radii, diameters, centers, and angles are detailed in Figure 20.17.

Symbols

Figure 20.18 shows the standard symbols used in theatrical drafting. These symbols should be used as substitutions for drawings of the actual objects.

Objects of nonstandard size, such as doorways, windows, platforms, archways, stairs, and ramps, should be drawn in their actual scale size using the conventions indicated by the symbols for those objects. According to this principle, a two-foot-wide doorway would use the convention for a doorway, but the width of the doorway would be drawn in scale to two feet, as shown in Figure 20.19A. In a similar manner, a four-foot-wide doorway would use the same convention, as shown in Figure 20.19B, but the scale width of the door would measure four feet. In both cases, the depth of the door casing would be drawn to its actual scale depth. Decorative detail on either the door or the door casing need not be indicated on the ground plan unless it alters the depth or width of the door or casing.

TYPES OF DRAWINGS

Ground Plan

The ground plan is probably the single most important mechanical drawing used in the theatre. Created by the scenic designer, it is a top view of the setting and shows the position of the set in relation to the physical structure of the stage and auditorium.

Depending on the complexity of the production, there may be one or several ground plans. If the play requires a simple single-set interior, a single plan may be able to show the three requirements of any ground plan: (1) the shape of the set, (2) the position of the set within the physical structure of the theatre, and

FIGURE 20.18
Technical production symbols.

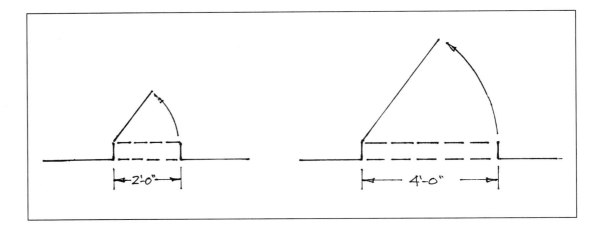

FIGURE 20.19
(A) A two-foot doorway and (B) a four-foot doorway. Notice that the symbol is the same, only the width varies.

(3) the location of the furniture and set pieces within the set. If the play is a complex multiset show, such as a musical, it may be necessary to have a separate ground plan for each set as well as a composite plan indicating the relationship of one plan to another. There is no hard and fast rule that dictates the number of ground plans necessary for any given production. The guideline that should be followed is that every drawing needs to be clear, consistent, and efficient.

Ground plans are usually drawn in a scale of one-half inch to one foot. Drawings in this scale are easy to read, and the size of the paper, usually twenty-four by thirty inches, is convenient for use in the shop. If you are working in a

FIGURE 20.20
Ground plan of
The Kitchen.

very large, or very small, theatre, it might be appropriate to use a larger or smaller scale for the ground plan. The ground plan shown in Figure 20.20 illustrates all the pertinent data that need to be included on the ground plan for a proscenium production.

The set line is a leader line that extends, parallel with the proscenium arch, across the farthest downstage point(s) of the set. The plaster line is a leader line that extends across the opening of the proscenium arch. The fixed point from which this line normally extends is the upstage edge of the proscenium arch, although any other permanent or semipermanent physical element of the stage or its equipment, such as the edge of the false proscenium, could also be used. The center line runs perpendicularly to the set line from the midpoint, or center, of the opening of the proscenium arch. It extends from the apron to the upstage wall of the stage. The margin line is an aesthetically pleasing line that is placed around the border of the plate approximately one-half inch from the edge of the paper. The margin line can be functionally useful as well. When computer drafting and printing on small paper, you'll know that something isn't missing if the margin line is neatly encircling your entire plate.

Procedurally, it is normally advisable and convenient to draw the structure of the theatre first, then draw the scenery, and finish the plate by drawing the furniture and the margin line. If you are designing for a thrust or arena stage, you will not have a proscenium arch to serve as a reference for your set line and center line. In this case, you still need to establish two reference lines that have an identifiable connection with some permanent element of the stage or auditorium space, as shown in Figure 20.21. Most designers prefer to establish two

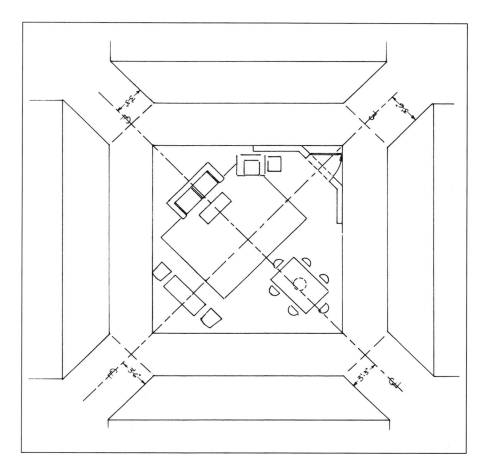

FIGURE 20.21
An arena ground plan.

intersecting lines that cross in the relative center of the set and then extend those lines until they intersect some element of the physical structure of the theatre. It then becomes a relatively simple matter to measure from that point of intersection to an identifiable element of the theatre's structure such as a door frame or exposed water pipe. On a proscenium, thrust, or arena stage, these intersecting lines (set and center) are used as the base lines for transferring the scenic designer's ground plan from the drawings to the actual stage floor.

Sectional Drawings

A sectional drawing provides a view of an object as though it had been cut along some imaginary plane. A scenic sectional, also called a hanging plot (Figure 20.22A), shows a sectional view of the stage with the cutting plane of the section being on the center line of the stage. This drawing is used to show the relative position of the set, masking, and various lighting instruments. It is used to help determine trim heights for masking, the heights of various scenic pieces, and similar tasks. A sectional drawing frequently provides the best way of explaining a shape with irregular surfaces, as shown in Figure 20.22B.

Other sectional drawings are used for a variety of purposes. The vertical and horizontal sectional drawings that are used for determining sight-line drawings are discussed in Chapter 21, *Perspective Drawing*, and the sectional drawings used in lighting design were discussed in Chapter 12, *Lighting Design*.

Front Elevations

A front elevation is a front view of the setting as it would appear if it were flattened out until it was in a single plane and viewed as though the observer

(A)

FIGURE 20.22
(A) Sectional drawing of a stage. (B) An irregularly shaped object can be explained with a sectional drawing.

PLAN VIEW

SECTION A-A'

SECTION B-B'

SECTION C-C'

(B)

UNIVERSITY OF ARIZONA
DEPARTMENT OF DRAMA
THE KITCHEN
FRONT ELEVATIONS
SHEET 1 OF 2
SCALE: 1/4" = 1'-0"
DESIGNER: M. GILLETTE

FIGURE 20.23
Front elevations of *The Kitchen*.

were standing exactly at right angles to it. The purpose of these drawings, usually drafted in a scale of one-half inch to one foot, is to show the location and measurements of all objects that cannot be recorded on the ground plan. As shown in Figure 20.23, the position, size, and arrangement of all structural elements such as walls, doors, and windows, as well as the location of any built-in items, are given on the front elevations. Decorative and trim features on the walls, such as pictures, baseboards, chair rails, wainscoting, cornices, and so on, are also indicated on the front elevations.

Rear Elevations

Rear elevations show the reverse side of objects depicted in the front elevations. This rear view allows the construction details—placement and dimensions of stiles, rails, toggles, and so forth—to be shown. Rear elevations, shown in Figure 20.24, are normally drawn in the same scale as their front-elevation counterparts. The outline of the flats for the rear elevations is easily produced by turning over the tracing paper that contains the front elevations, covering it with another piece of tracing vellum, and tracing the outline using your T square and triangles.

Although the responsibility for producing rear elevations is one of the genuinely gray areas of theatrical production, the need for these drawings isn't. Rear elevations must be drawn when the construction crew is inexperienced or just learning how to build scenery. In the professional theatre, where the construction is done by trained theatrical carpenters, rear elevations are not normally drawn for ordinary construction items such as flats and platforms. They are made only when the object to be built is unusual enough to warrant the precise explanation that the rear elevation provides. In those instances, the drawings are usually done by the scene-shop foreman in consultation with the scenic designer.

In educational theatre, the responsibility for the production of the rear elevations becomes fuzzier. Generally speaking, the rear elevations are the responsibility of the technical director. Due to a variety of circumstances, however, the drawing may be accomplished by the scenic designer or student assistant

FIGURE 20.24
Rear elevations of *The Kitchen*.

designers. Regardless of who actually draws the rear elevations, they are vital, as previously noted, to give student carpenters a precise guide for building every element of the setting. Rewards will be reaped in terms of reduced construction errors, better training techniques, lower costs, better use of time, and less frustrated (therefore happier) students.

Detail Drawings

Many times the scale of ½ inch to 1 foot normally used in drawing the front elevations reduces the size of some of the smaller set features to the point that it is difficult, if not impossible, to include all of the dimensions and notes necessary for a complete understanding of the object. In these cases, a larger scale, such as 1 inch or 1½ inches to 1 foot, is frequently used.

If the smaller features of the set are intricately detailed, it is usually both easier and faster to draw them full scale. This would certainly be the case with the design for a turned banister or the pattern for a wallpaper design. It is much easier construct this type of object from a life-size drawing than from one that has been proportionally reduced to a smaller scale.

Many features of a setting cannot be fully described by drawing them in top and front views alone. Three-dimensional objects normally require a third (usually side) view to supplement the other two. Objects that cannot be fully described with only a front, top, and side view, such as an elaborate fireplace or an intricately designed stained-glass window, can usually be well described through the use of orthographic projection, isometric drawing, oblique drawing, or cabinet drawing.

Orthographic Projection   Orthographic projection describes an object with a series of scale elevations showing each side of the article, as shown in Figure 20.25.

FIGURE 20.25
Orthographic projection.

The different views of the table are each represented by a separate drawing. Notice that each drawing shows the table as if the observer were standing at right angles to that side of the table.

Isometric Drawing Isometric drawing provides a fast and easy way of representing an object pictorially without becoming involved with perspective. These drawings are based on three lines called the isometric axes. Two of these axes, illustrated in Figure 20.26, are located at thirty degrees above the horizontal plane on either side of the third axis, which is perpendicular to the base line. Dimensions can be measured at their true length along any of the isometric axes or on lines parallel to them. Lines that are not located on or parallel to the isometric axes cannot be measured.

Since isometric drawing does not take into account the effects of foreshortening or the principles of perspective, it is inevitable that some finished drawings will appear to be distorted. This is especially true of large drawings; the larger the drawing, the more obvious the distortion becomes. Irregular shapes (those with nonsquare bases) are also difficult to draw and, if drawn, may seem to be misshapen.

FIGURE 20.26
Isometric drawing.

FIGURE 20.27
Oblique drawing.

Oblique Drawing Oblique drawing is a combination of the principles of orthographic and isometric drawing. In oblique drawing, one of the faces of the object is placed at right angles to the observer's line of sight (as in orthographic projection), and the other faces subscribe to the tenets of isometric drawing, as shown in Figure 20.27.

If the most complicated surface of the object being drawn is placed in the front view, then the distortion problems encountered with isometric drawing are minimized. The remaining two sides of the object are drawn to the right or left of the front view at angles of thirty or forty-five degrees.

Although the object being drawn will probably appear to be distorted, the advantage of the oblique-drawing technique is that it is possible to measure all elements of the drawing that are parallel to the vertical, horizontal, or base (30- or 45-degree) axes.

FIGURE 20.28
Cabinet drawing.

Cabinet Drawing   Cabinet drawing (Figure 20.28) and oblique drawing are similar in every detail except one: The depth or thickness measurements of a cabinet drawing are reduced by one-half or a similar ratio such as 1:4. This foreshortening is done in an attempt to reduce the pictorial distortion that occurs if the depth measurement is excessive.

Two precautions should be taken when using this drafting technique. Be sure to write the ratio of reduction in a conspicuous place on the drawing and to specify that the written depth dimension is its true length. The reversed 2 figure placed on either side of the dimension indicates that the length of the dimension line is not an exact scale measurement and that the stated figure is the correct dimension.

All mechanical drawings are created for one purpose—to provide clear, comprehensive visual communication. The standards and guidelines that have been suggested in this chapter are intended to help you reach that goal. But don't follow them blindly simply because they look like rules. Remember that it is the intended application of each drawing that dictates the appearance of that specific plate. For example, the general guidelines suggest that elevations are usually drawn in a scale of one-half inch to one foot. But common sense counsels that if another scale will provide a better representation of the object, that scale should be used. In addition to thinking about the purpose of each drawing, be sure to develop good drafting habits. Keep your work area and drafting equipment clean; use a "pig" to keep your drawings clean; practice and develop a clear and confident printing style based on single-stroke Gothic; apply consistent pressure to the pencil; and always, always keep your pencil sharp.

Chapter 21
Perspective Drawing

The process of perspective drawing provides a sketch with the illusion of realistic depth. The form of perspective drawing that will be discussed in this chapter provides you with an accurate, and fairly simple, method of sketching stage sets from a scale ground plan.

While computer drawing programs greatly simplify the process of creating accurate, scale perspective drawings, the reality is that you need to know how to hand-draw in perspective. Knowing both methods is even better. This chapter provides you with one method of creating accurate, scale, hand-drawn perspective drawings.

PRINCIPLES OF PERSPECTIVE

The craft of drawing three-dimensional objects on a flat plane so that they will seem to have depth is based on an understanding of **foreshortening,** the principle that receding parallel lines apparently converge into a single point, as illustrated in Figure 21.1. In this scene, we seem to be looking at a desolate highway stretching into the empty flatness of west Texas. Telephone pole A seems to be closer than telephone pole B because it is taller. The portion of the road at the bottom of the picture appears to be closer to us than the road at the horizon because it is wider. The fence on the right side of the road seems to get smaller as it recedes toward its **vanishing point** (VP) on the horizon. The apparent depth in this drawing is caused by the converging of the parallel lines (the tops and bottoms of the telephone poles, the sides of the road, the barbed wire strung between the fence posts, and so on) to a single vanishing point on the horizon.

The basic principles of any perspective drawing can be further illustrated through the drawing of an everyday object such as a table (Figure 21.2). Again, notice how all of the parallel lines recede to the same vanishing points on the **horizon line** (HL).

To draw an accurate perspective sketch, you have to know the following basic information:

1. the distance from the observer to the object being drawn
2. the height of the observer's eye above the object being drawn
3. the size and shape of the object

Figure 21.3 illustrates the interrelationship among these three facts.

foreshortening: Representing the lines of an object as shorter than they actually are in order to give the illusion of proper relative size.

vanishing point: The point on the horizon to which a set of parallel lines recedes.

horizon line: A line in a perspective drawing representing the meeting of the earth and the sky; normally drawn parallel to the top or bottom edge of the paper.

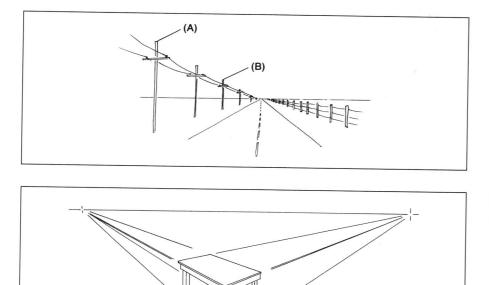

FIGURE 21.1
The principles of foreshortening.

FIGURE 21.2
Parallel sets of lines recede to the same vanishing point.

You also need to know the relative position of the object in relation to a vertical plane that is placed between the observer and the object, as illustrated in Figure 21.4. You might better understand the principles of this method of drawing if you think of this vertical plane as a transparent piece of glass. You are sitting in the auditorium looking through this "window" at the objects on the stage (in this case, the table illustrated in Figure 21.4B). A perspective drawing of this table would be created if its outline were to magically appear on this huge plate of glass, as shown in Figure 21.4C.

You don't need magic to create a perspective drawing; the following method provides you with the ability. It enables you to draw the outline of those objects on that vertical plane. The only significant differences are that the vertical plane is your drawing paper, not glass, and you don't have to be sitting in the auditorium looking at the stage to create the drawing.

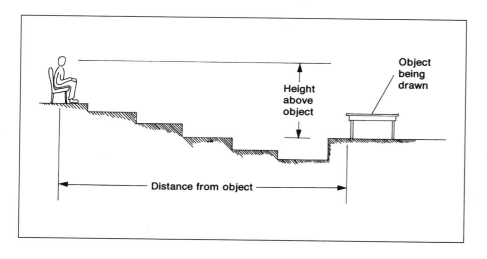

FIGURE 21.3
To draw in perspective, you need to know (1) the distance to the object, (2) your height above the object, (3) the size and shape of the object.

FIGURE 21.4
Perspective drawing is like drawing the outline of the object on a vertical pane of glass erected between you and the object you're observing.

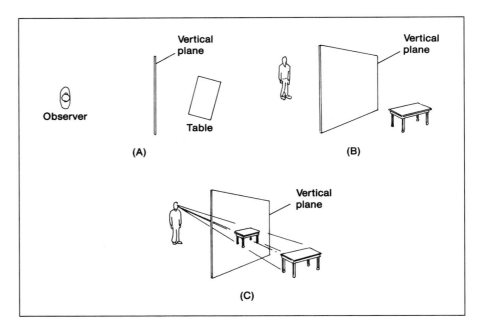

FIGURE 21.5
The vertical plane for the three forms of stage configuration is usually located in slightly different places.

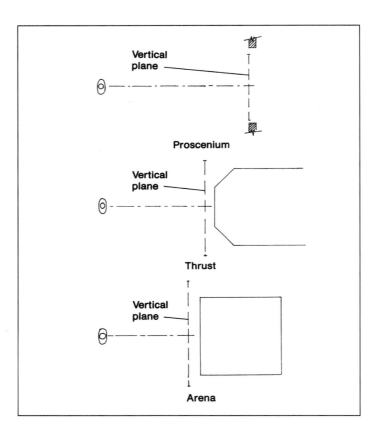

The location of this vertical plane is the only adjustment that needs to be made when applying this method of perspective drawing to proscenium, thrust, or arena theatres. As illustrated in Figure 21.5, the vertical plane in a proscenium theatre could be placed to coincide with the proscenium arch. For a thrust theatre,

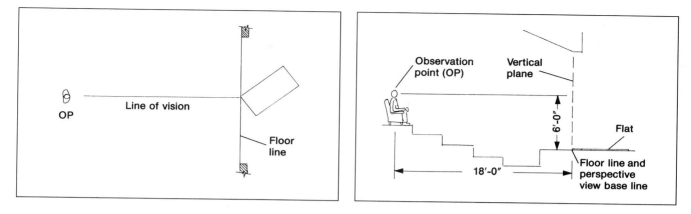

FIGURE 21.6
Plan and section layouts for the
practice exercise.

it would be more appropriate to locate the vertical plane just outside the auditorium end of the thrust. For an arena stage, it could be erected in the aisle just beyond the edge of the stage that is closest to the observer.

Experience really *is* the best teacher, so the easiest way for you to develop a full understanding of drawing in perspective is to create a drawing in mechanical perspective. Later in this chapter we'll go step by step through several practice exercises.

Creating a Perspective Drawing

Imagine that you are sitting in a proscenium theatre looking at a flat lying on the stage floor, as shown in Figure 21.6. Your seat (observation point [OP]) is in the center of the auditorium, eighteen feet from the proscenium arch, as shown. The flat is lying in the center of the stage floor with its near corner in contact with a line (the **floor line**) that has been drawn across the stage from the downstage edge of one side of the proscenium arch to the other. The sides of the flat make a forty-five-degree angle with the floor line. In this particular seat (OP), your eyes are six feet above the stage floor, which means that the horizon line (HL) is located six feet above the stage floor. Figure 21.7A shows how this information is used to lay out the basic grid used with this perspective method, which consists of only four lines—one vertical and three horizontal.

After you lay out the basic grid and the flat, the next thing you need to do is establish the vanishing points for the various sets of parallel lines. (Remember that in perspective drawing each set of receding parallel lines converges on a specific vanishing point located on the horizon line. The only exception to this rule is lines that are parallel to the floor line—they don't converge; they stay parallel to the floor line.) The flat in Figure 21.7A provides an example of this principle. There are two sets of parallel lines: AB and DC are parallel, and AD and BC are also parallel. Each of these systems of lines (AB/DC and AD/BC) has its own vanishing point on the horizon line.

To establish the vanishing point for lines AB/DC on the perspective grid, draw a very faint guide line, parallel to lines AB/DC, from OP until it intersects the floor line, as shown in Figure 21.7B. (Notice that this guide line for lines AB/DC angles to the right from OP.) From the point of intersection between the guide line for AB/DC and the floor line, drop a vertical line until it intersects the horizon line. This point of intersection between the dropped vertical and the horizon line establishes the vanishing point for line system AB/DC. The vanishing point for lines AD/BC is found in the same way. (The only difference is that the guide line for AD/BC angles to the left from OP.) Draw a very light guide

floor line: The base of the vertical plane in a perspective drawing; for a proscenium sketch, usually drawn across the stage in contact with the downstage edge of the proscenium arch; in a thrust drawing, normally placed just outside the auditorium end of the thrust; in an arena sketch, usually placed in the aisle closest to the observer.

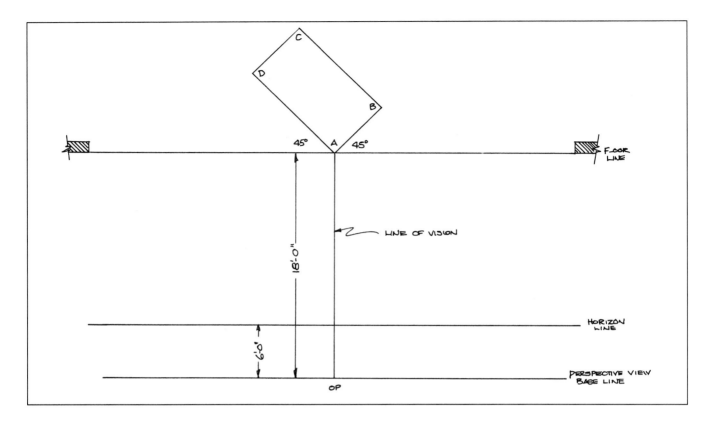

FIGURE 21.7A
Sequential layout of the practice exercise. See text for explanation of each drawing.

line of vision: The vertical line drawn from OP to the floor line in a perspective grid; represents the line of sight from the observer to the vertical plane.

perspective-view base line: The bottom edge of a perspective drawing.

line from OP (parallel with lines AD/BC—which is the same as the angle of intersection between AD and the floor line) until it intersects the floor line. From this point of intersection, drop a vertical to the horizon line. This point of contact will be the vanishing point for lines AD/BC.

A basic rule of this perspective method is that any point in contact with the floor line is unaffected by the laws of perspective. Pragmatically, this means that a line can be dropped (a vertical line drawn parallel to the **line of vision**) from any point on the floor line until it contacts the **perspective-view base line**. The reason any point in contact with the floor line is unaffected by the laws of perspective is that the floor line and the perspective-view base line are simply different views of the same line. The floor line is a ground plan view of an imaginary line drawn across the stage at some easily identifiable location such as the upstage edge of the proscenium arch. The perspective-view base line is the bottom edge of a vertical plane that is erected from the floor line.

Since point A of the flat is in contact with the floor line, a vertical line can be dropped from point A until it contacts the perspective-view base line at point A' (the prime points—A', B', C', and so on—will establish the perspective view of the object), as shown in Figure 21.7C. In this particular case, point A happens to be located in the center of the floor line, so the dropped vertical coincides with the line of vision and point A' coincides with the observation point (OP).

To find the perspective view of line AB, extend a light guide line from A' to the vanishing point for the line system AB/DC, as shown in Figure 21.7D. This gives you a perspective view of line A'B' extended, but it doesn't show you the location of point B'.

To find the location of point B' on line A'B' extended, draw a light guide line between OP and corner B on the flat, as shown in Figure 21.7E. Where this

FIGURE 21.7B

FIGURE 21.7C

FIGURE 21.7D

FIGURE 21.7E

FIGURE 21.7F

FIGURE 21.7G

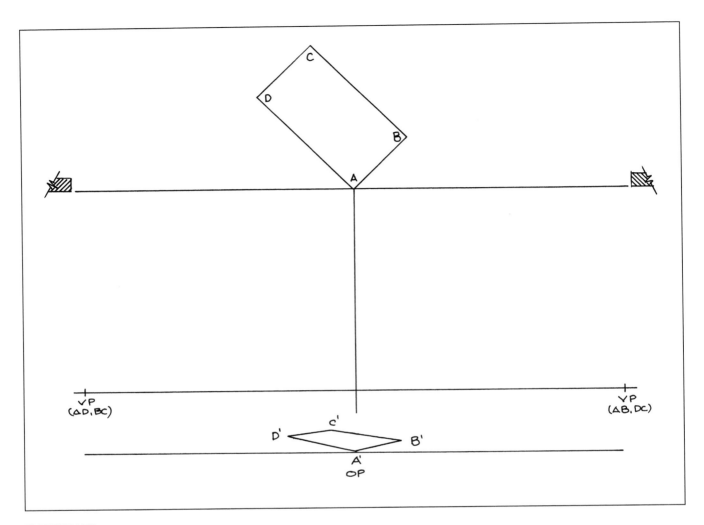

FIGURE 21.7H

guide line intersects the floor line, drop a vertical until it intersects line A′B′ extended. This is the location of point B′. (Remember that any point in contact with the floor line is unaffected by perspective, so a line parallel with the line of vision can be dropped from that point on the floor line to the perspective-view base line.)

To find the perspective view of line A′D′, repeat the process used to find the perspective view of line A′B′, but this time use the vanishing point for the line system AD/BC. Draw a light guide line from A′ to the vanishing point for line system AD/BC to form line A′D′ extended, as shown in Figure 21.7F. Next draw a light guide line between OP and corner D on the flat. Where this line intersects the floor line, drop a vertical until it intersects line A′D′ extended. This will be the location of point D′.

To find the perspective location of the last corner of the flat, point C′, use the same process you used to find the location of B′ and D′. Line D′C′ is parallel to line A′B′, so they have the same vanishing point (the vanishing point for line system AB/DC). To find line D′C′ extended, draw a light guide line from point D′ to the vanishing point for line system AB/DC, as shown in Figure 21.7G. To find the location of C′ on line D′C′ extended, draw a guide line from OP to C. Where that guide line intersects the floor line, drop a vertical until it intersects line D′C′ extended. This point of intersection will be the location of point C′.

Words of Encouragement

As you wade through the frequently frustrating complexities of learning to draw in mechanical scale perspective, take heart. Every major scenic designer has had the same kind of heartburn. They all had to learn how to draw in perspective. Some of them, such as Ming Cho Lee and Jo Mielziner, received their early training in art schools. Others, such as Peter Wexler, were formally trained as architects. Increasing numbers of rising designers are choosing university educational theatre training. All of them have a common bond—learning how to draw in perspective.

Assimilating the principles of any mechanical-perspective technique is difficult. But as with any craft, the more you practice, the easier it becomes.

In reality, the reason for learning any mechanical-perspective technique is to train your eye. As you practice, you learn how various objects are supposed to look when they are drawn. As you become adept at using mechanical perspective, you will also find that your freehand sketches will start to look better—more real. This is because you *are* training your eye. Eventually, you will find that you'll be able to sketch full sets freehand in accurate perspective, and you'll only occasionally need to use the perspective method to monitor or check your work. This kind of proficiency doesn't happen overnight; it comes with practice. But if you have a passion for drawing and designing, the practice won't be work, it'll be fun.

To complete the perspective view of the flat, you just need to play connect the dots between points B' and C', as shown in Figure 21.7H.

A Review of Perspective Procedure

Before moving on to the perspective exercises, you might want to review the procedure that is used to create these drawings.

1. All of the drawings are made on a basic grid composed of four lines, as shown in Figure 21.8A.

2. The vanishing point for any line or system of lines is determined by extending, from OP, a line parallel to the ground plan view of that particular line until it intersects the floor line, as shown in Figure 21.8B. From that point of intersection, a vertical line is dropped until it intersects the horizon line. That point of intersection is the vanishing point for that line system.

3. Any point in contact with the floor line is unaffected by the laws of perspective. Therefore, a line parallel to the line of vision can be dropped from that point to the perspective-view base line, as shown in Figure 21.8C.

4. A perspective view of a line can be established by extending a line from the point of contact with the perspective-view base line to the vanishing point for that particular line, as shown in Figure 21.8D.

5. To find the location of any point on the perspective view of a line, draw a sight line from the observation point (OP) to the ground plan view of that point, as shown in Figure 21.8E. From the point of intersection between that sight line and the floor line, drop a vertical until it intersects the extended line (A'B' extended and A'C' extended).

6. After all of the perspective points have been located using the techniques described above, connect those points to provide a perspective view of the object, as shown in Figure 21.8F.

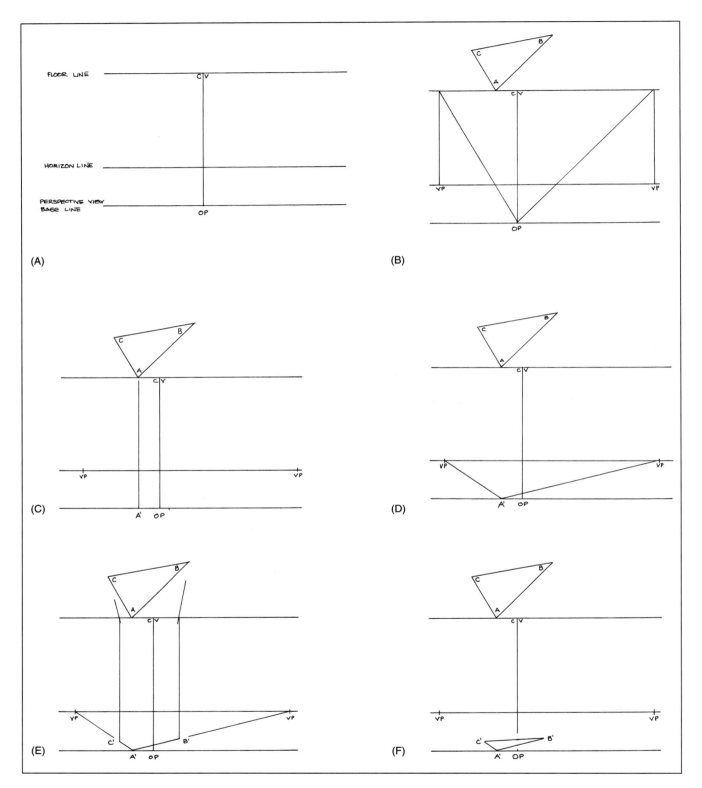

FIGURE 21.8
The perspective procedure.

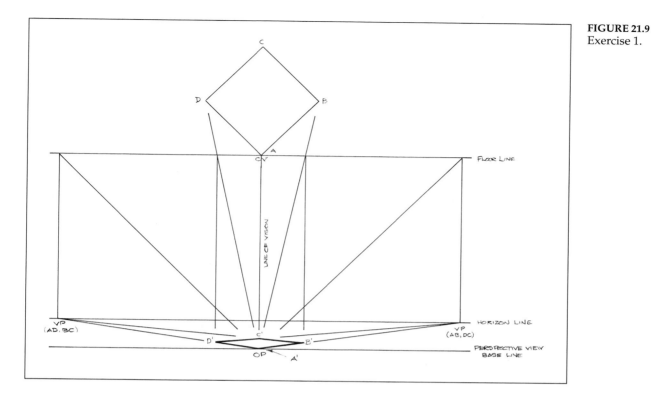

FIGURE 21.9
Exercise 1.

PERSPECTIVE EXERCISES

Craft is learned through doing. This perspective method is a craft. The following nine practice exercises, which are arranged in an ascending order of difficulty, provide specific examples of a variety of common situations and challenges frequently encountered in perspective drawing.

Exercise 1

The closer your eye level (horizon line) is to the stage floor in Exercise 1, Figure 21.9, the less you will see of the actual form of some object resting on the stage.

> **Scale:** ¼″ = 1′-0″
>
> **OP:** 36′-0″ right and 8′-0″ up[1]
>
> **Floor line:** 20′-0″ from **OP**
>
> **Horizon line:** 3′-0″ from **OP**
>
> **Perspective-view base line:** extends horizontally through **OP**
>
> **Object being drawn:** an 8′-0″ square resting on the stage floor with its sides at a 45-degree angle to the floor line and the near corner **(A)** in contact with the floor line at the line of vision.

[1] These dimensions are intended to help you center your drawing in the middle of a 12 × 18 sheet of paper. By measuring, in quarter-inch scale, 36′-0″ to the right of the lower left-hand corner and 8′-0″ up from the bottom edge of the sheet of paper, the observation point **(OP)** will be placed in a position that will center the perspective exercise in the middle of the paper. These dimensions don't have a thing to do with drawing in perspective; they just help to make the whole sheet look attractive and balanced. These exercises won't fit on a sheet smaller than 10 × 14, but if you are using paper larger than 12 × 18, just center the **OP** about one-quarter or one-third of the way up from the bottom of the sheet.

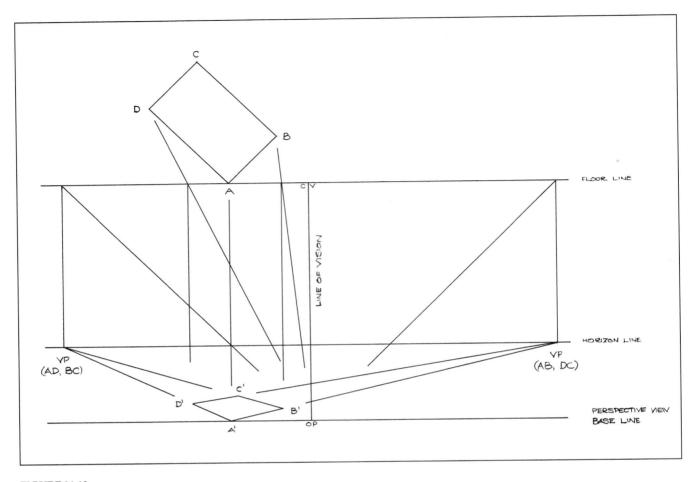

FIGURE 21.10
Exercise 2.

Procedure No new challenges have been introduced here, so you can follow the procedure summarized in the previous section to do this exercise.

Exercise 2

The second exercise shows what to do if an object contacts the floor line in some location other than the point of intersection between the floor line and the line of vision.

>   **Scale:** ¼″ = 1′-0″
>
>   **OP:** 36′-0″ right and 8′-0″ up
>
>   **Floor line:** 22′-0″ from **OP**
>
>   **Horizon line:** 7′-0″ from **OP**
>
>   **Perspective-view base line:** extends horizontally through **OP**
>
>   **Object being drawn:** a flat 6′-0″ by 10′-0″ with its sides at a 45-degree angle to the floor line. The near corner **(A)** is in contact with the floor line and 7′-0″ to the left of the intersection between the line of vision and the floor line.

Procedure Since the corner of the flat **(A)** is in contact with the floor line, it is unaffected by the laws of perspective. A vertical can be dropped from point **A** until it intersects the perspective-view base line, as shown in Figure 21.10. This point will be the perspective location of point **A′**.

After determining the location of **A'**, you can do the rest of the exercise using the procedure summarized in the previous section.

Exercise 3

Finding the perspective of an object that has height, as well as width and length, requires an additional step in the perspective procedure.

> **Scale:** ¼″ = 1′-0″
>
> **OP:** 50′-0″ right and 8′-0″ up
>
> **Floor line:** 23′-0″ from **OP**
>
> **Horizon line:** 8′-0″ from **OP**
>
> **Perspective-view base line:** extends horizontally through **OP**
>
> **Object being drawn:** a platform 8′-0″ square by 3′-6″ high is placed on the stage with its sides forming 30- and 60-degree angles with the floor line. Corner **A** is in contact with the floor line and 12′-0″ to the left of the intersection of the floor line and the line of vision.

Procedure   Any point in contact with the floor line is unaffected by the laws of perspective. Corner **A** of the platform is in contact with the floor line, so a vertical can be dropped to the perspective-view base line to determine the perspective location of **A'**. Since this point (**A'**) is similarly unaffected by perspective, it is possible to determine the height of the platform by measuring the true vertical distance from **A'**.

Along a light vertical guide line erected from **A'**, lay out, in scale, the 3′-6″ height of the platform. This distance will determine the perspective location of point **A″**, which is the top of the front corner of the platform.

Draw guide lines from both **A'** and **A″** to the vanishing point for the **AB/DC** line system. The perspective location of corner **B** of the platform will be the point where these lines (the guide lines drawn between **A'** and **A″** and the vanishing point for the **AB/DC** line system) are intersected by the vertical dropped from the point of intersection between the floor line and a sight line drawn between **OP** and **B,** as shown in Figure 21.11.

The perspective view of the other face (**A'D'/A″D″**) of the platform is determined in the same manner, except that you use the vanishing point for the line system **DA/BC.**

The perspective view of the two upstage edges of the platform (**B″C″** and **D″C″**) is determined by drawing lines between **D″** and the vanishing point for the **AB/DC** line system and between **B″** and the vanishing point for the **AD/BC** line system. Where these two lines intersect will be the location of **C″.**

Point **C″** can also be located in the conventional manner by drawing a sight line from **OP** to **C.** Where the sight line crosses the floor line, a vertical can be dropped until it intersects line **B″C″** extended or **D″C″** extended. This will be the location of **C″.**

Exercise 4

Drawing a perspective view of an object that is not in contact with the floor line adds one more step to the procedure but uses the same principles.

> **Scale:** ¼″ = 1′-0″
>
> **OP:** 40′-0″ right and 10′-0″ up
>
> **Floor line:** 20′-0″ from **OP**

FIGURE 21.11
Exercise 3.

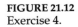
FIGURE 21.12
Exercise 4.

Horizon line: 8′-0″ from **OP**

Perspective-view base line: extends horizontally through **OP**

Object being drawn: a small flat, 6′-0″ by 10′-0″, lying on the stage floor with its sides at a 45-degree angle to the floor line. The near corner **A** is 4′-6″

to the left of the intersection between the floor line and the line of vision and 2'-6" upstage of it (Figure 21.12).

Procedure   Extend the line that forms one side of the flat **(DA)** until it intersects the floor line (**X**). Since any point in contact with the floor line is unaffected by the laws of perspective, a vertical can be dropped to the perspective-view base line to determine the perspective location of point **X'**. Draw a light guide line between **X'** and the vanishing point for line system **AD/BC.** The locations of points **A'** and **D'** are determined in the usual manner. Sight lines are drawn between **OP** and points **A** and **D.** Where those sight lines cross the floor line, verticals are dropped until they intersect the guide line drawn between **X'** and the vanishing point for line system **AD/BC.**

The perspective view of the rest of the flat is determined using the same principles used in the previous exercises. Guide lines are drawn between **A'** and **D'** and the vanishing point for line system **AB/DC.** Sight lines are drawn between **OP** and points **B** and **C.** Where those sight lines cross the floor line, verticals are dropped until they intersect the guide lines drawn between **AD** and the vanishing point for line system **AB/DC.** These points of intersection will be the location of **B'** and **C'.**

Exercise 5

Drawing a perspective view of an object whose sides are either parallel with or perpendicular to the floor line doesn't differ in principle from the procedures that have been previously established.

Scale: ¼" = 1'-0"

OP: 36'-0" right and 8'-0" up

Floor line: 20'-0" from **OP**

Horizon line: 3'-0" from **OP**

Perspective-view base line: extends horizontally through **OP**

Object being drawn: a large rectangular ceiling flat, 10'-10" by 14'-0", lying on the stage floor with its longer side parallel with, and 2'-0" upstage from, the floor line. Notice that the floor line has been placed at the outer face of the proscenium arch to facilitate your creating a perspective drawing of the arch. The proscenium arch is 32'-0" wide, 16'-0" high, and 1'-0" thick, as shown in Figure 21.13.

Procedure   Fortunately, creating a perspective drawing of objects whose sides are parallel with or perpendicular to the proscenium arch follows exactly the same procedure that has been used in the previous perspective exercises. First, find the vanishing point for the line system **AB/DC,** as shown in Figure 21.13A. From **OP** draw a line parallel to **AB** and **DC** until it intersects the floor line. From that point, drop a vertical until it intersects the horizon line. You will notice that this point happens to coincide with the intersection between the horizon line and the line of vision. Any line that is perpendicular to the floor line will always have this center vanishing point (CVP).

To find the perspective location of the lines that form the sides of the ceiling piece (**AB** and **DC**), extend those lines until they intersect the floor line. From those points, drop verticals until they intersect the perspective-view base line (points **X** and **Y**). From **X** and **Y,** draw light guide lines to the center vanishing point (vanishing point for line system **AB/DC**). You can determine the perspective

FIGURE 21.13
Exercise 5.

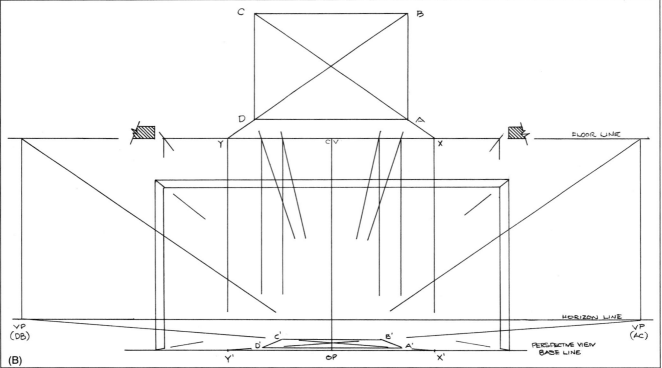

location of points **A** and **B** or **D** and **C** in the usual manner and connect the dots to form a perspective view of the ceiling flat lying on the stage floor.

An alternative method: Instead of using the center vanishing point, you can draw diagonal lines between **CA** and **BD,** as shown in Figure 21.13B. Extend those diagonals until they intersect the floor line, and then locate the vanishing point for those lines in the usual manner. The rest of the exercise can be done using the procedure as previously outlined.

Determining the perspective location of the proscenium arch is fairly easy, since the downstage edge of the arch is in contact with the floor line. From points **E** and **H,** drop verticals to the perspective-view base line. The vertical height of the proscenium arch can be measured from **E′** and **H′,** since those points are in contact with the perspective-view base line and are consequently unaffected by the laws of perspective. Locating the top of the perspective view of the proscenium arch is done by connecting the dots between **E″** and **H″.**

The perspective view of the depth of the proscenium arch can be determined by using the methods previously described. To locate the base of the stage-right side of the arch, draw a light guide line from **E′** (the downstage edge of the proscenium arch) to the center vanishing point. To locate **F′,** draw a sight line from **OP** to **F.** Where that sight line crosses the floor line, drop a vertical until it intersects the guide line drawn from **E′** to the center vanishing point. This will be the location of **F′.**

The top of the stage-right side of the proscenium arch is found by drawing a guide line from **E″** to the center vanishing point. Where this line intersects the vertical erected from **F′** will be the location of **F″.**

The other side of the proscenium arch is determined in the same manner. The top of the proscenium arch can be determined by connecting **E″** and **H″** as well as **F″** and **G″.**

Exercise 6

This exercise synthesizes all of the previous material and allows you to draw a perspective view of a full stage set.

Scale: ¼″ = 1′-0″

OP: 36′-0″ right and 6′-0″ up

Floor line: 22′-0″ from **OP**

Horizon line: 6′-0″ from **OP**

Perspective-view base line: extends horizontally through **OP**

Proscenium arch: 16′-0″ high, 36′-0″ wide, 1′-0″ thick

Object being drawn: a full stage setting, as illustrated in Figure 21.14

Procedure   Although the concept of drawing a full setting may, at first glance, be somewhat overwhelming, you can accomplish it by using the techniques described in this chapter. "Where do I begin?" is a logical first question. The answer isn't clear cut and absolute. Drawing the proscenium arch first provides a visual framework and reference that makes most designers feel fairly comfortable. After you've drawn the proscenium (refer to the instructions for drawing the proscenium arch detailed in Exercise 5, if you need them), start on the set. It is usually easiest to begin by drawing the set at one corner of the ground plan. Point **A,** which is the downstage end of the bottom of flat **AB,** provides a convenient beginning place.

FIGURE 21.14
Exercise 6.

Flat AB   To find the location of point **A**, you will need to set up the vanishing point for flat **AB.** This can be done by measuring, with a protractor, the angle of intersection between **AB** extended and the floor line, and duplicating that angle from **OP,** to lay out the vanishing point. The full perspective view of flat **AB** can then be drawn using the techniques previously described. The sides and top of the door opening can be drawn by using the same techniques that are used to locate the sides and tops of the flat.

Flat BC   Since flat **BC** is parallel to the proscenium (and the floor line), horizontal lines can be extended from the top and bottom of the upstage end of flat **AB** to create a perspective view of the top and bottom of flat **BC.** The onstage **(C)** end of flat **BC** is determined by drawing a sight line between **OP** and **C.** Where that sight line crosses the floor line, a vertical is dropped toward the perspective-view base line. Where that dropped vertical intersects the horizontal lines extending from the upstage end of the top and bottom of flat **AB** determines the location of the onstage edge of flat **BC.**

Flat CD   Because flat **CD** is perpendicular to the floor line, it will have a center vanishing point. Draw guide lines from the top and bottom edges of the onstage **(C)** end of flat **BC** to the center vanishing point to determine the perspective view of the top and bottom edges of flat **CD.** To find the upstage end of the flat, draw a light sight line from **OP** to **D.** Where it crosses the floor line, drop a vertical until it intersects the guide lines that define the top and bottom edges of flat **CD.**

Flat DE   Flat **DE** is parallel to the proscenium, so you use the techniques described for flat **BC.** To create a perspective view of the window, determine the height of the top and bottom edges of the window on either edge (**D** or **E**) of the flat, using the techniques described in Exercise 3. From those points, extend horizontal lines across the flat. Draw light sight lines from **OP** to the edges of the ground plan view of the window. Where those sight lines cross the floor line,

FIGURE 21.15
Furniture can be sketched fairly
easily if it is placed inside boxes.

drop verticals until they intersect the horizontal lines that describe the top and bottom height of the window. These lines will denote the sides of the window.

Flat EF   Since **EF** is perpendicular to the proscenium, use the techniques described for flat **CD.**

Flat FG   Flat **FG** is also parallel to the proscenium, so use the techniques described for flat **BC.**

Flat GH   You can find the perspective view of flat **GH** in one of two ways: Either (1) establish the vanishing point for the flat and proceed as usual, or (2) instead of working on flat **GH,** forget about it for the moment and move on to flat **HI.** If you draw flat **HI,** using the techniques described for flat **AB,** you can find the location of flat **GH** by simply connecting the tops and bottoms of flats **FG** and **HI.**

Flat HI   As mentioned, the perspective view of flat **HI** can be found by using the techniques described for flat **AB.**

Tormentors   The tormentors are the flats on either side of the stage connected to the downstage ends of flats **AB** and **HI** and extending behind, and parallel to, the proscenium arch. Because they are parallel to the proscenium, they can be drawn by extending horizontal lines from the tops and bottoms of the downstage ends of flats **AB** and **HI** until they intersect the sides of the proscenium arch.

Exercise 7

The drawing of furniture presents a significant challenge to many beginning scenic designers. Here is a technique that can help to visually anchor the furniture to the floor. Almost all furniture can be placed in a box, as shown in Figure 21.15. If these "furniture boxes" are placed around the furniture on the ground plan, it becomes fairly simple to draw them, in perspective, on the scenic sketch, as shown in Figure 21.16.

Scale: ¼″ = 1′-0″

OP: 36′-0″ right and 4′-0″ up

Floor line: 20′-0″ from **OP**

Horizon line: 6′-0″ from **OP**

Perspective-view base line: extends horizontally through **OP**

Proscenium arch: 32′-0″ wide, 16′-0″ high, 1′-0″ thick

FIGURE 21.16
Exercise 7.

Objects being drawn: a very simple set with 14'-0" walls, a 7'-0" door, a sofa, a chair, a table, and a rug. The sofa is 6'-0" long, 2'-6" deep, and 3'-0" high. The wingback chair is 3'-0" wide, 3'-0" deep, and 4'-0" high. The table is 2'-0" square and 3'-0" high.

Procedure   To give yourself a visual reference, you will probably draw the proscenium arch first. If you are a little hazy on the procedure for drawing the arch, refer to Exercise 5 for specific instructions.

Second, draw the walls of the set. It will probably be easiest to draw a perspective view of flat **AB** first and then flat **CD.** After these two flats have been laid out, you can connect the dots between their tops and bottoms, respectively, to create flat **BC.** Exercise 6 reviews the procedure for drawing the walls of a set.

Finally, put the "furniture boxes" on the set. The corners of the boxes coincide with the corners of the furniture that you are trying to draw. All of the furniture boxes are located on the set according to the instructions detailed in Exercises 3 and 4.

FIGURE 21.17
How to draw furniture in a box:
(A) Draw a box the height, width,
and depth of the overall dimensions
of the furniture item. (B) Sketch the
furniture on the faces of the box.
(C) "Uncrate" the furniture by erasing the box.

After you have drawn the furniture boxes (use light lines) on the perspective sketch, you can sketch the appropriate view of the furniture piece on each exposed face of the box, as shown in Figure 21.17.

Exercise 8

The perspective technique outlined in this chapter can also be used to create a mechanically accurate sketch of a scenic design done for an arena or thrust production. This exercise shows the procedure for creating a perspective sketch of an arena production and is illustrated in Figure 21.18.

Scale: ¼″ = 1′-0″

OP: 36′-0″ right and 6′-0″ above

Floor line: 15′-0″ from **OP** (Note that the floor line is placed 2′-0″ toward the audience from the edge of the stage. This placement allows you to create a drawing of the full stage.)

Horizon line: 8′-0″ from **OP**

Perspective-view base line: extends horizontally through **OP**

Object being drawn: a scenic design for an arena production

FIGURE 21.18
Exercise 8.

Procedure The procedure for drawing an arena design is exactly the same as for any other production. Although most scenic designs for arena stages are noticeably devoid of any tall vertical elements such as walls and doorways, the design may contain some low walls or cutaway doors. If these elements are present, they will provide the visual framework for the design and will consequently be an appropriate beginning point for drawing the sketch. After the visual framework has been established, the furniture and other set pieces can be drawn using the furniture-box technique described in Exercise 7.

Exercise 9

This exercise provides a demonstration of the perspective technique as applied to a play produced on a thrust stage. The exercise is illustrated in Figure 21.19.

> **Scale:** ¼″ = 1′-0″
>
> **OP:** 24′-0″ right and 14′-0″ up
>
> **Floor line:** 25′-0″ from **OP** (Note that the paper has been turned 90 degrees and the floor line is located just in front of the front edge of the thrust stage. This placement allows you to achieve a full view of the stage and the set.)

FIGURE 21.19
Exercise 9.

Horizon line: 7'-0" from **OP**

Perspective-view base line: extends horizontally through **OP**

Object being drawn: a scenic design for a thrust production. The flats are 14'-0" tall and the doors are 6'-9".

Procedure The procedure for drawing a perspective view of a design created for a thrust stage production is exactly the same as that for the other stages.

The understanding and use of the perspective method presented in this chapter should enable you to create accurate scale perspective drawings of scenic designs for proscenium, thrust, and arena productions. However, this mechanical method is just a tool to show you *how* to draw in perspective. Once you become confident in your ability to use this technique, you should wean yourself from it. Learn to sketch in reasonably accurate perspective. If you encounter a problem or if some element of your design doesn't look right, you can check its accuracy with this perspective method. But once you've learned how to use the method, try to work without it so that its necessarily mechanical processes won't inhibit the free flow of your design ideas.

Chapter 22
Drawing and Rendering

Drawing and rendering are the primary visual-communication methods used by theatrical designers. Every designer must be able to draw and render with ease and facility. During the production meetings, designers frequently communicate their ideas with quickly drawn pencil sketches—the costume designer's preliminary sketches and the scenic designer's thumbnail sketches. After the concepts have been discussed and developed, the designers create renderings that provide color representations of the appearance, character, and flavor of the designs.

It is also important that you learn how to draw and render on a computer. Both methods are important. But it is absolutely essential that you be able to draw and paint—well and with ease and facility—by hand. This chapter will demonstrate some of the materials and techniques that are common to this skill.

There are literally as many styles of drawing and rendering as there are designers. Every good designer will ultimately develop a distinctive style for creating scenic or costume sketches. Rest assured, however, that no beginning designer ever just sat down and magically began to draw and paint. Personal style develops after a great deal of time, practice, and effort. Before you begin to practice, you need to learn about the basic materials and techniques of sketching and rendering.

MATERIALS

Designers use a wide variety of materials to create their sketches and renderings. These materials can be roughly divided into two categories: the material being applied—pencils, inks, paint, pastels, or markers—and paper.

Pencils

Almost any pencil can be used for sketching, but different pencils have different characteristics. Hard-lead drafting pencils such as a 3H, 4H, or 5H make crisp, sharp-edged lines, whereas soft-lead drawing pencils such as the 3B or 4B make darker, wider, and softer-edged lines. Ordinary pencils such as the Number 2 tooth-marked Ticonderoga used for taking notes in class can also be used for sketching.

Which type of pencil you choose depends on the subject matter you'll be drawing, the type of paper on which you'll be working, and personal preference. However, it is important to practice with all types of pencils on all types of papers. Experimentation is the only way to learn about the different characteristics of each type of pencil and paper, which works well with which, and which ones you prefer.

There are two general types of colored pencils—hard and soft. As might be expected, the hard pencils produce sharp lines and are good for linear effects, whereas the softer pencils, such as Eagle Prismacolor, produce softer lines. Watercolor pencils can be used to produce a pigmented line which, when overlayed with a water wash, creates a tint of the same hue.

Inks

Some designers use inks for making preliminary and thumbnail sketches and outlining detail on renderings. Frequently, these ink drawings are made with inexpensive drawing and drafting pens such as those manufactured by Pilot, Expresso, and Itoya-Nikko. These pens are available in a variety of nib widths and flexibilities. Traditional artist's pens and inks are also preferred by some designers because of the larger variety of nibs that are available. Bottles of drawing inks, manufactured by Pelikan, Carter's, and Higgins, are available in a relatively narrow range of colors.

FIGURE 22.1
Watercolor pigment is available in tube, cake, and liquid forms.

Paint

Costumes and scenic sketches or renderings have traditionally been painted with transparent watercolor paints. Although this practice continues, most designers use other materials as well.

Watercolor   Watercolor paint is a pigment mixed with water to create a transparent paint. It is the traditional medium for theatrical rendering, because transparent watercolor provides the sketches with a luminescent quality which closely approximates the appearance that costumes and scenery will have under stage lights. If too much pigment is added to the mix, the watercolor becomes opaque, the dried surface of the painting will have an uneven gloss, and the luminescent quality of the rendering will be lost.

Watercolor pigments are available in three types—tube, cake, and liquid— as shown in Figure 22.1. The tube colors are emulsified pigments of approximately the consistency of well-chilled sour cream. The cake colors are manufactured in hard blocks of watercolor pigment. The liquid watercolors are packaged in small bottles of highly saturated hues.

Both tube and cake watercolors provide the same high-quality pigment, so the choice of which to use is basically a matter of personal preference. Tube colors are a little more convenient for painting a large expanse, such as a sky in a scenic rendering. Similarly, the cake colors are a little more convenient if you need only a small amount of paint to provide trim color on a costume sketch. The third type of watercolor shown in Figure 22.1, Dr. Martin's Watercolors, is a liquid of extremely strong saturation and brilliance. Because these paints are already liquid, they mix very easily and always remain transparent.

Designer's Gouache   Designer's gouache is an opaque watercolor. It is available in tubed form in a wide range of hues similar to those of transparent watercolor. Designer's gouache closely resembles the **matte** reflective properties and colors of scene paint. When thinned sufficiently, the paint becomes transparent. The primary differences between designer's gouache and transparent watercolor are that gouache has a matte finish regardless of whether it is mixed to an opaque or transparent consistency and that watercolors seem to have a little more **life**.

matte: Dull, nonreflective.
life: Brilliance, visual depth, and sparkle.

FIGURE 22.2
Pastels, colored pencils, and associated materials.

Acrylic   Acrylic paint is very versatile. It can be thinned with water to the consistency of watercolor and can be used for the same purposes. When it is used as a substitute for watercolor or designer's gouache, the only significant difference is that the acrylic leaves a slightly **glossy** surface whereas the watercolor and gouache finishes are matte.

Brushes   It is a truism that you should buy the best brushes that you can possibly afford. With this proviso in mind, most artists would agree that the best watercolor brushes are made from red sable. The next best alternative is the synthetic bristles made to duplicate the characteristics of sable, such as Sabline.

Red sable and high-quality synthetic bristles, such as most manufacturers' student line of brushes, carry watercolor pigment easily, have good **spine,** and cling together when wet. Brushes other than these do not have these qualities, and they will not allow you to do your best work. Consequently, you're wasting your money and your time if you buy them.

While the number and type of brushes that you purchase are matters of choice, you will need brushes of at least two sizes with which to begin. The size of artist's brushes is indicated by numbers—the higher the number, the bigger the brush. The number is normally printed on the handle of the brush. A No. 3 brush can be effectively used for most detail work, and a No. 7 can be used for laying in most washes. A No. 12 brush is very handy for creating large, smooth washes.

gloss: Highly reflective, mirrorlike.

spine: The relative stiffness of bristles; good watercolor bristles will flex easily but will also have enough spine to remain erect when fully saturated with paint.

Pastels

There are two primary types of pastel, chalk and oil, as shown in Figure 22.2. Colored pencils are also shown, because even though they are not made of pastel, they are used in basically the same manner. Ultimately, the way in which an artist uses any tool is a matter of personal choice, but each type of pastel has specific working characteristics.

Blending with Pastels

Both chalk and oil pastels can be blended using either paper or felt blending stumps. The figures show some blending techniques. In addition to the commercial paper and felt blending stumps, newsprint, toilet paper, facial tissues, or your fingers can also be used.

Chalk-pastel blending techniques.

FIGURE 22.3
Markers.

Chalk Pastels   Chalk pastels are formed into square or round sticks that have approximately the same consistency as blackboard chalk. The square sticks are about 3½ inches long, and the round sticks are about 6 inches. The square sticks are generally more useful for theatrical sketching, because you can draw a relatively sharp line with the edges of the stick as well as a smooth wash with the flat surfaces.

Chalk pastels are available in three hardnesses: soft, medium, and hard. The brilliance of the color is linked to its hardness—the harder the stick, the less brilliant its color. Soft- and medium-consistency chalk pastels are extremely useful for laying down a smooth background color or a graded wash (which smoothly varies in hue from top to bottom or side to side). Medium and hard pastels are useful for detail work.

Oil or Wax Pastels   Oil or wax pastels have a slightly greasy feeling, because they are manufactured with a soft wax binder. The wax makes them very easy to blend. If you are planning to use oil pastels in conjunction with watercolors, you will need to remember to "paint first and pastel second," because the wax prevents paint from adhering to the paper.

Markers

A number of different markers and marking pens are available. The principal differences are in the shape and material of the tip and the nature and characteristics of the paint or ink contained in the marker (Figure 22.3).

The majority of these markers, such as the Magic Marker brand, contain a permanent semitransparent ink that dries very quickly and is generally available in a limited range of colors. Several lines of artist's markers contain watercolor ink that is more transparent than this permanent ink. Watercolor markers are also available in a much wider range of colors. Both types of marker can be used very effectively for detail work on renderings.

Another type of marker contains a lacquer-base metallic paint. Generally available in silver, gold, bronze, and copper, these markers are very useful for applying metallic detail or highlights to renderings.

illustration board: Watercolor paper mounted on a pressboard backing.

hot-press finish: A slick, smooth texture achieved by pressing paper between hot rollers; this treatment leaves a thin layer of oil, which makes the paper unsuitable for use with transparent watercolor; works well with designer's gouache, acrylic, pencils, and markers.

cold-press finish: A slight surface texture achieved by pressing paper between cold rollers; no oil residue results, so the paper can be used with transparent watercolor, designer's gouache, acrylic, markers, or pencils.

rough finish: A pebble-grained texture achieved by cold-pressing paper with a textured roller or by other techniques; suitable for painted and pastel renderings having little intricate detail.

tooth: A term used to describe the surface texture of a paper.

pixel: A picture element; the smallest discrete part of an electronically projected picture, as on a computer monitor.

Paper

Most final scenic and costume sketches are drawn or painted on some type of watercolor paper or **illustration board.** Illustration board is simply watercolor paper that has been mounted on a stiff pressboard backing to keep it from bending or wrinkling. Other types of paper such as charcoal or velvet paper can be used for work with pastels, pencils, and markers, but they don't work well with paint.

There are three primary surface finishes for watercolor papers and illustration board. A **hot-press finish** is very slick and smooth. The **cold-press finish** has a slight texture similar to a heavy bond typing paper. **Rough-finish** paper has a very noticeable texture.

Your choice of which paper to use should be dictated by the medium in which you plan to work. The hot-press finish is good for opaque paints, pencils, and markers. The cold-press papers work well with all media. The rough-finish papers are particularly well suited for pastels and watercolor.

Matte boards (hot-press illustration board with colored surfaces) are also interesting surfaces for designer's renderings, particularly if you are planning on working with any of the opaque media such as designer's gouache, pastels, or pencil.

Newsprint is often used by both scenic and costume designers for their thumbnail and preliminary sketches. It is inexpensive, has a slightly roughened **tooth,** and is a receptive surface for softer pencils, soft-nibbed markers, and soft pastels.

To determine which paper is suitable for a particular project, you will need to develop an understanding of the characteristics of the various papers and their surfaces. This knowledge can be gained only by playing and experimenting with the various media on the different papers and illustration boards.

Computer Drawing

There are a variety of drawing programs, and they contain a number of features. Generally, they can be divided into two generic types: painting programs and drawing programs.

Painting Tools   Painting programs such as Adobe Photoshop (Figure 22.4A) and Fractal Painter (Figure 22.4B) are generally used for nontechnical drawings such as renderings and sketches. Technically, these programs create bitmap objects. A bitmap object is viewed by the computer as a collection of **pixels,** each pixel corresponding directly to one or more "bits" of computer memory including its color and location within the picture.[1] The structure of a bitmap image facilitates the creation of blended or soft-edged images commonly associated with sketching and painting.

Drawing Tools   Objects created with drawing programs such as Strata Studio Pro (Figure 22.5) and/or 3D Studio are object-oriented or vector images. A vector-based program views each object in a picture as a mathematical calculation. If you create a background, then draw other objects in the foreground, you can point and click on one of the foreground objects and move it around in the drawing without affecting the background. When an object is moved, the computer recalculates its position.[2] This quality enables the operator not only to

[1] Peter Jerram and Michael Gosney, *Multimedia Power Tools,* 2nd edition (New York: Random House/Verbum, 1995), p. 89.
[2] Ibid.

(A)

(B)

FIGURE 22.4
(A) On-screen view of Adobe Photoshop, an image editing program. Software: Photoshop by Adobe Systems Incorporated. (B) On-screen view of Painter, an image editing program. Software: Printer™ by MetaCreations Corporation.

change the position of the object within the picture but also to rotate the object about its various axes to see what it looks like from all sides. Vector programs can be used to create sketches and renderings, but their forte is in the creation of drawings which contain multiple objects that may need to be manipulated independently and that require relatively hard-edged lines.

Most of these drawing and painting programs contain both two- and three-dimensional functions in the same program. The actual drawing can be done with a mouse or with a **digitizing tablet** (Figure 22.6). The first digitizing tablets

digitizing tablet: An electro-mechanical device that converts the pressure of a stylus on a flat plate (tablet) into binary information that can be understood by the computer.

FIGURE 22.5
On-screen view of Studio Pro, a drawing/painting program. Software: Studio Pro by Strata, Incorporated.

scan: To use a digitizing scanner to convert existing artwork, photos, or drawings into binary information.

allowed you to draw lines on the pad with a stylus. The line you traced on the tablet was transferred to the monitor screen. You could erase, move, and redraw the lines. The drawings could be stored and/or printed. A new generation of digitizing tablets are pressure-sensitive. The pressure sensitivity permits a more natural drawing style closely akin to drawing with a pencil: The harder you press the stylus, the wider and darker the line; the lighter the pressure, the narrower and lighter the line. Both types of digitizing tablets are still available, and both are quite useful.

Most of the current drawing programs include color palettes ranging from a minimum of 256 hues to over 1.6 million specific colors. These programs also allow you to select specific surface textures (e.g., wood, paper, cloth, skin, plastic, and steel) to "wrap" around the objects you are drawing or modeling. The majority of drawing programs also allow you to design the lighting for your drawings. The software enables you to select the location and intensity of the light(s) that are illuminating the object you're drawing. This feature automatically results in the projection of shadows which aid the three-dimensional quality of the drawings.

FIGURE 22.6
A digitizing tablet, which can be used to "draw" images on the monitor screen.

Drawing programs can be used in several ways. Original sketches can be created with a program such as POSER, or hand-drawn sketches or research illustrations can be **scanned** into the computer. Various color combinations and textures can be quickly "tried out" on the sketches. 3D drawings allow you to see all sides of costumes and sets from any seat in the house. Computer-drawn sketches generally have not replaced hand-rendered drawings and designs at this time. But, as the technology advances, it is certainly possible that it will become more and more difficult to tell the difference between hand- and computer-drawn designs. The advantages that computer drawings offer the designer are many and ever-increasing. Which method is better? It really doesn't matter. The reality is that whichever method provides the best visualization of the designer's intention will be the appropriate method to use. But the caveat "know how to do both" still applies.

The Digitizing Scanner

A scanner is an electronic device that allows you to input an existing drawing/photo/picture into the computer. The scanner functions much like a copying machine. You put the picture into the scanner, which digitizes the information and transfers it into the computer and onto the screen. In addition to working with pre-existing artwork, you can create an original sketch by hand and scan it into the computer; then you can play with its color, outline, and texture to quickly see what effect these changes have on the overall design.

DRAWING AND RENDERING TECHNIQUES

The following suggestions will familiarize you with some of the basic techniques that are used with the various media. Try the suggested application techniques. Doodle with the pencils, paint, pastels, and markers. Have fun with them. After you've worked with each medium separately, try combining them. Whatever else, be sure that you have fun, because you will improve only with practice, and you will practice only if you're having fun.

Sketching

Scenic, costume, and property designers need to be able to make quick, clear sketches. Thumbnail drawings and preliminary sketches are presented and modified during the production meetings, and almost all renderings begin with pencil sketches.

Initially, almost everyone feels intimidated by the idea of sketching. But some simple hints may help you improve your ability to sketch.

In Chapter 5 we learned that lines are evocative, that they contain meaning. But what is that meaning, and how is it expressed? In theatrical sketching, the

Choosing a Watercolor Paper

If you are going to be rendering with watercolor, designer's gouache, or acrylic paint, you'll have a lot fewer headaches if you use watercolor board rather than watercolor paper. Although the board is more expensive, the backing prevents it from wrinkling and causing the paint to collect in little puddles.

Sometimes, however, it makes more sense to use watercolor paper—as when doing 50 costume renderings for a single show. The weight of that portfolio makes the use of watercolor paper much the better choice.

If you are going to use watercolor paper, you will need to prepare it. If you are going to be making large washes, mount the paper on some type of backing so that it won't wrinkle. Thumbtack or firmly tape the paper to a smooth board, such as a drawing board or smooth-finished plywood at least three-eighths of an inch thick. After you've attached the paper, and several hours before you plan to paint, thoroughly wet the paper and then let it dry. This will "relax" the paper and let it shrink before you start to paint.

Cold-press illustration board, such as Crescent 100 or Bristol board, or a rough-surface watercolor paper or board works very well for most scenic or costume renderings in watercolor.

lines that define the shape, texture, and detail of costumes, sets, and props are actually representations of the materials that will be used to build the designs. This is the first principle of theatrical sketching: Lines must reflect the qualities of the materials they represent. For example, the quality and character of the line(s) used to create a costume sketch should reflect the psychological qualities of the character as well as the weight, texture, and characteristics of the fabric and materials from which the costume will be made. Similarly, the lines used to describe a set should be evocative of the wood, metal, fabric, and so forth from which it is constructed. This first principle leads to a second: You must be intimately familiar with the physical characteristics of the materials you're drawing. To accurately sketch a chiffon blouse or heavy woolen cape, you must know the hand of those fabrics—what they feel like, their weight, their draping characteristics, and so on. Sets are made from various types of woods, metals, fabrics, and plastics, each of which has its own physical characteristics. Some are rigid, others flexible; some are rough, others smooth and polished. The set designer must know and understand those characteristics before he or she can create an accurate representation of them.

A related, third principle states that you must know what you're drawing before you can draw it. To draw a chiffon blouse, you must be able to see what it looks like—the shape and fullness of body, sleeve, collar, and cuff; whether it has button closure down the front or back or no buttons at all. To create a realistic Victorian drawing room, you have to know what one looked like. This type of understanding comes from doing the research described in the design process (Chapter 2).

When you follow these three principles, something magical happens as you begin to draw. Your brain, programmed with all the background information it needs, guides your hand and a finished representation of the concept, which actually looks like the object you envisioned, just seems to appear on the paper. But this magic doesn't happen instantly. It takes practice—lots of practice. But it is a skill that all designers must master, and it is only mastered through repetitive practice.

A sketch does not need to, nor is it supposed to, create a photographic likeness of a person or object. Sketching creates a simplified view that shows the basic appearance and, of equal importance, the spirit or character of the object.

A major stumbling block that many people encounter when learning to sketch is that they try to draw what they think they see rather than what they actually see. Figure 22.7A shows a photograph of a table. Because people know that the top of a table is its most useful surface, they tend to draw the top of the table as the most dominant visual element, as shown in Figure 22.7B. They're not drawing what they see. If you really look at the photo of the table, you'll see that the top is only a narrow sliver compared with the overall size of the table. Figure 22.7C is a sketch that was made after careful observation of the photo of the table. Notice that even though the sketch doesn't show every detail, it does provide an accurate representation of the table, and it also gives you a feeling about its nature or character.

All sketches are based on three principal elements: thematic lines; line angles and intersections; and proportions. Most objects are composed of more than one thematic or predominant line, like the rocking chair shown in Figure 22.8A. The intersection of these thematic lines allows you to use a fairly easy method to accurately lay out the proportions of an object. While you're noting the angle of intersection of the thematic lines (the chair back, legs, seat, rockers, and the floor), also note the relative position where those line intersections take place. On the rocking chair, notice that the seat intersects the back just a little more than one-third of the way up the back. Also notice that the seat itself is just a little bit longer than the distance from the seat to the rockers. This "ratio technique" generally reduces a beginning artist's anxiety (which allows you to be more creative), because it depersonalizes the sketching process. You're no longer "drawing a chair," you're simply observing lines of intersection and recreating them. An accurate sketch of the rocking chair, Figure 22.8B, can be made simply by using these observations as a guide. The rest of the detailing of the sketch, Figure 22.8C, is based on the same type of observational techniques. The locations of the various solid and spindle elements of the chair are determined by observing their relative positions on the model and then, using the ratio technique, drawing them on the sketch.

(A)

(B)

(C)

FIGURE 22.7
Draw what you see, not what you think you see (review the text for details).

Figure Drawing

It is imperative that designers be able to sketch the human figure easily. For costume designers, this requirement is obvious. If clothes are to fit the body in a natural and realistic manner, the costume designer must draw the figure so that it looks natural and realistic, then the clothes follow easily. For scenic designers, the figure-drawing requirement is less obvious, but many designers like to place a human figure or two in their sketches, models, or drafting plates to provide a readily understandable scale reference.

Some designers believe it is important that a figure have a readily identifiable face. Others do not. However, almost all costume designers agree that a visually dynamic sketch—one in which the figure, and consequently the costume, appears to be in motion—is an important aid in representing the character of the costume.

The quick figure sketch in Figure 22.9 is used to capture the flavor and personality of the character. Accomplished with just a few strokes, the quick sketch is the visual distillation of the designer's thoughts, ideas, and research about the character, and it provides a visual description of that character's personality. In costume design, the quick sketch can be considered analogous to

FIGURE 22.8
Sketching techniques (see text for details).

(B)

(C)

the lighting designer's lighting key in that it provides a touchstone to which the designer refers as the figure and subsequent costume design are being developed.

Every costume design needs to begin with a figure drawing. If the body doesn't look right—isn't in proper proportion, doesn't reflect the personality characteristics of the role—then the design of the clothes placed on that body will be similarly flawed. Proportion is arguably the single most important element in figure drawing. If the proportions aren't correct, the figure won't seem natural. Reasonably normal proportions are achieved if the male is about 8½ heads high and the female about 8 heads high, as shown in Figure 22.10. Study the distances and relationships between the various body parts. Notice that the center of the chest is about one head height below the chin, the shoulders are about two heads wide, and so on. A sense of balance and stability is achieved when the figure's head is directly above its center of support, as shown in Figure 22.11. Notice that this sense of balance is achieved because the body's mass is evenly divided on either side of the center of balance. Notice also that the body pivots around its natural hinge points—spine, shoulders, elbows, wrists, hips, knees, ankles, and so forth—to create this balance.

To provide the best possible view of the costume, designers draw most costume figures standing with one or both arms extended away from the body in a manner that will provide a view of sleeve detail. Naturally, the particular pose chosen should reflect the personality and nature of the character being portrayed. Deviations from this convention are appropriate when they will provide a better view or understanding of how the costume will look and work in the production.

FIGURE 22.9
Quick figure sketches use a few lines to capture the flavor and personality of the character.

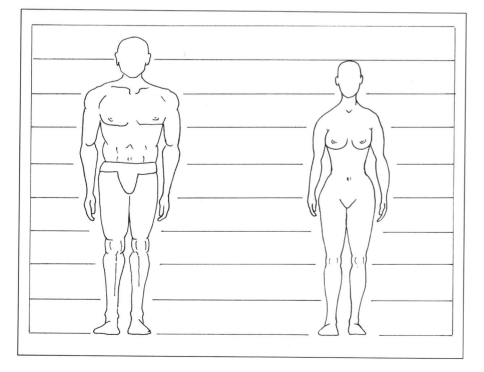

FIGURE 22.10
Proportions of male and female figures.

FIGURE 22.11
Costume design figures should appear to be dynamically balanced (see text for details).

graphite: A soft carbon similar to the lead in a pencil; sticks can be purchased in most art supply stores.

Proficiency in figure drawing is not achieved easily. It requires study and practice. Designers should become familiar with the skeletal structure of the body and how the various muscle groups work to animate it. And they must practice. Take life-drawing courses, carry a sketch pad, and draw during any idle time. For further study of basic anatomy and figure drawing, see the Selected References at the end of the book.

Graphite Transfers

Watercolor and pastel renderings and sketches usually begin with a pencil drawing. It is fairly standard practice to draw the design on tracing vellum, since the vellum is fairly rugged and will be able to sustain a fair amount of erasing as the sketch is modified. Figure 22.12 explains the process of graphite transfers. After the sketch is completed, turn the vellum over and cover the back side of the sheet with **graphite.** (A soft stick is used for this purpose.) To prevent smearing, set the

FIGURE 22.12
Graphite-transfer technique. Cover the reverse side of the sketch with soft graphite (A). Turn the drawing over and trace the sketch (B and C) to transfer the linework to the watercolor paper or board (D).

(A)

(B)

(C)

(D)

(A)   (B)   (C)

graphite by daubing thinned rubber cement over it. Use a cotton ball as your dauber. Tape the drawing, face up, to the illustration or watercolor board, and trace the outline of the sketch. (If you use a fine-point ballpoint pen with red ink, it will be very easy to see where you've been as you are tracing the drawing.) As you trace the outline of the sketch, you will be transferring the design to the illustration board.

You may be tempted to employ the carbon paper used for making copies in typing instead of going through the rather laborious task of "graphiting" the reverse side of the tracing vellum. If you are planning on using a transparent medium such as watercolor, try to resist this temptation, because the carbon paper graphite is very dark and will bleed through any transparent paint that you may apply to the paper. If you are planning on working with opaque media, however, the colored transfer papers typically used by costumers to transfer pattern outlines will work very nicely. Colored transfer paper is usually available at most fabric stores.

Watercolor

A **wash** can be laid down wet or dry. A wet wash is made by wetting the area to be painted with water before applying the paint, as shown in Figure 22.13. Using your brush, paint the outlined area with water, let it dry until the area has a uniformly dull finish, and then apply the paint. A wet wash conceals brush strokes a little better than a dry wash.

Since watercolor is a transparent medium, you'll need to remember that the whites and light colors are achieved by letting the paper show through. Because of this characteristic, it is normal procedure to build up a watercolor rendering from light to dark. This simply means that you paint the light areas first, then move to those of middle tone, and finish by painting the darkest details or objects. Applying each hue individually is also a normal technique in watercolor painting. After each coat has dried, additional layers can be built up over the original coat to deepen or change its hue or add texture or detail *if* the previous work has been sealed with a **workable fixative.** Fine detail work can either be applied over the watercolor washes after they have dried, and fixed, or the area where the detail is to be applied can be left unpainted when you are putting in the wash. Detail work can also be applied directly on top of a dried transparent wash with opaque media such as designer's gouache, acrylic, pastels, or markers.

If you have some intricate detail that will be silhouetted against a large wash area, you can "paint" the detail area with rubber cement before laying in the wash. After the wash has dried, peel off the rubber cement to expose the unpainted paper, and paint in the detail work.

FIGURE 22.13
Applying a wet wash with watercolor. First wet the area with water (A). When the water has partially dried (the paper will have a uniform dull sheen), smoothly spread the watercolor across the area (B) to create a smooth wash of color (C).

wash: The covering of a relatively large area with a smooth layering of paint; a smooth wash consists of only one color; a blended wash is created by smoothly segueing from one color to another.

workable fixative: A spray that seals colors in place. "Workable" indicates that paint can effectively be applied on top of the fixative.

(A)

FIGURE 22.14
Pastel-application techniques. (A) A straight line. (B) A smooth wash. Pastels can be used to lay down background washes (C). Be sure to use drafting tape to mask areas to be left "unwashed." Spray the drawing with workable fixative (D) to lock the pastel to the paper.

(B)

(C)

(D)

Pastels

The design can be transferred to the pastel paper or illustration board using the graphite-transfer technique.

Oil or wax pastels, which are very easy to blend, give a smooth, opaque finish that somewhat resembles a drawing done with crayons. Chalk pastels give a chalkier, luminescent finish. Most theatrical designers prefer working with chalk pastels, because they can be used with watercolor whereas oil pastels cannot. (The oil in the wax pastel causes the watercolor to bead up and dry in little blobs rather than a smooth wash.)

How you actually apply the pastel to the paper has a great deal to do with the finished appearance of the design. Chalk pastels will leave a definite line when applied using an edge, as shown in Figure 22.14. A smooth coverage over a large area can be accomplished by using a softer blend (soft or medium hardness) and the flat side of the pastel stick.

Once the pastel has been applied, it can be blended using felt or paper blending sticks, tissue, or your fingers. Stick pastel can also be erased (although not completely) with a kneadable or soft pink eraser.

If you don't want to get the pastel on a particular area of the drawing, mask off that space with drafting tape. Large areas can be effectively masked using paper held in place with drafting tape. Be sure not to use masking tape, which will leave a slightly gummy residue on the paper when it is removed. Additionally, the adhesive on masking tape is sufficiently strong that it can pull the finish surface layer right off the paper!

Chalk pastels are basically colored chalk. The image they leave on the paper is made of chalk dust and is very easy to smear. Although this characteristic is handy for blending two or more colors, a spray fixative is needed to prevent the picture from being smeared after it is finished.

A workable fixative enables you to create several layers on a pastel rendering. If you first draw and blend the background and then spray it with fixative, you can draw the foreground detail without smearing the background work. Each successive layer should be sprayed, and when the rendering is complete, it should be sprayed again. Be sure to use workable fixatives; their finish won't affect the application of additional layers of pastel.

Pencils and Markers

Colored pencils and pens as well as watercolor or oil markers can be used to good effect for both scenic and costume renderings.

The watercolor drawing pencils, which are hardened watercolor pigments, can be used to sketch in detail. The edge of the line can be softened by painting it with water, as shown in Figure 22.15.

Artist's markers are available in a full range of hues and saturations. The ink has the same transparent properties as watercolor paint, whereas the oil markers are generally translucent or opaque. Either type of marker can be used in a variety of ways to achieve any number of interesting effects.

Combined Media

To be able to select the appropriate visual expression for a specific design concept, a designer should feel free to use and combine a wide variety of rendering materials, styles, and techniques. The rendering for a soft, ethereal, dye-painted scrim is probably best achieved with chalk pastels, watercolors, or a combination of the two. The sketch for a costume with a sequined bodice and a long, flowing diaphanous skirt could be effectively realized with watercolor or designer's gouache and fine-line markers or pen and ink. A nonrepresentational setting of abstract forms in strongly contrasting colors might best be expressed by cutting the forms from colored construction paper and pasting them to a representation of the stage space. Ultimately, the selection of which medium, or combination of media, to use for a specific rendering is the designer's choice, and those choices will be more varied if the designer is familiar with a number of media and rendering techniques.

As with any craft, your personal ability to use this information about rendering will improve only with practice. Take courses in drawing, life drawing, pastel sketching, and watercolor painting in your school's art department to help you learn the many techniques and media that can be used to visually communicate your design ideas. As you become more familiar with the materials and techniques of sketching and rendering, you will discover that your ability to manipulate them is improving as well.

(A)

(B)

(C)

(D)

(E)

FIGURE 22.15
Combining media can produce interesting results. The building masked in the pastel drawing shown in Figure 22.14 is unmasked (A), and the detail is sketched in and colored with watercolor pencils (B), which are blended with a brush and water (C). After the water has dried, additional detail is sketched in with pens (D) and markers to create a drawing with an interesting appearance of depth (E).

Appendix A

LISTSERVS FOR THEATRE PRODUCTION[1]

Patrick Finelli

One of the most valuable features of the Internet is that, once you have an e-mail address, you can get in touch with others who have similar interests and specialized knowledge through listserv discussion groups. Listservs usually require members to subscribe, unlike newsgroups, which are available through your server's news reader (see "Welcome to Cyberspace," October 1994).

A listserv works like an electronic mail distribution list, and subscribers receive any mail that is posted to the group—most of which is germane to the basic subject matter the group serves. Members also may send messages to selected individuals or the entire group, simply by posting a message to the list.

There are hundreds of listserv discussion groups on the Internet. Here is some basic information about theater-related listservs and how to subscribe, along with some suggestions for future reference.

Joining a listserv is as simple as e-mailing a subscription message to the listserv address. For example, you may join the Theatre listserv by sending a subscription message to *listserv@pucc.princeton.edu*. All subscription requests follow the same format: you send a message to the listserv with the following body: subscribe [listserv name] [your first name] [your last name]. An example would be "subscribe theatre jane doe".

Some lists require that you send the subscription message to "listproc" (a computer list processor) and other listservs are subscribed through an individual who screens requests and manages the list. The first time you subscribe to a listserv you will receive a welcoming e-mail message from the server stating you have been added to the list and giving you other information about posting messages and unsubscribing. Often these messages are generated automatically. Save all your confirmation messages in a folder for future reference. It is a good way to keep track of your listserv subscriptions and other pertinent data, such as how to access each list's archives and unsubscribe procedures—especially if you subscribe to more than one list.

All this may sound complicated, but once you are officially subscribed, you may post a message simply by sending e-mail to the list. For instance, if you have subscribed to the Actor listserv, you would send a note to the list address "actor@talentnet.co". This is called "sending mail to the list," because your mail goes to a single address and then the listserv program distributes your note to all other subscribers.

Members receive e-mail messages whenever anyone posts a message to the list. You can read your listserv messages along with your other e-mail, save or delete individual postings, and respond either to the multiple subscribers on the list or privately to the person who posted the original message. When you post a message to the list, you get it back (unless you have disabled that feature) and everyone else gets a copy as well. Each message has an identifier in the heading which indicates the topic of discussion.

You may choose to follow selected topics and screen your mail by subject before reading. Usually there are multiple threads woven throughout a listserv discussion. Readers who want to add their own comments to the discussion make follow-up postings. Often the responses go far beyond the original question, which is part of the fun. Most listservs automatically archive the notes for future reference.

There are two main directories of theater listserv discussion groups and both are available through the University of Michigan's server: *ftp://una.hh.lib.umich.edu/ inetdirsstacks/theater:torresmjvk* or *ftp://una.hh.lib.umich.edu/ inetdirsstacks/theater:mccoy.*

Both lists include most of the listservs noted at the end of this column, but when I checked, McCoy's was updated more recently than Torres' list and also had a section devoted to new groups. I subscribe to several listservs and have created one for a theater history course I teach.

One of the most active listservs on my subscription list is the one for the American Society of Theatre Research. It is primarily for theater historians and scholars, although quite a few directors and scenographers subscribe. The range of topics in one recent week included questions about the origin of the "green room" and the "main curtain," the earliest printed plays, *commedia dell' arte* conventions, "sea plays" (e.g., early Eugene O'Neill),

[1] *Stage Directions*, March 1996, Volume 9, No. 3. Reprinted with permission of *Stage Directions*.

"American plays of the land," Jerry Rojo's scenic innovations, notices about drama anthologies, and notes on a play written about Paul Robeson.

It is not unusual to discover a question about a particular theater artist or production answered by someone who is either extremely knowledgeable or speaks from personal experience. The presence of experts on most listserv discussion groups and your ability to contact them without intruding is a valuable resource.

Depending upon the number of lists you join and their level of activity, you will increase substantially the volume of electronic mail in your inbox each day. Reading new items can be time consuming. I receive about 50 electronic messages a day, but may only read 40 of them and write about a dozen notes back. Consider joining one or two groups at a time at first until you get the hang of it. Otherwise, you will be overwhelmed with lots of messages.

Suppose you've joined a list and want to catch up on previous discussions, or search for a particular topic. You can query the list processor to find out if archives are available and what files may be obtained from the archives. When you join a list, you will learn if it supports search, index, and retrieval requests. Most of them do, and also support "help" requests for extensive information on the commands for listing and retrieving files.

Here are some helpful guidelines for listserv subscribers:

- Familiarize yourself with the discussion topics before jumping in with your own comments. Think of it as "listening" before "talking." This also is called "lurking."
- Keep your message brief and to the point.
- Use descriptive titles for an original post (for example, "green room").
- Respond to discussion items using the original header so others may follow the thread.
- Limit your number of listserv subscriptions.
- Unsubscribe when you are on vacation, otherwise your mailbox will be filled when you return.
- Remember who your audience is. Many lists include subscribers who are leading experts in their field.

The listserv gives you unprecedented access to knowledgeable individuals. Make the most of this opportunity and remember your netiquette. Listservs are a very good way to organize discussions and exchange ideas with others who share your particular interests. Here is a list of theater-related listservs to help you get started:

ACTOR (Actor discussion group)
subscribe: *listserv@talentnet.com*
post: *actor@talentnet.com*

ARS-DIGIT-L (Digital Technology and Performing Arts)
subscribe: *listproc@frank.mtsu.edu*
post: *ars-digit-l@frank.mtsu.edu*

ARTMGT-L (Arts Management)
subscribe: *listserv@bingvmb.cc.binghamton.edu*
post: *artmgt-l@bingvmb.cc.binghamton.edu*

ASIANTHEAT-L (Asian Performing Arts)
subscribe: *probert@uhunix.uhcc.hawaii.edu*
post: *asianthea-l@uhunix.uhcc.hawaii.edu*

ASTR-L (American Society for Theatre Research)
subscribe: *listserv@postoffice.cso.uiuc.edu*
post: *astr-l@vmd.cso.uiuc.edu*

ATHE_RT-L (ATHE Religion and Theatre Focus Group)
subscribe: *listserv@mtu.edu*
post: *athe_rt-l@mtu.edu*

CANDRAMA (Canadian Theatre Research)
subscribe: *listserv@unb.ca*
post: *candrama@unb.ca*

CERVANTES (Miguel de Cervantes Discussion List)
subscribe: *listserv@listserv.acns.nwu.edu*
post: *cervantes@listserv.acns.nwu.edu*

COLLAB-L (On-line Collaboration in Theatre and Musicals)
subscribe: *sas14@psuvm.psu.edu*
post: *collab-l@psuvm.psu.edu*

COMEDIA (Spanish Golden Age Theatre)
subscribe: *listserv@listserv.arizona.edu*
post: *comedia@listserv.arizona.edu*

F-COSTUME (Fantasy Costume)
subscribe: *majordomo@lunch.asd.sgi.com*
post: *f-costume@lunch.asd.sgi.com*

H-COSTUME (Historic Costume)
subscribe: *h-costume-request@andrew.cmu.edu*
post: *h-costume@andrew.cmu.edu*

LATHE (Latin American Theatre List)
subscribe: *lathe-request@kutztown.edu*
post: *lathe@kutztown.edu*

PERFORM (Medieval Performance)
subscribe: *listserv@iubvm.ucs.indiana.edu*
post: *perform@iubvm.ucs.indiana.edu*

PERFORM-L (Performance Studies)
subscribe: *listserv@acfcluster.nyu.edu*
post: *perform-l@acfcluster.nyu.edu*

PUPTCRIT (Puppetry)
subscribe: *mailserv@odie.ccs.yorku.ca*
post: *puptcrit@odie.ccs.yorku.ca*

QUEATRE (International French Theatre Discussion List)
subscribe: *listproc@uqam.ca*
post: *queatre@uqam.ca*

REED-L (Records of Early English Drama)
subscribe: *reed@epas.utoronto.ca*
post: *reed-l@epas.utoronto.ca*

SHAKSPER (Shakespeare)
subscribe: *hmcook@boe00.minc.umd.edu*
post: *shaksper@vm.utcc.utoronto.ca*

SHOW-FIRE (Special effects/pyrotechnics)
subscribe: *murr@vnet.net*
post: *show-fire@vnet.net*

STAGECRAFT (Technical Theatre)
subscribe: *stagecraft-request@jaguar.cs.utah.edu*
post: *stagecraft@jaguar.cs.utah.edu*

THEATRE (Theatre Discussion List)
subscribe: *listserv@pucc.princeton.edu*
post: *theatre@pucc.princeton.edu*

THEATRE-THEORY (Theory of Acting, Movement, Voice)
subscribe: *quijote@mit.edu*
post: *theatre-theory@mit.edu*

VASTAVOX (Voice, Speech, Dialects)
subscribe: *listserv@uci.edu*
post: *vastavox@uci.edu*

WTP-L (Women and Theatre Program Discussion List)
subscribe: *listserv@uhccvm.hucc.hawaii.edu*
post: *wtp-l@uhccvm.hucc.hawaii.edu*

Appendix B

A REVISED STANDARD GRAPHIC LANGUAGE FOR LIGHTING DESIGN[1]

Patrick Gill, Chair of USITT Lighting Graphic Standards Committee

Most lighting designers and electricians feel that standards in the nomenclature, characteristics and use of stage lighting equipment provide clear criteria for training and for professional use. However, in a large area like entertainment lighting technology, the task of creating such standards is both complicated and ongoing. There are many areas where standards can apply, from lighting equipment manufacturers' specifications to the system of communication between designers and electricians. It is also difficult to determine how much detail to include in a standards statement.

The work of a previous lighting graphics standards committee that culminated in 1985 with the publication of the current lighting graphics standards enabled USITT to offer a communication framework for lighting design information that was acceptable to the professional lighting community as a whole. However, as in all areas of technology, rapid change usually dictates a restructuring of guidelines. The current USITT lighting graphics standards committee includes professional designers and electricians from academic and commercial theatre. It became our task to update the existing lighting graphics standards by incorporating new technology, finding a method of accurate scale representation of symbols, and providing more concise drafting guidelines. Also, since it would be cumbersome to represent all manufacturers' instrument profiles on lighting templates, the USITT standard symbols continue to represent generic instrument types.

A point to stress is that young designers do emulate both the professionals who train them and those whose commercial successes they adopt as role models. In terms of the training and of the clarity of our industry practice, it is important that a common means of communication exist between all professionals that does not inhibit the development of a personal style of graphic representation. The current committee endeavored to solicit the opinion of all interested lighting professionals in USITT by generating and distributing a survey at the 1991 conference in Boston. What follows is an assemblage of the committee's work and the survey results.

THE LIGHT PLOT

A major reason for doing scale lighting drawings is to present a clear, consistent and efficient picture of the instruments and how they fit into the represented space. All electricians have tried to hang lighting instruments in places where the symbol will fit on the drawing but the real unit won't fit in the real space, or will just fit but then can't move in the desired direction for focus. Also, lighting drawings that are inconsistent or that have too much information on them just confuse the process and waste time.

The light plot is a horizontal offset section in which the cutting plane intersects the theatre at whatever level gives the most descriptive view of the instrumentation in the stage configuration. The only information clearly represented on the light plot and (usually) nowhere else is the actual position and size of the instrument. Even in a repertory situation, accurate pictorial information about instruments is critical for standard hangs and for special designs or to communicate unusual rigging ideas.

In the general description of the light plot there are several items essential to a clear understanding of the designer's intentions. These are the center line, transverse and/or longitudinal scales, a line-set index with designations, a representation of the apron, the edge of the stage or the edges of the playing area, the interior walls of the stagehouse or of the flexible theatre space, all masking, all architectural and scenic obstructions, the proscenium arch, the plaster line, the smoke pocket or other architectural details (in non-proscenium spaces) necessary to orient the lighting design, elevations of booms, torm ladders and other vertical positions, identification (name and plan location) of lighting positions, identification of critical sightlines, identification of lighting areas, the instrument key, and the titleblock.

The instrument symbols used on scale lighting plots should accurately represent the actual size of the instruments and use a standard identification mark for focal length or beam angle. Instruments require adequate spacing in layout to allow traverse during focus. Servo-

[1] Approved by the USITT Executive Committee, August 1991, Seattle, WA, and recommended for adoption by the Board of Directors at the Winter Business Meetings, November 1991, Reno, NV.

operated instruments should have their rotation area indicated. The standard information on the plot that should be included with the instrument symbol consists of an instrument number as an aid to location, a symbol for attached hardware (such as templates, irises, color scrollers, top hats, barn doors, etc.), the channel, the circuit and/or dimmer number or a space for the electrician to add the circuit and/or dimmer number, the color notation, a symbol for lamp axis alignment on PAR cans, and a standard technique for showing "two-fers." Strip lights should be shown actual size in scale and their notation should include the channel, the circuit and/or dimmer, a symbol for lamp axis alignment (where applicable), the color, and an indication of focus direction. The wattage and the focus notes are still included on the standard notation diagrams but for clarity should be kept only on the hook-up.

The accepted designation and numbering of hanging positions and instruments in proscenium configurations include the following conventions: Onstage electric pipes should number from downstage to upstage. Onstage booms should number from downstage to upstage. Box-boom or torm positions should number consistently within each plot. All lighting positions should designate by stage directions. Front of house (FOH) ceiling positions should number from the apron to the rear of the house as should FOH boom positions, side coves, ladders or ports. Balcony rails should number from the floor to the ceiling. Pipe grids in "black-box" type theatres should number on the "x" or "y" axis of the grid and letter on the opposing axis.

Non-conventional black-box lighting positions should identify by compass directions. Trim measurements should be from the stage floor or the deck to the pipe with a note on the plot to verify them that designates "stage floor" or "deck." Instruments on stage electric pipes should number from stage left to stage right. Instruments on booms should number from top to bottom. Strip lights should label (using numbers or letters) from stage left to stage right. Acceptable locations for titleblocks are in the lower right-hand or left-hand corners or centered on the bottom of the plate. The instrument key is a very important source of information. It should minimally contain standard identifications of all instruments and devices shown on the plot and controlled by the lighting console, the instrument manufacturer, the wattage (if typical for instrument type), and a representation of the typical instrument notation method.

THE VERTICAL LIGHTING SECTION

Vertical lighting sections should minimally contain batten and/or grid trim heights from the stage floor or the deck, with a note that designates from "stage floor" or "deck," identification of lighting positions including configurations for trusses and bridges, a scale view of a lighting instrument in each position, an indication of where the section is cut, the apron or edge of the playing area, the back wall of the stagehouse or the walls surrounding the playing space, all masking visible in the section, all architectural and scenic obstructions including masking, vertical audience sightlines, a sectional view of the scenery, an approximate representation of the lengths between the clamp and the bottom of an instrument, a scale representation of a human figure, and the titleblock. Vertical sections should also be in the same scale as the plot. In proscenium theatres, vertical sections should include the proscenium arch and the smoke pocket.

SYMBOLS

(See pages 558–560.)

LINE WEIGHTS

The adopted line weight standards are, for ink, a 0.010" to 0.0125" thin line and a 0.020" to 0.025" thick line and, for pencil, a 0.3 mm thin line and a 0.5 mm thick line. In terms of computer-aided design, these standards are well within the parameters of DM/PL and HPGL plotters. Guidelines for object emphasis in drawings are that instrument outlines should be darkest followed by architectural lines while the set lines shown for landmarks should be the lightest. Also, instrument outlines and information should take precedence over other objects in the plot. Lettering legibility, ease of use, and the allowance of rapid execution are the major attributes of good lettering. For hand lettering, the single stroke Gothic style in upper case meets these requirements adequately. In computerized drawing, legibility and consistency become the primary attributes in the choice of fonts.

COMPUTER-AIDED DESIGN (CAD) SYMBOLS STANDARDS

The symbols in this document are the product of a CAD program and should therefore answer the question of whether these symbols will work in a CAD environment. The ease with which more specific symbols libraries are created on a computer combined with the wish not to inhibit personal style should make the adoption and use of these guidelines more acceptable to the entertainment lighting community.

FUTURE STANDARDS

As already noted, this process is and should be ongoing. This standards document is not final and will continue to be revised as new technology and techniques are discovered. According to comments on the lighting graphics survey, it appears that the film and television area of lighting graphics will need to be considered next.

**THE GRAPHICS STANDARDS BOARD, LIGHTING
GRAPHICS STANDARDS COMMITTEE**

Patrick Gill, IES

Neil Jampolis, USAA

Richard Nelson, USAA

Rob Shakespeare, IES

William B. Warfel, USAA

Eric Schultz, IATSE

John Tissor, USAA

Chris Watts, ABTT

Advisory members:

Dawn Chaing, USAA

Mark Stanley, USAA

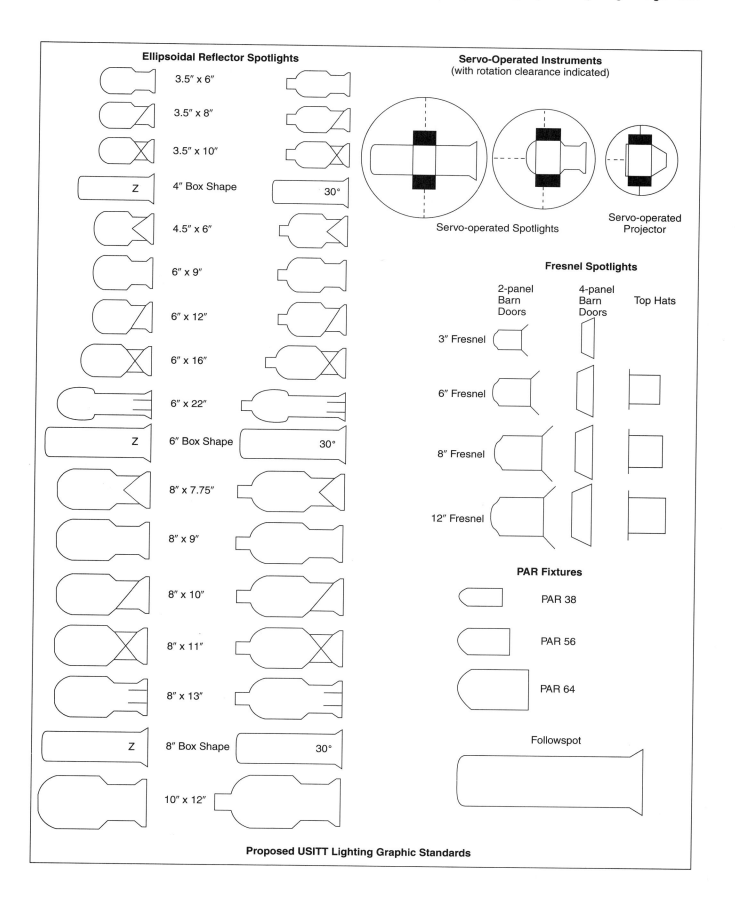

Ellipsoidal Reflector Spotlights

3.5″ x 6″

3.5″ x 8″

3.5″ x 10″

Z   4″ Box Shape   30°

4.5″ x 6″

6″ x 9″

6″ x 12″

6″ x 16″

6″ x 22″

Z   6″ Box Shape   30°

8″ x 7.75″

8″ x 9″

8″ x 10″

8″ x 11″

8″ x 13″

Z   8″ Box Shape   30°

10″ x 12″

Servo-Operated Instruments
(with rotation clearance indicated)

Servo-operated Spotlights

Servo-operated Projector

Fresnel Spotlights

	2-panel Barn Doors	4-panel Barn Doors	Top Hats
3″ Fresnel			
6″ Fresnel			
8″ Fresnel			
12″ Fresnel			

PAR Fixtures

PAR 38

PAR 56

PAR 64

Followspot

Proposed USITT Lighting Graphic Standards

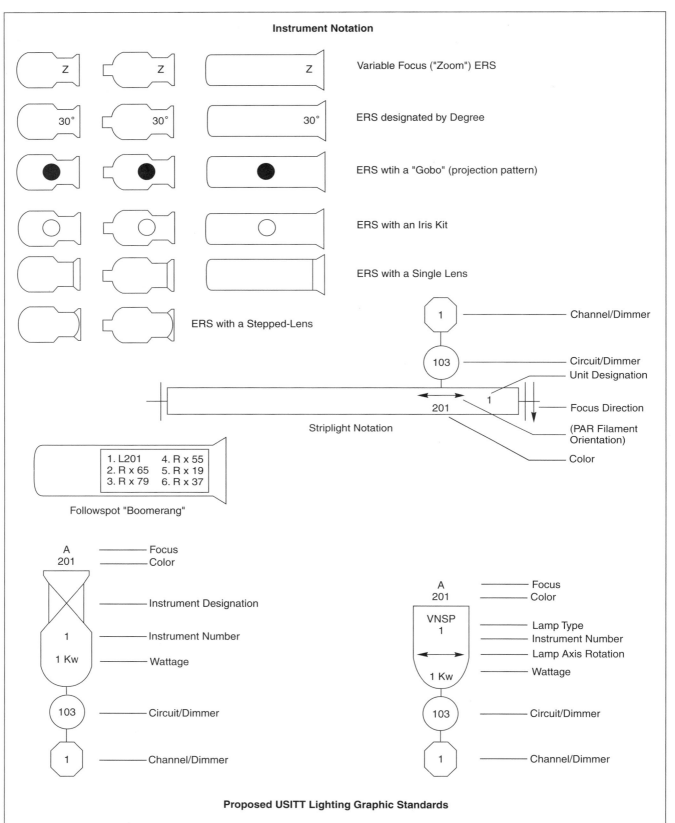

Instrument Notation

Variable Focus ("Zoom") ERS

ERS designated by Degree

ERS wtih a "Gobo" (projection pattern)

ERS with an Iris Kit

ERS with a Single Lens

ERS with a Stepped-Lens

Channel/Dimmer

Circuit/Dimmer

Unit Designation

Focus Direction

(PAR Filament Orientation)

Color

Striplight Notation

1. L201	4. R x 55
2. R x 65	5. R x 19
3. R x 79	6. R x 37

Followspot "Boomerang"

Focus
Color

Instrument Designation

Instrument Number

Wattage

Circuit/Dimmer

Channel/Dimmer

Focus
Color

Lamp Type
Instrument Number
Lamp Axis Rotation

Wattage

Circuit/Dimmer

Channel/Dimmer

Proposed USITT Lighting Graphic Standards

Glossary

Accessory: in costuming, anything other than clothing that is worn or carried, including wigs, hats, footwear, jewelry, and similar items.

Acoustics: the sound-transmission characteristics of a room, space, or material; also, the science that studies these qualities.

Acrylic: a plastic most readily identified by its trade name Plexiglas; available in rigid sheets and in liquid form (for use as a casting resin).

Acting areas: those areas of the stage on which specific scenes, or parts of scenes, are played.

Additive color mixing: the transmission of light of varying hues to the eye and the brain's interpretation of the ratio of the light mixture as a specific hue.

Adjustable arc-joint pliers: long-handled pliers with a series of jaw pivot points that provide a variety of jaw-opening ranges; used for gripping square and round objects with a great deal of leverage; also known as alligator pliers.

Adjustable-end wrench: generally known by the trade name Crescent Wrench, the adjustable-end wrench has smooth jaws that adjust to fit almost any small to medium-sized nut; used to tighten bolts and nuts.

Adjustable wood clamps: a wooden clamp with two adjustable faces; the jaws can be adjusted to various angles that are useful in holding furniture frames while the glued joints are drying.

Aerial perspective: an optical phenomenon in which objects that are farther away appear less sharply in focus and less fully saturated in color.

Air caster: a nonwheeled caster that lifts objects and holds them up using high-volume, low-pressure compressed air; three to four air casters are used to raise most objects; the one-foot-diameter air caster, load rated at 2,000 pounds, is the standard size used in theatrical production.

Aircraft cable: extremely strong, flexible, multistrand, twisted metal cable; eighth-inch aircraft cable is frequently used for flying heavy scenery because it has a breaking strength of approximately one ton.

Allen wrench: an L-shaped piece of steel rod with a hexagonal cross-sectional shape; used for working with Allen-head screws and bolts.

Alligator pliers: *see* adjustable arc-joint pliers.

Ambient: surrounding or background.

Ampere: the unit of measurement of electrical current.

Amplifier: a device used to boost the signal received from a transducer to a level that will drive a loudspeaker.

Amplitude: synonym for loudness.

Analog: in electronics, a circuit or device in which the output varies as a continuous function of the input.

Analogous colors: colors that are adjacent to each other on the color wheel; also known as related colors.

Aniline dye: transparent pigment made from aniline, a poisonous derivative of benzene; characterized by brilliant hues and full saturation; a strong solution can be made by putting one teaspoon of dye into a quart of boiling water.

Animal glue: a natural glue (a byproduct of the meat-packing industry) used for securing muslin to flat frames and as a binder in dry pigment and binder scene paint.

Anvil: a heavy, solid metal device with variously shaped faces; used in conjunction with a mechanic's or blacksmith's hammer for shaping metal.

Appliqué: a decorative item attached to a basic form.

Apron: the flat extension of the stage floor that projects from the proscenium arch toward the audience.

Arc: an electric current that leaps the gap between two closely placed electrodes.

Arc welder: a welder that uses an electrical arc to melt the metals being welded. The approximately ⅛-inch-diameter electrode melts and flows into the welding zone to provide filler metal.

Arena stage: a stage completely surrounded by the audience.

Armature: a basic skeletal form that holds the covering materials in the desired shape or alignment.

Artistic director: person responsible for the major artistic decisions of a theatrical production company—hiring of production personnel, selection of season, and so on.

Asymmetrical balance: a sense of equipoise achieved through dynamic tension created by the juxtaposition of dissimilar design elements.

Atom: the smallest particle of a chemical element that retains the structural properties of that element.

Atomic theory: a generally accepted theory concerning the structure and composition of substances.

Attenuate: to decrease or lessen.

Auditorium: the seating area from which the audience observes the action of a play.

Auger bits: spiral-shaped bits designed to be used with a brace; used for drilling holes (¼ inch to approximately 2 inches in diameter) in wood.

Backing: flats, drops, or draperies placed on the offstage side of doors and similar openings to prevent the audience from seeing backstage.

Backsaw: a fine-toothed (twelve to fourteen teeth per inch) crosscut saw with a stiffening spine on its back; used with a miter box to make accurate miter cuts.

Balance: the arrangement of parts of a composition to create a sense of restfulness; also, to adjust the loudness and equalization levels of individual signals while mixing, to achieve an appropriate blend.

Balanced line: a sound cable in which two insulated conductors are wrapped in a braided or foil shield.

Bald cap: a latex cap that covers a person's hair.

Ball peen hammer: a hammer made of hardened steel with a round ball on the back of its head; used for bending and shaping metal and seating rivets.

Baluster: a vase-shaped vertical member that supports the handrail of a staircase rail.

Band saw: a stationary power saw with a narrow continuous loop (or band) blade that passes through a table which supports the work; used for making curvilinear cuts.

Banister: the vertical member that supports the handrail of a staircase rail.

Bar clamp: similar to a pipe clamp except a notched bar is substituted for the pipe.

Barn door: an accessory for a Fresnel spotlight whose movable flippers are swung into the beam to control it.

Base coat: the first coat of the finished paint job; provides the basic color for the ensuing texture coats.

Bass-reflex speaker enclosure: an insulated box with a carefully designed hole or port in front that synchronizes the phase of the rearward speaker excursion with its forward excursion to reinforce the bass frequencies.

Baste: to temporarily stitch pieces of cloth together with long, easily removable stitches.

Batten: a wooden dowel or metal pipe (generally 1¼ to 1½ inches in diameter) attached to the onstage lines from a ropeset or counterweight system. Scenery is attached to the batten.

Batten-clamp drop: a drop that can be quickly attached to or removed from a batten by the use of batten clamps.

Battened butt joint: two pieces of lumber butted end to end with a small piece of similar width attached directly above the joint.

Beam angle: that point where the light emitted by an instrument is diminished by 50 percent when compared with the output of the center of the beam.

Beam projector: a lensless instrument with a parabolic primary reflector and a spherical secondary reflector that creates an intense shaft of light with little diffusion.

Belt clamp: a woven nylon belt with a ratchet device to tighten the belt around the work; used to clamp irregularly shaped objects.

Belt sander: a hand-held, portable power tool that uses belts of sandpaper for rapid sanding of (primarily) wood.

Bench grinder: a stationary stand- or bench-mounted power tool consisting of an electric motor with shafts extending from either end; various grinding and buffing wheels, as well as wire brushes, can be mounted on the shafts to perform a variety of grinding, buffing, and polishing functions.

Bench sander: a stationary stand- or bench-mounted, power tool that consists of a combination of a belt and a disk sander; used to bevel or smooth the surface or edges of wood and some plastics.

Bevel protractor: measuring device similar to the combination square except that the angle of the blade is adjustable; used for marking angles between zero and ninety degrees.

Bevel set: a measuring device similar to a tri square except that the angle between the blade and handle is adjustable; used for transferring angles from one piece of work to another.

Bidirectional: two directions; a microphone pickup pattern primarily receptive to the front and back.

Binder: an adhesive in paint that "glues" the pigment and fillers to the painted material after the vehicle has evaporated.

Bleeding: the characteristic of dyes and thinned paints to spread through cloth in the same way that water spreads through blotter paper; also known as spreading.

Blend: a combination of more than one type of fiber, blends are created to take advantage of the best properties of all fibers in the blend.

Blocking: the actors' movements on the stage.

Block out: in makeup, to cover with soap, spirit gum, wax, material, or preformed plastic film so that no hair is evident.

Block plane: a small plane with a shallow (approximately fifteen to twenty degrees) blade angle; used to smooth across the grain of wood.

Blueline: to copy drawings made on tracing vellum; the lines are printed in blue or, sometimes, in black; also known as the diazo process.

Blueprint: a drawing-reproduction technique in which the background is blue and the lines are white; frequently used as a misnomer for blueline.

Board foot: a unit of measurement equivalent to a piece of stock lumber that is twelve inches long, twelve inches wide, and one inch thick.

Board operators: the electricians who run the light board during rehearsals and performances.

Bobbinet: a transparent, open, hexagonal weave material; used as a glass substitute, diffusion drop, net backing for cutout drops, and similar applications.

Bodice: the upper part of a woman's dress.

Bogus paper: a heavy, soft, absorbent paper; similar to blotter paper.

Bolt cutter: heavy-duty shears with a great deal of leverage; used to cut through bolts and mild-steel round stock up to one-half inch in diameter.

Book: to fold hinged flats together so that they resemble a book.

Book ceiling: two large flats about the same width as the proscenium arch, stored in a booked position in the flies; when needed to create a ceiling, they are opened and lowered onto the walls of the set.

Boomerang: (1) a rolling scaffold with several levels; used for painting vertical scenery; (2) a device to hold color media in a followspot.

Borders: wide, short, framed or unframed cloth drops suspended over the stage to prevent the audience from seeing above the stage. In the Restoration theatre, borders normally matched the decorative treatment on the wings and drops. In modern practice, borders are frequently made of black, unpainted velour.

Bottom hanger iron: flying hardware; a metal strap iron with a D ring at the top and a hooked foot at the bottom; used at the bottom of heavy flats to support the load under compression.

Box: to pour paint back and forth between buckets to ensure a complete and uniform mix.

Box-end wrench: a wrench with a closed, toothed head that must be fit over the head of the bolt or nut; used to tighten bolts and nuts.

Box nail: nail with a narrower shaft than a common nail, to reduce the chance of splitting the lumber.

Brace: a hand-cranked drill used for turning auger bits; used for drilling large-diameter holes in wood.

Brace cleat: bracing hardware attached to the stile on the back of a flat to provide means for securing a stage brace to the flat.

Breathes: a term that defines a material's ability to transmit heat, air, and water vapor.

Brocade: fabric similar to damask but lighter in weight; woven patterns achieved by weaving high-luster yarn into a matte-finish background can be either raised or flat; used for making costumes, upholstery, and decorative drapery.

Bulb: the Pyrex glass or synthetic quartz container for a lamp filament and gaseous environment; synonymous with envelope.

Burn: to record on a CD.

Butcher paper: a medium-weight brown paper, available in 36-inch-wide rolls; also known by its trade name, Kraft paper.

Butt joint: a wood joint; two pieces of wood are square cut and fit together end to end, end to edge, edge to edge, end to face, or edge to face.

Butt weld: a welded metal joint; the pieces being welded are joined edge to edge.

Cabinet drawing: a type of detail drawing that subscribes to the principles of oblique drawing except that all depth measurements are reduced by one-half or some similar ratio, such as 1:4.

Call: to tell specific crew members when to perform their cues.

Capacitance: the electrical capacity of a condenser, or capacitor.

Cardioid: a heart-shaped pickup pattern that primarily picks up sounds in front of, and slightly to the sides of, the microphone.

Card stock: a thick cardboard, similar in thickness to three-by-five notecards and file folders.

Carpenter's level: a two- to three-foot piece of wooden, steel, or aluminum I beam with glass-tube spirit levels at either end and the middle; used to determine true horizontal and vertical.

Carpenter's rule: *see* folding wood rule.

Carpenter's vise: a vise for holding wood; attached to a workbench, one or both faces are covered with hardwood to prevent the vise from scratching, denting, or marring the surface of the work.

Carriage: the part of a stair unit that supports the tread and risers.

Carriage bolt: a bolt whose upper face has a rounded surface and whose underside has a slightly tapered square collar a little wider than the diameter of the bolt shaft; used to join wood to wood or wood to metal.

Cartooning: the process of transferring line work (and color blocks) from the painter's elevations to the scenery.

Casein: a natural or synthetically derived phosphoprotein—a chief component of milk.

Casein paint: a paint with a casein binder; has good covering power, is water-resistant when fully dry, and can usually be thinned with a ratio of between two and four parts water to one part paint concentrate.

Casket lock: a heavy-duty hidden lock used to hold platforms together and for similar applications.

Cassette tape: audio recorder tape, also used in computer storage.

Caster: a wheel/axle device attached to platforms and the like to make them roll; casters for theatrical use should have hard rubber tires, a load rating of at least 300 pounds, and sturdy construction.

Casting resins: any number of liquid plastics used for casting forms in molds.

Cavea: Roman term for auditorium.

C clamp: a clamp composed of a U-shaped frame with a threaded shaft; work is clamped between a pressure plate at one end of the U and the toe of the shaft; used for a wide variety of jobs, such as holding work together while parts are being assembled or while glue joints are drying.

Ceiling plate: flying hardware; a flat metal plate with an O ring in the center; attached to the primary structural members of ceiling flats to provide a means of attaching the flying lines to the ceiling.

Center line: a leader line that runs perpendicular to the set line from the midpoint or center of the opening of the proscenium arch.

Center-line sectional: a sectional drawing with the cutting plane located on the center line of the stage and auditorium; used to show the height of the various elements of the stage and theatre and any pertinent set pieces.

Center punch: a pointed tool made of hard steel; used for indenting shallow holes in wood and metal.

Centrifugal force: force that moves away from the center; for example, the circular motion of electrons spinning around a nucleus generates centrifugal force.

Chalk line: a metal or plastic housing holding a long piece of twine and filled with dry scenic pigment; used for marking straight lines.

Character: the distinctive qualities, traits, and personality of a person, place, or thing. Also, the emotional quality (e.g., soft, hard, harsh, sensuous) of a line.

Chiffon: a sheer, usually translucent, cloth frequently made from rayon or silk; used for scarves and diaphanous blouses and gowns.

Chopper: *see* shutter.

Chroma: *see* saturation.

Chuck: the adjustable jawed clamp at the end of a drill that holds the drill bits.

Circuit: a conductive path through which electricity flows; also, to connect a lighting instrument to a stage circuit.

Circuit breaker: a device to protect a circuit from an overload; it has a magnetic device that trips open to break circuit continuity.

Circular saw: a portable circular-bladed saw; the angle and depth of cut is variable; used to cross- and angle-cut as well as rip stock and plywood.

Claw hammer: a hammer with two sharply curved claws projecting from the back of its head that facilitates nail removal; used for driving nails.

Cleat: a piece of wood used to brace, block, or reinforce.

Clip art: digitized pictures that can be transferred, or clipped, from the original program into a document on which you are working.

Clothesline: a small-diameter cotton rope; not used for raising or suspending loads, but is the standard rope for lash lines and is used as the operating rope for traveling drapes (travelers).

Clout nail: a wedge-shaped nail made of soft iron used to attach cornerblocks and keystones to the frame of a flat; it is driven through the wood onto a steel backing plate, which curls the end of the nail back into the lumber.

Club: in context, refers to night clubs in which high-energy music (live or recorded) is the prime attraction.

Coated box nail: a box nail with an adhesive applied to the shaft that tightly bonds the nail to the wood.

Cobbler: one who makes shoes.

Cold chisel: a chisel made of hard steel; used for cutting or shearing mild steel and nonferrous metals.

Cold-press finish: a slight surface texture achieved by pressing paper between cold rollers; no oil residue results, so the paper can be used with transparent watercolor, designer's gouache, acrylic, markers, pencils, pastel, and so forth.

Collage: a picture made of various materials (e.g., paper, cloth) glued on a surface; can include drawn or photographic images as well.

Color: a perception created in the brain by the stimulation of the retina by light waves of certain lengths; a generic term applied to all light waves contained in the visible spectrum.

Color frame: a lightweight metal holder for color media that fits in a holder at the front of a lighting instrument.

Color media: colored plastic, gel, or glass filters used to modify the color of light.

Combination square: a twelve-inch steel rule with a movable handle angled at forty-five and ninety degrees; used for marking those two angles, and the rule can be used for measuring.

Commando: a lightweight cotton fabric with a short, feltlike, almost matted pile; available in two weights and widths, the heavy-weight is suitable for stage drapery; the material face is generally too susceptible to wear for use as an upholstery fabric; also known as duvetyn.

Common nail: nail with a large head and thick shank; used for heavier general construction.

Complementary: two hues that, when combined, theoretically yield white in light or black in pigment; colors that are opposite to each other on a color wheel. In practice, mixing complementary pigment colors results in complex dark grays, not true black.

Composition: an arrangement of parts to create a whole.

Compressor: a pump that drives air into a tank; the output pressure from the tank is controlled by a valve called a regulator.

Concert: in context, primarily refers to touring rock and country western shows.

Condensing lens: a device that condenses the direct and reflected light from a source and concentrates it on the slide-plane aperture of a projector.

Conduit: thin-wall metal (aluminum or steel) tubing; used as a housing for electrical wiring and decorative stage material.

Conduit bender: a tool for bending conduit.

Cones: nerve cells in the retina that are sensitive to bright light; they respond to red, blue, or green light.

Connecting strip: an electrical gutter or wireway that carries a number of stage circuits; the circuits terminate on the connecting strip in female receptacles.

Constructed sound: any sound created by editing, manipulating, or changing previously recorded sounds.

Construction calendar: a calendar that details when various technical elements of a production will be constructed.

Construction crew: those who build the set, move it into the theatre, and set it up on-stage.

Construction line: in a two-line-weight system, a thick line 0.5 mm thick (in pencil) or 0.020 to 0.025 inch thick (in pen).

Contact cement: an adhesive for bonding nonporous surfaces together; surfaces bond as soon as they come in contact with each other.

Continental parallel: a platform made of a folding framework of nonvariable height; the top and center supports are removable; the frame folds into a more compact unit than does the standard parallel.

Contrast: the juxtaposition of dissimilar elements.

Coping saw: a lightweight handsaw composed of a U-shaped frame with a narrow, fine-toothed (sixteen to eighteen teeth per inch) replaceable blade; used for making curvilinear cuts in thin plywood and lumber.

Corduroy: a cotton material whose pile ridges, called wales, alternate with a low-luster backing; available in a wide variety of wale widths and depths; heavier weights are used for upholstery, while lighter weights are used in costuming; waleless corduroy is similar to a short-nap velour, with similar uses.

Cornerblock: a triangular-shaped piece of quarter-inch plywood used to reinforce the joint between a stile and a rail of a flat.

Corner brace: a diagonal internal framing member that helps keep a flat square.

Corner plate: an L-shaped piece of one-sixteenth-inch galvanized steel, predrilled for use with flat-head wood screws; used to reinforce corners of doors, windows, and so on.

Corrugated fasteners: corrugated strips of metal used primarily to hold lightweight frames together.

Costume designer: person responsible for the design, visual appearance, and function of the costumes, accessories, and makeup.

Costumer: person responsible for the construction of the costumes and supervision of the costume shop.

Cotton canvas: a durable lightweight, coarse-weave material; used for covering platforms and making ground cloths.

Cotton duck: a lightweight cotton canvas; used more in costumes than scenic construction.

Cotton linters: the short hairs covering the cotton seed.

Cotton rep: a tough cotton fabric with a ribbed finish similar to a narrow, short-nap corduroy; good for stage draperies, costumes, and upholstery.

Counterweight arbor: a metal cradle that holds counterbalancing weights used in flying.

Crepe: a thin, crinkle-finished, soft cloth usually made from rayon, silk, or fine cotton; frequently used for women's blouses.

Crescent wrench: *see* adjustable-end wrench.

Crosscut saw: a handsaw with an approximately twenty-six-inch blade whose angle-sharpened teeth bend outward so that the kerf is wider than the blade; designed to cut across the grain of the wood. Crosscut saws with ten to twelve teeth per inch are suitable for most scenic purposes.

Crossover network: an electronic device that splits the signal from the amplifier into frequency ranges most appropriate for use by woofers, mid-range speakers, and tweeters.

Crowbar: a round metal bar with flattened metal claws similar to those on a claw or rip hammer on one end and a tapered wedge on the other.

Cue: a directive for action, for example, a change in the lighting.

Cure: to harden and reach full strength (in reference to adhesives).

Cut awl: a portable power saw with a reciprocating blade mounted in a swiveling head; available with a variety of blades to make intricate curvilinear cuts in materials ranging from fabric to wood, paper, and plastic.

Cut list: a list of the color media required for the lighting design for a particular production categorized by hue

and size; used to assist in ordering and cutting the color media for a lighting design.

Cutoff saw: a semiportable stand-mounted circular-bladed power saw that can be equipped with a wood or metal cutting blade for square and angle cutting of lumber or metal stock; can be set up for cutting either wood (wooden table without holding clamps) or metal (metal table with holding clamps); also known as a motorized miter box.

Cutout line: *see* silhouette.

Cutter: person who pins patterns to fabrics and cuts the material.

Cutting plane: the plane at which an object is theoretically cut to produce a sectional view.

Cyanoacrylate cement: a powerful, rapid-bonding adhesive that will bond almost anything; generically known by the trade names Super Glue, Krazy Glue, and so forth.

Cyc light: a lensless instrument with an eccentric reflector used to create a smooth wash of light on a cyc or skytab from a close distance.

Cyclorama: a large drop used to surround the stage.

Dado head: a specialty circular saw blade consisting of a set of toothed blades that sandwich a chisel-like chipper. The blades smooth-cut the outside edges of the kerf while the chipper gouges out the wood between the blades. The distance between the blades is variable; used with table and radial-arm saws.

Dado joint: a wood joint made by cutting a notch or groove in the face of one piece of lumber to receive the edge of another piece of stock.

Damask: a rich-appearing cloth with raised patterns of high-luster yarn that are normally woven into the matte finish of the background cloth; used for making costumes, upholstery, and decorative drapery.

Dart: a short, tapered seam resembling a narrow "V"; used to make clothes fit more closely.

Dead hang: to suspend without means of raising or lowering.

Decibel: a unit for expressing the intensity of sounds; an increase or decrease of one decibel is just about the smallest change in loudness that the human ear can detect.

Decking: the covering surface of a structure on which people will walk.

Decorative prop: any item that is used to enhance the setting visually but is not specifically touched by an actor, such as window curtains, pictures, doilies, table lamps, bric-a-brac, and so forth.

Demi-mask: a mask, normally mounted on a stick, that covers half the face.

Denim: a coarsely woven cotton or cotton blend twill.

Designer's cue sheet: a form used by the lighting designer to record pertinent information (dimmer levels, timing, "go" point, and so forth) about every cue in the production.

Design style: a recognizable pattern of compositional elements that provides a distinctive reflection of the social and political history of the time.

Detail drawings: drawings that describe the detail of objects. Usually drawn in a fairly large scale, normally between ¾ inch = 1 foot and 1½ inches = 1 foot.

Detailing: trim, appliqués, buttons, ribbons, braid, and so forth attached to a garment to enhance its appearance.

Diagonal cutters: pliers with beveled cutting faces on the jaw rather than flat gripping faces; used for cutting soft wire.

Diffuse: to soften the appearance of light by using a translucent filtering element to scatter the light rays.

Digital tape recording: a form of recording in which the audio information is stored on the magnetic tape as binary information rather than an analog signal.

Digitizing tablet: an electro-mechanical device that converts the pressure of a stylus on a flat plate (tablet) into binary information that can be understood by the computer.

Dimension: the relative length and width of a line.

Dimmer: an electrical device that controls the intensity of a light source connected to it.

Dimmer circuit: an electrical circuit terminating on one end at a dimmer. The other end terminates at either a patch panel or onstage. Synonymous with stage circuit when it terminates onstage.

Director: person responsible for interpreting the script, creating a viable production concept, and directing the actors.

Discrete: separate and complete; in context, pertaining to information represented by binary code.

Distress: to create a worn or aged appearance as with fabric, wood, or metal.

Double-headed nails: nails with two heads; they are driven into the wood until the lower head is flush with the surface, leaving the upper head exposed so that it can be pulled out easily; used for scaffolding or any temporary structure that needs to be dismantled quickly.

Double plano-convex lens train: two plano-convex lenses placed with their curved surfaces facing each other; creates a system that has a shorter focal length than either of its component lenses.

Double whip: a block and tackle configuration that provides a 2:1 mechanical advantage.

Douser: a mechanical dimming device used in followspots.

Dowel: a short cylinder of hardwood, usually birch.

Doweled joint: a butt joint that is internally supported by dowel pegs.

Drape: a vertical element of heavy fabric that frames the sides of a window or an archway.

Draw to scale: to produce a likeness that is a proportional reduction of an object.

Dremel tool: a hand-held router similar to a dentist's drill that can be equipped with a number of bits for grinding, cutting, or carving of wood, metal, and plastic.

Dress: to place decorative props such as curtains, doilies, knickknacks, or magazines on the set to help make the environment look lived in and provide clues to the personalities of the characters who inhabit the set. Also, to work with hair or a wig to create a specific style or look.

Dressers: costume-crew personnel who assist actors in putting on their costumes.

Dress rehearsal: a run-through with all technical elements, including costumes and makeup.

Drill press: a stationary bench or stand-mounted power drill with a variety of speeds. The chuck will generally hold bits up to one-half inch in diameter.

Drop: a large expanse of cloth, usually muslin or scenic canvas, on which something (a landscape, sky, street, room) is usually painted.

Drop box: a small connecting strip, generally containing four to eight circuits, that can be clamped to a boom or a pipe.

Dry brushing: a painting technique frequently used to create a wood-grain appearance; done by lightly charging a brush and lightly stroking it across the surface of the work.

Ducted-port speaker enclosure: a speaker enclosure similar in operational theory to the bass-reflex enclosure except that a tube of specific diameter and length is substituted for the open hole, or port; it reinforces bass frequencies.

Dust mask: a device covering the nose and mouth that filters particulate matter from the air.

Dutchman: a five- to six-inch-wide strip of cloth of the same material as the flat covering; used to hide the joints between flats in a wall unit.

Duvetyn: *see* commando.

Effects head: a motor-driven unit capable of producing crude moving images with a scenic projector.

Electric: any pipe that is used to hold lighting instruments.

Electrical current: the flow or movement of electrons through a conductor.

Electrical potential: the difference in electrical charge between two bodies; measured in volts.

Electric glue pot: a thermostatically controlled pot used for melting animal glue.

Electric hand drill: a portable, hand-held power drill; some models have variable-speed and reverse controls; it generally accepts bit shanks up to three-eighths of an inch in diameter.

Electricians: those who work on the stage lighting for a production.

Electrician's cue sheet: a form used by the board operator that contains the primary operating instructions for every lighting cue in the production.

Electricity: a directed flow of electrons used to create kinetic energy.

Electric screwdriver: a portable, hand-held power tool that resembles an electric hand drill; equipped with a variable-speed motor, a clutch, and a chuck that holds a screwdriver tip; used to insert and remove screws.

Electron: a negatively charged fundamental particle that orbits around the nucleus of an atom.

Electronics: the field of science and engineering concerned with the behavior and control of electrons within devices and systems, and the utilization of those systems.

Ellipsoidal reflector floodlight: a lensless instrument with a conical ellipse reflector; used for lighting cycs and drops; also known as a scoop.

Ellipsoidal reflector spotlight: a lighting instrument characterized by hard-edged light with little diffusion; designed for long throws, it is manufactured with fixed and variable focal-length lenses; the light beam is shaped with internally mounted shutters.

Emery cloth: fabric whose surface has been coated with abrasive grit; used for smoothing wood, metal, and plastic.

Enamel: an oil-, lacquer-, or synthetic-base paint that has a hard surface and excellent covering power. It is usually formulated so that it dries with a smooth satin or gloss finish.

Envelope: the Pyrex glass or synthetic quartz container for a lamp filament and gaseous environment; synonymous with bulb.

Epoxy: an extremely strong, waterproof plastic most frequently used in the theatre as an adhesive and casting resin.

Epoxy-resin adhesive: a two-part epoxy-base adhesive available in a variety of formulations that enable the user to do gluing, filling, and painting.

Equalizer: an electronic device that selectively boosts or attenuates specific frequencies or ranges of frequencies.

Eyebrow mask: a thin piece of plastic film or latex glued over the eyebrow; also known as an eyebrow block.

Fader: a device, usually electronic, that effects a gradual changeover from one circuit to another; in lighting it changes the intensity of one or more dimmer circuits; in sound it changes audio circuits or channels.

False proscenium: a rigid framework covered with drapery material that is used to adjust the height and width of the proscenium arch. Sometimes unframed drapes are used to create a false proscenium.

Felt: a material made by matting together short fibers by the use of heat, water, and light pressure.

Ferrule: the metal part of a brush that binds the bristles to the handle.

Field angle: that point where the light output diminishes to 10 percent of the output of the center of the beam.

Filament: the light-producing element of a lamp; usually made of tungsten wire.

Filler: a material that creates opacity (covering power) in paint.

Filler rod: a metal piece of the same composition as the material being welded; used to replace the metal lost during welding or to fill a hole or groove in the work.

Fillet weld: a welded metal joint; made when the edge of one piece is welded to the face of another; both sides of the joint should be welded.

Fill light: the light or lights that fill the shadows created by the key light.

Finish nail: a nail with a slender shaft and minute head; designed to be driven below the surface of the wood so that the nail head can be hidden.

First electric: the onstage pipe for lighting instruments that is closest, from the onstage side, to the proscenium arch.

Five-quarter lumber: a specialty lumber, straight grained and free from knots, that is 1¼ inches thick.

Fixture: *see* lighting instrument.

Flange weld: a welded metal joint; similar to a butt weld, except the edges of the material are bent up; the weld is made by melting the upturned flanges.

Flannel: a lightweight, loosely woven material usually made from soft-finish wool, wool blend, or cotton thread; used for men's and women's suits, trousers, and shirts.

Flat: a framework, normally made of wood or metal; usually covered with fabric, although a variety of other covering materials may be used.

Flat-head wood screw: common screw with a flat head that is beveled on the underside to easily dig into the wood; used for attaching hardware (hinges, doorknobs) and joining various wood elements together.

Flexible glue: animal glue with glycerine added.

Floor line: the base of the vertical plane in a perspective drawing. For a proscenium sketch, it is usually drawn across the stage in contact with the upstage edge of the proscenium arch; in a thrust drawing, it is normally placed just outside the auditorium end of the thrust; in an arena sketch, it is usually placed in the aisle closest to the observer.

Floor plate: bracing hardware; a block of wood with a nonskid material (foam, rubber) attached to the bottom; the foot of a stage brace is attached to the top of the floor plate, and weights (sandbags, counterweights) are piled on to keep it from moving.

Floor pocket: a connecting box, usually containing three to six circuits, whose top is mounted flush with the stage floor.

Floppy disk: a thin piece of plastic coated with metal oxide, used to record the information stored in a computer's memory.

Fluorocarbons: a family of tough, durable, low-friction, nonstick plastics best known by the trade name Teflon; used in the theatre as a bearing surface where its slippery qualities can be used to advantage.

Flush: smooth, level, even.

Flux: a chemical that reduces surface oxidation and thus aids in soldering or welding.

Fly: to raise an object or person above the stage floor with ropes or cables.

Fly cyc: a single drop, hung on a U-shaped pipe, that surrounds the stage on three sides.

Fly gallery: the elevated walkway where the pin rail is located.

Fly loft: the open space above the stage where the scenery and equipment are flown.

Focal length: the distance from the lens at which light rays converge to a point; for lenses used in stage lighting instruments, the focal length is usually measured in even inches.

Focus: to direct light from the lighting instruments to a specific area.

Folding wood rule: a six-foot wooden rule, composed of twelve segments that fold into a unit seven and a half inches long; used for measuring lumber in scenic construction.

Followspot: a lighting instrument with a high-intensity, narrow beam; mounted in a stand that allows it to tilt and swivel so that the beam can "follow" an actor.

Font: a particular style or design of typeface.

Forced perspective: a process that creates apparent depth in a set by angling the horizontal line.

Foreshortening: representing the lines of an object as shorter than they actually are in order to give the illusion of proper relative size.

Form: space enclosed within a line or lines that meet or cross; also, elements that have similar physical characteristics, such as arena theatres, thrust stages, proscenium stages, and so forth.

Found theatre spaces: structures originally designed for some other purpose that have been converted into performing spaces.

Framing square: a large steel L, typically sixteen inches on the bottom leg and twenty-four inches on the vertical leg; used for checking the accuracy of ninety-degree corner joints.

Free electron: an electron that has broken away from its "home" atom to float free.

French enamel varnish (FEV): made by dissolving aniline dye in alcohol and mixing that (one part to one part) with white shellac which has been reduced somewhat with alcohol.

Frequency: the rate at which an object vibrates; measured in hertz (cycles per second).

Fresnel lens: a type of step lens with the glass cut away from the convex face of the lens.

Fresnel spotlight: a spotlight that produces a soft, diffused light; the Fresnel lens is treated on the plano side to diffuse the light.

Front elevation: a front view of each wall segment of the set, including all detail such as windows, doors, pictures, and trim.

Front-of-house: the area in an auditorium that is close to the stage.

Front projection screen: an opaque, highly reflective, usually white material used to reflect a projected image; the projector is placed on the audience side of the screen.

Full-scale drawings: scale drawings made actual size.

Functional model: a three-dimensional thumbnail sketch of a scenic design; normally built on a scale of one-quarter or one-half inch to one foot; usually made from file folders or similar cardboard; also known as a white model.

Funnel: an accessory for a Fresnel spotlight that masks the beam to create a circular pattern. Also called a snoot or top hat.

Fuse: a device to protect a circuit from an overload; it has a soft metal strip that melts, breaking circuit continuity.

Garbage paint: any paint left over from previous paint jobs; the various paints are mixed and neutralized to create a medium gray or light-brown hue; frequently used for a prime coat.

Gel: (1) to put a color filter into a color frame and insert it in the color-frame holder of a lighting instrument. (2) generic name for the color media used in lighting instruments.

Gesso: plaster of paris in liquid state; approximately the consistency of sour cream; dries to a hard plaster finish.

Glaze: a transparent, usually lightly tinted, slightly glossy coating.

Gloss: highly reflective, mirrorlike.

Gobo: a thin metal template inserted into an ellipsoidal reflector spotlight to create a shadow pattern of light.

Graded base coat: a base coat that gradually changes hue or value over the height or width of the painted surface.

Grand drape: the curtain that covers the opening of the proscenium arch.

Grand rag: slang synonym for grand drape.

Grand valance: a teaser or border made of the same material as the grand drape. Used in conjunction with the grand drape, it masks the scenery and equipment just upstage of the proscenium arch.

Graphic equalizer: an equalizer with individual slide controls affecting specific, usually fairly narrow, segments of the sound spectrum; so called because the position of the individual controls graphically displays a picture of the equalization of the full sound spectrum.

Graphite: a soft carbon similar to the lead in a pencil; sticks can be purchased in most art supply stores.

Grid: a network of steel I beams supporting elements of the counterweight system.

Grid transfer: transferring a design from an elevation to the scenery by use of a scale grid on the elevation and a full-scale grid on the scenery.

Grommet: a circular metal eyelet used to reinforce holes in fabric.

Grommet set: a hole punch, a small anvil, and a crimping tool; used to seat grommets.

Ground plan: a scale mechanical drawing in the form of a horizontal offset section with the cutting plane passing at whatever level, normally a height of four feet above the stage floor, required to produce the most descriptive view of the set.

Ground row: generally low, horizontal flats used to mask the base of cycs or drops; frequently painted to resemble rows of buildings, hedges, or similar visual elements.

Gusset: a triangular piece of material used to reinforce a corner joint.

Hacksaw: an adjustable frame handsaw with an extremely fine toothed (twenty to twenty-five teeth per inch) replaceable blade; used for cutting metal.

Halved joint: a wood joint made by removing half the thickness of both pieces of lumber in the area to be joined so that the thickness of the finished joint will be no greater than the stock from which it is made; also called a halved lap joint.

Hand: the quality and characteristics of a fabric that can be evaluated or defined by a sense of touch.

Hand drill: a hand-cranked device used for spinning drill bits; used for making small-diameter drill holes in wood.

Hand power grinder: a portable, hand-held version of the bench grinder; useful on pieces that are too heavy or awkward to be worked with the bench grinder.

Hand power sander: a slightly less powerful version of the hand power grinder; equipped with a flexible disk that provides backing for sanding discs of varying grit; used for rough sanding of wood, metal, and plastic.

Hand prop: a small item that is handled or carried by an actor.

Handrail: the part of the stair rail that is grabbed with the hand; supported by the banister and newel posts.

Hanger iron: flying hardware; a metal strap with a D ring at the top; the hanger iron is attached to the top or bottom of the back of a flat, one end of a line is attached to the D ring, and the other end is attached to a counterweight batten.

Hanging: the process of placing lighting instruments in their specified locations.

Hanging cards: small segments of the light plot, typically pasted onto cardboard so it can be carried in an electrician's pants pocket, that detail all of the hanging information about a specific location such as the first electric or down left boom.

Hanging crew: those responsible for the hanging, circuiting, patching, focusing, and coloring of the lighting instruments;

they are under the supervision of the master electrician.

Hanging positions: the various locations around the stage and auditorium where lighting instruments are placed.

Hang out: in this instance, hang out means that most wrinkles will disappear from the fabric if it is hung up.

Hang tag: the small label usually attached to the cardboard core of a bolt of fabric that indicates the percentages of various component fibers.

Hardboard: generic term for composition sheet goods such as Masonite and particle board.

Hard teaser: the horizontal element of the false proscenium; usually hung from a counterweighted batten so that its height can easily be adjusted.

Hardware: the physical elements of the computer and the various electronic equipment, printed circuit boards, and so forth inside the computer.

Harmonics: frequencies that are exact multiples of a fundamental pitch or frequency.

Harmony: a sense of blending and unity that is achieved when the various parts of a design fit together to create an orderly, congruous whole.

Head: (1) a housing that holds scenic-projector lenses in fixed positions to project images of a specific size; (2) a high-quality electromagnet on a tape deck or tape recorder that is used to implant, retrieve, or erase electrical data from audio tapes.

Head block: a multisheave block with two or more pulley wheels, used to change the direction of all the ropes or cables that support the batten.

Header: a small flat that can be placed between two standard-sized flats to create a doorway or window.

Heat gun: a high-temperature air gun, visually similar to a hand-held hair dryer.

Heat welding: the use of a heat gun to fuse two pieces of plastic.

Heavy-duty hand drill: similar to the electric hand drill, but with a heavier-duty motor; the chuck will generally accept bit shanks up to one-half inch in diameter.

Hinged-foot iron: bracing hardware similar to the rigid foot iron but hinged so that it can fold out of the way for storage.

Hole saws: saw-toothed cylinders of hardened steel with a drill bit in the center that is used to center the saw in the work; used with a power drill to make holes from three-quarters of an inch to two inches in diameter in wood that is one and a half inches thick or less.

Home page: a site or addressable location on the Internet which contains information about (generally) a particular service, interest group, resource, or business.

Homespun: a coarse, loosely woven material usually made from cotton, linen, or wool.

Honeycomb paper: a manufactured paper product with a hexagonal structure similar to a honeycomb.

Hookup sheet: a sheet containing pertinent information (hanging position, circuit, dimmer, color, lamp wattage, focusing notes) about every lighting instrument used in the production. Also known as an instrument schedule.

Horizon line: in perspective drawing, a line representing the meeting of the earth and the sky; normally drawn parallel to the top or bottom edge of the paper.

Horizontal offset section: a section drawing with a horizontal cutting plane; the cutting plane does not remain fixed—it varies to provide views of important details.

Horn: a dispersion device attached to the front of a pressure driver to direct the sound emitted by the pressure driver into a specific pattern.

Hot-melt glue gun: a hand-held electric tool that heats sticks of adhesive to make rapid-hold bonds on a wide range of materials, such as wood, plastic, paper, cloth, metal, dirt, sand, and so forth.

Hot mirror: a glass dichroic filter that reflects the infrared spectrum while allowing visible light to pass.

Hot-press finish: a slick, smooth texture achieved by pressing paper between hot rollers; this treatment leaves a thin layer of oil, which makes the paper unsuitable for use with transparent watercolor. It works well with designer's gouache, acrylic, pencils, and markers.

Hot spot: an intense circle of light created when a projector lens is seen through a rear projection screen.

Hot-wire cutter: a tool for cutting foam; it consists of a wire that is heated to incandescence.

House: synonym for auditorium.

Hue: the qualities that differentiate one color from another.

Hypercardioid: a directional, narrow, elongated cardioid pickup pattern that all but eliminates pickup from anywhere except directly in front of, and for a short distance immediately behind, the microphone.

Illustration board: watercolor paper mounted on pressboard backing.

Image of light: a picture or concept of what the light should look like for a production.

Immersion heater: an electric heater that can be immersed in a bucket of liquid to heat it; used for heating water for starch mixtures, aniline dye, flameproofing solutions, and so forth.

Impact wrench: a power-driven tool that uses sockets to tighten or loosen bolts or nuts; may be either electric or pneumatic.

Impedance: resistance in an AC circuit; the only difference between impedance and resistance is that impedance is defined as resistance to the flow of an alternating current.

Improved stage screw: bracing hardware; an improved version of the stage screw consisting of a steel plug, threaded on the outside and inside, that is inserted into an appropriately sized hole drilled into the stage floor. The screw screws into the plug, and the plug can be removed and a piece of dowel inserted into the floor to fill the hole.

Infinite-baffle speaker enclosure: an airtight, heavily insulated box that absorbs the sound waves produced by the rearward excursion speaker; it is inefficient and requires a high-wattage amplifier to achieve satisfactory sound levels.

Inner above: the elevated area located directly above the inner below in the Elizabethan theatre.

Inner below: the curtained area at the upstage edge of the playing area in the Elizabethan theatre.

Instrument schedule: a form used to record all of the technical data about each instrument used in the production; also known as a hookup sheet.

Intensity: the relative loudness of a sound.

Iris: a device with movable overlapping metal plates, used with an ellipsoidal reflector spotlight to change the size of the circular pattern of light.

Irregular flat: a flat having nonsquare corners.

Isometric drawing: a scaled mechanical drawing that presents a pictorial view of an object on three axes; the primary axis is perpendicular to the base line and the other two project from its base, in opposite directions, thirty degrees above the base line.

Jack: a triangular brace.

Jog: a flat less than two feet wide.

Joists: parallel beams that support flooring.

Kerf: the width of the cut made by a saw blade.

Keyhole saw: a handsaw with a narrow, tapering blade of ten to twelve teeth per inch; used for making curvilinear cuts in plywood and lumber.

Key light: the brightest light on a particular scene.

Keystone: a wedge or rectangular-shaped piece of quarter-inch plywood used to reinforce the joint between a stile and toggle bar of a flat.

Keystoning: the linear distortion created when a projector is placed on some angle other than perpendicular to the projection surface.

Lacquer: refined shellac or varnish with quick-drying additives.

Lag screw: large wood screw with a hexagonal or square head; used in situations where bolts are not practical, such as attaching something to a wall or floor.

Laminate: to build up an object from several layers.

Lap joint: a wood joint made when the faces of two pieces of wood are joined.

Lap weld: a welded metal joint; made when the pieces being welded are overlapped.

Lashing: a method of joining scenery; a piece of quarter-inch cotton clothesline (lash line) is served around special hardware on adjoining flats to hold them together.

Lash-line cleat: lashing hardware secured so that the pointed end projects over the inside edge of the stile.

Lash-line eye: lashing hardware with a hole through which the lash line passes, attached to the inside edge of the stile.

Lash-line hook: used for same purposes as a lash-line cleat, but has a hook instead of a point; used on extra-wide stiles or in situations that preclude the use of a lash-line cleat.

Latch keeper: see S hook.

Latex: a natural or synthetic liquid plastic with the flexible qualities of natural latex or rubber; bonds well and is flexible.

Latex cement: a milky-white flexible cement.

Latex paint: a paint with a latex binder; has fair to good covering power, may or may not be water-resistant, and can be thinned very little, usually no more than one pint of water per gallon of paint.

Lathe: a stationary, stand- or bench-mounted, variable-speed power tool that rapidly spins wood so that it can be carved with the use of special chisels. Can be used to turn foam.

Leader line: in a two-line-weight system, a thin line 0.3 mm thick (in pencil) or 0.010 to 0.0125 inch thick (in pen).

Leaf: the movable flap of a hinge.

Legitimate theatre: refers to plays that rely on the spoken word to convey the message. Does not include musicals, reviews, dance, opera, or concerts.

Legs: narrow, vertical stage drapes used for masking.

Lensless projector: a projector that works by projecting a shadow image without a lens, such as the Linnebach and curved-image projectors.

Life: in rendering, the qualities of brilliance, visual depth, and sparkle.

Life mask: a plaster mask of a person's face. A negative mold is made by covering the person's face with plaster of paris or alginate. The negative mold is used to make a positive cast that is the life mask.

Lift jack: a jack equipped with swivel casters, used to pick up and move platforms.

Lighting area: a cylindrical space approximately eight to twelve feet in diameter and seven feet high; lighting areas are located within acting areas to facilitate creating a smooth wash of light within the acting area.

Lighting cue: generally, some type of action involving lighting; usually the raising or lowering of the intensity of one or more lighting instruments.

Lighting designer: person responsible for the appearance of the lighting during the production.

Lighting grid: a network of pipes, usually connected in a grid pattern, from which lighting instruments and other equipment can be hung.

Lighting instrument: a device that produces a controllable light; for example, an ellipsoidal reflector spotlight or a Fresnel spotlight.

Lighting key: a drawing that illustrates the plan angle and color of the various sources that are illuminating the image of light.

Lighting rehearsal: a run-through, without actors, attended by the director, stage manager, lighting designer, and appropriate running crews to look at the intensity, timing, and placement of the various lighting cues.

Lighting sectional: a composite side view, drawn in scale, of the set showing the hanging position of the instruments in relation to the physical structure of the theatre, set, and stage equipment.

Lighting template: a guide for use in drawing lighting symbols.

Light plot: a scale drawing showing the placement of the lighting instruments relative to the physical structure of the theatre and the location of the set.

Line: the wires in low-voltage control systems; frequently called "lines" rather than "wires."

Line level: a signal voltage range, approximately .75 to 1 volt; specified as a voltage range rather than one particular voltage because the voltage and current of the signal vary with the intensity and frequency of the sound.

Linen canvas: an excellent flat-covering material; extremely durable, it accepts paint very well and doesn't shrink much; expensive.

Line of vision: the vertical line drawn from OP to the floor line in a perspective grid; it represents the line of sight from the observer to the vertical plane.

Liner: in makeup, any saturated color that is used as rouge, as eye shadow, or to create other areas of highlight or shadow.

Lining: painting narrow, straight lines; done with lining brushes and a straightedge.

Livery: identifiable clothing associated with a specific occupation or trade.

Load: a device that converts electrical energy into another form of energy: A lamp converts electrical energy to light and heat; an electric motor converts electricity to mechanical energy.

Load-in: the moving of scenery and associated equipment into the theatre and their positioning (setup) on the stage.

Loading platform: a walkway suspended just below the grid where the counterweights are loaded onto the arbor.

Locking pliers: generally known by the trade name Vise Grip, locking pliers are available in a wide variety of sizes and configurations; used for gripping and holding, the size of the jaw opening and amount of pressure applied by the jaws are adjustable by the screw at the base of the handle.

Locking rail: a rail that holds the rope locks for each counterweight set.

Loft block: a grooved pulley mounted on top of the grid, used to change the direction in which a rope or cable travels.

Long-nose pliers: pliers with long tapering jaws; used for holding small items and bending very light wire; also called needle-nose pliers.

Loudspeaker: a transducer used to convert an electrical signal from an amplifier into audible sound.

Luan: also known as Philippine mahogany; one-eighth-inch luan plywood is strong and quite flexible; commonly used as a flat-covering material and for covering curved-surface forms.

MAC: the hardware, operating systems/software, and peripherals based on the Apple Macintosh computer.

Machine bolt: bolt with a square or hexagonal head used to attach metal to metal.

Machinist's vise: a vise with toothed steel faces; used to hold and clamp metal; can be used to hold wood, but the serrated steel faces will mar the surface unless protective blocks of wood are used to sandwich the work.

Main drape: synonym for grand drape.

Mallet: a hammer with a wooden, plastic, or rubber head; the wooden and plastic mallets are generally used for driving chisels; all three can be used for shaping thin metal.

Managing director: person responsible for the business functions of a theatrical production company—fund raising, ticket sales, box office management.

Manila rope: a strong, yet flexible rope; used in the theatre for raising and suspending loads and as the operating line for counterweight systems.

Mansions: small scenic representations of the standard locations (heaven, hell, garden, palace, etc.) used in medieval plays.

Margin line: an extra-heavyweight line that forms a border for the plate one-half inch in from the edge of the paper.

Mask: to block the audience's view—generally, of backstage equipment and space.

Masonite: a registered trade name for a sheet stock made from binder-impregnated wood pulp compressed into four-by-eight-foot sheets.

Mass: the three-dimensional manifestation of form.

Master electrician: person responsible for ensuring that the lighting equipment is hung, focused, and run according to written and verbal instructions from the lighting designer.

Master seamer: person responsible for costume construction and direct supervision of costume crews.

Matte: dull, nonreflective.

Matte knife: *see* utility knife.

Mechanical perspective: a picture, in scale, drawn with drafting tools, that provides an illusion of depth.

Mechanic's hammer: a hammer with a heavy, soft metal head; used for shaping metal.

Merrow machine: a machine that, in one operation, sews a seam, cuts both pieces of fabric about one-quarter inch from the seam, and makes an overcast stitch on the edge of both pieces of fabric to prevent raveling.

Metal file: any file with very fine teeth; used for smoothing metal.

Microcassette tape: audio recorder tape for use in small cassettes; used in computer storage.

Microphone: a transducer used to convert sound waves into electrical energy.

Mid-range speaker: a speaker designed to reproduce the middle range of audible frequencies—roughly 200 to 1000 Hz.

MIG (metal inert gas) welder: a welder that focuses a flow of inert gas (usually carbon dioxide or argon) on the welding zone to prevent or reduce oxidation of the weld; the electrode is a thin piece of wire automatically fed through the welding handle from a spool stored in the housing of the power unit.

Mike: (verb) to pick up a sound with a microphone; to place one or more microphones in proximity to a sound source (instrument, voice). (noun) microphone.

Mild steel: a medium-strength, easily worked ferrous metal that is easy to weld; the metal most commonly used in stage construction.

Milliner: one who constructs and styles hats.

Miter: an angle that is cut in a piece of wood or metal, usually in pairs, to form a corner.

Miter box: a guide used with a backsaw to make accurate angle cuts in wood.

Miter joint: similar to a butt joint, but the edges to be joined are angle, rather than square, cut.

Mix: to blend the electronic signals created by several sound sources.

Mixer: an electronic device used to mix the output of a variety of sources and route the blended signal(s) on to other equipment; it can be used for both recording and playback.

Model: an object that is being used as the subject of a mold casting.

Mold: a matrix used to create a form.

Molding cutter head: a heavy cylindrical arbor in which a variety of matched cutter blades or knives can be fit; used with a table or radial-arm saw to cut decorative molding.

Monkey wrench: a heavyweight, smooth-jawed adjustable wrench for use on large nuts or work that is too large for an adjustable-end wrench.

Monofilament line: a single-strand, transparent, monofilament line; sold as fishing line in sporting goods stores; also known as trick line.

Mood: the feeling of a play—comic, tragic, happy, and so forth.

Mortise: a square hole; used in conjunction with a tenon to make a mortise and tenon joint.

Mortise and tenon joint: a wood joint made by fitting a tenon (square peg) into a mortise (square hole).

Mortise drill bit: a drill bit housed inside a square hollow chisel; used with a drill press to make square holes.

Motorized miter box: *see* cutoff saw.

Mouse: an electro-mechanical device that controls the movement of a cursor on the computer screen; used by the operator to provide directives to the computer program.

Mullion: a vertical crossbar in a window.

Multiplex: (1) to transmit two or more messages simultaneously on a single channel or wire. (2) to carry out several functions simultaneously in an independent but related manner.

Muntin: a horizontal crossbar in a window.

Muslin: a flat-surfaced, woven cotton fabric.

Nail puller: a tool with a movable jaw on one end for grasping nail heads and a movable slide hammer on the other to drive the jaws into the wood to grasp the nail; used to pull nails out.

Needle-nose pliers: *see* long-nose pliers.

Neutralization: subtractive color mixing; the selective absorption of light as the result of mixing complementary pigment hues; the creation of gray.

Neutron: a fundamental particle in the structure of the nucleus of an atom; possesses a neutral charge.

Newel post: the post at the bottom or top of a flight of stairs that terminates the handrail.

Nicopress tool: a plierlike tool that crimps Nicopress sleeves onto wire rope or cable to make permanent, nonremovable friction clamps.

Nonrepresentational design: a style in which the portrayed elements do not represent physically identifiable objects.

Nonspecific musical effect: any sound effect that does not reinforce a readily identifiable source such as a doorbell or telephone.

Notched joint: a wood joint made by cutting a notch from a piece of lumber; the size of the notch is determined by the width and thickness of the other piece of stock that the notch will receive.

Noxious: harmful to one's health.

Nucleus: the central part of an atom, composed of protons and neutrons.

Nut driver: tool similar in appearance to a screwdriver with a cylindrical socket instead of a slot or Phillips head; used for tightening small hex (six-sided) nuts.

Objective lens: a device used to focus a projected image on a screen or other surface.

Oblique drawing: a scaled mechanical drawing with one face of the object, drawn as an elevation, placed at right angles to the observer's line of sight; the remaining faces project from the elevation to the right or left using a 30- or 45-degree base line.

Ohm's Law: the law that states: As voltage increases, current increases; as resistance increases, current decreases.

Oil stone: an abrasive composite stone, usually with different grits on opposite faces; used for sharpening knives, chisels, and other cutting tools.

Omnidirectional: in all directions; a spherical microphone pickup pattern.

On 1-inch centers: the centers of adjacent elements, such as holes, are spaced 1 inch apart.

Open-end wrench: a wrench with non-adjustable U-shaped jaws on both ends; the opening between the jaws is of a specific width to grip bolts and nuts of specific diameters; used to tighten bolts and nuts.

Orchestra: the circular area on which the majority of the action of the play took place in a Greek theatre.

Orchestra pit: the space between the stage and the auditorium, usually below stage level, that holds the orchestra.

Orthographic projection: a series of elevations, drawn to scale, that show each side or face of an object.

Overlay: a garment, usually made of lace or a similar lightweight, semitransparent fabric, designed to lie on top of another garment.

Oxford cloth: a flat-surfaced cotton or cotton-blend material frequently used for making shirts.

Oxidation: a chemical reaction between metal and air that forms a thin, discolored "skin" over the work that effectively prevents heat transfer. Oxidation adversely affects the strength and conductivity of both soldered and welded joints.

Pageant wagon: a staging convention used during the medieval period. Basically, a bare platform backed with a plain curtain mounted on a wagon. The wagon could be pulled from town to town.

Paint chip: a small rectangle of paper or thin cardboard painted in a specific hue.

Paint crew: persons responsible for painting the scenery and properties; they are under the supervision of the scenic artist.

Painter's elevations: elevations of a set painted to show the palette and painting styles to be used on the actual set.

Pan: to rotate an object about its vertical axis.

Paper clad: both sides covered with paper.

Papier-mâché: a process of building up a form by laminating wheat-paste-soaked strips of newspaper; also available commercially in a powdered form to make a paste suitable for forming in molds.

Parametric equalizer: an equalizer in which individual frequencies or custom-designed bands of frequencies can be programmed for boost or attenuation.

Paraskenia: long, high walls that extended on either side of and parallel with the skene of the Greek theatre.

PAR can: a holder for a parabolic aluminized reflector (PAR) lamp; creates a powerful punch of light with a soft edge; the PAR 64 is commonly used for concert lighting.

Particle board: a sheet stock composed of small wood chips and sawdust mixed with a glue binder and compressed into four-by-eight-foot sheets; it is quite brittle, so it cannot be used as a load-bearing surface.

Patch: to connect a stage circuit to a dimmer circuit.

Patch bay: a cross-connect or patch panel for sound.

Patch panel: an interconnecting device that allows one to connect any stage circuit to any dimmer.

Pattern maker: person who makes patterns based on information contained in the costume designer's sketch, notes, and instructions.

PC: the hardware, operating systems/software, and peripherals based on the IBM personal computer (PC).

Perspective-view base line: the bottom edge of a perspective drawing.

Phillips-head screwdriver: *see* screwdriver.

Photomontage: a composite picture made by combining several separate pictures; can include nonphotographic images as well.

Piano wire: extremely strong wire made from spring steel; frequently used for flying scenery because of its strength; should not be sharply bent as this significantly reduces its strength.

Picture-frame stage: a configuration in which the spectators watch the action of the play through a rectangular opening; synonym for proscenium arch stage.

Picture hook and eye: hooks and eyes that facilitate rapid hanging and removal of decorative draperies.

Piezoelectricity: voltage produced when pressure is placed on certain crystals.

Pig: a loosely woven bag containing powdered eraser material.

Pigment: material that imparts color to a substance such as paint or dye.

Pilot hole: *see* starter hole.

Pinch bar: a flattened metal bar configured like a crowbar.

Pin rail: a horizontal pipe or rail studded with belaying pins; the ropes of the rope-set system are wrapped around the belaying pins to hold the batten at a specific height.

Pipe: a counterweighted batten or fixed metal pipe that holds lighting instruments.

Pipe clamp: a threaded pipe with a movable end plate and an adjustable head plate; used for clamping furniture frames and similar wide objects. A bar clamp is similar except that a notched bar is substituted for the pipe.

Pipe cutter: a tool used for making clean right-angle cuts through steel tubing of half-inch and larger diameters.

Pipe wrench: similar in shape to the monkey wrench, the pipe wrench has jaws that are serrated to bite into the soft metal of pipes; used for holding or twisting pipes and their associated couplings.

Pit: (1) the ground in front of the stage where the lower-class audience stood to watch the play in Elizabethan theatres; (2) in twentieth-century theatres, a commonly used abbreviation for orchestra pit.

Pitch (print): the size of a particular typeface.

Pitch (sound): the characteristic tone produced by a vibrating body; the higher the frequency of vibration, the higher the pitch.

Pixel: a picture element; the smallest discrete part of an electronically projected picture, as on a computer monitor.

Plan angle: the ground-plan view of an object.

Plane: a knife-edged tool used to smooth or round the edges or corners of wood.

Plano-convex lens: a lens with one flat and one outward-curving face.

Plaster line: in drafting, a leader line extending across the opening of the proscenium arch.

Plate: a sheet of mechanical drawings, drawn to scale.

Platea: the open acting area in front of the mansions of the medieval stage.

Playback system: devices used to play recorded sound; usually composed of some combination of a turntable, a tape deck, a CD player, or a computer; an equalizer; an amplifier; and a speaker.

Playwright: person who develops and writes the script.

Plotter: a printer used to produce computer-generated drafting sheets and drawings on large paper.

Plug: a wooden insert used to replace a knothole or other imperfection in the surface layer of a sheet of plywood.

Plush: fabric similar to velveteen but with softer and longer pile; common drapery and upholstery fabric.

Plywood: a sheet stock made by laminating several layers of wood; its superior strength is created by alternating each successive layer so that its grain lies at a ninety-degree angle to the layers immediately above and below it.

Pneumatic nailer: a compressed-air-powered tool similar in appearance to a pneumatic stapler but using clips of adhesive-coated nails rather than staples.

Pneumatic stapler: a compressed-air-powered stapler capable of driving staples with legs up to one and one-half inches long; adhesive-coated staples are generally used for assembling flat frames, putting tops on platforms, and similar functions.

Pointing and clicking: pointing: using a mouse to move the on-screen cursor to a specific location; clicking: using a button on the mouse to initiate an action. Thus, "pointing and clicking" refers to using a mouse to initiate a specific action.

Polyethylene: a class of plastics that, in solid form, have a characteristically slick, waxy surface; polyethylene film is frequently used as a drop cloth and can be used as a projection surface; polyethylene foam, generally known by the trade name Ethafoam, is flexible and is available in sheets, rods, and tubes.

Polystyrene: a class of plastics with a variety of formulations useful in theatrical production; high-impact polystyrene sheeting has a hard surface and is moderately flexible, fairly strong, and somewhat brittle. It is used in vacuum forming; polystyrene foam is commonly known by the trade name Styrofoam; it is available in sheets and is frequently used as decorative trim.

Polyvinyl chloride: a family of plastics that are, in solid form, characteristically strong, lightweight, and rigid; PVC water pipe can be used for a variety of functional and decorative purposes; also available in sheet, rod, and other forms.

Polyvinyl glue: a white liquid adhesive that resembles white glue; has excellent adhesion to porous surfaces and good flexibility.

Pop riveter: a tool used to secure rivets in thin metal.

Position: relative placement of objects within a composition.

Potential: the difference in electrical charge between two bodies; measured in volts.

Power amplifier: *see* amplifier.

Power hacksaw: a stationary power tool for cutting metal; a horizontal reciprocating metal-cutting blade is used to cut through various types of metal stock.

Power pipe cutter: a stationary stand-mounted power tool for cutting and threading metal pipes with diameters from approximately one-half to two inches.

Preamplifier: an electronic device that boosts the level of a signal, without alteration or reshaping, to the requisite input signal level of the next piece of equipment in a sound system.

Preset sheet: a form used by the electrician to record the intensity levels for each dimmer during major shifts in the lighting.

Pressing cloth: a cloth placed between the iron and the fabric being pressed.

Pressure driver: a unit housing a large magnet that vibrates a thin metallic diaphragm to create mid-range and high-frequency sounds.

Primary colors: hues that cannot be derived or blended from any other hues. In light the primaries are red, blue, and green; in pigment the primary colors are red, blue, and yellow.

Prime coat: the first layer of paint; applied to all elements of the scenery to provide a uniform base for the rest of the paint job.

Producer: person who selects the script, finds financial backing, and hires all production personnel.

Production concept: the creative interpretation of the script, which will unify the artistic vision of the production design team.

Production design team: the producer, director, and scenic, costume, lighting, and sound designers who, working together, develop the visual/aural concept for the production.

Production manager: coordinator of production scheduling and administrative/logistic details of a multishow theatrical season.

Production meeting: a conference of appropriate production personnel to share information.

Production model: a scale model similar to a functional model but fully painted and complete with furniture and decorative props.

Production style: a recognizable pattern of elements, both visual and intellectual, based on social and political history, used to create the environment for the production of a particular play.

Production team: everyone working, in any capacity, on the production of a play.

Profile: *see* silhouette.

Prompt book: a copy of the script with details about each actor's blocking as well as the location, timing, and, as necessary, action, of all set, prop, light, and sound cues.

Propane torch: an open-flame torch powered by propane gas; used for heavy-duty soldering and heat shaping of thin-gauge steel.

Properties: such elements as furniture, lamps, pictures, table linens, bric-a-brac, and window draperies that provide the finished set with visual character.

Property crew: those who construct or acquire all props and run (organize, shift, store) props during rehearsals and performances.

Property master: one responsible for the design, construction, and finishing of all properties.

Prop table: a table, normally located in the wings, on which hand props are stored between onstage use.

Proscenium: a stage configuration in which the spectators watch the action through a rectangular opening (the proscenium arch) that resembles a picture frame.

Proskenium: a columned arch that supported a porchlike projection from the upper floor of the skene in the Greek theatre.

Prosthetic device: in makeup, a device such as a false nose, beard, or other appliance that is added to the face to change the actor's appearance.

Proton: a fundamental particle in the structure of the nucleus of an atom; possesses a positive charge.

Pull: to remove a costume from storage for use in a production.

Push-drill: a hand-powered drill that uses a springloaded shaft to spin the drill bit when one pushes downward on the handle; for light usage, it uses bits from $1/64$ to $3/16$ inch in diameter; useful for making starter holes.

Push-drill bits: steel bits with sharp points and straight fluted indentations running up the sides of the shaft; used with the push drill to drill narrow holes ($1/64$ to $3/16$ inch in diameter) in wood.

Pyroxylin: Celastic is the trade name for a pyroxylin-impregnated felt material that becomes extremely limp when dipped in acetone; when the acetone evaporates, the pyroxylin stiffens the felt so that it will hold its molded shape.

Quadraphonic: a sound system composed of four discrete sound channels.

Quality: the nature or intrinsic properties (e.g., straight, curved, jagged) of a line.

Radial-arm saw: a circular-bladed stationary power saw; the motor and blade are suspended from an arm above a table; the height and angle of the blade are adjustable. Primarily used for cross and angle cutting, this versatile saw can be used for ripping and trim molding as well.

Rail: a top or bottom framing member of a flat.

Raked stage: a stage that is higher at the back than the front.

Ratchet winch: a device used for hoisting that consists of a crank attached to a drum. One end of a rope or cable is attached to the drum, the other end to the load; turning the crank moves the load; a ratchet gear prevents the drum from spinning backward.

Rat-tail file: a file with a circular cross-sectional configuration; depending on surface finish it can be used for smoothing wood, metal, or plastic; also known as a round file.

Rear elevations: scale mechanical drawings that show the back of flats depicted on front elevations.

Rear projection screen: translucent projection material designed to transmit the image through the projection surface; the projector is placed in back of the screen.

Related colors: *see* analogous colors.

Representational design: a style in which the portrayed elements represent some recognizable object, such as a room, a forest, or a street corner.

Resistance: the oppositon to electron flow within a conductor, measured in ohms; the amount of resistance depends in part on the chemical makeup of the material through which the electricity is flowing.

Respirator: a mask covering the nose and mouth that filters out gases as well as particulate matter; the type of filtering medium used determines the type of gases removed from the air.

Reverberate: to reflect in a series of echoes.

Reverberation: a multiple reflection of a sound that persists for some time after the original source has decayed.

Revolve: large, circular platform that pivots on its central axis; also called turntable.

Revolving stage: generally refers to a revolve that is built into the stage floor as part of a theatre's permanent equipment.

Rhythm: the orderly and logical interrelationship of successive parts in a composition.

Rigid caster: a caster that cannot swivel or rotate.

Rigid foot iron: bracing hardware; an L-shaped piece of metal, one leg attached to the bottom of the flat, the other secured to the floor with a stage screw that is inserted through the ring at the end of the leg.

Rip bar: tool similar to a crowbar, but the nail-removing claws have more curl for better leverage.

Rip hammer: a hammar with two relatively straight claws projecting from the back of its head that can be used for prying or ripping apart previously nailed wood; used for driving nails.

Rip saw: a handsaw with an approximately twenty-six-inch blade whose chisel-sharpened teeth bend outward so that the kerf is wider than the blade; designed to cut parallel with the grain of the wood. Rip saws have fewer teeth per inch than a crosscut saw has.

Riser: the vertical face of a stair.

RMS wattage rating: a system (root-mean-square) providing an accurate picture of the energy-dissipation characteristics of sound equipment.

Rods: nerve cells in the retina that are sensitive to faint light.

Rope set: a counterbalanced flying system in which ropes are used to fly the scenery. Sandbags are tied to the offstage end of the ropes to counterbalance the weight of the scenery.

Rough finish: a pebble-grained texture achieved by cold-pressing paper with a texture roller or by other techniques; suitable for painted and pastel renderings having little intricate detail; can be worked with other media as well.

Roundel: a glass color medium for use with striplights; frequently has diffusing properties.

Round file: *see* rat-tail file.

Round-head wood screw: screw with a head that has a flat underside and a rounded upper surface; used when having the top of the screw flush with the surface of the work is not desirable, as when attaching thin metal or fabric to a wood frame.

Router: a portable, hand-held power tool that uses a chisel-like rotating bit (25,000 RPM) to shape or carve the surface or edge of the piece of wood; primarily used for shaping decorative moldings and trim pieces.

RTV (room temperature vulcanizing) silicone rubber: a compound used to make flexible molds.

Running: controlling or operating some aspect of production.

Running block: a block and tackle system that provides a 2:1 mechanical advantage.

Running crew: those responsible for operating lighting equipment and shifting scenery and props during rehearsals and performances.

Saber saw: a portable power saw with a reciprocating blade; used for making curvilinear cuts in wood and plastic.

Sandpaper: paper whose surface has been coated with abrasive grit; used for smoothing wood and plastic.

Satin: a stiff, heavy fabric with a smooth, shiny finish on the front and a dull finish on the back; if patterned, the design is usually printed on rather than woven in; used for making costumes, upholstery, and decorative drapery.

Saturated polyester: a plastic used to form the fiber from which polyester fabrics such as Dacron are made; also used to form films such as Mylar.

Saturation: the relative purity of a particular hue.

Scaenae frons: an elaborately decorated facade or wall that was located at the rear of the stage in the Roman theatre. Its historical antecedent was the skene of the Greek theatre.

Scale: a black, scaly coat that forms on iron when it is heated for processing.

Scan: to use a digitizing scanner to convert existing artwork, photos, or drawings into binary information.

Scarf joint: two boards joined lengthwise by making a shallow angle cut approximately eighteen inches long in the face of each board; the joint is secured by gluing and screwing or bolting.

Scene shop foreman: person responsible for supervising the crews who build and rig the scenery and some of the larger props.

Scenic artist: person responsible for the painting of the scenery and properties.

Scenic designer: person responsible for the design and function of the scenery and properties.

Scenic projector: a high-wattage instrument used for projecting large-format slides or moving images.

Scoop: *see* ellipsoidal reflector floodlight.

Score: to cut partially through.

Scratch awl: *see* scribe.

Screwdriver: a tool for inserting or driving screws; the standard screwdriver has a narrow blade for work with standard screws; the Phillips-head screwdriver has a four-flanged tip that matches the crossed slots of the Phillips-head screw.

Screw nail: nail with a threaded shaft that rotates as it is driven into wood; used for jobs that require greater holding power.

Scribe: a sharp metal tool used to mark wood, metal, and plastic; also called a scratch awl.

Scrim: a drop made from translucent or transparent material.

Scumbling: a blending of paints of several hues or values to create the appearance of texture; done with brushes.

Secondary colors: the result of mixing two primary colors.

Secrets: the name used to describe the stage machinery in medieval times.

Sectional: a drawing, usually in scale, of an object that shows what it would look like if cut straight through at a given plane.

Sectional angle: the angle of intersection between the axis of the cone of light emitted by an instrument and the working height—usually the height of an average actor's face (about five feet, six inches)—of the lighting areas.

Set: to prevent smearing or smudging. Once a greasepaint makeup design is finished, it is locked in place with a coating of powder.

Set line: in drafting, a leader line that extends, parallel with the proscenium arch, across the farthest downstage point(s) of the set.

Set prop: a large, movable item, not built into the set, that is used in some way by an actor, such as a sofa, floor lamp, table, and so forth.

Setting: to help lock the dye into the fiber of the fabric; to reduce or prevent the dye from being rubbed off the fabric.

Shade: a color of low value; usually created by mixing one or more hues with black.

Sharkstooth scrim: an open-weave material used to make transparent scrims.

Sheer: a thin gauze curtain that hangs across the opening of a window to soften the sunlight and obscure the view into a room.

Sheet-metal screw: a pan-head or hex-head screw used for joining sheets of metal.

Sheet stock: a generic term that applies to lumber products sold in sheet form, such as plywood, Upson board, and Masonite.

Shell: the basic form of a costume, basted or pinned together, which covers the torso, arms, and legs.

Shellac: a generally clear glossy coating made of resinous material (lac—the secretions of certain scale insects) suspended in wood alcohol; also known as spirit varnish.

Shift: to change the position of the scenery, props, or stage equipment.

Shift rehearsal: a rehearsal, without actors, where the director, scenic designer, technical director, and stage manager work with the scenery and prop crews to perfect the choreography and timing of all scenic and prop shifts.

Shim: scrap wood or metal used to raise adjacent parts so that they are level or fit together as designed.

S hook: an S-shaped piece of steel strap used to hold stiffening battens on the back of wall units that are made up of two or more flats; also called a latch keeper.

Show portal: a false proscenium that visually supports the style and color palette of a particular production.

Shutter: a lever-actuated device used to control the height of the top and bottom edges of a followspot beam; also called a chopper.

Shuttle stage: a long narrow wagon that moves back and forth across the stage, like a shuttle in a loom; used for shifting scenery.

Sight line: a sighting extending from any seat in the house to any position on stage.

Sight-line drawing: a scale drawing (plan and section views) of sightings that extend from the extreme seats (usually the outside seats on the front and last rows of the auditorium) to any position on the stage; used to determine how much of the stage and backstage will be visible from specific auditorium seats.

Silhouette: the general outline of form; frequently used to refer to the shape of a garment, set, or prop. The quality and character of the line determines the evocative characteristics of the resultant form. Also known as a profile or cutout line.

Sill iron: a strap of mild steel attached to the bottom of a door flat to brace it where the rail has been cut out.

Single-hand welding: a technique in which one hand holds the welding handle and the other hand is not used.

Single whip: a block and tackle configuration that changes the direction of travel of the line but provides no mechanical advantage.

Size coat: a paint coat used to shrink previously unpainted scenic fabric and to fill the weave of the fabric.

Size water: a mixture of approximately one cup of hot animal glue and one tablespoon of Lysol (or one cup of white glue) per gallon of warm water; the amount of binder in the size water depends on the weight of the pigments being used.

Skene: originally a wall or facade to hide backstage action in Greek theatres. By the end of the fifth century B.C., the wall had evolved into a two-story building.

Skid: a low-profile substitute for a wagon; usually a piece of three-quarter-inch plywood on which some small scenic element is placed.

Skin: a top or bottom plywood covering for a platform.

Sky drop: a large drop made to be hung flat, without fullness; used to simulate the sky.

Sky tab: synonym for sky drop.

Slide-plane aperture: the point in a projection system where a slide or other effect is placed.

Slide projector: a reasonably high output instrument capable of projecting standard 35 mm slides.

Slip-joint pliers: common pliers with an adjustable pivot point that provides two ranges of jaw openings; used for clamping, gripping, bending, and cutting light wire.

Slipstage: a stage wagon large enough to hold an entire set.

Sloper: a paper pattern for a costume.

Smooth base coat: a base coat that has no texture.

Smoothing plane: a large, heavy plane with a blade angle of approximately twenty-five to thirty degrees; used to smooth parallel with the grain of wood.

Socket set and ratchet handle: sockets are cylindrical wrenches used with a ratchet handle; the reversible ratchet handle allows one to tighten or loosen nuts without removing the socket from the nut; used to tighten or loosen nuts and bolts in confined spaces or where other wrenches might not fit.

Software: the programs (sets of electronic instructions) that perform various functions such as word processing, drafting, and three-dimensional modeling.

Solder: a metal alloy made of lead and tin.

Soldering: the process of forming a low-strength bond in metal by flowing a molten metal over a joint area.

Soldering gun: a quick-heating, trigger-activated soldering iron that physically resembles a pistol.

Soldering iron: a device to heat solder and the item to be soldered to the point where a good bond can be made.

Soldering pencil: a low-wattage soldering iron.

Sole: the bottom plate of a plane, with a slot through which the tip of the blade projects.

Sound crew: those who record and edit sound and who set up and run any sound equipment during the production.

Sound designer: person responsible for the design, recording, and playback of all music and sound effects used in a production.

Sound mixer: an electronic device used to adjust the loudness and tone levels of several sources, such as microphones and tape decks.

Sound plot: a list describing each sound cue in the production.

Sound-reinforcement system: the amplification of sound coming from the stage.

Sound scoring: background music and/or effects tracks that play at a low loudness level throughout a scene or scenes.

Source: the origin of electrical potential, such as a battery or 120-volt wall outlet.

Source light: the apparent source of light that is illuminating a scene or an object.

Spade bits: *see* wood bits.

Spattering: the process of applying small drops of paint to a surface; done by spraying paint with a garden sprayer or slapping a lightly charged brush against the heel of one's hand to throw paint drops at the scenery.

Specifications: clarifying notes that explain the building materials, textures, or special effects to be used in a design or other project.

Spectrometer: a device for measuring specific wavelengths of light.

Spidering: running a cable directly from the dimmer to the instrument; also known as direct cabling.

Spindle chuck: a device used to hold wood in a lathe.

Spine: the relative stiffness of brush bristles; good watercolor bristles will flex easily but will also have enough spine to remain erect when fully saturated with paint.

Spirit: the manner and style in which a play is presented to the audience.

Spoke shave: a small plane with a wide, narrow, slightly rounded sole and a steeply angled (approximately thirty to thirty-five degrees) blade; it is pulled rather than pushed across the surface of the wood; used to soften or round sharp edges rather than to smooth flat surfaces.

Spray cone: the shape or pattern of paint emitted from the nozzle of a spray gun.

Spray gun: a pistol-like device that shoots out a cone of paint.

Spreading: *see* bleeding.

Stage: the area where the action of the play takes place.

Stage brace: an adjustable wooden or aluminum pole that is attached to a brace cleat on the back of a flat to hold it vertical.

Stage business: a specific action, also known as a "bit," performed by an actor during the play.

Stage circuit: an electrical circuit terminating on one end in a female receptacle in the vicinity of the stage. The other end is connected to a dimmer or a patch panel. Synonymous with dimmer circuit when it terminates at a dimmer.

Stage crew: those who shift the sets and, sometimes, props during rehearsals and performances.

Stage house: the physical structure enclosing the area above the stage and wings.

Stage manager: person who assists the director during rehearsals and manages all backstage activity once the play has opened.

Stage screw: bracing hardware; a coarse-threaded, large, hand-driven screw used to anchor a foot iron or the foot of a stage brace to the stage floor; leaves ragged holes in the stage floor.

Standard parallel: a platform made of a folding framework of nonvariable height; the top is removable and the frame folds like a giant parallelogram for storage.

Staple gun: a tool with a spring-driven piston used to drive staples; used in upholstery, in attaching muslin to flat, and so forth.

Staples: U-shaped fasteners sharpened at both ends; used to attach wire, rope, cording, chicken wire, screening, and similar materials to supporting wooden frames.

Starter hole: a small hole bored into a piece of wood to hold the tip of a screw or drill bit; also called a pilot hole.

Stencil brush: a short, squat brush with a circular pattern of short, stiff bristles; the bristles are pressed onto, rather than stroked across, the work, to prevent the paint from bleeding under the edges of the stencil.

Stencil paper: stiff, water-resistant paper used for making stencils.

Step-down transformer: a transformer whose output voltage is lower than its input voltage.

Step lens: a plano-convex lens with the glass on the plano side cut away in steps that are parallel with the plano face.

Step motor: an electric motor whose movement consists of discrete, angular steps rather than continuous rotation. Precise movement is achieved by programming the motor to run, in either direction, for a specific number of steps.

Step-up transformer: a transformer whose output voltage is higher than its input voltage.

Stereo: two distinct sound channels; a stereo system is composed of two discrete monaural systems.

Stiffening batten: a length of 1 × 3 attached to a multiflat wall unit to keep it from wiggling.

Stile: a vertical side member of a flat.

Stippling: in scene painting, a texturing technique, similar in appearance to spattering, but leaves a heavier texture; stippling is done by touching a sponge, feather duster, or ends of a brush to the surface of the work. In makeup, a texturing technique in which makeup is applied by touching the skin with a textured surface, usually a stippling sponge. Similar to stippling in scenic painting.

Stitcher: one who sews costumes together.

Stock: regular-sized lumber that can be purchased from a lumberyard.

Stock furniture: furniture items owned by the producing organization and held in storage until they are needed for a production.

Stock set: scenery designed to visually support a generalized location (garden, city street, palace, interior) rather than a specific one.

Stop block: a small piece of scrap wood attached to the stile of a flat to prevent flats from slipping past each other when lashed together in an inside corner configuration.

Stop cleat: metal tabs used to prevent flats from slipping past each other when they are being lashed in an outside corner configuration.

Stove bolts: bolts smaller than carriage or machine bolts and with threads on the entire length of the shaft; used for attaching stage hardware, hinges, and similar items that require greater fastening strength than screws do.

Stovepipe wire: soft-iron wire approximately one-sixteenth of an inch in diameter and generally black; very flexible but has little tensile strength; used for tying or wiring things together; is not strong enough to be used for flying scenery.

Straightedge: a thin piece of wood, usually four to six feet long, with a handle attached in the center; used as a guide while painting straight lines.

Straps: rectangular strips of quarter-inch plywood used to reinforce butt joints on the interior support elements (toggle bars, diagonal braces) of flats; substitute for keystones.

Stream-of-consciousness questioning: asking whatever relevant questions pop into your mind in the course of a discussion.

Striplight: a long, narrow troughlike instrument with three or four circuits controlling the individual lamps; each circuit is normally equipped with a separate color; used for blending and creating color washes; also known as an x-ray.

Style: specific compositional characteristics that distinguish the appearance of one type of design from another; e.g., realism, expressionism, surrealism, and so forth.

Stylization: the use of specific compositional elements characteristic of a particular style or period that create the essence of that style or period.

Subtractive color mixing: the selective absorption of light by a filter or pigment.

Supernumerary: an actor, normally not called for in the script, used in a production; an extra; a walk-on.

Surform blade: a thin, disposable strip of spring steel honeycombed with sharp-ened protrusions projecting from its surface; the serrated blade face doesn't leave a smooth surface, so the wood generally has to be smoothed with sandpaper.

Surform tools: tools that use the Surform blade—planes, files, routing bits, and gouges.

Sweat off: when an actor's face perspires, some makeups will run. These makeups are said to "sweat off."

Sweep: a wooden curvilinear form frequently used to outline an arch or irregular form in door- and window-flat openings.

Swivel caster: a caster that swivels or rotates around a vertical axis; the bearing plate should have a ball-bearing swivel.

Symmetrical balance: correspondence in size, form, and relative position of parts on either side of a center dividing line; mirror-image balance.

Synthesizer: a musical instrument that creates sound electronically; can be used to create a close facsimile of instrumental, vocal, or natural tones.

Table saw: a circular-bladed stationary power saw; the blade projects upward from the underside of a table; the height and angle of the blade are adjustable; used to rip lumber, plywood, and other sheet goods.

Tack hammer: a lightweight hammer with a small magnetized head for inserting tacks and a large face for seating them; used only with tacks.

Tap and die: tools used to cut threads on pipe and rod stock; the tap is used to cut internal threads; the die cuts external threads.

Tape deck: a magnetic-tape transport mechanism used to record an electrical signal on magnetic tape; also used to play back that signal; does not contain a playback amplifier or speaker.

Tape measure: a retractable, flexible metal rule housed in a plastic or metal case; used for measuring in general stage work.

Tape recorder: a magnetic-tape transport mechanism used to record and play back an electrical signal on magnetic tape; it has a built-in playback amplifier and speaker(s).

Teaser: a short, horizontal drape used for masking the flies; synonym for *border*.

Technical director: person responsible for supervising the construction, mounting, rigging, and shifting of the scenery and properties.

Technical production: all organizational and procedural aspects of the construction, painting, and operation of scenery and properties.

Technical rehearsals: run-throughs in which the sets, lights, props, and sound are integrated into the action of the play.

Tenon: a square tab projecting from a piece of stock; used in conjunction with a mortise to make a mortise and tenon joint.

Texture: the relative roughness or smoothness of the finish of an object.

Theatrical gauze: a fine mesh weave, similar to cheesecloth, but the threads are thicker and the weave is slightly tighter; 72 inches wide; used for apparition effects and applications similar to sharkstooth scrim.

Theatron: the steeply raked seating area for the audience in a Greek theatre.

Theme: the repetitive use of similar elements to create a pattern or design.

Throw distance: the distance the light travels from its hanging position to the center of its focus area.

Thrust stage: a stage projecting into, and surrounded on three sides by, the audience.

Thumbnail sketch: a small, quickly drawn rough sketch, usually done in pencil, that shows the major outline, character, and feeling of an object but doesn't show much detail.

Tie-off cleats: special cleats used in pairs approximately thirty inches above stage level to tie off the line after the flats have been lashed together.

Ties: strips of material (usually 36-inch pieces of half-inch-wide cotton tape, or 36-inch shoestrings) used for tying stage drapes to battens.

Tilt: to rotate an object about its horizontal axis.

Timbre: the distinctive quality of a sound that distinguishes one voice, musical instrument, or sound from another of the same pitch and intensity.

Tin snips: scissorlike tools used for cutting thin metal.

Tint: a color of high value; usually created by mixing one or more hues with white.

Tip jack: two (or more) large interconnected jacks that are fitted with swivel casters; normally used for moving wall units.

Toggle bar: an interior horizontal framing member of a flat.

Tone: (1) a color of middle value achieved by mixing one or more hues with black and white; (2) a generic term referring to the intensity of the component frequencies contained in any particular sound.

Tooth: a term used to describe the surface texture of a paper.

Tormentor: the vertical flats that form the side elements of the false proscenium.

Toxic: poisonous.

Tracing paper: translucent paper used for drafting.

Transducer: a device that converts energy from one state into another, such as a microphone or loudspeaker.

Transformer: a device that changes voltage in an electrical system.

Travel: to move horizontally relative to the stage floor, as with a drape that opens in the middle and is pulled to the sides.

Traveler: any drapery that moves or opens horizontally; generally, travelers are composed of two sections of stage drapes covering the full width of the proscenium; the sections split in the middle, and each section retracts in an offstage direction.

Tread: the horizontal surface of a stair unit—the part on which you walk.

Trick line: *see* monofilament line.

Tri square: a small, rigid, hand square with a steel blade and steel, composition, or wooden handle; used as a guide for marking ninety-degree angles across narrow (under six inches) materials.

Truss: an engineered beam in which a downward force at any point on its top will be distributed over its full width by a series of interlocking triangles that channel and redirect the downward force into a horizontal force.

"Tubed" building adhesive: an adhesive product, such as Liquid Nails, packaged in a caulking tube and designed to be dispensed with a caulking gun.

Tubing cutter: a tool used for making clean right-angle cuts on steel and nonferrous metal tubing one-half inch and smaller.

Tumbler: a narrow (three-fourths inch thick by one inch wide, or 1×3) piece of stock used as a spacer when three or more flats are going to be booked.

Turntable: *see* revolve.

Tutu: the short, stiff skirt frequently worn by ballerinas.

Tweed: a rough-surfaced woolen fabric in plain, twill, or herringbone weave of two or more shades of the same color; used for men's and women's suits and trousers.

Tweeter: a high-frequency speaker generally designed to reproduce from approximately 1000 to 20,000 Hz.

Twill: a weaving pattern that results in parallel diagonal lines or ribs; a flat-surfaced, durable, heavy cotton fabric used for making dresses, men's suits, and work clothes.

Twist-drill bits: drill bits made of mild steel, filed to a point, with spiral indentations in the shaft to carry away material being removed from the hole; used for drilling holes of approximately one-sixty-

fourth to one-half inch in diameter in wood, plastic, mild to medium steel, and nonferrous metals.

Two-fer: an electrical "Y" that has female receptacles at the top of the "Y" and a male plug at the bottom leg of the "Y"; used to connect two instruments to the same circuit.

Two-hand welding: a technique in which the torch or welding handle is held in one hand and the filler rod in the other.

Unbalanced line: a sound cable in which a single insulated conductor is wrapped in a braided or foil shield.

Unbleached muslin: a cotton fabric commonly used to cover flats; available in a variety of widths from 72 inches to 33 feet; for scenic-construction purposes, it should have a thread count of 128 or 140 threads per inch.

Undercut: an indentation in a form that leaves an overhang or concave profile, such as the nostrils on a mask of a face.

Unified aniline dye: a coal-tar-derivative dye formulated to work on both animal- and plant-derivative fibers.

Unit set: a single set in which all of the play's locations are always visible and the audience's attention is usually shifted by alternately lighting various parts of the set.

Unsaturated polyester: a liquid plastic generally used as a casting resin and as the bonding agent to create the multipurpose material known by the trade name Fiberglas.

Upson board: a sheet stock composed of a paper pulp and binder compressed into four-by-eight-foot sheets.

Urethane: a class of plastics that have a variety of formulations: flexible foam, rigid foam, and liquid casting resin. Because of toxic fumes emitted when working with urethane foams, their use is not recommended.

Utility knife: a metal handle with a usually retractable replaceable blade; used for a variety of jobs including cutting cardboard and trimming fabric from the edges of flats; also called a matte knife.

Vacuforming: the process of shaping heated plastic, usually high-impact polystyrene, around a mold through the use of vacuum pressure.

Valance: a horizontal element at the top of a drapery arrangement that covers the curtain rod.

Valence shell: the outermost plane of orbiting electrons in the structure of an atom.

Value: the relative lightness or darkness of an object.

Vanishing point: the point on the horizon to which a set of parallel lines recedes.

Varnish: a transparent coating made of synthetic or natural resinous materials suspended in an oil (oil varnish), alcohol (spirit varnish), or synthetic (polyurethane, vinyl acrylic) vehicle.

Vehicle: the liquid medium—water, oil, lacquer, and the like—in which pigments, fillers, and binders are suspended to create a paint mixture; after the paint is applied, the vehicle evaporates.

Velour: a thick, heavy material with a deep pile; generally made of cotton or cotton/nylon blends; heavier weights are used for upholstery and draperies; lighter weights can be used in costuming.

Velum: an awning covering the cavea (auditorium) of a Roman theatre; also known as a velarium.

Velvet: a rich, lustrous material with a soft, thick pile; frequently made of rayon with a cotton or cotton-blend backing; used in dresses, coats, upholstery, and draperies.

Velveteen: fabric possessing the same general characteristics as velour but much lighter (six to eight ounces); used in upholstery and costumes.

Ventilate: a method of tying hair to the net foundation of a wig, mustache, or beard. The technique is similar to that used in hooking rugs.

Vinyl acrylic concentrates: highly saturated pigments with a vinyl acrylic binder.

Vinyl acrylic paint: paint made with a vinyl acrylic binder; in scene painting, thinned vinyl acrylic concentrates (two parts water to one part concentrate) are mixed with an opaque white base to create tints and are mixed with a transparent base for fully saturated hues; after curing for twenty-four hours, the paint is highly water-resistant; can be thinned with up to ten parts of water depending on particular application.

Void: an unfilled, empty space.

Volatility: in computers, loss of electronic data when a computer loses its power supply.

Volt: the unit of measurement of electrical potential.

Wafer board: a sheet stock composed of large chips of wood mixed with a binder and compressed into four-by-eight-foot sheets; stronger and cheaper than plywood; can be used for the same purposes as plywood.

Wale: visible, usually narrow, ridges in the surface of a fabric caused by a variation in the weaving pattern.

Walk the cues: to move about the stage as the light cues are being run so the light will be falling on a person rather than on a bare stage.

Wall pocket: a connecting box similar to a floor pocket but mounted so that its face is flush with a wall.

Wardrobe crew or staff: those crew members such as dressers and wardrobe-repair personnel who work during the dress rehearsals and performances.

Warp: the vertical threads in a fabric.

Wash: the covering of a large area with a smooth layer of paint. A smooth wash consists of only one color; a blended wash is created by smoothly segueing from one color to another.

Watch tackle: a block and tackle system that provides a 3:1 mechanical advantage.

Web browser: a software program that enables you to preview and access sites on the World Wide Web.

Weft: the horizontal threads in a fabric.

Welding: the process of making a high-strength bond in metal by heating the parts to be joined to their melting points and allowing the parts to become fused together.

Welding rod: a rod, usually coated with flux, that serves as the positive electrode in arc welding.

Wheat paste: a mixture of unrefined wheat flour and water; used for attaching dutchmen and for similar low-strength gluing.

White glue: commonly known by the trade name Elmer's Glue-All, white glue is a casein or milk-based glue used extensively in scenic and property construction.

White model: *see* functional model.

Whiting: a white powder extender, basically low-grade chalk, used to increase the covering power of dry pigment and binder paint.

Wigmaker: one who makes, styles, and arranges wigs.

Winch-driven system: a system that uses a motorized or handpowered winch to move a cable; frequently used to move wagons or skids across the stage or to turn small revolves.

Wings: (1) tall cloth-covered frames or narrow unframed drops that are placed on either side of the stage, parallel with the proscenium arch, to prevent the audience from seeing backstage. In the Restoration theatre, wings were usually painted to match the scene on the upstage drop. (2) The off-stage space adjacent to the stage in a proscenium arch theatre.

Wire-crimping tool: specialty pliers whose jaws are designed to pressure-clamp solderless connectors to electrical wire.

Wire frame: lines used to define the shape of an object.

Wireless microphone: a microphone system that uses a short-range FM radio transmitter and receiver instead of a cable to send the signal from the microphone to the mixer.

Wire nails: small finish or box nails with very slender shafts; used for attaching delicate decorative moldings or panels to larger scenic elements.

Wire strippers: specialty pliers used for removing insulation from electrical wires.

Wood bits: paddle-shaped bits primarily for use in drilling wood, although they can be used in some plastics; must be used in a power drill; also known as spade bits.

Wood chisel: a steel blade sharpened at a thirty-degree angle; used for gouging, paring, or smoothing wood.

Wood file: a file with medium-sized teeth; can be flat on both faces, flat on one face and curved on the other, or round; used for smoothing wood and plastic.

Wood rasp: an extremely coarse-toothed file; usually has one flat and one rounded face; used for rough shaping of wood.

Woofer: a low-frequency speaker with a frequency range from approximately 20 to 150–250 Hz.

Work: the object on which work is being performed.

Workable fixative: a spray that seals colors in place. "Workable" indicates that paint can effectively be applied on top of the fixative.

Working sectional: a drawing showing the sectional angle for a lighting instrument; used to determine its trim height; not to be confused with a lighting sectional.

Work light: a lighting fixture, frequently a scoop, PAR, or other wide-field-angle instrument, hung over the stage to facilitate work.

Worsted: a tightly woven, smooth-surfaced fabric of wool or wool blend; used for men's or women's suits and trousers.

Wrecking bars: generic name for the class of metal tools used to pry wood apart and remove nails.

X-ray: *see* striplight.

Zoom ellipse: an ellipsoidal reflector spotlight with movable lenses that allow the focal length and beam-edge sharpness to be varied.

Selected References

Acoustics and Architecture

Beranek, Leo L. *Music, Acoustics and Architecture.* Robert E. Krieger Publishing, 1979.

Burris-Meyer, Harold, and Edward C. Cole. *Theatres and Auditoriums.* Reinhold, 1949.

Burris-Meyer, Harold, and Lewis Goodfriend. *Acoustics for the Architect.* Reinhold, 1957.

Mullin, Donald C. *The Development of the Playhouse.* University of California Press, 1970.

Scenic/Property Design and Construction

Arnold, Richard L. *Scene Technology.* Prentice-Hall, 3rd ed., 1993.

Baldwin, John. *Contemporary Sculpture Techniques: Welded Metal and Fiberglass.* Reinhold Publishing, 1967.

Bay, Howard. *Stage Design.* Drama Book Specialists, 1974.

Bellman, Willard F. *Scene Design, Stage Lighting, Sound, Costume and Makeup.* Harper & Row, 1983.

Birren, Faber. *Creative Color.* Schiffer, 1987.

Bowman, Ned. *Handbook of Technical Practices for the Performing Arts.* Scenographic Media, 1975.

Bryson, Nicholas L. *Thermoplastic Scenery for the Theatre, Vol. 1: Vacuum Forming.* Drama Book Specialists, 1972.

Burris-Meyer, Harold, and Edward C. Cole. *Scenery for the Theatre.* Little, Brown, 1972.

Gillette, A. S., and J. Michael Gillette. *Stage Scenery.* Harper & Row, 3rd ed., 1981.

Glerum, Jay. *Stage Rigging Handbook.* Southern Illinois University Press, 2nd ed., 1997.

Gottshall, Franklin H. *How to Design and Construct Period Furniture.* Reprinted by Bonanza Books, original copyright 1937.

Kenton, Warren. *Stage Properties and How to Make Them.* Drama Book Specialists, 1978.

Meyer, Franz Sales. *Handbook of Ornament.* Dover Publications, 1957.

Meyers, L. Donald. *The Furniture Lover's Book: Finding, Fixing, Finishing.* Sunrise Books, E. P. Dutton, 1977.

Neuman, Jay Hartley, and Lee Scott. *Plastics for the Craftsman.* Crown Publishers, 1972.

Parker, W. Oren, Harvey K. Smith, and R. Craig Wolf. *Scene Design and Stage Lighting.* Holt, Rinehart and Winston, 6th ed., 1990.

Payne, Darwin Reid. *Theory and Craft of the Scenographic Model,* rev. ed. Southern Illinois University Press, 1985.

Pecktal, Lynn. *Designing and Drawing for the Theatre.* McGraw-Hill, 1994.

Taylor, Douglas C. *Metalworking for the Designer and Technician.* Drama Book Specialists, 1979.

Lighting Design and Production

Bellman, Willard F. *Lighting the Stage: Art and Practice.* Harper & Row, 1974.

Gillette, J. Michael. *Designing with Light.* Mayfield Publishing, 2nd ed., 1989.

Parker, W. Oren, Harvey K. Smith, and R. Craig Wolf. *Scene Design and Stage Lighting.* Holt, Rinehart and Winston, 6th ed., 1990.

Pilbrow, Richard. *Stage Lighting.* Drama Book Publishing, 1991.

Rosenthal, Jean, and Lael Wertenbaker. *The Magic of Light.* Little, Brown, 1972.

Warfel, William, and Walter A. Klappert. *Color Science for Lighting.* Yale University Press, 1981.

Costume/Makeup Design and Production

Anderson, Barbara and Cletus. *Costume Design.* Holt, Rinehart and Winston, 1984.

Barton, Lucy. *Historic Costume for the Stage.* Baker's Plays, 1963.

Corey, Irene. *The Mask of Reality.* Anchorage Press, 1968.

Corson, Richard. *Stage Makeup.* Prentice-Hall, 8th ed., 1990.

Cunningham, Rebecca. *The Magic Garment: Principles of Costume Design.* Waveland Press, 1994.

Ingham, Rosemary, and Elizabeth Covey. *The Costume Designer's Handbook.* Heineman, 1992.

Ingham, Rosemary, and Elizabeth Covey. *The Costumer's Handbook: A Complete Guide for Amateur and Professional Costume Designers.* Heineman, 1992.

Pecktal, Lynn. *Costume Design: Techniques of Modern Masters.* Watson-Guptill, 1993.

Prisk, Berneice. *Stage Costume Handbook.* Greenwood, 1979.

Russell, Douglas. *Costume History and Style.* Prentice-Hall, 1982.

Russell, Douglas. *Stage Costume Design: Theory, Technique and Style.* Prentice-Hall, 2nd ed., 1985.

Waugh, Norah. *The Cut of Men's Clothes 1600–1900.* Theatre Arts Books, 1964.

Waugh, Norah. *The Cut of Women's Clothes 1600–1930.* Theatre Arts Books, 1968.

Safety

Rossol, Monona. *The Artist's Complete Health and Safety Guide.* Allworth Press, 1994.

Rossol, Monona. *Stage Fright: Health and Safety in the Theatre.* Allworth Press, 1991.

Sound Design and Production

Collison, David. *Stage Sound.* Drama Book Publishers, 1982.

Davis, Gary, and Ralph Jones for Yamaha. *Sound Reinforcement Handbook.* Hal Leonard Corporation, 2nd ed., 1989.

Heil, Bob. *Practical Guide for Concert Sound.* Melco Publishing, 1976.

Drafting for the Theatre

Morgan, Harry. *Perspective Drawing for the Theatre*. Drama Book Specialists, 1979.

Payne, Darwin Reid. *Computer Scenographics*. Southern Illinois University Press, 1994.

Sweet, Harvey, and Deborah M. Dryden. *The Complete Guide to Drawing for the Theatre*. Allyn & Bacon, 2nd ed., 1994.

Warfel, William. *Handbook of Stage Lighting Graphics*. Drama Book Specialists, 1974.

Periodicals

Lighting Dimensions
Entertainment Design
Theatre Design and Technology

Credits

Chapter 7 p. 124 Adapted from Mel Gussow, "Onstage Magic with Water," *The New York Times,* July 28, 1998. Copyright © 1998 by The New York Times. Reprinted by permission. **Chapter 9 p. 224** Adapted from Si Morse, "Hooping It Up," *Stage Directions,* March 1999, pp. 9–11. With permission from the publisher. **Chapter 12 p. 292** Adapted from Arnold Wengrow, "Thomas Lynch: Far East Marks This Designer's Latest Scenic Transformation," *Entertainment Design,* March 1999, pp. 38–41. Copyright © 1999 Entertainment Design. Courtesy of Intertec Publishing Corporation, NYC. All rights reserved. Information: *http://www.etecnyc.net;* **p. 299** Lighting Graphic Standard reprinted with permission from United States Institute for Theatre Technology, Inc. **Chapter 16 p. 390** Adapted from "Designing Woman," *Time,* February 22, 1999. Copyright © 1999 Time Inc. With permission from the publisher; **p. 394** Adapted from Amy Reiter, "Designing Woman," *Entertainment Design,* May 1999, pp. 6–7. Copyright © 1999 Entertainment Design. Courtesy of Intertec Publishing Corporation, NYC. All rights reserved. For information: *http://www.etecnyc.net;* **p. 406** Adapted from David Barbour, "I Want My Mummy," *Entertainment Design,* February 1999, pp. 5–6. Copyright © 1999 Entertainment Design. Courtesy of Intertec Publishing Corporation, NYC. All rights reserved. Information: http:/www.etecnyc.net. **Chapter 20** Figs. 20.11, 20.12 Reproduced with permission from Diehl Graphsoft, Inc. **Chapter 22** Fig. 22.4a Reproduced with permission from Adobe Systems Incorporated. Adobe and Photoshop are trademarks of Adobe Systems Incorporated; Fig. 22.4b Reproduced with permission from MetaCreations; Fig. 22.5 Reproduced with permission from Strata, Inc. **Appendix B** Lighting Graphic Standard reprinted with permission from United States Institute for Theatre Technology, Inc.

Index